The International Guide to Nonprofit Law

NONPROFIT LAW, FINANCE, AND MANAGEMENT SERIES

The International Guide to Nonprofit Law

LESTER M. SALAMON

With the assistance of
STEFAN TOEPLER AND ASSOCIATES

John Wiley & Sons, Inc.

New York • Chichester • Weinheim • Brisbane • Singapore • Toronto

Copyright © 1997 by John Wiley & Sons, Inc.

Library of Congress Cataloging-in-Publication Data:

Salamon, Lester M.
     The international guide to nonprofit law / Lester M. Salamon with
  the assistance of Stefan Toepler and associates.
        p.   cm.—(Nonprofit law, finance, and management series)
     Includes bibliographical references.
     ISBN 0-471-05518-2 (cloth : alk. paper)
     1. Nonprofit organizations—Law and legislation.   I. Toepler,
  Stefan.   II. Title.   III. Series.
  K656.S25   1997
  346'.064—dc21
                                                                            97-7451
                                                                              CIP

Printed in the United States of America

10 9 8 7 6 5 4 3 2 1

Subscription Notice

This Wiley product is updated on a periodic basis with supplements to reflect important changes in the subject matter. If you purchased this product directly from John Wiley & Sons, Inc., we have already recorded your subscription for this update service.

If, however, you purchased this product from a bookstore and wish to receive (1) the current update at no additional charge, and (2) future updates and revised or related volumes billed separately with a 30-day examination review, please send your name, company name (if applicable), address, and the title of the product to:

Supplement Department
John Wiley & Sons, Inc.
One Wiley Drive
Somerset, NJ 08875
1-800-225-5945

For customers outside the United States, please contact the Wiley office nearest you:

Professional & Reference Division
John Wiley & Sons Canada, Ltd.
22 Worcester Road
Rexdale, Ontario M9W 1L1
CANADA
(416) 675-3580
1-800-567-4797
FAX (416) 675-6599

John Wiley & Sons, Ltd.
Baffins Lane
Chichester
West Sussex, PO19 1UD
UNITED KINGDOM
(44) (243) 779777

Jacaranda Wiley Ltd.
PRT Division
P.O. Box 174
North Ryde, NSW 2113
AUSTRALIA
(02) 805-1100
FAX (02) 805-1597

John Wiley & Sons (SEA) Pte. Ltd.
37 Jalan Pemimpin
Block B # 05-04
Union Industrial Building
SINGAPORE 2057
(65) 258-1157

ABOUT THE AUTHOR

Lester M. Salamon is a Professor in the Schools of Arts and Sciences and Hygiene and Public Health at the Johns Hopkins University and director of the Johns Hopkins Institute for Policy Studies. Prior to this, he was director of the Center for Governance and Management Research at the Urban Institute in Washington, DC and deputy associate director of the U.S. Office of Management and Budget in the Executive Office of the President. Before that, he taught at Duke University, Vanderbilt University, and, during the American civil rights struggle of the mid-1960s, at Tougaloo College in Tougaloo, Mississippi.

Dr. Salamon pioneered the empirical study of the nonprofit sector, first in the United States and more recently throughout the world. His 1982 book, *The Federal Budget and the Nonprofit Sector* (The Urban Institute Press), was the first to document the scale of the American nonprofit sector and the extent of government support to it. As director of the Johns Hopkins Comparative Nonprofit Sector Project, Dr. Salamon has extended this analysis to the international sphere, producing the first comparative empirical assessment of the size, structure, financing, and role of the nonprofit sector at the global level. The results of this work were published in 1994 in a book entitled *The Emerging Sector* (reissued as *The Emerging Nonprofit Sector* in 1996 by Manchester University Press).

In addition to his work on the nonprofit sector, Dr. Salamon is an expert on the tools of government action and on social welfare and urban development policy. He is the author or editor of more than a dozen books and has contributed articles to more than 50 different journals. His most recent book, *Partners in Public Service: Government and the Nonprofit Sector in the Modern Welfare State*, published in 1995 by the Johns Hopkins University Press, recently won the 1996 ARNOVA Award for Distinguished Book in Nonprofit and Voluntary Action Research.

Dr. Salamon received his B.A. degree in Economics and Policy Studies from Princeton University and his Ph.D. in Government from Harvard University. He is married, has two sons, and serves on the board of the International Society for Third-Sector Research and on the editorial boards of *Voluntas, Administration and Society,* and *Nonprofit and Voluntary Sector Quarterly.*

ABOUT THE CONTRIBUTORS

Takako Amemiya graduated from the law department of Keio University and completed her doctorate work in 1973. She specializes in civil and trust law, and currently teaches at Meijigakuin University and at Shoin College, where she is Dean of the Department of Business Management. She is a member of the academic committee of Japan Association of Charitable Organizations. Her publications include *Incorporation and Management of Charitable Organization, Fundamental Issues on the Philanthropy Tax System,* and *Legal Procedure of the Charitable Organizations.*

Nina Balyaeva, Ph.D., JD is with the Institute for State and Law in Moscow. She is also President of the Interlegal Charitable Foundation.

Gian Paolo Barbetta, Ph.D. teaches political economy at the Catholic University of Milan. He also directs research on nonprofit organizations at the Institute for Social Research. Dr. Barbetta's most recent publications include *Senza Scopo Di Lucro,* (Il Mulino, Bologna, 1996) a comprehensive analysis of the Italian nonprofit sector.

Hadara Bar-Mor, JSD (Tel-Aviv University) is the Vice Dean and Senior Lecturer at Netanya Academic College in Israel. Specializing in corporate and labor law, she is the author of a text book on company law and was the editor of the yearbook on labor law and social security. Currently, she is the chief editor of the periodical issued by the School of Law of Netanya Academic College. Dr. Bar-Mor also serves as a lay-judge in the National Labor Court and is a public representative in the national press council.

Blake Bromley, LLB devotes his professional practice to advising donors and charities on taxation and compliance issues in funding and operating charities. He has an extensive international practice that includes advising governments on drafting laws governing charities, which has taken him to Asia, Europe, Australia, Africa, and South America.

Marta Cartabia is a research scientist of public law in the Department of Political Science at the State University of Milan, Italy.

Sami Castro, Docteur en droit is currently the voluntary legal advisor of UNIOPSS in Paris, where he is the central representative body of health and social private institutions in France. He was director of social and cultural private institutions. Dr. Castro is a member of the board of the National Council of Voluntary Organizations in France, which is an official public body under the Prime Minister's authority.

Mel Cousins, Barrister at Law received a Barrister-at-Law degree from Kings Inns, Dublin in 1989 while working as Legal Administrator for Free Legal Advice Centres in Dublin. He currently works as an independent research consultant and has provided consultancy services to a wide range of groups including the National Social Service Board and Combat Poverty. His publications include reports on: Legal Structures for Voluntary and Community Organizations, Community Involvement in the Delivery of Legal Services and various guides to welfare payments in Ireland.

Susan L.Q. Flaherty, JD is a founding partner of Roha & Flaherty, Attorneys at Law, Washington, D.C., which serves as corporate and tax counsel to nonprofit organizations and tax counsel to individual and corporate philanthropists. She holds Juris Doctor and Master of Laws-Taxation degrees from George Washington University and speaks and writes frequently on the law of nonprofit organizations.

Emilio Carrillo Gamboa is a senior partner with the law firm Bufete Carrillo Gamboa in Mexico. Mr. Gamboa was formerly Mexico's Ambassador to Canada from 1987 to 1989. He is Chairman of the Board of Trustees of the Mexican Center for Philanthropy and the Antiguo Colegio de San Ildefonso. He is also a member of the Board of Trustees of the Bancomer Cultural Foundation. Mr. Gamboa serves as Chairman of the Mexican chapter of the North American Institute and is a member of the International Committee of the Council of Foundations of the United States and of the Advisory Council of the Mexican Center of the University of Texas at Austin.

Bruce R. Hopkins is a lawyer who specializes in the representation of nonprofit organizations. He has served as Chair of the Committee on Exempt Organizations, Tax Section, American Bar Association; Chair, Section of Taxation, National Association of College and University Attorneys; and President, Planned Giving Study Group of Greater Washington, D.C. Mr. Hopkins is the author of numerous publications, as well as *The Nonprofit Counsel*, a newsletter. He teaches a course on nonprofit organizations at the University of Missouri—Kansas City School of Law.

Amani Kandil, Ph.D. is a professor of political science at Cairo University and the National Center for Social and Criminological Research. She is currently working as a consultant at the Follow-up Committee for Arab NGOs. Her fields of interest include public policies, interest groups, nonprofit organizations, and the civil society in Egypt and the Arab world. Dr. Kandil has published several books and articles, mostly focused on the nonprofit sector, which include *Civil Society in the Arab World, Non-Governmental Organizations in Egypt,* and *The Democratization Process in Egypt*.

Jacek Kurczewski, Ph.D. is a professor and Chair of Sociology of Custom and Law at the University of Warsaw. Dr. Kurczewski was a member of both the Solidarity advisory councils and the round table talks on freedom of association. He is a member of the ICNL board and the 1996/1997 Senior Advisor on NGOs to UNDP in Uzbekistan.

Eva Kuti, Ph.D. is a senior researcher at the Research Project on Nonprofit Organizations. Dr. Kuti's main areas of research include giving and volunteering, state/nonprofit sector relationships, economics of culture, and the redistributional role of the nonprofit sector; she is the author of numerous publications on these topics. Dr. Kuti is also the local associate for the Johns Hopkins Comparative Nonprofit Sector Project; the head of section for the Hungarian Central Statistics Office's Section on Voluntary Sector Statistics; and an Associate Professor in Economics at Budapest University of Economics.

Leilah Landim, Ph.D. is a Research Coordinator at the Institute for Religious Studies in Rio de Janeiro, Brazil. She is a professor at the Federal University of

Rio de Janeiro, as well as an Associate Researcher at the Johns Hopkins Comparative Nonprofit Sector Project. She has published work on NGOs and Third Sector issues.

Mark Lyons, Ph.D. is an Associate Professor in the School of Management at the University of Technology, Sydney, Australia, and Director of the University's Centre for Australian Community Organizations and Management (CACOM). He is also Director of the Australian Nonprofit Data Project, a collaborative project between the university and the Australian Bureau of Statistics which is undertaking the first comprehensive study of the Australian nonprofit sector.

José Luis Piñar Mañas, Doctor of Law is the Dean of Law Faculty of the San Pablo-CEU University of Madrid. He is a member of the Real Spanish Jurisprudence Academy and Legislation. Mr. Perez specializes in foundations, and has given conferences throughout the world. He has published numerous books, including *Foundations in Latin America: Legal Regime, Scientific Research in Spain,* and *Law of Foundations: Regulatory Development.*

Daniela Mesini is a junior researcher and member of the research group on nonprofit organizations at the Istituto per la Ricerca Sociale (IRS), Milan, Italy.

Erik Nerep, Ph.D., JD is a professor of law at the Stockholm School of Economics. He was formerly a practicing lawyer from 1982 to 1986.

Klaus Neuhoff, Ph.D. is the Director of the Institute Foundation & Common Wealth at the University of Witten/Herdecke. He has done research in the areas of charity and foundations, both nationally and internationally. Dr. Neuhoff has written more than 100 articles and books in the field.

Amara Pongsapich, Ph.D. is currently the Director of the Social Research Institute and a Political Science faculty member at Chulalongkorn University in Bangkok, Thailand, where she teaches and carries out research on involvement by government and nonprofit organizations in social development activities. Dr. Pongsapich has been closely linked with nonprofit organizations as a founding member of registered foundations and associations and is presently a board member of a few nonprofit organizations. She is actively involved in campaigning for changes in legislation and regulations to enable nonprofit sectors to function more effectively for the benefit of the disadvantaged groups.

Alicia Real Pérez, Doctor of Law, is a professor of civil law at the Complutense University of Madrid, Spain, and also in San José, Costa Rica. A member of the Real Spanish Jurisprudence Academy and Legislation, she specializes on foundations and the given numerous conferences on this topic in Spain, Portugal and Latin America. Her publications include *Qualitative Intangibility of the Legit, Usufruct of the Widower Spouse,* and *Civil Law Bibliography.* She has also contributed to *Foundations in Latin America: Legal Regime.*

Francesco Rigano is associate professor of public law in the Department of Political Science at Teramo University, Italy.

Richard B. Rosenthal is a South African attorney and specialist consultant to major development bodies, including the IDT and DBSA. He works with numerous NGOs and CBOs and other nonprofit organizations. Mr. Rosenthal has drafted electoral legislation, has provided advice on constitutional issues and the development of policy proposals for land reform and communal tenure.

Siddhartha Sen, Ph.D. is an associate professor in the Graduate Program in City and Regional Planning at Morgan State University in Baltimore, Maryland. He has written several articles and book chapters on the nonprofit sector in India.

Sven-Erik Sjöstrand, Ph.D. is currently the Matts Carlgren Professor of Management at the Stockholm School of Economics, where he has been chairman of the board of its Research Institute since 1995. He is also a member of the Board of the Stockholm School of Economics and of large Swedish multinational companies. He has published numerous books, including *Organizational Myths, Institutional Change: Theory and Empirical Findings, On Economic Institutions-Theory and Applications,* and *The Two Faces of Management.*

Geraint W. Thomas, D. Phil. (Oxon.), is a Senior lecturer in Law at Queen Mary and Westfield College, a University of London, and Barrister at Law of 10 Old Square, Lincoln's Inn, London, England.

Stefan Toepler, Ph.D., is a research associate at the Johns Hopkins University Institute for Policy Studies in Baltimore, MD.

Jeffrey A. Trexler, Ph.D. (Duke), JD (Yale) is an Associate at the law firm of Gardner, Carton and Douglas in Chicago, Illinois, where he concentrates his practice on tax-exempt organizations in U.S. and Russian law. He is a former law clerk of the Hon. Dorothy W. Nelson, U.S. Circuit Judge, Ninth Circuit Court of Appeals.

Wino Van Veen, Ph.D. is currently an associate law professor at the Vrije Universiteit in Amsterdam. He is also affiliated with the Center for Government, in nongovernmental relations. Dr. Van Veen has authored numerous publications in the areas of private law, law on associations and foundations, and the relationship between government and NGOs.

PREFACE

This book is, to a significant extent, the product of serendipity.

As part of the Johns Hopkins Comparative Nonprofit Sector Project, which is analyzing the scope, structure, scale, and role of the nonprofit sector in countries throughout the world, a series of "field guides" was commissioned on the legal treatment of nonprofit organizations in thirteen project countries. As it turned out, however, this process yielded far more material than could effectively be used in the country monographs that constituted the project's principal products. At this point, John Wiley & Sons, Inc. fortuitously intervened with an intriguing proposal: approached about publishing the country monographs, Wiley proposed instead to publish a separate *International Guide to Nonprofit Law* that would draw on our Legal Field Guides but cover other countries as well. The great challenge, then, was to find a way to convert the Field Guides prepared for our project into a series of coherent chapters for a legal guide, and to develop comparable materials on other countries as well. For this, the Charles Stewart Mott Foundation came to the rescue with support that allowed me to commission chapters on additional countries, and to retain assistance in converting all of the materials into a coherent and readable form.

The result, I believe, is a highly useful guide to the basic law of nonprofit organizations in close to two dozen countries around the world. Such a guide has become increasingly important as interest in philanthropy and the nonprofit sector has mushroomed around the world, and as the scope of cross-border philanthropy and support of nonprofit organizations has grown.

Every effort has been made to ensure that this is as reliable and authoritative a guide to the law governing this newly exploding field around the world as possible. Thus, well-known national legal experts were recruited to prepare the initial country submissions. These submissions were then subjected to a rigorous review to identify gaps in coverage or ambiguities in phrasing or meaning. The original country rapporteurs were then asked to review revised language, respond to queries, and provide any missing information. Finally, as a further quality control, the chapters were submitted to the local offices of Price Waterhouse accounting firm for review.

Despite this effort, anyone who has worked in a cross-national context will understand the great difficulties attending the kind of task that was attempted here, particularly given the complex legal questions that were at issue. In such a context, no account, and certainly no account operating within the space constraints of this one, can aspire to definitiveness. We make no pretense, therefore, to portraying this volume as a substitute for detailed scrutiny of actual national legal provisions. Rather, the volume should be viewed as a layman's guide to local law, an initial map of terrain that has remained a no-man's land far too long. My hope, therefore, is not that it will settle all the issues it addresses, but that it will make the field of international philanthropy and nonprofit action far more accessible and hospitable than it has been up to now. In the process, I hope it will serve as a useful sourcebook for those active in the field, allowing them to learn, at least in general terms, how other countries have handled some of the central legal issues they are confronting.

I am deeply indebted to the national legal experts whose work provided the basic input to the chapters in this book; to Marla Bobowick and Martha Cooley, the Wiley editors who, respectively, first conceived and encouraged this project and then saw it through to completion; to the Charles Stewart Mott Foundation and its program officer, Suzanne Feurt, for the financial support that allowed us to broaden the coverage and undertake the detailed editorial work that was necessary; to Richard Larkin and his colleagues at Price Waterhouse for helpful technical reviews of the country chapters; and to Stefan Toepler, who steadfastly and carefully attended to the painstaking task of reviewing the country drafts, spotting potential problems, and suggesting possible revisions.

None of these individuals or organizations bears responsibility, however, for the basic structure of the chapters, for the selection of key issues, or for any errors of fact or interpretation that may remain. That responsibility is mine alone.

LESTER M. SALAMON

Baltimore, Maryland
April 30, 1997

CONTENTS

CONTENTS

CONTENTS

CONTENTS

CONTENTS

CONTENTS

15   Japan   197

19 The Russian Federation 255

CONTENTS

CONTENTS

CHAPTER ONE

Introduction

Lester M. Salamon

A massive "associational revolution" is under way at the global level at the present time. In the developed countries of Western Europe, Asia, and North America, in the developing countries of Asia, Africa, and Latin America, and in the former Soviet bloc, people are forming self-governing, private organizations outside the formal apparatus of the state at rates that would have been unimaginable only decades ago.[1] The product of widespread pressures for popular participation and of declining faith in the capacities of government to solve the interrelated problems of social welfare, development, and the environment, this global upsurge of organized private activity has stimulated tremendous interest in the legal structures within which nonprofit organizations operate in different parts of the world. This is so for at least three reasons:

- In the first place, the legal treatment of nonprofit organizations in most countries of the world is at best highly ambiguous, and often quite hostile. Nonprofit activists, philanthropic leaders, and policy makers interested in expanding the role of nonprofit organizations in various countries are therefore eager to learn how other countries deal with some of the common issues involved in the operation of these organizations.
- In the second place, the rise of multinational enterprises and the overall globalization of social and economic life have increased the levels of cross-border funding of nonprofit activity. Corporations, foundations, governments, and international organizations such as the United Nations (UN) and the World Bank are increasingly involved in funding nongovernmental organizations in different countries. Understanding the legal position of these organizations and the tax treatment of contributions to them in different countries has thus become increasingly necessary to facilitate this cross-border activity.
- Finally, nonprofit organizations themselves have become increasingly international in their activities. Thousands of transnational nongovernmental organizations are now in existence organizing regional or global approaches to common problems or working with international agencies to alter national policies.[2] Such organizations are consequently in need of

---

[1] Lester M. Salamon, "The Rise of the Nonprofit Sector," 73 *Foreign Affairs*, No. 4, 109, July/Aug. 1994.
[2] K. Skjelsbaek, "The Growth of International Nongovernmental Organizations in the Twentieth Century," in R. Keohane and J. Nye (eds.), *Transnational Relations and World Politics* (Cambridge:

guidance about how to establish counterpart organizations in various locales or handle resource flows among affiliates located in different countries.

Beyond this, the sheer scale of the nonprofit sector makes better understanding of the laws surrounding its operations increasingly important. Although solid data on this question have long been lacking, recent research has now made clear that the private, nonprofit sector is a major economic force in a great number of countries. The first systematic study of the scope and structure of the nonprofit sector at the international level, for example, revealed that in seven major countries—the United States, the United Kingdom, France, Germany, Italy, Hungary, and Japan—nonprofit organizations employed the equivalent of 11.8 million full-time employees as of 1990.[3] This was six times larger than the number of workers employed in the largest private corporation in each of these countries taken together (e.g., General Motors in the United States, Fiat in Italy, Hitachi in Japan). In addition, the volunteer effort contributed to these organizations represents another 4.7 million full-time equivalent workers. Overall, close to 5% of all workers in these countries are employed in the private, nonprofit sector, and the sector accounts for over 12%, or one out of eight, workers in the service sector.

Despite the scale and importance of the nonprofit sector and the resulting growing interest in the law of nonprofit, or nongovernmental, organizations throughout the world, precious little is known about this topic in any systematic way. Indeed, even within individual countries the law of nonprofit organizations is often imperfectly specified and understood. Almost completely lacking are accounts that cover the law in a variety of countries, and particularly that do so in a fairly comprehensive way.

§ 1.1 PURPOSE AND SCOPE OF THIS BOOK

The purpose of this book is to remedy this significant gap in information. More specifically, this book reviews the legal treatment of nonprofit organizations in a broad cross-section of countries throughout the world.

(a) Countries Covered

Covered within this volume are three different types of countries:

- *Developed countries* in North America, Europe, and Asia, including the United States, Canada, the United Kingdom, Ireland, France, Germany, Italy, the Netherlands, Spain, Sweden, Japan, Australia, and Israel
- *Developing countries* in Asia, Africa, and Latin America, including Mexico, Brazil, South Africa, Egypt, Thailand, and India
- *Former Soviet bloc countries* in Central and Eastern Europe, including Hungary, Poland, and Russia

Harvard University Press, 1972); Jackie Smith, Ron Pagnucco, and Winnie Romeril, "Transnational Social Movement Organisations in the Global Arena," 5 *Voluntas*, 2, 121–154.
[3] Lester M. Salamon and Helmut K. Anheier, *The Emerging Nonprofit Sector: An Overview* (Manchester: Manchester University Press, 1996).

Not only do these countries differ in level of development and geographic location, they also differ in basic legal systems. Thus, the United States, the United Kingdom, and Canada historically have been considered "common law" countries, basing their legal development on judge-made law formulated over time through the accretion of legal decisions. By contrast, the continental European countries and Japan have been considered "civil law" countries, in which rights and obligations are spelled out in explicit legal codes.[4] Because, in the common law tradition, the right to associate and form nonprofit organizations is thought to be an inherent right regardless of the existence of explicit legal provisions, there is some reason to believe that common law countries will offer a more hospitable clime for the emergence of nonprofit organizations.[5] At the very least, inclusion of countries from both legal traditions ensures the broadest possible array of options for the legal treatment of nonprofit organizations.

(b) Types of Organizations Covered

Not only does this book cover a broad array of countries, it also covers a broad array of types of organizations. The concept of the nonprofit sector is, of course, an ambiguous one, so much so that there are doubts in many quarters about whether it constitutes a distinctive sector at all. One reflection of this is the profusion of terms used to depict this set of organizations even within particular language groups. In English, for example, what we here refer to as "nonprofit organizations" are sometimes referred to as "voluntary organizations," "charities," "associations," "tax-exempt organizations," and the "independent sector."[6] At the international level the terminological tangle is even more complex. And not just terminology is at issue. The differences in terminology reflect differences in basic concepts about what this set of organizations really includes. Thus, the French concept of *économie sociale* differs markedly from the German notion of *Verein* and the Japanese concept of *koeki hojin*.[7] In fact, the question of what kind of entities are included within this sector in the different countries is one of the central issues we will examine in this book.

Although there are important differences about what is included within the "nonprofit sector" from country to country, and about what to call the resulting complex of organizations, some common elements also seem to be present from place to place, and these elements can be used to define the broad contours of the set of organizations that is of interest to us. In particular, recent international research has identified five such common elements or critical features that use-

---

[4] Rene David and John E.C. Briley, *Major Legal Systems in the World Today: An Introduction to the Comparative Study of Law*, 3rd ed. (London: Stevens, 1990).

[5] This argument is developed more fully in Lester M. Salamon and Helmut K. Anheier, "Caring Society or Caring Sector: Discovering the Nonprofit Sector Cross-Nationally," in Paul Schervish and Virginia Hodgkinson (eds.), *The Future of Caring and Service to the Community* (San Francisco: Jossey-Bass, 1994).

[6] For a further elaboration of these terms, see Lester M. Salamon, *The Nonprofit Sector: A Primer* (New York: Foundation Center, 1992), pp. 4–5.

[7] For further elaboration of this point, see Lester M. Salamon and Helmut K. Anheier, "In Search of the Nonprofit Sector I: The Question of Definition," 3 *Voluntas*, 2, 1992, 125–161.

fully demarcate the boundaries of a "third sector" outside the market and the state.[8] Included within this third sector, therefore, are entities that are:

1. *Organized*, that is, institutionalized to some extent
2. *Private*, that is, institutionally separate from government, even if they receive governmental support
3. *Nonprofit-distributing*, that is, not returning any profits they may generate to their owners or directors
4. *Self-governing*, that is, controlled according to their own internal procedures and not operated from outside
5. *Voluntary*, that is, noncompulsory and involving some meaningful degree of voluntary participation

Rather than focus on only a subset of such entities, such as "foundations" or "associations," this book covers virtually all entities that share these five features. This includes the following:

- Associations
- Foundations
- Mutual-benefit organizations
- Service-providing agencies such as hospitals, universities, and day care centers
- Advocacy groups
- Grass-roots development agencies
- Self-help groups

About the only exclusion from our coverage here is religious congregations and their religious support organizations. This is so because ecclesiastical law is quite specific in many countries and covering it in this volume would lead us far astray.

Generally speaking, we will use the terms *nonprofit sector* or *nonprofit organization* to refer to these covered entities. "Nonprofit" is not, of course, an ideal term since it emphasizes what these organizations are *not* rather than what they are. However, it seems far more precise than most of the alternatives since it focuses on what seems to be the most common defining feature of these entities throughout the world—the prohibition on their distribution of profits to owners or shareholders. By contrast, such terms as *civil society* and *nongovernmental organization*, while popular, are far less precise. "Civil society" is often interpreted to include a far broader array of organizations than is defined by the five features noted above, such as the media. "Nongovernmental organization," by contrast, is a more limited term, often referring only to the subset of nonprofit organizations involved in development work. What is more, the term "nonprofit sector" is the one that has been adopted by the United Nations in its International System of National Accounts. Under the circumstances, it seemed most appropriate to utilize this term here.

---

[8] Lester M. Salamon and Helmut K. Anheier, Supra n. 7.

(c) Issues Covered

Finally, this volume does not restrict itself to a narrow set of issues surrounding these organizations, such as the tax treatment of cross-border contributions or the taxability of organizational earnings. Rather, we examine the full range of issues most central to the formation and operation of these organizations in each national setting. In particular, ten broad issues, embracing 17 sub-issues are the principal focus of our attention. Included here are the following:

1. *The legal context.* That is, the general legal framework within which the organizations operate.
2. *Organizational eligibility.* The definition of what constitutes a nonprofit organization and how an organization comes to be officially registered or classified as a nonprofit entity, including:
   - The question of permissible *types of nonprofit entities*
   - The question of the *purposes* or *activities* eligible for nonprofit status
   - Other requirements organizations must meet (e.g., membership requirements or minimum resource requirements)
   - Registration procedures
3. *Governance.* This refers to restrictions on the internal structure and operation of nonprofit organizations.
4. *Tax treatment.* This includes:
   - Tax treatment of organizations
   - Tax treatment of contributions to domestic organizations
   - Tax treatment of contributions to foreign organizations
5. *Personal benefit restrictions.* Included here are any legal limitations on the personal benefits that employees, board members, and others can receive from the organization.
6. *Obligations to the public.* This embraces disclosure and other obligations that nonprofit organizations have to the public.
7. *Business activity.* This covers any limitations on business income or business activity on the part of nonprofit organizations.
8. *Other funding restrictions.* Included here are limitations on fund-raising methods or costs.
9. *Political activity.* Any restrictions on nonprofit engagement in political activity are included here.
10. *Key outstanding issues.* Major impending legal developments that might affect the nonprofit sector in a country are covered here.

§ 1.2   INTERNATIONAL GUIDE TO NATIONAL LAW VS. INTERNATIONAL LAW OF NONPROFIT ORGANIZATIONS

Before turning to these central legal issues, it is important to note that while this book focuses on the law of nonprofit organizations in a number of countries, it is *not* primarily about the international law of nonprofit organizations. "International law" is the body of legal rules that apply between and among sovereign states. As it turns out, there is relatively little such law in the nonprofit field so that a book focused on this topic alone would be fairly short indeed. For those interested in this topic, however, Chapter 3 traces the limited development of cross-national law in this field. As will become clear, this body of international law largely points to the importance of the law of the home jurisdiction of a non-profit organization. This underscores again the importance of clarifying what such national laws provide, which is the focus of the rest of this book.

§ 1.3 OVERVIEW

To set this discussion in context, Chapter 2 describes in more detail the ten broad issues that form the principal focus of our analysis. The intent of this chapter is not to offer a summary of national practice or to suggest an ideal way to address the particular issues raised. Rather, the intent is to explicate the issues, to identify what each involves and why it is important. The purpose, in other words, is to identify systematically the *questions* that nonprofit law must address in any country rather than the *answers* that should be, or have been, provided. Chapter 3, as noted, then offers a brief side-trip into the limited world of international law pertaining to the nonprofit sector.

With this as backdrop, the subsequent chapters then review how the ten broad issues we have identified are addressed in each of the 22 countries we cover. Much of the material in these chapters is drawn from legal field guides prepared by legal experts in the respective countries for use in the Johns Hopkins Comparative Nonprofit Sector Project. For countries not covered by this project, original chapters were prepared by local legal experts specifically for this volume. Most chapters were then reviewed by a team of accounting and legal experts assembled by Price-Waterhouse. A full list of those who have contributed to this elaborate process is provided in the Contributors' page at the front of this book, and the contributors to each chapter are noted as well in the respective chapters. For ease of presentation, each chapter is structured similarly to address each of the ten major topics in turn.

Finally, two appendices offer additional relevant material. Appendix A reprints *Toward a Vital Voluntary Sector: An International Statement of Principles* formulated by an international network of experts on the nonprofit sector assembled through the Johns Hopkins University International Fellows in Philanthropy Program. This statement represents the closest thing in existence to an agreed-upon set of guidelines both for government policies toward the nonprofit sector, and for the internal operations of nonprofit organizations. Appendix B then provides a summary of the Discussion Draft of a *Handbook on Good Practices for Laws Relating to NGOs* produced by the World Bank.

§ 1.4 CONCLUSION

Nonprofit organizations have grown increasingly important to the solution of societal problems and the promotion of democratic values throughout the world in recent years. What is more, it is increasingly clear that this sector has also become a major economic force with sizable expenditures and immense levels of paid and volunteer employment.

Despite their importance, however, nonprofit organizations remain largely invisible in both scholarly analysis and public debate, with the result that we know precious little about them in most places. This is certainly true in the field of law, where systematic accounts of the treatment of nonprofit organizations are largely lacking. The result has been to impede the development of the sector and the expansion of international support for it. Under the circumstances, clarifying the law of nonprofit organizations has become an urgent practical necessity.

Although no brief account of the sort offered here can do justice to the complexity of legal treatment of nonprofit organizations in any particular country, it is nevertheless my hope that this book will provide a basic introduction to national treatments for those beginning to reconnoiter the terrain. While hardly specifying every bump and turn in the road, the aerial map offered here can at least help orient new travelers to the basic lay of the land and therefore help them efficiently identify the more detailed charting that they will likely need to undertake.

CHAPTER TWO

Nonprofit Law: Ten Issues in Search of Resolution

Lester M. Salamon and Susan L. Q. Flaherty

As noted in Chapter 1, the laws and regulations governing nonprofit organizations in different countries can usefully be assessed in terms of how they address ten basic issues. To be sure, these are not the only issues relevant to nonprofit law. What is more, countries can address these issues in different ways or choose not to address them at all. But these issues are certainly among the most fundamental in the field, and they provide a useful framework in terms of which the separate national treatments of nonprofit organizations can fruitfully be compared. Specifically, these ten issues are as follows:

1. The overall legal context, including protections for the right to associate
2. Eligibility for nonprofit status
3. Internal governance requirements
4. Tax treatment of the organizations and of contributions to them
5. Personal benefit restrictions
6. Organizational obligations to the public, such as reporting and other requirements
7. Permissible business activities
8. Other funding restrictions
9. Permissible political activity
10. Key outstanding issues affecting the sector

The purpose of this chapter is to examine these issues more closely, to identify what they are, and why they are important. The focus, in other words, is on the *questions* that must be addressed in laws related to nonprofit organizations rather than on the *answers* different countries provide to these questions. No attempt is made here, therefore, to summarize the rich texture of national treatments recounted in the subsequent chapters. Nor is there any attempt to identify an "ideal" legal treatment of nonprofit organizations. Readers interested in advice on how at least some of these issues might be handled are referred to Appendices A and B, which present two recent efforts to develop such advice. Our purpose here, therefore, is the more limited one of making clear what the central issues are that must be resolved in developing a body of law about nonprofit organizations and what considerations each one entails.[1]

§ 2.1   LEGAL CONTEXT

(a) Rule of Law; Basic Rights

A first basic issue relating to the legal treatment of nonprofit organizations in a country involves not nonprofit law per se, but the broader legal context within which the legal treatment of nonprofit organizations is rooted. Of central concern here is the extent to which the rule of law is firmly established within a legal system. Also crucial is the extent to which there are guarantees of basic rights of citizens to speak freely, to associate or assemble for nonviolent purposes, to form associations, and to hold private property. These are fundamental to creating a legal space within which nonprofit organizations can function, a space that is clearly outside of the state and protected from arbitrary state action.

An important guarantor of such a space is the existence of an independent judiciary able to enforce adherence to law even on the part of the state. Where such a tradition is firmly established, the possibilities for an effectively functioning nonprofit sector are much greater.

(b) Common Law vs. Civil Law

Such broad legal protections can either be explicitly identified in constitutions and/or codes or embedded in legal traditions built up over centuries through case law. Generally speaking, the former is more likely in countries utilizing civil law systems and the latter in common law countries, where legal traditions have evolved through centuries of judicial interpretation.

Which of these two basic types of legal systems is most congenial to the establishment of a firm right to associate is difficult to determine a priori. In truth, both have advantages and disadvantages. The advantage of the common law system is that the right to associate is typically assumed to exist even in the absence of positive law explicitly permitting it. Because of this, common law countries are often considered more hospitable to the existence of nonprofit organizations.[2] At

---

[1] As noted in Chapter 1, we use the term "nonprofit organization" as shorthand to refer to a broad array of entities that meet five crucial requirements: they are organized, they are not part of the state structure; they do not distribute profits to their members, they are self-governing, and they involve some meaningful voluntary input. The exact specification of what constitutes a "nonprofit organization" as the term is used here, varies considerably from country to country, as the discussion throughout this book will show. What is more, the terminology used to depict the resulting organizations also varies widely. For our purposes here, however, we follow the terminology adopted by the UN System of National Accounts, which refers to "nonprofit organizations," and rely on the definition above merely to establish the general domain in which we are interested, recognizing that the precise specification of this domain is one of the central issues that has to be resolved in this field.

[2] Lester M. Salamon and Helmut K. Anheier, "Caring Society or Caring Sector: Discovering the Nonprofit Sector Cross-Nationally," in Paul Schervish and Virginia Hodgkinson (eds.), *The Future of Caring and Service to the Community* (San Francisco: Jossey-Bass, 1994).

the same time, however, the exact character of these protections may be more ambiguous in such systems. For example, the United States, traditionally considered a common law country, has long recognized the importance of protecting the right of citizens to associate freely in order to check undue concentrations of power and protect liberty.[3] Yet, this widely recognized right of association is nowhere explicitly mentioned in the U.S. Constitution or its amendments. Rather, it is a byproduct of other rights that are constitutionally rooted. One of the roots is the so-called "freedom of intimate association," which is derived from the right of personal liberty.[4] A second is the so-called "freedom of expressive association," which is derived from the right of free speech provided by the First Amendment to the U.S. Constitution.[5] Pursuant to this right of freedom of expressive association, individuals may band together, without government interference, to advance charitable, scientific, educational, and other ends short of violent overthrow of the government.[6] In other words, an inherent right to associate is assumed to exist in the United States regardless of whether specific legal provisions exist for it, but the exact scope and contours of this right are not spelled out very clearly in any constitution or code, but rather must be found scattered throughout numerous judicial opinions delivered over two centuries.

Traditionally, the situation in civil law countries is just the obverse. In such countries, no such inherent right to associate is acknowledged. Rather, such rights exist only to the extent that they are explicitly provided for in basic laws. As such, they can be hedged and conditioned. At the same time, however, once explicitly spelled out, they can be more precisely protected and defended.[7]

---

[3] Jerome A. Barron and C. Thomas Dienes, *Constitutional Law*, (St. Paul: West Publishing, 1986), pp. 242–262.

[4] For example, the U.S. Supreme Court has stated:

> It is beyond debate that freedom to engage in association for the advancement of beliefs and ideas is an inseparable aspect of the "liberty" assured by the Due Process Clause of the Fourteenth Amendment, which embraces freedom of speech.

See *National Association for the Advancement of Colored People v. Alabama*, 347 U.S. 449 (1958); see also *N.A.A.C.P. v. Button*, 371 U.S. 415 (1963). The "due process clause" of the fourteenth amendment states, ". . . nor shall any State deprive any person of life, liberty, or property, without due process of law. . . ."

[5] The First Amendment to the U.S. Constitution provides:

> Congress shall make no law respecting an establishment of religion, or prohibiting the free exercise thereof; or abridging the freedom of speech or of the press, or the right of the people peaceably to assemble, and to petition the Government for a redress of grievances.

[6] Bruce R. Hopkins, *The Law of Tax Exempt Organizations*, 6th ed. (New York: John Wiley & Sons, 1992), at § 1.5.

[7] In practice, the distinctions between systems of civil law and common law have narrowed considerably in recent years. Even countries traditionally thought of as common law countries, such as the United States, are no longer clearly so, since today large parts of U.S. law are also contained in codes. Further, in some civil law countries, parts of the law have been developed by courts without having been reduced to codes, and some civil law code provisions have been dominated by judicial interpretation. Today, the most significant difference between the two systems is characterized largely by modes of procedure and to some extent by the types of personnel by whom justice is administered. See generally, Rene David and John E.C. Brierley, *Major Legal Systems in the World Today: An Introduction to the Comparative Study of Law*, 3rd ed. (London: Stevens, 1990).

(c) One Law or Many

Beyond these broad legal structural issues, there is a basic question of whether the laws regulating nonprofit organizations will be in one code or in one or more codes (e.g., one code for creating nonprofit entities of various types, another code for beneficial tax status for nonprofits, etc.). Basic decisions must also be made about whether to embody the legal provisions relating to nonprofit organizations in a single body of law that relates more or less generally to the entire of class of such organizations or to provide special legal provisions for the many different types of entities that comprise this class. An example of the latter approach is that found in Japan, which, for the most part, separately authorizes the existence of nonprofit-type institutions in each of a variety of different fields (e.g., health, social services, education, research), but provides only limited general rights to form such organizations outside these fields. An example of a more integrated body of law is that afforded by France, where the Law of July 1, 1901 acknowledged a general right to form associations and mutual benefit organizations for a wide variety of purposes. While either approach can accomplish the same purpose, it is probably the case that comprehensive laws are more likely to provide the firmest and broadest protection for the right to associate and form nonprofit organizations. At the same time, such laws can also more efficiently limit the rights of nonprofit organizations. A set of general provisions supplemented by more specific guarantees to form nonprofit organizations for particular purposes may therefore be desirable in many circumstances.

(d) National vs. Local Approaches

Closely related to the question of whether nonprofit laws are embodied in one comprehensive code or in particular codes covering particular fields is the question of whether such laws are national in scope or vary by subdivisions. The answer to this question will likely be determined by the general legal and political structure of a country. In the United States, for example, nonprofit organizations are governed by both state and national laws—the former relating to the basic formation of nonprofit entities and the local taxation of them, and the latter to the national tax treatment of these entities. In France, by contrast, the legal treatment of nonprofit-type organizations is much more fully nationalized.

§ 2.2   ORGANIZATIONAL ELIGIBILITY

Regardless of whether a country is a civil law or common law country, or whether nonprofit organizations are covered by a single comprehensive law or a variety of separate laws, specific provisions must be made to recognize such organizations as legal or juridical "persons." This is so for the obvious reason that such organizations are typically afforded certain special privileges (and certain corresponding obligations), which makes it necessary or desirable for them to be recognized in law. It consequently becomes necessary to define the features that qualify organizations for such legal recognition. For the sake of convenience, we will refer to this as the issue of "organizational eligibility."

The issue of organizational eligibility, in turn, involves a number of sub-issues. Four such subissues, in particular, can be distinguished:

(a) The specification of the *types of entities* that can be recognized as nonprofit organizations
(b) The *types of purposes* for which nonprofit status is considered appropriate
(c) Any *other requirements* that must be met for an organization to be considered a nonprofit organization (e.g., membership requirements or capital asset requirements)
(d) The actual *registration procedures* that organizations must follow to be recognized officially as nonprofit organizations

(a) Eligible Entities

To be recognized in law, that is, to enjoy juridical personality with its accompanying rights and obligations, nonprofit organizations must first of all be "organizations." That is, they must have some institutional reality to them as reflected in regularized patterns of behavior, internal procedures, and presumably, governing officers. As the Internal Revenue Service has put it in the United States, "formless aggregations of individuals" cannot qualify for nonprofit status.[8]

In other words, some act must be undertaken that transforms the group of individuals into a formally constituted, legal or juridical person, distinct from those individuals.

However, the exact type of entity and the means of formally creating it can vary widely. For example, in the United States, the types of entities that may constitute nonprofit entities include corporations, unincorporated associations, and trusts. In Germany, foundations and public law corporations are included.

Nonprofit corporations are entities normally granted formal legal person status by some governmental body. The great advantage of corporations is that their liabilities can be limited to assets held in the name of the corporation, thereby protecting the assets of those directors or officers who act on behalf of the corporation from claims against the corporation.

An *unincorporated association* is essentially a group of people bound together for common purposes that are not profit-distributing in character. In some jurisdictions, where such a body complies with certain legal formalities, it may obtain juridical person status and will be able to enjoy certain rights of juridical persons, such as the right to sue and hold property.

Typically, it is not necessary to have government approval to create an unincorporated association. In the United States, for example, the group of persons merely writes a constitution or articles of association stating the name of the association, purposes, members of the initial governing body, whether the association will have members, what will happen to assets on dissolution, and certain other basic formalities, much the same as those contained in legal articles of incorporation. For such unincorporated associations, however, liability may not be limited to the assets of the association, and thus there would be little or no protection afforded to members of the association. Partly because of the unlimited liability

---

[8] *U.S. Internal Revenue Service Exempt Organization Handbook* (IRM 7751) §§ 315.1, 315.2(3), 315, 4(2).

feature of associations, some countries have enacted laws granting "quasi-corporate" status to certain types of unincorporated associations. In the United Kingdom, for example, "friendly societies" organized to provide for the relief or maintenance of members or their families during illness, old age, and so on, have been granted some of the legal prerogatives of corporations while still remaining unincorporated entities.

Another possible type of nonprofit entity is the *mutual society.* A mutual society is a type of association in which members join together to help themselves, for example, to advance the interests of a profession. In some countries, this class of associations is given special legal status. This is so, for example, in France, where "mutuals" are one of four types of nonprofit entities that are juridical persons, the other types being associations, cooperatives, and foundations.

In the United States and the United Kingdom, another type of nonprofit entity may be a *trust,* though not all trusts are nonprofit. A trust differs from an association in that it is less an aggregation of individuals than an aggregation of resources put into the hands of an individual or corporate trustee(s) to manage in pursuit of some specific purpose defined by the donor. The trust may be nonprofit where the purpose of the trust is a nonprofit purpose or the class of beneficiaries constitute a charitable class. Like the unincorporated association, in some jurisdictions a trust can obtain legal personality without resort to government, just by complying with certain legal formalities, but in other jurisdictions, a trust has no juridical personality, and its trustees remain legally at risk.

In many civil law jurisdictions, an entity known as a *foundation* operates in a manner similar to the trust. Like the trust, it has an endowment of its own, managed by directors to serve the common welfare. In some jurisdictions, a foundation may not be set up without a previous authorization of some governmental authority.

In addition to corporations, unincorporated associations, mutual societies, foundations, and trusts, nonprofit organizations can also take a variety of other legal forms. Civil law countries often distinguish, for example, between *public law corporations* and *private law corporations*—the former applying to public sector, and the latter to private, entities. Because nonprofit organizations are typically private in form but public in purpose, they can often be found in both forms in civil law countries. Thus, some private nonprofit organizations in Germany are registered under public law as public law corporations, while others are registered under private law as private law corporations.

In countries where even these general legal provisions for nonprofit organizations do not exist, things can often be even more complex. This is the case in Japan, for example, where separate laws exist for each major type of nonprofit organization—medical corporations (*iryo hojin*), educational corporations (*zaidan hojin*), or social welfare corporations (*shakaifukushi hojin*).[9]

How many different types of entities to specify as eligible for nonprofit status is difficult to determine in the abstract, of course. The more different types are

---

[9] For information on these various types of Japanese nonprofit corporations, see Lester M. Salamon and Helmut K. Anheier, *The Emerging Nonprofit Sector: An Overview* (Manchester: Manchester University Press, 1996), pp. 49–53.

permitted, the easier it is to calibrate the privileges or requirements each can enjoy or endure.

Until 1969, for example, U.S. tax law made no distinction between what have come to be known as "foundations"—nonprofit entities having endowments controlled by the family or corporation that originally contributed the endowment—and all other nonprofit charitable entities. Because of a variety of perceived abuses among private foundations, however, the U.S. Congress established a separate definition of foundations and subjected them to payout and excise tax requirements, as well as additional regulations and reporting requirements in order to ensure that their funds were indeed devoted to charitable, rather than private, purposes.

While allowing a multitude of types of entities to qualify for nonprofit status can make it easier to calibrate requirements and privileges, it can also vastly complicate the job of forming such organizations. Since this sector is preeminently designed to afford citizens an easy mechanism through which to join together to meet common goals, such complexity can easily become self-defeating. This argues for some middle course between overly detailed and unduly one-dimensional specification of the legal entities eligible for nonprofit status.

(b) Eligible Purposes

Closely related to the type of entity that is eligible for nonprofit status is the question of the type of purpose that the entity pursues and the disposition of any profit that it generates. As noted above, not all corporations are nonprofit organizations. What differentiates the nonprofit corporation from other corporations is the purpose that it pursues. More specifically, three types of purposes are commonly associated with nonprofit status. One of these is associated negatively and the other two positively.

In the first place, organizations pursuing primarily *commercial purposes* are typically not considered eligible for nonprofit status. The form that this prohibition takes can vary widely, however. On the one hand, organizations that engage in any commercial activity, including the collection of fees for their own services, can be considered "commercial" and therefore ineligible for nonprofit status. On the other hand, organizations can actively engage in business activities and still qualify as nonprofit organizations so long as the profits thus earned are used wholly to support a broader "public" purpose and are not distributed to the directors, officers, or members. There are thus "maximum" and "minimum" tests of this noncommercial purpose criterion. At a minimum, however, organizations that earn profits and distribute them to their directors or officers are normally considered outside the nonprofit sector.

Beyond this negative requirement that organizations can qualify for nonprofit status only if they are not involved at all, or primarily, in commercial purposes, a more demanding test often provided in law concerns the positive purposes that these organizations serve. Two broad types of purposes are common here.

The less demanding of the two is *mutual benefit*. Under the mutual benefit test, an organization can qualify for nonprofit status if it works to the benefit of the members of the organization. Such a purpose would embrace professional societies, unions, business interest groups, cooperatives, "friendly societies," social and sports clubs, and related organizations.

A more demanding test is the criterion of *public benefit*. Under this test, an organization can be considered nonprofit only if it benefits the whole community or an appreciable section of it. What this means in practice, however, is often difficult to specify. The definition of what constitutes a "public benefit" is therefore often left to the accumulation of case law or the evolving judgment of legislative bodies. Some guidance on the meaning of this test is available, however, in the common law notion of "charity" as developed in England.

According to English law, a purpose is considered "charitable" if it falls "within the spirit and intendment" of the preamble to the Charitable Uses Act of 1601.[10] This preamble contained a catalogue of charitable purposes that included:

> ... Relief of aged, impotent and poor People, maintenance of sick and maimed soldiers and mariners, schools of learning, free schools, and scholars in universities, repair of bridges, ports, havens, churches, seabanks and highways, education and preferment of orphans, relief, stock, or maintenance for house of correction, marriages of poor maids, aid or ease of any poor inhabitants ... setting out of soldiers and other taxes. ...

More generally, this list of charitable purposes, plus others added in subsequent case law, were summarized in a famous decision in 1891[11] under four broad headings: *first*, relief of poverty; *second*, advancement of education; *third*, advancement of religion; and *fourth*, "other purposes beneficial to the community," which includes a broad array of activities such as assistance to the disadvantaged, relief of the sick, preservation of culture or the natural environment, and protection of the welfare of animals. This English concept of "charity" so defined and elaborated has become a touchstone for the definition of "public purposes" in many parts of the world. The U.S. tax code, for example, uses the term "charitable purposes" as one of the defining features of the most important class of U.S. tax-exempt organizations, the so-called IRC 501(c)(3) organizations.[12]

The three broad classes of nonprofit purposes identified here—noncommercial, mutual benefit, and public benefit—potentially identify three broad classes of nonprofit organizations. These broad classes can in turn be accorded different treatment in tax and other laws or be subjected to different types of requirements. In the United States, for example, organizations that meet either the mutual benefit or public benefit test are eligible for exemption from corpo-

---

[10] See 43 Eliz. c. 4 (1601). This was repealed by the Charities Act of 1960, § 5.

[11] *Commissioners for the Special Purposes of the Income Tax v. Pemsel*, [1891], A.C. 531 (H.L.).

[12] U.S. Internal Revenue Code (IRC) § 501(a) provides for exemption from U.S. income taxation for organizations described in Code § 501(c)(3), which embodies certain restrictions:

> (3) [organizations] organized and operated exclusively for religious, charitable, scientific ... or educational purposes ... no part of the net earnings of which inures to the benefit of any private shareholder or individual, no substantial part of the activities of which is carrying on propaganda, or otherwise attempting, to influence legislation ... and which does not participate in, or intervene in ... any political campaign on behalf of (or in opposition to) any candidate for public office.

rate income tax and from property taxes in most states. However, only those meeting the public benefit test are eligible to receive tax-deductible gifts from the public.

Whether, and how fully, a country embodies these three purposes in its own legal structure can vary greatly, of course, depending on local circumstances and traditions. So, too, can the way in which the standard is applied. Thus, an organization can be considered nonprofit if just some or most of its activities are for "public benefit," or it may be necessary to show that it operates *exclusively* for "public benefit."

(c) Other Requirements

In addition to restricting nonprofit status to entities pursuing particular kinds of purposes, laws can also stipulate other requirements that entities must meet before they are granted nonprofit status. Two of the most common of these are *capital requirements* and *membership requirements*.

Capital requirements apply most commonly to trusts or foundations, which can be required to have a minimum level of resources in order to qualify for non-profit or foundation status. In addition, in the United States for example, while a foundation is not required to meet any minimum paid-in capital requirement, it may be required to pay out for nonprofit purposes an amount equal to a stated percentage of its assets, whatever they may be. The rationale for such provisions may be to limit the foundation mechanism to organizations that really have a meaningful level of resources to distribute on behalf of their intended beneficiaries, and to make certain that foundations actually distribute resources for public purposes. Otherwise, there is the risk that individuals will abuse the foundation form to gain the tax advantage it sometimes affords while essentially operating a private business rather than a true nonprofit.

Membership requirements perform a similar function with respect to associations, which can be required to have a minimum number of members in order to qualify for nonprofit status. Here, again, the intent is to reduce the chances that associations will function as mere "shells" or fronts for business organizations, benefiting from the tax and other legal privileges accorded nonprofit organizations without actually serving a constituency or membership of interested people.

Beyond these capital and membership requirements, nonprofit organizations can also be subjected to other requirements as a condition of recognition of nonprofit or beneficial tax status, or even of juridical personality. In Japan, for example, the responsible ministry in each field must explicitly give its approval for the formation of each nonprofit organization, certifying that the organization will meet a need that the ministry feels a nonprofit organization can appropriately address.[13] These latter requirements can, of course, have a chilling effect on the growth of nonprofit organizations in a country.

---

[13] Takayonhi Amenomori, "Defining the Nonprofit Sector: Japan," in Lester M. Salamon and Helmut K. Anheier (eds.), *Defining the Nonprofit Sector: A Cross-National Analysis* (Manchester, U.K.: Manchester University Press, 1997), pp. 195–206.

(d) Registration Procedures

Whatever the permissible legal forms, purposes, or other requirements that nonprofit organizations must possess, there remains the separate issue of how an organization's compliance with these requirements is verified.

(i) *Juridical Person vs. Beneficial Tax Status.*   The first thing to note about such compliance procedures is that they can apply at either, or both, of two separate stages in the process of identifying a nonprofit entity: first, at the point where juridical person status is established; and second, at the point where recognition of beneficial tax status of various kinds is established. As discussed above, juridical person status of a nonprofit entity in some instances requires no government approval, and in such cases, it is only with respect to beneficial tax status that government approval may be required. In other instances, however, recognition of juridical personality and beneficial tax status are combined. As will be discussed below, in either instance, certain documents may have to be prepared in prescribed form, forms completed, or fees paid.

(ii) *Exception Basis vs. Registration Basis.*   Regardless of whether eligibility requirements are imposed at the stage at which an entity acquires juridical person status, or at the stage at which it secures beneficial tax status, two broad approaches are available for ensuring compliance with these requirements. The first might be termed the "exception basis." Under this system, organizations that fit the requirements of the law are assumed to be valid nonprofit organizations unless challenged through established legal procedures. Such challenges can be entered by tax authorities, specially constituted legal entities such as the U.K. Charity Commissioners, or an Attorney General at the state level in the United States who is empowered to protect the public against falsely operating nonprofit organizations.

The alternative is the "registration basis." Here, all organizations seeking to operate as nonprofit organizations must register with a governmental authority and satisfy this authority that they comply with the requirements for nonprofit status.

Generally speaking, the exception basis has historically been most widespread in common law countries, where the right to form nonprofit organizations is presumed to predate any legislative enactment establishing such a right or governing its exercise. Organizations therefore may be free to operate as nonprofit organizations without explicitly registering with any governmental authority, in some instances even including beneficial tax status and other privileges. In civil law countries, by contrast, no such inherent right is assumed, making it far more essential for organizations to secure explicit recognition as nonprofit entities in order to function in this capacity.

Although common law countries have historically relied much more heavily on the exception basis in practice, the registration basis has come to be increasingly important in such countries as well. One reason for this is that the tax and other benefits available to nonprofit organizations have grown increasingly sizable, making it increasingly important for organizations to be certain of their eligibility for such benefits. Registration is one way to verify that eligibility. Thus, in the United States, nonprofit organizations having more than $5,000 aggregate revenues each year wishing to attract tax deductible contributions and to be attractive donees for private foundation grants find it desirable to seek recognition from the Internal Revenue Service within 27 months of formation. If recognition of tax exemption is not applied for within 27 months of creation, the organization may experience regular corporate or trust tax liability for the period from formation until the IRS recognizes exemption, and donors cannot deduct contributions during this period. While not required to seek such status, therefore, increasing numbers of organizations choose to do so. A similar situation exists in the United Kingdom, where associations seeking to benefit from tax privileges on donations find it in their interest to register as charities with the Charity Commissioners. Thus, the shape and character of registration procedures has become increasingly important even in common law countries.

(iii) Degree of Discretion. A variety of considerations must be taken into account in the design of such procedures. Perhaps the most important of these is the degree of discretion to vest in the authorities operating the registration process. At one extreme are systems that allow nonprofit organizations to self-define their purposes and vest in registering authorities only the discretion to verify that the claimed purposes are consistent with those stipulated in law or legal tradition and that the organization complies with minimum requirements as to legal form (e.g., that it has bylaws, an address, and designated officers). At the opposite extreme are systems that vest in registering authorities the power to determine whether a particular organization is needed in a particular field, regardless of whether its purposes are consistent with those stipulated in law.

(iv) Locus of Registration Authority. Closely related to the degree of discretion left to registration authorities is the locus of this authority. Several options are available here as well. Thus, registration authority can be vested in courts or in executive agencies. What is more, these can operate at the national or local level. If registration authority is vested in executive agencies, it can be vested either in authorities that specialize in overseeing nonprofit organizations, such as the Charity Commissioners in the United Kingdom, or in authorities that have other functions as well. So far as other authorities are concerned, these can either be tax authorities or specialized ministries with responsibility over particular functions (e.g., health, education, research).

The advantages and disadvantages of these various routes are difficult to specify in the abstract. As a general rule, however, court-based systems may be the most open, but they raise potential problems with regard to appeals since adverse judgments would normally be appealed to the courts. Among administrative systems, those that vest registration power in tax authorities seem likely to be most restrictive since tax authorities are likely to view nonprofit organizations as drains on the tax revenues that such authorities are responsible for raising. Similarly, functional ministries may be too jealous of their prerogatives to support the widespread emergence of nonprofit organizations in their spheres. That, at any rate, has been the experience in Japan, where such authorities hold a powerful strangle-hold on the registration of nonprofit organizations, frequently driving persons motivated by nonprofit purposes to operate completely outside the law, without benefit of registration, government funding, or beneficial tax status, and therefore unregulated and subject to abuse. A separate nonprofit registration authority may therefore be the most promising option and the easiest for nonprofits to use.

(v) Burdensomeness.   Another crucial dimension of the registration procedures for nonprofits concerns the degree of burdensomeness of the process. Included here is the extent of information required of the applying organization, the nature of the verification that must be provided, and the length of time involved. This is affected as well by the basic structure of the process. In practice, registration can entail one integrated process, or it can often entail several different steps, each involving a different authority. In the United States, for example, organizations must generally register at the state level to create a legal entity such as a nonprofit corporation, then go to the federal level for recognition of beneficial tax status, then return to the state level to a different agency for state and local beneficial tax status, and finally apply to yet a different state agency to register for charitable solicitation purposes. While none of these steps in and of itself is unduly burdensome, the combination can create a significant obstacle to the formation of voluntary grass-roots organizations.

(vi) Duration.   Closely related to the question of how long it takes to become registered for juridical person status, beneficial tax status, or both is the question of how long an organization remains registered. At issue here is whether registration should be granted permanently or for a limited period, with the right to renew. The virtue of the latter is that it provides a regular check on the compliance of organizations with their originally stated mission. The drawback is that it can give governmental authorities the opportunity to exercise inappropriate political control over organizations.

Quite apart from the question of whether government might terminate the eligibility of an organization as a nonprofit entity for legal person status or beneficial tax status is the question of the procedures for voluntary dissolution of an organization. What is important here is the specification of who has the right to terminate an organization's existence or beneficial tax status and by what legal acts and what will become of any organizational property. We return to these topics in Section 2.3 when we discuss organizational governance.

(vii) Appeal Procedures.   Finally, whatever the registration procedures in effect, attention must also be given to the question of how to handle appeals from adverse judgments by the registration authorities. This can be handled administratively, of course, but ultimate appeal to the courts is also an important option.

§ 2.3   INTERNAL GOVERNANCE

The issue of organizational registration and eligibility for juridical status is, in turn, closely related to a third crucial issue, that of *internal governance*. To be sure, a strong case can be made that matters of internal governance should be left wholly to nonprofit organizations themselves, with no interference from the state. After all, one of the defining features of these organizations is their "self-governing" character, their ability to control their own internal operations. There are, nevertheless, compelling reasons for establishing at least certain broad parameters of internal governance in law.

The first of these derives simply from the status nonprofit organizations acquire as legally constituted entities, as "legal persons" in the meaning of the law. In granting such status to any organization, the state has a right to insist that the resulting "person" make clear who can rightfully act in its name. As a consequence, legal codes typically contain provisions requiring specification of certain features of governance structure as a condition of creating any legal entity.

Such provisions are even more important for nonprofit organizations, however, for a second reason—their public character and the tax and other privileges they often enjoy as a consequence. As the private Commission on Private Philanthropy and Public Needs in the United States put it in the early 1970s, the special status of nonprofits under law, particularly their beneficial tax status and use of government funds, entails "an obligation to openness and accountability to the public for actions and expenditures."[14] This, in turn, requires internal governance arrangements that are at least clear and open.

Finally, the "voluntary" character of these organizations also has implications for internal governance structure. To preserve their voluntary character, nonprofit organizations must have internal governance procedures that provide meaningful opportunities for participation by members in the organization's operations.

In framing laws on the internal governance of nonprofit organizations, therefore, policy makers must balance two competing values: first, the value of autonomy and noninterference by the state in the internal affairs of the organization; and second, the need for these organizations to have understandable decision-making structures and to be publicly accountable.

(a) Laws vs. Governing Documents

One way to achieve this balance is to limit the statutory provisions governing the internal structure of nonprofit organizations to broad general requirements (e.g., the need to specify the locus of ultimate authority in the organization, to identify the role of directors and officers, and to establish operating procedures); and then leave it to the organizations to explain in a set of governing documents, or "bylaws," how it proposes to meet these broad requirements. The bylaws can then be judged in terms of their compliance with the broad requirements of the law while leaving considerable flexibility for organizations to shape their internal management in a way that makes sense in terms of their purpose and style. Thus, for example, laws may enumerate a range of possibilities for types of governing bodies of organizations or the locus of decision-making authority. The bylaws can then specify which is chosen in a particular case.

---

[14] Commission on Private Philanthropy and Public Needs, *Report of the Commission on Private Philanthropy and Public Needs: Giving in America—Toward a Stronger Voluntary Sector* [Filer Commission Report] (Washington: Commission on Private Philanthropy and Public Needs, 1975), pp. 21–26.

(b) Key Issues

Whether stipulated in laws, or left to governing documents, however, certain key issues must typically be settled at the time an organization is legally constituted. Four of these issues are particularly important:

(i) The locus of ultimate authority in the organization
(ii) The size, terms of office, and role of the governing board
(iii) The officers of the organization
(iv) The decision-making procedures the organization will use

(i) The Locus of Authority: Membership vs. Board-Managed Organizations. Perhaps the most basic legal issue concerning the internal management of non-profit organizations concerns the ultimate locus of decision-making power. As noted above, laws will typically require that such authority be clearly and unequivocally fixed. Two broad options are available in the case of nonprofit organizations, however, depending on whether the organization is membership based or not.

1. *Membership Organizations.*   In the case of *membership organizations*, ultimate authority rests with the "membership" of the organization. How the membership exercises this authority can vary significantly, however. For organizations with large numbers of members, for example, representative assemblies of members may exercise authority. In such cases, bylaws would have to spell out how the representatives are to be selected, what the attendance must be in order to constitute a "quorum" able to act on behalf of the organization, and whether a simple majority or some type of super majority is required to act on particular types of resolutions (e.g., a requirement for a three-fifths majority to change the organization's bylaws). Alternatively, meetings of the entire membership may be required in order for the organization to take action. In such cases as well, bylaws must specify what proportion of the membership must be in attendance to make the meeting official and what the voting procedures are.
Because of the cumbersomeness of convening members, even membership organizations often specify a smaller body that is empowered to act on behalf of the members between membership meetings. Such governing boards, or boards of directors, can either be elected or appointed, but they exercise their authority at the pleasure of the membership, and the members often retain for themselves the power over the most important decisions affecting the organization, such as the election of directors and officers and the approval or amendment of the basic organizing documents, or budgets.

2. *Board-Managed Organizations.*   Not all nonprofit organizations have members, however. In such cases, the ultimate authority in the organization lies with the board of directors, by whatever name known. In such *board-managed organizations*, the board has a similar function to that in membership organizations—to oversee the management of the organization. However, in this case, the board of directors is self-perpetuating and is not subject to the control of a membership. This is typically the case, for example, with foundations, but it is common among service organizations as well.

Due to the more limited outside scrutiny and accountability involved with board-managed organizations, stricter statutory rules may be required to ensure their openness and accountability.

(ii) Board Structure.   Whether in the case of membership or board-governed organizations, laws often address issues concerning the size and terms of office of governing boards of nonprofit organizations. In the first place, laws often require a minimum number of persons who must serve on such boards. This is done to ensure a degree of openness and accountability in the organization. Within limits, the higher the minimum, the greater the number of persons involved in decision making, and presumably, the more open and accountable the organization.

Laws also often require that the bylaws of the organization specify how many board members there will be beyond this minimum. This is done to ensure that it is clear who is authorized to vote on matters affecting the governance of the organization.

Finally, laws frequently require that the organization's bylaws address the length of service of board members, whether successive terms may be served, and if so, what the term limits are.[15] These provisions, too, are intended to ensure a degree of responsiveness in the organization and provide for orderly procedures for succession.

(iii) Officers.   A third issue of internal governance frequently addressed by laws has to do with the officers of the organization. Here, again, laws may stipulate the officers that are required and the powers of each, or leave this to be spelled out in the organization's bylaws. The central point, however, is to clarify who has the right to act for the organization, to enter into contracts on its behalf, to commit funds, and to convene meetings.

An officer is a person who is appointed or elected to take an active part in the administration or management of the nonprofit organization. Bylaws must typically specify the requirements or qualifications for office (e.g., whether officers must be members of the organization and, if so, for how long), the manner of election of officers, whether one person may hold one or more offices, the rights and duties of officers, and the authority they have to deal in financial matters and contracts, to keep records, to convene meetings, and the like.

The number and roles of officers can obviously vary widely. Typically, however, there is at least a chief administrative officer, such as a president or chairperson; a chief financial officer, or treasurer, who supervises the financial affairs of the organization; and a secretary, who handles all nonfinancial records of the organization and maintains records and minutes of all meetings.

---

[15] In the United States, many of the 50 states have adopted nonprofit corporation statutes dealing with many aspects of internal governance just discussed. Many of these states have based their nonprofit corporation statutes on the Model Nonprofit Corporation Act, which was developed by volunteers working on the Committee of Nonprofit Corporations of the Section of Corporation, Banking and Business Law of the American Bar Association. See *Revised Model Nonprofit Corporation Act: Official Text with Official Comments and Statutory Cross-References* (Clifton, N.J.: Prentice Hall Law & Business, 1988).

(iv) Decision-Making Procedures. In addition to stipulating that the authority structure of the organization be clarified, legal codes can also address the *decision-making procedures* the organization will use, or at least require that the organization establish such procedures. Among the procedural issues that typically may be addressed are as follows:

- The minimum frequency of meetings of the governing body
- Notice requirements for meetings
- Quorum requirements (i.e., the number of members or board members who must be present in order for the organization to conduct its activities officially)
- Voting procedures (e.g., whether voting must be in person or can be by proxy or written consent, or by use of telecommunications equipment)
- Whether voting is by simple majority for all issues, or whether "super majorities" are required on certain issues (such as changing the bylaws)
- The operating rules that will be used for the conduct of meetings

The choice among these various governance options may be left to nonprofit organizations themselves to resolve in their rules for internal governance, by whatever name these documents may be known. Where legal codes leave various procedural aspects for the organization to decide, governing bodies may want to specify informal schemes for democratic conduct of meetings such as those embodied in *Roberts Rules of Order*.[16]

(c) Summary

In short, although nonprofit organizations are "self-governing," crucial aspects of their internal governance are nevertheless appropriately the subject of public concern, and therefore an appropriate focus of law. A considerable range of options exists, however, for how rigidly such matters should be prescribed in law, as opposed to simply stipulating in law that organizations must address them in their own governing documents.

§ 2.4 TAX TREATMENT

One of the great advantages that frequently attaches to the nonprofit form of organization is the availability of beneficial tax treatment to some or all such organizations. To be sure, the extent of the tax advantages available to such organizations, and hence the importance of these advantages, varies widely around the world. The United States is an extreme case where nonprofit organizations are frequently, though incorrectly, understood to be a product of the federal tax code, and nonprofit organizations are primarily thought of as "tax-exempt enti-

---

[16] *Roberts Rules of Order: The Standard Guide to Parliamentary Procedure* (London: Bantam Books, originally 1876). These rules are derived from the customs and rules of the English Parliament, which were in turn devised in part from the Roman Senate. These rules are in essence a common law of deliberative assemblies and organizations far less formal. An example would be procedures for making a motion, seconding a motion, calling for a vote, and so on.

ties." Elsewhere, the tax benefits available to nonprofit organizations may be more limited. Almost everywhere, however, the question of whether to extend beneficial tax treatment to nonprofit organizations and, if so, how and to what extent, is a major issue of law and policy.

(a) Rationale for Beneficial Tax Treatment

Many theories have been offered to support beneficial tax status for nonprofit organizations.[17] One theory is that nonprofit organizations are entitled to beneficial tax status because they perform functions that are supportive of central values that a government wishes to encourage, or at least avoid discouraging. For example, it is often said that nonprofit organizations foster democracy, voluntarism, and pluralism and that these are values that should be promoted through a supportive tax policy.

A second line of argument justifies special tax advantages for nonprofit organizations on grounds that such organizations relieve government of burdens it would otherwise have to bear. According to this line of argument, nonprofit organizations provide "collective goods" that meet societal needs in such fields as health, education, care for the disadvantaged, or even recreation and culture, that are not likely to be met by for-profit businesses. To the extent a society wishes to have such needs met, it must either do so directly through governmental action or rely on private voluntary action and charitable contributions to do so instead. Tax subsidies to such private organizations can thus be seen as a way to encourage activity that helps relieve government of responsibilities and costs it would otherwise have to bear directly. The argument for tax subsidies for such activity is strengthened, moreover, by evidence that the increase in private contributions that is stimulated by such special tax advantages is greater than the loss of revenue to government, so that the subsidies are "cost-effective" in stimulating the desired behavior.[18]

Other theories treat beneficial tax status for nonprofit organizations as a mere technical problem. Since nonprofit organizations do not exist primarily to earn a profit and therefore do not compute their net cost of operation, it is sometimes difficult to define what the tax base really is for such organizations, especially for income taxation. What is more, at least some portion of the income and resources of such organizations is often contributed rather than earned, complicating taxation further.

Such theories are not without detractors, of course. Some object to use of tax policy to achieve policy goals and argue for equal taxation of all types of entities, whether nonprofit or otherwise. Others point to the opportunities for abuse when

---

[17] For an interesting review of tax theory as it relates to nonprofit organizations, see, e.g., Rob Atkinson, *Theories of the Federal Income Tax Exemption for Charities: Thesis, Antithesis, and Syntheses* (New York: New York University School of Law, 1991), and "Altruism in Nonprofit Organizations," XXXI *Boston College Law Review*, No. 3, 501 *et seq.* (May 1990); Laura B. Chisolm, "Exempt Organization Advocacy: Matching the Rules to the Rationales," 63 *Indiana Law Journal*, No. 2, 201, 260 & nn. 257 (1987–1988); Henry Hansmann, "The Role of Nonprofit Enterprise," 89 *Yale Law Journal*, 835 (1980).

[18] For a review of this evidence, see Charles T. Clotfelter and Lester M. Salamon, "The Federal Government and the Nonprofit Sector: The Impact of the 1981 Tax Act on Individual Charitable Giving," XXXV *National Tax Journal*, No. 2, 171 (1982).

one class of entities is exempted from tax obligations levied on other types of organizations, creating powerful incentives for taxed organizations to redefine themselves in ways that make them seem eligible for beneficial tax status. Even where the rationale for beneficial tax status is granted, moreover, important issues still remain concerning the structuring of this treatment.

(b) Types of Tax Treatment

In practice, the issue of the tax treatment of nonprofit organizations really involves two distinct subissues: (1) the tax treatment of the nonprofit organization itself; and (2) the tax treatment of contributions to these organizations by individuals, corporations, and others.

(i) Tax Treatment of Organizations.   With regard to the tax treatment of nonprofit organizations, several distinct questions must be addressed.

1. *Type of Organization.*   A first question that must be addressed in deciding on the tax treatment of nonprofit organizations has to do with the type of organization eligible to receive such treatment. As noted earlier in this chapter, there are many distinct types of such organizations—foundations, associations, trusts, corporations, and so forth. In addition, such organizations serve a variety of purposes, such as public benefit and mutual benefit. Given this diversity, beneficial tax treatment can either be made available to all types of nonprofit organizations or reserved, in whole or in part, just for some types.

Assuming that some differentiation of tax treatment is considered appropriate, this can be done either in terms of the type of organization or in terms of the type of purpose it serves, though in practice these may overlap. Thus, in some statutory schemes, only certain types of entities are eligible for favorable tax treatment. In the United Kingdom, for example, many special tax and other advantages are only available to persons or organizations which serve exclusively charitable purposes.

In other statutory schemes, the purpose of the organization, rather than the legal form, is the principal basis for determining tax status. For example, certain kinds of beneficial tax status can be reserved for organizations serving public, as opposed to mutual, purposes, or fulfilling functions considered to be especially critical for national health and welfare.

2. *Types of Taxes.*   Not only can different types of nonprofit organizations be treated differently for tax purposes, but also these differences can vary by the many types of tax (e.g., *income taxes* and *consumption taxes*).

Income taxes include taxes on various sources of organizational income. Such income can come from contributions, from earnings on property or investments, from the sale of such assets, from fees for agency services, and from related and unrelated business activities. Nonprofit organizations can be exempted from taxes on all income or only on certain classes of income. Thus, some income tax codes may allow beneficial tax status for some sources of income—such as gift income, income from carrying out nonprofit purposes, or interest, dividends, or other types of passive income from investment sources—while denying it for others. In the United States, for example, even public benefit organizations that are generally exempted from income taxation are nevertheless liable for taxes on income from business activities that are "unrelated" to the tax-exempt purposes of the organization.

Consumption taxes are taxes on various types of purchases that nonprofit organizations may make. Included here are sales taxes, value-added taxes, luxury taxes, property taxes, and import taxes or duties. Because nonprofit organizations purchase goods and services like other entities, they are sometimes exposed to these consumption taxes even though they may be exempted from the more formal requirements of income taxation. Since consumption taxes can be at least as burdensome for nonprofits as income taxes, it is necessary to pay close attention to these taxes as well.

Not only are there different types of taxes, but these types of taxes may be under the jurisdiction of different governmental entities. For example, in the United States and United Kingdom, it is not uncommon for income taxes to fall under the jurisdiction of a national government and property taxes under the jurisdiction of local governments. Tax treatment can therefore vary not only among types of taxes and types of organizations, but also among levels of government.

3. *Application for Beneficial Tax Status.* In addition to the basic structure and coverage of beneficial tax treatment, consideration must also be given to the process of applying for it. This can be done either as part of the basic registration procedure for "nonprofit" status described earlier in this chapter, or it can be done as a separate process.

Where beneficial tax status is treated separately from other types of registration, such as for creation of a nonprofit entity, there may be one or more governmental entities that administer beneficial tax status matters. For example, exemptions from income taxation may be extended by the national income tax authorities and exemption from import duties by the Foreign Ministry. To avoid conflicts, however, countries often establish procedures under which different taxing authorities defer to the judgments made by one central authority in granting other forms of tax benefits. For example, import tax exemptions may be extended automatically to all entities that have been granted income tax exemption.

Whether registration and the granting of beneficial tax status are handled together or separately, there are inevitably varying degrees of discretion vested in the authorities operating such processes. To monitor such exercise of authority and provide some recourse in case of controversy, it is therefore often necessary to establish some appeal process, either to an administrative body or a court of law.

In addition to processes for initial certification of eligibility for beneficial tax status, procedures must also be established for monitoring the continued appropriateness of such status for particular organizations. This can take the form of regular financial and activity reporting requirements. Frequency and detail of reporting are also factors to consider in statutory drafting, as voluminous or frequent reporting may be overly burdensome and costly to nonprofits and government, while insufficient reporting does not give government adequate information to enforce the law or to maintain widespread public confidence in the nonprofit sector.

Consideration is often given to exclusion of small organizations from either applying for beneficial tax status or reporting on such financial matters since the burdens imposed may exceed any likely gain to the government. In countries where there is a strong separation of church and state, consideration must also be given to the degree to which government should require religious entities to report to the state. In the United States, for example, nonprofit organizations are generally required to file an annual information report to the national income tax authority, but organizations having less than $25,000 in annual revenue are exempt from the reporting requirement, as are churches, mosques, synagogues, and other religious organizations. With respect to the monitoring of these returns, in the United States in any given year, it is rare for the federal tax authority to audit more than 1% to 3% of nonprofit organizations. It is generally agreed in the United States that this is a sufficient level of auditing to prevent serious abuse.

(ii) Tax Treatment of Contributions.   Quite apart from the question of whether nonprofit organizations themselves should pay taxes on all or a portion of their income or purchases is the question of how to treat the contributions made by the donors to such organizations so far as the *donor's tax liabilities*, rather than the organization's tax liabilities, are concerned. By permitting donors to deduct such contributions from their income, or otherwise extending beneficial tax status to them, governments can provide important incentives for donors to make contributions to nonprofit organizations. In a sense, such special tax advantages reduce the "cost" or "price" of the gift by reducing the tax liabilities that the donor would otherwise bear. Whether such tax incentives actually induce taxpayers to make charitable contributions or merely influence the timing and amount of such gifts is open to debate, but there appears to be compelling evidence that they have some effect at least on the timing and amount of gifts.[19]

As noted earlier, the rationale for such beneficial tax status for giving hinges on the notion that the gifts support essentially public purposes and thereby relieve government of burdens it would otherwise face. Donors contributing to such public purposes are therefore considered to be entitled not to be taxed on the income they devote to these purposes. Critics charge, by contrast, that such incentives are undemocratic since they vest in the hands of private persons decisions over how to allocate revenues that would otherwise come to the government in the form of taxes. Thus, for example, Prime Minister Vaclav Klaus of the Czech Republic denounced tax deductions for voluntary contributions in the early 1990s on grounds that such deductions are undemocratic and place the interests of the donor ahead of the general interests of the public, thereby substituting private preferences for public preferences.[20]

---

[19] For a summary of this evidence, see Charles Clotfelter, *Federal Tax Policy and Charitable Giving* (Chicago: University of Chicago Press, 1985). While taxation can influence the size of gifts, however, the basic impulse for giving may come from other sources. In the case of U.S. corporate giving, for example, historically the motivators have been characterized as moral imperatives, corporate good citizenship, and enlightened self-interest. See David Logan, *U.S. Corporate Grantmaking in a Global Age* (Washington: Council on Foundations, 1989).

[20] Lester M. Salamon, "The Nonprofit Sector and Democracy—Prerequisite, Impediment, or Irrelevance?" Paper Prepared for Presentation at the Aspen Institute Conference on Democracy and the Nonprofit Sector, December 1993.

Once a country has determined that beneficial tax status for contributions is appropriate, however, several additional questions must still be addressed. Three of these are particularly important: first, the types of organizations or purposes for which beneficial tax status for contributions is justified; second, the form such favorable treatment should take; and third, the types of entities or contributors that should be eligible for such favorable treatment. Let us consider each of these in turn.

1. *Eligible Organizations or Purposes.* A first question related to the beneficial tax status of contributions has to do with the types of organizations or purposes eligible for tax-privileged gifts. This is similar to the question raised above in connection with the tax treatment of organizations, though the arguments for the one are not necessarily identical to the arguments for the other. For example, it can be argued that both public benefit and mutual benefit organizations serve a public purpose and, therefore, should be granted tax exemptions. However, contributors to a mutual benefit organization typically receive some direct benefit in return for their contribution (e.g., participation in social events or assistance with home loans) whereas the benefits of public benefit organizations are distributed more broadly. Therefore, there may be a stronger argument for extending tax incentives to contributions to public benefit organizations than to mutual benefit organizations. This is the practice under U.S. tax law, for example, where all types of nonprofit organizations are exempted from federal income taxation, but contribution deductions are available only for contributions to public benefit organizations (so-called 501(c)(3) charitable organizations). Similarly, U.K. law restricts favorable tax treatment to contributions to persons or organizations whose purposes are exclusively charitable. In France, the limitations are far more severe, and deductibility of contributions is permitted only for a narrow set of organizations judged to be "public utility corporations" by the Council of State.

Tax treatment of contributions can also vary depending on whether the recipient organization and/or its activities are domestic or foreign. Thus, in the United States, for example, the federal income tax code subjects corporate charitable contributions to a "domestic organization restriction" (DOR).[21] Contributions generally are not deductible unless the donee was created or organized in or under the laws of the United States, its possessions, any state or territory, or the District of Columbia.[22] The code also subjects corporate gifts to a "domestic use restriction" (DUR). Generally, in order for a corporate contribution to an unincorporated entity, such as a trust, community chest, or other such fund, to be deductible, the contribution must be restricted to use within the United States or its possessions.[23]

---

[21] IRC § 170(c)(2)(A).

[22] Only the Canadian, Israeli, and Mexican tax treaties alter this result in limited circumstances. See Stanley S. Weithorn, *Tax Techniques for Foundations and Other Exempt Organizations* (New York: Matthew Bender, 1975), at § 63.03 [2].

[23] IRC § 170(c)(2). A corporate contribution to a charity organized in the United States as a corporation (rather than as an unincorporated trust, association, etc.) is not subject to DUR, however. Thus, often DUR can be avoided by giving to a charity organized in the United States in corporate form. See Weithorn, *supra* n. 22.

The policy rationale behind the DOR and DUR rules derives from the "substitution" argument discussed earlier. As the Congress put it:

> The exemption from taxation of money or property devoted to charitable and other purposes is based upon the theory that the Government is compensated for the loss of revenue by its relief from financial burden which would otherwise have to be met by appropriations from public funds, and by the benefits resulting from the promotion of the general welfare. *The United States derives no such benefit from gifts to foreign institutions, and the proposed limitation is consistent with the above theory.*[24]

More recently, the DOR and DUR rules have been justified on grounds that U.S. authorities have "virtually no way to make a foreign voluntary organization accountable and assure that money going abroad would be used for the philanthropic purpose."[25] Whether these rationales still hold in the global economy of the present is open to question.

2. *Types of Tax Treatment.*   Whatever the type of nonprofit or activity judged to be worthy of beneficial tax status for contributions, important choices must still be made about such issues as the structure of the tax advantage, the types of gifts that are eligible for such advantages, and the extent or level to which such advantages should be permitted.

With respect to the *structure of the tax advantage*, a number of options are available depending on the nature of the tax system that exists. Two common types are *tax deductions* and *tax credits*. In an income tax context, tax deductions permit taxpayers to deduct all or a portion of their contributions from their income before computing their income tax liabilities. The value of the income tax savings of the deduction is then computed as the value of the gift times the tax rate that applies for a given taxpayer. Tax credits, by contrast, permit taxpayers to deduct all or a portion of the value of their contributions, not from their income, but from their actual tax liabilities. Tax credits are generally, therefore, worth more to the taxpayer than are tax deductions.

Yet, another form of tax advantage delivers the benefit of favorable tax treatment not to the donor, but to the recipient organization. Under the "covenant" system in the United Kingdom, for example, taxpayers making charitable contributions pay their regular taxes, and the Treasury then sends the tax that would normally be paid on the contribution to the designated charity.

Different treatment is also sometimes accorded different types of gifts—for example, whether a gift is in cash or in kind, whether a full interest or just a partial interest in property is donated, the length of time the property may have been held by the donor, or whether the donor receives something in return. In the case of donations of property (e.g., works of art, real estate, or stocks and bonds) important issues arise about how to value the property for purposes of calculating tax benefits. Questions of substantiation and record keeping of contributions

---

[24] U.S. House of Representatives, H. Rept. 1860, 75th Cong., 3rd Sess. (1938). (Italics supplied.)
[25] Gabriel Rudney, "Tax Rules and Overseas Philanthropy," *Philanthropy Monthly* 16, 17 (Aug. 1978).

must also be considered, both in terms of records to be kept by the contributor as well as records to be kept by the recipient nonprofit organization.

Even where tax laws provide for beneficial treatment of contributions, such treatment can be subjected to certain limits. An 11-country survey recently highlighted the following wide-ranging deduction limits: Austria—10% of taxable profits for firms, for scientific research only; Belgium—5% of income; Hungary—no limits; Israel—35% of gifts that are less than 25% of taxable income; Italy—generally 0.8% to 2%; Spain—20% of gifts that are less than 30% of taxable income, firms 10%; Taiwan—20% of income for individuals, 10% of profits for firms; and United Kingdom, no limits of gifts of capital (as opposed to current income).[26] In Japan, there are no percentage limitations on corporate contributions to the government and certain designated entities, while other corporate donations are generally deductible only up to the limit of one half of the sum of 2.5% of current net profits plus 0.25% of paid-in capital and capital surplus, with certain limited exceptions.[27]

(c) Classes of Donors

A final issue in the design of beneficial tax status for contributions concerns the types of donors eligible to receive such favorable treatment. Such donors can be individual citizens or businesses of various types (e.g., corporations, partnerships, cooperatives, etc.). As suggested above, tax laws can allow beneficial treatment of contributions for all of these but vary the extent of such treatment. In the United States, for example, the federal tax code makes a distinction between individuals and corporations, generally allowing deductions for contributions of roughly 10% of income for corporations and 50% for individuals.

Ideally, the twin objectives of simplicity and fairness considered in constructing any tax regime should be kept in mind by statutory drafters as they ponder these questions. But as the reader will see, different countries resolve these questions in myriad ways, few of which are simple.

§ 2.5 PERSONAL BENEFIT RESTRICTIONS

One of the essential characteristics of nonprofit organizations, as Chapter 1 pointed out, was that they are "nonprofit-distributing," that is, they do not return profits to persons who control the organization. Rather, any such profits must be used to advance the purposes for which the organization was created. This is a key distinction between nonprofit and for-profit organizations and has been variously characterized as the "nondistribution constraint,"[28] the prohibition on private benefit, the prohibition on private inurement, or the personal benefit restriction. For purposes of this discussion, we will use this latter term, "personal

---

[26] Burton A. Weisbrod, "Tax Policy Toward Non-Profit Organizations: An Eleven-Country Survey," 2 *Voluntas*, No. 1, 3 (1991).

[27] Susan L. Q. Flaherty, "The Voluntary Sector and Corporate Citizenship in the United States and Japan," 2 *Voluntas*, No. 1, 58 (1991).

[28] Hansmann, *supra* n. 17, p. 838.

benefit restrictions," to refer to a broad set of limitations on the diversion of non-profit income or assets for a private purpose.

The law concerns itself with this issue of personal benefit in order to ensure that nonprofit assets serve a public, rather than a private, purpose, and that beneficial tax status and other favored status are indeed warranted. Further, such laws place restrictions on use of nonprofit assets in order to maintain public confidence in and support for the nonprofit sector.

Obviously, many persons benefit incidentally from nonprofit assets and earnings. For example, a nonprofit organization may provide social services to a large class of low-income individuals. The provision of these social services to a charitable class is the reason the nonprofit was formed and granted beneficial tax status and is perceived to result in a public benefit, even though particular low-income individuals benefit from receipt of low- or no-cost services. Laws regulating private benefit do not typically attempt to capture incidental or *de minimis* occurrences of private benefit.

Nor do such laws commonly prohibit payment of salaries to employees of nonprofit organizations or expenses of board members for attendance at regular meetings or other organizational functions. Some laws even permit the payment of fees to board members, though this practice is less common.

What is commonly prohibited, however, are conflict-of-interest situations in which directors or officers use their position of trust to further their own private interests to the detriment of a nonprofit organization they manage. Some of the types of transactions from which such prohibited personal benefit may result include the following:

- A loan of money or other valuables by a nonprofit to a private individual
- Assumption by the nonprofit of liabilities of an individual
- Payment to an individual or a business of amounts in excess of what would be normal, reasonable compensation for goods or services provided to the nonprofit organization
- Granting a private person permission to use or purchase a nonprofit's facilities or office supplies and equipment at no cost, or low-cost
- Use of the nonprofit form to operate a for-profit business or to serve business purposes (e.g., allowing a foundation to invest in a business controlled by a board member)

Such transactions amount to an intentional, wrongful diversion to a private individual of nonprofit assets or income, a diversion from public to private purposes, often solely by virtue of that individual's relation to the nonprofit.

Among the critical questions that must be settled in law are the types and extent of such personal benefit restrictions. Typically, such restrictions apply particularly to individuals in positions of control in the organization. These include members of boards of directors and key officers and managers of the organization. In some countries, restrictions of this type may be greater for some classes of nonprofits than for others.[29] These matters may also be dealt with in general

---

[29] For a detailed discussion of private inurement and private benefit under U.S. law, see Hopkins, *supra* n. 6, Chapter 13, pp. 264 *et seq.*; for discussion of unreasonable compensation as pri-

criminal codes covering theft, embezzlement, and the like, instead of, or in addition to, a separate code for nonprofits or a tax code.

§ 2.6 OBLIGATIONS TO THE PUBLIC

Closely related to restrictions on utilizing nonprofit resources for private benefit are a set of broader responsibilities to the public at large that laws often place on nonprofit organizations and those who oversee them. Two broad sets of such responsibilities can be distinguished: first, *fiduciary responsibilities*, which refers to the responsibility for handling money or property not one's own for the benefit of another, in this case a nonprofit organization; and second, obligations for *openness and transparency* in the management of the organization. Such provisions are designed to further enhance accountability and transparency, and consequently public trust in nonprofit organizations, and to ensure that assets that receive beneficial tax treatment remain dedicated to public benefit. Let us examine each set in turn.

(a) Fiduciary Responsibilities

Laws relating to the fiduciary responsibility of those who manage nonprofit organizations may focus on such matters as the handling of nonprofit assets, the degree of personal financial responsibility assumed by individual members of governing bodies and staff of nonprofit organizations, and the breadth of responsibility board members have for other facets of organizational operations. Such laws may also consider restrictions on personal benefit, such as compensation limitations on members of governing bodies and standards for conflicts of interest and self-dealing.

Some countries will choose to subject persons having fiduciary responsibility to nonprofits to the same general obligations as apply to persons acting in fiduciary capacity in the business sector, and issues of fraud or criminal conduct may be governed in general laws rather than laws specific to the nonprofit sector.

The common law has a number of useful principles developed in the law of trusts to guide those who hold fiduciary positions of trust and who administer funds in that capacity. While the concept of a trust is not used in the civil law, provisions developed in the common law of trusts to guide those who hold funds in trust for charitable purposes are useful conceptual bases to consider in the regulation of fiduciary duties and in developing standards for obligations to the public. Moreover, these provisions are subject to codification (and in fact have been codified, for example, in some laws in various U.S. states). We consider these principles briefly here.

(i) *Three Basic Duties* Historically at common law, judges of courts of law charged those responsible for the management of charitable organizations with three basic duties.

vate inurement/benefit, see U.S. Internal Revenue Service, *Exempt Organizations Continuing Professional Education Technical Instruction Program*, 16th ed. (Washington: Internal Revenue Service, 1992), pp. 191 *et seq.*

- *Duty of Care.* The first of these is known as the *duty of care*. Those in charge of the operation or management of a nonprofit organization, by whatever name such persons are known (e.g., directors or trustees), are entrusted with stewardship of assets for the benefit of the public served by the nonprofit organization. Directors must act with that level of care that a reasonably prudent person would use in similar circumstances. This duty requires not only reasonableness with respect to matters submitted to them for approval, but also requires reasonable inquiry and monitoring of affairs of the nonprofit and informed decision making.
- *Duty of Loyalty.* In addition to the duty of care is the *duty of loyalty*. Directors must avoid conflicts of interest and are absolutely prohibited from using their position of trust to further their own private interests, as discussed in Section 2.5 personal benefit restrictions.
- *Duty of Obedience.* Finally, there is the *duty of obedience*. Directors are required to adhere to applicable laws and the terms of the nonprofit organization's governing documents, by whatever name known. Nonprofit organizations are often subject to a host of laws with which directors may not be familiar initially; for example, laws regulating charitable solicitation and fund-raising, legislative and political activity, and unrelated business activities. The duty of obedience holds that directors must familiarize themselves with such laws and abide by them. There is also a need for those operating nonprofits to be familiar with other laws that may apply, such as laws on occupational safety and health or environmental regulation.

(ii) Business Judgment Rule. At common law, a defense to alleged breach of these duties is the *business judgment rule* (BJR). To obtain the benefit of a BJR defense in any lawsuit, directors must have acted in good faith and with a reasonable basis for believing that their conduct furthered the organization's lawful purposes. In addition, directors must have exercised honest business judgment after due consideration of what they reasonably believed to be all relevant information. This rule recognizes that reasonable people may reach different conclusions on the same facts. What is required is that the action be reasonable in the circumstances.

Consistent with BJR, it has been said that governing boards as a whole and directors as individuals achieve their optimal level of performance of duty when they exercise their responsibilities primarily by asking good and timely questions rather than by attempting to "run" programs or implementing their own personal policies or agendas.

(iii) Personal Liability. After setting forth the rule that the operation of the nonprofit shall be vested in certain persons and then setting forth the duties of those in that position of trust, some laws may impose "personal liability" for wrongdoing in connection with a nonprofit organization; that is, a person guilty of wrongdoing with nonprofit assets may be required to reimburse the nonprofit from his or her own assets. In many U.S. states, so as not to discourage volunteer activity, laws are being adopted that limit the personal liability of volunteers, particularly where the entity itself carries certain minimum liability insurance.

Clearly, however, no law can tell a member of a governing body how to do that job well. This is where self-education and self-policing can play an important role in training volunteers and staff on their duties in their respective capacities. At a minimum, those who work with a nonprofit organization should at the start of their tenure be presented with the organization's fundamental documents and become thoroughly familiar with them. They should also be eager to prepare and publish annual reports of activities and finances and to make certain that all legal requirements are complied with.

(b) Reporting and Disclosure Requirements

In addition to fiduciary standards, laws relating to nonprofit obligations to the public may also specify public reporting and disclosure requirements. These reporting and disclosure requirements may be in a separate code, or they may be consolidated with beneficial tax status administration. However structured, the purpose of such requirements is to provide a means of confirming, through periodic reporting and disclosure, that a nonprofit organization is in fact conducting activities consistent with its purposes and beneficial tax status and devoting its financial resources to fulfillment of those purposes.

One common way of ensuring such openness is to require public access to certain records of a nonprofit organization, such as an annual report of activities or list of governing board members. Laws may indicate who has access to these records and under what circumstances. These measures are designed to enhance transparency and increase public confidence.

§ 2.7   BUSINESS ACTIVITY

In addition to their nonprofit activities, nonprofit organizations also often engage in a variety of "business" activities in order to generate income.

(a) Related vs. Unrelated Business

Broadly speaking, two types of nonprofit business activity can be distinguished: *related business* and *unrelated business*. Related business is commercial activity closely related to fulfillment of the basic purposes of a nonprofit organization. For example, a nonprofit day care center that charges fees to at least some consumers of its services could be said to be engaged in a related business. Similarly, a nonprofit university that operates a book store selling textbooks is also engaged in a related business activity.

An unrelated trade or business, by contrast, is one not closely related to fulfillment of the purposes of a nonprofit organization, or perhaps not related at all. For example, a nonprofit day care center that runs a laundry on the side can be considered to be operating an unrelated business, even if the income from the business goes to support the day care center. Definitions of unrelated income vary and many exclusions and exceptions are possible, such as exclusion of income from business conducted by volunteers or using donated goods, or in some cases, conducted for the convenience of patrons of a nonprofit, such as housing and cafeterias for university students or restaurants for patrons of museums. Indeed, some laws regard any fee-for-service activity, even a related one, as in essence a business activity that is unrelated to the mission of the organization and treat only income from donations as "related" income.

Some decision must be made as to whether nonprofit organizations are to be permitted to conduct unrelated businesses at all, and if so, to what extent. In some contexts, there may be no other reasonable sources of income, so that conduct of unrelated business becomes a necessity.

Assuming the law permits the conduct of unrelated trade or business, there may be limits on the portion of income derived from, or activities devoted to, unrelated businesses or on the ownership of business subsidiaries. Consequences that may be incurred if these limits are exceeded can include fines, complete loss of beneficial tax status, and payment of regular income taxes.

(b) Source vs. Destination of Income

Even if unrelated business activity is permitted, important decisions still remain about how to treat it for tax purposes, particularly where nonprofit organizations themselves are exempted from all or some taxes. Broadly speaking, two approaches exist for resolving this issue.

The first approach is to focus on the *source* of the income, that is, whether it derives from related or unrelated businesses. Thus, in some statutory schemes, related income is given the same beneficial tax status as other nonprofit income, while unrelated income, though permitted, is taxed in the same manner as the income of businesses. The rationale for this approach is that it puts nonprofit businesses on the same footing as for-profit businesses in the same field and thereby avoids charges of "unfair competition" from the business community. Even where this is done, of course, important issues still arise in determining taxable income from unrelated businesses due to varying methods of allocation of costs and overhead to unrelated activities,[30] and also from the use of tax-deductible capital in the form of charitable donations to capitalize a business.

A second approach for dealing with nonprofit business activity focuses not on the source of the income, but on its ultimate *destination* (i.e., the purpose for which the income is used or destined). Under this approach, if the income is used for nonprofit purposes, then the source or activity that generates that income is irrelevant. Australian law, for example, employs this destination principle and exempts from taxation income from any business activity—related or unrelated—so long as it is used for nonprofit purposes. This so-called destination principle was also in use in the United States until the 1950s when an "unrelated business income tax" was imposed on nonprofits.

There are many theoretical questions about whether failure to tax unrelated income (even if destined for nonprofit purposes) causes economic disparities and inefficiencies in the cost of raising capital and whether inequities result between nonprofit and for-profit organizations. The basic question for governments, however, is whether to leave open an important potential source of income for non-

---

[30] See, e.g., Henry Hansmann, "Unfair Competition and the Unrelated Business Income Tax," 75 *Virginia Law Review*, 605 (1989), and Ole Gjems-Onstad, "The Taxation of Unrelated Business Income of Nonprofit Organizations," *International Charity Law Conference Papers* (London: National Council of Voluntary Organisations, Sept. 1994).

profit organizations, whether to grant or withhold a tax subsidy for such income, and, if so, to what extent.

§ 2.8   OTHER FUNDING RESTRICTIONS

Because nonprofit organizations are frequently engaged in soliciting contributions from the general public, the possibility of fraud and abuse always exists. To reduce this, laws often impose a variety of restrictions or requirements related to such nonprofit solicitations and to other financial transactions in which nonprofit organizations may engage.

(a) Solicitation of Funds

For the nonprofit sector to remain able to secure contributions, it is imperative that public trust in the sector be protected. This can be done in part through the disclosure and private benefit restrictions noted above, through the adoption of voluntary codes of conduct, or even by incorporating higher-than-required standards in governing documents. At the same time, legal provisions are also sometimes considered necessary, particularly in the sensitive area of solicitation to minimize the chances that charlatans will solicit funds for allegedly nonprofit purposes, and then use the funds for illegitimate purposes to the detriment of donors and the nonprofit sector, generally.

Such laws can take a variety of forms. For example, they can require registration of organizations or persons holding themselves out as professional fund-raisers or fund-solicitors before permitting them to solicit funds.[31] Such laws might also require accountability to donors and the public with respect to the use of funds. This may be accomplished through measures such as disclosing to donors the amount of funds collected and the portion of funds actually devoted to nonprofit purposes as opposed to spent on fund-raising or administrative activities. Alternatively, laws can establish a ceiling on fund-raising or administrative costs such that these expenses may not exceed a certain percentage limitation (e.g., 15% to 35% of amounts received from the solicitation).

Laws may also consider means of making sure that gifts solicited or given for particular purposes are used for the purposes intended by the donors. This can be done by requiring that organizations secure advance approval from some public or private agency for major solicitations. Under such a system, organizations must disclose their identity, their purposes, the purposes for which funds are being solicited, how much is to be solicited, who will conduct the solicitation, the amount of anticipated costs of the solicitation, and confirmation that they are currently in compliance with applicable laws. On this basis, a license to solicit is then issued for a stated period. Typically, there are exemptions to such laws for

---

[31] A "professional fund-raiser" may be defined as "a person who for a flat fixed fee under a written agreement, plans, conducts, manages, carries on, advises or acts as a consultant, whether directly or indirectly, in connection with soliciting contributions for, or on behalf of, any [nonprofit] charitable organization," or several charitable organizations, but "who actually solicits no contributions as a part of such services." See generally, Bruce R. Hopkins, *The Law of Fund-Raising* (New York: John Wiley & Sons, 1991), at § 4.1, pp. 258–259.

solicitations by church organizations of their congregations, by membership organizations of their members, and by schools and colleges of their alumni.

Such solicitation laws are prevalent in the United States. Thus, each state has one.[32] They have received much attention due to multi-million-dollar scandals where some television evangelists solicited money for allegedly religious purposes, but in fact used the funds to support lavish lifestyles.

(b) Other Financial Responsibilities

In addition to the solicitation restrictions, legal provisions can also be made for other facets of nonprofit financial operations. Thus, in some instances, state regulatory authorities can require that generally accepted principles of financial accounting for nonprofit organizations (developed jointly by the accountancy profession and a governmental agency) be used by nonprofits to prepare their financial statements.

In addition, other codes may also come into play. For example, in the United States, some types of gifts may involve insurance and securities laws, such as charitable gift annuities. In the charitable gift annuity transaction, an individual makes an irrevocable transfer to charity of property such as securities. The charity contracts to pay the donor or other beneficiaries a guaranteed annuity for life. Because the property transferred has a value larger than the value of the annuity, the transaction is in part the purchase of an annuity and in part a contribution. If this type of gift is permissible in a particular country, consideration may be given to its regulation under other generally applicable bodies of law (such as insurance company law), or under laws designed for the nonprofit sector.

Finally, to make any of these restrictions effective, laws must include enforcement mechanisms as well. For example, some laws may establish civil or criminal penalties for misdeeds of directors or fraudulent solicitation or solicitation without complying with registration requirements. At the same time, to avoid discouraging volunteer involvement, laws can relieve volunteers of liability for unintentional wrongdoing where the entity for which they volunteer carries certain minimum levels of liability insurance coverage.

§ 2.9   POLITICAL ACTIVITY

The roles of "advocate and improver of social systems, empowerer of citizens, and critic and monitor of government policies and programs" are widely viewed as crucial functions of the nonprofit sector.[33] Thus, legal restrictions on these roles must naturally be approached with great care. Nevertheless, some legal structures, particularly those in the common law tradition, place limits on certain facets of nonprofit involvement in political activity.[34]

Underlying such restrictions is the belief that government should not underwrite participation in political debate, particularly partisan political debate, but

[32] See *supra* n. 31.
[33] Chisolm, *supra* n. 17, at 205 & nn. 27–29.
[34] Anita Randon and Perri 6, "Constraining Campaigning: Legal Treatment of Advocacy," 5 *Voluntas*, No. 1, 27 (1994).

should remain neutral, and that taxpayers should not be required to finance, through tax subsidies, views with which they disagree.[35] To the extent that non-profit organizations and contributions to them enjoy beneficial tax status, the involvement in direct political activity by such organizations can be construed as indirect public support for such political activity. To the extent that such concerns are present in a country, the great challenge is to frame laws that limit objection-able forms of political involvement on the part of nonprofit organizations with-out in the process destroying the ability of such organizations to perform their important advocacy functions.

(a) Forms of Political Activity

One mechanism for doing so is to differentiate among several types of "political" or advocacy activity. Three such types can usefully be identified: (1) *political cam-paign activity*, (2) *lobbying*, and (3) *policy advocacy*.

(i) **Political Campaign Activity.** Political campaign activity generally refers to activity designed to assist or prevent particular candidates from achiev-ing public office. This type of activity raises the most serious public policy ques-tions since it presents in the most direct form the phenomenon of public subsidies being used to affect the prospects of particular candidates for public office. In the United States, therefore, nonprofit organizations that qualify for tax-deductible charitable donations are absolutely prohibited from engaging in such political campaign activity and subjected to severe penalties if they do.[36]

(ii) **Lobbying.** A second type of political activity involves not promoting or opposing particular candidates for public office, but promoting or opposing the passage of particular pieces of legislation under consideration by some govern-mental body. Here, again, concerns about the use of public funds to subsidize par-ticular political views may lead to limits on the extent to which nonprofits that receive favorable tax treatment can engage in such lobbying activity, whether it takes the form of direct communication with legislators or indirect communica-tion through attempts to influence the opinion of members of the public toward particular pieces of legislation. Thus, in the United States, nonprofit organiza-tions that are eligible for receipt of tax-deductible contributions are not permitted to devote a "substantial part" of their activities to such lobbying or influencing

---

[35] Chisolm, *supra* n. 17 at 249.

[36] If a nonprofit charitable organization makes an expenditure for a political activity it may lose its tax-exempt status. If it does so, it is ineligible for tax-exempt status as any other type of non-profit organization.

It may also be subjected to an excise tax on "political expenditures." The initial tax is 10% of the amount of the expenditure, and a tax of 2.5% is imposed on the organization's managers (such as directors and officers) where it was known at the time of the expenditure that the expen-diture constituted a political expenditure. If the initial tax was imposed and the expenditure was not corrected in a timely manner, i.e., any recoverable amount was not recovered, safe-guards were not put in place to prevent future political expenditures, etc., a further tax is imposed at 100% of the amount of the political expenditure. Other penalties can be imposed as well. IRC §§ 501(c)(3) and 4955.

legislation. While the definition of "substantial part" is far from clear,[37] this limitation discourages many nonprofit organizations from active involvement in the legislative process and encourages those that wish to engage in such lobbying to establish special subsidiaries that are nonprofit but not "public benefit" in character.

(iii) Policy Advocacy. Even where campaign activity and direct involvement in the legislative process are constrained by law, it may still be possible to leave unfettered a substantial area of nonprofit involvement in policy advocacy more broadly conceived. Such advocacy can take myriad forms, including conducting and publishing research on important problems being overlooked in public policy, educating the public and elected leaders about such problems, engaging in peaceful assembly or free speech to protest, or promote, government actions, conducting seminars and distributing materials, and a host of other related activities. These activities can be vitally important in bringing new issues to the attention of the public though they stop one step short of direct lobbying. As such, they may raise fewer of the concerns that lead to constraints on nonprofit lobbying and a prohibition on nonprofit participation in campaigns for public office.

(b) Types of Nonprofit Organizations

In addition to differentiating among types of nonprofit activities, laws on nonprofit political involvement can also differentiate among types of organizations to which political limitations apply. Logically, the distinctions that make sense here are the ones that correspond most closely with the tax laws that are in effect. Since the major objection to having nonprofit organizations engage in political activity is that such activity constitutes a form of government subsidization of private political decisions, the restrictions can usefully be limited to the organizations that receive the greatest subsidies. In the common law tradition, for example, the limitations on political activity apply most directly to public-benefit organizations, which are eligible to receive tax-deductible gifts from the general public. By contrast, mutual benefit organizations can engage in lobbying activities without limitation. While there is a certain irony in this, since the public-benefit organizations may have the most interest in general public-interest questions, their substantial tax advantages make it somewhat inappropriate for them to be too directly involved in affecting the policies and personnel of the government that helps

---

[37] What constitutes a "substantial part" has been the subject of much controversy with the U.S. Internal Revenue Service and in the courts. Whether legislative activity rises to the level of a "substantial part" is a test of facts and circumstances, where often an attempt is made to measure the percentage of the organization's spending allocable to its efforts to influence legislation.

Because of the difficulty with the term "substantial part," nonprofit charitable organizations that engage in legislative activities often find it preferable to elect to be governed by a newer test based on expenditures for legislative activities. The newer test is based on permitted level of expenditures, called the "lobbying nontaxable amount," beginning with 20% of the first $500,000 of an organization's expenditures for tax-exempt nonprofit charitable purposes, 15% of the next $500,000, 10% of the next $500,000, and 5% of any remaining expenditures, not to exceed a total amount spent of $1 million. See IRC §§ 501(h) and 4911(c)(2); Treas. Reg. §§ 1.501(h)-3(c)(2) and 46.4911-1(c)(1).

finance them. Thus, in the United States, it is only the public-benefit nonprofits, the 501(c)(3)s, that are limited in their involvement in lobbying activities.

§ 2.10 KEY TRENDS

In addition to the nine broad issues confronting drafters of nonprofit laws that have been outlined, the nonprofit sector faces enormous changes in the years ahead that may also pose legal challenges for the sector. In this section, we identify some of the most salient of these changes and note some of the challenges they pose to nonprofit law.

(a) Growth and Diversification

Perhaps the central trend affecting the nonprofit sector around the world is the vast expansion of the demands being placed upon it and the resulting enlargement of its role and diversification of its basic structure. A veritable "associational revolution" appears to be under way at the global level, as citizens and policy makers have begun looking to nonprofit organizations to help resolve the multiple crises of the welfare state, development, socialism, and the environment.[38] As a consequence, the scope of the nonprofit sector has expanded massively and its internal differentiation has grown significantly.

Inevitably, this growth brings with it immense challenges of sectoral definition. Laws designed to accommodate charitable institutions providing relief to the indigent must be rethought in the context of organizations seeking to help the poor start their own businesses. Are the latter business enterprises not entitled to the tax and related privileges accorded charitable institutions? Or are they really charitable institutions pursuing their missions through a different route? Increasingly, nonprofit law must come to terms with a far more diverse set of institutions and purposes.

(b) Government-Nonprofit Relations

One of the principal factors helping to explain the expansion of the nonprofit sector on the global level is the increasing tendency of government to turn to nonprofit organizations to assist it in carrying out a wide variety of functions, from the provision of social welfare to the promotion of economic development. As citizens and political leaders alike have come to question the wisdom of sole reliance on government to meet the social welfare and development demands they face, attention has turned to mechanisms for forging partnerships between the state and the voluntary sector. Elaborate contractual relationships have consequently been forged between governmental authorities and nonprofit institutions in countries throughout the world, and the likelihood is that these relationships will grow in importance in the years ahead. In the process, important new legal challenges will arise as both government and the nonprofit sector search for ways to cooperate with each other while still retaining the features that make each distinctive.

---

[38] Lester M. Salamon, "The Rise of the Nonprofit Sector," 73 *Foreign Affairs*, No. 4, p. 109 (July/August 1994).

Thus, new contracting arrangements, vouchers, reimbursement systems, and provisions for sorting out indirect costs will come to the forefront and demand legal resolution.

(c) Commercialization

In their efforts to respond to pressing needs, as suggested above, nonprofit organizations will also increasingly turn to fees and charges for their activities and enter a variety of businesses to raise funds for their programs. In the process, they will come into increasing contact with private businesses operating in the same or related fields. The result will be increased demands for legal definition of the borders between these two sectors. Already, such demands are widespread in the United States, leading to a frontal assault on the whole concept of a nonprofit sector in some quarters. It seems reasonable to assume that similar challenges will arise in other settings, as well. This will intensify the concerns about nonprofit business activity identified earlier and raise new questions about the treatment of even the "related" service income that nonprofit organizations receive.

(d) New Forms of Private Giving

Another striking trend likely to affect the nonprofit sector around the world is the expansion of new forms of giving to nonprofits. Increasingly, giving is becoming institutionalized and planned. Impulse giving and collection box giving is being joined increasingly by "planned giving" involving charitable remainder trusts, charitable annuities, and other complex forms of contributing to charities.[39] The United Kingdom is even experimenting with a "charity card," a kind of charitable credit card with which donors can charge their charitable gifts. As these new forms of giving gain currency, legal structures will need to be adapted to make room for them.

(e) Professionalization and Formalization of Ethical Standards

As nonprofit organizations come into greater contact with both government and the business sector, new demands will arise for attention to the ethical standards under which these organizations operate and the level of professionalism they bring to their work. This will in turn stimulate debates about the relative virtues of *self-regulation* vs. *government regulation* to ensure that nonprofit institutions abide by the highest ethical standards and carry on their activities in a professional fashion. To the extent that nonprofit organizations recognize these demands and respond accordingly, cumbersome regulatory controls can be avoided. Given the peculiar character of this set of institutions, this would likely be a highly desirable outcome. However, it seems likely that legal action will be required in numerous circumstances as well, if only to guarantee openness and accountability.

---

[39] Under a charitable annuity, an individual contributes a block of stock or other property to a charity, receives the tax deduction that this gift affords, and then receives from the charity a guaranteed annuity income each year. This gives the donor the opportunity to benefit from the tax advantage such a gift involves while still having the benefit of the income that the asset that is given away provides.

(f) Globalization

Finally, the nonprofit sector seems likely to face increased demands of globalization and cross-national activity as a product of the broader globalization of the world economy, worldwide disillusionment with governmental capacity to deal with problems, a general decline in public sector resources, the dramatic and historic collapse of communism, the increasing prominence of multinational corporations, and the growing globalization of many of the issues with which nonprofits have been concerned, such as the environment and health.

To cope with this new development, the law of nonprofit organizations will have to become increasingly international in the years ahead. Thus, for example, more favorable legal provision will have to be made for cross-national grantmaking and for nonprofit organizations in various countries to operate across national borders. Drafters of nonprofit law, no less than drafters of laws for commercial activity, must be increasingly sensitive to the international dimensions of the activity they are regulating and, therefore, increasingly aware of the range of national treatments in this field.

§ 2.11 CONCLUSION

The ongoing nonprofit "revolution" requires changes in the law in just about every country. Some countries have the opportunity to start afresh, developing codes for regulation of the nonprofit sector based on a sampling of the best the world has to offer, adapted to local conditions and traditions. In so doing, they must resist the temptation to assume that any existing model contains the right mix of features that are appropriate to the new context.[40] Rather, important work needs to be done to fashion a new international model containing key elements that could be the subject of treaty or other international agreements.

While the details of such a law will need to be developed in line with national traditions, the goal legislative drafters everywhere may wish to consider is to create legal systems that allow the start of nonprofit organizations as a matter of right upon compliance with a limited set of statutory formalities and that guarantee these organizations a significant degree of autonomy and independence. Purposes should be stated broadly and in a flexible manner. Beneficial tax status should be a matter of right for entities organized and operated for appropriate purposes set forth in the law. Reporting should be significant enough to allow openness, transparency, and monitoring by public and government alike, but not be overly burdensome or intrusive. And cross-border giving and nonprofit activities should be facilitated through mutual recognition by treaty. All of this should ideally operate in the context of the rule of law with independent courts to provide meaningful enforcement of rights where necessary. Laws drawn or revised in this manner will contribute to the growth of a truly effective international nonprofit sector.

---

[40] See generally, E. Blake Bromley, "Exporting Civil Society: Confessions of a 'Foreign Legal Expert,'" *International Charity Law Conference Papers* (London: National Council of Voluntary Organisations, Sept. 1994).

CHAPTER THREE

International Law of Nonprofit Organizations

Susan L.Q. Flaherty

"International law" is the body of legal rules that apply between sovereign states. The term is equivalent to the term "law of nations" and its equivalents in other languages.[1]

We consider briefly much of the body of international law that exists with respect to nonprofit organizations, mainly for the purpose of illustrating that this body of international law still points to the importance of the law of the home jurisdiction of a nonprofit organization, yet holds promise for the future of a more international nonprofit sector. In the field of international law, the literature reflects the choice of terminology as "nongovernmental organizations" (NGOs), which we will treat as approximately equivalent to "nonprofit organizations" for purposes of this discussion.[2]

What follows is not intended to be an exhaustive survey of international law as it affects nonprofit organizations. We will first look at some United Nations (UN) structures, then some European arrangements, and finally, some North American arrangements.

Regarding the UN, in countries where there may be no firm legal support for the existence of NGOs, it has been suggested that official recognition by the UN might be a mechanism for preventing potentially hostile governments from shutting down operations.[3] Chapter X of the UN Charter dealing with the Economic and Social Council (ECOSOC) provides in Article 71:

---

[1] The term "international law" was first used by Jeremy Bentham in his *Introduction to Principles of Morals and Legislation*, 1789.

[2] For example, the UN has defined NGOs as follows:

> Non-governmental organizations (NGOs) are non-profit citizen's voluntary organizations organized nationally or internationally. NGOs are diverse in structure, membership and financial support. Some are active in information and education; others are operational and are engaged in technical projects, relief, refugee and development programmes.
>
> Examples of NGOs are: professional, business and cooperative organizations; foundations; trade unions; religious, peace, and disarmament groups; youth and women's organizations; development, environmental, and human rights groups; research institutes and associations of parliamentarians.

The United Nations and Non-Governmental Organizations (New York; United Nations, no date given).

[3] Fred Starr, "The Third Sector in the Second World," 19 *World Development* p. 65 (U.K.: Pergamon Press, 1991). Starr describes the experience of the "Polish Jazz Society and the so-called Jazz Section in Czechoslovakia," which in his view demonstrated:

The Economic and Social Council may make suitable arrangements for consultation with non-governmental organizations which are concerned with matters within its competence. Such arrangements may be made with international organizations and, where appropriate, with national organizations after consultation with the Member of the United Nations concerned.

Pursuant to Article 71, ECOSOC Resolution 1296 provides the procedures by which NGOs may obtain recognition as consultative organizations of the UN. The resolution also discusses principles to be applied in the establishment of consultative relations.

The types of organizations permitted to establish consultative relations with the UN include:

international economic, social, cultural, educational, health, scientific, technological and related matters and to questions of human rights, the purposes of which are in conformity with the spirit and purposes of the UN Charter.[4]

The resolution also indicates that such consultative organizations undertake to support the work of the UN. The resolution goes on to describe the necessary organizational and governance aspects of such an organization, as well as the means of funding, in the main either from national components of the organization or from individual members. ECOSOC Resolution 1297 goes further and recommends that the Secretary-General of the UN accord immediate and sympathetic consideration to applications of NGOs from "inadequately represented regions of the world."

There is an additional UN status as well, known generally as association with the UN Department of Public Information (DPI). However, the main purpose of association with DPI is to disseminate information to advance public understanding of the UN, which purpose is somewhat limited in scope and therefore in usefulness.

In the European arena, we first look at some international law with respect to nonprofit organizations developed by the Council of Europe. The Council of Europe, established in 1949 and having its headquarters in Strasbourg, is an organization primarily of western European states formed for the purpose of promoting European unity, protecting human rights, and facilitating social and economic progress. It has special bodies and expert committees, including the European Commission on Human Rights and the European Court of Human Rights. In some 40 years, the Council has developed over 100 conventions in vari-

astonishing boldness and organizational agility, inspiring tens of thousands of enthusiasts in other areas of activity to follow suit in their own fields of interest.

Both of these organizations "managed to get themselves registered with the United Nations as branches of an 'International Jazz Federation.' " He stated further that:

This entity may have existed largely on paper, but its official recognition by the UN long stymied the efforts of communist authorities in the two countries to suppress the jazz societies.

Presumably the status described is the Article 71 status.
[4] United Nations, ECOSOC Resolution 1296 (XLIV), Part I, ¶¶ 1, 2.

ous fields of international law. The Council's conventions are not for the member states of the European Union, but rather for those members of the Council that have chosen to ratify the conventions.

Like the UN, the Council has adopted consultative status for certain international nongovernmental organizations.[5]

The Council's Convention for the Protection of Human Rights and Fundamental Freedoms has been in force since 1953 and acts as a collective guarantee of human rights by its signatories. Article 11(1) of this Convention proclaims the "right to freedom of peaceful assembly and to freedom of association with others, including the right to form and to join trade unions for the protection of his interests." Articles 9 and 10 protect freedom of thought, conscience, and religion, and freedom of expression and opinion, respectively. Article 25 allows for the right of petition by "any person, nongovernmental organization or group of individuals claiming to be the victim of a violation by one of the High Contracting parties of the rights set forth in this Convention." These petitions are processed by a commission that determines whether the petition should be forwarded to the European Court of Justice. The development of this case law is in its relative infancy.[6]

The Council's European Convention on the Recognition of the Legal Personality of International Non-Governmental Organizations (Convention 124) was concluded in Strasbourg in 1986, after 75 years in the making.[7] It entered into force in 1991. Countries ratifying Convention 124 include Austria, Belgium, Greece, Portugal, Slovenia, Switzerland, and the United Kingdom. Under Convention 124, it is required that any NGO must first constitute itself under the law of a participating state and must have an international purpose. Once so constituted, the legal personality and capacity that an NGO has acquired in its state of origin are recognized in other participating states, and registration formalities are dispensed with.

This convention's simple proposition of recognizing entities across borders eliminates a host of problems of translation of one type of legal entity into terms understandable in another legal system. However, the convention is limited to legal recognition of NGOs. As useful a starting point as that may be, it leaves much to be done as it does not consider other legal matters such as taxation or labor law, which must be addressed by individual NGOs operating across borders.

Along these lines, in 1971, a draft European Convention on the Tax Treatment in Respect of Certain Non-Profit Organizations was submitted to the Council.[8] The draft does not attempt to harmonize tax legislation across borders, but instead would extend existing tax concessions in one country to foreign nongovernmental organizations coming into that country. The draft has not been adopted by any Council members.

[5] See Council of Europe, Committee of Ministers, Resolution (72) 35, adopted Oct. 16, 1972, and Resolution (93) 38, adopted Oct. 18, 1993.
[6] See generally, Christiane Duparc, *The European Commission and Human Rights* (Brussels: Commission of the European Communities, 1992).
[7] *European Treaty Series No. 124*, Strasbourg, Conseil de l'Europe (Aug. 1990).
[8] *Draft European Convention on the Tax Treatment in Respect of Certain Non-Profit Organizations: Report Presented to the Council of Europe* (Geneva: Interphil, March 1971).

In addition to provisions of the Council, provisions of the European Union are also of interest to nonprofit organizations operating across borders. The European Union differs from past national and international models in that it has power to enact laws directly binding throughout the territory. Its structures are inherently evolutionary and designed to allow for gradual development of European unification.[9]

In the context of the European Union, a proposed regulation has been developed on the subject of a European association, which would enable associations to take advantage of the single market in the same way that business companies hope to, and thus operate and be recognized across Europe. There are also proposed regulations on European cooperative societies and European mutual societies.

Like Convention 124, the proposals do not deal with fiscal or tax matters.[10] It is unclear whether the proposals will be adopted in whole or in part. The parallel proposed regulations on European business companies have been buried for a quarter of a century, and this does not bode well for action on this particular package.

As "regulations," if and when adopted these would be binding on all member states of the European Community. A regulation is European law unto itself and does not depend upon further implementation through legislative acts of the member states.[11]

Another source of international law on nonprofit organizations is the Hague Conference on Private International Law, which deals with a variety of legal topics selected by participating states. Of particular interest is a treaty concluded in the structure of the Hague Conference, Convention XXX on the law applicable to trusts and their recognition. Convention XXX was concluded in 1984, but its ratification is uncertain. While the Convention is limited in scope and would recognize a trust only when no important policies of the recognizing jurisdiction are involved, still it represents a solid start in clarification for civil law countries exactly what is a charitable trust in common law countries, namely that a trust is a relationship where a trustee is a legal representative of property for various purposes, but the property is not the trustee's beneficially.

In the North American arena, tax treaty provisions that the United States has with its neighbors raise tantalizing possibilities of what might be accomplished through additional bilateral or multilateral treaties. For example, the U.S.–Mexico tax treaty went into effect January 1, 1994.[12] Pursuant to Article XXII of the treaty, there is mutual recognition not only of juridical person status but of income tax exemptions for the two countries' qualifying charities.

---

[9] See generally, European Commission Delegation to the United States, *The European Union: A Guide*, Washington, D.C., 1994.

[10] See *Proposal for a Council Regulation on the Statute for a European Association*, in COM(91) 273 final—SYN 386–391 (Brussels: Commission of the European Communities, March 5, 1992).

[11] See Ole Gjems-Onstad, "The Proposed European Association: A Symbol in Need of Friends," and Frits Hondius, "Charities and International Law," *International Charity Law Conference Papers* (London: National Council of Voluntary Organisations, Sept. 1994); Paines, Aninous "Charities and Europe," *Solicitors Journal* Supplement (Apr. 24, 1992).

[12] *Tax Treaties* (Washington: Commerce Clearing House), ¶ 5903.

The treaty also allows limited charitable deductions to nationals of one country for gifts to charities in the other country, within certain limits. In addition, U.S. foundations may make grants to Mexican charities free of certain burdensome administrative procedures normally required for such grants.

Pursuant to the Canada–U.S. tax treaty in Article XXI, under certain circumstances, individuals may obtain tax deductions in their own country for gifts made to charities in the other country. The tax exemption of organizations in one country may also be recognized upon application to the tax authority in the other country.[13]

The United States has only one treaty outside the hemisphere with similar provisions. The Israel–U.S. treaty, which entered into force January 1, 1995, permits U.S. individuals deductions for contributions to charities organized in Israel.[14]

The U.S. officials have strongly suggested that future U.S. bilateral tax treaties are unlikely to contain similar provisions, and in fact, such a provision was rejected in the Brazil–U.S. treaty.[15]

As can be seen, the international law pertaining to nonprofit organizations is in its infancy, at a low level of achievement in terms of any grand goal of harmonization or unification of law as it applies to nonprofit organizations. International law is not limited to any particular subject, but rather limited only by the willingness of states to adopt it by relinquishing their sovereignty on certain matters. The applicability of much of the existing international law pertaining to nonprofits still depends on a nonprofit organization being recognized in its home jurisdiction for various purposes, which in turn, points to the importance of the subject matter we are about to consider in the following chapters.

[13] *Tax Treaties* (Washington: Commerce Clearing House), ¶ 1903.
[14] *Tax Treaties* (Washington: Commerce Clearing House), ¶ 4603.
[15] For an excellent discussion of the Canadian, Israeli, and Mexican treaties with the United States, see Harvey P. Dale, "Foreign Charities," 48 *Tax Lawyer* No. 3, at 665 *et seq.* (1994).

CHAPTER FOUR

Australia[*]

§ 4.1 LEGAL CONTEXT

The six states which comprise the Commonwealth of Australia were founded during the late eighteenth and early nineteenth centuries as English colonies and as a consequence inherited English law. In common with other countries that have inherited the English legal system, Australia has two sources of law: acts of parliament (statute law), and common or case law. The latter refers to law made by judges in the course of passing judgment on cases where statute or previous case law does not directly apply. In addition, Australia has a federal system, with a national parliament, six state parliaments, and two territorial parliaments. This means there are separate judicial systems and separate systems of legislation concerning the incorporation of nonprofit associations at the national level and in the separate states and territories.

In Australia, two or more people are free to form an association to pursue any purpose, providing that purpose is not illegal. If the object of the association is other than to make a profit, there is no requirement to register it with any government authority. At the same time, more formal governmental registration is required when organizations seek various types of public protection. The result is a generally quite open environment for nonprofit activity, but also a very complex and varied one.

§ 4.2 ELIGIBILITY

(a) Types of Organizations

As noted, the most common form for nonprofit activities is the unincorporated association. However, there are a variety of other legal forms available, the more important of which are trusts, companies, and incorporated associations.

(i) Unincorporated Associations. Unincorporated associations are formed to pursue myriad goals and interests, from arranging a baby-sitting roster to organizing mass protests against a government policy; from raising funds for a local hospital to organizing opportunities for members to pursue a particular enthusiasm such as lawn bowling, or the propagating of native plants, or campanology (i.e., the ringing of chimes or bells). Usually, they have some form of constitution or written rules, although there are no requirements for such.

*Country Rapporteur: Dr. Mark Lyons, Associate Professor, School of Management, University of Technology, Sydney, Australia.

While there is no obligation on such associations to incorporate and thereby gain legal personality, there are several good reasons for doing so. For instance, it is not possible for an unincorporated nonprofit association to hold property or to receive testamentary gifts. Neither can an unincorporated association enter into an enforceable contract. For this reason, governments now generally require an organization to be incorporated before it can receive government grants. An unincorporated association cannot seek legal redress for any wrong done to it, while at the same time the members of its management committee are personally liable for any obligations that might arise as a result of a legal judgment against the association. Finally, it is difficult for the courts to intervene in cases of disagreement between an unincorporated association's members, and it is often difficult for such an association to be wound up and its assets disposed of without the intervention of the courts.[1]

There are a number of legal forms and devices available to members of unincorporated nonprofit associations to address these problems. With the exception of trusts, they require the association to obtain a legal identity by incorporating.

(ii) *Trusts.*   A trust is essentially an obligation assigned to an individual or group to administer property for a given purpose. Two types of trusts exist: private and public. The latter is by far the most relevant to the nonprofit sector.

A public, or charitable, trust is a trust formed to serve a public purpose, rather than the interests of a particular set of individuals. Such a trust is an obligation enforceable in equity which involves the designation of a person (the trustee) as legal owner of some specific property (the trust property) to deal with that property for the advancement of certain charitable purposes. A charitable trust differs from other sorts of trusts in that it may be for purposes, rather than identifiable persons, and may exist in perpetuity, rather than for a limited time. More specifically, charitable trusts can be formed under any of the four heads of charity identified in the common law tradition: relief of poverty, advancement of education, advancement of religion, and other purposes beneficial to the community.

While a corporation may be a trustee, a charitable trust is not a legal entity with a separate persona. It is the trustees, as the legal owners of the property, who would sue or be sued on behalf of the trust and enter into contractual relations on behalf of the trust. The charitable trust is better characterized as an obligation or legal relationship than an entity. Each state and territory has an Act which deals with trusts, including charitable trusts.

Although charitable trusts are not legal persons, they may be incorporated (and thus given a legal identity) under certain circumstances. Generally, this is done by a special act of parliament. In Australia, many religious denominations, such as the Catholic or Anglican church, acquire a legal identity in a particular state through state legislation incorporating a trust to hold their property. Many quite large health, education, and social service organizations that are sponsored or "owned" by churches or religious orders similarly claim a legal identity by virtue of such acts.

---

[1] A.S. Sievers, *Associations and Club Law in Australia and New Zealand.* 2nd ed. (Sydney: Federation Press, 1996).

Although the public or charitable trust is most common for nonprofit purposes, private trust arrangements are also adopted by many unincorporated nonprofit associations, especially sporting clubs, to serve the interests of members. Such arrangements remove the requirement that the property of an unincorporated association be held in the name of all members of the association. Instead, only the trustees bear the responsibility.[2]

(iii) Companies. A more secure way for a nonprofit organization to attain legal status is to incorporate. This can be done most commonly through two routes: (a) by becoming a company or (b) by becoming an incorporated association. The companies route, in turn, can take either of two forms: (1) companies limited by shares, and (2) companies limited by guarantee. The first of these is primarily used for profit-making ventures. Such companies may be proprietary companies, in which case their shares must not be distributed among more than 50 people and must not be publicly traded. Alternatively, they may be public companies, whose shares are publicly traded, and which may raise capital by further share issue. Public companies are much more closely regulated and publicly accountable than are proprietary companies.[3]

Although the company limited by shares form is used mostly by for-profit firms, a number of sporting and social clubs in Australia have been incorporated as nonprofit proprietary companies, largely, it seems, because the lawyers and accountants responsible for incorporation were unaware of the company limited by a guarantee form of incorporation, or of the far more common form of incorporated association (though this latter form has existed in some states and territories for only twenty years).

The *company limited by guarantee* is another form of company that is available and commonly used to incorporate nonprofit associations (it is also sometimes used to incorporate for-profit associations such as insurance companies). This form of company has no share capital and, thus, is unable to limit its liability to the value of its shares. Instead, its members guarantee to pay a certain sum (generally very small) if the assets of the company are insufficient to discharge its debts upon dissolution.

(iv) Incorporated Associations. The most common form of incorporation for nonprofit organizations is the *incorporated association*. Such associations can be formed in all Australian states and territories. In most states, it is possible for a group of people who wish to form an incorporated nonprofit association to do so from the outset, without forming an unincorporated association as a first step. The first associations incorporation legislation was passed in South Australia in the late nineteenth century. This legislation was framed to create an easier method for nonprofit associations to incorporate than was available at the time under the companies law. Several other colonies followed suit. Legislation with a similar purpose was introduced by the other states and territories in the mid-to-late twentieth century. Those states and territories that have not recently introduced asso-

---

[2] Sievers, *supra*, p. 19.

[3] J.V. Gooley, *A Guide to Corporations and Associations Law* (Sydney: Magna Carta Press, 1989), p. 66.

ciations legislation, have, over the past 20 years, reviewed and amended their legislation, generally to make it easier to incorporate, but also to make the responsibilities attached to incorporation a little more demanding.

The incorporated association form of incorporation is available only to nonprofit associations and is by far the most popular. In Australia, in 1991, there were almost 80,000 incorporated associations, compared to less than 9,000 companies limited by guarantee.[4]

(v) *Other Forms.*   Several other forms of nonprofit organizations also exist. One of these is the *cooperative*. The cooperative form is generally used by groups of producers (e.g., dairy farmers) to market their product, or consumers (e.g., wine fanciers or book buyers) to leverage a lower price for their favored products. In both cases, members seek by cooperation to increase their market power. Whether these organizations are nonprofit is a matter of definition. However, in Australia's two largest states, New South Wales and Victoria, associations formed for what are clearly public purposes (such as to run a refuge or manage low-income housing) might incorporate as community advancement cooperatives.[5]

Another form of association, more common in the nineteenth century, is the *friendly society*. These are associations of workers or other groups to pool funds, provide social welfare protections, and for related purposes. They were governed by friendly society acts but such legislation did not usually provide incorporation. Friendly society legislation still exists in most jurisdictions and several hundred friendly societies still exist in Australia. But as a form of association it has fallen into disuse and it is rare for a new friendly society to form.

In order to encourage the development of community infrastructure among Aboriginal and Torres Strait Islander people, the Aboriginal Councils and Associations Act was passed in 1976 to facilitate the incorporation of *Aboriginal corporations* (i.e., associations formed by these people). In 1990, there were 1,200 Aboriginal corporations registered under the Act.[6]

The Aboriginal Councils and Associations Act is an example of legislation formed to provide corporate identity to groups of people sharing a common characteristic. Other legislation creates corporate forms for people who have associated to pursue a particular purpose. For example, in some Australian states and nationally, registration as an *industrial organization* (a trade union or employer association) with the relevant industrial court gives the benefit of incorporation. Strata title legislation in each state and territory provides for the creation of a *body corporate* comprised of the owners of apartments or offices in an apartment or office building which becomes responsible for maintaining the common areas and generally looking after the collective interests of individual owners.

There are many other pieces of legislation that have been passed at different times to facilitate incorporation for particular classes of organizations. For example, under the Queensland Religious, Charitable and Educational Institutions Act of 1861, there are still some 700 organizations registered as incorporated

---

[4] M. Lyons, "Australia's Nonprofit Sector," in S. Saxon-Harrold and J. Kendall (eds.), *Researching the Voluntary Sector*, 2d ed. (London: Charities Aid Foundation, 1994).
[5] D.R. Magarey, *Guide to the NSW Cooperatives Law* (Sydney: CCH Australia, 1994).
[6] Lyons, *supra* 4.

trustees. In the same state there is also a Sporting Bodies Property Holding Act of 1975, and a Hospitals Foundations Act of 1982. In most states, legislation governing public education provides for the incorporation of parents associations attached to individual schools.

Finally, two other methods of incorporation are available to nonprofit associations, but are rarely used. These are *incorporation by royal charter* or by a *special act of parliament*. These methods have been used in the past, but only by organizations which were well established and which had achieved a high social standing.

(b) Types of Purposes

Generally, the variety of methods by which nonprofit associations seek incorporation suggest that any nonprofit association, provided it is not formed for illegal purposes, can incorporate and obtain the status, benefits, and responsibilities of a legal personality. In three states, associations incorporation legislation explicitly permits any association formed for a lawful purpose other than for trading or generating a profit for its members to apply for incorporation. Legislation in the other three states and the two territories sets out a range of purposes. An association seeking incorporation must demonstrate that it shares one of these purposes. However, each of these more specific pieces of legislation allows the relevant minister to extend the privileges of incorporation to associations whose purposes fall outside the range set out in the legislation. A refusal to permit incorporation to such an association is rare. The only explicit prohibition in most states' legislation is to prevent from incorporating as associations nonprofit groups formed for special purposes (such as trade unions or building societies) for which more specialized forms of incorporation are available.[7]

So far as charitable trusts are concerned, though not bodies corporate, they are required to serve purposes that fall within the "four heads" of charity: relief of poverty, advancement of education, advancement of religion, and other purposes beneficial to communities.

(c) Other Requirements

There are few, if any, membership or capital requirements to incorporate a nonprofit organization. In most states, incorporated associations may be formed with as few as five members. Five members also suffice to incorporate a company limited by guarantee. In two states, application for incorporation can be made on behalf of any group of five people, as well as existing unincorporated associations; in other states and territories it is assumed that it is an unincorporated association which is applying for incorporation and evidence must be provided that the majority of members approve the application and proposed rules. In two states, incorporated associations are required to take out public liability insurance. Companies limited by guarantee must also have a registered office.

---

[7] Sievers, *supra*, p. 88.

(d) Registration Procedures

(i) Incorporated Associations.   To establish that they are genuinely non-profit organizations, incorporated associations are required to have a clause in their constitution stating that neither members nor office holders can receive any direct benefit from the activities of the association. In four of the eight states and territories, associations legislation, however, permits the distribution of the surplus assets of an association among its members upon dissolution of the association, provided its members have specially resolved to do so.[8] However, if the association wishes to claim tax exempt status (and most do), it is required to have a clause prohibiting this possibility and indicating clearly that any assets left upon dissolution of the organization will be passed to another tax-exempt organization with similar objects.

The process of registration varies among jurisdictions, but all provide a set of model rules and require associations to follow these in drawing up their constitutions. This ensures that a constitution addresses such matters as membership qualifications and dues and procedures for electing a committee and office holders, for calling a general meeting, for amending the rules, for disciplining members, and for winding up the association. All that is required is that members lodge an application to incorporate along with a copy of its rules (or constitution).

In some jurisdictions, the name and address of the committee of an association seeking incorporation must be provided, in others only the name and address of an applicant. In all but one jurisdiction, the association must appoint a person, or provide an address, to act as a contact between the association, the government, and the wider community. Under associations legislation this person is known as a "public officer." Frequently, a solicitor or an accountant who helped the association to form becomes the public officer.

In some states, provided requirements are fully met, the registrar must grant a certificate of incorporation. In several jurisdictions this might be refused if the registrar considered that the association might be better incorporated under some more specialized legislation or, because of its size or reach, as a company limited by guarantee.

Each act allows the registrar to refuse incorporation to an association under a name which might be confused with another association's name or might be considered offensive. In most states and territories, the regulation of business names provides protection to certain names that might imply an association has a charitable character. The term "foundation" has been given such protected status and in most states is permitted only to nonprofit associations (in Australia, foundations do not exist as a distinct legal type).

(ii) Companies.   Associations seeking to incorporate as companies limited by guarantee are required to have at least five members. They are furthermore required to lodge the names of directors and office holders with the Australian Securities Commission (ASC), which regulates all companies. Changes in directors or office holders must be immediately reported to the ASC where they are

---

[8] Sievers, *supra*, p. 153.

kept in an electronic database which can be searched by any member of the public for a fee. All companies are given an *Australian company number* (ACN), and are required to provide this on all correspondence, publicity, and so on. This is designed to make it easier for any member of the public who wishes to seek further information on the company to do so.

An association applying to be registered as a company limited by guarantee does not need to state a purpose or object unless its objects are for purposes beneficial to the community and it wishes to drop any reference in its name to the fact that it is an incorporated company. However, most such companies will include a statement of purpose in their constitution as they are required to indicate their purpose to gain an exemption from paying income tax. Generally, the requirements for incorporation as a company limited by guarantee are similar to those of incorporated associations. Thus, companies also need to include a benefit restriction clause in their constitution. The main difference is that the paperwork is more onerous and the subsequent reporting requirements are more rigorously enforced.

One unresolved debate concerns the circumstances in which one or the other of the two most common forms of incorporation—unincorporated associations or company limited by guarantee—is appropriate. It is generally thought that an association that has members, or which conducts its business, in more than one state or territory should incorporate under national companies legislation as a company limited by guarantee. It is also argued that associations with large trading income, such as some sporting bodies or large social clubs, should do so also. The provision exists in association incorporation acts in most states for the relevant minister to transfer the registration of an incorporated association to the ASC, thus changing it to a company limited by guarantee, but this power is rarely invoked.

Many types of bodies corporate created by state or territory legislation, such as incorporated associations, cooperatives, and special act nonprofit bodies, are defined under the Corporations Law as "registerable local bodies." A registerable local body that carries on business outside its state of incorporation is required to register with the ASC as a "registerable Australian body." Registration is by lodgment of documents with the ASC. Such a body receives an Australian Registerable Body Number (ARBN), which must be displayed on public documents.

§ 4.3 INTERNAL GOVERNANCE

In most jurisdictions, legislation providing for the incorporation of nonprofit associations sets out certain requirements for the governance of the organization. In all cases, it requires that the organization have a constitution or memorandum and articles of association, and that these documents spell out the relationship between the management committee or boards of directors and the membership of the organization. Generally, the two common forms of incorporation create a conventional organizational model, where members elect a board to govern the organization, and where that board is in theory accountable to them via regular elections.

In most jurisdictions, legislation does not set out the composition, duties, or length of term of management committee members. This is generally left to the members to decide. Generally, the founding members draw up the constitution and determine the size of the governing body and the requirements for elections, annual meetings, and reports to members. The constitution also sets out procedures whereby a majority of members can demand special meetings.

One requirement shared by both common forms of incorporation is that board members are not permitted to be paid directors' fees unless this is specifically authorized in the association's articles or rules. However, organizations are able to insure them against certain claims which might flow from some failure in their responsibility as directors, and reimburse them for out-of-pocket expenses incurred in performing their duties as directors.

Although the member/board organizational structure is the norm, in all jurisdictions except Queensland and South Australia, incorporated associations which are committed to collective forms of governance are able to bend the conventional board/member model of governance to match their values. Other variations of the conventional membership model of organization also exist. Many church-sponsored organizations are incorporated by the church body or religious order, which acts as the trustees. These trustees appoint the board and, generally, retain ownership of the real property.

§ 4.4   TAX TREATMENT

The tax treatment of nonprofit associations in Australia reflects the haphazard and, generally, uninformed approach to nonprofit associations in Australian public policy. The laws do not appear to embody any consistent principle but to have developed haphazardly in response to problems and special pleading. Case law is no more consistent and neither is the administration of these laws by the Australian Taxation Office (ATO).

(a)   Tax Treatment of Organizations

(i) Income Tax.   The various subsections of Section 23 of the Income Tax Assessment Act of 1936 (ITAA) exempt most nonprofit associations from paying tax on their income. In defining exempt organizations, the starting point of Section 23 is whether an organization is a charitable institution (or, in the case of a trust, if it has been established for a charitable purpose). The key subsection is Section 23(e), which exempts the income of "a religious, scientific, charitable or public educational institution." However, the term "charity" is not defined in legislation and relies on case law for its meaning. As noted, the Australian courts recognize as charitable any nonprofit organization whose purpose falls within one of the four heads of charity set out in nineteenth-century English case law: relief of poverty, advancement of education, advancement of religion, and other purposes beneficial to community. The fourth head of charity, "other purposes beneficial to the community," has generally been given a wide interpretation by the

ATO and the courts.[9] Other purposes which can qualify a nonprofit organization for a tax exemption, such as promoting the development of aviation or encouraging music, art, science, or literature, have subsequently been added.

Among those awarded tax-exempt status under these provisions are arts and culture organizations and many business and trade associations (those that represent groups in industries which the government wishes to foster, such as agriculture and manufacturing). Many sporting and some recreational associations are also fully exempt and so too are social clubs provided they include a sporting facility. But the law is vague and its interpretation is sometimes bizarre. For example, until a recent amendment, nonprofit associations that organize horse or dog races were exempt but those that arranged motor vehicle or yacht races were not. All are now exempt. However, some sporting and recreation associations, and some trade and most professional associations, are not exempt. But even for those bodies, the application of the mutuality principle exempts membership subscriptions from the calculation of income for taxation purposes.[10]

The ATO is relatively lax in its administration of Section 23. If an organization applies for exemption, it may have to alter its constitution to comply with the views of the particular clerk who handles the application, but once granted, it is told that it should not contact the ATO again. It is not required to file a return, nor to supply any other information. Many organizations assume they are tax exempt and never contact the ATO. With recent moves by the ATO to self-assessment, this would appear to be acceptable, although an organization may be required to prove that it fell within one of the exempt categories should it ever be audited.[11] However, unless the organization employs staff and therefore submits to the ATO withholding taxes deducted from employees' wages, an audit is unlikely since the ATO will have no record of the organization on file. By law, banks and other financial institutions where a nonprofit association has an account are required to tax any interest earned by that account, unless they see proof that the organization has been exempted from tax. In practice, some financial institutions ignore this requirement and treat as tax exempt the accounts of associations the manager or staff believe to qualify. It should be noted that whether or not nonprofit associations are incorporated has no bearing at all on their taxation status.

Although income tax exemption also applies to income in the form of capital gains, goods or property bequeathed to nonprofit organizations are not exempted from the application of the capital gains tax, which is payable by the trustees out

---

[9] A. Verick, and J. Lamerton, "Tax Concessions for Charitable Bodies and Philanthropies: Administration of the Tests," in R. Krever and G. Kewley (eds.), *Charities and Philanthropic Organizations: Reforming the Tax Subsidy and Regulatory Regimes.* (Melbourne: Monash University and Australian Tax Research Foundation, 1992).

[10] The position is more complex for nonprofit financial institutions such as friendly societies, credit unions, and cooperative building societies. Over the past decade, these have had tax exemptions, which they had enjoyed for many years, withdrawn. Many people, however, do not consider these true nonprofit associations.

[11] S. Rodman, and M. McGregor-Lowndes, "Income Tax Exemptions for Nonprofit Associations," in M. McGregor-Lowndes, K. Fletcher, and A. Sieves (eds.), *Legal Issues for Nonprofit Associations.* (Sydney: LBC Information Services, 1996), p. 131.

of the residue of the estate. This creates something of a disincentive for bequests to nonprofit associations.

(ii) Other Taxes.   Some nonprofit associations are exempt from other forms of tax. The exemptions vary, but in all cases are available chiefly to what are called public benevolent institutions (PBIs). Although the term "PBI" is used extensively in legislation, it has been left to the courts to define it. Basically, an organization is a PBI if it primarily engages in providing identifiable forms of relief to persons who are clearly deserving and needing of assistance. There is a requirement that such aid be provided directly, which excludes organizations that are confined to advocacy for classes of persons. The recipients of aid must also be in need of help, which precludes organizations primarily providing preventative assistance, such as marriage counseling or community development. Broadly, the term PBI seems to apply to organizations which would qualify as a charity under the first head of charity, "the relief of poverty."

PBIs are exempt from paying Australia's wholesale *sales tax,* which is levied on the wholesale price of many goods sold in Australia. PBIs, as well as public hospitals and religious institutions, are also exempt from the *fringe benefits tax,* which is payable by an employer on the value of certain benefits provided to an employee (e.g., the private use of motor vehicles, the payment of entertainment costs, free or subsidized housing or housing loans, and the payment of private school fees).[12]

Various groups of nonprofit associations are exempted from taxes levied by state government authorities, such as *payroll tax, land tax, stamp duty and bank charges,* together with rates levied by local government authorities. PBIs are in all cases exempt, while nonprofit schools, public hospitals, religious institutions, and less commonly, all charities, are exempted from some taxes in some jurisdictions. Each taxing authority is entitled to develop its own interpretation of terms used in the legislation and defined by the courts. In many cases, state authorities are happy to accept the ATO determination; in other cases they are not and occasionally anomalies are created whereby the same organization is considered a PBI by the ATO, but not by a state government authority.[13]

(b) Tax Treatment of Contributions—Domestic Organizations

The Australian taxation system allows donors to certain groups of nonprofit associations to claim their donations as a tax deduction; that is, to deduct the value of their donation from their taxable income before computing their tax obligations. Gifts may be made by real persons or by legal persons, such as companies. Testamentary gifts are not tax deductible. Section 78 of the ITAA defines the categories of organizations for which such tax deductibility is available. Included are: PBIs, school building funds, public museums, public libraries, and relief to per-

---

[12] G. Noakes, and A. Carrabs, "Charities, Philanthropies and Nonprofit Organizations: The Impact of Other Taxes," in R. Krever and G. Kewley (eds.), *Charities and Philanthropic Organizations: Reforming the Tax Subsidy and Regulatory Regimes* (Melbourne: Monash University and Australian Tax Research Foundation, 1992).

[13] Industry Commission, *Charitable Organizations in Australia,* Report No. 45, (Melbourne: Australian Government Publishing Service, 1995), p. 307.

sons in necessitous circumstances. Section 78 of the ITAA also lists some 90 organizations which do not qualify under any of the above categories for which donations are tax deductible. In addition, donations to appeals held by organizations registered with the Sports Foundation or to organizations on a Register of Environmental Groups or a Register of Cultural Organizations are also entitled to tax deductibility.[14]

Entitlement to tax deductibility for donors is thus more closely defined than is organizational exemption from income tax in Australia. Indeed, two main classes of charitable organizations—those formed for the advancement of religion and for "purposes beneficial to the community"—are excluded from being able to give a tax deduction to their donors. This means that many organizations which receive tax exemption are unable to provide tax deductibility to their donors. Not surprisingly, such arrangements produce anomalies. In a few cases, nonprofit organizations which are not tax exempt, such as some sporting bodies, may be able to give tax deductibility to donors to particular appeals for funds.

Generally, to be deductible, gifts have to be of a philanthropic character: membership fees, the purchase of raffle tickets, or participation in other fundraising events where there is the possibility of a beneficial return to the donor, are not eligible. Donations have to be at least two dollars in value, but there is no upper limit on what can be deducted. Gifts may be in kind, provided they are goods traded by the donor or they were purchased within the past twelve months. Companies, of course, also have the opportunity to obtain a deduction for assistance they provide nonprofit associations by writing it off as a business expense, as marketing or promotion expenditures.

One exception to these generalizations concerns political parties. Gifts to political parties of up to $100 per year are tax deductible, but only if they are made by individuals, not by companies.

Many trusts and foundations that are established to be grant making are restricted in their deed of trust to giving to PBIs, largely because in past years, when they were established, estate duties, which applied in all Australian states (and have in the last 20 years been abandoned), gave a favorable treatment to trusts which were restricted in this way. In the case of trusts and foundations that are both grant seeking and grant making, tax deductibility is only available to donors if their trust deeds or objects clearly state that the organizations that they assist with their grants are capable of giving a tax deduction.

---

[14] The Foundation and the two registers mentioned here were developed over the past few years to make it easier for nonprofit sporting, environment, and cultural organizations to obtain tax-deductible status. Before then, organizations favored by government, but not in one of the eligible classes of organizations could be added to the long list of organizations individually recorded in the legislation, but this required regular amendment of the Act. New sporting, cultural, and environmental organizations can now obtain similar status by meeting a few simple requirements such as being incorporated and having a separate fund to receive donations governed by people with standing in the community. The approval of the relevant portfolio minister and the treasurer must also be obtained before they can be added to the register. In 1993, there were about 150 organizations registered with the Sports Foundation, 390 with the register of cultural organizations and 35 with the register of environmental organizations (which had only recently been formed). See M. Lyons, *Tax Deductibility of Donations to Community Welfare Organizations. A Report of a Survey*, CACOM Working Paper No. 17 (Sydney: University of Technology, 1993).

Grant-making trusts and foundations are also faced with another restriction on their independence imposed by the ATO. Unless such organizations wish to run down their principal, they rely on interest or dividends as their revenue source. In some cases, trustees may wish to restrict their giving in order to build the principal, particularly during years when interest rates are high. In order to retain their tax-exempt status, however, charitable trusts and foundations that are designed to be exclusively grant making are not permitted to accumulate income on their assets indefinitely. Rather, the ATO requires that they spend 85% of their revenue on grants in the year in which it is earned.[15]

(c) Tax Treatment of Contributions—Foreign Organizations

In general, the rules about deductibility of donations apply only to organizations or funds that are established and operate within Australia. Australian branches of international bodies, such as the Red Cross, fall within this description. Indeed, gifts to all organizations or funds that provide relief to residents of developing countries and which have been approved by the Minister for Foreign Affairs and the Treasurer are tax deductible.

§ 4.5   PERSONAL BENEFIT RESTRICTIONS

In keeping with the general laissez-faire attitude of Australian governments toward nonprofit associations, few restrictions are placed upon their operation. Nevertheless, board members are prohibited from receiving any remuneration (other than out-of-pocket expenses) for exercising their governance responsibilities. Board members who are in companies limited by guarantee are required to declare any other directorships they might hold.

§ 4.6   OBLIGATIONS TO THE PUBLIC

In all but one state, *incorporated associations* are expected to file annual reports with their relevant state or territory government authority. However, these governments devote fewer resources than the ASC to ensuring compliance and many organizations do not file returns or do so sporadically. Only two states appear to be reasonably diligent in following up with nonfilers. No attempt is made to record financial data and, indeed, in most states, while financial reports must be presented to an organization's members, they are not considered part of the public record.[16] Only recently, moreover, have some jurisdictions moved to include some basic data on incorporated associations in an electronic database.

Unlike the United States or Canada, where reports to taxation authorities are public documents, in Australia the ATO specifically discourages nonprofits from submitting annual returns. The suggestion that any tax record might be a public document would be totally anathema to privacy-obsessed Australians.

---

[15] Industry Commission, *supra* 13, pp. 316–317.
[16] Industry Commission, *supra* 13, p. 203.

In contrast to incorporated associations, *companies limited by guarantee* face more restrictive reporting requirements. In particular, such companies are required to submit audited annual financial statements along with summary financial details to the ASC. These must all have been passed by the annual general meeting before transmittal. The summary financial details are also entered in the electronic file and are publicly available. The ASC is quite rigorous in ensuring that company data is up to date and uses a system of fines and deregistration to ensure compliance. However, the reporting requirements are framed with the far more common public companies (limited by shares) in mind and the information held in the ASC files is of limited value to anyone seeking to assess a nonprofit company. For example, it provides no information on the sources of the organization's funds, where those funds are expended, or the cost of fund raising.

While the general reporting requirements for nonprofit organizations are relatively limited, government departments that subsidize the activities of such organizations through grants and contracts often require extensive reports, but these generally relate only to the subsidized activities and are also not public documents. They may, however, be obtained under freedom of information legislation, for a fee. Only a few departments publicly report the grants they make.

§ 4.7 BUSINESS ACTIVITY

Many nonprofit associations raise revenue by pursuing various business activities. These activities may be classified in several ways. Some nonprofit associations charge a fee for their services; others use the profit from separate or unrelated business ventures to add to the income they apply to their core activities. In Australia, unlike most other countries, if an organization is given exemption from income tax, then all income it receives is exempt from tax. This includes any surplus or profit from unrelated business activities.[17]

The only restriction imposed on a nonprofit association to curb its unrelated business activity is an administrative rule applied by the ATO which says that the association's activities must be predominantly of an exempt character, which the ATO interprets to mean that if unrelated activities exceed 15% of the association's revenues, then the association is at risk of losing its exemption.[18] But, given the lack of any regular scrutiny by the ATO of exempt organizations, organizations could easily exceed this limit without fear of retribution. In effect, the rule means that the larger an association, the larger might be its unrelated business activities, provided, of course, that all the profits of that business are applied to the main purpose of the association. The position may now be even more benign. In a recent case, the court ruled that a bowling club was still exempt even though 92% of its income was generated from poker machines and only 6% of its expenditures was devoted to bowling.[19] The ramifications of this for nonprofit associations in other industries have yet to be tested.

---

[17] A recent inquiry into charitable organizations conducted by the Industry Commission examined this exemption and recommended that it be maintained. (See Industry Commission, *supra* 13, p. 316).

[18] Verick and Lamerton, *supra*, p. 39.

[19] Rodman and McGregor-Lowndes, *supra* 11, p. 124.

§ 4.8   OTHER FUNDING RESTRICTIONS

One area where there is extensive regulation is fund raising. All but one Australian state has in place legislation and consequent regulations governing fund raising by many nonprofit associations. Ostensibly introduced to protect the public from fraudulent appeals, the legislation imposes some severe restrictions on those classes of nonprofit organizations which are unable to claim an exemption. Regulations vary from state to state, making it difficult to conduct national appeals. Some classes of organizations are exempt from this regulation, but the list of exempt classes varies from state to state though it generally includes government departments, nonprofit hospitals, schools, and church-sponsored organizations. Regulations once closely specified even the way the organization was to manage its finances (to the extent of specifying the size of a petty cash float). However, these laws have mostly been reviewed and modernized over the past 15 years, though they continue to impose often unrealistic requirements. For example, in New South Wales, the cost of conducting any particular fund raising appeal is not permitted to exceed 40% of the revenue raised. If applied rigorously, this would prohibit any donor acquisition appeals. In some states, associations are required to report some of the details of their fund raising in annual reports; in others they are merely required to submit reports to the relevant authority. In only one state are these considered public documents.

For several decades, these charitable collection acts (as they were all once called), shaped the popular public perception of a charity. Charities were those organizations that sought to raise funds from the public by way of appeal. Registration under the act neither conferred a legal identity nor did it qualify an organization for any of the various tax concessions available to charities or the more limited set of PBIs, yet many, including board members and managers of these organizations, believed it did both.[20]

§ 4.9   POLITICAL ACTIVITY

English case law restricting the political activity of charities applies in Australia, but is rarely invoked by the taxation authorities. Many nonprofit associations engage in activity that could probably be construed as lobbying and many more certainly engage in advocacy for particular interests and to support or oppose particular government policies. Some tax-exempt organizations go so far as to endorse particular parties at election time and even to stand their own candidates without imperiling their tax-exempt status. Yet, there have been a few cases where less extensive political activity has led to loss of tax-exempt status. It would appear that organizations whose primary purpose is to seek legislative changes are most at risk, although it also appears that the ATO acts only if they receive a complaint from an aggrieved politician. It seems probable that the reason why there is so little concern to enforce case law prohibiting political activity by charities is a belief on the part of government officials that very little rides on it. Charities that are PBIs would lose a lot if they lost their charitable status. However,

---

[20] Lyons, *supra* 14.

few of these do any advocacy and for those that do, it is clearly incidental to their main purpose. Most nonprofit advocacy organizations are charities but are not PBIs. All they would lose if they lost their charitable status is their tax exemption. As most have little surplus income, this would matter little to them. Therefore, the threat of loss of charitable status carries little weight and there is little point in wielding it.

§ 4.10   KEY OUTSTANDING ISSUES

Australia has many nonprofit associations and most Australians belong to or support several. But Australians are generally unaware of the size and importance of these organizations as a class. Consequently, the legal and regulatory treatment of nonprofit associations is lax and muddled. In general, this helps nonprofit organizations to flourish, but it also means that widespread misunderstanding of this set of organizations and resulting comparatively low levels of giving persist.[21]

Generally, there is little likelihood of any of the legal arrangements outlined above being changed dramatically before the next century. A major inquiry by the Industry Commission into nonprofit social service organizations (inaccurately called charitable organizations) recommended some changes to current forms of incorporation available to those organizations, designed to make them more directly and clearly accountable to the public, but the government response has been unenthusiastic. The government has responded similarly to the Industry Commission's recommendation to remove or review some of the tax exemptions for these organizations. If the government were to adopt the Industry Commission's recommendations, this would have ramifications for most or all nonprofit associations and not just those that were the subject of the inquiry. It would have ramifications for state and territory governments as well. It is too big an issue for one government, let alone nine, to handle.

Several other reforms being pursued more enthusiastically by governments will have some effects on nonprofit associations, but these effects will be largely unintended. In the health and social services fields, governments seem determined to strengthen and extend the use of market approaches in the way they finance the provision of human services.[22] This may lead to widespread amalgamation of smaller nonprofit associations and to the creation by large associations of for-profit subsidiaries to compete for government contracts. In addition, what is called the simplification of company legislation seems likely to create strong incentives for nonprofit associations to seek to incorporate as small proprietary companies. This is because both the cost of doing so and the reporting requirements are far less onerous than they are even under associations legislation. This will legitimize a form of incorporation which draws no distinction between for-profit and nonprofit associations.

[21] M. Lyons, *Private Donations and Australia's Welfare State*, CACOM Working Paper No. 15 (Sydney: University of Technology, 1993).
[22] M. Lyons, *Reforming Australia's Community Services: A Review of Proposals*, CACOM Working Paper No. 28 (Sydney: University of Technology, 1995).

CHAPTER FIVE

Brazil*

§ 5.1 LEGAL CONTEXT

Brazil is a civil law country in the Roman law tradition with a codified body of written laws (Civil Code) based on a set of abstract principles which form the legal doctrine. In general, the Civil Code distinguishes among three types of legal corporations: *internal public-law corporations*, which may be established by the federal, state, or municipal governments, federal districts, or the autonomous administrative entities known as autarchies; *external public-law corporations* established by foreign entities; and *private law corporations*. All legal corporations including public-law entities are subject to the norms of private law once they conduct activities of a civil or business nature. Nonprofit organizations are formally recognized in the Civil Code[1] as private law corporations.

The rights and liberties of some kinds of nonprofit organizations are furthermore explicitly mentioned in the federal constitution, which also guarantees a general freedom of association.

§ 5.2 ELIGIBILITY

(a) Types of Organizations

Article 16 of the Civil Code distinguishes between two broad categories of private law corporations: (1) those with economic ends (commercial organizations); and (2) those with noneconomic ends (civil, religious, charitable, ethical, scientific, or literary societies, and public interest associations and foundations). It is the latter set of organizations that are of concern to us here. They can, in turn, be divided into two groups: (a) associations/societies; and (b) foundations.

Associations are organizations based on a contract freely entered into among individuals to exercise common activities or defend common interests. They have their own internal interests, goals, and means which pertain exclusively to the membership. The members of an association may change the organization's goals and purposes and are involved in creating the organization's assets.

Foundations are organizations established to manage assets supplied by a founder in accord with the founder's wishes. They are generally directed toward external beneficiaries and pursue goals that are set by their founders and that are long lasting and not changeable.

* Country Rapporteur: Dr. Leilah Landim, Research Coordinates, Institute for Religious Studies, Rio de Janerio. Based on a legal field guide of the Johns Hopkins Comparative Nonprofit Sector Project.
[1] Law No. 3107 of January 1, 1916.

Unincorporated associations. In addition to the registered or incorporated organizations, which enjoy formal status as legal persons, there are a substantial number of unregistered or unincorporated organizations in Brazil. The Civil Process Code recognizes these organizations as "de facto" or "irregular" organizations and accords them some responsibility before the law. More specifically, unincorporated associations may be sued by third parties if they neglect to fulfill their obligations. If the property of the association is not sufficient to cover incurred obligations or debts, the members of the association become liable with their personal property proportionally to their share in the association.[2]

(b) Types of Purposes

The fifth article of the federal constitution establishes "total freedom of association for licit purposes, with groups of a paramilitary nature prohibited." This reference to licit purposes is repeated in article 17 of the constitution in regard to the organization of political parties. Licit purposes are generally those purposes which are not illegal, immoral, or contrary to the public or social order.

While associations and foundations can pursue a wide array of purposes, the law does distinguish a subclass of "public interest organizations." Included here are associations and foundations that are not primarily member serving, but rather provide services for the public at large. They, thus, pursue goals that are not only noneconomic, but also of public or social benefit. Classification as a public interest organization requires formal recognition by the appropriate organs and carries with it certain tax and other benefits. Thus, for example, the federal constitution stipulates that only organizations related to *education*, defined as community, confessional, or philanthropic schools,[3] and those providing *social assistance*[4] are eligible to receive governmental resources. Other benefits available only to public-interest organizations are noted in this chapter.

(c) Other Requirements

In the case of foundations, the supervisory agency needs to determine whether a foundation's assets are sufficient to allow the organization to pursue its goal in a reasonable manner.

(d) Registration Procedures

The current federal constitution in its fifth article states that the creation of associations does not depend on government authorization. Moreover, the government is prohibited from interfering in their operation (which, if it should happen, could lead to a dual responsibility on a political-administrative or criminal level on the part of the public authorities). The constitution and the Law of Public Registries prohibit the registration of articles of incorporation for corporations only when they are illegal, immoral, or contrary to public or social order. Moreover, corporations acting in such a matter, while already in operation, may be disbanded on the initiative of any citizen or agency of a government ministry. They

---

[2] Articles 1381 and 1396 of the Civil Law Code.
[3] Article 213 of the constitution.
[4] Article 195 of the constitution.

may also be suspended temporarily by the president of the Republic should they be carrying out an activity that is illicit or contrary to public order. However, while no explicit government authorization is necessary, associations and foundations do have to satisfy some formal registration requirements in order to attain a legal personality.

(i) Associations.   To register an association, a founding general assembly of members must approve a charter and elect a board, which may be either provisional or permanent; and prepare minutes of the founding meeting, including the names and identification of founding members. The legal existence of nonprofit law corporations begins with the filing of the charter or articles of incorporation or registration with the agency holding jurisdiction—in this case, the Registration Office for Corporations. The association's articles or charter must include (1) the name, any social funds, purposes, the association's office address, and the duration of the organization; (2) provisions on the administration and representation of the association, both actively and passively and legally and commonly; (3) stipulations concerning procedures for amending the charter or similar governing documents with respect to the administration of the association; (4) provisions regarding the liability of members; (5) rules concerning the winding up of the association and the destination of assets in the event of the dissolution; and (6) the names of founding and board members showing nationality, marital status, and profession. Registration requires the publication of abstracts of the organization's bylaws in the government bulletin *Diario Oficial.* Further required are minutes of the founding meeting, a list if the organization's directors, and a list of its founding associates.[5]

(ii) Foundations.   According to articles 24 and following of the Civil Code, a foundation is created at the time the founder issues a public document or last will which freely and clearly allocates property to a specific purpose. If desired, the founder may also state the manner in which the foundation is to be administered and name a third person to set up the foundation's statutes. If the donor fails to do so, the establishment of statutes falls within the responsibility of the Public Ministry, in which case court approval within the following six months becomes necessary. The Public Ministry of the state in which the proposed foundation is to be located is responsible for verifying that all clauses of the statutes are observed, and that the funds are sufficient in regard to the proposed goals. The Public Ministry must also approve the foundation's internal arrangements.

(iii) Foreign Organizations.   Foreign nonprofit private-law corporations that wish to set up agencies in Brazil must comply with the legal procedures set forth in article 11, first paragraph, of the Introductory Law to the Civil Code, which states:

> Organizations intended to operate in the public interest, such as societies and foundations, shall comply with the law of the State in which they are founded. They may not have affiliates, agencies or establishments in Brazil

---

[5] Article 114 of Public Registration Law No. 6015/73.

until their articles of association have been duly approved by the Brazilian government, and shall be subject to Brazilian laws.

§ 5.3 INTERNAL GOVERNANCE

Under Brazilian law, neither associations nor foundations are subject to any stipulations regarding the administration and management of the organization. The only legal requirement is that governance structure and procedures be explicitly specified in the organization's charter. However, in the case of foundations, the internal arrangement needs to be approved by the Public Ministry.

§ 5.4 TAX TREATMENT

(a) Tax Treatment of Organizations

According to article 150, paragraph VI, of the federal constitution, the central government, the states, the federal districts, and municipalities are prohibited from levying taxes on the assets, revenues, or services received or provided by political parties, including their foundations, workers' unions, and nonprofit educational and social welfare institutions, so long as these assets, revenues, and services are related to the essential aims of the organization in question.

In accordance with articles 126 and 130 of the Income Tax Regulations, these organizations—referred to as "educational and social welfare institutions, societies and foundations of a philanthropic, beneficent, charitable, scientific, cultural, instructive, literary, recreational or sports related nature, and associations and unions"—are not required to submit a declaration of income when the necessary conditions are met. These conditions are spelled out in article 130 of the Income Tax Regulation as "nonremuneration of directors, nondistribution of profits of any type whatsoever; total application of funds for maintenance and development of the corporate objectives; entering of revenue and expenses on the books, respecting conventions that ensure their respective accuracy; and provided that they furnish tax assessors with the information required by law and collect withheld income tax they may have paid." These organizations are directly controlled by the Federal Tax Bureau, however, and are obliged to present annually, every June, the Declaration of Exemption of Income Tax for Law Corporations.

(b) Tax Treatment of Contributions—Domestic Organizations

Public interest organizations, a subset of all nonprofit organizations, are also entitled to favorable tax treatment of private donations as well as eligibility for government support. A public interest organization, or public interest civil association in the language of the Civil Code, is a nonprofit organization considered to be operating for the general public benefit, thereby justifying financial assistance from the state. In addition to eligibility for government assistance and the tax exemptions generally enjoyed by all nonprofit organizations, public interest organizations benefit from a number of mechanisms through which they may obtain financial support from individuals and corporations.

The preconditions for public interest status were originally spelled out in Law No. 91 of 1935, but the issue has recently been taken up again in a new directive by the National Secretary of Citizens' Rights and Justice of June 13, 1990, aimed at clarifying some of the regulatory matters involved. According to this directive, "federal public interest" status is granted to organizations which (1) provide necessary services in fields such as social welfare, medical care, scientific research, and education and culture (purely religious organizations are explicitly excluded); (2) carry out these services in a fashion similar to the operation of governmental agencies, without regard to race, creed, color, or political convictions; and (3) do not have profit making as an objective. Furthermore, organizations are only eligible after being in operation for at least three years, a fact which must be confirmed by the respective local authorities.

Public interest organizations enjoy the following prerogatives:

- Exemption from the employer's contribution to the social security system
- Eligibility for receiving donations from the federal government and its independent agencies
- Deductibility of donations from the donors' gross income for income tax purposes up to a limit of 10% of net income if the donor is a private citizen
- Eligibility for receiving revenue from federal lotteries
- Eligibility for organizing raffles (under authorization by the Ministry of Finance)
- Exemption from monthly deposits into the Severance Payment Fund

In addition, according to article 79 of the Income Tax Regulations, donations and contributions from corporate taxpayers are limited to 10% of gross income. They may not, however, exceed 5% of operating profits.[6]

Besides these federal regulations, states and municipalities have established their own criteria for recognition of public interest or utility organizations with respect to nonfederal taxes and requirements.

(c) Tax Treatment of Contributions—Foreign Organizations

There are no particular tax benefits for gifts to charities operating outside Brazil. All income must be used within the Brazilian territory.

§ 5.5   PERSONAL BENEFIT RESTRICTIONS

Members of the boards of directors and administrative councils of public benefit organizations cannot receive remuneration or any distribution of profits, bonuses or other benefits.

---

[6] Article 246 of the Income Tax Regulations.

§ 5.6 OBLIGATIONS TO THE PUBLIC

As long as the necessary conditions of article 130 of the Income Tax Regulation are met (see section 5.4), nonprofit educational and social welfare institutions do not have to file income declarations, although they are legally obliged to furnish required information to tax assessors and present an annual Declaration of Exemption from Income Tax for Law Corporations to the Federal Tax Bureau. There are no other reporting requirements or disclosure obligations under Brazilian law.

§ 5.7 BUSINESS ACTIVITY

Nonprofit organizations are permitted to engage in business activities in Brazil. However, the proceeds of these activities must be used exclusively to advance the purposes of the organizations and not distributed to members or directors. In addition, as article 150 of the federal constitution implies, such income is not exempt from taxation like other nonprofit income unless it is generated from activities that are related to the essential, public benefit aims of the organization in question.

§ 5.8 OTHER FUNDING RESTRICTIONS

No legal regulation of fund raising exists in Brazil.

§ 5.9 POLITICAL ACTIVITY

The purposes of nonprofit organizations must be strictly of public interest, and such organizations may not participate in any political or partisan activities. However, nonprofit organizations do engage in lobbying activities in Brazil and there are no explicit legal prohibitions on that.

§ 5.10 KEY OUTSTANDING ISSUES

The current Brazilian constitution is still fairly recent, having been promulgated in October 1988. The prior one was promulgated in 1967 during the height of the military regime that lasted from 1964 to 1984. Democratic institutionalization was only fully reestablished in December 1989 with direct elections for the presidency of the Republic. Accordingly, it is important to point out that Brazil still is in a transitional phase, especially with respect to a series of legal matters. Although the rights and liberties of some types of nonprofit organizations have been firmly amplified by the new constitution, there remain a lot of unresolved issues that call for future regulations.

One of these issues regards the creation of more suitable regulations governing nonprofit associations in Brazil, the revision of various bureaucratic regulations that currently exist at the federal level, and the consolidation of existing laws by act of parliament. For instance, the registration procedures for obtaining tax benefits and eligibility for public subsidies are unduly bureaucratic and do not appear to take into account the control and evaluation of the public interest or the convenience and usefulness of the services rendered by nonprofit organizations. Organizations trying to register for these benefits face a number of successive and cumulative administrative barriers that all too often are a disincentive to seek legal recognition. However, government has recently begun to acknowledge this problem and first discussions between officials and civil society organizations on how to reform the system are underway.

One item that is needed but still missing on the legal agenda concerns a more precise and updated definition of different types of nonprofit organizations, which, so far, are treated more or less generically. Ideally, future legislation should develop clear and concise legal criteria to distinguish different types of organizations and establish a progressive balance between benefits granted and obligations imposed on such different types of organizations, depending on the organization's purpose, social function, and degree of complementarity with government policies.

CHAPTER SIX

Canada[*]

§ 6.1 LEGAL CONTEXT

Canada is a federal country with a national parliament as well as parliaments for each of the provinces and territories. This means that it is difficult to make countrywide generalizations about the legal environment for nonprofit organizations as they can be incorporated under a variety of statutes in individual provinces as well as under federal legislation. In addition, there is a constitutional separation of power between the federal and provincial governments under which the power to regulate activities such as education and health theoretically resides in the provincial governments whereas taxation of income is a federal power. In actual practice, however, extensive sharing of powers is the norm.

The supreme statutory law of Canada is the *Constitution Act*, which applies throughout the country and guarantees a high level of freedom through the *Charter of Rights*, which is an integral part of the constitution. Under these general rights and freedoms, it is possible for any citizens to come together to establish a society, corporation, or foundation for any social, political, religious, or other legal purpose as a matter of right upon complying with minimum requirements.

The legal environment is further complicated by the fact that Canada is primarily a common law country but has one province, Quebec, which is a civil law jurisdiction. After 25 years of revision, an entirely new *Civil Code of Quebec* took effect on January 1, 1994. It introduced a new concept of a civil law foundation that is different from the common concept and also has a sophisticated "social trust," which incorporates into the civil code many trust and equity features of the trust as used in the common law. Not enough time has elapsed to understand the differences, if any, this new Civil Code of Quebec will bring to the legal environment of nonprofit organizations.

The reason that it is difficult to predict the impact of the new Civil Code of Quebec is that the tax privileges given to registered charities in Canada are granted under the *Income Tax Act*, which is a federal statute applying throughout the entire country. It applies the common law definition of charity to organizations to which it grants tax privileges irrespective of whether or not they are in Quebec. At a pragmatic level, tax laws are the most important component of the legal environment for most charities as they determine the benefits available to donors and the privileges available to charities.

---

[*] Country Rapporteur: Blake Bromley, Esq., Barrister and Solicitor, Vancouver, Canada.

§ 6.2   ELIGIBILITY

(a) Types of Organizations

There are two broad classes of charities in Canada: *charitable organizations* (or operating charities) and *charitable foundations*. A foundation can be exclusively an operating charity, but because a charitable organization is prohibited from giving more than 50% of its income to other charities it cannot be exclusively a grant-making charity. It is very important to distinguish the legal treatment of these two types of charities from the tax treatment. In legal terms, charitable organizations can take three different forms: they can be unincorporated associations, incorporated entities, or trusts. Charitable foundations, however, can take only two forms: trusts or corporations.

The term "registered charity" is an Income Tax Act term that includes both "charitable foundations" and "charitable organizations." By contrast, the Income Tax Act defines a "nonprofit organization" as something which is not a charity. A Canadian nonprofit organization is exempt from tax on its own income, but donations to it are not tax deductible by donors for tax purposes. Consequently, in tax terms a nonprofit organization is not nearly as advantageous as a registered charity; but most charities are properly referred to as nonprofit corporations in terms of their legal incorporating statutes.

As noted, a charitable organization is an operating charity and it can take any of three forms. The first of these is an *unincorporated association.* Such an organization does not have the status of a legal person and need not register with any court or government body. However, it must have a constitution and bylaws, though no statute dictates any minimum compliance requirements.

A charitable organization can also be constituted as a *trust*. If a charity chooses to be constituted as a trust it must have exclusively charitable purposes as Canada does not recognize noncharitable purpose trusts. A trust is not a legal person at law but is deemed to be a legal person under the Income Tax Act. In Quebec, a trust would be constituted as a "social trust" under article 1270 of the Civil Code of Quebec.

Finally, a charitable organization can be legally incorporated. The overwhelming majority of charities in Canada are incorporated as societies or nonshare capital corporations. It is possible to incorporate under a federal statute, the *Canada Corporations Act*, as a nonshare capital corporation which authorizes the corporation to operate in all ten provinces as well as the territories. In addition, all provinces have provincial legislation governing incorporation. The statutes and regulations vary significantly depending upon the province. In Ontario, a charity incorporates as a nonshare capital corporation while in British Columbia it would incorporate as a society. In Alberta, the charity has the option to incorporate as either a society or a nonshare capital corporation as well as incorporating under the for-profit corporation statute. While a for-profit statute is an option at law, Revenue Canada would require the shares to be held in trust and this option is seldom used.

Unlike charitable organizations, charitable foundations must be constituted either as corporations or trusts. Although it can be an operating charity, a charitable foundation is generally understood to be a passive repository of income-generating assets, which income is then distributed to charitable organizations that are actively engaged in charitable work. If a charitable foundation receives more than 50% of its capital from one or related sources or if 50% of its directors are related persons it will be designated as a private foundation. A private foundation has much stricter rules on how it functions than does a public foundation.

(b) Types of Purposes

Under the incorporating statute, the purposes that a society or nonshare capital corporation may pursue must in the broadest possible terms be for some charitable, educational, patriotic, community, or public benefit purposes. The only restriction is that the primary purpose must not be to operate some business, professional, or other for-profit activity. However, the statutes frequently require permission from ministries other than the one responsible for corporations if the activity is regulated. For instance, a society wanting to provide hospital care in British Columbia would need the approval of the provincial Minister of Health. Consequently, while there is a constitutional freedom to associate, there are regulatory restrictions on operating universities or hospitals through incorporated societies without the express prior permission of the government ministry responsible. In some provinces, such societies cannot even be incorporated until that regulatory permission is granted, and any subsequent changes to the constitution and bylaws of such societies require prior approval by the ministry responsible before they will be processed by the government officials responsible for corporate registration.

The Income Tax Act imposes other restrictions on organizations seeking exemption from taxation. In particular, charitable organizations are prohibited from carrying on unrelated business activities and must devote all of their resources to charitable activities.[1]

The law of charities denies charitable status to many worthy activities beneficial to the community, such as sports. Canada circumvents some of these problems by special provisions which extend the same privileges which charities receive to such purposes. One example is the creation of a special category called *registered Canadian Amateur Athletic Associations.* While such organizations are not registered charities, they are tax exempt and donations to them receive exactly the same treatment as donations to registered charities.

A similar procedure was adopted in 1991 in relation to arts organizations. Prior to this time, there was a legal problem in registering organizations exclusively devoted to promoting the arts as charities in Canada because they were usually primarily operated by and for artists themselves. Therefore they failed to meet the legal definition of charity. Canada solved the problem in favor of the artists by having the Minister of Communications (which is the Department responsible for promoting cultural activities) designate certain bodies to be "national arts service organizations" and amended the Income Tax Act to require them to be treated as if they were registered charities. Therefore, donors receive

---

[1] The Income Tax Act has an interesting anomaly in that it uses an activities test for the definition of a charitable organization and a purposes test for a charitable foundation. Technically, this means that there is no legal requirement that a charitable organization have exclusively, or indeed any, charitable purposes as long as all of its resources are devoted to charitable activities carried on by the organization itself.

the same tax incentives in making gifts to a national arts service organization as to a registered charity.

(c) Other Requirements

All incorporating statutes in Canada require nonprofit organizations to have members as well as directors. The minimum number of members required to incorporate ranges from three to five persons depending on the statute. However, once incorporated, the minimum number of members falls to three or even one person depending on the statute. In some statutes, such as the *Ontario Corporations Act*, it is required that directors be, or become within six months, members of the corporation. In most statutes, however, it is a matter of choice to be set out in the bylaws as to whether directors are members. (In trusts, of course, there are no members and the care and control is the legal responsibility of the trustees.)

Most statutes require something in the name of the corporation which indicates that it is an incorporated body. Name searches are required prior to incorporation to help prevent one society from passing itself off to the public as another of a similar name. Some provinces require a name search on a national basis and others only require a search within that province. Corporate name searches, however, do not include names of unincorporated associations or trusts.

There is no minimum amount of capital required to form a foundation. Nor is the fact that a corporation has the word *foundation* in its legal title an indication that for tax registration purposes it is a charitable foundation rather than a charitable organization. Charities without endowments carrying on charitable activities directly can at law call themselves a foundation.

(d) Registration Procedures

There are no registration procedures at law for an unincorporated association; but such associations do not become legal persons able to protect their members or directors from personal liability for the association's obligations. Nor are there any formal requirements for a charitable trust to register: the trust is constituted once the deed of settlement is signed and any property of any value is settled on the trustees.

In the case of incorporated associations, an application must be filed with the government ministry in charge of all corporate registrations. The name varies according to the province, but it is almost always a suboffice in the ministry responsible for incorporating for-profit corporations. The government official must certify that the association's constitution and bylaws meet the minimum requirements set out in the incorporation statute with regard to members, directors, and other requirements. Once this is done, incorporation is granted as a matter of right for any legal purposes without any discretion granted to the government to deny registration because it dislikes the purposes or organization. However, as previously noted, if the proposed purposes indicate an activity regulated by another ministry, then approval will be required from that ministry prior to incorporation. The costs of incorporation range from fifty to several hundred dollars. Once incorporated, the corporation is a legal person empowered to carry on its purposes. The members and directors are not personally liable for the lawful actions and liabilities of the corporation.

Tax privileges are granted as a subsequent step by Revenue Canada. The application documents are very simple and there are no registration fees. The same application applies to charitable organizations and charitable foundations. Questions are asked about proposed activities, whether the primary activity will be to make grants, and whether the funding comes primarily from a single source, all of which enables Revenue Canada to determine which designation should apply. The applicant must submit a detailed statement of proposed activities as well as a budget. This can lead to prolonged correspondence justifying the activities proposed and providing assurances that they will be restricted to exclusively charitable purposes. All applications from all parts of Canada are processed in one office in Ottawa.

Tax registration therefore requires meeting first a test that all of the objectives of the organization seeking tax privileges qualify the organization as being charitable and then a test that the proposed activities will actually be carried out in a way the law regards as charitable. While registration is theoretically a matter of right, it is a more subjective process because of the activities test. If registration is denied, the applicant has a right to appeal to the Federal Court of Appeal. Once registration is granted, however, it is not done on a provisional or subsequent review basis and is effective until revoked for cause and then the charity again has full rights of appeal to the courts.

§ 6.3   INTERNAL GOVERNANCE

Once incorporated, the care and management of the corporation is by law the responsibility of the directors. The ultimate function of the members is that they have the right to change the bylaws and, therefore, to set the rules which determine how the directors are elected or appointed. Most commonly, the directors are elected by the members. Most statutes give the members a statutory right to remove any director notwithstanding the particular provisions of the bylaws. There usually is a statutory minimum of three directors. The directors are normally given the right to hire and fire the officers, although the bylaws can provide contrary provisions.

In addition to legal requirements related to governance, one must consider the tax rules. Thus, the tax law stipulates that a "charitable organization" must have at least 50% of its directors deal at arm's length with each other and not more than 50% of the organization's capital can be contributed or otherwise paid into the organization by one person or members of a group of persons who do not deal with each other at arm's length. These governance and funding rules are to make sure that the extra privileges available to charities under the tax laws are only available to charities that are publicly funded and controlled.

§ 6.4   TAX TREATMENT

(a) Tax Treatment of Organizations

All charities that have applied to Revenue Canada and been registered as charitable organizations, public foundations, or private foundations are completely exempt from all tax on income whether the income is from donations; earned by way of interest, dividends, or capital gains from passive investments; or earned from active businesses carried on by the charity. There is no excise tax payable by private foundations on earned income. There is also a wide range of exemptions on consumption, land, and import taxes, but these vary according to provinces and even municipalities.

Registered charities also receive favorable treatment under Canada consumption tax. Canada has followed the example of many countries in applying a comprehensive consumption tax, but in Canada this has taken the form of a Goods and Services Tax (GST) rather than the Value Added Tax (VAT) or Business Transfer Tax (BTT) implemented in many other countries. In order to understand the impact and mechanics of the GST, one must understand the terminology used. Unfortunately, some of the technical terms used are the same as used with regard to income tax, but the result is much less favorable.

The provision of almost every property and service is considered a taxable supply subject to GST unless there is a specific exclusion in the legislation. A taxable supply is defined as a supply that is made in the course of commercial activity, but does not include an exempt supply. Such taxable supplies are subject to a tax (GST) equal to 7% of the value of the consideration for that supply. The GST is paid by the purchaser of the taxable supply and generally collected on behalf of the government by the vendor and so is effectively passed on to the consumer. GST paid on purchases made by a charity for or in the course of its commercial activities (typically activities whereby the charity is making taxable supplies) may be refunded or credited to the charity by a mechanism referred to as input tax credits, as long as the charity is registered for GST purposes.

An exempt supply is not subject to GST. Exempt supplies include all supplies made by charities (and certain other public institutions) except for a small number of itemized supplies which are intended to be supplies of a type usually made by commercial business. Therefore, a charity cannot pass on to the consumer, the cost of the GST it has incurred in purchasing or producing the supplies which turn out to be exempt when supplied by the charity. GST paid on purchases made by charities which are not in the course of its commercial activities, i.e., its "exempt" activities, cannot be refunded or credited through the input tax credit mechanism, thus the GST rewards commercial activities (through the input tax credit mechanism) and penalizes exempt activities. Charities are only required to absorb one-half of the GST on exempt supplies as they can claim a rebate from Revenue Canada equal to one-half of the GST paid on purchases for their "exempt" activities. While a 50% rebate may not be as good as being zero rated or a 100% rebate, Canada is possibly the only country in the world which provides any such rebate on consumption type taxes. Public sector bodies such as universities and hospitals get a GST rebate of up to 83%.

There are two other concessions made to charities. Gifts to charities are generally not subject to GST because the consideration paid for the supply is deemed to be nil. As well, there is an exemption for small traders whose annual taxable supplies do not exceed $30,000 and a special exemption for charities whose annual taxable supplies do not exceed $250,000. As the commercial activities for many small charities will be less than this amount, they do not have to comply with costly administration of GST and need not add GST to the purchase price and recover it through input tax credits.

In 1993, the government made Revenue Canada the agency responsible to collect and administer the GST, whereas previously it was done by a different government body. It is too early to determine the ramifications of this consolidation, which means that Revenue Canada will determine the result of having certain activities of a charity categorized as "commercial" for purposes of claiming the input tax while the same charity simultaneously claims that the same activities are exempt from income tax on profits because they are a "related business" of the charity.

(b) Tax Treatment of Contributions—Domestic Organizations

Canada is the first country other than Israel to move to a system of tax credits for charitable donations from individuals. The government was persuaded that the tax-deduction system formerly used in Canada provided an unfair advantage to wealthy donors because the higher marginal tax rate on their income meant that the net cost of a gift was lower to them.[2]

In 1988, Canada changed its tax system to give all individual donors, regardless of their personal marginal tax rate, a tax credit at the lowest combined federal and provincial rate for the first $250 gifted in a year. All individual taxpayers then receive a tax credit calculated at the highest combined federal and provincial rate for the value of donations in excess of an aggregate of $250 in the year. The result is that the cost to the national treasury is the same for all donors. In 1994, the threshold for the high tax rate was lowered to $200.

Canada presently has a progressive system of taxation of income with three marginal rates of federal tax for individuals—17%, 26%, and 29%. The tax credit provides a positive tax incentive to individual donors in the 17% and 26% federal marginal rate classes who give over $200. For example, since the tax credit is computed at the 29% rate, all donors with a 17% federal marginal rate receive a 12% federal tax net benefit for all donations in excess of $200 (i.e., they pay taxes at 17% and receive a credit of 29% on all donations). This net benefit remains constant whether they give $206 or $10,000. However, as the credit is nonrefundable, it has a practical upper limit. This federal tax net benefit decreases to 3% (29% – 26%) when the donor's federal marginal rate is 26%. The benefit disappears entirely when the donor's federal marginal rate climbs to 29%. These federal credits are increased by the value of the respective applicable provincial taxes.

Canada retains deductions for donations from corporations and only uses the tax credit system for individuals. This has resulted in some debate and suspicion as to which system is superior. Having a $200 threshold before moving to the maximum tax credit means that the majority of donors do not benefit because they donate less than $200 a year.

In Canada, an individual receives the 29% tax credit against the full amount of his or her charitable donations. In any one year, however, an individual can

---

[2] A wealthy donor pays tax of 54 cents of every dollar when provincial taxes are added to federal tax. Consequently, every dollar donated to charity effectively costs that donor only 46 cents. By contrast, for a low-income donor who pays only 26 cents of every dollar in tax, each dollar donated effectively costs that donor 74 cents.

only use those tax credits up to a maximum limit of 77%[3] of his or her taxable income. However, the individual is able to carry forward any excess tax credit for an additional five years.

Canada has no inheritance, gift, estate, or generation-skipping taxes, so donations need no exemption from such taxes. However, every person is deemed to have disposed of all of his or her property immediately prior to death and so may have triggered capital gains taxes. A special provision enables an executor to avoid those capital gains if property is given to charity in the will. In addition, a gift in the will is deemed to have taken place in the deceased's terminal tax return, so the tax credit is allocated to the period when the tax relief is needed. The March 6, 1996 Federal Budget increased the maximum limit of a charitable donation in a will to 100% of the testator's taxable income. Further, a testamentary charitable gift can be carried back one year to provide relief in the prior year. This provision is not available to corporations or to gifts during the donor's lifetime.

In Canada, a corporation receives a tax deduction for 100% of the aggregate amount of its charitable donations. Apart from being a deduction rather than a credit, a corporation's position is the same as an individual with a maximum limit of 75% of its taxable income and the ability to carry forward any excess tax deduction for an additional five years. The ability for corporations to make charitable donations is not only important to large corporations, but is very important to wealthy individuals who hold most of their wealth in private holding companies.

Canadian donors receive the same tax benefit whether they give to a charitable organization, a public foundation, or a private foundation, and it does not matter whether the donor is giving cash or assets. A gift of assets, however, is a taxable disposition and will trigger capital gains taxes if the value of the asset has appreciated. Special rules allow the donor, whether a corporation or an individual, to elect the cost amount of the asset as the amount of the gift to avoid capital gains taxes.

(i) Gifts of Capital Property.   Donors of capital property can elect as the proceeds of disposition any amount which is not greater than the fair market value (FMV) of the property and not less than its adjusted cost base (ACB) to the donor at that time. The limit on the charitable tax credit of gifts of capital property is 100% of taxable capital gains triggered by the donation. Therefore, the donor will almost always elect to make the gift at the fair market value of the capital property because the donor will get $1.00 of tax credit for $.75 of tax liability because Canada only taxes 75% of capital gains. The February 18, 1997 Federal Budget increased the donor's donation limit to allow the donor to completely avoid taxation on the recapture of the value by which the property had been depreciated. The February 18, 1997 Federal Budget also proposes to reduce the amount of the taxable capital gain included in the donor's income to 37.5% from 75% when the capital property donated is a security listed on a prescribed stock exchange. This donation incentive does not apply if the recipient charity is a private foundation.

---

[3] The Canadian Parliament will enact the necessary legislation to give effect to the February 18, 1997 Federal Budget that raises the limit to 75% for all donations which take place after January 1, 1997.

(ii) Special Status for Cultural Gifts. Canada has special tax incentives to encourage gifts of cultural property. This is designed to encourage Canadians to gift valuable Canadian art and other cultural property to leading Canadian cultural institutions such as art galleries and museums and have these national treasures remain in Canada rather than selling them on the international market and having them leave Canada. There is a Canadian Cultural Property Export Review Board which reviews the cultural significance and appraised value of a particular object which the donor proposes to gift. If the object is determined to be significant enough to meet all of the criteria set out in the relevant legislation, it is certified to be cultural property.

It is not enough that the object be certified cultural property for the donor to receive enhanced tax incentives for the gift. The gift must be made to a designated Canadian institution or public authority which is an appropriate recipient for the object in question. These designated institutions are the leading art galleries, museums, and universities in the country who have specifically applied for and been granted this status. They almost always are also registered charities.

A gift of certified cultural property to a designated institution is treated under the Income Tax Act as a "cultural gift" rather than as a "charitable gift." Two important tax advantages accrue to the donor. First, the donor can claim a tax credit for the entire fair market value of the gift without the requirement which applies to other gifts of appreciated property of bringing the amount of the appreciation into the donor's taxable income. Second, the donation can be utilized in the year of the gift up to 100% of the donor's taxable income and any excess can be utilized up to 100% of income in the following five years. This is the most advantageous tax incentive given to donors in Canada and is specifically designed to protect and retain in Canada cultural property rather than simply encourage charitable giving.

There is concern that these valuable tax privileges could be abused by having the recipient-designated institution simply sell the national treasure for cash, thereby frustrating the purpose of the special tax privileges. Consequently, a designated institution faces a special tax equal to 30% of the fair market value of the certified cultural property if it disposes of the property within five years of the date it was certified unless it is disposed of to another designated institution.

(iii) Gifts of Art by Artists. Canada provides a smaller, but still significant, incentive to artists themselves to gift their work to ordinary charities. An artist is exempted from any income on the appreciation of a work of art created by him or her if the work is gifted to charity, and the artist can take a tax credit for the cost of the work to him or her. This does not need to be art of a caliber capable of being certified as cultural property and it can be gifted to any charity without any requirement that it be held by that charity. Therefore, it can be gifted to the charity and immediately auctioned or otherwise sold by the charity to raise cash. This special provision is designed to specifically benefit artists, but also benefits charities at the same time.

(iv) Crown Gifts Donation Benefit Limits. Canada has an interesting donation benefit which has encouraged many multimillion-dollar gifts in recent years. An individual's 100% tax credit and a corporation's 100% tax deduction in any

one year can be utilized up to a maximum limit of 100% of taxable income if the gift is made to "Her Majesty in right of Canada or a province." That is a technical way of saying the federal government or a provincial government and is known as a "Crown gift" rather than a "charitable gift." Any excess unused donation receipt can be carried forward for an additional five years.

Many provinces have created by statute foundations for public universities, hospitals, libraries, and arts groups which were explicitly designated in the incorporating legislation as "an agent of the Crown." While these foundations are not charities and by law all of their directors are appointed by the government, there entire function is to raise funds for charities. Charities without a related Crown Foundation fell at a competitive disadvantage and lobbied the government to "level the playing field." Consequently, the February 18, 1997 Federal Budget proposes to reduce the limit for Crown gifts to 75%.

(v) Alternative Minimum Tax.   Alternative minimum tax (AMT) was introduced in 1986 to allay the concern that some high-income earners were taking advantage of tax incentives and deductions to shelter virtually all of their income.

AMT is computed by calculating the "adjusted taxable income" of the taxpayer. The adjusted taxable income is the taxpayer's income for the year adjusted to include some deductions and tax-preference items which would otherwise be excluded. For example, the exempt portion of a capital gain is included in adjusted taxable income, as are certain contributions to registered pension plans and taxable dividends received from Canadian corporations (with no gross-up or dividend tax credit). An individual is entitled to a basic credit of $40,000 against the individual's adjusted taxable income. The individual may then apply certain tax credits, such as credits for charitable gifts, against the adjusted taxable income. The balance is subject to tax at 17%.

A taxpayer who makes a charitable gift in a year in which he or she has no taxable income may be subject to AMT. Unfortunately, the charitable donation tax credit applicable in that year is limited to 75% of taxable income as calculated prior to adding back the tax preference items which are included in calculating the adjusted taxable income.

(c) Tax Treatment of Contributions—Foreign Organizations

(i) Qualified Donees Outside Canada.   Canada is generous in its tax treatment of donors to certain categories of foreign organizations. Such donors receive exactly the same tax privileges for giving directly to such qualified donees as for giving to a Canadian charity. It is not necessary to use a registered Canadian charity as an intermediary or conduit to receive tax benefits for the donation. Because the fiscal benefits are so generous, however, the categories of foreign organizations which are "qualified donees" for this purpose are restricted. In particular, the foreign "qualified donees" are the United Nations or agencies thereof; prescribed universities outside Canada, the student body of which ordinarily includes students from Canada; and charitable organizations outside Canada to which the government of Canada has made a gift in that year or the previous year.

The important distinction between making a donation under these provisions and any tax benefit which can be claimed under any bilateral tax convention is that the donation credit applies against any Canadian source income without any corresponding requirement that the donor have source income from the recipient country where the donation is to be utilized. If universities which normally include students from Canada apply to Revenue Canada and qualify to be included on the prescribed list, then a Canadian donor can make a gift to them with all the fiscal privileges attached to a gift to a Canadian registered charity. Unlike some bilateral tax conventions, there is no provision restricting this privilege to donors who are alumni of that university and their families. The fact that the United Nations or agencies thereof are "qualified donees" is an even more generous tax provision because the United Nations or its agencies do not specifically benefit Canadians in a domestic sense.

The most intriguing category of foreign "qualified donees" are charitable organizations outside Canada to which the government of Canada has made a gift in that year or the previous year. This provision is little understood or utilized, but it has the potential to move the decision-making process in determining which foreign charities can become "qualified donees" away from the officials in Revenue Canada to the field officers of the Canadian embassy in foreign countries. If the Canadian Ambassador makes a small grant out of the discretionary funds provided by the Department of External Affairs to a charity in that foreign country, it is hard to deny that the government of Canada has made a gift to that charitable organization. At that point and for the following year, a government official on location in a foreign country who is not reporting to Revenue Canada has, advertently or inadvertently, created a qualified donee. The status can be renewed by gifts in subsequent years.[4]

(ii) Cross-Border Commuter Gifts. Canada has another interesting tax provision related to donations to foreign organizations which is an intermediate step between full domestic recognition of gifts to foreign qualified donees and the very limited tax relief provided to gifts to foreign charities under certain bilateral tax treaties. Canada has a long friendly border with the United States and many people reside in Canada and commute to the United States to work. The Canadian Income Tax Act allows any individual (not just a Canadian citizen) residing in Canada near the border with the United States who commutes to his or her principal place of business or employment in the United States which forms the chief source of that individual's income to make gifts to American charities eligible under the U.S. Internal Revenue Code and claim a deduction exactly as if the individual made a gift to a Canadian charity.

---

[4] This provision was not intended to operate in this decentralized way. The Canadian government makes certain gifts from Ottawa to a very small list of charities selected in Ottawa. The most recent publication of that list, in 1989, recorded only eight foreign charities (Information Circular 84-3R4). There is no requirement in the statute, however, similar to the requirement with regard to universities outside Canada that foreign charities be on a "prescribed" list. There are government officials in Ottawa who believe that this provision may even extend to all foreign charities that have received a gift from organizations such as the Canadian International Development Agency that are arms of the government.

(iii) Foreign Activities of Charities.   The tension and conflict between the common law definition of charity and the more restrictive statutory fiscal policies regulating charities is most evident in the policies governing the foreign activities of Canadian charities. Nothing in the common law concept of charity imposes a geographic limitation as to where a charity can carry on its operations; but there is a reluctance to have tax-supported donations be used outside the country. The Income Tax Act has no geographic limitation on charitable operations, although it does require that a registered charity be established in Canada and continue to be resident in Canada.

Nevertheless, Canada has developed a policy which effectively allows Canadians through Canadian charitable organizations to carry on charitable activities anywhere in the world. Because charitable organizations have an "activities" definition, their ability to carry on international philanthropy is not significantly restricted, whereas nonoperating charitable foundations are effectively restricted to making grants to qualified donees.

Although there is no stated requirement that Canadian charitable organizations expend their funds in Canada, there is an effective policy requiring funds to be expended by Canadian charities. While there is no explicit geographic limitation on where a Canadian charity can carry on its operations, Revenue Canada gives great emphasis to the wording in the Income Tax Act that defines a charitable organization as "an organization, whether or not incorporated, all the resources of which are devoted to charitable activities carried on by the organization itself." This definition of a charitable organization, which provides that its charitable activities must be carried on by the charity itself, is used to prevent grants to foreign charities. Therefore, if a Canadian charitable organization wants to make a grant to a foreign charity, it is necessary for the Canadian charitable organization to establish an agency or contractual relationship with the foreign charity and to characterize its expenditure of funds as an activity of the Canadian charity. It is not possible for a charitable foundation or a charitable organization to simply mail a donation to a foreign charity or make an outright grant in the way that it could if the recipient charity was also registered in Canada.

The result is somewhat different for Canadian charitable foundations. Because foundations do not have a definitional component that "all the resources of which are devoted to charitable activities carried on by the organization itself," it can make an outright grant to a foreign charity. The problem which a charitable foundation faces is that grants to foreign charities which are not "qualified donees" do not count toward the foundation's disbursement quota. Consequently, while grants to foreign charities may be technically possible, they are effectively barred unless the foundation has first made all the grants to qualified donees necessary to fulfil its disbursement quota. Further, Revenue Canada has changed its administrative policy to forbid such foreign grants and is considering legislative amendments to back up its policy in this regard.

§ 6.5   PERSONAL BENEFIT RESTRICTIONS

Canada has a restriction in the statutory definition in the Income Tax Act of a charity which states that no part of the income may be payable to, or otherwise available for, the personal benefit of any member, trustee, or settlor of the charity. Although on the face of it, this wording would prohibit paying any form of compensation; in practice it is acceptable to pay reasonable compensation for services rendered by members and directors.

While this is the position under the Income Tax Act, some provinces take a stricter interpretation under the general principles of the law of charity and forbid trustees and directors (but not members) from taking any compensation, no matter how reasonable. In those provinces, the result is to prohibit any paid staff members from being on the board of directors of a charity.

§ 6.6 OBLIGATIONS TO THE PUBLIC

Every registered charity must file a Public Information Return Form T3010 within six months of completing its fiscal year. This return requires significant disclosure as to the income and expenditures of the charity, but only has two pages of questions as to how much income has been received from donations, fees, business activities, and so on, and how much has been expended on charitable activities, fund raising and administrative costs, and so on. This information is available to the public if they request it from Revenue Canada Charities Division. However, Charities Division only has an office in Ottawa and there are no requirements to file this public information return and make it available at any local Revenue Canada offices or at the charity's own office. The February 18, 1997 February Budget will also require Revenue Canada to allow the public to have access to a charity's governing documents, names of directors and any other information that it was required to provide in applying for registration, as well as any conditions of its registration and, where the registration has been revoked, the grounds for revocation.

The charity must file a comprehensive set of financial statements with the public information return but Revenue Canada is forbidden by law from making these financial statements available to the public as they are not an integral part of the public information return. In recent years, Canada has made considerable effort to simplify the public information return and make it user friendly to charities. In 1997, however, charities will have to disclose considerably more information on their business, political, and foreign activities through new schedules being added to the T3010 return.

In addition to the Revenue Canada filings, an incorporated charity must make annual filings with the government ministry under which it was incorporated. This is a very simple filing, which usually requires only information on the number of members and who the directors are. In some jurisdictions it is necessary to file financial statements with the report. If filed, these financial statements are available to the public. The annual filing fees are nominal.

In one province, Ontario, the Public Trustee takes an active role in monitoring the activities of charities under the provisions of the Charities Accounting Act. The Public Trustee reviews the financial statements and also investigates complaints made to it by members of the public about the charity's activities. No other province has similar legislation mandating such a role for the Public Trustee or a comparable government official.

§ 6.7   BUSINESS ACTIVITY

The Income Tax Act allows charitable organizations and public foundations, but not private foundations, to carry on related businesses. "Related business" is defined as "a business that is unrelated to the objects of the charity if substantially all of the people employed by the charity in the carrying on of that business are not remunerated for such employment." This is essentially an authorization to carry on unrelated businesses so long as they are operated by volunteers, such as a gift shop in a hospital run by the women's auxillary.

The statutory definition of related business allows, but does not explicitly contemplate or authorize, what might be called the common sense or common law definition of a related business. Although the common law requires a charity to be constituted or instituted exclusively for charitable purposes, it has interpreted "exclusively" broadly enough to allow purposes which are merely incidental to the charitable purposes. Many charitable endeavors are substantially run as businesses and recover revenues from fees for services. These include examples such as universities, which obtain much of their revenue from student fees and contracts for research.

The extent to which Revenue Canada adopts a liberal interpretation of what constitutes an allowable related business is very important because Canada does not have a concept of imposing an unrelated business income tax on charities. A charitable organization and a public foundation may carry on a related business. All income received from this business is exempt from tax. Should the business become so extensive and commercial that it cannot be characterized as related, the charity has the possibility of having its registration revoked. Until such time as revocation is completed by Revenue Canada, it remains exempt from tax.

The Income Tax Act does not explicitly set out how broadly or narrowly "related" should be defined. A recent court decision which went up to the Supreme Court of Canada applied what the United States would call the "destination test." Basically, the court held that if the income was ultimately used for charitable purposes, it did not matter how it was earned. The decision was not unanimous and there is a lot of doubt as whether the court would hold the same way if it were faced with a different fact pattern. However, charities in Canada have significant legal authority for carrying significant business activities unrelated to the purposes of the charity as long as the proceeds are used entirely for the charity's purposes.

§ 6.8   OTHER FUNDING RESTRICTIONS

Two further funding restrictions apply to registered charities in Canada.

(a) Disbursement Quota

The first of these involves rules that the Income Tax Act imposes on how much of a charity's funds it must expend or disburse in each year. The mechanism, known as the disbursement quota, prevents a charity from accumulating all of the income it earns and retaining all the gifts it receives. If a charity does not meet its disbursement quota, it can have its registration with Revenue Canada revoked. A charitable organization has a significantly lower disbursement quota than a charitable foundation because its disbursement quota does not include income earned from investments.

The first component of the disbursement quota of a registered charity is that it must distribute 80% of all amounts for which it issued an official charitable receipt in the immediately preceding taxation year. If a charity does not issue an official receipt for a gift, the donor cannot claim the gift for purposes of a charitable donation tax credit and the charity does not include that gift in its disbursement quota. A charity must retain a duplicate copy of all official donation receipts which it issues and retain this duplicate for audit purposes. The aggregate value of all such receipts issued must be determined and disclosed by the charity in Public Information Return Form T3010. This total of "receipted income" is the number used to calculate the 80% of receipted income disbursement quota. Income from investments, fees, services, or business activities is not included in receipted income and the disbursement quota. This component of the disbursement quota applies to all charities and is intended to restrict the amount of income used for administrative and fund-raising expenses.

If there was no relief from this 80% requirement, it would be virtually impossible to build an endowment fund as the capital would necessarily be substantially distributed in the following year. Consequently, there is an exception to this disbursement quota if the gift is received subject to a trust or direction to the effect that the property given, or property substituted, therefore, is to be held by the charity for a period of not less than 10 years. The majority of such directions are to the effect that the property should be held in perpetuity, but it is adequate if the property is to be held for only 10 years. Such a direction should be given by the donor, preferably in writing, and not simply imposed on the gift by the charity itself.

If the charity receives a testamentary bequest of capital, then it also can avoid the 80% disbursement quota even though the 10-year direction provision may not appear in the wording of the bequest. This exception is simply an extension of the 10-year direction which recognizes that if the testator failed to have the direction included when the will was drafted, it is impossible to remedy that oversight after the testator has died. Since the majority of testamentary capital bequests are presumed to be intended to form endowments, the testamentary capital bequest exception was added to facilitate such endowments.

(b) Four and One-Half Percent Return

The 10-year direction provision allows a donor to make a large capital gift to charity and take a charitable receipt without requiring the charity to distribute the capital. While the charity can retain the capital, it must begin the following year to distribute income earned from this capital if it is a charitable foundation. A charitable foundation, but not a charitable organization, has an additional disbursement quota. Prior to 1984, a foundation had to distribute 90% of its income earned. This test was unsatisfactory and the Income Tax Act introduced a disbursement quota requiring a foundation to pay out an amount equal to a 4½% return on the capital value of its investment assets.

A private foundation must also be concerned about the property in which it invests. Certain restrictions, which do not apply to a public foundation or a charitable organization, are imposed on a private foundation when it invests in a "non-qualified investment." In general terms, a nonqualified investment is a debt or a share (other than either a share listed on a prescribed stock exchange or a common share) or a right to acquire such a share that is issued by persons who are in a position to control or influence the private foundation. This would include a loan by the foundation to a related person or a preferred share purchased by the foundation in one of the companies controlled by related persons. A private foundation must ensure that it receives a minimum rate of return on a nonqualified investment loan or there will be a special penalty tax. This penalty tax, however, will not be on the private foundation, but will apply to the person or corporation which is deemed to have received a taxable benefit to the extent the actual return paid to the private foundation on the loan or share is less than a fair market return.

Registration of any charity will be revoked if it fails to expend its disbursement quota. A foundation primarily meets its disbursement quota by way of gifts to registered charities and other "qualified donees." It is possible, however, to have a private foundation become an operating charity and meet its disbursement quota by carrying on its own charitable activities.

§ 6.9   POLITICAL ACTIVITY

Prior to 1985, there was no explicit allowance in the Income Tax Act for political activity of any kind by charities. The common law rule, as generally accepted, was that political purposes were not charitable. Nevertheless, a charity could engage in some limited amount of ancillary and incidental political activities in pursuing its charitable purposes. While most people can agree on the common law's position on political activities, there was doubt as to whether an organization registered with Revenue Canada as a "charitable organization" could engage in such ancillary political activities. The problem stemmed from the particular wording in the definition of a charitable organization in the Income Tax Act. A charitable organization is defined as "an organization, whether or not incorporated, all the resources of which are devoted to charitable activities carried on by the organization itself." As the definition is tied to the "activities" of the charity rather than its purposes, a reasonable argument could be made that the common law rules did not apply. The common law never converted political activities into charitable activities; it simply allowed groups with exclusively charitable purposes to carry on some incidental and ancillary political activities. Significance was attached to the difference in wording of the Income Tax Act definition of a "charitable foundation" which only had to be "constituted and operated exclusively for charitable purposes" and had no reference to "activities."

The uncertainty generated by this particular problem was alleviated by amendments to the Income Tax Act that took effect for the 1985 tax year, which read as follows:

(6.2) For the purposes of paragraph (1)(b), where an organization devotes substantially all of its resources to charitable activities carried on by it and

(a) it devotes part of its resources to political activities,

(b) such political activities are ancillary and incidental to its charitable activities, and

(c) such political activities do not include the direct or indirect support of, or opposition to, any political party or candidate for public office,

the organization shall be considered to be devoting that part of its resources to charitable activities carried on by it.

Many charities interpreted these amendments as a signal that the law had changed to allow direct political activities, as long as they only involved a minor portion of the charity's budget. Revenue Canada's view was that these amendments did not change the common law position, but only remedied a problem resulting from the wording in the definition in the statute.

In February 1987, Revenue Canada released Information Circular 87-1, which sets out categories of political activities allowed or denied to registered charities. Paragraph 8 states:

8. Activities that are clearly charitable at law are not subject to any limitation under the *Income Tax Act*. This remains so even if the activity has some political element or flavour to it, provided the activity is fundamentally charitable.

Paragraph 9 says that the Department views the following activities as charitable, so long as they are intended to inform and educate rather than to influence public opinion or generate controversy, and so long as devotion of resources to such activity is reasonable in the circumstances:

(a) oral and written representations to the relevant elected representatives . . . or a public servant to present the charity's views or to provide factual information,

(b) oral and written presentations or briefs containing factual information and recommendations to relevant government bodies, commissions or committees, and

(c) the provision of information and the expression of non-partisan views to the media.

The Information Circular then sets out the category of political activities which it considers prohibited to registered charities:

10. A charity may not oppose or endorse a named candidate, party or politician. The charity's resources may not be devoted directly to such activities, or devoted indirectly through provision of resources to a third party engaged in partisan political activities.

11. A charity may not engage in any illegal activity (i.e., any activity in Canada or elsewhere which contravenes or would, if such were carried on in Canada, contravene the law in Canada).

Beyond this, Information Circular 87-1 identifies other activities that, while not charitable in themselves, will normally be allowed so long as they are subordinate to bona fide charitable purposes, and so long as the two expenditure limit tests (discussed in section 6.9(a)), are met. Included here are publications, conferences, workshops, advertisements, public meetings, lawful demonstrations, mail campaigns, and other forms of communication which are designed to attract interest in, or gain support for, a charity's position on political issues and matters of public policy.

(a) Expenditure Limitations

There are two expenditure limitation tests which a registered charity must meet in order for its political activities to be allowable under the Income Tax Act. The first is the general disbursement quota, which requires a charity to spend at least 80% of its receipted unrestricted donations of the previous year on charitable activities. The Income Tax Act explicitly excludes an expenditure on political activities from being included in expenditures for the purposes of calculating the charity's disbursement quota.

The second expenditure limitation is that a registered charity must devote "substantially all" of its "resources" to charitable activities. Revenue Canada relies on the words "substantially all" to regulate the amount of money which a charity can spend on political activities. It interprets "substantially all" to mean "90% of," but will allow the "90% test" to be averaged over five years. There is nothing in the Income Tax Act which provides that "substantially all" is to mean "90% of"; but that is what the term is interpreted to mean when it is used elsewhere in the legislation. Similarly, averaging the "90% test" over five years is an administrative decision rather than a statutory provision. The result is that a registered charity cannot expend more than 10% of its resources on political activities.

Information Circular 87-1 states that "resources" include financial, physical, and human resources. A registered charity which has no problem meeting its financial disbursement quota because it has very little receipted income is therefore prevented by this provision from devoting an inordinate amount of human resources to political activities. Nor can it utilize its facilities and equipment to accomplish a political activity rather than simply spending money on that political activity. The regulation of the devotion of nonfinancial resources to political activities is much more difficult than determining how much money was spent on political activities.

§ 6.10 KEY OUTSTANDING ISSUES

One of the key outstanding issues is whether Revenue Canada will seek interim sanctions against charities which do not comply with its regulations. As demonstrated when discussing business activities, the only penalty which Revenue Canada can apply is to revoke charitable registration. This is a draconian step which it is reluctant to undertake when the solution is corrective action and recovery of tax benefits rather than to force the charity to cease all operations. Further, if the charity chooses to fight Revenue Canada in the courts, revocation will take place only after, and if, Revenue Canada succeeds, so several years may have passed.

Another reason that revocation is unsatisfactory is that the charity has twelve months after revocation to distribute all of its assets to another charity of its choosing. There is nothing to prevent the directors of a charity whose registration has just been revoked from transfering all of its assets to another charity controlled by them. In fact, they could have newly created another charity specifically for the purpose of receiving these assets.

Consequently, Revenue Canada is considering devising interim sanctions which could be applied to both charities and their directors in order to give them more effective regulatory powers.

CHAPTER SEVEN

Egypt[*]

§ 7.1 LEGAL CONTEXT

Egypt is a civil law country with a restrictive system of laws governing nonprofit organizations. The heart of this system is Law No. 32 of 1964, which restricted the establishment of associations, subjected many of their activities to close scrutiny by the state, and authorized public authorities to disband nonprofit organizations at will. Enacted during the consolidation of Nasser's one-party state, this law rescinded earlier provisions enacted in the period 1923 to 1952, which had granted legal status to a wide variety of political, economic, and social organizations. What is more, it runs counter to the long tradition of nonprofit activity that is deeply embedded in the religious and civil life of this country as reflected in the longstanding Islamic tradition of *Al Wakf*, or charitable bequest, as well as in the religiously inspired tradition of *Al Zakat*, or obligation to contribute to the poor. As such, it reflects the fear of autonomous political and religious organizations on the part of the Egyptian state. Governmental attitudes toward nonprofit organizations have softened considerably since 1964, however, Law No. 32 remains in effect today, creating a continuing climate of distrust between nonprofit organizations and the state. Nonprofit organizations are also regulated by a number of other, more specific laws. For example, professional groups must secure specific legal authority in order to attain legal status. Thus, specific laws exist authorizing each of the 22 professional groups and six business associations in existence in Egypt.

§ 7.2 ELIGIBILITY

(a) Types of Organizations

There are five main types of nonprofit organizations in Egypt: (1) associations, (2) foundations, (3) professional groups, (4) business associations, and (5) clubs and youth centers.

   (i) *Associations and Foundations.*   Associations and foundations are both governed by Law No. 32 of 1964. In fact, this law treats foundations as a sub-group of associations. In particular, according to this law, an *association* is "any organized group composed of individual or legal persons operating for a certain period of time with an aim other than achieving profit." A private *foundation*, on

---

*Country Rapporteur: Dr. Amani Kandil, Professor of Political Science, Cairo University, Cairo, Egypt and Consultant for Follow-up Committee for Arab NGOs. This chapter is based on a legal field guide of the Johns Hopkins Comparative Nonprofit Sector Project.

the other hand, is a type of association that is "established by the dedication of an amount of money [either by individual or legal persons] for an unspecified period of time to pursue religious, scientific, social welfare, or public benefit goals."[1] The principal difference between foundations and associations is thus that foundations operate on the basis of an endowment, like the historic Islamic *waqf*, whereas associations depend on current income from membership fees, donations, and grants.

(ii) Professional Groups.   Professional groups constitute a third type of nonprofit organization. The formation of such groups is expressly protected in the Egyptian Constitution, which declares that "the establishment of syndicates and unions on a democratic basis is a right provided by the law." Nevertheless, each such group must secure a separate law authorizing its existence before it can operate as a legal entity. These laws stipulate certain duties that are common for all professional groups, however, including: (1) to develop and further the respective profession; (2) to protect the rights of members and develop a spirit of cooperation; (3) to serve society; and (4) to participate in the planning of general policies relating to the profession. Membership in these groups is a precondition for practicing the respective profession (e.g., physicians, engineers, pharmacologists, and teachers) and the different laws usually place some membership requirements on the groups, such as, a certain educational status, Egyptian nationality, and a requirement that the member be free of any previous crimes.

(iii) Unions.   Unions share many of the features of professional associations except that they lack some of the self-governing powers that professional associations enjoy.

(iv) Business Associations.   A fourth type of nonprofit organization in Egypt is the association of businesspersons. Only a handful of such associations exist. Their main objectives are to improve the business climate, to strengthen the economic activities of their members, to promote commerce between Egypt and other countries, and to advise government in the development of economic policies. In contrast to the Chambers of Commerce and Industry, which have been transformed into quasi-governmental institutions, business associations are characterized by their financial and administrative independence. The legal basis for this type of organizations varies from case to case. Some associations, such as the American Egyptian Council in 1975 and the American Chamber of Commerce in Cairo in 1981, attained their legal status by presidential decree. The Economic Committee for Businessmen in Alexandria (established in 1983) gained legal status by declaring itself a branch of the Chamber of Commerce in Alexandria. Others are registered under Law No. 32 of 1964, such as the Egyptian Business Association, the Association of Investors and Businessmen of the *City of the 10th of Ramadan*, and the Association of Investors of *City of the 6th of October*.

(v) Youth Centers and Clubs.   Youth centers and clubs are a fifth type of nonprofit organization under Egyptian law. Law No. 77 of 1975 defines a youth

[1] Article 2 of Law No. 32 of 1964.

center as "an organization which has buildings and facilities, built by the state or local councils or individuals—either in co-operation or independently—and based in cities and villages aiming at developing youth of different ages and providing opportunities to practice social, spiritual, national, and sport-related activities under the supervision of professional leaders during their leisure time."[2] Youth centers often operate in poor areas, are specifically geared toward the poor, and are usually characterized by strong government involvement in their establishment and operation even if a center was founded by private individuals.

Youth clubs have purposes similar to those of youth centers, but legally constitute a distinctly different type of organization. Law No. 77 of 1975 defines such clubs as organizations "established by a group of people, with the aim of developing youth in an integrated way through sports and socialization taking social, psychological, spiritual and health aspects into account."[3] Youth clubs usually depend on membership fees for income and are not supported by government.

Membership in clubs and youth centers is by law open to the public but, in the case of youth centers, members have to live in the respective center's area in order to be eligible. Governmental and nongovernmental associations are allowed to join the membership of clubs and youth centers.

(vi) Civil Companies.   Because of the restrictions of Law No. 32, a class of associations known as *civil companies* has emerged in the 1990s. These nonprofit organizations have been established as companies under the civil law to avoid the complicated procedures involved in registering under Law No. 32. Organizations that choose to take this form are most often human rights and, women's and liberal rights groups, and research organizations.

These organizations are eligible neither for tax exemption, nor for other privileges enjoyed by organizations registered under Law No. 32. In the last few years, there have been many confrontations between the government and these emerging civil companies caused by the government's questioning of the accountability systems of the civil companies, which are mainly funded by foreign donors, but not subject to government supervision.

(vii) Foreign Organizations.   Generally, there is no unified status for foreign organizations in Egypt. Some foreign organizations, such as the Fulbright Commission, the American Research Center in Egypt, and CARE, operate in Egypt based on special protocol agreements between the organizations and the Egyptian government through the Ministry of Foreign Affairs, Cultural Relations, and Technical Cooperation Departments. Each organization has a different agreement with the government and the terms may differ among organizations. Others might be registered with the Ministries of Social Affairs or Cultural Affairs depending on their activities. Such organizations do not enjoy the same diplomatic status and privileges as those that are registered with the Ministry of Foreign Affairs. Another is to seek recognition as a local branch of an international organization and register according to Law No. 32.

---

[2] Article 98 of Law No. 77 of 1975.
[3] Article 72 of Law No. 77 of 1975.

(b) Types of Purposes

As a general rule, all types of nonprofit organizations are prohibited from pursuing for-profit goals;[4] usually have to pursue aims that are of general public benefit, although primarily member-serving associations are allowed; and are generally nonpolitical and nonreligious. Prohibitions against political and religious activities are either directly or indirectly expressed in the laws governing specific types of nonprofit organizations. Direct prohibitions, for instance, are found in Law No. 32 authorizing associations in general, whereas the laws on professional groups, youth clubs, and centers contain indirect prohibitions. However, both associations and foundations may pursue religious aims. Other purposes associations and foundations may pursue include scientific, technical, charitable, and social-care purposes, as well as other goals which are for the benefit of the general public.

(c) Other Requirements

Article 1 of Law No. 32 of 1964 requires associations to have at least ten members, but there are no capital requirements, since associations are mainly financed out of membership fees and voluntary donations.

There are also no capital requirements for foundations, but article 69 of Law No. 32 defines foundations as an allocation of capital to pursue eligible goals, so foundations are clearly based around a source of funding. This capital must be formally registered, specifying the amount of money, the objectives, the activities of the foundation, and the specifics of the administration.[5]

(d) Registration Procedures

(i) Associations. Associations attain legal personality only after explicit government permission and a formal announcement. Registration is mandatory. The specifics of this process are laid down in Law No. 32, which details the announcement procedures, the required documents, the time frame for government decisions relating to the establishment of associations, and the rules for appealing such decisions. Specific registration requirements include:

1. The proposed bylaws signed by a minimum of ten founding members
2. The association's name
3. Proposed activities
4. Area of operation
5. The names and positions of founding members
6. The sources of funding
7. Specifications pertaining to membership, the selection of members, and rights and duties of members
8. The governing bodies
9. Decision-making procedures

An application fee is required to begin the process of registration.

[4] Article 1 of Law No. 32 of 1964.
[5] Article 70, of Law No. 32 of 1964.

Within sixty days of the registration request, the Ministry of Social Affairs must announce the legality of the association, register it, and publish its formation in the official newspaper, *Egyptian Events*. In the case of refusal of registration, the Ministry of Social Affairs must announce its refusal, with documented reasons, within sixty days. Article 12 of Law No. 32 specifies the grounds on which the Ministry may refuse to approve the formation of an association. Specifically, approval may be denied (1) if there is no need for the proposed services or other organizations already provide such services, (2) if the proposed activities affect security issues, (3) if the area where the services are proposed to be rendered is deemed unfit, or (4) if the association is established to revive a previously outlawed organization. After legal personality is granted, associations are subject to tight control by the Ministry of Social Affairs, which has the right to directly control the activities of an association, to examine documents and control budgets, and to disband the organization.

(ii) Foundations.   Foundations must also seek legal status through registration.[6] The registration procedures are essentially the same as those for associations, except that the bylaws must be accompanied by an official document testifying to the donation of the endowment and specifications as to how and to which objectives the foundation's funds will be allocated. As in the case of associations, the Ministry of Social Affairs has the authority to refuse the establishment of a foundation on the grounds spelled out above and the right to supervise the activities, and check the documents, of the foundation.

(iii) Professional Groups.   No general law exists for the establishment of professional groups. Rather each such group is required to secure a special enactment approved by both the government and the People's Assembly (Parliament), and there are many cases of proposed professional groups that have been rejected by the government and parliament.

(iv) Youth Centers and Clubs.   Like associations, youth clubs and centers also require permission and formal announcement before attaining legal personality. According to Law No. 77 of 1975, applications must be filed with the Youth Administration Department, which is part of the High Council for Youth and Sports. The application must include:

1. An application form signed by the director of the organization
2. A contract pertaining to the establishment of the organization
3. A list of the names of board members
4. A list of the members of the general assembly
5. Proposed bylaws
6. A list of facilities and activities
7. A registration fee

To be recognized as legal entities, youth clubs and centers must meet certain conditions as spelled out in Decree No. 222 of 1975 of the President of the High

---

[6] Article 73 of Law No. 32.

Council for Sports and Youth, concerning, for example, overall health and clean-liness conditions, standards pertaining to medical assistance, and building design.

§ 7.3   INTERNAL GOVERNANCE

(a) Associations and Foundations

Law No. 32 of 1964 specifies a board of directors and the general assembly as the main governing bodies of associations and foundations. The *general assembly* con-sists of all the members of the organization. A general meeting must be held at least once a year during the first three months of the year, for the purposes of approving the budget, reviewing financial accounts and the reports of the board of directors, and holding elections.[7] Meetings must also be held on request of the board of directors, on petition signed by at least 25% of the assembly members, or to respond to the Ministry of Social Affairs.[8] Invitations to general meetings of members must be accompanied by an agenda. Decisions are made by a majority (51%) of the members attending the meeting. Minutes of the meeting must be sent within fifteen days to the Ministry of Social Affairs.

Whereas the general assembly largely performs supervisory functions, the *board of directors* is the focal point of governance according to Law No. 32. The board is responsible for the general administration of the organization and has the power to make decisions on behalf of the organization, except for those types of decisions for which the bylaws explicitly require the approval of the General Assembly. More specifically, the board is generally responsible for:

1. Directing the technical and administrative affairs of the organization
2. Establishing committees and identifying their responsibilities
3. Hiring staff
4. Preparing annual final accounts and the budget
5. Identifying the responsibilities of the appointed director
6. Inviting the general assembly for meetings
7. Preparing financial reports for the review of the general assembly
8. Representing the organization before the government and the courts

Details regarding the functions of, and elections to, the board must be speci-fied in the bylaws.[9] However, there are a few general legal requirements: the board must be composed of at least five members, but may have no more than fifteen members; board members serve three-year terms and members may be reelected; and the board must meet at least once a month.[10]

Quite importantly, the government in the form of the Ministry of Social Affairs retains the right to substantially interfere in the decision-making pro-cesses of both associations and foundations. In particular, the Ministry may

[7] Article 38 of Law No. 32 of 1964.
[8] Article 36 of Law No. 32 of 1964.
[9] Article 45 of Law No. 32 of 1964.
[10] Article 52 of Law No. 32 of 1964.

(1) revoke or change internal decisions that it deems in opposition to either Law No. 32, any other law, or to Egyptian morals in general (article 33); (2) nominate up to half of the board members of any association (article 48); (3) order and enforce mergers of organizations; and (4) dissolve an organization under certain circumstances. Mergers may be ordered if two organizations pursue the same objectives and the merger would lead to a better coordination of the services provided or, if this is required, to readjust the organizations to changing needs of the environment. The dissolution of an organization is permitted by article 57 of Law No. 32 of 1964 in four cases: (1) if the organization proves unable to achieve its aims; (2) if the organization diverts organizational finances to activities that have no relation to the organization's objectives; (3) if the general assembly of the organization has not met for two consecutive years; and (4) if the organization violates any laws.

(b) Professional Groups

The respective laws governing professional groups usually grant these organizations a greater degree of independence in terms of internal governance and management than is the case for associations. Professional groups are thus governed by their boards and members and are largely free from external governmental interference. However, the government opposes political activities of such groups.

(c) Youth Groups and Centers

Youth groups and centers are governed by committees elected by the membership, which have full responsibility for the administration of these organizations. However, in some cases, the High Council of Youth and Sports may nominate representatives for two or three seats on these committees.

§ 7.4   TAX TREATMENT

(a) Tax Treatment of Organizations

All nonprofit organizations are eligible for some form of fiscal relief. In addition, some types of organizations also qualify for other privileges, such as direct government support and technical assistance.

   (i) Associations and Foundations.   Except for sales taxes, associations and foundations are generally exempted from taxes. They are further exempted from stamp duties and tariffs for imported tools, equipment, and other production requirements, and are eligible for a 25% discount on the transportation of equipment and machinery and a 50% discount on the consumption of water and electricity. Besides these reliefs and discounts, associations are eligible for direct government support through the Fund for Special Organizations and Associations, to which both the government and private banks and companies contribute. However, direct financial assistance from the government is only symbolic in nature for most organizations. In addition, organizations may also receive support in the form of personnel paid by the government.

(ii) Professional Groups.   Professional groups are exempted from taxes as well, on their current income and their liquid assets, long-term investments, and pension and donation funds. They also receive direct government support, but the extent of this support varies greatly among different professional groups.

(iii) Youth Centers and Clubs.   Youth centers and clubs are also exempted from taxes and receive technical and financial support from government. This is particularly true of the youth centers, which receive a higher degree of financial support from the government because they provide services for the children of low-income families.

(iv) Foreign Organizations.   Certain nonprofit organizations operating programs on behalf of international donor organizations can receive tax exempt status and may be even exempted from sales tax, as is the case with the Fulbright Commission in Egypt administering an English training program funded by USAID.

(b) Tax Treatment of Contributions—Domestic Organizations

(i) Associations and Foundations.   Individuals or companies may deduct donations to nonprofit associations, foundations, public hospitals, youth centers, and other types of nongovernmental organizations (NGOs) from income tax up to certain specified limits. These limits vary not only between individuals and companies, but also between different income groups, and have been relatively restrictive.

(c) Tax Treatment of Contributions—Foreign Organizations

Donations from Egyptian nationals to such foreign organizations are not covered by law, leaving the tax treatment in this regard unclear.

§ 7.5   PERSONAL BENEFIT RESTRICTIONS

Members of the Board are not allowed to distribute any profit among themselves, or to be remunerated. Board members are furthermore not allowed to work as salaried staff for the association. In addition, organizations are required to deposit their funds in a bank or savings fund in the name of the organization.

§ 7.6   OBLIGATIONS TO THE PUBLIC

According to articles 14 and 16 of Law No. 32 of 1964, both the members and the government have the right to closely examine, control, and revise an organization's accounts and books. In the case of associations and foundations, the Ministry of Social Affairs appoints inspectors to supervise budgets and to investigate whether the budgets conform with the objectives and activities of the respective organization. To ensure further transparency, articles 17 and 18 of the law require boards of directors to submit final accounts to "a legal auditor" if the organizations' receivables or payables exceed 1,000 Egyptian Pounds, and to distribute both accounts and the auditor's report to all members before the meeting of the general assembly.

However, many organizations prepare very simple accounts, such as budgets showing sources of income and expenditures. In fact, it is often foreign donors that require indigenous organizations to disclose more sophisticated financial accounts as a prerequisite for funding.

§ 7.7   BUSINESS ACTIVITY

Business activities are recognized as a source of funding for associations and thus generally permissible. Profits from such activities are subject to sales tax, but not to other types of taxes so long as they are used to promote the public purposes of the organization.

§ 7.8   OTHER FUNDING RESTRICTIONS

Nonprofit organizations in Egypt are subject to a variety of fund-raising restrictions. The most important of these restrictions is that private donations and grants as well as other revenue received from certain parties (i.e., domestic and foreign donors) or lotteries need explicit government approval. Similarly, article 23 of Law 32 of 1964 stipulates that the government may prohibit the receipt of any financial support from foreign individuals and organizations. An exception from this rule has recently been granted to the American Development Agency, which, based on a special agreement between the Egyptian and American governments, has been granted the right to choose on its own Egyptian organizations to be supported and carry out the supervision of these grants.

Funding restrictions, however, do not only concern external funding, but internal revenue sources as well. Many professional groups, for instance, have to lobby the government to modify the laws authorizing the group in order to be able to significantly increase membership dues and other internal fees. As an additional funding restriction, professional groups are not allowed to invest capital in the stock market, but are obliged to place it in state banks. However, to circumvent this prohibition, some groups established private market companies funded by the groups to carry on stock market investments. This trend is currently being debated as a potential violation of the prohibition on profitmaking.

Besides the fund-raising limitations that the law imposes on nonprofit organizations, the government in the past has tried to gain control over the management of the traditional religious philanthropic institution of *Al Wakf*. However, the government's attempt to take over the administration of the *Al Wakf* funds in the 1950s resulted in a significant drop in bequests and donated funds, forcing the state to reinstate nonprofit Islamic organizations in control of the administration of these funds.

§ 7.9 POLITICAL ACTIVITY

In general, nonprofit organizations in Egypt are prohibited from pursuing political activities. The various laws affecting specific nonprofit organizations or specific types of nonprofit organizations state this prohibition either directly, as in the case of professional associations, or indirectly, as is the case with business associations, clubs, and youth centers.

Noteworthy in this context is that the establishment of religious political parties is prohibited by law. This prohibition, however, has contributed to efforts by Islamic activists to enter the nonprofit sector, through which they attempt to realize goals which would otherwise appear political. Notwithstanding the restrictions established by Law No. 32, or perhaps because of them, a high percentage of nonprofit organizations subject to this Law are Islamic associations formally registered as providing cultural and social services.

§ 7.10 KEY OUTSTANDING ISSUES

The main legal issues in Egypt concern the reform of the association law as well as a rethinking of the overall legal framework for the nonprofit sector; the issue of tax exemption; and the government's attempts to exert political influence on the sector.

(a) Reform of Law No. 32 of 1964

The major outstanding legal issue concerning nonprofit organizations in Egypt has to do with the restrictivity of Law No. 32 of 1964. Since the law's implementation, Egypt has undergone major changes both politically (i.e., the introduction of a multiparty system), and economically (i.e., the inauguration of economic open-door policies) from the 1970s on. However, the resulting substantial societal changes have not yet led to a revision of the severe restrictions imposed by the law on civic activities, reflecting the continued mistrust of the state toward the nonprofit sector. Nevertheless, there are a few tentative signs that a reform might be in the offing, as the issue of modifying the law has recently been debated in the parliament as well as in the mass media and government officials are beginning for the first time to acknowledge the important contribution of nongovernmental organizations in some areas.

(b) Standardization of the Overall Legal Framework

With the overall regulatory framework for all types of nonprofit organizations being too inflexible and rigid, some voluntary initiatives are increasingly avoiding formal nonprofit status and choosing the legal form of a civil company instead, thereby forgoing tax reliefs as well as other privileges afforded by law to nonprofit organizations. Furthermore, other organizations, such as the Egyptian human rights organizations, do not seek any legal status at all. Although there has not been a major backlash on the part of the government toward such organizations, they are in effect operating illegally and their operations are also negatively affected by the lack of an appropriate legal status. Together with the patchwork character of the multitude of laws authorizing and governing either specific nonprofit organizations or some subgroups of organizations, it would appear that a general revision and standardization of the overall framework for nonprofit activity in Egypt would be appropriate in addition to the repeal of the major restrictions imposed by Law No. 32 of 1964 on associations and foundations.

(c) Reliefs and Privileges Granted to Nonprofit Organizations

Another group of issues affecting the nonprofit sector relates to the inadequacy and relative volatility of tax exemptions and other privileges granted to the sector as a whole. In recent years, the government has been switching back and forth on this issue. A case in point here is the sales tax, which has been imposed on otherwise tax-exempted organizations. The imposition of this tax has been primarily motivated by the government's interest in increasing tax revenue during economic recession. One implication is that nonprofit organizations cannot take exemptions and privileges afforded to them by the law for granted anymore so long as the government subordinates such privileges to larger economic considerations.

Similarly problematic, is the issue of deductibility of donations or, more specifically, the complications involved in determining the actual percentage limits. Generally, different limits apply to "different income sectors," and currently, there is no one law governing the issue of deductibility of donations, but rather a total of 28 different laws governing deductibility limits for nonprofit organizations.

(d) Government Interference

In general, the government continues to attempt to exert direct influence on nongovernmental organizations and professional groups to achieve political objectives unrelated to the basic functions of the nonprofit sector. This has become very clear with Law No. 100 of 1993, also known as the Law of Professional Groups, which sought to severely limit the influence of Islamic authorities on these groups. This law, in effect, impeded the elections of governing committees of some professional groups or led to the postponement of internal elections for more than a year in other organizations, including the syndicates of engineers and physicians.

CHAPTER EIGHT

France[*]

§ 8.1 LEGAL CONTEXT

France is a civil law country in which the right to associate has been firmly enshrined in law. The legal position of nonprofit organizations in French law is of relatively recent vintage, however. Such organizations were outlawed at the time of the French Revolution on grounds that they represented partial interests that were potentially opposed to the "general interest" embodied in the democratically elected French state. In addition, severe limits were placed on endowments to prevent the perpetuation of centers of economic power not responsive to the democratic will of the people. Not until 1901 was the hold of this "Rousseauist tradition" broken and the right to associate firmly established in law. The resulting Law of July 1, 1901 established a broad right for French citizens to form "associations," organizations that do not distribute profits to their members. At the same time, however, this law retained the ambivalence toward such organizations that had long characterized French legal treatment: while granting French citizens a broad freedom to form associations, this law limited the rights of the resulting organizations to ward off the risk of secret or rebellious groups and to prevent the creation of organizations controlling large and immutable patrimonies (*biens de main-morte*), both of which were viewed as a potential danger to the political or economical peace of the country. Thus, for example, the Law of July 1, 1901 prohibited French associations from owning real estate other than that needed directly for their own operations.

Apart from the Law of July 1, 1901, associations, as civil groupings, are subject to the civil law for their internal operation and external relations, to the rules of public law (where associations perform tasks normally carried out by a public entity), and to the commercial law (for business-type activities, if there is no specific civil law to apply). Fiscal and labor laws also apply to nonprofit activities.

§ 8.2 ELIGIBILITY

(a) Types of Organizations

There are five basic types of nonprofit organizations in France: associations (*association*); mutual friendly societies (*mutuelle*); cooperatives (*cooperative*); foundations (*fondation*); and trade unions (*syndicat*). It should be noted, however, that, in general, the French legal system considers as a nonprofit organization

---

[*] Country Rapporteur: Dr. Sami Castro, legal advisor of UNIOPSS, Paris, France. This chapter is based on a legal field guide of the Johns Hopkins Comparative Nonprofit Sector Project.

any organization the constitution or bylaws of which prohibit any kind of direct or indirect sharing of profit. This differentiates nonprofit organizations from the only other type of organization traditionally recognized formally in France—the for-profit firm, known in France as the "society," or *société*. According to the French Civil Code, articles 1832 and following, the *société* is a contract instituted by two or more persons who hold in common property and labor in order to share out the resulting profits or savings. The definition of the *société* provides the backdrop against which the definition of the nonprofit organizations has proceeded.

(i) Associations.   Although the association is one of five types of nonprofit organizations in France, it is the main legal form of such organizations. In fact, the legal status of organizations with bylaws that prohibit the sharing of profits equals that of associations for all practical purposes, notwithstanding the other four types of organizations mentioned in section 8.2. According to the Law of July 1, 1901, an association is an agreement by which two or several persons permanently pool their knowledge or their activity for any purpose other than the sharing of profits. The wording of the law clearly lays down the principle that the basic character of associations is contrary to the for-profit character of the *société*: by definition, associations cannot engage in profit sharing. Although the regulation of associations is less complex than that of for-profit societies, associations enjoy fewer rights, especially with respect to (1) ownership of real property, which is restricted to ownership of property directly needed for the operation of the association; and (2) receiving legacies (only associations which obtain the fiscal designation of *reconnaissance d'utilité publique* or those whose exclusive aim is charitable [*associations de bienfaisance*] can receive legacies). Recently, associations whose aims are scientific and medical research also became eligible for this benefit.

Although, as noted more fully below, associations are allowed to engage in economic activities and to earn profits, business activity is not permitted to be their principal aim and activity. In addition, a characteristic feature of associations is their capacity to receive private donations and to engage the energies of *bénévoles*, that is, benevolent, nonpaid, volunteers.

(ii) Mutual Societies and Cooperatives.   Mutual societies and cooperatives are organizations that engage in economic activity but not with the primary motive of maximizing profits for a set of owners. Rather, they share with associations an essentially nonprofit objective. Thus, their property is owned collectively by their members and controlled on the basis of the number of members rather than the amount invested ("one person, one vote"). Similarly, if profits accrue, they are shared among the members rather than distributed on the basis of invested capital.

(iii) Foundations.   A fourth distinct type of nonprofit organization in France is the foundation. In contrast to associations and other types of organizations, which are groupings of persons or partners, a foundation is a grouping of capital or property earmarked to well-determined nonprofit aims of public benefit. Foundations were not separately defined legally until 1987, however, with the passage

of the Law of July 23, 1987,[1] followed by a second Law of July 4, 1990.[2] According to these laws, a foundation is the legal act by which one or several individual persons or legal entities irrevocably transfer estate, rights, or resources to the realization of an action of public benefit. Before 1987, foundations had been administratively recognized by the government as *reconnues d'utilité publique*, albeit with no legal basis to it.

There are two basic types of foundations. A foundation is either *reconnue d'utilité publique*, or a *fondation d'entreprise* (company-sponsored foundation). These two types of foundations differ with respect to the life span of the organization and their legal capacities. While the period of existence of *fondations reconnues d'utilité publique* is generally indefinite, *fondations d'entreprise* must terminate after five years with the possibility of renewal. Similarly, *fondations reconnues d'utilité publique* have a very wide legal capacity; they may, for instance, in contrast to the *associations reconnues d'utilité publique*, own real estate with no limitations. Also, they can receive donations and legacies, according to precise formalities and with a large privilege of tax exemptions. The *fondations d'entreprise*, on the other hand, have the same limited capacities as associations.

(iv) Trade Unions. A final type of nonprofit organization in French law is the trade union or professional association. Like other nonprofit organizations, trade unions are prohibited from sharing profits among their members. Their activities are further restricted to the protection of the rights of professions and workers. Although unions have been legally recognized since 1884, they have been considered to be a particular type of association since 1901.

(b) Types of Purposes

Given the broad freedom of association that was established by the Law of July 1, 1901, French nonprofit organizations can pursue a wide range of lawful purposes. Thus, such organizations are not restricted to pursuing aims of public or social utility but may also serve the nonmaterial or even material needs of their members alone. Only two types of purposes are prohibited: unlawful activities and the sharing of profits among the membership. Should such a prohibited case occur and constitute a grievance to any public person, such as the fiscal administration, or private person, such as a competitor firm, generally it has to be brought before the courts. If there is sufficient evidence, the judges may then decide to reclassify the association as a *société*, and/or stipulate the loss of preferential tax treatment.

Although a wide array of objectives are open to nonprofit organizations in France, only organizations that serve public interest purposes are eligible for special treatment. This special treatment takes the form of tax advantages for both the organizations and their donors and eligibility for government funding. Eligible for such treatment are organizations that serve the broader public rather than their members alone or that take on tasks that would otherwise fall within

---

[1] *Loi n° 87-571 du 23 juillet 1987 sur le développement du mécénat.*
[2] *Loi créant les fondations d'entreprise, et modifiant les dispositions de la loi n° 87-571 du 23 juillet 1987 sur le développement du mecénat relatives aux fondations.*

the responsibility of the state. This generally includes organizations working in the fields of education and research, health and social services, environment, development and housing, advocacy, philanthropy, international activities, or professional and business associations. Such organizations are often designated by state authorities as *organismes exercant des activités d'intérêt général* or *dont la gestion est désintéressée* to indicate the public benefit aim and nonprofit character of the organization, respectively.

(c) Other Requirements

Associations can be formed with as few as two people.

So far as capital requirements are concerned, no such requirements exist for associations. In the case of foundations, a minimum capital of FF 5 million is required for foundations *reconnue d'utilité publique*, while no such requirement exists for a *fondation d'enterprise*. However, the latter are prohibited from engaging in fund-raising activities.

(d) Registration Procedures

Since the freedom of association is one of the fundamental rights explicitly guaranteed by the constitution to the French people, the procedures for establishing an association and investing it with legal personality status are not very restrictive in France. No formal "incorporation" process or system of governmental approval exists. Indeed, attempts to introduce a priori registration controls for nonprofit associations into the French legal system have been firmly rejected, most recently by the *Conseil Constitutionnel* in its decision of July 16, 1971. At the same time, the state does take a stronger hand in the recognition of certain types of nonprofit organizations through a system of special agreements (*agrément*) or authorizations (*autorisation*). These are more specifically delineated in the following:

(i) *Associations.* In keeping with the principle of freedom of association as stipulated by the Law of July 1, 1901, there are no special formalities for associations to obtain legal entitlement other than to file a declaration with the respective regional department (*Préfecture du département*) and to publish in the *Journal Officiel* the name, location, founding date, and aims of the organization, and the names of the founders. Upon this publication, the association is then an *association déclarée et publiée* (or usually simply *association déclarée*) and thus a *personne morale*, or legal person. As associations cannot formally incorporate (and thus may not register in the *Registre de commerce et des sociétés*), no further procedures are required. Furthermore, the declaration is not compulsory. Undeclared associations are legal, but are considered informal assemblies of members without legal personality and thus without legal collective means of action.

(ii) *Foundations.* The registration requirements for foundations are somewhat stricter and differ between the two types of foundations. Like declared associations, both types of foundations have to publish the necessary details in the

Journal Officiel. A *fondation reconnue d'utilité publique* must be approved by the *Conseil d'Etat*. It thus receives its legal personality at the time when the *Journal Officiel* publishes the announcement that the *Conseil d'Etat* grants it the status of *reconnaissance d'utilité publique*. The *fondation d'entreprise*, on the other hand, receives its legal personality either by direct authorization given by the administration, or by default on the administration's side, within a period of four months after publication. When a *fondation reconnue d'utilité publique* is created by one or several companies or public concerns (*établissements publics à caractère industriel et commercial*), its denomination may be the name of at least one of them.

(iii) Special Authorizations for Public Benefit Organizations.

Under certain conditions, further authorizations in the form of an agreement (*agrément*) or authorization (*autorisation*) are either necessary or at least desirable for nonprofit organizations active in specific fields. In any case, they bring with them a range of significant benefits with respect to eligibility for public funding and/or permission to operate in certain fields.

In general, the *agrément* is an official recognition of the quality of activities performed by organizations in special fields, but also a means of very close state control. Under the agreement, an association becomes a private legal entity that is governed by special public rules for parts of its activities. Agreed associations (*associations agréées*) are subject to high standards of morality, financial solvency, and insurance; their membership has to accept special statutes and bylaws; in some cases, the president of the association is appointed by a minister; and the books, activities, and general operation of the organization are audited by controllers of the state administration. On the other hand, agreed organizations become eligible for public funding and other privileges. For instance, only agreed sports clubs are eligible to receive public funds. Furthermore, *associations agréées* may receive donations and legacies, even if they are not *reconnues d'utilité publique*; for the *centres de gestion agréés*, which help their membership keep their books, there are special tax privileges for the members; and most importantly, the *agrément* allows some associations to bring actions before the court for advocating causes relating to their aims, which is a very special exception to the French legal principle that no one is allowed to advocate somebody else's cause before court (*nul ne plaide par procureur*). Associations which are granted this privilege under the agreement include, among others, public morality organizations;[3] consumers' organizations;[4] and environmental organizations.[5]

While most organizations may seek the status of an agreed association voluntarily, a few specific activities may only be carried out by agreed organizations, including, for instance, nonprofit travel agencies;[6] hunter's federations;[7] youth

---

[3] *Associations de défense de la moralité publique*—décret du 24 janvier 1956.
[4] *Associations de défense des consommateurs*—loi du 27 décembre 1973.
[5] *Associations de défense de la nature, de l'environnement et de l'amélioration du cadre de vie*—loi du 10 juillet 1976.
[6] *Associations organisant des séjours et des voyages*—Law of July 11, 1975.
[7] *Fédérations départementales de chasse*—arrêté du 18 septembre 1975.

organizations;[8] fishers and fish-culture organizations;[9] and associations active in the fields of environment.[10]

The *autorisation valant agrément*, or authorization equal to an agreement, on the other hand, is obligatory in the area of health and social services in order to control the standard of quality of the activities performed, such as kindergartens, day nurseries for babies, housing of young workers or the elderly, education of handicapped or juvenile offenders, and so on. The authorization amounts to a grant of quasimonopoly in the respective field as only authorized agencies are allowed to provide such services. In return, however, the organizations must meet quality and performance standards set by the state. Organizations seeking to operate in these fields need to submit requests for *autorisations* to the *Préfet* of the *Département*, who may either decide directly or forward the case to the qualified ministry.

§ 8.3   INTERNAL GOVERNANCE

In general, there are no legal provisions relating to the internal governance of associations. Associations are therefore free to determine the governance structure in their bylaws. This also applies to general meetings of members. Only certain kinds of associations, such as *associations reconnues d'utilité publique*, *associations sportives affiliées à une fédération sportive, fédérations sportives*, and *associations émettant des obligations*, are required by law to hold an annual general meeting of members, which has to approve an activity report and a financial report. However, in practice, there are no controls and this rule is not always followed. Annual meetings, where not required by law, are generally stipulated by the statutes.

As there are hardly any specific regulations concerning the internal governance of associations, the real law ruling the life and operation of an association is its constitution, bylaws, and statutes. These provisions, which include rules on the internal organization of its governing bodies (the board of directors, the presidency, commissions, etc.), are determined by the founders of the organization, bearing in mind the two prohibited aims. This does not mean, however, that associations are governed by fewer rules than other types of organizations and individual citizens of the country. Rather, they are subject to the general legal network of rights and obligations ruling the life of every citizen or resident in France, including, where applicable, the civil, public, commercial, labor, and fiscal laws. In addition, the *associations agréées*, as noted in section 8.2(d), are subject to more stringent restrictions on the powers of the members as opposed to the government.

In contrast to associations, however, *fondations reconnues d'utilité publique* and, in a minor measure, *fondations d'entreprise*, are subject to the state's tutelage, due

---

[8] *Associations de jeunesse*—décret du 7 juillet 1977.
[9] *Associations de pêche et de pisciculture*—arrêté du 23 mars 1982.
[10] *Associations de protection de la nature, de l'environnement et du cadre de vie*—décret du 7 juillet 1977.

to their special privileges. Only part of the administrators of a foundation can thus be appointed by the founder, while about a third are appointed by the state.

§ 8.4 TAX TREATMENT

As noted earlier, nonprofit status in France is not necessarily reserved for organizations engaged in public benefit activity, even if it is the case that both the nonprofit and public benefit concepts are linked in the aims of many associations.

Nevertheless, French tax laws, especially those relating to income taxation and the value-added tax, do take account of this distinction, granting certain tax advantages to all organizations that are nonprofit (even if they do not bear the title of *association*), but reserving some additional privileges for organizations that also serve some public benefit. The French fiscal legislation also grants partial income tax exemptions to those who make charitable contributions to nonprofit organizations. Finally, *associations reconnues d'utilité publique* enjoy even greater tax-exemption privileges, especially in matters of legacies and donations.

Notwithstanding the present moves toward decentralization in France, most tax laws of relevance to nonprofit organizations are national laws. This applies to income tax on individuals and corporation tax on legal persons; value-added tax; license and apprenticeship tax; tax on wages; capital gains tax; and the tax on capital. Local authorities also collect some taxes such as land taxes, residential taxes, and building taxes, but in most cases these do not carry exemptions for nonprofit organizations.

(a) Tax Treatment of Organizations

While emphasizing the need for neutrality on the part of the state with respect to the taxation of various economic activities, French law nevertheless grants special privileges for organizations that either serve some public benefit, such as providing services not supplied by other organizations, or are managed in a nonprofit spirit.[11] In particular, the present fiscal situation[12] is the following:

(i) Corporation Tax. According to article 206-1 of the *Code Général des Impôts* (CGI), every organization engaged in activities in order to make a profit is subject to a tax on this profit. Because they do not seek a profit, nonprofit organizations are exempt from this tax. To qualify for the exemption, however, nonprofit organizations must fulfill five conditions established by the courts and/or the tax administration:

- The organization has to be of some social utility (*utilité sociale*), that is, it answers to needs which are not normally, or not sufficiently, taken care of by the market.

[11] These fundamental criteria have been expressed in the *Conseil d'Etat's* decision of November 30, 1973: "Association hospitaliére Saint-Luc, Clinique du Sacré Coeur," *Rev. trim. de Dr. sanit. et soc.*, 1974, p. 552.
[12] Only Income and Corporation Taxation and VAT will be discussed here, but similar observations can be made about other relevant taxes as well.

- The organization's management must not grant direct or indirect material profit to its founders, leaders, or members.
- The activities performed must be related to the nonprofit activity of the organization and contribute to the achievement of its aims.
- Surplus revenue must not be sought in a systematic way, such as through the use of business methods, moderated prices, balanced management, and so on.
- Any revenue surplus has to be reinvested in the organization.

While organizations that meet these conditions are exempted from corporation income tax, however, they are still liable for capital gains tax at a rate of 24% or 10%, but only on patrimonial revenues, such as revenues generated from real estate, investments, and so on.

(ii) Value-Added Tax.   Articles 256-1 and 256-A of the CGI state that this tax has to be paid by natural and legal persons who, usually or occasionally, deliver goods or services that are not free of charge. Exemptions from the value-added tax are available, however, either on the basis of the kind of services organizations provide or on the basis of the kind of organization involved.

So far as the *kinds of services* exempted from VAT are concerned, three types are identified: (1) social, educational, cultural, and sports organizations, but also philosophical, religious, political, patriotic, civic, and trade-union type organizations for services rendered to their membership, excluding food and shelter; (2) services performed by social, philanthropic, or medical organizations for the benefit of all people if either the fee structure is regulated by the authorities or the services provided are not usually performed by the for-profit sector; and (3) goods and services delivered at the occasion of "charity and support parties" (up to a limit of six a year), which include activities and events such as cultural performances, balls, dinners, charity sales, lotteries, and so on.

Beyond these specific types of services, nonprofit organizations must also meet the following conditions to be exempted from VAT:

- The organization must be managed and administered by unpaid officers who neither directly nor indirectly (via intermediaries) benefit from the financial results of the activity.
- The organization must not directly or indirectly share profits in any way.
- The organization's members or their beneficiaries cannot be declared assignees of any share of the assets.

If these criteria are met, organizations will be exempted from levying value-added tax on the services and goods they provide. However, this also means that they cannot deduct VAT paid by themselves on investments and equipment purchases. In practice, therefore, VAT exemption may be disadvantageous. This is particularly so in view of the fact that VAT-exempted organizations are bound to pay a tax on wages, which, until some thirty years ago, had to be paid by all employers, but which is presently levied on only a few professions and on VAT-exempted organizations. In some cases, and especially with associations that have many employees, paying the tax on wages instead of VAT can be more costly.

Unfortunately, however, the fiscal administration often links the corporation tax exemption with the VAT exemption so that, with few exceptions, individual organizations are often not allowed to choose whether or not to be subjected to VAT once they qualify for exemption from the corporation tax. The linkage between these two exemptions has thus become a contentious issue.

(b) Tax Treatment of Contributions—Domestic Organizations

The privileged treatment of charitable contributions to nonprofit organizations is a rather recent phenomenon in France. Until the 1980s, there was only a symbolic exemption on the income tax and corporation tax paid by individuals or organizations for contributions to a well-defined small group of associations or foundations.[13]

Even now, deductibility of contributions to nonprofit organizations is available only for cash donations and only for contributions to organizations that serve the public benefit in one way or another. In addition, it is available only up to rather narrow limits, described below:

(i) Individual Donations. Taxpayers are entitled to the following tax advantages for contributions to different types of nonprofit organizations:

1. A *credit* of 40% of the contribution against the taxes owed by the taxpayer, up to 5% of taxable income, for contributions to:
   - *Associations reconnues d'utilité publique* (or *associations dont la mission est reconnue d'utilité publique* in the departments of Alsace-Moselle) or to *fondations reconnues d'utilité publique*[14]
   - The parochial associations of the three recognized monotheistic faiths (Christian, Jewish, Moslem) authorized to receive gifts and legacies
   - Relief and charitable organizations
   - Catholic religious communities (*congregations*), legally recognized for the laic nature of their public benefit activities, which have gotten permission from the public authorities to receive gifts and legacies
   - The recognized public churches (*établissements publics des cultes reconnus*) in the three French departments of Alsace-Moselle; and

---

[13] Such deductions were permitted mostly for legacies and significant one-off donations to *associations reconnues d'utilité publique* (or *associations dont la mission est reconnue d'utilité publique* in the departments of Alsace and Moselle, which are still partly covered by the German Empire Law of 1908). Such contributions were generally exempted from probate duty (or inheritance tax) and the associations also only had to pay a reduced purchase tax on buildings if they are active in the fields of welfare, charity, or social service.

[14] The term *reconnaissance d'utilité publique* is a very official label and a kind of special recognition, which is generally only granted by the government, on the *Conseil d'Etat's* advice, to relatively few associations on their request. These associations have to provide certain evidence of the importance of their activities, the seriousness of their operation, the quality of their performance, and their reputation, and the government is entitled to withdraw this recognition for serious failures. Since 1933, associations whose only aim is charity or relief (*associations de bienfaisance*), even if they are not *reconnues d'utilité publique*, also get the same tax privilege. The privilege was extended to associations active in scientific and medical research in 1987.

- Those registered and published associations (*déclarées et publiées*), that have opened an intermediary account in the books of a *reconnue d'utilité publique* association or foundation.

2. A *credit* of 40% of the contribution against the taxes owed by the taxpayer, up to 1.25% of taxable income, for contributions to all other organizations serving any kind of public benefit, such as philanthropy, education, welfare, family, humanitarian causes, science, sport, culture, enhancing of the artistic patrimony, the environment, and diffusion of culture, language, and know-how. According to special provisions of the fiscal law and under special conditions and controls, individual contributions to associations whose aim is to finance election campaigns or to financial agents are also eligible for preferential treatment in this category.

3. A credit of 50% up to a total of FF 520 for contributions to organizations serving meals free of charge or providing assistance with emergency housing.

If an individual chooses to give to organizations in several of these categories, the total preferential treatment claimed for contributions cannot go beyond a total of 5% of the taxable income of the said taxpayer.

(ii) Corporate Donations.   All corporations can claim the following tax advantages:

1. Deduction of contributions up to 0.3% of the annual business turnover to associations and foundations *reconnues d'utilité publique* (or to organizations *reconnue d'utilité publique* in Alsace-Moselle), or to *associations de bienfaisance* according to the 1933 law. The same privilege exists for donations to associations *déclarées* which have opened intermediary accounts in the books of an association or a foundation *reconnue d'utilité publique*; to public or private schools teaching art or to higher grade education as far as they are nonprofit organizations; to the parochial associations of the three monotheistic faiths authorized to receive gifts and legacies; to recognized public churches in the French departments of Alsace-Moselle; and to Catholic religious *communutés* legally recognized for laic activities serving the public benefit.

2. Deduction of contributions up to 0.2% of the annual turnover to other nonprofit organizations serving a public benefit as listed under individual donations above; to approved organizations providing enterprise development; and to approved public or private organizations or bodies engaged in scientific or technical research. The special provisions concerning individual contributions to organizations whose aim is to finance election campaigns or to financial agents are also applicable to corporate donations.

The total of contributions to all organizations cannot go beyond 0.3% of the business turnover of the tax year of a given taxpayer. However, the amounts may be carried forward over five consecutive years.

(c) Tax Treatment of Contributions—External Organizations

Contributions by French individuals or corporations to nonprofit organizations operating in other countries are not deductible. However, contributions to French organizations operating in other countries are deductible.

§ 8.5 PERSONAL BENEFIT RESTRICTIONS

Restrictions on the personal benefit that can be claimed by founders, administrators, and members of associations in France are governed by the general prohibition on profit-sharing by associations laid out in article 1 of the Law of July 1, 1901. In particular, civil law courts as well as the tax administration generally test the reality of the profit-sharing prohibition by observing the kind and level of salaries and compensations for expenses paid to such officials. According to the judge-made rules, salaries and wages paid on a normal and usual scale to persons performing a real and well-defined job in the service of an association are not to be considered as profit or benefit and are, therefore, permissible. Nevertheless, since this general rule leaves a high degree of ambiguity, the civil and administrative High Courts have also recommended various additional rules in order to prevent both officers and members of associations from performing paid jobs in their organizations.

With respect to executive salaries, for instance, it has been ruled that "the association cannot pay a salary to a member of the organization for his activity in pursuit of the aims of the association. But the association is entitled to pay wages to people who are not members of the organization, for the services rendered by them."[15] This assumes that these services have actually been rendered, and that the level of the wages is appropriate for the kind of services rendered. Comparatively high wages might suggest a fraud against article 1 of the Law of July 1, 1901.

On the more general question of whether or not members, officers, or administrators of an association may, at the same time, also be salaried employees, the law is in considerable flux, with different interpretations under civil law and tax law.

Under the civil law (*droit civil*), the general principle is that officers and administrators cannot receive salaries for their official duties. They are entitled only to reimbursements or compensations for expenses in the service of the organization (this provision appears in almost all the statutes of French associations). According to a recent doctrine of the *Conseil d'Etat*, however, employees of an association can become members of the board of directors without losing their jobs, provided that the paid jobs have no link with the nonpaid offices and that the number of administrators who are also employees of the organization is not "preponderant" on the board.[16] Nevertheless, the same doctrine forbids having paid employees occupy one of the offices of Chairman, Vice-chairman, Secretary

---

[15] *Rép. du ministre de l'Intérieur et de la Décentralisation, Journ. Officiel, Débats à l'Assemblée Nationale,* 21 mai 1984.

[16] *"Avis" du Conseil d'Etat,* October 22, 1970, *Rev. trim. de droit sanit. et soc.* 1972, 547, n. 32.

General or Treasurer.[17] But recent Court decisions have even dismissed this prohibition in some cases[18] as long as the number of employees on the board is not preponderant. Furthermore, although members cannot receive salaries for activities directly linked with the aims of the association, they may, as long as they are not officers, nevertheless become employees of the organization for performing "technical" jobs, which could be performed as well for a similar salary in any other concern.[19]

So far as *tax law* is concerned, the principal concern is to check that salaries paid are comparable with those of similar jobs elsewhere, that compensations cover real expenses, and that the level of the wages or compensation paid is in line with the tasks performed and they do not represent, directly or indirectly, a kind of profit for a member of the board of directors, or a member of the organization, or any other individual.[20]

There are no self-dealing restrictions under French law. However, since associations are required to invest any capital in bonds and are thus prohibited from owning stocks, self-dealing problems seldom arise.

§ 8.6   OBLIGATIONS TO THE PUBLIC

The legal liability of nonprofit organizations and their boards rests on two provisions of the French civil code and on the jurisprudential constructions of the Courts. In general, associations as legal entities bear the responsibility of the acts performed on their behalf by their officers. On the basis of articles 1382 and following of the French Civil Code, however, officers and board members of *any* kind of legal entity are nevertheless personally responsible for the shortcomings and mistakes performed in their capacity and are subject to corresponding penalties. However, on the basis of article 1992 of the same code, the liability of unpaid board members (as is generally the case in nonprofit organizations) is judged less strictly than that of paid board members. In general, until a few years ago, there was no penal liability of legal entities as such (*non-responsabilité pénale des personnes morales*) and, therefore, no penal liability of the boards as a body, but only of individual officers. This applied to for-profit and to nonprofit boards. Very recent provisions of the law, however, established the new legal principle (for France) of direct liability of legal entities (*responsabilité des personnes morales*), which may either lead to fines or Court-decided dissolution.

Articles 1382 to 1386 of the French Civil Code have been the foundation on which the Courts have built a very important and complex system of liability rules (*droit de la responsabilité*). Among the many types of liabilities of board members and the organizations they operate are as follows:

1. *Civil responsibility (responsabilité civile).* A general obligation of carefulness and care in their operations and activities toward their members or third

---

[17] "*Avis*" *du Conseil d'Etat*, October 21, 1987 (*Juris-associations, n° 36, nov.–dec. 1988.*

[18] *Cour de cassation*, February 26, 1986 and December 17, 1987, in Henri Blaise, "Une transaction sans concessions, "*Droit social*, no. 5, 1988, pp. 432–438.

[19] *Cour d'Appel Versailles*, February 13, 1987.

[20] *Droit administratif*, n° 3A-3151, February 15, 1987.

parties. Board members can therefore be responsible to the association, to its members, or to any other third party possibly harmed by the organization.

2. *Penal responsibility (responsabilité pénale)*. If a board member in his or her official capacity commits illicit acts, he or she can be sued for them.

3. *Labor responsibility (responsabilité sociale)*. Board members are responsible for the application of the labor laws, including, for instance, the payment of all labor taxes (*cotisations sociales*) by their organization.

4. *Tax responsibility (responsabilité fiscale)*. Since 1980, officers and board members of nonprofit organizations are responsible for the tax-related requirements of their organization.

5. *Expenditure liability* in case of insolvency and bankruptcy (*cessation de paiements; faillite personnelle*). Since 1967, and more generally since 1985, board members of nonprofit organizations engaged in economic activities are subject to the same rules as their counterparts in any other type of organizations such as commercial firms and companies. This involves practically all nonprofit organizations today. The law provides inter alia that penalties can be imposed on officers and board members: their personal patrimony may be affected; civil and penal sanctions can be taken against them (interdiction of serving as officer of any organization, fines, etc.). Finally, personal bankruptcy (*banqueroute*) may be decided against a board member, possibly involving substantial fines and imprisonment.

§ 8.7 BUSINESS ACTIVITY

The basic French law on nonprofit associations, the Law of July 1 1901, establishes no restrictions on the ability of associations or other nonprofit organizations in France to conduct business activities, provided that neither direct nor indirect profit sharing be the aim of the organization and/or that no such profit-sharing take place. The ability of associations to engage in business activities has since been confirmed in a series of decisions of the Supreme Civil Court, the *Cour de Cassation*, which has ruled that associations can carry out permanent commercial activities to achieve their nonprofit goals.[21]

Not only may nonprofit associations engage in commercial activities, however, but also they may own all or a substantial portion of other business enterprises. In fact, many associations which do not wish to create ambiguities between their nonprofit aim and their business-type activities, choose to take a partnership in a for-profit subsidiary company or companies [*filiale*(s)] to which they delegate the performance of business-type activities. Profits generated from such affiliates will be transferred back to the association and used to help the association carry out its nonprofit aim. An association may play either the role of a parent organization of a group, or the role of a subsidiary daughter company (*filiale*).

---

[21] "Comité des fêtes de Lizine," May 13, 1970, *Dalloz* 1970, 644; "Institut musulman," March 17, 1981, *Bulletin civil* IV, no. 149, p. 117; "Club de chasse du Vert-Galant," February 12, 1985, *Bulletin civil* IV, no. 59, p. 50; and most recently: "Merens," September 27, 1989, *Semaine juridique éd. gle., sommaires de jurisprudence*, 1989, p. 375; and "Cottigny," June 27, 1990, *Semaine juridique, éd. gle., sommaires de jurisprudence*, 1990, p. 323.

Associations that pursue economic activities are, however, subject to the overall economic and business regulations relating to these economic activities, especially with regard to competition with other economic agents.[22] This applies particularly to the tax treatment of the business activity. Associations carrying out business activities can maintain the tax privileges they enjoy as nonprofit organizations (especially with regard to the corporation tax), but only if they bring evidence to the fiscal authorities that the activities in question are needful and unavoidable for reaching the nonprofit aim of the organization. In addition, they must comply with the criteria listed by the fiscal administration with respect to the *gestion désintéressée* (disinterested management), and the *intérêt général* (public benefit) or the *utilité sociale* (public utility) of their activities to get the benefit of tax exemption on corporation tax and VAT.

When the business activities are carried out by a *filiale* (subsidiary), taxes on the subsidiary's activity (especially the corporation tax) are the same as imposed on any other company performing the same type of activity. The profits earned by the company and transferred to the association are subject to a residual tax only (to avoid a double taxation). However, the fiscal administration often considers nonprofit parent organizations and for-profit subsidiaries as a group of organizations to which taxation should be applied as a whole. In these cases, the authorities might question the disinterested management or even the nonprofit aim of associations engaged in such activities and impose full taxes on the whole of the associations' revenues should the investigation lead to the conclusion that the nonprofit criteria are not strictly respected. Such investigations focus on the following:

- The relative extent and the type of businesses in which an association and/or its subsidiaries are engaged
- The more or less complementary character of these activities with regard to the aim of the association
- Whether the organization could have met its budgetary needs without resort to commercial activity

In cases where the business-type activities have neither a direct nor indirect link with the aim of the association, and the organization's budgetary needs might be met by other means; the tax authorities would deprive the association of any nonprofit tax privileges in order to avoid unfair competition and preserve equal treatment under the tax laws. In this sense, profits generated by activities related to the mission of the organization are more likely to be exempt from taxation than profits generated from activities that are unrelated to the aim of the association. The tax law (*droit fiscal),* on this point as on many others, is more restrictive than the civil law (*droit civil).*

---

[22] The most important of these regulations include the *loi du 1er mars 1984, relative au réglement amiable et à la prévention des difficultés des entreprises; loi du 25 janvier 1985 sur le redressement et la liquidation judiciaires des entreprises; loi du 11 juillet 1985 permettant à certaines associations d'émettre des valeurs mobilières; ordonnance du 1er décembre 1986 relative à la liberté des prix et de la concurrence; circulaire du Premier ministre du 10 mars 1979, relative à la lutte contre les pratiques contraires à une concurrence loyale dans le domaine du commerce et de la distribution;* and *circulaire du Ministre de l'Economie des Finances et de la Privatisation relative à la lutte contre les practiques paracommerciales.*

With respect to the *value-added tax*, associations are vulnerable to losing their VAT exemption if they engage in unrelated business activities. Naturally, activities carried out by a for-profit subsidiary (*filiale*) are subject to the VAT tax payment the same way as those of any other company or individual tradesman or businessman.

§ 8.8   OTHER FUNDING RESTRICTIONS

Fund-raising by nonprofit organizations on a large scale is a comparatively recent phenomenon in France. Accordingly, the question of fund-raising controls has only recently received significant attention. In 1991, many charitable and humanitarian organizations created a joint committee to establish a charter in order to voluntarily insure their operations' transparency with respect to operations, revenues, and expenditures. As important as this attempt to introduce voluntary self-control might be for the associations concerned and the public at large, there are also legal regulations that have very recently been consolidated in a chapter of the Law of August 7, 1991.[23]

According to this law, national appeals or fund-raising campaigns have now to be announced beforehand and accounts on the utilization of funds raised are subject to control by the *Cour des comptes*. However, litigation on this subject by donors, for instance, has to be brought before Court under the rules of the general civil law (*droit civil*) and not under the auspices of some special law governing nonprofit organizations.

Also under French law, company-sponsored foundations cannot engage in fund-raising and donative appeals.

§ 8.9   POLITICAL ACTIVITY

French law places no prohibitions on nonprofit political activity, so long as the activity is not seditious and that the bylaws of the respective association state that the aim and the activities of it are at least partly political. Indeed, most political parties in France have the legal form of associations.[24] Given these principles, nonprofit organizations can engage in a variety of political activities, such as:

1. Active participation in legitimate campaign activities
2. Active lobbying for legislation with the government or Parliamentarians
3. Raising money for political campaigns[25]

---

[23] *Loi no. 91-772 relative . . . au contrôle des comptes des organismes faisant appel à la générosité publique.*

[24] However, political parties do not necessarily have to be *déclares* since no rules compel them to do so. Accordingly, undeclared parties have no legal personality, but are, nevertheless, de facto commonly accepted as such, even by official authorities or the courts, as is the case with the *Parti Communiste*.

[25] On this particular and delicate issue, however, a series of rules have been established for legalizing such operations in the wake of recent scandals related to methods used by political parties to finance their election campaigns. Under these new rules, public funding will be provided to

Furthermore, candidates for political office who hold positions in nonprofit organizations are, in principle, free to do so. The custom, however, is that these candidates resign their positions in their respective organizations once they are elected. Persons holding office in nonprofit organizations usually also resign if appointed to important official posts or elected to an official political assembly. However, there are usually no resignations if the nonprofit organization is the political party of the person newly elected or if the political office is a minor one.

In this context, it should also be noted that political parties sometimes help to support a variety of "affiliated" associations, such as certain workers' unions, cooperatives, or friendly societies, which effectively constitute a kind of idealistic, philosophical, and also a strategic and tactical base for their corresponding parties.

§ 8.10   KEY OUTSTANDING ISSUES

Among the most important outstanding issues relating to nonprofit organizations in France are (a) the legal capacities granted to associations, (b) the regulations and restrictions imposed on nonprofits receiving governmental support, and (c) the issue of unfair competition with for-profit firms. A fourth issue, relating to the tax treatment of donations to nonprofit organizations, was a serious challenge until the 1980s, but has since been partly resolved as noted above.

(a) Incorporation

Given the increased development of economic or business-type activities performed by associations and the special challenges posed by the development of the European Common Market, there are discussions on remedying the current lack of provisions for any kind of incorporation for associations by introducing registration or incorporation procedures, at least for some types of associations. Some legal scholars have proposed the introduction of an option to voluntarily register in the *Registre du Commerce et des Sociétés* for those associations engaged in business activities. Although a voluntary registration would put certain constraints on associations, it would also have several advantages, as it would strengthen an association's credibility and clarify relations with bankers, clients, suppliers, partners, or competitors. On a more concrete level, a voluntary registration option would also ease transactions such as renting office buildings since the French law favors the renting of shop or office premises to corporate entities registered in the *Registre du Commerce et des Sociétés*.

(b) Regulations Associated with Government Support

The evolving partnership between nonprofit organizations and the government in France has spurred a variety of questions regarding the proper roles of each

political parties for their elections campaigns under certain criteria, while campaign expenses are subject to controls and may not exceed a certain maximum. On the other side, new tax-exemption rules were established in favor of those taxpayers wishing to make donations to political campaigns.

side in these partnerships and the issue of accountability for public funds, which subsequently have been addressed by a series of legal and administrative rulings concerning the modalities and methods of the cooperation between associations and the state. In practice, each government department develops its own guidelines and rules (*arrêtés ministériels, circulaires*, etc.) within the general framework of the law, which, however, are periodically synthesized in official government orders (*décret, décret-loi, ordonnance, circulaire du Premier ministre*, etc.). Generally, these regulations detail the way services have to be performed and attach technical and administrative controls. Often, these rules and regulations also prescribe the wording of statutes and bylaws of nonprofit organizations applying for public funding as well as decision-making and board election procedures, methods of spending the public funds, and those types of board decisions reserved for government appointees on the associations' boards. Nonprofit organizations naturally express concern about the extent of public control that comes to be exercised over associations as a consequence, as an entire system of a priori regulation has been established.

(c) Nonprofit–For-Profit Competition

The business activities of nonprofit organizations are a third major issue with respect to the French nonprofit sector. While this issue raises ethical questions on the one hand, it has also and even more importantly been discussed on the level of unfair competition with the for-profit sector. In fact, the government has repeatedly issued orders in an effort to solve this problem under pressure from businesses fearing competition from nonprofit organizations that enjoy both the privilege of tax exemption and access to unpaid, voluntary workers.[26]

While the problem is less severe where the economic activities of nonprofit organizations are restricted to either members or particular populations otherwise underserved by the business sector, the problem becomes acute when nonprofits produce marketable goods and services for the population at large. One case in point are associations employing handicapped or disadvantaged persons in an effort to reintegrate them into the production process while providing the necessary care and attention to their specific physical, intellectual, or social needs.[27] Since the additional financial burden of the educational activities of these organizations as well as the comparatively low productivity of the workers seldom really create competitive advantages that would allow them to unfairly undercut for-profit competition, unfair competition suits brought to the courts under this situation are more often than not dismissed. Similarly, the tax authorities seldom revoke tax privileges in such cases. However, as nonprofit organiza-

---

[26] *Circulaire du Premier Ministre du 10 mars 1979 relative à la lutte contre les pratiques contraires à une concurrence loyale dans le domaine du commerce et de la distribution*, and also the *Ordonnance du 1er décembre 1986 (JO du 9 Décembre 1986, p. 14773) relative à la liberté des prix et de la concurrence*, especially in its art. 37, al. 2; *Circulaire du 12 Août 1987 du Ministre de l'Economie des Finances et de la Privatisation relative à la lutte contre les pratiques paracommerciales" (JO du 23 août 1987, p. 9704 et s.).*

[27] These organizations usually bear the generic name of *entreprises intermédiaires, entreprises d'insertion, associations intermédiaires*, or *centres d'aide par le travail.*

tions broaden their involvement in business activities, as is increasingly the case, challenges from the business sector are likely to grow.

In order to counter these problems, nonprofit organizations have, where feasible, established commercial subsidiaries despite the potential problems with the tax authorities as described above. Nevertheless, the general question of business-type activities performed by associations remains a permanent ethical concern for the legal authorities, for the specialized lawyers, and for the leaders of these organizations, since such activities have become almost unavoidable for most associations and neither law nor Courts forbid it. How to achieve the right balance between "ethics" and "needs," between "nonprofit" and "business," between "making profits" and "sharing profits," and between "public benefit" and "private aim" thus remains unresolved.

CHAPTER NINE

Germany[*]

§9.1 LEGAL CONTEXT

According to the federal constitution (*Grundgesetz*—GG), German citizens enjoy the basic rights to assemble peacefully and to form associations and societies. They may also voice their concerns freely in speech and writing. In this, the GG provides an encouraging framework for nonprofit and charitable activities. More generally, two distinct legal systems exist in Germany: first, the private law system regulates the interactions among private individuals or organizations; and second, the public law system, which governs the relationships between the state and individuals or juridical persons, as well as the relations and interactions among public institutions themselves.

The private law system embraces civil law, which is mainly incorporated in the Civil Law Code (*Bürgerliches Gesetzbuch*—BGB) of 1896/1900; commercial law, which is concentrated in the Commercial Law Code (*Handelsgesetzbuch*—HGB) of 1897/1900; as well as several specialized codes for corporations, companies, or cooperatives which were separated in the past from the HGB or regulate legal matters never considered by the HGB, such as labor law, trade law, or copyright law. The public law system comprises constitutional law (*Staatsrecht*); the administrative laws (*Verwaltungsrecht*) of the federal, state, and local levels of government; as well as—among others—fiscal or tax law (*Steuerrecht*) and church law (*Kirchenrecht*).

This sharp division between private law and public law entities is far from complete, however. Thus, for the sake of simplicity, or economy, or for reasons of efficiency, private law can govern some transactions of public bodies. Similarly, private individuals have the option of creating institutions under public law if the state approves. Accordingly, the German nonprofit sector comprises not only private independent organizations, but also a variety of mixed public-private institutions.

The political structure of the Federal Republic of Germany features a strong federalism. In many cases, the regulation of nonprofit organizations is left to the individual states, or *Länder*. In the following, the term *state* will refer to the level of the *Länder*.

---

* Country Rapporteur: Dr. Klaus Neuhoff, Director of the Institute Foundation & Common Weal, University of Witten/Herdecke, Germany. This chapter is based on a legal field guide of the Johns Hopkins Comparative Nonprofit Sector Project.

§ 9.2 ELIGIBILITY

(a) Types of Organizations

The civil law recognizes two main types of nonprofit organizations: corporate bodies (associations, corporations, and cooperatives) and foundations and trusts. In addition, there are three selected types recognized under public law: public law corporations (including cooperatives), institutions (Anstalten), and foundations.

(i) Civil Law

1. *Associations.* Associations are the most common form of nonprofit organization. Although the BGB does not explicitly define an association, such organizations are generally understood to be voluntary alliances of a number of individuals or juridical persons to jointly accomplish a certain goal for a longer period of time. Associations receive the status of a juridical person or persona at law through registration, after fulfilling certain norms. However, registration is not mandatory. Section 54 BGB allows unregistered associations which are considered to be a body of rights. Although they can receive legacies and donations, and hold property (in co-ownership), unregistered associations cannot hold title to real estate. Furthermore, with the exception of political parties and trade unions, these organizations are not capable to sue in the courts themselves, but can be sued. Furthermore, they can be subject to distraint, and fall into bankruptcy.

2. *Foundations.* Foundations are instruments of Civil Law (Sections 80 through 88 BGB), to be used by private individuals or juridical persons, and to be endowed with private wealth. Foundations can be defined as autonomous bodies of assets which are permanently dedicated to a specific purpose or purposes. The assets may either consist of financial capital or institutions such as hospitals, nursing homes, or museums. The relevant laws do not distinguish between operating and grant-making foundations. Several other specific types of foundations recognized in the law are community foundations, church foundations, and family foundations. In contrast to the liberal registration procedures for nonprofit associations, the establishment of foundations requires a special act of the respective state authority, granting a concession for the foundation to become a juridical person.

3. *Trusts.* A trust is essentially an unincorporated version of a foundation that comes into existence when an individual donates resources for a public purpose. Not being a legal entity itself, the German-style trust has to rely on a natural or juridical person to carry out its purposes. Assets are to be held by that person as owner, but in trust. While there is a system of regulation for unincorporated foundations held in trust by public law bodies, there is almost no regulation regarding private law trustees.

4. *Corporations.* The types of organizations provided by commercial law have only relatively recently been recognized as an option for carrying out non-

profit activities. Both limited liability companies/closely held stock corporations and public stock corporations can be set up for nonprofit purposes. While both types of corporations face only minimal registration requirements and limited public oversight, the limited liability company is a rather useful legal form for nonprofit activities due to the more or less nominal capital of DM 50,000 required to be invested and the simple organizational structures that must be observed.

5. *Cooperatives.*   Cooperatives aim at enhancing the economic undertakings of their members such as small businesses, craftsmen, or farmers. Despite their being engaged in business activities, the legal order, historically, did grant cooperatives nonprofit status, since they lack the profit motive. Cooperatives have traditionally been active in the farming, housing, banking, and insurance industries. However, most cooperatives have changed into businesses.

(ii) Public Law.   Nonprofit-type institutions also exist under public law in Germany. Federal and state governments basically have four types of legal institutions at hand to organize public interest activities outside their own bureaucracy. These are public law corporations (*Körperschaften*), cooperatives (*Genossenschaften*), institutions (*Anstalten*), and foundations (*Stiftungen*). In the majority of cases, these entities of public law are intended for the use of public authorities. While individuals are not excluded from making use of them, they do not have a legal claim to do so. Instead, private individuals have to seek the consent of the authorities concerned in order to get their intentions through the respective registration or approval processes. However, this has often been done and such institutions as the major German churches, the Salvation Army, universities and colleges, chambers of commerce, and professional associations are formally established as public law corporations.

(b) Types of Purposes

The laws allow a wide freedom in choosing purposes for nonprofit activities, as long as these are in line with the law in general or not in contradiction with good morals. However, there are certain restrictions relating to tax exemption (see below). In addition, public law bodies are typically held to a more stringent public interest test than are associations and foundations more generally.

(c) Other Requirements

Associations need to have at least seven members as a prerequisite for registration, and, principally, membership needs to be open. However, the bylaws of the association may restrict the total number of members or require certain qualifying characteristics. Associations must also have boards of directors, though no minimum size is required. Although capital asset requirements are not codified, in practice, most state authorities require a reasonable amount of assets (usually at least DM 100,000) before granting the concession for the establishment of a foundation. A startup capital of 50,000 marks is formally required to incorporate limited liability companies.

(d) Registration Procedures

(i) *Associations*.   According to Section 21 BGB, a nonprofit *association*, or *Idealverein*, needs only to register in order to become a legal person.[1] The registration authority is vested in the local civil court, or *Amtsgericht*, at the place where the association has its seat though incorporation papers must normally be certified by a notary public in advance to verify compliance with the general norms set out by the law. After reviewing the lawfulness of the procedures of establishment, the court is responsible for entering the association in a special register (*Vereinsregister*) which confers juridical person status to the entity. Although associations may be founded freely and independently from state interference according to this system of normative rules, the federal Law of Associations (*Vereinsgesetz*) of August 5, 1964 grants both special state authorities and the Federal Ministry of the Interior a mandate to check applications to the local courts handling the registration procedures, and postpone registration until possible objections have been cleared. In cases like that, the group applying for registration has to be notified about the objections raised, and is entitled to bring the case to court. Exempted from this provision are political parties and religious groups. Trade unions and employer's federations also enjoy special privileges.

(ii) *Foundations*.   With respect to *foundations*, Section 80 BGB stipulates that there has to be a special act of a state authority to confer legal personality (concession system). The basic legal elements that need to be observed for creating a foundation in law require a donor to lay down a declaration of intent which implies that the organization is intended to come into existence for a period of great length, and that the donor is legally committed to transfer adequate resources to the foundation. The founding document has to state the purpose or purposes of the organization, and there has to be some organizational setup which is to be elaborated in the statutes, or bylaws, as the governing body of the foundation. In general, the concession-granting state authorities enjoy a considerable degree of discretion. Although more recently, the courts have restricted the authorities' power to grant or not to grant juridical personality, thus narrowing the gap between the liberal normative system under which associations receive legal personality and the concession system that rules foundations, there is still some room for discretion.

(iii) *Limited Liability Company*.   A *limited liability company* or close corporation is acceptable for registration with any purpose not illegal or against common morals. One individual as a founder is sufficient. The company's governing instrument has to be certified by a notary public and filed with the Commerce Register. The term *GmbH* has to be added to the company's name. Furthermore, the founder's name and the content of the intended business have to be dis-

---

[1] Since associations are eligible for registration after complying with a certain set of general norms, no specific authorization of the state is required. In the legal literature, this is referred to as the "normative system," as opposed to the "concession system," under which explicit state concessions are required in order for an organization to acquire legal personality.

closed. The minimum amount of a founder's share is DM 500, while the share capital must be at least DM 50,000. (A down payment of only DM 25,000 is acceptable.)

§ 9.3 INTERNAL GOVERNANCE

As for the internal organization, associations enjoy a wide freedom of action (*Vereinsautonomie*) which implies that the operating rules have, internally, the quality of laws. As a minimum requirement for the conferment of legal personality, the BGB stipulates that an association must have two internal organs, a membership or general assembly, and a board of directors. Provisions concerning these two organs must be included in the organic statute or bylaws of the organization. Ultimate authority lies with the membership assembly, which may be held annually or biannually. As far as the assembly's decision-making procedures go, the principle of majority rule is to be applied with each member having one vote. Proxies are allowed if respective provisions are laid down in the statutes. The assembly elects the board of directors, whose responsibility it is to represent the association in outside transactions. However, according to the law, this function can be assumed by a single person only.

In the case of foundations, a board of directors or trustees is the only necessary organ. Again, according to the BGB, one person may be sufficient.

§ 9.4 TAX TREATMENT

(a) Tax Treatment of Organizations

Tax-exempt status is granted by the local tax authorities, which also have to approve changes of purposes, and the procedures of dissolving a tax-exempt organization. Tax exemption is generally granted to those nonprofit organizations that pursue public benefit activities (*Gemeinnützigkeit*), regardless of the type of organization or its legal status. The rules relating to public benefit status are spelled out in Sections 51 through 68 of the *Abgabenordnung* (AO), or General Tax Code of March 16, 1976. The act distinguishes three categories of tax-privileged purposes: (1) charitable or public benefit purposes (*gemeinnützige Zwecke*); (2) benevolent purposes (*mildtätige Zwecke*); and (3) church-related purposes (*kirchliche Zwecke*).

According to Section 52 AO, *public benefit purposes* are those purposes that—materially, spiritually, or morally—promote the well-being of the public at large, as opposed to small and exclusive groups such as a family, company employees, or the members of a social club. The section includes the following purposes in this category:

1. The support of science and research, education, arts and culture, religion, international understanding, development aid, preservation of the environment, nature and monuments, and local and regional history and lore
2. Support of youth activities, of the aged, public health, welfare, and amateur sports

3. Support of civic activities
4. Support of animal breeding, plant cultivation, hobby gardening, carnival activities and local folklore, care of servicemen, amateur broadcasting, miniature airplane building and flying, and dog walking and guiding

According to the General Tax Code Regulation (*Anwendungserlaß zur Abgabenordnung*) of September 24, 1990, the first two groups describe only the most important purposes eligible for a preferential tax status, and are, therefore, not meant to be exclusive. In fact, various other administrative rulings have identified other specific classes of charitable organizations. Thus, Exhibit 7 to Section 111 of the Income Tax Act Guidelines lists 22 recognized benevolent purposes, and Section R 111(2) of the Income Tax Act Guidelines itself lists 59 recognized organizations.

As spelled out in Section 53 AO, tax exemption is also available to organizations pursuing benevolent purposes, which involves supporting individuals who are unable to care for themselves due to handicaps, mental illness, or poverty. In contrast to public benefit purposes, the criterion of the well-being of the public at large need not be applied under this category. Finally, the third category of tax-exempt purposes relates to church-related purposes. As defined in Section 54 AO, this applies rather narrowly to the construction and maintenance of churches, the support and promotion of religious services, and the upkeep of church property and personnel.

Sections 55 to 57 AO spell out additional principles which organizations have to observe in order not to lose tax exemption. According to these rules, purposes should be fulfilled in a disinterested manner (see issue 5), exclusively, and directly, by the charity itself. Section 58 AO details some minor exceptions from these principles.

Nonprofit organizations that qualify for public benefit status are generally exempt from corporate income tax.[2] They are also exempt from inheritance and gift taxes,[3] provided that their tax-exempt status lasts for another ten years after the inheritance. However, there is no general exemption from value-added tax which nonprofit organizations have to pay for most of their market transactions such as purchases of goods and services.[4] According to Section 3, No. 6, Local Business Tax Act (*Gewerbesteuergesetz*—GewStG), nonprofit organizations are generally exempt from trade tax. According to Section 3(1) of the Net Wealth Tax Act (*Vermögensteuergesetz*—VStG), they are also exempt from net wealth tax.

With regard to oversight, nonprofit organizations have to periodically file activity reports, usually in the form of annual reports, with the local tax authorities. In principle, the tax authorities are supposed to audit every tax-exempt organization every third year. In practice, however, the procedure of periodic checkups is not always observed due to lack of time or an overload of work.

Generally speaking, to be eligible for tax exemptions, an organization, whether juridical person or not, must undergo an exemption process only for cor-

---

[2] Section 5(1), No. 9, Law on Corporation Income Tax (*Körperschaftsteuergesetz*—KStG).
[3] Section 13(1), No. 16, Inheritance Tax Act (*Erbschaftsteuergesetz*—ErbStG).
[4] Sections 4, No. 18; 12(2), No. 8 Value-added Tax Act (*Umsatzsteuergesetz*—UStG).

porate income tax. Public-law organizations, however, are automatically tax-exempt.

(b) Tax Treatment of Contributions—Domestic Organizations

Both individuals and corporations are eligible to claim tax benefits for cash donations or in-kind gifts to certain nonprofit organizations. The benefit takes the form of deductions from pretax income up to a certain percentage. In exchange for the donation, the donee organization issues a certificate of deductibility (*Spendenbescheinigung*) which donors must file along with their tax returns. According to Section 10b of the personal Income Tax Law (*Einkommensteuergesetz*), individuals may deduct donations to organizations with benevolent, church-related, religious, and specifically recognized public benefit purposes up to 5% of pretax income. For scientific, benevolent, and specifically recognized cultural purposes, the ceiling has been raised to 10%. The criterion of specifically recognized purposes refers to 22 types of purposes, as listed in Exhibit 7 of Section 111 of Income Tax Act Guidelines (*Einkommensteuerrichtlinien*). Donors who wish to make tax deductible gifts to nonprofit organizations not entitled to receive such gifts under these regulations need to transfer their donation to a public sector body such as a municipality which will pass it through to the organization of the donor's choice and issue a certificate of deductibility to the donor.

The same restrictions and ceilings also apply to corporate donors. However, corporations, as well as entrepreneurs and self-employed individuals, may choose an alternative ceiling of two thousandths (2/1000) of turnover plus the sum of wages and salaries. Under this alternative provision, the ceiling for deductibility of donations may be substantially higher than 10%, especially in the case of large corporations.

Individual donors may deduct large donations in excess of DM 50,000 (approximately $35,000) to scientific or cultural organizations, not only in the current year, but they can also opt for a carryback for the two previous years and a carryover for the following five years, effectively spreading the deduction over eight tax years.[5] Corporations may carry over large donations for the following seven years.

(c) Tax Treatment of Contributions—Foreign Organizations

The German laws do not favor donations to foreign nonprofit organizations, since the inland tax authorities cannot monitor the orderly use of funds abroad. Accordingly, certificates of deductibility from foreign organizations are not acceptable. However, German nonprofit organizations are allowed to pass funds through to foreign "parent bodies" or otherwise related organizations for use abroad. In these cases, the German organization has to exercise some kind of expenditure responsibility. However, bequests in favor of foreign churches and charities may be tax exempt if the respective country had entered into a reciprocity agreement with the Federal Republic of Germany.[6] So far, there are only five of those agreements, the most important among them being those with the United States and with some Swiss cantons.

---

[5] Section 10b of the Income Tax Act (*Einkommensteuergesetz*—EStG).
[6] Section 13 of the Inheritance Tax Law.

§ 9.5   PERSONAL BENEFIT RESTRICTIONS

Regulations pertaining to personal benefit restrictions are mostly laid out in the above-mentioned Section 55 AO, which stipulates that tax-privileged purposes must be pursued in a disinterested manner. Among other things, this stipulation prohibits the distribution of surplus or profit to members or directors; unreasonable payments to officers, employees, or consultants for rendering services; and the return of donated or accumulated capital or other assets to members or donors when dissolving the organization. Instead, remaining assets at the point of dissolution need to be transferred to another charitable body.

However, there are a variety of minor exceptions. Members and officers may receive small gifts or may enjoy other usual amenities; staff and facilities can be made available to other tax-exempt organizations; foundations may use up to one-third of net income to provide financial support for the donor and his or her family, to preserve the memory of the donor, or to maintain the donor's graveside; and foundation capital may be returned to donors, when this was agreed upon in the beginning (though no tax exemptions are permissible at the time of the donation under this circumstance).

§ 9.6   OBLIGATIONS TO THE PUBLIC

In general, income and tax matters of individuals as well as juridical persons are thought to be a private preserve, and therefore strictly confidential. Since this applies to nonprofit organizations as well, there are no requirements concerning the disclosure of information to the public except for limited liability companies. Although the local tax authorities keep records of what has been donated to charity, this information is not available to the public at large and is reported only in aggregate in the official statistical tax series of the Federal Statistical Office.

With regard to the responsibilities of nonprofit Boards of Directors to the public, associations and foundations are basically free to determine those responsibilities in their statutes. The responsibility of managing the organization and representing it externally rests generally with the board. However, paragraph 30 BGB allows for some functions to be executed by other internal organs such as advisory or supervisory councils. Moreover, in the case of larger governing bodies, the statutes may stipulate that the legal responsibilities rest with a small group of officers or even one single person only (*Vorstand*). However, the external transactions such officers undertake in the name of the organization are valid only if the respective stipulations in the statutes have been filed with the Association Register at the local court.

§ 9.7   BUSINESS ACTIVITY

As with other facets of German nonprofit operations, two broad bodies of law govern the business activities of nonprofit organizations: basic civil law and tax law. According to the civil law, registered associations are not supposed to engage in commercial activity. However, commercial activities are tolerated so long as they serve the nonprofit purposes of the organization (*Nebenzweckprivileg*).

Tax law in Germany is somewhat more lenient toward nonprofit business activities. The tax laws distinguish between two spheres of a charity's material interests: the "ideal" sphere and the sphere of self-interest. The ideal sphere comprises acceptable business activities in the area of the charity's statutory purposes such as the collection of membership dues, donations, and public subsidies, and income derived from the administration of assets. Also acceptable are *related* business activities that promote the organization's charitable purposes. Related business activities include entrance fees for cultural, educational, and similar charitable events, entrance fees for sports events of less than 60,000 marks, lottery income, and fees for services rendered in hospitals, schools, nursing homes and the like (income from *Zweikbetrieb*).

The accumulation of capital, the distribution of benefits, and—at the termination of a charity—the distribution of remaining assets to members or donors, as well as unrelated business fall within the sphere of self-interest. While some exceptions are tolerable, the accumulation of assets beyond a ceiling of 25% of investment income and the distribution of benefits and assets are generally forbidden. Unrelated business activities, including the operation of museum shops, club restaurants, societal events, as well as advertisements in charity magazines, entrance fees for sports events exceeding 60,000 marks, and revenue from business sponsorships, are acceptable, but—in contrast to the activities within the ideal sphere—income derived from such activities is taxed like regular corporate income.[7]

§ 9.8   OTHER FUNDING RESTRICTIONS

Since 1966, legal regulations pertaining to street and door-to-door charitable collections as well as certain kinds of fund raising by mail have been left to state law. Reflecting a prior pattern of centralized control, however, state laws on charitable solicitation have a certain communality. Thus, these laws uniformly stipulate that public collections have to be announced beforehand, and need prior authorization by the State Minister of the Interior or a subordinate authority for the area where the collection is to take place. Collections in private homes, churches, among the work force of a company, or among the members of an association do not need this permit. If the *ordre public* is assumed to be violated, or if the orderly procedures in collecting, handling, or using the funds raised for the purpose stated in the appeal seems not to be guaranteed, permission cannot be granted. While the authorities originally had the mandate to deny permission when, for example, too many collections were planned in a given region at the same time, the courts more recently restricted the authorities' discretion, also advising them to refrain from value judgments and not to interfere with the purposes of a collection.

As with charitable solicitations, charitable lotteries also need prior authorization from state governments. Unlike most lotteries, charitable lotteries are exempt from the lottery tax. However, legal regulations stipulate the maximum rate of

---

[7] Section 64 of the General Tax Code (AO).

return to the participants and the share of the proceeds that must be reserved for public benefit purposes.

No ceiling for fund raising or administrative costs exists in German charity regulations, neither in civil, public, nor fiscal law. However, based on a specific court case which resulted in a special ordinance of the regional fiscal authority of Nuremberg (*Oberfinanzdirektion Nürnberg*) of August 1, 1991 (S 2223-278/St 21), one may assume that 15% of income spent on expenses is an acceptable figure. Expenses beyond that amount have to be justified in detail.

§ 9.9   POLITICAL ACTIVITY

According to the tax laws, charities are not supposed to engage in political activities, nor are they allowed to raise money or to divert funds for political action or parties. However, they are entitled to lobby in behalf of legislation that supports their aims. In doing so, they may address their membership and the public at large. For that, they may employ their own publications or the media. There is no ceiling concerning the amount of income spent on such public activities. At the same time, in pursuit of their missions, charities must carefully avoid the impression that they are joining a specific political campaign in favor of one party or candidate for political office. However, interlocking board membership (politicians holding offices in charities) is permitted. In turn, even chief executives of charities can hold public office.

Depending on the specific regulations, political involvement of non-public-benefit nonprofit organizations might also be possible. In promoting their members' vocational interests, for example, chambers of commerce or other comparable professional public law corporations with compulsory membership may side with political factions or even pledge funds for political action or to political parties (up to 10% of total income).

§ 9.10   KEY OUTSTANDING ISSUES

In general, the relationships between the state and the nonprofit sector as well as the general public's attitude toward this sector have been very positive in the past and there are no signs of major changes in the near future. However, there remain a few contentious issues concerning the general legal framework for the nonprofit sector. The more important of these issues include (a) the overall trend to regulate fields of societal activity in a process called legalization, (b) the reform of charity law, and (c) issues involving business sponsorships and unrelated business income.

(a) Legalization

One interesting development of the past two or three decades has been a gradual increase of regulation of charitable or nonprofit activities by federal or state governments. In this process of legalization, or *Verrechtlichung*, of societal affairs, lawmakers have increasingly assumed legal responsibility in matters of public interest and/or financial responsibility for certain fields of nonprofit activity by providing subsidies or fiscal privileges for organizations operating in such fields.

This trend toward legalization has affected activities as diverse as the protection of animals[8] and of monuments (state laws), day care (state laws or ordinances), nature conservancy,[9] and development aid.[10]

On the other hand, there are only a few instances of delegalization. The most important incident in this respect was the termination of the Charitable Housing Act (Wohnungsgemeinnützigkeitsgesetzl—WGG) which granted fiscal privileges and subsidies to low-cost housing companies and expired at the end of 1989. The system was phased out because of its inefficiency, some highly publicized scandals, and its interference in the construction and housing market. Some nonprofit development companies, however, were able to keep charitable status.[11]

(b) Reform of Charity Law

Since the late 1960s, there have been numerous attempts to improve the legal situation of the nonprofit sector. The most recent such attempts are "Law in Support of Associations" of 1989 and "Law in Support of Culture and Foundations" of 1990, and a new legal initiative, which will expand fiscal privileges for welfare charities, and allow those nonprofit organizations, that until now, could not issue to donors a certificate of deductibility to do so in the future.

However, these various (fiscal) initiatives basically aimed only at incrementally changing certain sections of the tax laws gradually, giving the German charity law a patchwork character, rather than attempting a fundamental reform of the tax laws on charities and nonprofits as called for by a commission appointed by the Federal Minister of Finance in 1988. However, the Chancellor promised in his inaugural address on March 18, 1987 (renewed in 1991) that there will be a serious review of the whole situation. Although the process of German unification has so far prevented parliamentary action on this issue, there are indications that the parliament will take up again the reform of charity law in the near future. Other related issues that are currently debated concern the reform of the law on political contributions and the possibility of including the protection of the environment as a civil right in the constitution.

(c) Sponsorships and Unrelated Business Income

Over recent years, business support for nonprofit activities has increasingly taken the form of sponsorships, especially in the fields of sports and arts and culture. Given the substantial amounts involved, the tax authorities have begun to scrutinize this source of income more closely and issued new restrictions with the basic argument that a business expense (e.g., for advertising purposes), on the side of the sponsoring firm, must necessarily be taxable unrelated business income for the sponsored organization. Such stipulations have been contested by nonprofit

---

[8] Tierschutzgesetz of July 24, 1972 and amendments.

[9] Bundes-NaturschutzG of December 20, 1976.

[10] Entwicklungshelfer-Gesetz of June 18, 1966, which provides a definition of private development aid organizations and which benefits individuals may be entitled to who are willing to serve as development aid personnel.

[11] According to the Reichssiedlungsgesetz of August 11, 1919.

organizations involved and a final regulation of this issue is still to be worked out. A compromise solution has been offered by the Senator of Finance of the city-state of Berlin in 1995, which would define sponsorship income as tax-free income from the administration of rights for the sponsored organization. Under this scenario, the sponsoring company could use the logo, the name, and the cooperation of the charity for their advertising and marketing purposes, while the charity would only be allowed to, more or less, incidentally mention the sponsor in its publications.

In general, there is a certain uneasiness with related and especially unrelated activities of basically nonprofit entities on the part of the lawmakers. This is especially true with regard to those borderline cases where nonprofits engage in business activities to finance their nonprofit aims, thereby competing with local small businesses, which are also a somewhat protected species in the tax laws. A typical example would be a small neighborhood restaurant being in competition with a professionally or volunteer-run sports club-cafeteria or dining facility nearby.

While growing financial pressures as well as highly trained staff and dedicated volunteers have been the driving forces behind some nonprofit organizations' decision to engage in such activities, this approach to generate additional income for charities is increasingly seen as unfair competition with businesses, due to the nonprofits' ability to use tax-exempt funds and perhaps even donations. This is a point where the tax laws as well as the civil law have to find a solution. So far, for example, the country's insurance industry was not successful in the courts in stopping the (nonprofit) General German Automobile Club (ADAC) from entering into their business field by offering insurance services (via taxable subsidiaries).

CHAPTER TEN

Hungary[*]

§ 10.1 LEGAL CONTEXT

Hungary is a civil law country in the Roman law tradition, which provides a constitutional guarantee of the *right of association, opinion and religion*. This right is then further elaborated in the II/1989 Law on Associations. According to this right, people are free to form voluntary organizations for any purpose that does not explicitly contradict fundamental human values and does not endanger the democratic political order.

In addition to the constitutional guarantees, legal provisions pertaining to foundations reappeared in the Civil Code in 1987,[1] and additional provisions relating to nonprofit organizations were enacted after the demise of the Communist regime in 1989 in the Hungarian Civil Code, in a number of special laws governing distinct kinds of nonprofit organizations, and in the tax laws.

Generally, the legal framework developed for nonprofit activity in Hungary in the immediate aftermath of the downfall of the Communist regime was very supportive. For instance, the association law[2] treated voluntary associations as essential elements of a democratic society. The minister's introductory explanation, which accompanied the law proposal, explicitly stated that voluntary associations provide the basis for the self-organization of society and their presence is a necessary condition for the healthy development and functioning of any community either at the local or at the national level.[3] Similarly, the II/1990 Law on the Modification of the Civil Code reflected the conviction that foundations could and should play an important role in the democratization of decisions, and the denationalization and deregulation of the Hungarian economy.[4] Reflecting this, foundations received generous and practically unconditional tax advantages in the first period of their development.

More recently, more restrictive provisions have been introduced. However, the general legal framework for foundations and nonprofit organizations remains generally favorable.

---

[*] Country Rapporteur: Dr. Éva Kuti, Senior Researcher, Research Project on Nonprofit Organizations, Hungary. This Chapter is based on a legal field guide of the Johns Hopkins Comparative Nonprofit Sector Project.
[1] Decree 11/1987.
[2] II/1989, Law on Associations.
[3] G. Kozma and F. Petrik, *Társadalmi szervezetek, alapítványok létrehozása és gazdálkodása. Jogszabályok, bírói gyakorlat és ezek magyarázata* (Budapest: UNIÓ Lap - és Könyvkiadó, 1990).
[4] T. Sárközi, "Az alapítványok jogi szabályozása Magyarországon," in É. Kuti (ed.), *Alapítványi Almanach.* (Budapest: Magyarországi Alapítványok Szövetsége, 1991).

§ 10.2   ELIGIBILITY

(a) Types of Organizations

There are five basic legal forms for nonprofit organizations under Hungarian law. Three of these are essentially private law forms and two are public law.

(i) *Private Law.*   The Hungarian Civil Code in articles 57 through 64 and 74 makes provision for three types of private nonprofit organizations: voluntary associations, foundations, and public benefit companies.

1. *Voluntary Associations.*   According to the Civil Code, voluntary associations are autonomous organizations formed voluntarily for a purpose agreed upon by their members and stated in their founding articles. Associations must have registered members who organize to actively pursue the associations' aims. Although membership organizations are not necessarily called voluntary associations and special laws and government decrees apply to some of them, the basic legal regulation of voluntary associations nevertheless applies to all such organizations, including societies, clubs, self-help groups, federations, unions, chambers of commerce, trade unions, mass organizations, social organizations, and so on. Such organizations can be formed around common hobbies, personal problems, age, interests, residence, support for particular institutions, concerns, professions, or occupations.

2. *Foundations.*   Foundations are organizations with endowments established to pursue durable public purposes. Their founders can be either private persons or organizations with legal personalities. Unlike associations, foundations do not have members. They can take many different forms, however: (1) operating foundations (e.g., foundations operating schools, nursing homes, health and cultural institutions; providing social services; publishing books and journals; managing cable television networks and local radio stations, etc.); (2) "fund-raising" foundations exclusively supporting public institutions such as libraries, theaters, museums, schools, universities, hospitals, or research institutes that established them; (3) "fund-raising" foundations pursuing particular aims or projects such as the creation of monuments, organization of festivals, or development of art collections; (4) grant-making foundations that support either projects or organizations; and (5) corporate foundations mostly supporting present or former employees of the company.

3. *Public Benefit Companies.*   Public benefit companies are organizations established by individuals and private organizations to produce public goods and meet public needs. Although such companies are subject to the basic economic regulations that apply to for-profit limited liability companies, they cannot distribute profits among their owners. This legal form generally applies to nonprofit service providers, which cannot reasonably be organized as either foundations or voluntary associations.

(ii) *Public Law Organizations.*   In addition to the private law organizations, the Hungarian Parliament in 1993 authorized the establishment of two public law types of nonprofit organizations: (1) public law associations and (2) public law foundations. The establishment of these two forms was justified as facilitating the process of privatization of current state functions by creating a class of semipublic, semiprivate organizations that can take on certain formerly state-run functions.

1. *Public Law Associations.*   Public law associations are self-governing membership organizations that are created by a specific law passed by the Parliament. The Academy of Sciences, the chambers of commerce, and the chambers of some professions (e.g., doctors, lawyers, architects, etc.) have been transformed into public law associations since the creation of this legal form. Although the legal regulation of voluntary associations generally applies to public law associations as well, the government has vested additional authority over their members in this kind of association, such as official registration, quality control, and the issuance of licenses.

2. *Public Law Foundations.*   Public law foundations are foundations established by the Parliament, the government, or municipalities to take over certain tasks that are defined in law as government responsibilities, including education, health care, and public safety. Public law foundations are financially accountable to the State Comptroller's Office and can be dissolved by their respective founders if their function can be more efficiently fulfilled by another type of organization. The property of a dissolved public law foundation reverts to its founder. Apart from these special provisions, the basic legal regulation of private foundations applies to public law foundations as well.

(b) Types of Purposes

Generally, private nonprofit associations in Hungary may pursue any purpose other than those considered harmful to democracy or public order. These latter include the promotion of racism, violence, armed attack against the constitutional order, or discrimination.[5] Also, associations cannot predominantly operate for-profit organizations.

Unlike associations, foundations must demonstrate that they have some "durable public purpose" in order to qualify for registration. The legal definition of public purpose has been quite general, however.

(c) Other Requirements

In the case of associations, the only other requirement is that the organization have ten members in order to acquire legal personality.

In the case of foundations, there is a requirement that the endowment establishing the organization be sufficient to allow the organization to pursue its goals. However, the legislation does not specify what amount that is.

---

[5] Kozma and Petrik, *supra* 3, pp. 63–64.

(d) Registration Procedures

Private nonprofit organizations attain legal personality through registration with the county or capital courts. Such registration is necessary if activities involve property and other transactions with third persons. Accordingly, voluntary organizations which are not registered cannot enter into any contract and are, furthermore, not eligible to receive direct or indirect state support.

(i) Voluntary Associations.   Voluntary associations can be registered if they have (1) at least ten founding members; (2) a set of articles specifying internal procedures; and (3) elected administrative and representative organs. A statutory meeting must precede the application, which must contain the articles of association and the minutes of the statutory meeting. The courts may not refuse registration if all legal requirements are fulfilled and can only order the dissolution of a voluntary association if the association's activities are unlawful or infringe upon other persons' rights and freedom.[6]

(ii) Foundations.   Foundations can be registered so long as they demonstrate that they have (1) a durable public purpose; (2) a founding statute; and (3) an endowment which is large enough to enable the foundation to pursue its goals. In the founding statute, the founder can determine rules concerning the operation and governance of the foundation. It is possible to name an organization as trustee in the founding statute. If a founder fails to determine such arrangements, it is the court's duty to name trustees.

Foundations must pass a "public benefit" test before the courts grant registration. However, the test is very loosely constructed. At the time of registration, the courts have only the information they can acquire from the founding statutes. They do not know anything about the actual plans and activities of the nonprofit organizations. If the documents presented to them are in accordance with the requirements of the law, the courts do not have the right to refuse registration. Later on, they can dissolve the foundation at the attorney's request if its purpose cannot be fulfilled any longer, if the law changes, or if the trustees do not comply with the foundation's aim.

(iii) Public Benefit Companies.   Public benefit companies must register with the Company Court, which keeps the official register of for-profit companies.

(iv) Public Law Associations and Foundations.   Public law associations and foundations are subject to the same registration procedures as voluntary associations and private foundations.

§ 10.3   INTERNAL GOVERNANCE

Hungarian law imposes few, if any, requirements on voluntary associations with respect to internal governance. The major requirement is that the organization

---

[6] Article 20 of the II/1989 Law on Associations.

develop its own formal procedures for internal governance, including the identification of governing bodies and decision-making procedures in a formal set of "articles" or "bylaws." In addition, the governing organs must be elected by the members.

Foundations must also have a founding statute that specifies governance procedures. In the case of foundations, the governing body is a trustee, which can be named by the founder or, in case of the founder's death, by the court. The founder can also set the rules on joining a foundation and on its operation, but is not allowed to institute controlling majorities on the foundation's board.[7] The court retains the right to appoint new trustees if the original trustees do not comply with the foundation's stated purpose. A foundation can only be dissolved at the attorney's request if (1) its purpose cannot be fulfilled any longer; (2) its registration ought to be refused because of changes in law; and (3) the trustees' activities do not comply with the foundation's aim, and the (living) founder does not appoint another trustee.[8] Public law foundations can be dissolved at the founder's request.[9]

§ 10.4 TAX TREATMENT

The original laws on the tax treatment of nonprofit organizations in Hungary were passed in the immediate aftermath of the demise of Communist rule in 1989 and were quite liberal.[10] Since then, somewhat more restrictive measures have been introduced to limit the tax benefits available and tie them more closely to public purposes.

(a) Tax Treatment of Organizations

(i) *Voluntary Associations.* Only selected types of voluntary associations are exempted from corporate income tax under Hungarian law, namely those engaged in scientific and technical research, culture, environment protection, sports, health care, social help, and child and youth care. Originally, all business income earned by such associations was exempted from taxation so long as the income was used for the charitable purpose. Membership fees and donations even to such organizations are not automatically exempted by law, but can be if approved by government authorities.

Laws LXXXVI/1991 and LXXXVII/1991, which came into force in January 1992, tightened these provisions, limiting the exemption for business income to 10% of the organization's whole income, up to a maximum of 10 million Hungarian forints. For the purposes of this law, moreover, business income was defined to mean income from activities that are not closely related to the public purposes

---

[7] Article 74/C of the Civil Code.
[8] Article 74/E of the Civil Code.
[9] Article 74/G of the Civil Code.
[10] Government Decree 16/1989 issued in 1989; Law XCI/1990.

served by nonprofit organizations. The legislation specified a list of such public purposes.[11]

(ii) Foundations. The tax advantages available to foundations under Hungarian law were originally more favorable than those available to associations. Foundations were automatically exempt from corporate income tax so long as they met the minimal "durable public purpose" test. This exemption applied to business income as well as other income so long as it was used directly for the charitable purpose laid down in the founding statute.

Laws LXXXVI/1991 and LXXXVII/1991, which went into effect in January 1992, tightened the tax treatment of foundations, however. Henceforth, registration as a foundation is no longer a guarantee of full exemption from corporate taxation, since the business income of foundations is now subject to corporate tax if it exceeds 10% of total income or 10 million HUF.

(b) Tax Treatment of Contributions—Domestic Organizations

(i) Voluntary Associations. Donations to voluntary associations are not tax deductible unless the Tax Authority specifically declares otherwise on a case-by-case basis. The same is true of membership fees.

(ii) Foundations. *Individuals* may deduct 30% of their contributions to foundations from their tax liability if (1) the recipient foundation is engaged in the fields of culture, education, research, social care, preventive medicine, health care, religion, environment, protection of the cultural heritage, sports, public security, human rights, support to the legislation, providing care for children, young people, the elderly, the poor, ethnic minorities, refugees, or the Hungarian minorities in foreign countries; and (2) the donors do not receive any direct or indirect compensation for their contribution. *Corporate donations* are tax deductible up to 20% of taxable income under the same preconditions. Foundations are subject to occasional audits and may be fined if found not to be operating in these fields or otherwise in violation of these requirements.

(iii) Public Law Foundations. Individual contributions to public law foundations are subject to the same deductibility limits and conditions as donations to private foundations. Corporations, however, can deduct the full amount of contributions to public law foundations if the recipient foundation is engaged in the fields of culture, education, social care, health care, religion, environment, sports, or the care of children and young people.

(c) Tax Treatment of Contributions—Foreign Organizations

Contributions to Hungarian organizations that operate in the fields specified in section 10.4(b), but are working outside of Hungary are still eligible for deduct-

---

[11] Thus, under the terms of Laws CXIV/1992 and CXV/1992, the following are considered to be public purposes: health care, social services, education, social tourism and recreation, research and development, environmental protection, sports, libraries, museums, exhibitions, archives, theaters, music, dance, protection of monuments, amateur sports, and employment procurement for unemployed people.

ibility. This is particularly true of foundations working with Hungarian minorities in other countries. Foreign donations to Hungarian foundations and voluntary associations are tax exempt. Hungarian contributions to non-Hungarian organizations working in other countries are not deductible.

§ 10.5 PERSONAL BENEFIT RESTRICTIONS

As the regulatory framework for the nonprofit sector is still very much in flux in Hungary, many of the specific personal benefit issues concerning nonprofit organizations and their founders and directors have not yet been touched by lawmakers. However, there are a number of general legal principles that influence the decision to grant legal personality. Specifically, it is generally required that organizations must become independent from their founders. In the case of associations, relationships the organization may have with third parties must be separated from the relationships that its individual members have with the same third parties. In the case of foundations, the endowments donated to the foundations must become completely and definitively separated from the private properties of the founders or donors.

§ 10.6 OBLIGATIONS TO THE PUBLIC

Nonprofit organizations are obliged to prepare financial accounts. However, and in contrast to for-profit firms, there is no obligation to submit such accounts to the financial authorities or to open financial reports to public scrutiny. There are no requirements concerning the preparation of activity reports.

§ 10.7 BUSINESS ACTIVITY

Nonprofit organizations cannot be established for the main purpose of running for-profit businesses, but associations and foundations serving public purposes are allowed to own and operate businesses in order to increase their revenues if this revenue is used to achieve their charitable aims.

However, as noted above, the tax laws place limits on the amount of business income that is exempt from taxation. For this purpose, "business income" is defined as income from businesses that are not closely related to the public purposes of the organizations (see note 11 above for a list of the "closely related" types of businesses). Both associations and foundations are exempt from taxes on such income up to 10% of their total income or HUF 10 million.

If unrelated business income exceeds these limits, the organization loses its tax exemption on all income for the year in question. As a consequence, large foundations with substantial unrelated business activities have begun to spin off these activities into separate for-profit subsidiaries. The transfer of the profits generated by these subsidiaries to the parent nonprofit organization counts as a donation and the unrelated business income limits do not apply.

§ 10.8   OTHER FUNDING RESTRICTIONS

No restrictions exist on fund-raising costs or other facets of nonprofit operations in Hungary.

§ 10.9   POLITICAL ACTIVITY

Hungarian law does not limit or prevent nonprofit organizations from engaging in political activities. Although some discussion of potential conflicts between tax deductibility and political action has surfaced, the authorities have so far been averse to considering restrictions on the political activities of nonprofit organizations.

§ 10.10   KEY OUTSTANDING ISSUES

Numerous issues remain unresolved within the body of law affecting nonprofit organizations in Hungary. However, five major issues have recently attracted particular attention: (a) the tax treatment of foundations, (b) the emergence of public law organizations as legal forms, (c) the development of government-nonprofit partnerships in the provision of welfare services, (d) the political involvement of nonprofit organizations, and (e) private benefit and other ethical standards.

(a) Tax Treatment of Foundations

Hungarian legal and tax authorities are still struggling with the question of how best to provide tax privileges for nonprofit organizations. The original laws stipulated that foundations must serve a "durable public purpose" to be registered and then provided tax exemptions and tax deductions to all registered foundations. For a variety of reasons, this approach was found to be too open to fraud and abuse, partly because the definition of "public purpose" was rather vague and the only basis available to authorities to judge it was the founding declaration of the organization, and founders were quite able to devise language that would meet the letter of the law even for foundations with essentially private objectives.

To avoid this problem, two alternatives are available. One is to develop an exhaustive list of fields and activities that can guarantee organizations involved in them tax exemption and tax deductibility for contributions. The other is to vest in government agencies the authority to decide which purposes are validly "public purposes" and therefore eligible for tax exemptions and tax-deductible gifts. The first of these options can be more costly to the state budget, but avoids arbitrary governmental decisions. The second can be more targeted and limited, but opens nonprofit foundations to state control.

To date, Hungarian law has opted for the first of these options. Thus, Laws XV/1991 and XVI/1991 provided lists of "public" purposes. While all nonprofit organizations are legally protected, only those that primarily engage in the specified public purposes are eligible to receive favorable tax treatment.

While clear and precise, however, this arrangement has not been without its problems. Foundation leaders thus complain about a second "public benefit" test.

Many foundations consider it to be irrational that every foundation has to serve a public purpose, but that only some of them are considered of "public benefit" and are thus eligible for tax deductions on donations. An additional problem is that some very important fields of nonprofit activity, such as services to unemployed persons, neighborhood development programs, and the promotion of entrepreneurship, are missing from the list of the preferred activities. This has not only hurt some prestigious foundations, but is also seen as somewhat unjustified, since there are a number of large public foundations in these fields established by state authorities that receive substantial support from the government. This suggests that such fields are useful, "of public benefit," and important enough to be directly supported from the state budget, but not enough to get tax-deductible private donations. Further evolution of Hungarian law on this question thus seems highly likely.

(b) Emergence of Public Law Organizations Among the Legal Forms in the Nonprofit Sector

Until 1993, associations and foundations were accorded legal status in Hungary only under "private law." This had the very useful effect of emphasizing the "private" character of nonprofit organizations as entities existing outside the apparatus of the state. In 1993, however, a bill was passed by the Parliament that introduced into the Civil Code, the legal forms of public law foundations and public law associations, both of which are common in the German legal tradition. The very emergence of these two public law organizations has broken the clearly "private" character of the Hungarian nonprofit sector. Although some of these private nonprofit organizations have never been completely independent of state support, their "private law" status was—if not a guarantee—at least some demonstration of their legal independence from the government and its institutions. The public law foundations and the public law associations will be definitely closer to the government than their private law counterparts. Otherwise, there would not be any reason to create these legal forms. The official reasoning for their creation is that both public law foundations and public law associations will serve as structures for privatizing some functions that are currently performed by the state. It remains to be seen how this will work in practice, how many and what kinds of public law foundations and associations will be created, how severe their government control will be, and whether they will be favored over private law foundations and associations so far as state subsidies and favorable tax treatment are concerned. So far, the financial authorities have made several efforts to change the tax treatment of nonprofits in favor of the public law organizations. Most of these efforts, however, have failed due to the resistance of nonprofit umbrella organizations and their political allies. The only point where the tax treatment of public law foundations has become more favorable concerns the tax deductibility of corporate donations, as noted above.

(c) Government Contracting with Nonprofit Providers

Another recent development of immense importance to the evolution of the nonprofit sector in Hungary is the emergence of contracting relationships between nonprofit organizations and the state. Purchasing and contracting out of services were almost unknown methods under state socialism. Public institutions literally monopolized the provision of government-financed welfare services. This monopoly was ended, however, by parliamentary decision in December 1992. According to this decision, nonprofit organizations providing basic social, educational, and cultural services have the right to get exactly the same per capita subsidies as are given to the state-owned institutions. This decision was then confirmed by the XXXVIII/1992 Law on Public Finances, which officially stated that the provision of public welfare services was not the monopoly of public institutions.

These decisions represent a breakthrough for Hungarian nonprofit organizations, particularly given the limited potentials for growth in private giving in Hungary.

Unfortunately, however, significant challenges still confront the growth of government contracting with nonprofit organizations. Thus, for one thing, the law did not expressly address the definition of the "nonpublic" service providers that are the possible contractors of the state authorities. Beyond this, there are great uncertainties about how to manage such contracts, how to ensure the quality of services, what the terms and conditions should be, and other related matters. Considerable work consequently remains to be done to develop the contracting mode more fully.

(d) Political Activity

A fourth key issue under debate in Hungary is the permissibility of political activity on the part of nonprofit organizations. Because of the heritage of authoritarianism, political leaders are wary about putting legal limits on political and lobbying activity by nonprofit organizations. At the same time, the concept of providing tax exemptions and tax deductions for support of political activities has prompted concerns in some quarters.

(e) Ethics

A final concern that has begun to surface in debates on the nonprofit sector in Hungary concerns a variety of ethical issues ranging from executive salaries and compensation of board members to fund-raising costs, insider trading, and self-dealing. Some foundations and associations have begun to frame self-regulatory ethical codes on these matters, but there is also some interest in establishing legal regulations to avoid abuse.

CHAPTER ELEVEN

India[*]

§ 11.1 LEGAL CONTEXT

India has a statute and case law system with a set of statutory laws governing various types of nonprofit organizations.[1] The most important of these laws include the Societies Registration Act of 1860, the Indian Trusts Act of 1882, the Charitable and Religious Trust Act of 1920, the Cooperative Societies Act of 1904, the Trade Union Act of 1926, and the Companies Act of 1956.

In addition, many of the Indian states have enacted their own laws modifying or adding to the central legislation. Thus, for example, some states have added other categories to those eligible for registration under the national Societies Registration Act.

More generally, the right of all citizens to form associations or unions is laid down in article 19(1)(c) of the Constitution of India.[2]

§ 11.2 ELIGIBILITY

(a) Types of Organizations

Under Indian law, there are five types of nonprofit organizations: societies, trusts, cooperatives, trade unions, and companies.[3]

(i) Societies. Societies are basically governed by the central Societies Registration Act of 1860 as well as various state amendments to this Act, where appli-

---

[*] Country Rapporteur: Dr. Siddhartha Sen, Associate Professor, Graduate Program in City and Regional Planning, Morgan State University, Baltimore, Maryland. This chapter is based on a legal field guide of the Johns Hopkins Comparative Nonprofit Sector Project.

[1] The entire chapter is based on Noshir H. Dadrawala, *Handbook on Administration of Trusts* (Bombay: Centre for Advancement of Philanthropy, 1991); Noshir H. Dadrawala, *Management of Philatrophic Organisations* (Bombay: Centre for Advancement of Philanthropy, 1996); PRIA (The Society for Participatory Research in Asia), *Forms of Organisation: Square Pegs in Round Holes* (New Delhi: PRIA, 1987); PRIA, *Management of Voluntary Organisations* (New Delhi: PRIA, 1989); PRIA, *Manual on Financial Management and Account's Keeping* (New Delhi: PRIA, 1990) and interviews with officials of Indian nonprofit organizations, bureaucrats, and researchers, unless otherwise stated.

[2] P.D. Mathew, *Law on the Registration of Societies* (New Delhi: Indian Social Institute, 1994).

[3] Some nonprofit organizations prefer to register as partnerships under the Partnership Act of 1932 if they aim to generate business income. While this Act does not accord nonprofit status, the rates of taxation for partnerships are relatively low (i.e., between three and 24% of its business profit). Legal requirements and oversight are, on the whole, less for partnerships.

cable. The Act of 1860 initially allowed the registration of literary, scientific, and charitable societies that do not primarily serve their own members. Societies have legal personality and can thus sue and be sued. The liability of their members is limited and their private assets cannot be confiscated to satisfy the society's liabilities.

State amendments have since broadened the scope of organizations that can be registered under the Act. Not withstanding variations at the state level, the types of organizations that may generally register as societies include development and empowerment-oriented nonprofit organizations, clubs, cultural and literary societies, professional associations, educational institutions, as well as scientific and medical institutions. There are also some government-sponsored nonprofit organizations, such as the National Labor Institute and the National Dairy Development Board, that have been registered under the Act.

(ii) Trusts.   Trusts are grants of property for specified purposes. There are two basic types of trusts in India: public and private trusts. Public trusts are generally created for public religious or charitable purposes, while private trusts can be created for the benefit of one or a number of private individuals. While there is no central law for public trusts,[4] private trusts are governed by the Indian Trust Act of 1882. This law provides for creating trusts for the purpose of managing property for private, religious, public, and charitable uses. More specifically, the Act defines a trust as "an obligation annexed to the ownership of property, and arising out of a confidence reposed in and accepted by the owner, or declared and accepted by him, for the benefit of another or of another and the owner."[5] The person who declares the "confidence" is the donor and the person who accepts the "confidence" is called the trustee. Most private trusts pursue religious, charitable, communal, and educational purposes,[6] although some development and empowerment-oriented organizations have also used the Act to form organizations.

Under the Act, the trustees are required to manage the trust and are liable with their private property and assets for breach of trust and for losses. Trustees cannot withdraw from their responsibilities unless they resign or retire. The Act also allows the trustees to approach the court to seek advice about the management and functioning of the trust.[7]

---

[4] However, there are state laws governing public trusts, such as the Bombay Public Trust Act of 1950, which is applicable to the states of Maharashtra and Gujarat. Under this Act, a public trust is defined as a trust for religious and/or charitable purposes and includes religious or charitable societies registered under the Societies Registration Act of 1860. In Maharashtra and Gujarat, a registered society created for a charitable purpose must, therefore, also register under the Bombay Public Trust Act, rendering the registration procedures somewhat burdensome.
[5] PRIA, 1987, p. 8.
[6] Educational trusts include both research institutions and grantmakers funding research or education in general. Communal trusts are formed for the benefit, a particular community or caste. See Dadrawala, 1991, supra 1.
[7] Other legislation governing trusts in India includes the Charitable Endowments Act of 1890, the Charitable and Religious Trust Act of 1920, Section 92 of the Code of Civil Procedure, and the Official Trustee Act of 1913.

(iii) Cooperatives.   Although there is no clear legal definition, a cooperative may be defined as an institution which aims at the economic and social betterment of its members and an enterprise which is based on mutual aid conforming to cooperative principles. All states and union territories have their own laws governing cooperatives, and institutions registered as cooperatives are expected to abide by these laws, which can vary considerably from state to state.

Under the Delhi Cooperative Societies Act of 1972,[8] for example, an organization formed with the objective of promoting the economic interests of its members may be registered as a cooperative provided it adheres to a set of cooperative principles. Such principles include (1) *voluntary membership* (i.e., membership must be open to all interested persons, irrespective of social, political, and religious beliefs or racial origins); (2) *democratic decision-making structures*, in which the administrators are elected or appointed democratically and all members participate in decision making; (3) *limitations on interest*, meaning that the rate of interest on share capital, if any, must be strictly limited; (4) *equitable distribution* of economic results; (5) *cooperative education* mandating the provision of education about principles and techniques of cooperation to members, officers, and employees and to the general public; and (6) *mutual cooperation* defined as cooperation with other cooperatives at the local, national, and international levels.

(iv) Trade Unions.   Trade unions are governed by the Trade Union Act of 1926, which defines a trade union as a temporary or permanent institution formed for regulating the relations between workers and employers, among workers, or among employers. The Act also allows for a federation of two or more unions. In contrast to all other forms of nonprofit organizations, trade unions are allowed to use their general fund to remunerate staff and to fund legal procedures, educational activities, and the welfare of its members. Trade unions are also allowed to have separate funds for promoting civil and political interests of their members.

(v) Companies.   Although the Companies Act of 1956 is primarily intended to govern profit-making entities, Section 25 of the Act allows the possibility to obtain nonprofit status for companies. A company may obtain such nonprofit status if (1) the Memorandum of Association of the company expressly declares it to be nonprofit, (2) the income of the company is exclusively applied to the promotion of charitable objectives, and (3) the members do not get any dividends or other profits. Such companies are known as charitable companies and can hold property for charitable purposes. However, if the company is intended to hold such property, it must be stated in the Memorandum of Association and the central government has to grant a license. Generally, the company form is only very rarely used for nonprofit purposes.

(b) Types of Purposes

The Societies Registration Act of 1860 lists literary, scientific, and charitable purposes as eligible purposes for nonprofit organizations. However, as noted above,

---

[8] This Act is a good illustrative example because several provisions are similar to those applicable in other states.

state amendments have enlarged the scope of eligible purposes. For instance, the promotion of industry and agriculture has been added in the state of Bihar, and in Uttar Pradesh, organizations that promote *Khadi*, or village industry, and rural development are also allowed to register under the Act.

To qualify for tax exemption, organizations must be either religious or charitable in nature. The definition of charity includes (1) relief of the poor, (2) education, (3) medical relief, and (4) other purposes of general public utility (see below).

Article 35A of the Constitution (Eightieth Amendment) Bill of 1993 suggested that the Parliament be vested with the authority to legally ban any organization or body of individuals if they promote, or attempt to promote, disharmony or feeling of enmity, hatred, or ill-will among citizens of India on grounds of religion by words, written material, or by signs or visible representations.[9]

(c) Other Requirements

(i) Membership Requirements.   Regarding *societies*, a minimum of seven persons must subscribe to the Memorandum of Association before the society can be registered. Furthermore, the membership of a society must be open to everyone who subscribes to its aims and objectives. Ten persons from different families are necessary to form a *cooperative*, according to the Delhi Societies Cooperative Act of 1972. Furthermore, agricultural cooperatives must reserve half of the membership for scheduled castes (i.e., the lower castes in India), and in cooperatives in which the central government shares capital, up to one-third of the managing committee members can be nominated by the government. The Indian Trust Act of 1882 does not specify membership requirements. The minimum membership requirements for trade unions and public companies is seven, while that of private companies is two.

(d) Registration Procedures[10]

(i) Societies.   According to the main provisions of the Societies Registration Act, seven persons must subscribe to a Memorandum of Association in order to be able to register a society. The Memorandum must include (1) the name of the society; (2) its objectives; (3) the names, addresses, and occupations of those members subscribing to it; and (4) the members of its governing body.

In addition to the Memorandum, a society must also file a set of governing rules and regulations with the Registrar of Societies. These rules and regulations must contain the following:

1. The name and address of the registered office of the society
2. The manner, criteria, and procedures for enrolling and removing various categories of members
3. The rights, obligations, and the length of membership for the members

---

[9] Social Action, The Constitution (Eightieth Amendment) Bill 1993: A Bill further to amend the Constitution of India, 44 *Social Action*, no. 1, 1994, 142–147.

[10] For a detailed discussion on registration procedures of other types of nonprofit organizations, see PRIA 1987, 1989, *supra* 1.

4. The criteria, manner, and procedures of forming the governing body
5. The manner in which meetings are conducted
6. The notice period for such meetings
7. The designation, manner of election, and removal of officers
8. The powers and rights of members
9. The procedures for conducting the annual general body meeting and special meetings
10. Accounts and audit procedures
11. The manner in which the objectives and rules and regulations of the society can be changed
12. Other provisions as required by state acts

The Registrar ensures that the various provisions of the Act have been met and that no other society is registered with a similar name before granting a certificate of registration. According to the central Act, as a further requirement, societies must submit a list of the members of the governing body after the annual general meeting each year.

(ii) Trusts. The Indian Trust Act is extremely flexible and minimizes government interference. Thus, there are no requirements pertaining to the number of trustees and the procedures for creating the legal entity are very simple. Under the Bombay Public Trust Act of 1950, for example, the requirements include the names and addresses of the trustees and managers, the mode of succession into the office of trustee, a list of the movable and immovable trust assets and their approximate value, the gross average annual income of the trust, expenditures, and a permanent address.

(iii) Companies. The registration procedures for companies are elaborate and require the submission of a printed Memorandum of Association and Articles of Association to the Register of Companies. Such companies can have directors who are also the trustees. Directors or trustees manage the company and can be reimbursed for their management activities, but cannot accept remuneration or share a profit, which creates problems in employing staff.

§ 11.3 INTERNAL GOVERNANCE[11]

(a) Societies

Societies must have democratic organizational structures that allow for the periodic election of a governing body, which is entrusted with the management of the society and accountable to the society's general membership. Apart from this requirement, the law allows a high degree of flexibility with respect to amendments to and changes of internal rules and regulations. However, in some states,[12] the Registrar of Societies has the power to amend the rules of a society.

[11] For a discussion on internal governance of other types of nonprofit organizations, see Dadrawala, 1991, 1996 PRIA 1987, 1989, 1990, *supra* 1.
[12] For example, Karnataka, Madhya Pradesh, Tamil Nadu, and West Bengal.

(b) Trusts

The governance and administration of private trusts is affected by a variety of laws, including the following:

- The Charitable Endowments Act of 1890, which regulates the transfer and administration of property held by the trust for charitable purposes, and the conditions under which government officials can intervene to ensure the proper management of trust property.
- The Charitable and Religious Trusts Act of 1920, providing for the administration of such trusts, approaching the court to seek advice on managing the trust, and auditing and examining the trust under Section 92 of the Code of Civil Procedure.
- Section 92 of the Code of Civil Procedure provides several aspects related to breach of trust. These include regulations pertaining to the appointment and removal of a trustee, vesting of property in a trustee, directing the trustee to deliver the possession of any property, directing accounts and inquiries, and so on. The law also allows the alteration of the original purpose of a religious or charitable trust under specified preconditions.

According to the Indian Trust Act of 1882, "the trustees must take due care for the management of the affairs of the trust and act in a serious, careful and impartial manner."[13] The Act also states that trustees are fully liable with their private property and assets for any losses that occur due to breach of trust. In cases where there is more than one trustee, trustees are both individually and collectively liable.

The Act further states that "trustees cannot delegate their responsibility and accountability, nor can they renounce their trusteeship"[14] except under certain conditions, such as resignation or retirement. Furthermore, trustees may not use the trust for private, personal profit or benefit, though they may charge expenses incurred in the course of the management of the trust. The Act also provides for the possibility of third parties to approach the court of law to seek information about the management and functioning of the trust.

(c) Cooperatives

The general body of members of the cooperative has the ultimate authority with respect to the management of the institution and the law requires regular elections of committees. Further legal requirements include stipulations regarding general meetings, annual audits, and accounting procedures. Cooperative societies are allowed to transfer liabilities and assets to other such societies or to split themselves into two or more societies. The Registrar and two-thirds of the members must, however, approve such a decision. At the same time, the Registrar has the power to direct amalgamation, division, or reorganization of a cooperative when the public interest is affected. The Registrar has also the right to supersede elected committees, order new elections, or appoint one or more administrators

---

[13] PRIA, 1989, *supra* 1, p. 16.
[14] PRIA, 1989, *supra* 1, p. 16.

who must be remunerated from the funds of the committee. The Act limits annual net profit to 5%, which, in addition, must be used for the cooperative's educational purposes. Finally, the Act prohibits a cooperative from providing loans to persons other than its members.

§ 11.4   TAX TREATMENT

The tax regulations regarding charitable giving and tax exemption for nonprofit organizations are found in Sections 10 through 13 and Section 80G of the Income Tax Act of 1961. Sections 10 through 13 regulate the exemptions for organizations and Section 80G covers the tax preferences for donations. Tax-exempt status is a prerequisite for Section 80G deduction.

(a) Tax Treatment of Organizations

Sections 10 through 13 of the Income Tax Act of 1961 define organizations eligible for tax-exempt status generally as "religious and charitable" organizations. These religious and charitable organizations fall into two groups: (1) organizations that are totally exempt from taxation due to their nonprofit status, and (2) organizations that can acquire income tax exemptions if they satisfy certain requirements.
The first group includes:

1. Scientific and research associations
2. Universities, colleges, or other educational institutions pursuing exclusively educational purposes
3. Hospitals or medical institutes that are not profit making and exist solely for the provision of medical care to suffering persons
4. Organizations exclusively promoting sports like cricket, hockey, football, etc.
5. Organizations existing solely for the protection or encouragement of *Khadi* and village industries registered with the *Khadi* and Village Industries Commission

These organizations are fully exempt from income tax as long as they continuously pursue their objectives and apply all of their income to these objects.[15]
Organizations that are "charitable" in nature but not included in this list can still acquire tax exemptions. According to Section 2(15) of the Income Tax Act of 1961, the term "charitable purpose" includes "relief of the poor, education, medi-

---

[15] Once an organization is registered, it has to apply to the Income Tax Authorities within one year to obtain tax exemption. Upon acceptance of the application, the Income Tax Department issues a registration number. After acquiring the registration number, the organization must file a return of income form (Form 3(A)) under Section 139(2) of the Income Tax Act every year before June 30. The Income Tax Authorities review this return as well as other papers and records that they may request and, if satisfied as to the nonprofit character of the organization, will issue an exemption certificate.

cal relief, and advancement of any other object of public utility not involving the carrying on of any activity for profit."[16]

(i) *Relief of the Poor.*   Relief of the poor includes the provision of food, assistance in the preparation of marriages, and gifts. Gifts for the relief of the poor can take the form of (1) direct cash assistance; (2) nonfinancial assistance through the establishment of institutions, such as a home for the destitute; and (3) support for nonprofit organizations that are helping the poor if the latter are public in nature, meaning that "relief of the poor must not be relief to a body of private individuals, but must have a public character."[17]

(ii) *Education.*   Education is defined as "systematic instruction, schooling, or training given to the young in preparation for the work of life."[18] This heading covers mainly institutions, such as schools, colleges, and universities. Other qualifying activities include vocational training, providing scholarships, and running libraries or nonformal schools.

(iii) *Medical Relief.*   This category includes the provision of medical relief, nursing care, and medical facilities. Organizations qualifying under this heading are allowed to cater to the needs of other social classes as well, provided that the charitable character of the organization is not endangered. The services offered must, however, be available to the general public.

(iv) *General Public Utility.*   The concept of general public utility includes any activity that is carried out for the benefit of the public, in general, and not for any particular group of people without further definition. For example, the digging of wells and ponds, the construction or maintenance of community centers, or the establishment of cultural societies fall under the realm of public utility. However, organizations must fulfill the following conditions or abide by the following regulations to acquire income tax exemption:

1. Income-generating property must be held by a trust.
2. Property should belong to a charitable organization that is eligible for tax exemption.
3. Trusts cannot be for the benefit of any particular caste or community or utilize any part of their income for the benefit of the trustees.[19]
4. Only that part of income that is used or accumulated for charitable purposes is entitled for exemption.
5. Accumulated income can only be applied within India.
6. Income of trusts involved in business activity are calculated on the basis of Section 11(4A) of the Income Tax Act of 1961.
7. Trusts qualifying for income tax exemption must register under Section 12(A) of the Income Tax Act of 1961 with the Income Tax Commissioner within a year of their existence.

[16] PRIA, 1990, *supra* 1, p. 164.
[17] PRIA, 1990, *supra* 1, p. 164.
[18] *Id.*
[19] Only applicable to trusts created after April 1, 1962.

8. Trusts with an annual income of Rs 25,000 (approximate 1992 value = Rs 270,762 or US $10,447) or more need to conduct annual audits.[20]
9. Trusts are required to invest their accumulated income with nationalized banks or government enterprises.
10. Trusts are required to apply 75% of their total annual income for charitable purposes during the same year.[21]

These organizations are exempt only from income taxes. They have to pay other taxes such as property taxes, sales taxes, and custom duties.

(b) Tax Treatment of Contributions—Domestic Organizations

Section 80G of the Income Tax Law of 1961 specifies that any donation paid to an organization that is exempted under Section 80G entitles an individual or corporate donor to a 50% tax deduction on the donated amount. To qualify for deductions, donations must not be less than Rs 250 (approximately Rs 2,708 or US $105 in 1992 value) and may not exceed Rs 500,000 (approximately Rs 5.3 million or US $204,395 in 1992 value) or 10% of the total income of the donor.

With respect to donations from industry, the Financial Act of 1983 has limited the funds that nonprofit organizations may receive from businesses by removing a 100% deduction for corporate donations to rural development projects that was introduced in 1977 under Section 35CCA of the Income Tax Act. As an alternative policy, the government established the National Fund for Rural Development. Corporate donations to this paragovernmental body are still deductible.

(c) Tax Treatment of Contributions—Foreign Organizations

Under the Foreign Contributions Regulations Act (FCRA) of 1976, as amended in 1985, all nonprofit organizations receiving foreign funds must register with the Home Ministry, get a foreign contributors account number, receive all donations to one account, and notify the Ministry of the account number and the amount of each donation. Even if the organization is already registered with the Home Ministry, prior permission may be needed for receiving foreign funds. Alternatively, a nonprofit organization which has not registered with the Home Ministry may receive foreign funds after obtaining prior permission from the government for each remittance.

§ 11.5 PERSONAL BENEFIT RESTRICTIONS

Under the Indian Trust Act of 1882, trustees are not allowed to use the trust for private personal profit or benefit, but may charge expenses incurred while man-

---

[20] Although all rupee figures have been converted to 1992 values, the government has not built in inflation and increased the amount to its present values.

[21] If a trust is unable to apply 75% of its total income for charitable purposes, then the balance can be set aside for specified application within the next ten years under Section 11(12) of the Income Tax Act. A notice should, however, be sent to the income tax officer on Form 10 of the Income Tax Act within four months or June 30, whichever is later. Errors in Form 10 may lead to taxation at the rate of 62.25%.

aging the trust. Since a trustee cannot enjoy any benefits from the trust, trustees cannot be staff members at the same time. In the case of companies, directors or trustees may receive reimbursements for their management activities, but no remuneration or shares of profit. The property of societies are vested on its governing bodies and cannot be used for the personal benefit of its members.

§ 11.6   OBLIGATIONS TO THE PUBLIC[22]

Trusts.   The official Trustee Act of 1913 generally outlines the rights and obligations of trustees and further obligations are laid down in state laws. Requirements of the Bombay Public Trust Act, for instance, include informing the Charity Commissioner's office within 90 days of any changes in the rules and regulations or bylaws of the trust. Other obligations include proper account keeping and an annual audit by a chartered accountant. The Charity Commissioner must also sanction the sale, mortgage, exchange, or gift of immovable property, as well as leases exceeding ten years for agricultural land and three years for nonagricultural land and buildings belonging to a public trust.

§ 11.7   BUSINESS ACTIVITY

Nonprofit organizations in India are generally not permitted to engage in both business and other income-generating activities. Even related income is not eligible for tax exemption, but taxed at the maximum rate applicable. Section 11(4A) of the Income Tax Act allows exemptions for business income of charitable trusts only if (1) the business consists of the publication of religious books or other wholly religious activities allowed by the government or (2) the business is carried out by the beneficiaries of the trust wholly for charitable purposes. In both cases, separate accounts for the trust and the business activities must be maintained.

§ 11.8   OTHER FUNDING RESTRICTIONS

The Foreign Contributions (Regulation) Act of 1976 was enacted by Parliament to maintain a surveillance of nonprofit organizations receiving foreign funds. The Act was amended in 1985, requiring a mandatory registration of all nonprofit organizations receiving foreign funds with the Home Ministry. These organizations must have a foreign contributions account number, place all foreign donations in one account, and notify the ministry of the account number and the amount of each donation (see above).[23] The act empowers the state to ban any organization from receiving foreign contributions, should the state consider the organization not to be politically neutral.

---

[22] For a detailed discussion on obligations to public for other types of organizations, see PRIA 1987, 1989 *supra* 1.

[23] Alternatively they may get prior permission for each duration.

§ 11.9   POLITICAL ACTIVITY

No political activity of any kind is allowed for nonprofit organizations in India. According to the Religious Institutions (Prevention of Misuse) Act of 1988, the term "political activity" is defined as "any cause, issue or a question of political nature."[24]

§ 11.10   KEY OUTSTANDING ISSUES[25]

Reform of the Societies Registration Act.   The Societies Registration Act of 1860 was initially formulated for organizations providing services to beneficiaries that are not members. However, this creates a number of problems and legal complications for more modern forms of nonprofit organizations, such as member-serving organizations. For example, the Registrar in the State of Andhra Pradesh and the Union Territory of Delhi are continuously lobbying for a declaration that the activities of a society should not benefit its members.

Another problem is the prohibition on paying salaries to society members who are also employees. Although the payment of salaries to society members has been accepted by Registrars of most states and union territories, some states, such as Tamil Nadu, continue to prohibit this practice. What is more, paying members working as staff involves the risk of a possible loss of tax-exempt status under the Income Tax Act of 1961. Although this is not the rule, some income tax officers have indeed revoked tax exemption for societies in which most of the members of the governing body are also paid staff.

---

[24] Upendra Baxi, The "Struggle" for the Redefinition of Secularism in India: Some Preliminary Reflections, 44 *Social Action*, no. 1, 1994, 13–30.

[25] Note that there is a general need to reform all laws regarding registration of, taxation of, and contributions to nonprofit organizations. For a detailed discussion see PRIA 1987, 1989 *supra* 1.

CHAPTER TWELVE

Republic of Ireland*

§ 12.1 LEGAL CONTEXT

Ireland is a common law country but has a written constitution which is recognized by the courts. The general right to form associations is guaranteed by article 40.6.1(iii) of the Irish Constitution, which provides that the state guarantees "the right of citizens to form associations and unions." This right is subject to the protection of "public order and morality" and the constitution provides that laws may be enacted for the regulation and control of this right in the public interest. The more detailed provisions concerning the right to form associations or nonprofit organizations are set out in legislation passed by the Irish parliament.

Irish legislation governing commercial and nonprofit organizations is derived from, and closely related to, United Kingdom law. This concerns mainly the Companies Acts of 1963 to 1990, which provide for companies limited by shares (mainly for commercial purposes) and companies "limited by guarantee," which are normally used by nonprofit organizations.

A different type of legal status for organizations was also established in the nineteenth century to meet the needs of the cooperative movement. This type of structure is known as an Industrial and Provident Society. Most Industrial and Provident Societies are commercial bodies, but this structure is also used on occasion by nonprofit organizations.

An area of the law which is also relevant to nonprofit organizations is that concerning charities. In contrast to England, however, there is no "Register of Charities" in Ireland. Organizations can apply to specific bodies in relation to specific issues; that is, an organization can apply to the Revenue Commissioners, who are the body responsible for the implementation of the general Tax Code in Ireland, for exemption from certain taxes and/or to the Valuation Office for exemption from rates on buildings. But there is no general-purpose Charity Commission as in the United Kingdom.

§ 12.2 ELIGIBILITY

(a) Types of Organizations

The company limited by guarantee and the Industrial and Provident Society are the two main legal structures for nonprofit organizations in Ireland. However, such organizations can also take the form of unincorporated associations, trusts, friendly societies, and incorporated schemes under the Charities Act. With the

* Country Rapporteur: Mel Cousins, Barrister at Law and independent research consultant, Dublin, Ireland.

exception of the incorporated scheme under the Charities Act, none of these latter structures provides a separate legal status for the organization, however.

(i) Company Limited by Guarantee. According to the Companies Act of 1963 and its subsequent amendments, a group of people can come together in accordance with the rules laid down in the Companies Act and form a company that acquires its own legal status entirely separate from the legal status of its members. Two major types of companies are provided for in law: first, companies limited by shares, the type used for business purposes; and second, companies "limited by guarantee," which is the type normally used by nonprofit organizations in Ireland. For the company limited by guarantee, there are no shares and the members simply guarantee to pay a certain (usually nominal) amount toward the debts of the company if it is wound up and unable to pay its debts from its own capital.

Some companies limited by guarantee may be granted permission by the Minister for Enterprise and Employment to omit the word "limited" from their title in order to avoid its commercial overtones. The objects of such a company must be the promotion of commerce, art, science, religion, charity, or any other useful object and the applications of its profits or income must be confined to these objects. The company therefore must not be able to distribute any profits to its members.

(ii) Industrial and Provident Society. In addition to companies limited by guarantee under the Companies Acts, nonprofit organizations in Ireland can also be incorporated as Industrial and Provident Societies. Although the origins of such societies are different from those of the limited company, the rules which have to be satisfied to become an Industrial and Provident Society are quite similar in many ways to those which apply to a company limited by guarantee. However, to become an Industrial and Provident Society, the organization must intend to carry on an "industry, business or trade." Whether an organization satisfies this requirement is decided by the Registrar of Friendly Societies on a case-by-case basis based on the objects of the organization as set out in its Rules. The relevant legislation is set out in the Industrial and Provident Societies Act of 1893, as amended.

(iii) Incorporated Schemes Under the Charities Acts. In addition to the two major types of nonprofit organizations noted above, bodies that are recognized as having "charitable" status for purposes of tax treatment can apply to the Commissioners of Charitable Donations and Bequests[1] to be incorporated, that is, to be granted separate legal status. There are only about twenty-five such schemes

---

[1] The Commissioners of Charitable Contributions and Bequests are appointed by the government and give their services voluntarily. They act as trustees for some charitable trusts and hold the funds on behalf of others. They can invest and authorize charity trustees to invest in securities outside the ordinary range of trustee securities. They have a range of other functions, including the appointment of new trustees, the authorization of sales of charity property, and the incorporation of schemes referred to in the text. Unlike the U.K. Charity Commission, they do not have any general supervisory role in relation to charities and have no role in relation to tax exemption.

in Ireland. In order to apply for incorporation the body must (1) draw up a draft Deed of Trust; (2) get a Barrister's opinion that the Trust is of a charitable nature; and (3) be granted charitable status by the Revenue Commissioners. This option is relevant only to bodies whose objects are entirely charitable and might be suitable for some bodies which have already been recognized as having charitable status by the Revenue Commissioners. However, for any body which had not previously obtained charitable exemption, it is a relatively slow and expensive process.

(iv) Unincorporated Associations.   Many small nonprofit organizations that choose not to incorporate formally may, nevertheless, draw up a written constitution. This has the advantage that they do not have to be registered with any government organization and there are no specific rules as to what can and cannot be included in the constitution. In legal terms, the constitution is a contract between the members of the organization to abide by the terms of the agreement. However, while the constitution is legally binding between the members of the organization, it has no effect in relation to nonmembers. Thus the organization does not have a legal personality of its own. Anything which, in practice, is done by the organization is, in law, done by all the individual members. So the members are all responsible for any activities of the organization including paying debts, and so on. It is difficult for such an unincorporated body to own property such as land or buildings because the property would have to be purchased by all the individual members.

(v) Trusts.   A Trust is an arrangement whereby one or more persons operating under a legal document known as a Deed of Trust holds funds or property on behalf of another person or persons. This system is sometimes used by nonprofit organizations, particularly in relation to the ownership of property. A Trust may also arise where one or more persons act on behalf of a wider group without any formal Deed of Trust being enacted. A Trust can be quite cumbersome and undemocratic in that the Trustees, once appointed, are difficult to remove and so the organization may have only indirect control over its own property. In addition, the Trust is only of relevance to the specific property covered by the Deed of Trust. It does not provide a legal personality for the general work of the organization and the members of the organization would still be individually responsible for any other activities of the organization.

(vi) Friendly Society.   This type of body is related to the Industrial and Provident Society and falls within the remit of the Registrar of Friendly Societies. In legal terms, the Friendly Society is separate and distinct from the Industrial and Provident Society. In fact, there are three types of Friendly Society: the Friendly Society, the Cattle Insurance Society, and the Benevolent Society. The Benevolent Society would be the type applicable to voluntary organizations. It is not an incorporated body and, thus, does not give a separate legal status to the organization. The Friendly Society dates from the nineteenth century, when many small, mutual insurance and assurance bodies provided benefits for their members and for others. There are only about 100 Friendly Societies in Ireland and this form of organization would appear to have little relevance for nonprofit

organizations as the structure is quite cumbersome and does not give a separate legal status to the organization.

(b) Types of Purposes

Similar to England, there are no general restrictions as to the purposes nonprofit organizations may pursue. In order to be eligible for beneficial tax treatment as detailed below, however, organizations must be engaged entirely in "charitable purposes." The definition of charitable purposes has been established by a series of legal decisions dating back several centuries and includes: (1) the relief of poverty; (2) the advancement of education; (3) the advancement of religion; and (4) other purposes beneficial to the community, which covers objects such as the relief of illness and disability, the provision of welfare services, and the advancement of knowledge.[2]

(c) Other Requirements

The details of membership for *companies limited by guarantee* are generally set out in the company's required Memorandum and Articles. However, there must be at least seven members. There is no maximum number, although organizations will often set out a maximum number for their own particular circumstances. The details of who can become a member and who decides on the membership will be set out in the Articles. The membership can be entirely open or can be confined to a specific group (e.g., women's organizations) or to a specific geographical region. The decision on applications for membership will normally be left to the committee of the organization (or the board of directors as it is described in the Acts), but it could be left to a general meeting of the full membership. Details as to the termination of membership will also be set out in the Articles, and again, there is a degree of flexibility about the arrangements which can be made.

Concerning *Industrial and Provident Societies*, the details on membership must be set out in the Rules and can be changed according to the wishes of the organization. There must be at least seven members and there is no maximum number. There are no relevant restrictions in the legislation on who can become a member. The Rules normally provide that the management committee may at their discretion decide on membership, but an alternative arrangement can be made (e.g., that all the members decide on applications for membership at an annual general meeting).

(d) Registration Procedures

There are different provisions for the incorporation of companies and Industrial and Provident Societies.

(i) Companies Limited by Guarantee. In order to register as a company, one must draw up a constitution setting out the objects of the company (i.e., the aims

---

[2] The interpretation of Charitable Law in Ireland is similar to the interpretation adopted by the U.K. courts. However, there are many differences of detail. See J. Wylie, *Irish Land Law* (Butterworths, 1986) for a detailed discussion of charitable trusts.

of the organization) and the rules and regulations by which it will be run.[3] This is contained in two documents known as the *Memorandum* and the *Articles of Association*. The Memorandum contains the name of the company, and the objects, and sets out the amount which the members must contribute if the company is wound up. It will also state that the liability of the members is limited and will set out the names of the first members.

The Articles are usually much longer than the Memorandum because they contain the detailed rules about membership, control of the organization, appointment of officers, and so on. They also contain procedural details such as how meetings can be called, proceedings at meetings, and so on. Many of these rules are set out in the Companies Acts and cannot be altered. However, other rules can be adapted to suit the particular circumstances of the organization. A standard form of Articles is set out in the Companies Act of 1963 and this (or some variation on it) is normally used when setting up a company. Some of the issues covered in the standard Articles include:

1. The details of membership
2. The method of holding meetings
3. Voting details
4. The appointment and removal of a management committee (board of directors)
5. The powers and duties of the committee
6. The provisions for the audit of accounts and appointment of auditors

The body responsible for overseeing the operation of the Companies Acts is the Companies Office in Dublin Castle. This office is responsible for ensuring that applications for registration as a company comply with the requirements of the Acts and for ensuring that companies comply with the ongoing requirements under the legislation, such as making annual returns, submitting annual accounts, and so forth. The government Department with the overall responsibility for the regulation of companies is the Department of Enterprise and Employment.

(ii) Industrial and Provident Societies.   Like a company, an Industrial and Provident Society must also have a constitution. In this case, the constitution is simply known as the Rules of the Society. The legislation does not set out any standard form of Rules although several bodies, including the Co-operative Development Society (CDS) and the Irish Co-operative Organizations Society (ICOS), have drawn up standard Rules for cooperatives.[4]

The Industrial and Provident Societies legislation provides that the Rules must contain provisions covering a wide range of issues including:

---

[3] The charge for registering a new company limited by guarantee is currently £165. This is only the registration fee and does not include solicitor's charges.

[4] The Registrar of Friendly Societies accepts applications in the form of these standard Rules at a reduced registration charge of £20. The organizations involved charge for the use of their model Rules, although this charge includes assistance with adapting the Rules to the particular circumstances of the organization and also includes the registration charge. An organization can also draw up its own Rules, although in this case the registration charge is £100.

1. The objects, the name, and the registered office of the society
2. The terms of admission of members
3. The method of holding meetings, voting details, and the ways of amending the Rules
4. The appointment and removal of a committee of management and of officers
5. The powers and remuneration of the committee and officers
6. The provisions for the audit of accounts and appointment of auditors

The range of issues covered is quite similar to those covered in the Memorandum and Articles of a company limited by guarantee. However, because the Industrial and Provident Societies legislation generally requires only that the Rules should cover an issue, rather than setting out in detail what the provision must contain (as in the Companies Acts), the Industrial and Provident Society has a greater degree of flexibility.

The person responsible for overseeing the operation of this legislation is the Registrar of Friendly Societies. This officer ensures that applications to register an organization as an Industrial and Provident Society conform with the rules set out in the legislation and also ensures that the ongoing requirements of the legislation are complied with (e.g., making returns, etc.).

§ 12.3   INTERNAL GOVERNANCE

(a) Control and Management of the Company

The theory of control of a company limited by guarantee is that the members, by way of the annual general meeting or other general meetings, are in overall control of the company. Each company must have at least two directors. A board of directors is appointed by the membership and it is responsible for the management of the company subject to the overall direction of the members. In some smaller voluntary organizations, all the members may also be directors. In practice, in many companies, the board of directors will control the operation of the company and the holding of an annual general meeting is just a formality. However, the Articles themselves allow for a system of representative democracy in the running of the company and the extent to which this works (or does not work) is dependent on the actual membership rather than on any limitations in the Articles.

However, there are a few restrictions on persons acting as directors. Persons convicted of a serious offense in relation to a company or one involving fraud or dishonesty are automatically disqualified for five years from acting as a director or other officer of a company or from being involved in the management or formation of a company. This applies only in criminal proceedings, but a court can also disqualify a person from being involved in a company if a person has been guilty of fraud in relation to a company, has been guilty of a breach of duty as an officer of the company, has been declared personally liable for the company's debts due to fraudulent or reckless trading, and in related situations. In addition, any director of a company which is being wound up and which cannot pay its debts must be disqualified unless he or she can satisfy the court that his or her actions were honest and reasonable. These provisions were not specifically directed at the operations of nonprofit organizations and, in most cases, it should be possible for directors of such companies to prove that they acted honestly and reasonably. However, it should be noted that once an insolvent company is being wound up, the onus is then on the director to show that he or she acted honestly and reasonably—otherwise he or she will be disqualified for up to five years from acting as a director or being involved in the promotion or management of a company.

The standard Articles provide for the election of the board of directors at the annual general meeting. It will be necessary to change the standard Articles if an organization wants to ensure that specific groups have a certain number of representatives on the board, for example, if there is a balance between statutory and voluntary representatives or between representatives from different areas.

(b) Control and Management of an Industrial and Provident Society

The structure which is adopted for an Industrial and Provident Society is quite similar to that of a company limited by guarantee with the management committee being responsible for the management of the Society subject to the overall control of the annual general meeting. However, the balance of power between the management committee and the members depends on the specific Rules adopted and the way in which the Society operates rather than on the legislation. Persons who are bankrupt or who have been convicted of serious offenses involving fraud or dishonesty cannot be members of the management committee nor can they be involved in the establishment or management of a society.

§ 12.4   TAX TREATMENT

Generally speaking, the same tax treatment applies to nonprofit organizations as to commercial bodies. Some types of nonprofit organizations are specifically exempt from various taxes, however. These include credit unions; bodies promoting human rights which have consultative status with the United Nations or Council of Europe; athletic and amateur sporting bodies; and certain Friendly Societies. In addition, organizations that pursue charitable purposes are eligible to receive charitable exemptions from the Revenue Commissioners, the body responsible for the implementation of tax legislation in Ireland.

(a) Tax Treatment of Organizations

With respect to direct taxation, only charitable organizations in the legal sense of that term and those organizations listed in the previous paragraph are eligible for exemption.

(i) *Charitable Status.*   In order to be recognized as having charitable status, the objects of the organization must be entirely "charitable" as defined through years of case law (see section 12.2.b above). Since there is no official register of charities in Ireland, organizations must apply to the Revenue Commissioners for exemption from certain taxes. In order to be recognized by the Revenue Commissioners, an organization must already have some form of constitution and must be "the subject of a binding trust for charitable purposes only"; that is, the constitution or rules of the organization must contain a binding clause which guarantees that any money received by the organization will be used only for charitable purposes. This can be achieved through the constitution of a company limited by guarantee or through the constitution of an unincorporated body or a Trust. Since the purpose of an Industrial and Provident Society is to allow the profits made by the society to be distributed among the members, this is probably not the most appropriate legal form to use for an organization wishing to apply for charitable status. It is, however, possible to do so if the rules of the society are worded correctly.

Any of these bodies can be recognized as having charitable status for the purposes of the tax code by the Revenue Commissioners. The consequence of such a recognition is that certain tax exemptions apply to the property and income of the organization. In addition, some funding bodies—particularly in the United Kingdom and the United States—will only provide grants to charitable bodies so that persons who make contributions to the funders can themselves claim tax relief on the donations.

In particular, the taxes from which a charitable organization may be exempt include income tax, corporation tax (in the case of organizations), capital gains tax, deposit interest retention tax, capital acquisition tax, and stamp duty on a transfer or lease of land. There is no exemption, however, from value-added tax and employees of a charity are liable to income tax under the PAYE (pay-as-you-earn) system and are also liable to pay related social insurance contributions.

Organizations which are granted exemption from certain taxes on this basis must provide annual accounts to the Revenue Commissioners on request and such organizations cannot alter their constitutions without the permission of the Revenue. In practice, however, the level of monitoring of such bodies by the Revenue is minimal.

(ii) Indirect Taxation. Although nonprofit organizations are subject to value-added taxes, article 13 of the European Union 6th VAT Directive sets out some specific exemptions from VAT which are of relevance to nonprofit organizations. The specific exemptions relevant to organizations in Ireland (including those required by the 6th VAT Directive) include:

1. School or university education and vocational training or retraining
2. Hospital and medical care or treatment provided by a hospital, nursing home clinic, or similar establishment
3. Services for the protection or care of children and young persons
4. Supply of goods and services closely related to welfare and social security by nonprofit organizations
5. Supply of services and goods for the benefit of their members by nonprofit organizations whose aims are primarily of a political, trade union, religious, patriotic, philosophical, philanthropic, or civic nature

In addition, some items are zero rated, which may be of relevance to nonprofit organizations. These include medical equipment and appliances.

(b) Tax Treatment of Contributions—Domestic Organizations

The tax incentives for charitable giving in Ireland are quite limited. There is a "covenant system" in place, in which the taxes donors would pay on income used for gifts pledged to nonprofit organizations are rebated to the donors. However, this provision applies only to donations to universities and colleges for (1) research; (2) teaching natural sciences; and (3) to human rights bodies having consultative status with the United Nations or the Council of Europe. From 1996, only 5% of a taxpayer's total income is allowable for tax purposes by way of covenant.

Gifts by individuals and companies may also be subject to limited tax relief in some other special circumstances. One of the main reliefs of relevance to the nonprofit sector is that gifts of between £100 and £10,000 to certain educational establishments may be entitled to relief.[5]

(c) Tax Treatment of Contributions—Foreign Organizations

The Finance Act of 1995 has recently provided that certain Third World charities can receive payment from the Revenue Commissioners of the income tax paid by qualifying donors on donations between £200 and £750 per year. However, the donor does not receive any tax relief on his or her donation. The effect of this is that if the donor contributes, say, £730, the charity receives an additional £270 from the Revenue (providing the donor has paid income tax of at least that amount). To be designated a Third World charity, an organization must be established for charitable purposes only; have been granted charitable tax exemption for at least three years prior to the date of application for designation; prepare and furnish annual audited accounts; and have as its sole object relief and development in a country or countries listed by the OECD.

Apart from Third World charities, there are no specific provisions concerning non-Irish bodies. In principle, the general provisions of Irish law would therefore apply to them as well.

§ 12.5 PERSONAL BENEFIT RESTRICTIONS

An organization which is accepted as having charitable status must include in its constitution a clause providing that payment of reasonable and proper remuneration is allowed to any officer or servant of the company or to any member of the company in return for any services actually rendered to the company. In addition, payment of interest at a rate not exceeding 5% per annum on money lent or reasonable and proper rent for premises may also be made to any member of the company. However, the constitution must include a clause providing that no member of the management committee of the company shall be appointed to any salaried office or to any office paid by fees and that no remuneration or other benefit in money or money's worth shall be given by the company to any member of

---

[5] This provision applies to third-level establishments providing education in relation to architecture and the arts, including film and theater. The Revenue Commissioners have published a list of about 100 approved establishments.

the management committee, except repayment of out-of-pocket expenses and interest as set out above or reasonable and proper rent for premises. The purpose of this restriction is, of course, to prevent an abuse of the charitable status.

§ 12.6   OBLIGATIONS TO THE PUBLIC

For *companies*, there are a variety of specific responsibilities of directors. In particular:

- *Acting in the best interests of the company.* The directors of a company (i.e., the members of the management committee) are under a legal duty to act in the best interests of the company, of the members, and of the employees of the company. They cannot take unfair advantage of their positions for personal gain. However, this does not mean that the directors cannot be paid fees and expenses and it does not mean that an employee of the company cannot be a director. The Articles will normally set out some details as to whether this will be allowed in individual cases. For example, it is generally possible to have members of staff on the management committee of the company. However, in the case of companies that wish to be recognized as charities by the Revenue Commissioners, it is not possible to pay directors (except for legitimate expenses; interest on money lent to the company and rent for premises). Thus, in the case of a charity only, it is not possible to have a member of staff on the board of directors.
- *Liability for company debts.* The Companies Acts set out rules about the liability of directors where a company is unable to pay its debts. As we have seen, the company and the members of the company are separate legal entities and neither the directors, nor the ordinary members are generally liable for any liabilities incurred by the company. However, in some limited cases, this rule is changed so that directors are made personally liable for debts. The Companies Acts provide that a director (or any other person involved in the company) who is responsible for fraudulent trading is both guilty of a criminal offense and personally liable for debts arising from the fraudulent trading. Obviously, this only applies in extreme cases where a person knowingly sets out to defraud. Since 1990, if a person is knowingly involved in running the business of a company in a reckless manner, that person may be made personally liable for the debts of the company (if the company cannot itself pay the debts). Reckless trading involves a situation where, having regard to the knowledge, skill, and experience of the director, he or she may reasonably be expected to have known that his or her actions would cause a loss to the creditors of the company, or where the director did not honestly believe on reasonable grounds that the company would be able to pay its debts. This would apply only where the director should have known that the company would not be able to pay its debts, but went on running up further debts.[6]

---

[6] This legislation was not introduced with nonprofit bodies specifically in mind. In fact it was brought in to prevent fly-by-night businesspersons from running up large debts, going into liq-

- *Tax returns.* From the 1992–1993 tax year, directors of companies and the spouses of directors are liable, in most cases, to make self-assessment returns for income tax purposes. Persons who make late returns are liable for a surcharge of 10% of their total tax liability. However, although this applies to the directors of companies limited by guarantee, it appears that this will not be pursued in practice against such directors. The Minister of Finance has said that "voluntary unpaid directors of companies established for social, cultural, or charitable purposes are not the intended target of this measure. It is not the intention of the Revenue Commissioners to apply the surcharge where such directors, who do not hold other directorships, fail to make timely returns of income."

- *Ongoing obligations.* General obligations are set out in the Companies Acts and specific obligations may also be imposed in the Articles. [See also § 12.4(a)(i) the section of charitable status for specific obligations for such bodies.] The main ongoing obligations of companies are as follows:

  1. To keep a register of members and directors
  2. To keep minutes of all meetings
  3. To hold an annual general meeting within 18 months of being incorporated and at least every fifteen months after that
  4. To make an annual return to the Companies Office within 60 days of the annual general meeting
  5. To keep proper accounts and submit audited accounts with the annual return
  6. To notify the Companies Office of any special resolutions and of any changes to the Memorandum and Articles
  7. To notify the Companies Office of any changes in the directors, the secretary, the auditors, or the registered office within 14 days of the change and of any change in the name (which must be approved by the Minister)

- *Ongoing management.* The directors are generally responsible for ensuring that the ongoing obligations of the company are complied with, for example, making annual returns. In many cases, it is an offense if these requirements are not complied with and the directors may be liable for such offenses. Therefore, it is important to ensure that the annual returns and other ongoing obligations of the company are in order. Every company must also have a company secretary or someone else who may be a member of the management committee. The company secretary is often given specific responsibility for ensuring that the following are done:

  1. Keeping the company registers of members and of directors up to date

uidation, and opening up again somewhere else. It had proved extremely difficult to show that such businesspersons were acting fraudulently since there was often a lack of documents about the company's operation. So the new concept of reckless trading was introduced as this should be much easier to prove. In theory, this could apply to nonprofit bodies that continue to accrue debts even where they should know that there is no hope of getting funding to meet the debts, but in practice it is unlikely that this legislation would be applicable in most cases concerning such organizations. However, it would obviously apply where such a body was operating in a quasifraudulent way.

2. Making sure that the annual general meeting is held on time and that proper notice is given
3. Calling general meetings in accordance with the details set out in the Articles
4. Keeping minute books
5. Sending annual returns and other documentation to the Companies Office

With respect to *Industrial and Provident Societies,* committee members have the following responsibilities:

- *Acting in the best interests of the society.* Members of the management committee of an Industrial and Provident Society are in a similar position to the directors of a company limited by guarantee in that the general obligation to act in the best interests of the Society and of the members also applies to them. A member of a management committee should therefore not take advantage of his or her position for unfair personal gain.
- *Liability for debts.* Members of the management committee are not generally liable for the society's debts. The restrictions on company directors which have been strengthened in recent years in relation to reckless trading do not apply to the management committee of an Industrial and Provident Society. A member of a management committee which goes into liquidation will, therefore, not normally be faced with any restrictions on becoming involved with another Industrial and Provident Society in the future.
- *Tax returns.* The Rules in relation to tax returns which have been set out above in relation to limited companies also apply to the management committee members of an Industrial and Provident Society. Again, however, it is not clear how this will be enforced in practice.
- *Ongoing obligations.* The responsibilities of an Industrial and Provident Society are set out in the legislation and in the rules of the Society. The main ongoing obligations are as follows:

1. To make an annual return (including accounts) to the Registrar before March 31 each year
2. To make a special return at least every three years
3. To provide the Registrar with any other information and returns which he or she thinks necessary
4. To keep proper accounts and have them audited by a public auditor
5. To seek the Registrar's approval of any proposed changes to the Rules and of any change in the name
6. To notify the Registrar of any changes in the registered office within fourteen days of the change

- *Ongoing Management.* The members of the management committee are generally responsible for ensuring that the ongoing obligations of the society (set out above) are carried out. They may be convicted of an offense if these obligations are not complied with.

§ 12.7   BUSINESS ACTIVITY

There is no specific limitation on the ability of nonprofit organizations to carry on commercial activity. However, as set out above, in the case of organizations classified as charities, the organization must guarantee that any money received will be used only for charitable purposes. In addition, the main objects of the organization must be charitable and it is unlikely that an organization which had any considerable commercial objectives would be accepted as being charitable by the Revenue Commissioners.

So far as the taxation of business income is concerned, a charity is taxable on trading profits unless the profits are applied solely for the purposes of the charity, and either the trade is exercised in the course of carrying out the primary purposes of the charity or the work in connection with the trade is mainly carried on by beneficiaries. In sum, charities that earn money from business activities will be taxed on the income unless (a) the activities are related to the charitable purposes and (b) the income is used for a charitable purpose.

§ 12.8   OTHER FUNDING RESTRICTIONS

There is no general legislation in relation to fund-raising activities in Ireland. There is also no requirement for organizations which raise funds from the public for charitable purposes to account to any authority in relation to them. However, there is a range of separate pieces of legislation which have been developed in a fairly ad hoc way to address specific aspects of fund-raising. In particular:

- *The Street and House to House Collections Act of 1962.* This Act contains controls on fund-raising by means of street collections and house-to-house collections undertaken both for charitable and noncharitable purposes. Fund-raising, falling within the scope of the Act, must be authorized by the senior police officer in the area.
- *The Gaming and Lotteries Act of 1956.* This Act sets out a series of controls in relation to gaming and the promotion of lotteries.
- *The National Lotteries Act of 1986.* The main purpose of this Act is to provide a statutory framework for holding of a National Lottery, at least part of the proceeds of which are distributed to nonprofit organizations.

The lack of any overall control of fund-raising activities and the odd ad hoc nature of existing statutory provisions led to the establishment of a Committee on Fund-Raising Activities by the Minister for Justice in 1989. The findings of the Committee are discussed below in section 12.10.

§ 12.9   POLITICAL ACTIVITY

Nonprofit organizations are permitted to engage in activities of a political nature in Ireland. However, such activity is not allowed for organizations seeking charitable status and the exemptions it brings. At the very least, the inclusion of any political objectives in the organization's constitution would result in its rejection as a charity by the Revenue Commissioners.

§ 12.10   KEY OUTSTANDING ISSUES

(a) Basic Legal Structure

The number of nonprofit organizations in Ireland has grown considerably in recent years. The Programme for Economic and Social Progress, agreed between the government, employers, trade unions, and farming organizations in 1991, states that "having regard to the contribution which voluntary organizations make in delivering services and combating poverty, the government will draw up a charter for voluntary social services in Ireland which will set out a clear framework for partnership between the State and voluntary activity and develop a cohesive strategy for supporting voluntary activity. A White Paper outlining the government's proposals in this area will be prepared." Subsequent to this announcement, an extensive period of consultation was entered into by the government with the voluntary sector and considerable work was done on preparing such a Charter and White Paper. In 1997, a Green Paper (i.e., discussion document) was published on the community & voluntary sector and its relationship with the state. It suggests a review of the position concerning the recognition of charities for tax purposes and tax treatment of charities.

The Combat Poverty Agency (a statutory body whose role is to advise the Minister for Social Welfare in relation to poverty issues) commissioned a report by this author which was to document the current legal structures for community and voluntary organizations in Ireland, to suggest changes which would be appropriate to the needs of such organizations and to document the advice and support provision which currently exists in this area. This report, entitled "Legal Structures for Community and Voluntary Organizations," was submitted to the Combat Poverty Agency in September 1993. Arising from this report, a Guide to Legal Structures for Community and Voluntary Organizations was published by the Combat Poverty Agency in 1994. It does not appear that there are any immediate proposals to reform the legal structures as set out above in relation to nonprofit organizations.

(b) Fund-Raising Law

The law in relation to fund-raising is an area of relevance to many nonprofit organizations. As noted earlier, a committee was established by the Minister for Justice in 1989 to examine the adequacy of the existing statutory controls over fund-raising for charitable and such other purposes and to make recommendations. This committee reported in 1990 and recommended the introduction of a system of registration for all organizations raising funds for charitable purposes and a range of other reforms. No action has been taken to date to implement these proposals although a conference was organized in 1995 by the Department of Justice to discuss these recommendations. Subsequently an Advisory Group on

Charities/Fund-Raising Legislation was appointed and reported in 1996. It is unclear whether, and if so when, this will lead to significant reforms.

(c) Tax Relief for Donations

One other area of relevance is that concerning tax relief on donations to charitable organizations. As a result of lobbying by charities working in the Third World, recent concessions have been granted to these bodies. These do not, however, apply to charities working in Ireland and this has given rise to considerable concern for such organizations arising from their fear that the recent change may lead to donations going to Third World charities rather than Irish-based bodies.

CHAPTER THIRTEEN

Israel[*]

§ 13.1 LEGAL CONTEXT

Israel is a country with a mixed legal structure resulting from the fact that its legal system is influenced both by common and civil law. Moreover, the Israeli legal system has also been shaped by the Ottoman and British occupations which predated the establishment of the state of Israel. Many organizations, including many nonprofit organizations, formed under a pre-1948 Ottoman Law have consequently found themselves in a complex legal situation often requiring reregistration and reconstitution to claim benefits available only under the Israeli legal code.

Notwithstanding its mixed legal structure, the right to form a nonprofit organization is considered to be a basic human right in Israel, inherent in the basic democratic character of the regime. This right is not explicitly codified, however.

Seven distinct bodies of law govern the operation of nonprofit organizations in Israel. Three of these—the Nonprofit Organizations Law of 1980 (5740), the Companies Ordinance [new version] of 1983 (5743), and the Trust Law of 1979 (5739)—relate to the establishment of the juridical status of such organizations as nonprofit entities. While the first two enactments relate to incorporated bodies, the Trust Law governs the formation of nonincorporated "public endowments."[1]

The other four bodies of legislation with relevance for the nonprofit sector are the Income Tax Ordinance, the Value-Added Tax Law of 1975 (5735), the Property Tax and Compensation Fund Law of 1961 (5721), and the Capital Gains Tax on Real Estate Law of 1963 (5723). These laws regulate the tax treatment of nonprofit organizations and of private contributions to these organizations. In addition, separate legal provisions apply to trade unions and political parties.

§ 13.2 ELIGIBILITY

(a) Types of Organizations

Three broad types of nonprofit organizations are provided for in Israeli law.

---

[*] Country Rapporteur: Dr. Hadara Bar-Mor, Vice Dean, Senior Lecturer, School of Law, Netanya Academic College, Israel.

[1] There is also the possibility of forming a nonprofit organization under the Co-operative Societies Act of 1933. This ordinance does not provide a special legal arrangement for such a cooperative and it does allow a limited distribution of profits. However, the organizers of a cooperative society may voluntarily agree not to distribute profits and a provision to this effect should be included in the articles of association. In practice, this option is rarely used.

(i) Nonprofit Organization.   The first are organizations incorporated under the Nonprofit Organizations, or Amutot, Law of 1980 (hereafter the NPO Law). *Amuta* is a special Hebrew word derived from the noun *amit*, which means "colleague" or "friend." An *amuta* is an association of people gathered to achieve public, cultural, or social purposes without any personal profit-sharing intent. This law replaced an earlier Ottoman law which regulated the registration and management of nonprofit organizations. Previously registered organizations were required to reregister under the new law or risk losing their tax exemption and their elimination from the register of nonprofit organizations. The only types of nonprofit organizations exempted from the NPO Law are trade unions and employers' unions registered prior to passage of the NPO Law, and political parties, which are governed by the Political Parties Law of 1992.

Generally speaking, registration under the NPO law is the preferred status for associations formed for purposes other than the profit of their members. The nonprofit association title ("amuta" in Hebrew) added to an association's name instead of the word "company" seems to contribute to its credibility as well as to the ease with which it can acquire tax exemptions.

(ii) Nonprofit Company.   The second broad type of nonprofit organization provided for in Israeli law is the nonprofit company incorporated under the Companies Ordinance. This ordinance is the general law regulating the establishment and operation of limited liability companies in Israel. Companies formed for purposes other than the profit of their members are one type of such companies. If such companies are formed for the promotion of commerce, art, science, religion, charity, or any other beneficial purpose and use their income solely for the promotion of these objects and do not pay dividends to their members, they are designated as "public utility companies" and can delete the word "Limited" from their names, thus improving their external image. They may also avail themselves of the tax exemption privilege.

Of the various types of corporate entities permitted under the Companies Ordinance, nonprofit companies typically assume the form of "companies limited by guarantee" with or without share capital. Such companies can be registered either as public companies or as private companies. The major differences between these two are that (a) public companies must have a minimum of seven members to register, whereas private companies may register with as little as two members; and (b) private companies may not issue securities for sale to the public.

(iii) Unincorporated Associations.   In addition to the two types of incorporated nonprofit organizations, Israeli law also provides for the existence of unincorporated associations. Such organizations are not separate legal entities, however, which means that their members are personally liable for the organizations' activities.

(iv) Public Endowments.   Another type of unincorporated organizations is the "public endowment," which, as spelled out in the Trust Law of 1979, is a trust fund that need not be registered as a body corporate. Such funds should have as their primary goals, the promotion of public interest purposes. Public endow-

ments are created either by a testament or by a contract between the donor of the endowment and the trustee or by a special writ of endowment. These written documents should include (1) the expressed intention of the donor to form a trust, (2) the purposes and beneficiaries of the endowment, (3) a description of the property allocated to the endowment, and (4) the terms according to which the endowment should be managed. The terms should also specify the personality of the trustee, and his or her rights, duties, and obligations. The trustee of a public endowment is usually a nonprofit organization incorporated under the NPO law, or a "public utility company" incorporated under the Companies Ordinance. However, physical persons may also serve as trustees.

(b) Types of Purposes

Aside from the prohibition on profit seeking, there are no further limitations under the NPO law regarding the selection of purposes for nonprofit organizations. The law explicitly declares that two or more persons who wish to incorporate for any legal purpose other than profit seeking are free to do so. However, registration is prohibited if proposed purposes include the denial of the existence of the state of Israel, or its democratic character, or if the association serves as a front for illegal activities.

Similarly, the Companies Ordinance and the case law interpreting it also do not stipulate any specific purpose restrictions on the formation of companies, with the exception of prohibitions concerning the legality of the selected purposes and acceptance of the state of Israel. To enjoy the privilege of excluding the word "Limited" from a company's name, however, the company must be formed for public benefit purposes such as the promotion of commerce, art, science, education, religion, and charity. Although purpose restrictions do not apply to the basic incorporation of nonprofit organizations, they do apply to the granting of favorable tax treatment, as will be detailed below.

Public endowments created according to the Trust Law do, however, have to aim at the promotion of public benefit purposes, which include the promotion of commerce, art, science, religion, charity, or any other purpose and use beneficial to the public.

(c) Other Requirements

Nonprofit organizations established under the NPO Law can be formed by two or more persons and no minimum contributions or resource requirements exist. Permissible as members are adult individuals and corporations. For individual members, the membership is personal and cannot be transferred or bequeathed. Other membership requirements such as rules regarding the terms of acceptance or removal of members are usually matters of the organization's internal law, as laid down in the organization's articles. However, the law stipulates that a member should not be removed from the organization before receiving a proper chance to present his or her arguments. The NPO law in its Appendix A provides a standard model of such articles, which serve as a default alternative if an organization chooses not to register its own articles. The standard form contains the following stipulation: any person who wishes to join the organization must apply for membership to the board of directors. The applications must include a declaration to abide by the organization's articles and the decisions of the general meeting. The power to grant or deny membership lies with the board of directors. Rejections, however, can be appealed to the general meeting.

In the case of nonprofit companies, there are certain membership requirements. Private companies must have at least two, but no more than 50 members, while public companies have to have at least seven members with no restriction on the maximum membership. However, the Companies Ordinance does not contain any further special requirements for nonprofit companies. Any person can be a member of such a company, provided he or she guarantees to contribute to the assets of the company in the event of liquidation. The amount of the guarantee fee has to be specified in the company's memorandum at the time of registration, and cannot be increased or reduced. However, the Companies Ordinance does not provide minimum or maximum limits, and it is possible that different members subscribe to different guarantee fees. The amount that the members have agreed to contribute is not considered assets of the company while it is a going concern and thus may not be mortgaged or charged by the company.

(d) Registration Procedures

(i) Nonprofit Organizations.   To obtain registration for nonprofit organizations, an application must be filed with the Registrar of Nonprofit Organizations. The application must state (1) the name of the organization; (2) the organization's objectives; (3) the place of its registered office; and (4) the name of its founders, their addresses, and identity numbers. The articles of association which specify internal arrangements and management procedures may also be included in the application. If no articles are included, the standard articles provided in Appendix A of the NPO Law will be in effect.

Upon receipt of the application, it is the duty of the Registrar to determine whether the statutory requirements have been complied with. Specifically, the Registrar has to determine (1) whether the name of the organization would not mislead or offend public feelings, be against public policy, or duplicate the name of an already registered corporation in Israel; (2) whether the organization is formed for a legal purpose as specified above; and (3) whether the application contains all the necessary details and is signed by all founders. After the Registrar is satisfied that all these statutory requirements and the laws, in general, are complied with, and after payment of a registration fee, the organization is entered into the nonprofit organization register. Upon registration, the Registrar issues a certificate of incorporation and, from the date stated therein, the organization comes into existence as a legal person, separate and distinct from its members. A notice of the issue of the certificate of incorporation is then published in an official gazette. If the Registrar refuses to register the organization, the applicants may appeal before the district court within thirty days of notification of the refusal.

In the special case of organizations which are specifically formed to save the life of a certain person, the Registrar has to make a decision within two weeks. If he or she fails to do so, the applicants may ask the Minister of the Interior to order registration within fourteen days. This special registration is valid for only one year, during which the organization has to fulfill all the registration requirements as prescribed by the law.

(ii) Nonprofit Companies. To obtain registration for a nonprofit company limited by guarantee, the following documents are required:

1. A *memorandum of association* stating the name of the company, the objectives, the limited liability of its members, and a clause declaring that each member will contribute to the company's assets a sum which will not exceed a specified amount in case the company is dissolved while he or she is a member, or within one year after he or she ceases to be a member. The amount of the guarantee has to be stated in the memorandum. If a company wishes to exclude the word "Limited" from its name—which is usually the case with nonprofit companies—it has to prove to the Companies Registrar that it intends to promote public benefit purposes as defined in section 13.2(b).
2. *Articles of association* detailing internal management procedures. Although the standard form of articles, as provided in Appendix B of the Companies Ordinance, does not automatically apply, the relevant parts may be used as a model.
3. A statement of the names(s) of the intended first director or directors. Such a statement must be signed by, or on behalf of, the subscribers of the memorandum, and must contain a consent to act, signed by each of the persons named as directors.
4. A statutory declaration by a solicitor who was engaged in the formation of the company that the requirements of the Ordinance with respect to the registration are complied with.

After examination of the application and the receipt of a registration fee, the Registrar will sign and issue a certificate declaring that the company is incorporated and limited by guarantee. Notice of the issue will be published in an official gazette. From the date of issue, the subscribers of the memorandum, as well as other persons who become members afterward, will be a body corporate by the name laid down in the memorandum. That body corporate is then capable of exercising all functions of an incorporated company, but with such liability on the part of its members to contribute to its assets in the event of its dissolution as is stated in the memorandum.

(iii) Public Utility Companies. If a nonprofit company is registered and designated as "a public utility company," it must, according to the Trust Law, inform the Endowments Registrar within six months. The title of a "public utility company" is granted, according to the Trust Law, to a nonprofit company on the fulfillment of any one of the three following preconditions:

1. It is registered as a "company for public utility" under the Companies Ordinance.

2. It has been exempted from paying income tax under the Income Tax Ordinance; property tax under the Property Tax and Compensation Fund Law; and capital gains tax under the Capital Gains Tax on Real Estate Law.
3. A court declared that it is a "public utility company" whose main purposes are for public benefit.

(iv) Public Endowments.   As soon as a trustee (either a physical person or a body corporate) is appointed, the trustee has to register with the Endowments Registrar within three months of the appointment by providing specific details relating to the endowment and to the trustee. The trustee is required to deliver copies of the annual accounts to the Registrar, who is also authorized to demand the delivery of any other documents concerning the management of the fund.

§ 13.3   INTERNAL GOVERNANCE

Like other features of Israeli law, the requirements regarding internal governance of nonprofit organizations differ between nonprofit associations and companies.

(i) NPO Law.   According to the NPO Law, nonprofit organizations must have two organs, a general meeting of members and a board of directors. Furthermore, an audit committee is required, though by decision of the general meeting it may be replaced by either a single accountant or any other body specifically created for this purpose and approved by the Registrar.

While the distribution of power between the general meeting and the board of directors is generally left to respective stipulations in the association's articles, the law provides that, in absence of other provisions, the board of directors will have the residual power to manage the organization. The few powers which are by law exclusively reserved for the general meeting include the modification or alteration of articles, the appointment and removal of directors and the audit committee, and the voluntary dissolution of the association. As a result, although the ultimate control lies with the general meeting by virtue of the power to appoint and remove directors, members have usually very limited immediate control over the board. Again, in absence of stipulations in the articles to the contrary, this usually means that the general meeting cannot override decisions of the board of directors, or exercise direct control over the exercise of their powers. Monitoring of the management is a function reserved for the audit committees which, in practice, are usually not very effective in this respect. In general, members may bring a legal action on behalf of the NPO against the directors and officers, although the incentive to do so is very small.

According to the law, the general meeting must convene at the dates fixed in the articles, but not less than once a year. If the organization fails to convene the general meeting, the Registrar has the power to either call, or direct the calling of, a meeting, and give directions to the effect that one member present in person may be deemed to constitute the meeting. Additional general meetings (i.e., meetings other than the annual one) may be convened by the board whenever the board sees fit, but must be convened on the written request of the audit committee or of members representing not less than one-tenth of the membership.

According to the standard articles of Appendix A of the NPO Law, a quorum of members is required to be present at the beginning of any meeting. If a quorum is not present, the meeting shall be adjourned to the same day in the following week. If at the adjourned meeting, again a quorum is not present, the members present shall form a quorum. If membership exceeds 2,000 members, the general meeting may take the form of an agents assembly. Decisions at the general membership meeting are normally by majority vote, except for voluntary dissolution of the organization, which requires a two-thirds vote of the members present.

The audit committee, which is elected by the membership at the general meeting, has the responsibility to audit the financial and economic affairs and the bookkeeping of the organization and recommend approval of the financial statements. No member of the board may serve on the audit committee. The board must deliver annual financial statements, including a balance sheet and a profit and loss account, to the audit committee within two weeks before the annual meeting or within any other earlier date if the articles so specify. Copies of the financial statements must also be made available to the general meeting.

(ii) Company Ordinance. Nonprofit companies normally have at least two governing bodies, a general meeting and a board of directors. As is the case with nonprofit organizations, the division of power between the general meeting and the board of directors is left to the articles. The powers reserved for the general meeting are, *inter alia,* the authority to alter the memorandum and articles, to appoint or remove directors, and to pass a resolution to dissolve the company. Although the directors have the residual power to manage the company—subject to the provisions of the Ordinance, the memorandum, and the articles—and the general meeting has few opportunities to intervene in management, ultimate control of the company resides, nevertheless, with the meeting, since it has the power of management displacement. Generally problematic is the monitoring function. Given the nondistribution constraint, the general meeting will have few, if any, incentives to scrutinize management.

The Companies' Ordinance also requires the appointment of an audit committee or audit body, but only for publicly owned for-profit companies. In the case of guarantee companies, the appointment of an audit committee is not required, although the company's members may institute such a committee if they see fit. However, the law does require the appointment of an auditor who may not simultaneously serve as an officer of the company. Finally, companies registered as "public utility companies" have to comply with the Trust Law's requirement to deliver annual financial and business accounts to the Registrar.

Annual meetings are called by the board of directors, and must be held at intervals of no more than fifteen months. If default is made in holding an annual meeting, the court may call, or direct the calling of, the meeting on request of any member of the company. Additional meetings may be called by the board at its discretion or on the request of members holding not less than one-tenth of the voting rights. Under the standard articles of Appendix B of the Companies Ordinance, no business may be transacted at the general meeting unless an effective quorum of members is present. Usually, a quorum is achieved when two members are present in person. If a quorum is not present, the meeting will be adjourned to the same day the following week. According to the standard articles, votes shall be by show of hands with one vote per member, unless a poll is demanded. On a poll, the voting power is distributed according to the amount of the guarantee individual members have subscribed to. According to the standard form articles, polls may be demanded before a vote by show of hand, but also immediately after the votes' results are known, thereby nullifying the prior vote.

The position of the board of directors in companies limited by guarantee is largely similar to the board position in associations. Directors are usually sovereign in the exercise of their powers, and the general meeting is not entitled to override board decisions. The minimum number of directors depends on the type of company in question: public companies must have at least two directors, while one director is sufficient for private companies. The determination of the maximum number of directors, however, is in both cases left to internal regulation of the company's articles. Furthermore, in contrast to the regulations of the NPO Law, the only persons disqualified from holding office as director in a company are undischarged bankrupts. Stipulations regarding annual accounts constitute another difference. In each financial year, the board of directors has to present copies of its annual accounts to the general meeting. If the guarantee company is registered as a public company, the Companies Ordinance further requires that a balance sheet, audited and annotated by an independent auditor, as well as a copy of the auditor's report approved by a director of the company must be added to the annual accounts. Companies registered as a "public utility company," regardless of whether they are public or private companies, also have to comply with the above-mentioned audit requirements of the Trust Law.

(iii) Trust Law.   As detailed above, public endowments are managed by a trustee, which is usually a nonprofit association or a nonprofit company. The duties of the trustee are to protect and preserve the property of the trust, to manage and develop it, and to aim at achieving the purposes of the trust. The trustee is authorized to do whatever is required to ensure the successful fulfillment of his or her duty. However, trustees are not allowed to confer any of their duties on somebody else, although they may hire employees to help them carry out their duties.

Unlike other trustees who have to report to the fiduciaries, a trustee of a public endowment must report annually to the Registrar of Endowments, according to the requirements mentioned above. Furthermore, a trustee of a public endowment has to open a special bank account under his or her name, give notice about serving as a trustee of this public endowment, and deposit in this account all money received in the course of his or her duties. Any cash not immediately needed has to be efficiently invested to preserve the capital and maximize returns.

§ 13.4   TAX TREATMENT

Under the tax laws in Israel, there is no difference between nonprofit organizations and companies. For tax purposes, both types are treated equally.

(a) Tax Treatment of Organizations

There are two main bodies of law affecting the tax status of nonprofit corporations or entities: the Income Tax Ordinance, which regulates both individual and corporate income taxation; and the Value-added Tax Law of 1975, which taxes final consumer expenditure. Two other laws—the Property Tax and Compensation Fund Law of 1961 (5721) and the Capital Gains Tax on Real Estate Law of 1963 (5723)—are also relevant to nonprofit organizations, although to a lesser degree.

(i) *Income Taxation.* The Income Tax Ordinance exempts the income of any "public institution" from tax on its income (defined as corporation tax) insofar as such income is not derived from any trade or business carried on by the organization or by another association that it fully controls. For tax purposes, a "public institution" is defined as either an association of at least seven persons, the majority of whom are not related to each other, or an endowment where the majority of its trustees are not related to each other, and that exists and operates exclusively for a public purpose.[2] Public purposes are defined as religious, cultural, educational, scientific, health, welfare, and sports-related purposes, and any other purpose approved by the Minister of Finance. Additional purposes approved by the Minister of Finance include the prevention of accidents and the prevention of unemployment. Any use of property or revenue other than for the promotion of its public purposes will subject the institution to tax liabilities. In sum, nonprofit associations, public endowments, and companies will be exempted from income and corporation tax if they satisfy the definition of a "public institution," do not receive income derived from trade or business, and use their income for exempt public purposes. Since there is much ambiguity with regard to the definition of income from trade or business, however, a considerable body of case law exists interpreting these requirements and many "public institutions" whose expenses exceed their income, nevertheless, find themselves subject to taxation because the Tax Authorities consider some of their income to be derived from business or trade. However, since only that part of total income is taxed that is derived from business activities, this limitation of the tax exemption is only partial.

Organizations exempt from income and corporation taxes are subject to oversight exercised by the Minister of Finance. He or she may annul the privileged status as a public institution as defined in the Income Tax Ordinance if an organization (1) has failed to file annual accounts with the Revenue Tax Authorities for two consecutive years, (2) does not keep its books according to the law, or (3) pursues activities that do not aim at achieving public purposes.

(ii) *Value-Added Taxation.* The exemption from corporation taxation under the Tax Ordinance does not automatically exempt nonprofit organizations from value-added tax (VAT) as well. The Value-added Tax Law grants tax exemptions

---

[2] In principle, it is legally permissible for an unincorporated association to obtain tax exemption. However, the tax authorities usually demand incorporation as a prerequisite for recognizing a "public institution" with respect to granting tax credits to contributors or for the purpose of exemption from Capital Gains Tax on Real Estate.

to each of the following types of institutions, designated as "not-for-profit institutions" under the law:

1. The state, local authorities, and associations of cities
2. Bodies or associations of persons, whether incorporated or not, that are not profit seeking, and that are not financial institutions
3. Corporations other than a company, partnership, or cooperative society
4. Pension funds exempted from income tax

While the first category relates to national or public nonprofit institutions, the other three categories define private nonprofit institutions mainly supported through public funding. In order to qualify for value-added tax exemption, "not-for-profit institutions" must meet the following requirements:

1. The organization must be an association of persons, incorporated or unincorporated.
2. The organization must not carry out a business for profit.
3. The organization cannot be a financial institution.

The VAT exemption is only partial. While exempted organizations do not have to charge VAT on goods and services they sell, they are, however, not allowed to recover VAT paid on goods and services they purchased. Moreover, any "not-for-profit institution" exempted from VAT is obliged to pay a wage tax levied on all wages and salaries the institution pays its employees.[3] Under certain circumstances, this constellation leaves VAT-exempted "not-for-profit institutions" with higher tax liabilities than those imposed on for-profit corporations. The Department of "not-for-profit institutions" within the Revenue Service is authorized to monitor the financial activities of any organizations classified as "not-for-profit institutions" for VAT purposes.

(iii) Capital Gains Tax on Real Estate.   The Capital Gains Tax on Real Estate Law of 1963 exempts gifts of real estate to "public institutions" from capital gains tax duties, even if it defines this donation as a "sale." Likewise, a sale of real property by a "public institution" is tax exempted if the property was held by the "public institution" for at least one year and was directly used for the institution's purposes for at least 80% of the time the property was held by the institution.

(iv) Property Tax.   The Property Tax and Compensation Fund Law of 1961 generally exempts "public institutions" from property tax liabilities.

(b)   Tax Treatment of Contributions—Domestic Organizations

Any person, individual or body corporate, who contributes a minimal sum, not exceeding a certain amount,[4] to a public institution as defined in the Income Tax

---

[3] Another tax imposed on "not-for-profit" institutions is the employers tax, which any employer qualifying as an "exempted institution" has to pay, according to the Employers Tax Law of 1975 (5735).

[4] The amount is subject to change on a year-to-year basis. The maximum amount was NIS 327,000 (approximately $106,169) in 1994 and NIS 335,000 (approximately $108,766) in 1995.

Ordinance, will enjoy a tax credit of 35% of the amount of the contribution, provided this does not exceed 30% of the total taxable income of the contributor. However, the Minister of Finance may annul the privileged classification of an organization as a "public institution" if the organization has failed to file annual accounts for two consecutive years, does not keep its books as legally prescribed, or does not direct all of its activities toward public purposes. The value of gifts of real property is computed as the cost of acquisition.

(c) Tax Treatment of Contributions—Foreign Organizations

Tax credits are granted for contributions to domestic organizations which qualify as "public institutions." Contributions to foreign organizations, however, may be exempted from tax if the foreign organization obtains a certificate from the Israeli tax authorities qualifying it as a "public institution."[5]

§ 13.5 PERSONAL BENEFIT RESTRICTIONS

The NPO Law contains no limitations on the remuneration of members of the board of directors. The determination of board member remuneration is, therefore, left to the general meeting. The Law does state, however, that persons who are employed by the organization cannot serve on the board. There are also no restrictions on personal benefits for staff members. However, as a general rule, salaries should not exceed a reasonable sum in order not to be considered as distributed dividends, which could potentially endanger the tax-exempt status of the organization, since the Department of "not-for-profit institutions" is authorized to annul tax exemption if wages are exceptionally high.

According to the Companies Ordinance and the standard form articles of its Appendix B, directors of guarantee companies are not employees as such of the company, and thus, in principle, not entitled to any payments for their services unless, as is usual, there are respective provisions in the articles. The standard articles contain a clause according to which directors shall be entitled to such remuneration and emoluments as the company may determine by ordinary resolution at the general meeting. The terms of service of any director and his or her terms of employment, in case he or she also holds a salaried position as an officer, shall be approved by the audit committee if such a committee exists, the board of directors, and the general meeting. The Companies Ordinance contains no restrictions on personal benefits for salaried employees or for salaried officers employed in guarantee companies.

According to the Trust Law, as a general rule, trustees are not entitled to payment for their services unless the fulfillment of their duties as trustee is part of

---

[5] Furthermore, the Capital Gains Tax on Real Estate Law contains one reference to a "public institution" that is a foreign resident. According to these regulations, a foreign public institution may be exempted from "acquisition tax" pertaining to shares in a real estate corporation which the foreign institution received as a gift, if the Minister of Finance confirms that (1) a tax is imposed on the reception of such shares in the country of origin of the foreign public institution; and that (2) that country also exempts Israeli residents from any taxes on the receipt of shares in real estate corporations.

their business. In that case, their remuneration should be fixed either in the writ of endowment or by the creator of the endowment or by the court. Trustees are allowed to use the trust property to pay themselves remuneration and expenses and may even detain the property as a guarantee to ensure the reimbursement of the debts owed to them. Trustees are also entitled to reimbursement of expenses incurred in the course of duty.

§ 13.6   OBLIGATIONS TO THE PUBLIC

(a) Fiduciary Responsibilities

On the issue of the duties of directors, the stipulations of the NPO law are somewhat vague and unsatisfactory and do not fully specify the whole set of duties necessary to regulate the behavior of directors of a nonprofit organization whose nondistribution constraint reduces the monitoring incentive of members. In particular, the law states only that a director of a nonprofit association shall discharge his or her duties as a director acting in the best interests of the organization within the framework of its purposes, and in accordance with the articles and the decisions of the general meeting. However, both the general law and common law rules dictate the duties of bona fide behavior and the duty to act with the care and skill which an ordinarily prudent person in a like position would exercise under similar circumstances. There are three individual fiduciary responsibilities of directors that may be derived from these general norms. First, a director is under the duty of disclosure, which means that he or she has to disclose any possible conflict of interests between him or her and the association. Second, he or she may not make a secret profit or divert an opportunity from the organization to himself or herself. Third, directors are forbidden to abuse any of their powers.

Compared to the unsatisfactory arrangement of the NPO law regarding the duties of directors, the Companies Ordinance provides a very specific set of rules concerning the duties of officers and directors. According to the Companies Ordinance, directors and officers shall discharge their duties as directors and officers (1) in good faith, (2) with the care an ordinary prudent person in a like position would exercise under similar circumstances, and (3) in a manner the director reasonably believes to be in the best interests of the company. Furthermore, directors should not put themselves in a position in which their duties to the company may be in conflict with their personal interests. In cases of ordinary commercial misjudgments, the Companies Ordinance permits a business-judgment-rule defense. Although the duties are owed to the company as a whole, other constituencies may have a right to sue the directors and officers under certain circumstances.

The Trust Law stipulates that a trustee must discharge his or her duties in good faith and with the care and diligence an ordinarily prudent person in a like position would exercise under similar circumstances. Trustees should not put themselves in a position of conflict of interest between their personal interests or the interests of another trust they might serve and the interests of the present trust. A trustee has to submit to the Registrar an account concerning the current matters of the endowment. However, a trustee of a public endowment does not have to report to any fiduciaries unless a regulation to that effect appears in the writ of endowment.

(b) Reporting Requirements

According to the NPO Law, nonprofit organizations have to keep the following documents at their registered offices open for inspection by members: (1) a register of members, including names, addresses, identity numbers, the date at which each person was entered into the register as a member, and the date at which any person ceased to be a member; (2) a register of directors, including names, addresses, identity numbers, the date at which each director was appointed, and the date he or she vacated the office; and (3) minutes of all proceedings of general meetings.

In addition, the following documents must be kept for inspection by the general public:

1. The application to register as a nonprofit organization, including the name, objectives, and address of its registered office
2. The name of the founders, their addresses, and identity numbers
3. The articles
4. Any notifications to the Registrar regarding changes in address, directors, members, or articles
5. Minutes of the general meeting ratifying the financial statement and the financial statement itself
6. Any notice of a claim filed against the nonprofit organization or against any director of the organization
7. Any decisions of the general meeting to voluntarily wind up the organization and the name of the liquidator

Furthermore, notifications on the following changes and decisions must be furnished to the Registrar within fourteen days: (1) changes of address, election of new members, appointment of a new director or member of the audit committee, or any vacation of office on the board or in the audit committee; and (2) changes in objectives, name, articles, or the names of the new directors authorized to bind the organization.

According to the Companies Ordinance, every company must keep at its registered office, open to inspection by members and the public at large, a register of members and a register of directors similar to the respective registers of nonprofit organizations. Furthermore, companies have to keep minutes of all proceedings of general meetings open to inspection by members, and have to notify the Registrar of changes in the memorandum or the articles.

With regard to public endowments, the Trust Law stipulates that the trustee must furnish to the Registrar within three months a notification of changes of (1) the name and the address of the creator of the endowment, (2) the creation date, (3) the purposes, (4) the property of the endowment, (5) the name and address of the trustee, and (6) any other matters as specified by the Minister of Justice.

As detailed above, the NPO Law requires nonprofit organizations to install an audit body to provide internal financial oversight, whereas the Companies Ordinance holds no such provisions for guarantee companies. However, while the financial reports of a guarantee company must be audited by an external auditor, the NPO Law does not impose such a duty on an NPO.

(c) Investigations

Investigations into internal affairs of nonprofit organizations, companies, and public endowments may be ordered by the Registrar. The Registrar may appoint an inspector to investigate a nonprofit organization and report on the investigation on application by either one-fourth of the membership or the audit committee. Such appointments may also be made on the Registrar's own initiative, usually initiated by complaints filed by the public. In case of religious organizations, the Registrar has to consult the Ministry of Religions before initiating an investigation. In contrast to the NPO Law, the Companies Ordinance does not authorize the public to request such investigations of nonprofit companies. Here, the application of one-fifth of registered members is necessary along with evidence that the applicants have good reasons for requesting an investigation. With respect to public endowments, the Registrar of Endowments is authorized to open an investigation when he or she suspects a violation of the Trust Law, a breach of the writ of endowment, or a false report to the Registrar.

§ 13.7   BUSINESS ACTIVITY

With respect to business activities of nonprofit organizations, a sharp distinction must be made between the treatment under the Income Tax Ordinance and that under the VAT. The VAT law stresses the criterion of "profit seeking" as the main test for determining whether an institution is considered a "not-for-profit institution" exempted from taxes. A "not-for-profit institution" that occasionally conducts business activity would thus have to pay value-added tax on the commercial part of its activities. Such activities with a commercial character would include the occasional selling of goods or deliverance of services. The Income Tax Ordinance, by contrast, stresses the criterion of "public purpose" as the main test for determining tax exemption. Under the Income Tax Ordinance, therefore, nonprofit organizations will be exempted from corporation tax if their activity is fully aimed at achieving public purposes and they do not distribute dividends to their members. The sources of the funds used to support the institution are not important, however, except that in this respect exempted institutions must avoid conducting a "business." The problem, however, is that the Ordinance does not define the word "business," which has thrown the matter to the judiciary. Although far from precise, the main criteria used by the courts to define a "business or trade" are the recurrence or frequency test, which focuses on whether business-type revenue occurs only occasionally or is recurrent; and the management test, which examines the identity of the body that controls and manages the business. However, in practice, the ambiguity and lack of an exact definition of the word "business" has led to the reclassification of some "public institutions" whose expenses have not exceeded their income as nonexempt institutions on the grounds that they conducted a business or trade instead of promoting their public purposes.

Generally speaking, however, under the Income Tax Ordinance, nonprofit organizations are permitted to engage in business activities and will not lose their exemption from corporation taxes under the Income Tax Ordinance if profits resulting from these activities are immediately and exclusively used for the organization's public purposes. Thus, the possibility exists that a body corporate can, be exempted from corporation tax while still being obliged to pay value-added tax, even if its profits from business activity are used for public purposes.

§ 13.8 OTHER FUNDING RESTRICTIONS

Generally speaking, there are no specific funding restrictions in the relevant laws. However, nonprofit organizations that derive substantial portions of their revenues from contributions in the form of very long term "loans," most of which are actually never paid back, are likely to find themselves classified as business associations carrying out the business of a financial institution.[6] Therefore, nonprofit organizations in danger of reclassification must limit the number and amount of such "loans" they arrange in a given period.

Another problem with respect to funding restrictions is that recurrent contributions to a nonprofit organization may be classified as taxable income from "commercial" activity for the organization, if they meet the tests of recurrence and frequency.

Apart from these issues, there are requirements relating to the registration and bookkeeping of donations. According to Income Tax Authorities' bookkeeping regulations of 1992, a "public institution," whose turnover exceeds NIS 500,000 (approximately $162,338) or which employs at least 10 employees, must register the names of its donors. Every donation has to be registered and a receipt given to the donor. Likewise, local and foreign donations have to be registered as well.

§ 13.9 POLITICAL ACTIVITY

Neither the NPO Law nor the Companies Ordinance contain any restrictions on political activities by nonprofit organizations or companies, respectively, except that such activities may not be illegal. Political parties may not incorporate under the NPO Law, but must register in compliance with the Political Parties Law of 1992. According to this Law, a candidate is forbidden to receive donations from domestic or foreign corporations within nine months before the election day. However, this prohibition shall not apply to the support offered by a party to its members who are candidates in the campaign.

§ 13.10 KEY OUTSTANDING ISSUES

(a) Revision of Companies Law

In the fall of 1995, a draft of a new Companies Law was published and approved by an interministerial committee dealing with legislative affairs. This proposal, if

---

[6] These donations are defined as "loans" following a Jewish custom of a secret donation—the "rich" and "well-off" contribute to charity-funds established in synagogues and gain the satisfaction of doing a *Mitsva* (good deed). The "poor" receive this money as a "loan" and avoid the shame of admitting their inability to pay back.

accepted by Parliament, will adjust the legal framework for companies to modern business realities and recent developments.

More specifically, the proposed law intends to deal exclusively with commercial companies. Therefore, the provisions governing public utility companies in the present law would be cancelled. Consequently, the possibility of dropping the suffix "Limited" from the name of public utility companies would be annulled. Although a company could still be formed as a limited nonprofit company without share capital, it would not be entitled to the presently granted preferential treatment anymore. However, the new law would not be retroactive, meaning that existing public utility companies would still be governed by the legal arrangement currently in force. In addition, this change would not necessarily affect the tax status of the organization. Thus, for tax purposes, the tax authorities might recognize limited nonprofit companies registered without share capital as corporations which comply with the criteria established for "public institutions" and "nonprofit organizations." Thus, the NPO law will remain the sole legal arrangement to regulate the formation and administration of nonprofit organizations.

(b) New Proposal of Public Endowments Law

In the winter of 1996, a draft of a new Public Endowments Law was published. Its main principles are as follows:

1. A registered public endowment will have to be an incorporated and separate entity.
2. All registered public endowments will be exempted from paying income tax and property tax.
3. Trustees are awarded remuneration as of right. Yet, they are exposed to closer monitoring.

CHAPTER FOURTEEN

Italy[*]

§ 14.1 LEGAL CONTEXT

Italy is a civil law country that provides strong constitutional guarantees for the right to associate and a number of specific laws for nonprofit activities, but no general body of legislation directly applicable to the whole nonprofit sector. Rejecting Italy's fascist past, the Italian Constitution of 1948 explicitly acknowledges[1] that people belong to different social groupings and guarantees freedom of association,[2] religious freedom,[3] freedom of trade unions, and legitimacy of political parties.[4] While the constitution confers primary responsibility for the provision of such important services as health care and social insurance on the state,[5] it also expressly sanctions private institutions to provide such services as well.

Beyond these constitutional provisions, nonprofit organizations are affected by the general regulations on private organizations laid down in the Civil Code (*Codice Civile*), in tax legislation pertaining to noncommercial enterprises enacted in 1986, and in two recent laws pertaining, respectively, to "voluntary organizations"[6] and social cooperatives.[7] These latter laws have in turn been supplemented by regional legislation filling in details that the national laws left open for local determination.

§ 14.2 ELIGIBILITY

(a) Types of Organizations

Reflecting the absence of any overarching law on nonprofit organizations, such organizations take a wide variety of forms in Italy. Most organizations adopt structures similar to the basic forms of private organizations spelled out in the Civil Code. These include associations, both "recognized" and "unrecognized"; foundations; and cooperatives. However, in addition to these basic forms there are other types of nonprofit organizations. The most important of these are the IPABs (*Istituzioni Pubbliche di Assistenza e Beneficenza*) or Public Welfare and Char-

* Country Rapporteurs: Dr. Marta Cartabia, Stobe University of Milano, Italy; Dr. Francesco Rigano, Teremo University, Italy; Daniela Mesini, Instituto per la Riceica Sociale of Milano, Italy; and Dr. Gian Paolo Barbetta, Catholic University of Milano, Italy. This Chapter is based on a legal field guide for the Johns Hopkins Comparative Nonprofit Sector Project.
[1] Article 2.
[2] Article 18.
[3] Article 19.
[4] Article 49.
[5] Articles 32 and 38.
[6] Law 266 of August 11, 1991.
[7] *Cooperative sociali*—Law 381 of November 8, 1991.

ity Institutions, which are part public and part private institutions. In addition, recent legislation has carved a new type of organization out of these others, namely the "voluntary organization," and has established a new type of cooperative called a *social cooperative*, which is closer to a nonprofit organization than the traditional cooperative.

(i) Unrecognized Associations.   Associations are groups of people who join together to pursue a common aim. They are covered by Book I of the Civil Code, Title II, articles 11 to 42. Associations assume legal existence as soon as they are formed and are under no obligation to register with any public authority. In fact, most of Italy's associations, including some of the best known ones, are not recognized. One reason for this is that the privileges secured by gaining recognition are not deemed sufficiently strong to justify the effort.

(ii) Recognized Associations.   While legal recognition is not common among Italian associations, associations may acquire legal personality (*personalità giuridica*) status by securing "recognition" from the President of the Republic, the President of the region, or the Prefect (who represents the national government at the provincial level). In this way, they gain limited liability for the organizations' members, officers, and board. (For a discussion of the procedures for recognition, see section 14.2(d)).

(iii) Foundations.   Foundations are organizations based on a bequest or similar donation provided for the pursuit of a specific purpose laid down in an act of constitution. Although the Civil Code is not entirely clear on the question of whether a foundation may be established without having sought and obtained official recognition, such recognition is necessary to establish the legal personality (*personalità giuridica*) of a foundation, which opens the possibility of receiving bequests and limits the liability of those managing the organization (*responsabilità limitata*).[8] Besides the general definition of the Civil Code, many different laws, most of them passed before the approval of the Civil Code (1942), regulate particular types of foundations with specific aims. These include *family foundations*, regulated by Royal Decree 99 of 1891, whose aim is to provide social and educational services to the members—or the offspring—of one or more families; *educational foundations*, regulated by Royal Decree 1297 of 1928 and by Presidential Decree 3 of 1972, whose aim is to provide economic support to deserving students in financial difficulty; *university foundations*, regulated by Royal Decrees 1592 of 1933 and 1269 of 1938, whose aim is to increase attendance at universities and to support deserving students with loans and subsidies; *military foundations*, whose aim is to support the members of the army and their families in case of economic hardship; *religious foundations*, regulated by the Concordat of 1929 and the laws—approved in 1985—amending the Concordat, including many different types of organizations with religious or social welfare aims; and *bank foundations*, created in 1990. (See section 14.10 of this chapter.)

(iv) Cooperatives.   A cooperative is essentially a mutual aid organization designed to help its members, usually in material rather than monetary terms,

---

[8] F. Galgano, *Le associazioni, le fondazioni, i comitati* (Padova: Cedam, 1987), p. 135.

for example, by providing work, goods, or services for their members under better conditions than are available on the open market. Cooperatives are thus a hybrid type of organization, not pursuing profit yet delivering benefits to a particular class of people (their members) rather than to society at large. Reflecting this, the Civil Code describes them as a "third type" (*tertium genus*) of organization between businesses and associations.[9]

While cooperatives have been viewed by some scholars as more economic than social in focus and therefore not really appropriately a part of the nonprofit sector, in fact the cooperative form has also been used to carry out social objectives as well. In fact, Law 381 of 1991 explicitly established the category of "social cooperatives" (*cooperative sociali*), cooperatives that extend beyond "mutual help" to "pursue the general interest of the community by helping people and encouraging social integration." Such social cooperatives are free to operate in the fields of health and education, and can operate in other fields as well so long as the focus is on helping disadvantaged people, defined as the physically or mentally handicapped, ex–drug offenders, and alcoholics. Social cooperatives must register with the regional authorities and subject themselves to inspection by the Ministry of Employment and Social Security. In turn, they enjoy a variety of tax and other privileges that will be outlined more fully below.

(v) *Voluntary Organizations.* Law 266 of 1991 established a cross-cutting category of nonprofit organizations called "voluntary organizations." Voluntary organizations do not enjoy any special legal status and can opt for any legal form compatible with the social ends that they pursue.[10] This implies that they cannot register as business organizations or opt for any of the commercial legal forms covered by Book V of the Civil Code. Moreover, Circular 3 of 1992 of the Department of Treasury established that voluntary organizations cannot register as cooperatives because this legal status is not compatible with the altruistic and solidaristic aims that the voluntary organizations must pursue. In line with these restrictions, voluntary organizations typically take the legal form of association.[11]

What differentiates "voluntary organizations" is less their legal form than their voluntary character. In particular, they are defined as organizations that (1) work toward some social end; (2) have more volunteers than paid employees; (3) operate without profit motive; (4) have democratic organizational structures; (5) are open, free of charge, to anyone interested in their aims; and (6) provide services free of charge.[12]

Organizations that meet these conditions are required to sign on to a register of the appropriate region or autonomous province, providing an organizational governing statute or other document that verifies that the above conditions are being met. Once registered, organizations are entitled to a number of special benefits. Specifically, in contrast to other nonrecognized associations, voluntary organizations can acquire real estate necessary for the conduct of their activities, regardless of whether they have legal personality or not. They may also accept

---

[9] Book V of the Civil Code, Title VI, articles 2511 to 2548.
[10] Law 266 of 1991, article 3(2).
[11] Book I of the Civil Code.
[12] Law 266 of 1991, article 3(2).

bequests and donations as long as these are used for the organization's statutory aims.[13] Furthermore, once registered for at least six months, voluntary organizations are allowed to subcontract for services with the state, the relevant region, provinces, or local authorities. Finally, as detailed more fully below, voluntary organizations are entitled to certain tax advantages not available to other noncommercial associations. Further details about the operation of "voluntary organizations," for example, the definition of the fields in which voluntary work can be undertaken, have been left to the regional governments.

(vi) *Public Welfare and Charity Institutions (IPABs).*   A fourth type of nonprofit organization in Italy are the so-called *Istituzioni Pubbliche di Assistenza e Beneficenza* (IPABs). IPABs were originally Church-sponsored private organizations known as *Opere Pie* engaged in charity work at the community level. They were converted to "public" status under the Crispi Law in 1890[14] as part of a more general effort by the secular authorities to limit the influence of the Church in Italian life. While imposing "public status" on these organizations and subjecting them to public regulation, however, the Crispi Law permitted them to retain much of their former private character in order to avoid infringing on the intentions of their benefactors. Many even continued to be operated by Church personnel, in fact, though this varied by region. In addition to the rules establishing state control over the IPABs, therefore,[15] other rules encourage private involvement. Recently, however, the Italian Constitutional Court ruled[16] that the Crispi Law was not constitutional and that the IPABs should be given the opportunity to reconvert to private status, but on a case-by-case basis. This process of conversion is now underway, at least in some regions.

(b) Types of Purposes

Nonprofit organizations are generally required to be organized for purposes other than the pursuit of profit. However, this is not a formal requirement of the law, but more a logical consequence of it. Indeed the Italian Civil Code does not distinguish between nonprofit and for-profit organiztions, but only between organizations established for money-making purposes[17] and organizations established for purposes other than the pursuit of profit.[18] Another form that, under certain circumstances, is suitable to nonprofit activity is the cooperative.[19]

In addition, article 18 of the constitution grants freedom of association for purposes that are not against the law. In accordance with this article, secret associations and associations that carry out, even indirectly, political purposes with a military structure are forbidden. Moreover, public control of the activity and purposes of associations comes through the process of recognition of the legal personality. (See section 14.2.d of this chapter).

[13] Law 266 of 1991, article 5.
[14] Law 6972 of July 17, 1890.
[15] For example, articles 44 to 50 of Law 6972 of 1890; articles 23 and 24 of Royal Decree 2841 of 1923.
[16] Ruling 396 of April 7, 1988.
[17] Book V of the Civil Code, Title V, articles 2247 to 2510.
[18] Book I of the Civil Code, Title II, articles 11 to 42.
[19] Book V of the Civil Code, Title VI, articles 2511 to 2548.

The law does not require nonprofit organizations to serve people other than members. In fact, Italian nonprofit organizations can be divided into organizations that pursue the benefit of their members and organizations that benefit the whole community or an appreciable section of it. The border between these two categories is not easy to define, in fact, organizations can help both thier members and society at large (e.g., a social or a sport club). Moreover, what constitutes "public benefit" is often difficult to specify and can vary greatly, depending on local circumstances and traditions.

In the case of foundations, the Italian Civil Code does not prescribe or list any specific aims that a foundation should pursue, except the purpose must be of "public interest."

More specific eligibility requirements are imposed on particular types of organizations. Thus:

- *Voluntary organizations* are required to work toward some social end and to do so without a profit motive.[20] However, article 1 of Law 266 of 1991 also mentions the intention to encourage projects not just in the social, but also in the "civil, and cultural spheres," suggesting a broader set of purposes. These purposes can then be further refined by regional and local authorities.
- *Cooperatives* operate according to a "mutual" principle, allowing them to focus primarily on the needs of their members rather than others in the society.
- *Social cooperatives* as defined by Law 381 of 1991 are required, unlike regular cooperatives, to pursue not just the interests of their members, but "the general interest of the community by helping people and encouraging social integration."[21] Such organizations may operate automatically in the fields of health and education, and may also operate in other fields so long as they provide significant benefits to the "disadvantaged," defined as the physically or mentally handicapped, ex–drug addicts, and alcoholics.

(c) Other Requirements

There are no explicit guidelines concerning member or capital requirements for creating associations or foundations under Italian law. However, if an organization chooses to seek recognition, that is, legal personality, the relevant authorities have considerable discretion to reject an application on the grounds of insufficient members or financial base to carry out the intended aims.

(d) Registration Procedures

(i) *Associations and Foundations.* If an association or foundation seeks legal personality, it must apply for recognition, which may be granted by the President of the Republic or by the President of one of the twenty regions in Italy

---

[20] Law 266 of 1991, article 3(2).
[21] Law 381 of 1991, article 1.

if the organization will only operate within the area of the respective region.[22] Law 241 of 1990 describes in detail the procedure that associations and foundations must follow in order to be "recognized." The application, addressed to the proper Minister, must be submitted to the Prefect of the province where the organization is going to operate with the following documents: (1) four copies of the charter; (2) a report, in four copies, on the activity that the organization is going to undertake; (3) a report, in four copies, of the economic and financial situation of the organization; (4) budgets and final balances approved over the last three years, or before the submission of the application, if the organization already operated as an unrecognized association; and (5) a list of board members and the total number of members (in case of associations).

Acceptance of an application for recognition is at the discretion of the relevant authority. The most frequent cause for rejection is that the association or foundation is deemed to be ill-equipped to carry out its stated function due to either too few members or insufficient financial base.[23] Once recognized, the association or foundation must enroll on the *registro prefettizio delle persone giuridiche* (Prefect's Register of Legal Bodies), as detailed in article 33 of the Civil Code.

(ii) Voluntary Organizations.   Article 6 of Law 266 of 1991 states that qualifying voluntary organizations have to sign on to the register of the appropriate region or autonomous province. Registration involves filing the statute or other documents clearly stating that the conditions, as outlined in article 3(2) of the Law, are being adhered to. The registering authority is responsible for monitoring registered voluntary organizations and can delete organizations from the register in the event of irregularities.

(iii) IPABs.   There are no separate registration procedures for IPABs. In fact, IPABs that remain in the public domain are, more or less, considered to be public bodies. On the other hand, IPABs that have truly broken away from the public sector and have requested private incorporation are not treated differently from other associations and foundations as defined by the Civil Code. Therefore, the documents that must be filed for recognition are those listed above.

§ 14.3   INTERNAL GOVERNANCE

Italian law provides only general rules about the internal governance of nonprofit organizations and leaves detailed regulations to the charter and the bylaws of the organization itself.

The organizational structure of foundations is based on directors, who exert the ultimate authority and oversee the management. They can be appointed either

---

[22] The Civil Code originally stated that only the President of the Republic could grant recognition, unless he delegated this duty to another competent body. Traditionally, the prefects of the Italian provinces were given the right to recognize organizations whose operations were restricted to a specific province. After the creation of regions in 1977, this power was transferred to the regional Presidents by Presidential Decree (DPR 616 of July 24, 1977).

[23] M. V. De Giorgi, "Associazioni—Associazioni riconosciute," In *Enciclopedia giuridica Treccani*, vol. III, Roma, 1988.

by the founder or by third parties and their responsibilities are regulated by articles 18, 19, and 33 of Book I of the Civil Code. Election procedures for directors, their number, roles, and powers must be specified in the charter and the bylaws of the organization. In addition to the board of directors, the charter can also provide for other organs, such as executive or auditors' committees.

Broadly speaking, similar internal governance provisions apply to associations (and therefore for voluntary organizations and IPABs). However, while foundations are based on endowments, associations are based on members. Accordingly, the board of directors is elected or nominated by the members and exercises its authority at the pleasure of the membership, which often retains power over the most imporotant decisions. The membership can convene when necessary or upon written request of one-tenth of the members. A member can resign at any time. However, members can be expelled for only serious reasons. Members leaving an association cannot reclaim subscription fees nor can they lay claim to the assets of the association.[24]

Social cooperatives have three distinct types of members: the so-called *soci prestatori*, members who work in the cooperative; *soci fruitori*, members who can satisfy their needs thanks to the activity of the cooperative; and *soci volontari*, volunteers. At least 30% of the people working in a social cooperative must be disadvantaged people (physically or mentally handicapped, ex–drug addicts, alcoholics) and, when possible, they should be members of the cooperative.[25]

§ 14.4 TAX TREATMENT

(a) Tax Treatment of Organizations

Under Italian tax law, the absence of a profit motive has never been a rationale for granting tax exemption to organizations. Nonprofit organizations, therefore, do not automatically enjoy a privileged position as far as liability for Italian taxation is concerned. Rather, the key to whether an organization is liable for tax is whether it carries out commercial activities, as defined in article 2195 of the Civil Code. According to this article, the following activities are considered as "commercial": (1) industrial activities aimed at the production of goods and services; (2) brokering for the circulation of goods; (3) land, sea, and air transport; and (4) activities that are auxiliary to the former. Activities other than those listed are considered as noncommercial. The exact application of this principle varies considerably by type of tax and type of organization, however.

(i) Corporate Income Tax. The Italian Fiscal Law 917 of December 22, 1986 (the so-called *Testo Unico delle Imposte sui Redditi*) deals with all income taxes for both individuals and businesses (IRPEF, IRPEG, ILOR).

Regarding corporate income tax, the legislation does not distinguish between nonprofit and for-profit organizations, but rather between commercial and non-

---

[24] Article 24 of the Civil Code.
[25] Law 381 of 1991, article 4.

commercial bodies as well as commercial and noncommercial activities.[26] The crucial distinction between commercial and noncommercial activities, addressed in this law, is based on article 2195 of the Civil Code, described above. Generally, commercial bodies include organizations regulated by Book V of the Civil Code (public stock companies, limited liability companies, and cooperatives) and organizations regulated by Book I of the Civil Code (associations and foundations) that carry on business regularly. On the other hand, noncommercial bodies include both public- and private-sector organizations whose objects do not include carrying on a commercial activity. The law assumes that commercial bodies carry out commercial activities and therefore taxes their whole income, whatever its origin. Noncommercial bodies can carry out either commercial or noncommercial activities. Income produced from commercial activities is taxed, even if these activities are carried out by noncommercial bodies; income generated by noncommercial activities is not taxed when the following three conditions are met: (1) the activity is in line with the stated aim of the organization; (2) services are supplied without any specific organizational structure (that is without a professional structure able to operate continually in a competitive market); and (3) the fees for the services do not exceed the actual costs of producing them.[27]

In addition to these general regulations, there are a number of special provisions for *associations* under Italian law. Thus, for example:

- Associations and other organizations offering social or cultural services or operating sporting facilities are exempt from taxation even on commercial activities, and even when their fees exceed their costs, so long as these activities are carried out for the benefit of their members or members of organizations with a similar function; and if both organizations are members of a local or national association. However, these concessions have been reduced for nonrecognized cultural or sports associations by Law 537 of 1993.[28]
- Charitable and cultural organizations may claim a 50% reduction on any income tax due.[29]
- The activities of nongovernmental organizations are not considered to be commercial as long as the organization is recognized by the state or the European Union. The same is true of volunteer associations of blood-donors, notwithstanding the conditions stated in article 111 of the 1986 law. This article deals with the distinction between commercial and noncommercial activities of noncommercial organizations that take the form of associations. According to this article the following activities should be considered as "noncommercial:" (1) activities, in line with the stated aim of

---

[26] Article 87 of the *Testo Unico*.

[27] Article 108 of the *Testo Unico*.

[28] In particular, services for adult members are exempted only if (1) these members have voting rights with regard to amendments of the constitution concerning internal governance issues; and (2) they have the right to a share of the proceeds in the event the association is dissolved, unless such proceeds are devoted to social aims.

[29] Article 6 of Presidential Decree 601 of 1973.

the organization, carried out toward the members of the association; and (2) associative subscriptions or contributions (paragraph 1).[30]

- *Voluntary organizations*, under Law 266 of 1991, are granted exemption from corporate tax (IRPEG) and ILOR (a local income tax) on those parts of their income derived from occasional production and commercial activities if these are clearly intended to further the aims of the organization itself.[31]
- Law 398 of 1991, which originally applied only to voluntary sports associations, was extended to all nonprofit organizations and to so-called pro-loco organizations working locally for the development of tourism and cultural activities. Under this law, organizations with commercial income not exceeding one hundred million Lire are exempted from filing a full tax declaration, which would determine their corporate tax, VAT, and local income tax liabilities, but can declare a token amount.

The tax treatment of *foundations* does not differ from that of nonprofit organizations in general. Accordingly, income produced from commercial activities is subject to regular corporate income taxation, while income generated by noncommercial activities is not taxed so long as the three conditions stated by article 108 of the Testo Unico are met.[32] In effect, foundations enjoy some special advantages: for example, according to article 6 of Presidential Decree 601 of 1973,[33] foundations that carry out activities in the areas of social services, hospitals, education, research, and culture enjoy a 50% reduction of their corporate income tax. Moreover, income generated from parks and gardens that admit people free of charge, as well as income generated by buildings used as museums, libraries, art galleries, or archives are tax exempt. As a further incentive, foundations can deduct costs incurred for "maintenance and restoration of the artistic and cultural heritage" from their income.

(ii) Value-Added Tax. Services provided by nonprofit organizations are generally exempt from VAT, unless these services are provided on a regular basis as part of a commercial activity. In addition, according to Presidential Decree 633 of 1972, contributions and membership fees to associations, as well as financial contributions made by public bodies, are also exempt from VAT, unless these contributions represent payments for services. Nonprofit organizations always have to pay VAT on their purchases.

---

[30] On the other hand, notwithstanding the regulations of article 108, assignments of property and the provision of services to members for which fees are charged, together with additional subscriptions or contributions, are considered as "commercial" activities (par. 2), except if provided by political, religious, charitable, cultural, sportive associations, and labor unions (par. 3). Paragraph 4 of article 111 lists activities that are always subject to taxation, including the sale of new goods; water, gas and light distribution; and the administration of meals, even if carried on by organizations described in par. 3.

[31] Law 266 of 1991, article 8(4).

[32] However, there is a slight difference in the treatment of associations and foundations. More specifically, the 1986 fiscal law introduces a particular distinction between commercial and noncommercial activities of associations, but it does not provide an analogous section for foundations.

[33] Amended by article 66 of Decree 331 of 1993.

(iii) Invim.   Invim, a tax based on the increase in real estate values, was abolished in 1993. It used to be paid when the real estate was sold or after ten years of possession of real estate. The functioning mechanism of Invim, however, will keep it alive until December 31, 2002. Until then, noncommercial organizations will have to pay this tax (even if they are eligible for a 50% discount) on buildings which are not used for institutional purposes.

(iv) Other Taxes.   Nonprofit organizations also enjoy other fiscal benefits. Presidential Decree 131 of 1986 established total exemption from registration tax for donations and bequests to organizations not engaged in commercial activities; Legislative Decree 504 of 1992, article 7, stated that real estate used by noncommercial bodies for recreational, charitable, health, religious, cultural, and sportive activities is not subject to taxation.

Additional tax advantages are provided by special legislation for voluntary organizations and social cooperatives. More specifically, Law 266 of 1991, article 8 provides exemption from stamp duty for the charters and other legal documents and tax exemption for all donations and bequests to voluntary organizations, in addition to exemption from VAT, IRPEG, and ILOR. Law 381 of 1991, article 7, paragraph 2, grants a reduction to 25% of all taxes arising from mortgages and property taxes of buildings or land acquired by social cooperatives in the pursuit of their aims. Article 3 of Presidential Decree 637 of 1972, Law 381 of 1991 also exempts social cooperatives and recognized associations and foundations from tax for donations and bequests.

(b) Tax Treatment of Contributions—Domestic Organizations

Tax deductions for charitable contributions are a relatively recent, and still limited, phenomenon in Italy. According to the 1986 law on tax treatment of associations,[34] *individuals* may generally set against income tax donations up to a maximum of 2% of net income, but only for donations to recognized associations operating on a nonprofit basis that are involved in (1) study, research, or documentation to promote cultural or artistic endeavors; (2) the promotion of cultural activities, such as theaters; and (3) improving conditions or sponsoring cooperation projects in developing areas.

According to article 65 of the *Testo Unico, corporations* can deduct donations to (1) legal persons working toward educational, recreational, research, or religious ends as well as those providing social or health services and (2) nongovernmental organizations up to a total of 2% of their income. Moreover, corporations can also deduct donations to (1) universities; (2) legal persons based in southern Italy, conducting research; and (3) bodies undertaking activities in the field of performing arts up to an additional 2% of their income for each category. In addition they can deduct donations to private foundations, associations or cooperatives operating community radio stations up to an additional 1% of their income. Donations to bodies promoting cultural and artistic events can be deducted without any limits.

The 1991 Law on Voluntary Organizations (par. 3) authorizes much broader deductions for contributions to this special class of organizations. According to

---

[34] Articles 10 and 13-bis of the *Testo Unico.*

this law: (a) individuals will be able to write off up to two million Lire a year against their income tax; and (b) companies can write off 50% of the amount donated up to 2% of the company's declared income or 100 million Lire. However, these concessions have not yet come into force.

In addition to these general deductions, the recent Concordat with the Catholic Church and the respective pacts with other churches offer financial incentives for religious giving. For example, the 1985 Concordat allows citizens to deduct up to two million Lire per year for donations to the clergy[35] and similar measures are in effect for the Seventh-day Adventist Church and Pentecostal Churches.[36] Moreover, since 1989, Italian taxpayers have the option to designate 8/1000 (0.08%) of their actual income tax liability to either the Catholic Church, the Assembly of God, the Seventh-day Adventists, or the Valdese Protestants. Other faiths may join this list. To make such a designation, a form must be signed and filed with the annual tax return. If this form is not signed, the money will automatically be divided between the government and the Catholic Church.

As far as the Jewish faith is concerned, the *Unione delle comunità israelitiche* (Union of Jewish Communities) decided not to take part in the "eight per thousand" program. However, donations to the Jewish Communities are tax deductible up to 10% of declared income to a maximum of 7.5 million Lire per annum.

(c) Tax Treatment of Contributions—Foreign Organizations

Article 16 of the preliminary provisions of the Civil Code states that foreign recognized organizations must be treated like Italian ones. Therefore, donations and contributions made by Italian individuals or corporations to foreign recognized organizations can be deducted from the taxable income of the donors following the rules established by articles 10 and 65 of the *Testo Unico*. Foreign organizations, however, must be legally recognized and should pursue social aims. Contributions made to Italian organizations by foreign individuals or corporations are treated according to the law of the donors' country.

§ 14.5 PERSONAL BENEFIT RESTRICTIONS

At present, the law does not prohibit distribution of personal benefits to members of nonprofit organizations, with the exception of general criminal laws covering theft, embezzlement, and so on. Some restrictions are included in a new bill (the so called Zamagni bill) now under discussion. When passed, the new law would prohibit (1) the payment of annual wages to officers higher than those stated by the law for the president of the syndacal committee of joint-stock companies; and (2) payments to third parties for activities not directly in line with the stated aim of the organization for an amount higher than 10% of the income of the accounting period.

---

[35] Law 222 of 1985, article 46.
[36] Articles 30 and 21 of the respective agreements.

What is more, Italian law does not generally prohibit the distribution of profits to members or shareholders, even in the case of associations. That said, it is generally understood that organizations created for purposes other than making profit (such as associations, foundations, legally recognized ecclesiastical bodies, and voluntary organizations) should not distribute any net returns. Profit distribution is explicitly prohibited only for professional football clubs, which are not considered part of the nonprofit sector, and for cooperatives (although to a limited degree). According to Presidential Decree 601 of 1973, cooperatives cannot distribute dividends greater than the legal rate of interest (10%), if they want to enjoy some fiscal advantages. Moreover, a recent law[37] states that this limit can be increased to 12% in the case of a particular class of members (the so-called *soci sovventori*, members who are allowed to invest a higher share of capital compared to normal members). Cooperatives not willing to exploit fiscal advantages are not subject to any restriction in the distribution of profits, but they have to put 20% of their annual profit into statutory reserves. Thus, even though the law sets limits to the distribution of profits, those limits are reasonably high.

In the case of voluntary organizations, volunteers may not have employment contracts; nor can they have any claim to the assets of the organization for which they are volunteering.[38] However, volunteers may be reimbursed for expenses incurred.

§ 14.6   OBLIGATIONS TO THE PUBLIC

Closely related to personal benefit restrictions and to limitations on the purposes of nonprofit organizations are responsibilities toward the public. Generally, nonprofit organizations entering into contractual relationships with public bodies are subject to controls and inspections aimed at evaluating their performance and their expenditures. Something more is then provided by the special legislation.

However, specific laws create additional provisions for certain types of organizations.

- *Voluntary organizations.* Article 6 of Law 266 of 1991 states that voluntary organizations should be recorded in a regional register. Registered organizations will be controlled by the regional authorities and could be dissolved when they do not follow the law. Only registered voluntary organizations can enter into contractual relationship with public bodies.
- *Social cooperatives.* Each cooperative shall have a registered constitution, as laid down in article 2518 of the Civil Code. Moreover, Law 381 of 1991, article 9, states that social cooperatives must enroll in a special section of the cooperatives register.

All cooperatives are subject to inspection by representatives of the Ministry of Employment and Social Security as set out in Decree 1577 of 14 December 1947. Social cooperatives are subject to inspections at least once a year. Should viola-

---

[37] Law 59 of 1992.
[38] Law 266 of 1991, article 2.

tions be discovered, the Ministry may work with the relevant regional authority to establish what is to be done and within what time-scale.[39] In the event that the violations are not put right by the members of the cooperative itself, the Ministry can order the cooperative to be struck off the Prefect's register, which means that it loses its tax and other concessions.

§ 14.7   BUSINESS ACTIVITY

Under Italian law, nonprofit organizations (except cooperatives) must principally pursue noncommercial activities. Nevertheless, business activities are permissible, but income from commercial activities is subject to taxation. Income produced by noncommercial activities, however, is tax exempt as long as the conditions stated in article 108 of the *Testo Unico* are met (see section 14.4(a) of this chapter).

§ 14.8   OTHER FUNDING RESTRICTIONS

So far, the Italian law has not established any ceilings on fund-raising or administrative costs. The proposed Zamagni bill, mentioned above, however, provides for the creation of a national authority that will be in charge of ensuring the use of gifts and donations for the purposes intended by the donors.

§ 14.9   POLITICAL ACTIVITY

Generally, there are no restrictions concerning political activities of nonprofit organizations under Italian law. Although, historically, nonprofit organizations have rarely independently engaged in political activities, individual organizations are increasingly beginning to perform advocacy functions to obtain collective benefits (such as the removal of architectural barriers, or obtaining transport services for the physically handicapped) or the recognition of rights that do not seem sufficiently guaranteed by existing laws (such as the right to free treatment for persons suffering from a variety of diseases, or the fight for the right not to be discriminated against by HIV-positive persons). The most well-known examples are the *Tribunale dei diritti del malato* (Tribunal for the Rights of the Sick) and the numerous specialized associations that limit themselves to a single form of handicap such as the muscolar distrophy, multiple sclerosis, and Alzheimer's disease associations, and so on. Another example is the *Forum del Terzo Settore,* or Third Sector Forum, which represents the first real attempt of Italian nonprofit organizations to associate together in defense of their own interests in a politically autonomous role.

---

[39] Law 381 of 1991, articles 3 and 6.

§ 14.10   KEY OUTSTANDING ISSUES

(a) New Legislative Initiatives

Over the last few years, a number of new laws promoting nonprofit activities, such as Law 266 of 1991 on voluntary organizations and Law 381 of 1991 on social cooperatives, have been enacted in Italy. This development is important in two respects. First, it demonstrates that the Italian legislature has begun to acknowledge the existence as well as the importance of the nonprofit sector and the need for an improved legislative structure for it. Second, however, developments to date indicate that Italy's lawmakers are not so much interested in assisting the nonprofit sector as a whole but in fostering certain areas of its operation, particularly those that have a social output as is the case with voluntary organizations and social cooperatives. Indeed, a new law on organizations with a "public utility" purpose is now under consideration.

In fact, in December 1996, the Italian Parliament directed the government to issue, within nine months, a Legislative Decree aimed at reorganizing the tax treatment of nonprofit organizations. This decree will probably follow the so-called Zamagni bill, promoted by the government in the last legislature. The bill aims at: (1) simplifying the tax treatment of nonprofit organizations, in coordination with other laws; (2) improving incentives for donations made to some nonprofit organizations; (3) granting fiscal advantages to some nonprofit organizations; and (4) simplifying the registration procedures.

The bill also introduces a new category of organizations, called ONLUS (*Organizzazioni Non Lucrative di Utilità Sociale*) and states that only these organizations are eligible to receive tax privileges. Generally, foundations, associations, social cooperatives, and other private organizations, recognized and unrecognized, except commercial bodies, with a solidaristic and a public utility purpose and carrying on charitable, cultural, sportive, educational, research, artistic, or naturalistic activities can qualify for ONLUS status. The bill grants special fiscal advantages to these organizations: (1) exemption from IRPEG for income produced through commercial activities, if in line with the aims of the organizations; (2) exemption from stamp duties for charters and other legal documents; (3) exemption from Invim; and (4) tax exemption for all donations and bequests. Moreover, ONLUS would be charged with the lowest rate (4%) of VAT on registered real estate and personal property they purchase. The Zamagni bill further proposes that directors should be responsible for the activities undertaken by the organization and establishes the ultimate authority of the membership. It also imposes a well-defined nondistribution constraint and creates a national authority in charge of supervising the performance of the organizations and the transparency of their fund-raising procedures.

(b) Bank Foundations

Bank foundations represent a new type of organization in the world of Italian grant-making institutions. They are the outcome of the transformation of many semipublic-sector banks into stock companies, set in motion by Law 218 of 1990 (the so called "Amato law," after the name of the Treasury Minister who promoted it) and some following decrees. Affected by this law were about one hundred *Casse di Risparmio* (savings banks) and a few *Istituti di Credito di Diritto Pubblico*—registered associations or foundations—which represented a strange hybrid of banking and charitable activity. While acting much like normal banks, their charters forced them to donate large percentages of their profits to charity.

The process of transformation, started by the Amato law and still to be completed, created two different sets of organizations: (1) some new banks with the legal status of joint stock companies able to compete on an equal footing with ordinary private banks and (2) a significant group of foundations (now about 80) whose endowments consist of the stocks of the new banks. These foundations should act as grant-making bodies funding activities in the fields of health, social services, culture, recreation, research, and so on. These banking foundations should be considered as public bodies, but the process of transformation into fully private foundations is underway, along with the process of diversification of their endowments now almost exclusively represented by stocks of the banks.

(c) Privatization of IPABs

A second key issue in Italian nonprofit law concerns the status of the IPABs created under the Crispi Law of 1890. The Italian Constitutional Court's ruling in 1988,[40] revoking the Crispi Law's effort to absorb all the IPABs into the public sector, has produced a complex process of institutional remetamorphosis that the courts are attempting to handle by means of a judicial review on a case-by-case basis. The result is a considerable degree of ambiguity about the rights and responsibilities of this important set of institutions and the relationships they bear to the rest of the nonprofit sector.

(d) Treatment of Cooperatives

A peculiar feature of the Italian nonprofit scene is the widespread presence of cooperatives and mutual societies, many of them now performing what in other countries would be considered "charitable" functions. A key issue in any further development of nonprofit law in Italy will therefore concern how to treat these cooperatives. Since many of them adhere to a "mutuality" principle rather than a "nonprofit distribution" principle, use of the "nonprofit distribution constraint" as a way to define the nonprofit sector is not likely to work in Italy. At the same time, it will be necessary to continue the process begun by Law 381 of 1991 to differentiate between those cooperatives serving essentially public purposes and those serving essentially the private purposes of their members. This may be a politically charged process in Italy, however, given the strength and influence of the cooperatives.

[40] Ruling 396 of April 7, 1988, point 4.

CHAPTER FIFTEEN

Japan[*]

§ 15.1 LEGAL CONTEXT

Japan is a civil law country that requires, in article 33 of its Civil Code, that private juridical persons, whether profit-making or nonprofit, "cannot be established without sanction of the Civil Code and other statutes." However, there is no single body of law that authorizes the creation of nonprofit organizations. Rather, separate bodies of law exist for various types of such organizations. These include: article 34 of the Civil Code for "public-interest corporations" (*koeki hojin*), which include incorporated foundations (*zaidan hojin*) and incorporated associations (*shadan hojin*); and separate laws for nonprofit medical corporations, social welfare corporations, private school corporations, and others.

The establishment of such organizations is not considered to be a right in Japan. Rather, it is more like a privilege granted by the government. This is reflected in the legal principles of *permission* and *approval*, which essentially hold that the establishment of nonprofit organizations requires the specific approval, and is at the discretion, of the relevant authorities even if the legally prescribed conditions are satisfied.

In addition to the Civil Code, permission for setting up public-interest corporations and the supervision of such organizations are spelled out in government and ministerial ordinances prescribed by competent authorities.

§ 15.2 ELIGIBILITY

(a) Types of Organizations

The main legal types of nonprofit organizations in Japan are the *public-interest corporations* (which include both incorporated associations and foundations), *private school corporations, social welfare corporations, religious corporations* and *medical corporations.*[1]

(i) *Public-Interest Corporations.* The public-interest corporation (*koeki hojin*) is the generic form of a nonprofit organization in Japan. It is essentially an

---

* Country Rapporteur: Dr. Takako Amemiya, Professor of Law and Dean, Department of Business Management, Shoin College, Atsugi City, Japan. This chapter is based on a legal field guide of the Johns Hopkins Comparative Nonprofit Sector Project.
[1] Originally, private school corporations, social welfare foundations, religious corporations, and so on, were included in the "public-interest corporations" category. However, the enactment of the Private School Law, the Social Welfare Service Law, and the Religious Corporation Law after World War II separated these types of organizations from the general category.

organization that is formed to serve the public good in the sense of serving many, unspecified people; that is not intended to earn a profit; and that has the approval of the competent ministry in its proposed area of activity.

Two types of such public-interest corporations exist in Japan: (1) associations (*shadan hojin*); and (2) foundations (*zaidan hojin*).

1. *Incorporated Associations (shadan hojin).* The *shadan hojin* is a group of persons pursuing a public-interest purpose that has been authorized by a competent governmental authority. Once registered and incorporated, it has a will as an organization separate from the will of individual members, exists regardless of changes in the size of its membership, and acts as a single legal entity. The *shadan hojin* operates under a Charter of Association and is governed by the general assembly of all the group members (*shain sokai*), which is the highest decision-making organ.

2. *Incorporated Foundations (zaidan hojin).* Unlike a *shadan hojin*, which is formed by its members, a *zaidan hojin* is essentially formed around a pool of assets and comes into existence to ensure that an endowed fund donated for a public-benefit purpose will be maintained and managed in order to serve the purpose stipulated by the donor. Since a *zaidan hojin* does not have members, it is governed by a board of directors in accordance with the basic rules laid down by its founders in the charter of the foundation.

(ii) Private School Corporations. Private School Corporations, which usually take the form of incorporated foundations, are juridical persons set up under the Private School Law[2] for the purpose of founding private schools and are the only agencies authorized to found schools besides the state or local governments.[3] Such corporations must have necessary facilities and equipment or sufficient funds to obtain them as well as sufficient property to operate a school.[4] As long as these requirements are fulfilled and the Charter of Association conforms with the law, private school corporations will be approved.[5]

(iii) Social Welfare Corporations. According to the Social Welfare Services Law,[6] social welfare corporations are corporations that are established to benefit society by providing either of two broad types of social welfare services: first, any of a list of so-called Type I services that only government agencies or social welfare corporations can provide (e.g., relief or rehabilitation facilitates, infant orphanages, homes for the aged); or second, any of a list of 12 additional types of social services that can be provided by a broad range of organizations, including social welfare corporations (e.g., the provision of daily necessities, the operation of maternity clinics, the operation of welfare centers for the aged). (For a more complete listing of these allowable services, see section 15.2(b)).

---

[2] Law No. 270 of 1949.
[3] School Education Law, Section 2(1).
[4] Private School Law, Section 25.
[5] Private School Law, Sections 30, 35–50, etc.
[6] Law No. 45 of 1951.

(iv) Religious Corporations.   Religious corporations are religious organizations (*shukyo dantai*) that have become corporations under the Religious Corporation Law[7] to gain legal competency in order to facilitate the maintenance and management of their assets, including facilities for worship, and the fulfillment of their organizational purpose. The Religious Corporation Law defines religious organizations as organizations whose main purposes are to propagate religious teachings, perform rituals, and teach and foster a group of believers. Included are (1) shrines, temples, churches, monasteries, and similar organizations, as well as (2) religious denominations, schools, orders, churches, dioceses, and similar organizations.

(v) Medical Corporations.   Medical corporations (*iryo hojin*), as defined by the Medical Law,[8] are incorporated associations and foundations that, with the official approval of a prefectural governor, establish and operate hospitals, clinics staffed by full-time physician(s) or dentist(s), or health facilities for senior citizens.[9] Medical corporations can also engage in (1) educating people in medical services; (2) the establishment of medical and dental study facilities; and (3) duties related to other hygienic matters. Under the medical law, for-profit corporations are prohibited from providing medical treatment, leaving the management of hospitals and clinics entirely to nonprofit medical corporations. However, in operating such institutions, medical corporations are not required to adhere to the same "public-interest" standard of Section 34 of the Civil Code which other nonprofit corporations are subject to. As will be noted below, the tax law reflects this and treats medical corporations as "ordinary corporations."

(b) Types of Purposes

As a general rule, public-interest corporations as defined in the Civil Code, article 34, may pursue any of a variety of purposes that are not profit-seeking and for the benefit of society in general or for many and unspecified persons. As examples of such "public-interest" activities, article 34 of the Civil Code lists "worship, religion, charity, academic activities, and art and craft." In addition, there are a number of other activities or services, such as health improvement, environmental preservation, international exchange, and so on, that are also considered to be for public benefit.

Since such corporations must actively serve the interest of many, unspecified people,[10] the establishment of a public-interest corporation is not approved for mutual benefit purposes, such as (1) fostering mutual friendship, communication, and exchange of views among the members of an alumni association or asso-

---

[7] Law No. 126 of 1951.

[8] Law No. 205 of 1948, Sections 39 and 44.

[9] "Hospital" refers to a facility that can house 20 or more patients, in which physician(s) or dentist(s) provide medical or dental service to the public or unspecified citizens. Similarly, "clinics" are facilities offering medical or dental services to the public or unspecified citizens having either no in-patient accommodations or the capacity to house fewer than 20 patients (Medical Law, Section 1D).

[10] See "The Standards for the Permission of Establishment and Guidance of the Management of Public-Interest Corporations" adopted September 20, 1996 by the Cabinet directive.

ciation of like-minded persons, (2) promoting the welfare and mutual relief of members of a specific organization or a specific occupation only, or (3) extending spiritual and/or economic support to specific individuals.

Furthermore, purposes that, in the judgment of the competent government authorities, undermine the law and order of the country are also not considered to be of "public interest" even if favored by the public at large. Examples include efforts to promote the building of nuclear shelters and to educate people about the collapse of the capitalist system. Indeed, the determination of whether a purpose is eligible for public-interest status is ultimately at the discretion of the competent governmental authority, which must approve each separate application for public-interest corporation status.

In addition to these general definitions of eligible purposes, more specific purposes are spelled out in the laws authorizing each of the separate types of public-interest corporations. Thus, as we have seen, for example, the eligible purposes for social welfare corporations are spelled out in a complex set of social welfare laws.[11]

---

[11] Generally, Japanese law differentiates among a number of social welfare service types. The main ones, however, are Type I services, which only the national and local governments and social welfare corporations may conduct, and Type II services, which may be conducted by a wider range of organizations, including social welfare corporations. In contrast to Type I services, organizations engaged in the provision of Type II services do not face limitations on their operations, as long as they notify the governor of the prefecture where such services are being rendered (Social Welfare Services Law, Section 64).

Type I social welfare services include the operation of (1) "relief facilities" (*kyugo*), "rehabilitation facilities" (*kosei*), or other institutions designed to provide asylum and livelihood relief for those in need, either free of charge or at low cost, or to support the burial of the indigent according to the National Assistance Law; (2) infant orphanages (*nyujiin*), homes for fatherless families (*boshiryo*), centers for the protection of neglected or abused children (*yogo*), institutes and day-care centers for mentally handicapped children, facilities for blind, deaf, and mute children, physically weak or handicapped and severely handicapped children, as well as institutions for short-term medical care of children suffering from emotional disorders, and juvenile reformatories (*kyugoin*) in accordance with the Child Welfare Law; (3) homes for the aged (*yogo rojin homu*), special homes for the aged (*tokubetsu yogo rojin homu*), and low-cost homes for the aged (*keihi rojin homu*) under the Welfare Law for the Aged; (4) institutions for rehabilitation, medical care or vocational training of the disabled, and homes for the physically handicapped as described in the Physically Handicapped Welfare Law; (5) rehabilitative institutions or vocational aid centers for the mentally handicapped according to the Mentally Disabled Welfare Law; (6) "protective homes for women" (*fujin hogo*) under the Anti-Prostitution Law; (7) public pawnshops, vocational training facilities, and institutions providing loans to those in need, either free of interest or at low interest; and (8) community chests.

Among the twelve items listed as Type II services (Social Welfare Services Law, Section 2(3)), the major ones are (1) the provision of daily necessities, including food and clothing, (at their homes) or the money necessary to obtain them, to the needy, or counseling related to problems of daily life; (2) the operation of maternity clinics, day care centers or children's welfare facilities (including after-school day-care centers) as well as the provision of counseling for the promotion of children's welfare as described in the Child Welfare Law; (3) the operation of fatherless families' welfare facilities in accordance with the Mother and Children and Widows Welfare Law; and (4) the operation of welfare centers for the aged under the Old-Age Welfare Law.

Social welfare corporations dedicated to community chest activity, which is a Type I service under the Social Welfare Services Law, Section 72(1), are called "Community Chest Socie-

(c) Other Requirements

(i) *Membership and Capital Requirements.*   There are no laws on membership and capital requirements of Japanese nonprofit organizations. However, *private school corporations* must have the necessary facilities, equipment, and funds to operate a school, and *social welfare corporations* must possess assets required to undertake social welfare services.[12] The same applies to medical corporations.

In addition, on September 20, 1996, the ministerial cabinet adopted a resolution, entitled "Standards for the Permission of the Establishment and Guidance of the Management of Public Interest Corporations." Generally, these standards require public-interest corporations to have a solid financial basis to be able to sustain activities to achieve their missions. In the case of public-interest corporations incorporated as associations, the standards require associations to have sufficient income from membership dues and capital assets to manage their activities. The number of members and the amount of capital assets necessary depend on the association's purposes and activities and are not specified in the standards. However, in administrative practice, associations are required to have at least a few tens of millions of yen at their disposal. Similarly, public-interest corporations incorporated as foundations must have sufficient income from the initial endowment as well as sustained income from financial contributions. Although there is no lower limit for assets specified by law, the standards suggest that the endowment should be large enough to allow the corporation to operate. In the light of the currently low interest rates in Japan, the administration requests initial endowments of at least several hundred millions of yen.

(ii) *Permission Requirements.*   As indicated above, public-interest corporations are subject to the rule of permission, which is set forth in article 34 of the Civil Code. Explicit permission from the competent authorities is thus required for the establishment of such corporations. In this context, "competent authorities" refers to national government agencies, that is, the Prime Minister's Office or the ministry with jurisdiction over the public-interest activity of any given corporation. For example, if the main area of activity is international exchange, the competent authority is the Ministry of Foreign Affairs. The competent authority in the realm of culture, arts, and science is the Ministry of Education, Science and Culture, and that in the realm of welfare is the Ministry of Health and Welfare, and so forth. If a corporation serves purposes that come under the jurisdiction of two or more agencies, permission must be obtained from each competent ministry. Such cases are called *kyokan* ("joint jurisdiction"). The authority to grant permissions may be delegated by government ordinance to the heads of the national government's local departments, prefectural governors, or prefectural boards of education.[13]

ties" (*kyodo bokin kai*) and are the only type of organizations allowed to engage in community chest activities [Social Welfare Services Law, Section 72(2), (3)]. The Japanese Red Cross Society is a public-interest corporation under the Japanese Red Cross Society Law (Law No. 305 of 1952), but it is regarded as a social welfare corporation under Section 7 and other provisions of the Social Welfare Services Law.

[12] Social Welfare Services Law, Section 24.

[13] Article 83A of the Civil Code.

(d) Registration Procedures

(i) Public-Interest Corporations. An application for permission to establish a public-interest corporation involves the submission of a number of specified documents to the government agency with jurisdiction over the activities the corporation intends to engage in.[14] Each competent agency has its own rules and regulations concerning the establishment and supervision of public-interest corporations as well as the documents required for application. Generally, however, the major documents necessary are the following:

1. A prospectus specifying the significance of, and purposes for setting up, the proposed corporation and the proposed activities
2. A Charter of Association or Charter of Foundation specifying the corporation's name, location of offices, purpose, nature of activities, board members, property managers, rules for convening meetings, and so on
3. A list of assets by type and their total value (differentiated among property already owned, property to be donated to the organization after its establishment, and expected revenue)[15]
4. A certification regarding the title to assets and their value, which must also include a record of contributions, a bank certification of deposits, and certified copies of real property registration
5. A written plan of activities and financial estimates for the first two years
6. Names, addresses, and brief resumes of founders and directors and their written acceptance of appointment[16]
7. For associations, a list of charter members as well as a list of people to join the organization after its establishment with an application form attached
8. The minutes of the founding general meeting for associations or charter member meeting for foundations
9. An outline and balance sheet if the organization has already engaged in activities

If an existing voluntary organization is dissolved, in order for a new association to take over its activities, the activity reports, balance sheets, and financial statements of the last three years should be submitted.

Whether or not to grant permission is entirely at the discretion of the competent authority. Once permission is granted, registration is no more than a condition for asserting its establishment vis-à-vis third parties.

[14] Prior to the establishment of public-interest and other nonprofit corporations, an association or foundation must be set up. In the case of foundations, an endowment must be established and a charter of the organization prepared. Associations must prepare a Charter of Association at a founding general meeting before a representative can apply for permission for establishment.

[15] In the case of foundations, the endowment is divided into core endowment and operating assets.

[16] In the case of associations, a list of persons present at the founding general meeting (charter members) and of the names of directors and auditors appointed after the founding must be included. In the case of foundations, the names of the founders (charter members) as well as directors and auditors named after the founding is necessary. If a board of trustees is set up, a list of trustees must also be attached.

(ii) Private School Corporations.   Applications for approval of the establishment of a private school corporation must include a Charter of Association specifying:

1. The purpose of its founding
2. The name of the private school corporation
3. The name of the private school to be founded
4. The location of its administrative offices
5. Bylaws
6. Regulations relating to trustees and the board of trustees
7. Stipulations concerning property and accounts
8. Types of proposed activities and rules for the conduct of profit-making activities if intended
9. Stipulations regarding abolition or dissolution
10. Regulations concerning changes in the Charter of Association
11. Means of public notification

In addition to the Charter of Association, the application must also include:

1. A prospectus
2. A specification of the endowment
3. A list of property
4. Written resolutions of founding
5. A plan of operations and budget for the first two years of operation
6. The school location, the arrangement of school grounds, and the layout of buildings, dormitories, and so on
7. Documents certifying the title to real estate and other major properties
8. An appraisal of the value of real estate and other major properties
9. Documents testifying to the authority of the representative founder
10. Resume and identification papers of the founder
11. Written statements of acceptance of appointment, resumes, and identification papers for the members of the board (directors and auditors)
12. Documents showing that for each member of the board, there is no more than one other member related by blood (third degree) or marriage to that member
13. School regulations
14. A form recording the endowment

The competent authorities, that is, either the Minister of Education or the prefectural governor, decide upon approval or disapproval after examining, among other matters, whether the proposed private school corporation has sufficient property to meet the requirements spelled out in Section 25 of the Private School Law, and whether the content of the Charter of Association conforms with the law. In this process, the competent authorities must consult either the Council for Private Schools (*Shiritsu Gakko Shingikai*) or the Council for University Chartering and School Juridical Persons (*Daigaku Settchi/Gakko Hojin Shingikai*). If all requirements are satisfied, approval may not be withheld.

After receiving the approval of the Minister of Education or the prefectural governor, a private school corporation comes into existence upon completion of the required registration procedures at the registration office with jurisdiction in the district, where the corporation's main office is located in accordance with the Association Registration Ordinance.

(iii) Other Corporations. Similar requirements and procedures apply to the other types of nonprofit corporations.

1. *Social Welfare Corporations.* Social welfare corporations must file a Charter of Association very similar to those of private school corporations as listed above, and apply for approval of establishment to the governor of the prefecture where they are located or to the Minister of Health and Welfare if they will operate in two or more prefectures.[17] Applications are approved after the competent authorities determine that (1) the assets of the proposed social welfare corporation conform with Section 24 of the Social Welfare Services Law stipulating that a corporation "has sufficient assets to undertake social welfare activities"; (2) the content of the Charter of Association fulfills the requirements set down in law; and (3) the procedures followed in applying for approval of establishment do not violate the laws. In contrast to private school corporations, a consultation with a third party is not necessary.

A social welfare corporation comes officially into existence by registering after receiving approval at the locality of its main office. As in the case of private school corporation, registration is a condition of establishment, and approval is assured as long as legal and other requirements are satisfied.

2. *Religious Corporation.* In order to receive legal status as a religious corporation, an organization must draw up bylaws as prescribed in the Religious Corporation Law and present them, along with other required documents, to the prefectural governor with jurisdiction over the area where the organization's main office is located, or to the Minister of Education if the religious corporation embraces religious corporations in other prefectures. Only after these bylaws are approved by the competent authority can a religious corporation be founded.[18]

When the decision is made to deny approval, or insufficient documentation makes it impossible to confirm whether the requirements for approval have been fulfilled, the applicant will be given an opportunity to provide clarification within a certain period of time. If the competent authority is the Minister of Education, a denial of approval may be made only after consulting with the Religious Corporation Council.[19]

3. *Medical Corporation.* A medical corporation may be founded only after obtaining the official approval of the prefectural governor. An "extended area medical corporation" (*koiki iryo hojin*), which is a medical corporation planning to

[17] Social Welfare Services Law, Section 28A; and Section 29.
[18] Religious Corporation Law, Section 12.
[19] Religious Corporation Law, Section 14(1)–(3).

operate hospitals in two or more prefectures, must be approved by the Minister of Health and Welfare. Applications for approval must be submitted to the governor of the prefecture where the main office is to be located, or to the Minster of Health and Welfare, and must include, in addition to the standard materials mentioned above, documentation pertaining to the kind of medical care to be provided and the number of regular staff to be employed in the hospital or clinic to be founded, as well as the location and a map of the grounds, the layout of facilities, floor plans of buildings, and a plan of operation and budget for two years after opening.

Prior to arriving at a decision on approval or disapproval, the prefectural governor or Minister of Health and Welfare should consult the Prefectural Medical Council, or, in the case of the MHW, the Council on Medical Service Facilities (*Iryo Shingikai*). Approval must be granted for the founding of a medical corporation as long as the content of the application fulfills the prescribed requirements.

§ 15.3   INTERNAL GOVERNANCE

The Japanese civil code stipulates that the internal governance of an incorporated association must be specified in a Charter of Association, which spells out the relations between the association and its staff, the role of representatives, the management of general meetings of the members, quorum requirements, the procedures for care of organizational property, and related matters. The code also defines the general assembly of all members of the association as the highest decision-making organ and stipulates that decisions must be by majority vote. Similar Charters are required of most other types of nonprofit corporations, though the details may vary slightly.

In the case of foundations, where no members exist, management authority is vested in a board of directors, subject only to the basic rules, charter of foundation laid down by the founders.

Beyond this, the only explicit provision of the Japanese Civil Code pertaining to internal governance issues of nonprofit organizations is the stipulation that every incorporated association and foundation must have a board with more than one member. However, the "Standards for the Permission of the Establishment and Guidance of the Management of Public Interest Corporations," as adopted by the ministerial cabinet on September 20, 1996, provides further guidelines. According to these standards, the number of board members should appropriately reflect the size and activities of the organization; the boards of incorporated associations should be elected by the general assembly and, as a rule, a board of counselors should select the board members of incorporated foundations;[20] in cases where several members of the same family or company, or officials of the competent ministry, serve on a board, their number should not exceed one-third of total board members. The standards also require the appointment of more than one auditor.

---

[20] Boards of Counselors also appoint auditors and, more generally, serve in an advisory function.

These guidelines supplement the more specific provisions of the special laws governing the respective types of nonprofit corporations. The social welfare services law stipulates that social welfare corporations must have more than three board members and more than one auditor and a board of counselors at least twice the size of the board of directors. Similarly, private school corporations are legally required to have more than five board members, more than two auditors, and also a board of counselors twice the size of the board of directors. The medical law stipulates more than three board members and more than one auditor for medical corporations. In the case of religious corporations, the law does not require a board of directors, but more than three executives, one of which must legally represent the corporation and be responsible for its activities.

§ 15.4 TAX TREATMENT

(a) Tax Treatment of Organizations

(i) Public-Interest Corporations. Nonprofit corporations that engage in activities for the benefit of society as a whole rather than the pursuit of profits are given favored treatment in tax law in Japan. Most significantly, such corporations are exempt from corporate income tax except for income derived from profit-making activities.[21] Such activities include 33 specific types of activities named in article 5(1) of the Enforcement Ordinance of the Corporation Tax Law. Although such activities are taxed, however, the rate is set at 27%, which is substantially below the 37.5% rate imposed on for-profit corporations. This is done to balance the tax burden between public-interest corporations and profit-making corporations while taking account of the fact that nonprofit corporations set aside the gains from such activities for public-interest purposes while for-profit corporations are free to split up the profits among the owners of the corporation.

In addition to the lower tax rate on income from business activities, public-interest corporations are also permitted to exempt up to 20% of such income from even the lower tax rate if they use them for so-called "constructive contributions" (*minashi kifukin*), that is, contributions to expand their activities for the public good.[22]

Public-interest corporations are also exempt from tax on the dividends and interest they earn from their endowment funds and from stamp duties levied on *teikan* (the Charter of Association). Furthermore, no tax is levied on the registration of titles to real property, such as school buildings, used directly for educational purposes or on real property for use in relief and rehabilitation programs. However, public-interest corporations are subject to consumption tax, securities transaction tax, local taxes, and other indirect taxes.

(ii) Other Specialized Public-Interest Corporations. The basic provisions applicable to general public-interest corporations also apply to the more specialized public-interest corporations such as social welfare corporations, private

---

[21] Corporation Tax Law, articles 4 and 7.
[22] Article 37(4).

school corporations, and religious corporations, albeit with some exceptions. Thus, for example, in contrast to public-interest corporations, private school corporations and social welfare corporations are allowed to deduct the higher of 50%, or ¥2 million, of the income they earn from their profit-making activities as "constructive contributions" exempt even from the reduced business income tax. Similarly, the lists of business activities that different types of corporations can engage in vary somewhat among the different types of corporations. Thus, for example, under the Private School Law, the competent authorities can stipulate—after consultations with the Council for Private Schools (*Shiritsu Gakko Shingikai*), the Council for Private Universities (*Shiritsu Daigaku Shingikai*), or the Council for Vocational Colleges (*Koto Senmon Gakko Shingikai*)—lists of profit-making activities for private school corporations that are not necessarily identical with the list in the Enforcement Ordinance of the Corporation Tax Law. Thus, for example, agriculture and fisheries are considered "profit-making activities" permissible under the Private School Law, but are not included among the 33 types covered by the corporation tax. They are therefore tax-free. Similarly, for *religious corporations* the rental of burial grounds is not considered a profit-making activity even though the rental of real estate generally is one of the 33 types of profit-making business activities as listed in article 5 of the Corporation Tax Law Enforcement Ordinance.[23]

(iii) Medical Corporations.   Generally, medical corporations do not enjoy the same tax incentives as other nonprofit corporations. Rather, they are taxed like for-profit corporations. Therefore, they are subject to full corporation tax,[24] corporate residence tax, business tax, and fixed property tax. However, business tax does not apply to medical fees reimbursed by the social insurance system.

An important exception are so-called "special medical corporations" (*tokutei iryo hojin*).[25] These are medical corporations that the Finance Minister finds to make such a considerable contribution to the promotion of medical care, social welfare, and other causes in the public good as to warrant the same tax treatment accorded to other public-interest corporations. For these organizations, the corporate tax rate is set at 27%. These corporations are also exempted from the inheritance tax and from tax on real estate acquisitions for nurses' training facilities.

---

[23] For social welfare corporations, the following profit-making activities are not taxable:

(1) Profit-making activities supporting the livelihood of physically handicapped or mentally retarded workers or workers on relief if more than half of the social welfare corporation's workers fall in these categories

(2) Activities conducted during the term of redemption by a child and maternal welfare organization of a loan from child and maternal welfare funds under the Child and Maternal Welfare Law (*Boshi fukushi ho*), or such activities as vendor sales within public facilities undertaken by women without spouses or by a child and maternal welfare organization

(3) Medical and health-related services conducted by a social welfare corporation or the Japanese Red Cross Society

[24] The corporation tax rate is 37.5% for corporations with a capital of ¥100,000,000 or more and 28% for corporations with a capital of less than ¥100,000,000 earning not more than ¥8,000,000 per year.

[25] Article 67A of the Exceptions to Tax Laws Act.

(b) Tax Treatment of Contributions—Domestic Organizations

The tax treatment of contributions in Japan varies by the type of donor, the type of donation, and the type of recipient organization and purpose. In addition, while the tax treatment is outlined in law, much is also left to the discretion of governmental authorities, particularly the Minister of Finance.

(i) *Cash Donations by Individuals.* Generally, individual donors may deduct from their taxable income each year cash contributions, known as "public-interest contributions" (*koeki kifukin*), that do not exceed the equivalent of 25% of their total annual income minus ¥10,000. Such contributions are only deductible, however, if they are directed to any of three types of organizations: (1) units of national or local government; (2) organizations designated by the Minister of Finance for so-called "designated contributions" (*shitei kifukin*); or (3) "special public-interest-promoting corporations" (*tokutei koueki zoshin hojin*).[26]

1. *Designated Contributions.* Designated contributions are contributions to public-interest corporations and other corporations and organizations that undertake activities for the public good and that, in the judgment of the Minister of Finance, meet certain additional requirements. According to article 78(2)-[2] of the Income Tax Law, these requirements are that the contributions (1) are raised from the public at large and (2) are certain to be used to meet urgent needs in the promotion of the public good, such as furthering education, science, and culture, or improving welfare services. Before designating contributions as eligible for this treatment, moreover, the Ministry of Finance must examine the activities to be supported by the contributions the organization is soliciting, the target amount to be raised and from whom, and the period during which the contributions will be raised. If the Ministry is satisfied, it then announces that the contribution qualifies as a "designated contribution" eligible for deduction up to the limit noted.

2. *Contributions to "Special Public-Interest-Promoting Corporations."* Contributions to "Special Public-Interest-Promoting Corporations" are contributions made to a special set of corporations identified in article 217 in the Enforcement Ordinance of the Income Tax Law. These "special public-interest corporations" are different from the "public interest corporations" defined in article 34 of the Civil Code. Included are the following:

1. Twenty-six corporations based on special laws, such as the Japan Safe Driving Center, the National Institute for Research Advancement, the Japan Foundation, and the Japan Scholarship Society
2. The Japan Amateur Sports Association, the Institute for International Studies and Training, and nine other specified public interest corporations
3. The organizations designated under article 11(2)-[7] of the Enforcement Ordinance of the Japan Scholarship Association Law
4. Private school corporations

[26] Income Tax Law, article 78(2)-[3].

5. The organizations for providing relief and rehabilitation programs (for criminal offenders) as defined in Article 2(2) of the Rehabilitation Protection Law[27]

6. Social welfare corporations

7. Those public-interest corporations authorized by article 34 of the Civil Code that, in the judgment of the Minister of Finance, have appropriate management and accounting systems, achieve reasonable results on a sustainable basis, do not provide directors and employees any special benefits from the contributions raised, and principally devote their energies to any of a specified list of activities, including:

   (i) Conducting experiments and research in the natural sciences

   (ii) Making grants to persons engaged in experimentation and research in the natural sciences

   (iii) Providing general education and dissemination of knowledge and ideas on the natural sciences

   (iv) Making grants for outstanding nationwide research in natural science

   (v) Assisting education at schools defined in article 1 of the School Education Law

   (vi) Making grants or giving loans for student school expenses or for setting up and managing dormitories

   (vii) Establishing and operating lodging and training facilities for teachers and students from many of the universities and colleges defined in article 1 of the School Education Law

   (viii) Conducting wholesome social education for young people on a national scale

   (ix) Promoting appreciation of the arts

   (x) Preserving and utilizing of "cultural properties" as defined in Article 2(1) of the Cultural Properties Protection Law,[28] or of historic sites as defined by Article 2(2) of the Special Measures Law Concerning the Preservation of Historic Sites in Ancient Capitals[29]

   (xi) Extending economic (and technological) cooperation to overseas regions in the process of economic development

   (xii) Extending overseas economic (and technological) cooperation and managing public facilities located in regions to which the Japanese government provides gratuitous aid

   (xiii) Promoting understanding of Japan overseas

   (xiv) Making grants to those engaged in "promoting the understanding of Japan overseas" as mentioned above and so on.[30]

---

[27] *Kosei Hogo Jigyo Ho*, Law No. 86 of 1995.

[28] Law No. 214 of 1950.

[29] Law No. 1 of 1966.

[30] In addition to those listed, other types of activity qualifying a "public interest corporation" as a "special public interest corporation" eligible for tax deductible gifts include:

   (xvi) Volunteer guidance and counseling for law offenders, inmates of juvenile rehabilitation schools, and others nationwide

   (xvii) Nationwide legal action support programs for the poor

Altogether, 900 Civil Code public-interest corporations have been identified as meeting these requirements and therefore eligible for tax deductible gifts as special public-interest-promoting corporations.

While private school and social welfare corporations are considered special public-interest-promoting corporations eligible for tax-deductible gifts as specified above, donations to religious and medical corporations are not deductible.

(ii) Donations of Individually Owned Property. Donations of individually owned property to public interest corporations are generally subject to transfer income tax as if the owner received income calculated at the market value of the property.[31] Such a property donation can be exempted, however, if (1) it is made to the national or local government;[32] or (2) it is made to a public-interest corporation or another corporation engaged in public-benefit activities that are specifically declared tax exempt by the Commissioner of the National Tax Administration Agency on grounds that (a) the donation makes a substantive and direct contribution to the promotion of education, science, culture, social welfare and other areas of public benefit; (b) the donated property will serve, or is likely to serve, the public-interest purpose of the donee within two years from the date of contribution; and (c) the contribution will not unreasonably lessen the income tax burden of the donor or the inheritance or donation tax burden of the donor's relatives or persons with special relationship with the donor.[33]

The requirement that the contribution "directly" serve the public-interest purpose is especially strictly enforced. Thus, if such property is used to produce income for the donee's public-interest purpose (e.g., rental income from a donated apartment building) but is not directly used in the conduct of the public-interest purpose, the Commissioner of the National Tax Administration Agency will not consider the donation as tax exempt and the donor will be liable for transfer income tax.

(iii) Donations of Inherited Property. If recipients of inherited property or recipients of properties under the will of deceased persons donate such properties to a public-interest corporation, they are exempted from inheritance tax as long as the contributions are made to qualified public-interest corporations.[34] As

(xvii) Preservation and breeding of wildlife for protection of the natural environment if commissioned by the national or local government

(xviii) Preserving and utilizing important natural environments

(xix) Promoting reforestation of national lands

(xx) Discouraging drug and other stimulant abuse as part of crime prevention campaigns, and preventing juvenile delinquency and encouraging healthy growth of young people nationwide

(xxi) Nationwide rescue operations for sea disasters

(xxii) Conducting two or more types of the activities listed above in combination

[31] By contrast, corporations may donate property as general contributions and deduct the donation within the limits described above.

[32] Exceptions to Tax Laws Act, first half of the provision of article 40(1)

[33] Exceptions to Tax Laws Act, second half of the provision of article 40(1).

[34] Article 70(1), Exceptions to Tax Laws Act.

defined in article 40B of the Enforcement Ordinance of the Exceptions to Tax Laws Act, the qualified public-interest corporations here are essentially the same as the special public-interest-promoting corporations defined above, with a few exceptions. In particular, this benefit also extends to corporations that found and operate libraries as defined in article 2(1) of the Libraries Law, and museums as defined in article 2(1) of the Museums Law. However, special public-interest-promoting corporations engaged in (1) student and teacher training, (2) guidance and counseling for law offenders, and so on, and (3) rescue work in sea disasters, cannot qualify for this tax benefit.

(iv) Corporate Donations.   The tax treatment of corporate contributions is even more complicated than that for individual contributions. Three types of contributions are distinguishable:

- First, contributions to government as well as "designated contributions" as defined above are entirely deductible without limits.
- Second, contributions to special public-interest-promoting corporations as defined earlier are subject to a deductibility limit, which varies among different types of corporations. For regular business corporations, the deductibility limit is determined by a formula that takes both the size of the corporation as well as its disbursement capacity into account.[35]
- Third, corporate donors also have the additional option to make "general contributions" (*ippan kifukin*), which are contributions not directly related to their business activities. These general contributions are not restricted to public benefit purposes, but may also be given to other types of activities, such as political fund-raising events. Maximum deductible amounts are determined through the same formula that applies to contributions to special public-interest-promoting corporations. However, the maximum amount for general contributions is computed separately from that of contributions to special public-interest-promoting corporations, meaning that the maximum amount effectively doubles if a business makes both types of contributions.

(c) Tax Treatment of Contributions—Foreign Organizations

As there are no special legal provisions concerning the deductibility of donations to foreign nonprofit organizations, the same restrictions that apply to contributions to domestic organizations apply to foreign organizations. In practice, this means that individuals cannot claim deductions for such donations, since foreign organizations do not fall within the three categories of entities eligible for such deductions as specified in article 78 of the Income Tax Law (see above). However, business corporations have the option to deduct such donations to foreign organizations as general contributions.

---

[35] More specifically, the maximum deductible amount equals half of the sum of .25% of the corporation's capital discounted by the share of the year the capital is held plus 2.5% of the income for the term. Corporations having neither capital nor invested funds may deduct up to 2.5% of their income.

Grants from foreign organizations to Japanese nonprofit corporations are tax exempt on the grounds that only income from profit-making activities is subject to taxation. Similarly, so long as these organizations meet the standards of Japanese nonprofit law, no limits apply to Japanese public interest corporation grants to foreign nonprofit entities. Finally, grants from foreign organizations to Japanese individuals can be tax exempt as is the case with the Nobel Prize.

§ 15.5 PERSONAL BENEFIT RESTRICTIONS

Public interest corporations are prohibited from distributing accrued profits among members. The laws governing the other major types of nonprofit corporations (i.e., the Private School Law, the Social Welfare Services Law, and the Religious Corporation Law) impose similar restrictions. Also, Section 54 of the Medical Law stipulates that surpluses of funds cannot be divided among the employees, who are contributors to the medical corporation. Finally, the laws on charitable tax deductions stipulate that contributions to special public-interest corporations are deductible only if the directors and employees of the recipient organization do not receive any special gains from the contributions raised.

More generally, article 57 of the Civil Code stipulates that board members of public interest corporations shall not represent the organization in transactions, in which these board members have private interests. In such cases, a special representative must be appointed to handle the transaction in the place of the board member in question.

§ 15.6 OBLIGATIONS TO THE PUBLIC

Incorporated associations and foundations are required to submit to the appropriate ministry annual activity and financial reports for the past year as well as planned activities reports and budget estimates for the coming year. However, neither the ministry nor the organization is obliged to make such reports available to the public at large. The only type of organizations that must publicize their activity and financial reports annually are charitable trusts.

Religious corporations are legally obliged to inform both stakeholders and members of their faith about the establishment, any disposition of assets, mergers, dissolution, and the like.[36] Social welfare corporations must publicize mergers and bankruptcies and notify creditors at the time of dissolution of the organization.

§ 15.7 BUSINESS ACTIVITY

(a) Public-Interest Corporations

In Japan, public-interest corporations are allowed to engage in profit-making activities, though, as noted earlier, the proceeds of such activity are taxed, albeit

---

[36] Articles 12, 23, 34–6, Religious Corporation Law.

at a lower rate than corporate income generally. In addition, according to the Standards for the permission of the Establishment and Guidance of Management of Public-Interest Corporations (adopted on September 20, 1996), the profit-making activities of a public-interest corporation must meet the following conditions:

1. The scale of for-profit activities must be restricted to allow no more than an appropriate growth of the public-interest activity (the competent authorities usually provide administrative guidelines to the effect that the profit from business activities should not exceed half of total revenue).
2. The kind of for-profit activities undertaken may not breach the social trust in a public-interest corporation.
3. Proceeds accruing from such activities in excess of the amount necessary for the healthy management of the activities must be used for the core public-interest activities.
4. Profit-making operations must not impede the activities conducted for the public good.

For tax purposes, "profit-making activities" consist of 33 types of business named in article 5(1) of the Enforcement Ordinance of the Corporation Tax Law, but public-interest corporations are also permitted to earn profits from their public-interest activities and from "concomitant" business activities.

(b) Private School Corporations

Section 26(1) of the Private School Law states that a private school corporation may undertake profit-making business activities and use the proceeds accruing from those activities for the management of private schools so long as such activities do not infringe upon the educational mission of the school. However, there are limitations on the types of profit-making businesses that private school corporations may engage in. More specifically, the law obliges the competent authorities to specify and notify in consultation with the Council for Private Schools and other concerned parties what types of businesses private school corporations are allowed to conduct. Furthermore, Sections 26(2) and (3) of the Private School Law stipulate that profit-making activities must be "special accounts." Thus, the law permits activities that yield profits, but such profits are not to be divided up for private use and must be set aside for the benefit or the management of the school.

(c) Social Welfare Corporations

The Social Welfare Services Law allows social welfare corporations to undertake profit-generating activities to be utilized for the operation of social welfare services as long as such activities do not obstruct the provision of welfare services. Profit-making activities must be handled in "special accounts."[37]

(d) Religious Corporations

Section 6 of the Religious Corporation Law holds that religious corporations may not only undertake public-service activities but also "other" activities, as long as

---

[37] Social Welfare Services Law, Section 25(2).

such other activities do not run counter to the purpose of the corporation. Religious corporations may thus engage in profit-generating activities, but the proceeds must be used for their religious or public-service activities. This may be interpreted to mean that the proceeds are not to be divided for private acquisition by individuals.

(e) Medical Corporations

Section 54 of the Medical Law stipulates that if the annual settlement of accounts shows a surplus of funds, these funds cannot be divided among the employees, who are contributors to the foundation. As the purpose of a medical corporation is not to make profit, excess funds must be reserved for, and used to, improve facilities and other conditions. While the Corporation Tax Law treats medical corporations like for-profit corporations, Section 54 of the Medical Law stipulates that the Corporation Tax Law provision for taxation of internal reserve funds does not apply to medical corporations.

§ 15.8 OTHER FUNDING RESTRICTIONS

An important funding restriction in Japan relates to the issue of ownership of corporate stocks by public-interest corporations. Generally, the government only allows public-interest corporations to hold stocks that are secure and yield high returns. Public-interest corporations are permitted, however, to receive corporate stocks that do not qualify along these requirements if such stocks are donated as part of an endowment. In either case, public-interest corporations may not hold more than half of the total stock of a company.

The other major funding restrictions in Japan apply to fund raising, particularly so-called "designated contributions." Organizations seeking to have their contributions identified as designated contributions, which makes them eligible for unlimited corporate support, must satisfy the Minister of Finance that the contributions are being raised from the public at large and that they are certain to be used to meet urgent needs in the promotion of the public good, such as upgrading education, science, and culture or improvement of welfare services. In addition, the Minister must examine the purposes to which the organization proposes to put the contributions, the sources and amounts targeted, the period during which the contributions will be raised, the purposes and activities of the organization, and the cost of the activities.

§ 15.9 POLITICAL ACTIVITY

The Japanese Civil Code does not prohibit political activities of public-interest corporations per se. As a general rule, nonprofit corporations may pursue a wide range of activities, including political activities, as long as they do not deviate from the activities laid down in the articles of associations or foundation charters and approved at the time of incorporation.

§ 15.10   KEY OUTSTANDING ISSUES

(a) Exclusiveness of Nonprofit Laws

It has been argued that the legal system for the nonprofit sector in Japan is some-what deficient. More specifically, many types of nonprofit organizations, includ-ing societies, alumni associations, hobby associations, and small-scale volunteer organizations (i.e., those that cannot meet the requirements for associations or foundations) cannot attain legal personality because of the absence of a special authorizing law. For this reason, a discussion is currently underway to introduce an NPO bill to the diet session which would grant legal status to smaller citizens' organizations active in a wide spectrum of social areas.

(b) Deductibility Limits for Corporate Contributions

As mentioned above, the calculation of maximum deductible amounts for gen-eral contributions and the contributions to special public-interest-promoting cor-porations of business corporations takes corporate size and disbursement capacity into account. However, the current formula is too restrictive, since it does not allow corporations with small capitalization to obtain a larger deduction maxi-mum for their contributions, no matter how much their income grows. Therefore, it would appear beneficial to introduce a limit of 2.5% of total income for all kinds of corporations, as is already the case with business corporations without capital or invested funds.

In this context, it seems also unfair that "constructive contributions" by pri-vate school corporations and social welfare corporations are deductible to a limit of 50% of their income from profit-making activities (or ¥2 million; whichever is larger), whereas such contributions by general public-interest corporations and nonprofit corporations under special laws are deductible only to a limit of 20%.

CHAPTER SIXTEEN

Mexico*

§ 16.1 LEGAL CONTEXT

Mexico is a civil law country with a decentralized regulatory system for philanthropic activities. Charitable organizations had historically been established under the umbrella of the Catholic Church until the second half of the nineteenth century, when, due to the separation of the Church and State, the government began to take a more active role in defining and regulating philanthropy. After passing a law to confiscate Church properties, the State took steps to regulate philanthropic organizations to prevent Church properties from being transferred to private individual control.

This gave birth to what are still known as Private Assistance Institutions, or *Instituciones de Asistencia Privada* (IAP), which are closely regulated by the Private Assistance Board, an official body on which both government officials and private individuals are represented. Also present within the Mexican nonprofit sector are so-called "civil associations" or *Asociaciones Civiles* (AC), as well as a number of other nonprofit organizations, such as Unions, Chambers of Industry and Commerce, political parties, and so on, which are incorporated under specific laws pertaining to such activities.

Reflecting this diverse structure of nonprofit institutions, there are five different authorities involved in the regulation of the nonprofit sector in Mexico:

1. The Private Assistance Board (*Junta de Asistencia Privada*) at the State level, for the regulation of the IAP
2. The Ministry of Finance and Public Credit (*Secretaria de Hacienda y Credito Publico*) for all tax matters
3. The National Council on Science and Technology (*Consejo Nacional de Ciencia y Tecnologia*) for the approval of institutions in the National Register of Science and Technology and the Register of Foreign Universities for scholarship purposes
4. The Ministry of Education (*Secretaria de Educación Publica*) for the approval of educational institutions under the Education Law
5. The Ministry of External Affairs (*Secretaria de Relaciones Exteriores*) for the approval of the names of the Institutions and the issuance of the permits to incorporate

* Country Rapporteur: Emilio Carillo Gamboa, Esq., Senior Partner, Bufete Carrillo Gamboa, Mexico.

§ 16.2   ELIGIBILITY

(a) Types of Organizations

Nonprofit organizations in Mexico can be incorporated as either Private Assistance Institutions (IAP) or as civil associations (AC). Occasionally, trusts are also used for this purpose. However, many organizations operate without formal incorporation, either because their volume of activity is small or because they are working on an informal basis on very specific activities in particular communities, such as providing aid to the poor. Such organizations are not subject to regulation, but are not eligible for special tax exemptions either.

(i) Private Assistance Institutions.   IAPs are defined as legal entities that perform humanitarian assistance acts, utilizing private assets. Such institutions may not aim at making profit or serve only a specific group of designated beneficiaries. The federal government plays no role in the regulation of these private assistance institutions, which is left to State Laws on Private Assistance. So far only the Federal District of Mexico, where the Capital of Mexico City is located, and seventeen other states have passed such laws.[1]

Private Assistance Institutions can take the form of either foundations or associations. *Foundations* are designated as legal entities utilizing private assets to perform their humanitarian acts, whereas *associations* are entities comprised of individuals or volunteers who periodically contribute to the institution and provide personal services. Generally, assets committed to an institution cannot be returned to their donors.

(ii) Civil Associations.   According to the law, a civil association (AC) is a group of individuals who associate permanently in order to perform a common purpose, which must be neither unlawful nor primarily economic in character. Only the State Laws on Private Assistance mention the word "foundation" but it is common that civil associations be called foundations. Civil associations are governed by the respective Civil Codes of each of the different states of the Republic.[2]

Although there are specific differences between private assistance institutions and civil associations in terms of the kind of activities they pursue, the boundaries between these two classes of nonprofit organizations have become blurred. Thus, many new associations have the choice between becoming an IAP or a civil association. This decision invariably involves a trade-off: IAPs are closely regulated, but enjoy immediate tax exemption and tax deductibility for donations, whereas civil associations enjoy a higher degree of independence in terms of administration, but are subject to the Treasury's discretion with regard to beneficial tax treatment.

(iii) Trusts.   Mexican law allows the establishment of trusts that are governed by trustees to fulfill a legal purpose, whether private or philanthropic.

---

[1] The existing law regulating these institutions in the Federal District was published on January 2, 1943.
[2] For the purposes of this chapter, we only refer to the Civil Code of the Federal District, which is, however, generally applicable.

Trusts may be established for up to 30 years by any person with the trust department of a financial institution of Mexico. In the case of philanthropic trusts, the trustees nominate a technical committee, whose task it is to instruct the trust institution to proceed with the application for tax-exempt status for the trust and, more generally, to provide charitable assistance in accordance with the purposes established by the trustees or donors. Once the 30-year term elapses and a new trust is not established to substitute for the previous one or, alternatively, when the trustees represented on the technical committee so decide, the trust may be liquidated. When this occurs, any assets remaining after paying off the liabilities must be distributed among other institutions pursuing the same purpose.

(b) Types of Purposes

Generally, the purposes of nonprofit organizations must be lawful and not aim at profit making. The purposes of *private assistance institutions* are restricted to human assistance or charitable activities. While *civil associations* may engage in such activities as well, they are also used for other types of nonprofit purposes and include member-serving organizations, such as social and athletic clubs, and other private benefit or service organizations.

(c) Other Requirements

Civil associations must have at least two members. There are no membership or capital requirements for trusts or IAPs.

(d) Registration Procedures

There are different registration requirements in effect for IAPs and ACs.

(i) *Private Assistance Institutions.* In order to establish an IAP, the founders must submit a petition to a Board of Private Assistance, or *Junta de Asistance Privada* (JAP), stating:

1. The name and address of founders
2. The name, social purpose, and office address of the institution to be established
3. The kind of assistance activities that will be provided and the areas where they will be performed
4. The assets allocated to these activities or, alternatively, the means by which funds will be raised
5. The persons who will serve on the Board of Trustees (*Patronato*)
6. The intended life span of the institution (whether permanent or temporary)
7. The main rules regarding its administration

The JAPs are organized at the state level and have the responsibility:

1. To authorize the establishment of private assistance institutions and to approve their bylaws

■ 218 ■

2. To promote the creation of special tax incentives for such institutions
3. To approve the operating budgets of the institutions as well as their investments
4. To approve the annual report of the institutions
5. To approve the dissolution of institutions
6. To assist the governing boards of the institutions in the promotion and establishment of good management practices

In the Federal District of Mexico City, for example, the Private Assistance Board is comprised of four aldermen named by the government representing the Department of the Federal District, and the Treasury, Health and Education Ministries. The member Institutions (IAP) appoint another five aldermen, who must have special expertise in the fields of infant care, elderly care, medical care, educational assistance, and other kind of services, respectively. These privately appointed aldermen do not necessarily have to be drawn from the boards of trustees of the member institutions, but they may not be public officials.

The Board (JAP) is headed by a chairman, who is appointed by the Mayor of Mexico City from a list of three candidates presented to him by the aldermen representing the member Institutions and nine other members of good standing. The Chairman of the Private Assistance Board has the duties (1) to inspect and audit the institutions; (2) to propose the election of an Executive Delegate of the Board, who acts as Secretary; and (3) to appoint the personnel of the Board.

The Board is financed by a fee of six per thousand of the gross income levied on each member institution. In Mexico City, this Board (JAP) reports to the Head of the Department of the Federal District (*Jefe del Departamento del Distrito Federal*) who is an appointed official named by the President of the Republic and who acts as Mayor of Mexico City. On July 6, 1997, for the first time the citizens of Mexico, D.F. elected the Mayor who will be called Head of Government of the Federal District. He will take office December 3 for a three-year term ending in the year 2000; then it will be elected for six years.

Once the Board (JAP) approves the petition for the formation of a Private Assistance Institution, the founders must appear before a Notary Public within 30 days to sign the incorporation and the bylaws of the institution, which must include:

1. The name of the institution
2. The goods and properties owned by it
3. The kinds of activities intended to obtain the funding required for the institution
4. The institution's premises
5. Eligibility criteria for beneficiaries
6. The persons appointed to the board of trustees and the rules for succession

An IAP receives its legal personality on the day the Board (JAP) approves the petition to incorporate. In cases where such an institution is to be created through a Last Will or Testament of a person donating property or goods for charitable purposes, the Board (JAP) takes part in the execution of the will. If the deceased has not specified detailed purposes, the Board can supplement the will and take appropriate measures to assure an execution in accordance with the deceased's wishes.

(ii) Civil Associations. In order to establish a civil association, the founders have to apply for a permit from the *Secretaria de Relaciones Exteriores* (Foreign Affairs Ministry) indicating the intended name of the association. The Ministry verifies that the name is not being used by another association and it is customary to submit three options to the Ministry to assure that one of them will be approved. Such a permit is usually granted in less than one week and issued under the condition, established by the Mexican Constitution, that members of foreign nationalities agree to abide by Mexican legal jurisdiction and not seek diplomatic protection of their governments in case a legal conflict arises with the association with the government.

Furthermore, members must draw up a founding contract in writing, which must be notarized to be valid externally and to be eligible for registration in the Public Registry. When these requirements are satisfied, the association receives its own legal personality separate from the members.

§ 16.3 INTERNAL GOVERNANCE

(a) Private Assistance Institutions

Although IAPs are self-governed institutions, issues relating to the internal governance are closely regulated. The main legal provisions relate to the rights and duties of the original founders, board responsibilities, and procedures for dissolution of the organization.

The original founders are entitled (1) to determine the kind of services the institution shall provide, (2) to determine the kind of persons eligible for assistance, (3) to name and substitute the board of trustees,[3] (4) to approve the bylaws of the institution, and (5) to serve as trustees during their lifetime. Apart from these rights and duties, the founders of the IAP, once having established the institution, delegate the day-to-day operations to a board of trustees appointed by them.

The main responsibilities of the board of trustees are as follows:

1. To assure that the founder's purpose is accomplished
2. To preserve and improve the assets of the institution
3. To appoint the necessary personnel
4. To govern the institution according to the Law
5. To assure that the documents required by the Private Assistance Board are delivered
6. To legally represent the institution
7. Not to borrow in any way against the institution's properties without the prior authorization of the Board of Private Assistance (JAP) or to lease such properties for more than five years, or receive rents for future use for more than two years, without the authorization of the Board

---

[3] The only restrictions on board membership relate to persons legally impeded, government officials, and corporations or persons that have been removed from another board.

8. Not to appoint persons personally related to the president, treasurer, or auditor of the institution
9. Not to pay an account not yet due, or deliver monies or goods without adequate receipt, or to sell any goods or properties of the institution to a person with family relationship, except in a public auction
10. To obey the instructions of the Private Assistance Board issued to correct malpractice

Generally, given the organization's separate legal personality, board members are not personally responsible for the actions of the institution. However, they might nevertheless incur civil or criminal liabilities for the activities they commit or approve. Personnel handling financial matters must be adequately insured.

Regarding the dissolution of an IAP, such institutions may be dissolved by a decision of the founders or the board of trustees or by a resolution of the Private Assistance Board (JAP). In the latter case, a dissolution may be legally ordered if (1) the institution's revenue is not sufficient to sustain the services provided, (2) if the institution is established in contravention to the law, or (3) if the services provided are no longer considered to be of public interest. In these cases, the Board (JAP) may determine that the assets be allocated to another institution serving a similar purpose. Alternatively, it can also determine that a new institution be created.

To carry out a dissolution, the board of trustees and the Board of Private Assistance (JAP) each appoint a liquidator to (1) prepare an inventory of the institution's properties, (2) to receive from the board of trustees a detailed account of the financial condition of the institution, (3) to submit to the Board (JAP) a monthly report, and (4) to collect all amounts due and make all the payments for which the institution is liable. Once the assets have been allocated, the institution is formally declared dissolved.

When an inspection or audit of an institution is ordered, the Board's representatives have full authority to review all documents, files, and other information of the institution in order to review its financial matters as well as to evaluate whether the provision of assistance activities is adequate. If an Institution is served notice of any judicial proceeding, it must advise the Board within ten days of such an instance and keep it informed of any developments. The Board (JAP) may appoint a special representative to participate in these proceedings. The Board is also empowered to remove any member of the board of trustees of any Institution with due cause. Notaries, consulate and similar officials, shall not certify any contract or document relating to an IAP that has not been previously approved by the Board (JAP).

(b) Civil Associations

According to the civil code, the members' meeting is the supreme governing body of the association. However, there are no further rules concerning the internal governance and the administrative structure is largely left to the particular bylaws. Usually, associations are administered by a general administrator or by a board of directors if more than three administrators are designated by the founders or members' meeting. However, there are certain provisions relating to the bylaws, members' meeting, and the dissolution of civil associations that need to be taken into account.

The bylaws must specify:

1. The names of the persons that establish the association
2. The name of the association, which can be either a person or family name or a name not related to any of these
3. The purpose, which, according to the Tax Law, must be irrevocable; the intended life span; and the address of the association
4. The assets, if any, and the amount each member must contribute
5. The name of administrators or directors and the powers granted to them
6. Membership categories and, if relevant, any specific responsibilities granted to members[4]
7. That, in case of liquidation, all patrimony shall be allocated to other associations that are also tax exempt and authorized to receive tax-deductible donations[5]
8. That no member shall receive any benefit from the association and that remuneration to any member shall be paid only for work executed
9. The way in which the ordinary and extraordinary members' meetings are to be conducted and the issues to be discussed
10. Other clauses that the founders establish to create governing bodies within the association, such as special committees or an auditing board

Regarding member meetings, such meetings must be convened at the time stipulated by the bylaws, which, in the case of ordinary meetings, is normally within the first four months of a calendar year. They can be convened by the chairman, the secretary, or the director general of the association or on the request of 5% of the membership.

In general, members' meetings are legally empowered to decide on (1) the admission or exclusion of members; (2) the dissolution of the association or an extension of its duration beyond the time originally stipulated in the bylaws, where applicable; (3) the appointment of directors, when such an appointment has not been regulated otherwise in the bylaws; (4) the revocation of the appointments made; or (5) any other matters referred to in the bylaws.

Except when all members are present, a members' meeting can discuss only matters specified in an agenda published in the Official Gazette or a daily newspaper circulating in the city where the association resides.

Decisions on the dissolution of the association or the amendment of the bylaws are often reserved to the extraordinary meetings, whereas ordinary meetings customarily decide on the appointment of the board of directors and the auditor, or any other committee established by the bylaws; the admission of new members and the exclusion of them; and the approval of the financial statements of the association.

Members are entitled to ascertain that their dues are used entirely for the association's objective and, therefore, they may review the accounts of the asso-

---

[4] Common categories are founding members with or without special privileges and active (regular) members. Occasionally, honorary members are appointed, whose voting power in the members' meetings, however, is normally restricted. The liability of members is generally understood to be limited to the amount contributed to establish the association, although the law is not fully clear on this issue.

[5] This clause is required by the Tax Code and is irrevocable.

ciation. Usually, an auditor is designated to perform an adequate audit of the association's accounts and, if the organization has tax-exempt status, to provide to the tax authorities the required information and reports.

As indicated above, the decision to dissolve and liquidate an association is the responsibility of the member meeting. However, a dissolution can also occur in case the purpose becomes obsolete or when the competent authority so decides in keeping with the law. If the decision is made, the member meeting has to appoint one or several liquidators, who must establish an inventory of properties, pay the debts owed by the association, collect whatever accounts are due, and transfer the remaining assets to another association of the same kind, and if possible, of the same purpose. If the dissolved association did not obtain tax exemption, remaining properties may be distributed among the partners or members of the association. Once all these procedures are concluded, the liquidators apply for the cancellation of the register entry in the Public Registry.

§ 16.4   TAX TREATMENT

(a) Tax Treatment of Organizations

By law, private assistance institutions are automatically granted exemption from corporate income taxation. However, in the case of civil associations, the application for tax-exempt status is handled separately from the registration for legal personality. In particular, institutions wishing to obtain tax-exempt status must apply in writing to the Ministry of the Treasury, Undersecretary of Revenues, Area of Donations or, alternatively, to the Local Legal Administration of Revenues of the same Ministry. This application must include (1) the section of the law declaring the proposed activities to be eligible for tax exemption; (2) a copy of the institution's bylaws with all the requisites mentioned above; (3) evidence of the activities performed; and (4) a copy of the registry in the Science and Technology Registry or in the Education Ministry, if applicable. The Treasury authorities publish an annual list in the Official Gazette of all the institutions that have obtained this benefit and that are currently in compliance with their obligations. The tax exemption is granted permanently and there is no need for periodic reapplications.

Trusts, patrimonies (*patronatos*), and other entities established as civil associations, which support other associations authorized to receive tax-deductible donations, may also be tax exempt if (1) all income is used for this purpose, and (2) their patrimony will be distributed among associations authorized to receive tax-deductible donations in case of liquidation. These associations must also comply with the restrictions applicable to other tax-exempt associations, as detailed above.

Any tax-exempt institution is also exempted from the tax on assets Mexican corporations are subject to. This assets tax is a 1.8% levy on the value of fixed assets.

There are certain circumstances in which tax-exempted institutions are nevertheless subjected to paying the 34% corporate income tax even if any excess of income over expenditures is not distributed. This is usually the case if institutions fail to register all of their income or undertake unrealized or inadequately registered purchases or if they make expenditures that do not qualify as tax deductible under the law. This penalty tax is due in February following the closing of the fiscal year.

Tax-exempt organizations are relieved of the following:

1. Income tax on donations and on income from sales or services, although the latter is still subject to a 15% VAT charge
2. Import duties on in-kind donations received from foreign noncontributing organizations subject to additional conditions
3. VAT on foreign in-kind donations

Institutions regulated by the *Junta de Asistencia Privada* are furthermore eligible for lower rates on taxes on acquisitions, real estate, water, raffles, and so on.

(b) Tax Treatment of Contributions—Domestic Organizations

The maximum tax rate in Mexico is presently 35% for individuals and 34% for corporations, and there are no limits for the deduction of donations from taxable income. This means that any person or corporation can give to a charitable institution all its taxable income and fully deduct it, without any tax being due after the donation. Furthermore, there are no inheritance taxes, neither at the federal nor the state level, for properties transferred from the deceased to their heirs, including nonprofit institutions, although in some cases property transfer taxes apply. However, there are certain differences between IAPs and civil associations in terms of eligibility for such preferential treatment.

(i) *Private Assistance Institutions.* The Law of Private Assistance specifically stipulates that donations made to all IAPs are tax deductible and that these institutions must issue receipts to the donors, which they can deduct from their taxable income.

(ii) *Civil Associations.* By contrast, the extension of this privilege to civil associations lies entirely at the discretion of the Treasury Department (*Secretaria de Hacienda y Credito Publico*). The Federal Income Tax Law declares to be tax exempt those associations authorized to receive tax-deductible donations, which do not have individually designated beneficiaries and perform the following activities:

1. Provision of care to persons who are unable to satisfy their basic needs due to their economic or physical condition
2. Support of specialized institutions for minors or the elderly who have been abandoned or are without any protection, and for disabled persons of lesser means
3. Provision of legal or medical assistance, or social orientation/counseling services, or funerary services to persons of limited resources, especially minors, the elderly, and disabled
4. Resocialization of convicted criminals
5. Rehabilitation of drug addicts of limited resources

6. Teaching that is authorized or recognized officially under the terms and conditions of the Federal Education Law
7. Promotion of culture
8. Scientific or technological research carried out at institutions recorded in the National Registry of Scientific and Technological Institutions
9. Libraries and museums open to the public
10. Granting of scholarships
11. Native conservancy activities in national parks and natural reserves so declared by the federal government

In order to be considered eligible for the receipt of tax-deductible donations, these associations must also:

1. Receive a substantial part of their funding from federal, state, or municipal governments, or from private donations, or from income derived from their social purpose, provided they do not receive excessive amounts from leases, interest, dividends, royalties, or activities that are not related to their social purpose.[6]
2. Primarily perform activities directly related their social purpose, without intervening in political activities or propaganda or influencing legislation.
3. Use their assets exclusively for the fulfillment of their social purpose, without using net income to provide any benefit or payment to any person except for services provided; in addition, administrative expenses must not exceed 5% of donations received.
4. Distribute their assets among other institutions authorized to receive tax-deductible donations if liquidated.
5. Maintain open for public inspection the documentation pertaining to the authorization to receive tax-deductible donations and showing their compliance with the tax regulations according to the rules issued by the Treasury Department.

Scholarship organizations, in order to be authorized, are in addition required to grant such scholarships (1) only for study in institutions duly authorized in Mexico or, if in foreign countries, recognized by the National Council of Science and Technology; and (2) through open public competition taking into consideration the merits of the applicants.

(c) Tax Treatment of Contributions—Foreign Organizations

In terms of cross-border donations, Mexico has entered into a Double Taxation Treaty with the United States under which Mexican institutions can receive donations from U.S. donors that are tax deductible in the United States if they comply with certain rules to assure that these institutions are in compliance with provisions of the U.S. law. However, the U.S. Internal Revenue Service generally recognizes the authorizations granted by the Mexican Federal Tax authorities as sufficient evidence of deductibility from U.S. taxable income. This benefit applies to institutions providing the following services:

[6] There is no definition of what constitutes an excessive amount.

1. Medical or legal assistance to the poor or disabled, counseling and reso-cialization of convicted criminals, or the rehabilitation of drug addicts of lesser income. However, this does not apply to institutions whose main purpose is to provide medical research or education, unless these activities directly involve the provision of medical assistance to patients and the research or education is part of such assistance.
2. Education in learning institutions, schools, colleges, or universities officially recognized by the Education authorities and having a regular faculty and pupils.
3. Medical research carried out at institutions registered in the National Registry of Science and Technology and conducting continuous research jointly with a hospital, but only if all the donations are employed exclusively in innovative research within five calendar years of the receipt of the donation.
4. Restoration and preservation of governmental archaeological, artistic, historic, or patrimonial monuments according to the law.
5. Promotion of the fine arts.
6. Research on technological development in institutions that are registered with the National Registry of Science and Technology.

All these institutions must provide audited financial statements, which should be open for public inspection for three years following the fiscal year to which they refer, as well as a list of all administrators and employees to whom they paid more than 192.500 new pesos (subject to adjustments for inflation) during the year.

The authorization to receive tax-deductible donations from across the border is granted by the Mexican Treasury if:

1. The institution receives at least one-third of its income from federal, state, or municipal grants or donations from the general public;[7] or
2. If the institution receives at least 10% of its income from such sources, provided it complies with the additional requirements
   a. that it is established and operates in a way that allows for a continuous flow of new funds (i.e., that it is a permanent institution); and
   b. that it can prove to the Tax authorities
      (i) that the board of directors is broadly representative of society;
      (ii) that their installations are used permanently for services to be provided directly to the public;
      (iii) that services are provided by specialized personnel;
      (iv) that the institution operates under a continuous work program; and
      (v) that it receives significant donations from other institutions authorized to receive tax-deductible donations.

---

[7] For this purpose, only donations that do not exceed 1% of the institutions' income are counted.

The Treasury Department is empowered to decide on whether any given organization has to comply with all or just some of these requirements before issuing the authorization.[8]

By way of reciprocity, Mexican tax authorities recognize U.S. organizations classified by the U.S. Internal Revenue Service as 509(a)(1) and 509(a)(2) as eligible recipients of Mexican donations. However, Mexican individuals and corporations can claim deductions for donations to U.S. nonprofit organizations only against income received from the United States and the same applies to U.S. corporations and individuals, which can only claim against Mexican income which is a substantial limitation. Since the U.S.-Mexican treaty is the only such treaty currently in force in Mexico, Mexican donations to nonprofit organizations in other countries are generally not deductible.

§ 16.5   PERSONAL BENEFIT RESTRICTIONS

Personal benefits for members of nonprofit institutions are severely limited to assure that the resources of such institutions are indeed utilized for their chartered purposes. Accordingly, institutions authorized to receive tax-deductible gifts and issue tax-deductible receipts (1) must not have individually designated beneficiaries, (2) may not distribute profits among their members, (3) must apply their patrimony exclusively to their chartered purposes, and (4) must transfer their patrimony to other institutions that are authorized to issue tax-deductible receipts in case of liquidation.

§ 16.6   OBLIGATIONS TO THE PUBLIC

(a) Special Fiscal Obligations of IAPs

The accounting books of Private Assistance Institutions are to be kept current and the board of trustees must forward copies of all its financial information, prepared under the JAP's procedures, to the Private Assistance Board on a monthly basis. Furthermore, Private Assistance Institutions must submit their operating and investment budgets as well as their work programs for the following year to the Board of Private Assistance (JAP) no later than December 1. The approval of these documents is subject to the conditions that administrative expenditures do not exceed the cost of the services being provided and that any excess of rev-

---

[8] However, institutions receiving more than one-third of their income from donations, sales of goods or services, or rents may also qualify, provided that this income is related to the social purpose of the institution. For the determination of whether an institution receives one-third of income from such sources, donations from government sources, donations from individuals in excess of 32.000 new pesos a year and from "nonqualified donors" may not be included. Nonqualified donors are, for instance, administrators of the institution, persons holding more than 20% of the stock of a corporation that contributes more than 32.000 new pesos a year, and relatives of such persons. (All peso amounts are subject to adjustments for inflation.) Moreover, such institutions must not receive more than one-third of their annual income from leases, interest, dividends, or royalties, or from profits obtained from activities not substantially related to its social purpose. These limitations on funding do not apply to institutions dedicated to educational purposes.

enues over expenditures is maintained as retained earnings within the Institution. Private Assistance Institutions must abide by the investments and expenses detailed in the approved budget and any other extraordinary item cannot be contracted or paid for without the previous consent of the JAP. Similarly, the cancellation of bad debts likewise needs the previous authorization of the Board. If an institution violates any articles of the law, the members of the board of trustees may be subjected to the penalty of removal if they consistently ignore, or do not abide by, the resolutions of the Private Assistance Board.

(b) Accounting

In addition to the special reporting requirements imposed on IAPs, all tax-exempt organizations are required to have a simplified accounting system in the form of an accounting book, in which the institutions, as minimum requisites, must (1) identify every operation, action, or activity and relate it to the appropriate documents; (2) maintain proper documentation of income received from sales, services, or leases; and (3) identify their investments with appropriate documents and apply the authorized depreciation percentages on them.

(c) Tax reports

For income tax purposes, exempted institutions must file the following reports:

1. An Information Report listing the donations received in the preceding year, which is due in the month of February.
2. A Tax Report detailing taxable income, if any, due in the month of March.
3. An auditor's opinion in a simplified form no later than July. According to this requirement, which is mandatory for medium and large corporations and all tax exempt institutions, a Certified Public Accountant must submit to the Treasury Authorities a document containing
   (i) the auditor's opinion regarding the institution's compliance with the tax laws;
   (ii) an income and expense statement;
   (iii) a list of donations received, both in cash and in kind;
   (iv) the administrative expenses of the institution;
   (v) a list of donors and donations comprising 90% of the Institution's income from this source;
   (vi) taxes paid or withheld;
   (vii) a list of the real estate properties of the institution;
   (viii) an assessment of the income tax, if any, to be paid; and
   (ix) a list of other tax-exempt institutions that gave or received donations from the association.

In addition, tax-exempt institutions, as any other registered taxpayer, must file all reports required from all individuals and/or corporations regarding, for instance, sales taxes, withholding taxes, social security, and so forth.

(d) Public Information

The law requires tax-exempt institutions to publicly display at their offices the tax reports filed for the last three years as well as any documents that the Institution filed with the Treasury authorities in order to receive its tax exemption. However, IAPs are exempted from this requirement.

§ 16.7   BUSINESS ACTIVITY

Nonprofit institutions in Mexico may engage in business activities. However, the Income Tax Law stipulates that such institutions may not receive "substantial" parts of their income from such activities, to prevent unfair competition with for-profit corporations. Since the law does not define what constitutes a "substantial" part of income, the determination is left to the discretion of the authorities. As a general rule of thumb, business income should not exceed one-third of total annual revenue. As long as income from business activities does not exceed this threshold and is fully applied to the organization's purposes, it is subject only to VAT, but exempted from income tax.

§ 16.8   OTHER FUNDING RESTRICTIONS

Private Assistance Institutions face a variety of restrictions concerning their investment behavior and other funding methods. In terms of securities invest-ment, for instance, IAPs are restricted to publicly listed securities approved for investment purposes by the National Securities Commission.

While IAPs may engage in mortgage lending, such activities are closely regu-lated. Institutions can lend no more than 50% of the appraised value of homes or 30% of specialized buildings. Buildings must be fully insured during the term of the loan, which must not exceed 10 years, and mortgage payments have to be made in accordance with procedures approved by the JAP.

While IAPs may only acquire real estate necessary for their operations, they may invest in housing construction with previous authorization of the Board, pro-vided the construction plans are also approved by the Board and houses will be sold within two years.

In terms of other funding restrictions, Board of Private Assistance (JAP) authorization is necessary for raffles, festivals, and public campaigns. The JAP must furthermore approve the terms on which such activities are to be announced to the public.

No such provisions exist for civil associations.

§ 16.9   POLITICAL ACTIVITY

According to Section II of article 70-B of the Income Tax Law, organizations that have obtained tax-exempt status are prohibited from intervening in political cam-paigns, engaging in propaganda, or attempting to influence legislation. However,

Section II also holds that "the publication of an analysis or research paper that does not have any purpose of gaining members for a cause, or technical assistance for a governmental agency that has requested it in writing" does not constitute an attempt to influence legislation.

§ 16.10 KEY OUTSTANDING ISSUES

The most important recent trends concern the enactment of a new law for philanthropic and charitable activities and the tax treaty with the United States relating to cross-border donations.

(a) Demands for a New Law

Currently, demands are increasing for a new Philanthropy Law in order to provide a clearer and more secure framework for philanthropic and charitable activities. Some advocates have even proposed a constitutional amendment to facilitate the participation of civil society organizations in matters of public interest, following the path of the different laws on philanthropy recently approved in Spain and in other parts of Latin America, such as Colombia and Argentina. With the inauguration of the administration of President Zedillo on December 1, 1994, preliminary talks on a draft law have started and the president has publicly announced his support for a greater participation of civil society organizations.

(b) Tax Treaty with the United States

The Tax Treaty between the United States and Mexico that has been in force since January 1, 1994 holds provisions that will increase the flow of funds between Mexico and the United States, allowing individuals or foundations of one country to directly donate to institutions of the other country. This important advancement is only now being fully understood by Mexican institutions. Many organizations are therefore beginning to apply for public charity status, accepting the various limitations on activities and funding that come with this status in order to be eligible for the benefits of increased donations from the United States. However, although the treaty brought many improvements, some misgivings remain since it affects only public charities. Foundations, whether grant making or operating, are not eligible for the benefits of cross-border philanthropy.

CHAPTER SEVENTEEN

The Netherlands[*]

§ 17.1 LEGAL CONTEXT

Generally, the Netherlands Constitution (Grondwet voor het koninkrijk der Nederlanden) guarantees the freedom of speech,[1] of association,[2] and of assembly,[3] although the freedom of association can be restricted by law in the interest of the public order.[4] The freedom of assembly and demonstration can be restricted by law in the interests of public health, traffic, and to prevent disorder.

The legal culture of the Netherlands belongs to the (Roman) civil law tradition, as opposed to the Anglo-American common law tradition. Accordingly, a clear distinction is made between public law and civil law. For example, while tax regulations are a matter of public law, issues concerning the legal form of an organization, its governance, and so on are matters of civil law.

The civil law is laid down in the Netherlands Civil Code (*Nederlands Burgerlijk Wetboek*, hereafter BW), the second Book of which, under the heading "Legal Persons," spells out a general framework of organizational law for nonprofit organizations. It covers matters of legal personality, establishment, organizational structure, decisionmaking (including procedural and majority/quorum requirements for certain decisions, such as altering statutes and dissolution), registration, the position of the board and other organs within the organization, as well as the legal position of third parties.

Within the limits of this framework, there is ample room for individual organizations to determine through statutes and bylaws their own internal structure and rules for decision making, representation, and other conduct of affairs.[5] The discretion allowed by the Civil Code in this respect differs depending upon whether the organization is a membership or nonmembership organization. The Civil Code contains more elaborate regulation for membership than for nonmembership organizations.

---

[*] Country Rapporteur: Dr. Wino van Veen, Associate Professor, Vrije Universiteit, Amsterdam.
[1] Article 7.
[2] Article 8.
[3] Article 9.
[4] According to the European Convention on Human Rights, restrictions are only permissible on limited grounds if prescribed by law and *necessary* in a democratic society (see Articles 10 and 11 ECHR).
[5] The terms statutes and bylaws are used in this chapter for the regulation of legal persons in the following way: *Statutes* are the main regulations, which are usually part of the deed of establishment (charter). Special requirements are necessary for the amendment of these regulations. *Bylaws, on the other hand,* are internal regulations of the legal person that have lower status than statutes. They are issued by some organ of the legal person, and may be amended or recalled by the same organ.

Although fiscal law does not play an important role in the process of establishing nonprofit organizations, it recognizes the social importance of nonprofit organizations by granting tax exemptions or other facilities, and by providing incentives such as tax deductibility of donations to promote private giving.

§ 17.2 ELIGIBILITY

(a) Types of Organizations

In the Netherlands, there are three main types of nonprofit organizations: associations (*vereniging*), foundations (*stichting*), and churches. While churches are governed by their own regulations, associations and foundations are governed by the Civil Code.[6]

(i) Associations. Associations are essentially membership-based organizations.[7] As such, the members hold important organizational powers within the association. The bond between members and the association goes beyond a contractual relationship and involves a special relationship of mutual responsibility, in which members in their membership capacity must consider the interest of the association and its members as such and obey the regulations and decisions regardless of their individual consent. Thus membership also creates a bond between the members.

There are two different types of associations in the nonprofit sector: formal and informal associations (*vereniging*). An informal association can be formed without any formal action and its statutes are not laid down in a notarial deed and are not necessarily written down. Such an association is a legal person, but has limited legal competence. It cannot, for example, be heir to an inheritance or acquire real estate or other registered goods. Most importantly, the members of the board of an informal *vereniging* are all personally liable for the activities and obligations of the *vereniging*,[8] although this liability may be tempered through registration of the association in the Trade Register. Registration, however, is not obligatory for informal associations.

Formal associations are associations that are established by a notarial deed, and informal associations can become formal associations once their statutes have been laid down in such a deed. Formal associations have full legal competence and their board members are shielded from personal liability for the associations' obligations unless the registration requirements are not met (see below).

(ii) Foundations. A foundation is defined in article 2:285 BW as "a legal person created by a legal act which has no members and whose purpose is to realize an object stated in its articles using capital allocated to such purpose." By

---

[6] In contrast to the Anglo-American countries, the Dutch legal system does not know the concept of the trust—which is not an organization, but rather a specific type of legal relationship between (legal) persons and property. For purposes similar to the trust, the foundation is a suitable and effective legal form.

[7] Article 2:26 BW: 1.

[8] Article 2:30 BW.

definition, foundations cannot have members. This does not imply, however, that, apart from members of the board, no other persons can be granted organizational powers within a foundation. Rather it means that those persons cannot have the same democratic powers as the members of associations have.[9]

(b) Types of Purposes

There are few restrictions on the types of purposes that are eligible for nonprofit status. The only significant restriction, applicable to both associations and foundations, is that they cannot have as their purpose the provision of financial benefits to their members, persons appointed to their organs, or, in the case of foundations, to their founders. Beyond this, foundations and associations, like all other legal persons, are forbidden to have as their purpose, or perform, activities that are against the basic principles of the state under rule of law and will lead to disruption of society.

Within these broad boundaries, a wide range of possible purposes and activities are eligible for nonprofit status, such as providing housing, food, medical, technological or legal help; setting up and supporting orphanages, hospitals, or nursing homes; the advancement of music, drama, and other arts; providing schools, libraries, and museums; financial support; worker training; research facilities; family help; and other purposes beneficial to the community or certain groups in society, including, for example, professionals, unions, political parties, and others.

(c) Other Requirements

With respect to associations, there are no capital requirements. Interestingly, the same applies to foundations. Although a foundation is a legal person whose purpose is to realize certain objectives by using capital allocated to these purposes, there are no capital requirements for the formation of a foundation. A foundation may thus be established without any means. However, the Civil Code in article 2:301 BW contains a provision according to which a foundation can be dissolved by court order on request of a third party with a justified interest, or on request of the public prosecutor, when the foundation lacks sufficient means to realize its purpose and there are no prospects for future acquisitions. Cases based on this article, however, are extremely rare.

(d) Registration Procedures

Significantly, no governmental bodies are involved in the establishment of associations or foundations. Rather, the law merely stipulates the formal steps those forming such organizations must take to acquire legal entity status. Thus, for example, for the formation of an association, a multilateral legal act of at least two persons is required. The founders of an association usually also become mem-

---

[9] A foundation's statutes can grant to organs other than the board the power to alter statutes or bylaws, to appoint or dismiss board members, to approve certain board decisions, or to exercise general oversight over the board (e.g., check the annual report). See P. Dijk and T.J. Van der Ploeg, *Van vereniging en stichting*, cooperatie en onderlingewaarborgmaatschappij 3e ed. (Arnhem: Gouda Quint, 1997), p. 20 f.f.

bers of the association. However, in theory, it is possible that certain founders do not enter into a legal bond with the association. Foundations, on the other hand, can be established by the legal act of one person only. This can also be done in a last will. In practice, founders quite often also become members of the board of the foundation. This, however, is not necessarily the case, since a founder does not have to enter into a legal relationship with his or her foundation.

In the Dutch legal system, nonprofit organizations must satisfy certain requirements to become a legal person. These requirements differ among formal associations, informal associations, and foundations. In addition, there are separate registration procedures, though these are handled by the Chambers of Commerce and Industry, not by a government department. Registration does not affect the legal personality of an organization, but it has certain consequences in respect to matters relating to the issue of board member liability.

(i) Informal Associations.

(i) Informal Associations. Informal associations are established without any formalities. To become a legal person with limited legal competence, an adequate expression of the will to work together as an association is sufficient. This may be done explicitly or implicitly, that is, by acting together in an organized way that is comparable to the functioning of an association. This involves creating two organs, the board and the general meeting of members, as well as being publicly active as a unity.[10] A consequence of the informal status is that board members are jointly and severally liable for the association's obligations, unless the association chooses to register voluntarily. Informal associations have the option to change their status to formal citation by laying down their statutes in a notarial deed.

Although registration with the *Handelsregister*, or Trade Register, is not compulsory for informal associations, if informal associations do register, board members are only liable for obligations of the association if the other party involved proves that the association will not keep its obligation toward him or her.[11] Any association—whether formal or informal—that also has commercial activities must be entered into the Trade Register.[12]

(ii) Formal Associations.

(ii) Formal Associations. Formal associations are established by the execution of a notarial deed. The difference between informal and formal associations is that the latter have full legal competence, and can thus receive inheritances and acquire real estate and other registered goods. Furthermore, members of the board of a formal association are not personally liable for the obligations of the association if the association is registered in the trade register. When an association is established by notarial deed, the deed must contain the statutes of the association, which in turn must include: (1) the name; (2) the municipality in which the association has its registered office; (3) the purpose; (4) the obligations of the members toward the association or the manner in which those obligations can be imposed; (5) the manner of convening the general meeting of members; (6) rules

---

[10] P. Dijk and T.J. Van der Ploeg, *Van vereniging en stichting, coöperatie en onderlinge waarborg maatschappij*, 3e ed. (Arnhem: Gouda Quint, 1997), p. 33 f.f.

[11] Article 2:30 BW.

[12] Article 4(3), *Handelsregisterwet 1996*.

concerning the appointment and dismissal of board members, and the allocation of surplus after winding up the association or the manner in which such allocation shall be determined.[13]

Formal associations must register in the public Trade Register, which is held by the Chambers of Commerce and Industry. Information that needs to be published in the Trade Register includes (1) the notarial deed containing the full text of the statutes; (2) the full names and addresses of board members as well as those of other persons whom the statutes authorize to represent the association; and (3) details about the limits of this representive authority.

(iii) Foundations.

(iii) Foundations. Foundations must also be established by the execution of a notarial deed containing the statutes. The statutes must include (1) the name of the foundation with the word *stichting* in the name; (2) the purpose; (3) rules concerning the appointment and dismissal of board members; (4) the municipality where the foundation has its registered office; and (5) the allocation of the surplus after termination of the foundation or the manner in which such allocation shall be determined.[14]

For the registration of foundations in the Trade Register, the following information must be published: (1) the notarial deed containing the full text of the statutes; (2) the names of the founders; (3) the full names and addresses of the members of the board and other persons whom the statutes authorize to represent the *stichting*, and details about the limits of their competence to represent the organization. Such registration is compulsory and if these requirements are not met, the notary public is liable for damages caused by this negligence.

As mentioned above, registration is not necessary for obtaining legal personality. It has only certain consequences for the liability of board members. As long as registration has not taken place, not only the foundation itself, but also the members of the board are each personally liable for the obligations of the *stichting*.[15]

§ 17.3   INTERNAL GOVERNANCE

The Civil Code presents a framework within which an association or foundation can develop its own internal structure. The freedom to do so, however, differs depending on the type of legal person in question. There are, for instance, more compulsory stipulations concerning associations than foundations. In general, both associations and foundations must have a governing body which is called the *Bestuur*, or board, and which is in charge of the management, the setting of general policies, and legal representation. The number of board members is prescribed in the statutes, not mandated in the Civil Code. In principle, the board can consist of one person, although this is not very common, especially for associations. The board is free to exert its authority to manage the organization within

---

[13] Article 2:27 BW.
[14] Article 2:286 BW.
[15] Article 2:289 BW.

the limits of the law and the statutes. Organizational law also allows for the establishment of additional organs which may have advisory or supervisory powers or even competence to make decisions in respect to certain matters independently from the board, providing this ability is laid down in the statutes.

(a) Associations

The governance structure of the *vereniging* is shaped both by the Civil Code and organizational statutes. Generally, the Civil Code guarantees the right of members to speak freely and vote in the general meeting and grants the members and the general meeting of members, respectively, specific rights and powers within the association. The general meeting is thus an important countervailing power to the board.

Thus, the general meeting must check and approve of the annual account which the board has to submit to the general assembly within six months after the end of the financial year.[16] For this purpose the meeting must convene at least once every year. The meeting also has (1) the competence to amend statutes;[17] (2) the authority to appoint and dismiss at least half of the members of the board;[18] (3) the final authority to decide on admission of a member when the board has refused to do so,[19] or on the termination of a membership;[20] (4) the power to decide on dissolution of the association;[21] and (5) the authority to decide on all matters that according to the law or statutes do not fall into the competence of any other organ.[22]

This does not mean, however, that the general assembly is the ultimate locus of authority in an association: Each organ is bound by the law and the statutes and therefore has to respect the authority of other autonomous organs in the exercise of their legal and statutory tasks.

(b) Foundations

For the foundation, the board is the only organ required by the Civil Code. However, it is not uncommon that the statutes of a foundation provide for a supervisory organ or an organ for consultation. As a rule these organs must be informed, consulted, or asked for approval before decisions in certain matters are made. Furthermore, the statutes may give these organs autonomous competencies with regard to certain matters. This may involve important issues such as altering the statutes or bylaws; checking the annual account; or the appointment or dismissal of board members. If no organ other than the board is given the competence to appoint or dismiss members of the board, statutes usually empower the board itself to do so by cooptation. If there is a deadlock situation concerning the appointment of new members of the board, the courts may also appoint new members of the board on request of interested persons or the public prosecutor.[23]

[16] Article 2:48 BW.
[17] Article 2:42 BW.
[18] Article 2:37 BW.
[19] Article 2:33 BW.
[20] Articles 2:35 and 36 BW.
[21] Article 2:42 BW.
[22] Article 2:40 BW.
[23] See article 2:299 BW.

Changes of the purpose of a foundation require an amendment of the foundation's statutes, since the purpose of a *stichting* is determined in its statutes. However, such an amendment is possible only if the statutes allow a change of purpose. If the statutes contain no such regulation, no organ is empowered to do so.[24] Indeed, in some cases, the statutes explicitly prohibit a change of purpose.

Even in such cases, however, if circumstances arise under which the continuation of the statutory purposes would lead to consequences contrary to the original founder's intentions, the founder(s), the board, or the Attorney-General may petition the Court to amend the statutes. If changing the purpose is found necessary, the court will determine a new purpose that is as close as possible to the original one. The court may also decree an amendment that deviates from the one requested.[25]

(c) Participation Requirements

With respect to internal management and governance, additional regulations pertaining to nonprofit organizations are found in various laws on participation which are not incorporated in the Civil Code. Participation laws, for instance, grant participation rights to employees and, in the field of education, to staff, parents, and pupils.[26] These laws apply to any organization regardless of whether it is a commercial or a nonprofit organization. Even where these laws on participation do not apply, participation structures may be adopted by organizations since those structures are often a precondition for receiving subsidies from government. The diverse laws on participation all have a similar structure, and give participants in organizations a say in matters that are of direct concern to them. They can exert these rights through a council formed by themselves or their (legal) representatives. The management of the organization is obliged to give such a council the information it needs to carry out its functions effectively. In matters that directly affect the participants, the management must secure the concurrence of the council before putting a decision into effect. In more general matters, the council has more of an advisory role.

(d) Inquiry Procedure

Finally, since January 1, 1994, formal associations and foundations are subject to the so-called inquiry procedure. The inquiry procedure is to be found in the second Book of the Civil Code[27] and is designed to combat mismanagement and misconduct of affairs in an organization that is a legal person. The inquiry procedure

---

[24] Article 2:293 BW.

[25] The court may also amend the statutes to avoid the dissolution of the *stichting* when its purpose is not in accordance with the legal definition of the *stichting*, or when there is lack of sufficient property. See article 2:294 BW.

[26] A fairly new law in the field of participation is the *Wet Medezeggenschap Cliënten Zorginstellingen* (Staatsblad 1996, 204), which allows the participation of admitted clients in health and nursing care institutions (i.e., hospitals, homes for the elderly). Additional such laws are currently being drafted, for instance, in the field of youth care. However, these laws only apply to institutions that receive government funding. For a treatise on this subject see W.J.M. van Veen, "Gesloten of open overlegstelsel," in Van Eijk et al. (eds.), *SDU juridische en fiscale uitgeverij* ('s-Gravenhage, 1993), p. 111 a.f.

[27] Article 2:344 a.f. BW.

applies only to nonprofit organizations if the organization is by law obliged to set up a works council (*Ondernemingsraad*). The procedure begins with a written complaint lodged against an organization by appropriate complainants, which can be a trade union that has members among the employees of that organization, the Attorney-General at the Court of Appeals in Amsterdam, or, in the case of an association, at least 300 members, or 10% of the members or of the votes at a general meeting. Grounds for such complaints can be general mismanagement, poor bookkeeping, conflict-of-interest situations, organizational deadlock, and the like. In the event an organization fails to respond adequately to a complaint, the complainants can petition the Court of Appeal in Amsterdam (Chamber for Enterprise) to conduct an inquiry procedure. At the end of the inquiry, if the organization still does not correct any irregularities found, the Court can overturn a decision of an organization's board or general assembly, dismiss board members, or take other appropriate action.[28]

§ 17.4   TAX TREATMENT

Several taxes are of importance with regard to nonprofit organizations. These include taxes on the organizations and their activities, on the one hand, and taxes on the contributions to the organizations, on the other. The first category involves the company tax, the value-added tax, and gift and death duties. The second involves tax deductibility with regard to personal income tax and company tax.

(a) Tax Treatment of Organizations

(i) Company Tax.   In the Netherlands there are two different taxes on regular income. The first is income tax, which is imposed on individuals. The other is company tax, which applies to organizations with legal personality. Associations or foundations are not subject to the company tax. However, economic activities which are economically speaking, in direct competition with businesses and generate at least a modest profit, will be subject to taxation.

Only the net profit of such activities is taxable. Other sources of income of nonprofit organizations such as donations or contributions, and investment revenues so long as they are not related to economic activities, however, are not subject to taxation. This is an important difference between the tax treatment of nonprofit organizations and other types of corporations, since the latter are subject to company tax for their total income and gains. If the for-profit and nonprofit activities of an association or foundation are so entangled that net profit of the taxable activities cannot be determined, the taxable profit will be estimated.[29]

Furthermore, there are certain exemptions for nonprofit organizations from the general rules described above. If an organization pursues a purpose of general interest and the pursuit of profit is only of marginal importance, the organization may be exempt from company tax by the Ministry of Finance.[30] Exempt-

---

[28] Article 3:356 BW.
[29] Supreme Court, Decision of November 15, 1989, BNB 1990/48.
[30] Article 6 of the Law on Company Tax.

are institutions involved in curing and caring for (mental) patients, institutions providing care for elderly people or orphans, and institutions that provide occupation for socially maladapted people. The condition for this exemption is that at least 90% of their activities consist of providing the actual services, and under the further condition that the profits are used only for exempted organizations or in the general interest.[31] Further exempted from company tax, for instance, are recognized housing corporations and public libraries (Art. 5, Law on Company Tax).

(ii) Value-Added Tax.   Nonprofit organizations are in principle also subject to value-added tax for services and goods that they provide on a regular basis for which they charge their clients activities are not subject to VAT. Also, when there is a clear and direct link between a granted subsidy and certain activities (e.g., a government contract), it is taken that value-added tax is due with regard to the subsidy.[32] There are, however, a number of activities—many of them in fields where nonprofit organizations operate—that are exempt from this tax. These include caring for patients admitted to an institution and the provision of food and medicine to such patients as long as these activities are not undertaken to earn a profit; services performed by (para)medics, such as ambulance services; recognized organizations in the field of youth work; social and cultural activities as long as these activities do not substantially compete with businesses in the field; and education. Fund-raising activities by nonprofits on behalf of exempt activities are often also exempt from value-added tax as long as they do not exceed certain amounts. At the moment, the amounts are Dfl 150,000 for deliverance of goods and Dfl 50,000 for services (Dfl 70,000 for services by sports organizations). Furthermore, if nonprofit organizations jointly establish an independent organization in order to lower administrative costs through synergy effects, such organizations are also generally exempt, except for salary-related and financial services.

(iii) Gift and Death Duties.   Like other organizations, nonprofit organizations are also subject to gift and death duties, which are imposed on gifts, legacies, or inheritances obtained from a resident of the Netherlands or a person that has left the Netherlands as his residence for less than ten years. However, the rates paid by nonprofit organizations that serve the public interest are lower than those paid by other recipient organizations. For other organizations, the general rate for gift and death duties differs according to the worth of the acquisition from 41% up to 68%. Churches, charitable, cultural, and scientific institutions, as well as institutions that serve the general interest—defined as activities that, do not aim at benefiting a single individual or a limited group of individuals, but serve

---

[31] Decision August 20, 1971, Staatsblad 558 and December 18, 1990, Stb. 1990, 638.

[32] See F.J. Oomen, *Stichting & Vereniging* (Deventer: Kluwer, 1990), p. 127 a.f. According to a recent statement of the Ministry of Finance further clarifying this matter, VAT is not due if the government subsidy supports the provision of services that are exempted from VAT in general or if the subsidy is not intended to lower fees for clients receiving a particular service (see *Vakstudie Nieuws*, (Deventer: Kluwer, February 2, 1995), p. 506 (ff).

the interest of the public—are subject to a more favorable rate of 11%.[33],[34] These "11%-rate organizations" also benefit from a provision that sets the threshold above which gifts are actually subject to gift or death duties higher for them than for other types of organizations. Although foreign organizations are, in principle, not eligible for the favorable 11% rate, foreign organizations serving the general interest in an international perspective are generally granted remission of gift and death duties. Thus, they are treated like domestic organizations serving the general interest. Apart from this, remission may also be granted in individual cases under special circumstances.

Oversight of these various tax provisions is performed by the tax authorities. Any (legal) person must make its books available to the tax authorities on request. This applies also to nonprofit organizations. Tax authorities, however, check only whether or not the fiscal laws are being obeyed properly. They do not review the management of an organization as such. In case of misconduct, only fiscal sanctions can be imposed upon the subject.

(b) Tax Treatment of Contributions

Dutch fiscal law allows tax deductions for both individuals and companies for gifts to domestic institutions such as churches, charitable, cultural, and scientific institutions as well as institutions that serve the general interest. General interest for this purpose means any purpose not intended to benefit a particular person or restricted group of persons, but the public in general. Eligible fields include education, art, development aid, animal protection, social work, health care, child protection, and so on. Political parties are also considered to serve the general interest and are treated accordingly in terms of tax benefits. Though an organization must be a domestic organization to be eligible for tax-deduction, there is no restriction as to where the activities of the organization are performed.

To be eligible for deductions from personal income taxes, individuals must contribute at least 1% of gross income to such organizations. The maximum deductible amount is 10% of gross income. If, however, donations can be regarded as expenses related to a profession or business of the taxpayer, there is no limit on the deductibility. Furthermore, donations by notarial deed comprising at least five annual installments are deductible without any limits.

With regard to the deductibility of donations made by corporations that are liable to the company tax, a distinction must be made between donations as costs and donations as gifts. Donations made by corporations or enterprises for essentially business purposes—for example, corporate sponsorship for which the corporation receives advertising—can be considered to be costs and are deductible without any limits. Enterprise donations that are gifts are only deductible if they exceed the amount of Dfl 500 and can be deducted up to a maximum of 6% of the taxable profit of that year.

---

[33] The 11%-rate status can be applied for at the Inspector of Registration and Succession. If the decision of the Inspector of Registration and Succession is contested, the final ruling lies with the courts.

[34] Article 24, subsection 4, *Successiewet* 1956.

§ 17.5   PERSONAL BENEFIT RESTRICTIONS

Under Dutch law, nonprofit organizations face some restrictions in respect to the distribution of benefits. In particular, associations are prohibited from dividing any profits or benefits they generate among their members.[35] Foundations may not have as part of their purposes to benefit their founders, members of their governing bodies, or other persons unless, with regard to the latter, the benefits have an idealistic or social character. If violations of these restrictions occur, the court can dissolve the association or foundation on the request of the Public Prosecutor or other person with an interest.[36] On the other hand, members of the board or other organs may receive reasonable compensation and reimbursement of costs for the work they do for the organization.

§ 17.6   OBLIGATIONS TO THE PUBLIC

In the Netherlands, nonprofit organizations, like other legal persons, have an obligation to keep books and prepare annual accounts.[37] The obligation to keep books implies that the board must, at any time, be able to present an overview of the rights and obligations of the legal person involved. The accounts must be kept available for at least ten years. There is, however, neither a controlling agency to which the annual reports must be sent or published, nor an obligation for the board to make such information available to interested persons. This is not so much a point of concern for associations since the annual report must be presented to, and be approved by, the general meeting of members.

For foundations, however, the lack of an obligation to report is a matter of more concern since foundations do not necessarily have a controlling organ unless one is constructed in the statutes of the organization. The legal structure of foundations and the lack of an obligation to publish annual accounts thus means that supervision of the actions of foundation boards is quite limited. Therefore, some powers are given to the public prosecutor, who is in charge of maintaining the law in general. The public prosecutor can ask the board for information if he or she has serious doubts if the law or the statutes of the foundation are being observed faithfully, or if he or she doubts that the foundation is being managed properly.[38] In principle, however, the members of the board have no obligation to the authorities as long as they have not been asked for specific information.

While there is no general public disclosure requirement, however, the government often only agrees to grant subsidies to associations or foundations if books are kept properly, and insight in the annual account is given.[39] Sometimes

---

[35] Article 2:26 BW.

[36] Article 2:21 BW. Also, monies received in violation of the nondistribution constraint qualify as undue payment and thus have to be restituted.

[37] Article 2:10 BW.

[38] Article 2:297 BW.

[39] At current, legislation is being prepared that would subject certain foundations and associations (commercial associations and foundations with a turnover of Dfl 6 million or more) to the same regulations for accounting and publication of annual accounts that apply to for-profit organizations (TK 24 255). In addition, special laws on accounting procedures apply to certain types of nonprofit organizations, such as hospitals and housing corporations.

the right to visit board meetings or meetings of the supervising organ is stipulated. Finally, as detailed more fully below, associations and foundations engaged in fund raising from the public have additional public scrutiny obligations administered by municipal governments and a nongovernmental Central Bureau on Fundraising.

With the Law of June 29, 1994, Staatsblad 1994, 506, implemented September 1, 1994, the Chambers of Commerce and Industry have also been given a role in controlling legal persons, especially with regard to inactive organizations. This new law, incorporated in the Civil Code in article 2:19a BW, is designed to enable the Chambers of Commerce to close down legal persons, including associations and foundations, under certain circumstances described in the law when the organization is considered to be inactive.

§ 17.7   BUSINESS ACTIVITY

In Dutch law, there are no restrictions as to which sources of income a nonprofit organization may seek to exploit. Nonprofit organizations may therefore be commercially active in support of their noncommercial activities. If nonprofit organizations perform economic activities *on a regular basis,* such as selling souvenirs, running a restaurant, and so on, to support their nonprofit activities, these activities are in principle subject to company tax, regardless of the "nonprofit" character of the organization. However, as noted earlier, company tax is imposed on nonprofit organizations only when they engage in business activities that are in competition with businesses. Even in these cases, however, organizations engaged in general interest purposes can be exempt from this tax (see above).

§ 17.8   OTHER FUNDING RESTRICTIONS

To protect the public interest in ensuring that fund raising is conducted properly and that the proceeds are used as intended, nonprofit organizations are subject to some reporting requirements and other restrictions at the local level. More specifically, for door-to-door or on-the-street solicitations a permit from the municipal government is required. However, there are practically no requirements and restrictions for all other types of solicitations.[40] To partly remedy the potential pitfalls that might result from the lack of such regulation at the local and national level, the Central Bureau on Fundraising (CBF) (the foundation was established in 1925), a foundation in which fund-raising organizations,[41] large grant makers, and the Netherlands Association of Municipalities cooperate, has been created. The distribution of competencies and the composition of its key organs guarantee

---

[40] Except for provisions in criminal law and consumer protection prohibiting fraud, misrepresentation and other forms of deceit. Selling of goods by telephone is prohibited when it is suggested or implied that (part of) the proceeds will benefit some public interest serving organization. See article 435e Netherlands Criminal Code.

[41] In this context, fund raising organization means a nonprofit organization that depends on free contributions from the public.

independent and objective decision making, involving one or more members of the academia, certified public accountants, magistrature, and other disciplines. In addition the CBF is supervised by the Netherlands Council for Accreditation (Raad voor de Certificatie). The purpose of the CBF is to ensure the responsible conduct of fund-raising activities aiming at soliciting donations from the public at large by charitable, cultural, scientific, and other legal persons which are serving the general interest.[42] One of the main instruments the CBF has developed is a system of accreditation. The first form of accreditation is a "Declaration of Supportworthiness." The second form is an official "Seal of Approval," which can be obtained only by organizations which are in existence for more than three years and have proven that their fund-raising activities meet the highest standards. Once the Seal of Approval is granted, an organization is allowed to use the *CBF-Keur* logo in their activities. A fund-raising organization can apply for accreditation to the CBF. The system of accreditation helps municipal governments to decide whether to grant certain organizations the permission to hold collections, and the public to determine whether a fund-raising organization is worthy of support. The CBF is also involved in designing a national plan for collections. This plan is meant to prevent organizations from organizing national collections at the same time. The organizations submit themselves voluntarily to this plan, thus respecting each others' collection periods. In sum, while municipal governments have the right to grant or deny permission for collection activities, fund-raising regulation is largely left to self-regulation by the nonprofit organizations in cooperation with (local) government and representatives of several disciplines.

§ 17.9   POLITICAL ACTIVITY

There are no restrictions on nonprofit organizations in the Netherlands with regard to lobbying, advocacy, or other political activities. Organizations that are involved in these activities receive the same tax treatment as "other" nonprofit organizations. The only limitation is that it is forbidden to have a purpose or perform activities that undermine the public order. Beyond this, organizations directly engaged in electoral activity must register as political parties with the Central Bureau of Elections, and must have full legal competence as formal associations.

§ 17.10   KEY OUTSTANDING ISSUES

(a) Government-Nonprofit Relations

Governments have historically relied heavily on nonprofit organizations in the Netherlands to provide services and have subsidized them for this purpose. However, this relationship is currently in a process of rapid and erratic change. In par-

---

[42] See M.J. Wester, "Central Bureau on Fund Raising and how is fund raising organized in the Netherlands," In T.J. van der Ploeg and J.W. Sap, *Rethinking the Balance, Government and Nongovernmental Organizations in the Netherlands* (Amsterdam: VU University Press, 1995), p. 139.

ticular, and partially due to the decentralization of certain financial responsibilities from the central governments to local municipalities, over the last five years the government has used the power it exercises over nonprofits as a consequence of these subsidies to force mergers of nonprofit organizations such as schools, hospitals, and welfare institutions. The trend appears to be that governmental bodies view subsidized nonprofit organizations as mere instruments at their disposal to pursue their policies. This poses significant risks to the independence of nonprofit organizations and their ability to respond to private initiative. This raises important questions about how far government authority should actually reach, and what opportunities the civil law offers to prevent further damage to the subsidized portion of the nonprofit sector.

The traditional relationships between government and the nonprofit sector are also undergoing change as a consequence of government moves to establish private law foundations to take over certain public tasks, such as education. This essentially eliminates democratic control over an important municipal activity and circumvents legal procedures provided by constitutional and administrative law to control improper governmental conduct of affairs.

(b) Commercialization and Privatization

Due to declining financial support from the government, nonprofit organizations are increasingly forced to charge fees for services where revenues can be expected, and to use such revenues to cross-subsidize activities that are not supportable through fees. However, this trend increasingly creates direct competition between nonprofit organizations and commercial enterprises offering the same services, and potentially leads to disputes regarding the fairness of competition when some competing organizations enjoy the privileges of nonprofit status. If such disputes take full effect and legal action is taken to remedy this situation, nonprofits might lose the opportunity to gain additional income from the provision of "lucrative" services, and thus return to financial dependence on government largesse.

This development may become even more problematic if the nascent practice of using subsidies under contract becomes more widespread in the Netherlands. This is so because there are legal arguments to treat such contracts as transactions that, under European Union law, are subject to the rule of public tender. This would also increase the ability of commercial firms to compete for such "business."

Also important has been an accelerating trend toward the shifting of governmental functions to the for-profit business sector. This trend is a product of budgetary pressures on government in the Netherlands. As gaps are created, for-profit corporations have moved in increasingly to meet the demands that exist, in some cases displacing nonprofit organizations that were active in the field.

(c) Professionalization and Formalization of the Participation Process

The above-mentioned wave of mergers under way in the Netherlands is also leading to greater professionalization, since larger organizations generally need a more professional management. However, there are considerable risks associated with this trend, as these large and professionalized organizations can become increasingly bureaucratic, making citizens feel less involved and thus reducing volunteerism.

The new participation laws that give clients a voice in the management of care facilities may offer relief from this problem. However, the establishment of a code of conduct is left to self-regulation by individual organizations, and the interpretation of the participation laws will depend on the development of case law.

(d) Globalization and Internationalization

The formation of the European Union (EU) is going to affect the functioning of nonprofit umbrella organizations in the Netherlands. The current relationship between government and nonprofits at the national level can best be described as a consultancy model in which government and umbrella organizations share in shaping public policies. With the formation of the EU, however, many issues formerly decided at the national level are now being resolved in Brussels and it is uncertain as of yet how this will ultimately affect the position of umbrella organizations in the Netherlands. An interesting option for umbrella organizations will be European-association status as a legal form of cooperation. The law regarding European association, is, however, still in development.

CHAPTER EIGHTEEN

Poland[*]

§ 18.1 LEGAL CONTEXT

Poland belongs to the continental family of predominantly civil law countries. As a reflection of the division of Poland between its neighboring powers during the nineteenth century, Polish law was a conglomerate of different aspects of French, German, Austrian, and Russian law, which had all been in force in various parts of Poland before Polish law was largely codified and thus unified before World War II. The introduction of the Soviet-style system in the aftermath of World War II was followed by further adjustments in the law, which, however, have never been completed.

The gaps and contradictions that remained in the legal system led to an even more complex state of affairs after the reintroduction of the market economy and the rule of law in 1989. Not surprisingly, this transformation led to changes in law, in regulation, and in practice that are still not complete especially with regard to the complex set of relationships between fiscal authorities and various types of nonprofit organizations and institutions.

Although there are many types of nonprofit organizations which are recognized under Polish law, there is no single, unified body of legislation or other binding interpretation that would treat these organizations as one single type of legal entity. Similarly, while the concept of nonprofit activity appears in some parts of the legislation, it is under change and not necessarily consistent across the whole body of law.

Although many types of nonprofit activities were recognized in Polish law prior to the establishment of the communist system, some institutions fell into disuse under communism, some were co-opted into the totalitarian Party-State's control structure, and some were formally abolished. After the dismantling of the Communist political system and its legal instruments in 1989, not all of the legal forms that other civil law countries often provide for nonprofit activities were reinstituted in Poland. Instead, two legal forms were reestablished for nonprofit organizations in laws passed in the 1980s: first, foundations, authorized by the Law on Foundations enacted in 1984 in order to provide a legal mechanism for the transfer of foreign aid to nongovernmental structures in Poland, while the country was still under communist rule; and, second, associations, authorized by the new Law on Associations, which was enacted in 1989 by the Communist-nominated Parliament after Round Table discussions that were part of the reintroduction of democracy in Poland. In addition, the new Constitution of 1997 provides safeguards for the freedom of "trade unions, farmers unions, associa-

---

[*] Country Rapporteur: Dr. Jacek Kurczewski, Chair of Sociology of Custom and Law, University of Warsaw, Warsaw, Poland.

tions, civic movements, other voluntary organizations and foundations" (Art. 12) and generally guarantees the freedom of association (Art. 58). Art. 59 deals specifically with trade unions and farmers' and employees organizations.

§ 18.2   ELIGIBILITY

(a) Types of Organizations

Polish law acknowledges two broad types of nonprofit organizations: associations and foundations. In addition, there are several other types of nonprofit organizations that are regulated either by other general legislation or by individual legal acts. The former category includes political parties (Law on Political Parties) and trade unions (Law on Trade Unions); whereas the latter category includes churches, which are regulated by specific legislation on the relations between the state and any given church, the Polish Red Cross, and some other organizations. While all of these different organizations might be subsumed under the category of nonprofit organizations, the focus here is on associations and foundations as the major types.

(i) Associations.   The Polish Law on Associations of April 7, 1989 (LA 1989) and subsequent amendments defines associations (*stowarzyszenia*) as "voluntary, self-governing, enduring groupings of people (*zrzeszenie*) for nonprofit purposes,"[1] then further distinguishes between two types of associations: (1) full associations, which must involve at least 15 individual members and which enjoy legal personality; and (2) associations simple, which must involve only three people and do not have legal personality. It is important to note here that the right to form associations pertains only to physical persons. The only exceptions are unions of associations, which may have legal persons as members, although legal persons pursuing profit cannot be full members of such unions either.

(ii) Foundations.   Unlike associations, foundations are estates usually established by a single founder for more or less specifically defined nonprofit purposes. Once established, foundations are managed by a board. The legal basis for this type of nonprofit organization is the Law on Foundations of April 6, 1984 (LF 1984) with further amendments. Although the law does not provide a general definition of foundations, it does specify specific rules for setting up, registering, and starting such organizations. However, since 1989, two foundations have been established by specific acts of parliament.

(b) Types of Purposes

Under Polish law, *associations* enjoy a wide range of eligible purposes. According to article 1.2 of the Law on Associations, any restrictions of the right to associate must be introduced by legislation and are permissible only for reasons of national security, maintaining public order, the protection of public health and morality, or the protection of the rights and freedoms of other persons.

---

[1] Article 3.1, LA 1989.

Regarding foundations, however, the Law on Foundations is more stringent and states that foundations may be established only "to fulfill socially or economically useful purposes" in "accordance with the basic interests of the Republic." As legitimate purposes, the law lists health care, economic and scientific development, education, culture and science, social care and assistance, and the conservation of the environment and historical monuments. The registration court has the power to interpret the charters of applying foundations to determine whether the drafted purposes are in line with the law.

(c) Other Requirements

As mentioned above, *full associations* must have at least 15 individual members and *associations simple* at least three. Unions of associations may have legal persons as members, although profit-making organizations are barred from full membership.

Foundations, whose statutes allow economic activities, are required to demonstrate founding assets of at least 1,000 zlotys.

(d) Registration Procedures

Both foundations and full associations must register with government authorities, although the respective procedures are somewhat different.

(i) Associations. In the case of full associations, at least 15 founding members must approve the statute and elect the founding committee which represents the membership in the registration process. The committee must file (1) the statute; (2) a list of founders including names, birth dates, addresses, and signatures; and (3) a report on the internal elections and the provisional address of the association with the registration court whose jurisdiction area includes the seat of the association in the respective *voivodship*.

The statutes must specify the following:

1. A proper and unique name for the association
2. Territorial scope of activities and the location of the association
3. The purposes and means for pursuing them
4. Procedures for joining the association and for revoking membership, a list of potential reasons for revoking membership, and the rights and duties of members
5. The governing bodies of the association, their respective competencies, and procedures for the election of these bodies
6. Specifications concerning the external representation of the association and the authority for, and validation of, transactions with third parties involving external obligations on the side of the association
7. Provisions concerning the funding of the associations and the assessment of membership fees
8. Rules for amending the statute
9. Stipulations for the dissolution
10. Provisions for structuring local chapters and the ways such chapters may be established

The registration court must decide within three months and cannot refuse registration as long as the formal requirements stipulated by the Law on Associations of 1989 are met. After the application is filed, the court must inform the local administrative authorities about the application, which, in turn, have 14 days to express their opinion before the court. Associations are also required to set up governing boards and an internal controlling authority.

Associations simple, which do not acquire legal personality, only have to inform the territorially relevant administration of pertinent facts regarding the association, including the name, purpose, area and intruments of activity, location, and details concerning the association's external representation. The local administration or the public prosecutor has the option of applying to the registration court in order to prohibit the establishment of an association simple. If the association simple has not received a prohibition order within 30 days of informing the authorities, it may assume its functioning.

(ii) Foundations. With respect to foundations, the founder, or alternatively the board, must file with the territorial court in Warsaw the statute for the foundation as well as relevant information pertaining to the establishing capital. At least 1,000 zlotys in capital must be available if the foundation in its statute provides for economic activities. In contrast to the registration courts for associations, which are decentralized in the *voivodships*, there is only one national register for foundations and the registering court resides within the court in the capital, Warsaw. For registration purposes, the founder must file a declaration of intent to establish the foundation, certified by a notary, unless the foundation is established by last will. Furthermore, the founder must specify the purpose of the foundation and the material assets designated for the purpose and determine the foundation's statute which must include the name, location and the assets of the foundation, its purpose, internal regulations, the form and scope of its activities, the structure and composition of the governing board, the way the board is set up, and the rights and duties of the board members. In addition to these mandatory provisions, the statute may stipulate additional rules pertaining to the economic activities the foundation may engage in, provisions for possible mergers with other foundations, changes in purpose and amendments to the statutes, and other organs of the foundation in addition to the board of directors. The founder may also specify a Ministry to provide appropriate oversight of the foundation, depending on the scope of its activities.

§ 18.3   INTERNAL GOVERNANCE

(a) Associations

According to the Law on Associations of 1989, associations are free to decide on their own internal "organizational structures."[2] However, the law does put some limits on how this freedom is executed. In particular, the law stipulates that associations have to be governed by elected officers. Therefore, the statute has to provide for election procedures, specify the form of internal government, and make provisions for the replacement of officers. The supreme power within an associa-

[2] Article 2.1, LA 1989.

tion rests with the general assembly of members, which holds the power to decide on organizational affairs in all matters in which the statute does not grant jurisdiction to other specified internal authorities.[3] The general assembly of members may be substituted by an assembly of elected delegates if the number of members passes the threshold (if any) specified in the statute. In addition, associations must also have a board and an "internal controlling organ," which must be separate from the board. In the model statute which is not legally binding, a Review Commission as well as a Court of Peers are listed, as these have traditionally been considered to be the necessary institutions even though the Law on Associations of 1989 does not explicitly mention either. Both the Review Commission and the Court of Peers are composed of members of the association, who must be elected by the general membership or by its elected delegates. The purpose of a Review Commission is to assess the actions of the Board, especially in financial matters, while a Court of Peers handles disputes between the members of the association should such a dispute be brought before it by a member involved.

(b) Foundations

With regard to foundations, the Law on Foundations of 1984 only stipulates that the "board of the foundation directs its activity and represents the foundation externally."[4] Article 5 of this law further confers on the founder the responsibility of drawing up the statute, which must include, *inter alia*, provisions on the composition and organization of the board; the manner in which it is set up; and the duties and rights of the board and its members. The statute may also provide for additional internal organs.

§ 18.4   TAX TREATMENT

(a) Tax Treatment of Organizations

The general principle of Polish law is that all legal actors, including associations and foundations, are treated equally in matters of taxation. Accordingly, tax exemption is not granted to specific types of organizations per se, but is rather related to the pursuit of specific eligible activities. All legal entities are therefore formally obliged to pay income tax, commodities and services tax, tax on real property, and so on.

An exception to this general legal principle was introduced by the Law on Foundations of 1984, which originally exempted bequests or gifts of cash and other movable property or property rights made to foundations from inheritance and gift taxation. Although this exemption was annulled in 1989, the Law of January 31, 1989 granted exemption from income taxation for all legal personalities, including associations and foundations, whose statutory aims are scientific and scientific-technical activities; education; culture; sports and recreation; the protection of the environment; charity; health protection; social assistance; occupational and social rehabilitation of the handicapped; and religious practice. Only that part

---

[3] Article 11.1, LA 1989.
[4] Article 10, LF 1984.

of the income that is actually allocated to these statutory purposes in the current or the following tax year is exempted, however. Since then, this law has been subject to several amendments and "support of economic initiatives aiming at the development of roads and telecommunication in the countryside and water supply" have been added to the list of tax-exempted activities. Since the tax legislation in this regard continues to be subject to change, further adjustments and extensions are to be expected.

(b) Tax Treatment of Contributions—Domestic Organizations

Both individuals and corporations are eligible to claim tax benefits for cash or in-kind donations to foundations and associations for up to a fixed percentage of the gross income if the donation is to serve the above-listed purposes and the recipient is not pursuing these purposes through economic activities. The limits, determined in the annual review of tax legislation, have recently increased to from 10% to 15%.

(c) Tax Treatment of Contributions—Foreign Organizations

Polish tax law does not differentiate betwen domestic organizations and foreign organizations registered in Poland concerning the issue of tax benefits for donations.

§ 18.5   PERSONAL BENEFIT RESTRICTIONS

Regulations pertaining to personal benefit restrictions are explicitly laid out in the Law on Associations of 1989, which prohibits associations from distributing any income among their members and further obliges the association to use all income for the statutory, nonprofit goals.

§ 18.6   OBLIGATIONS TO THE PUBLIC

Polish associations are not required by law to prepare and submit annual or other reports to local or other authorities or to the public. However, the Law on Associations of 1989 places associations under the supervision of the local authority in whose jurisdiction the association operates. The local government authorities have the right to check the books and all other relevant documents of the associations under its jurisdiction, order the submission of copies of all decisions passed by the general assembly, and order the officers of the association to provide the necessary information. If these authorities have reason to conclude that an association is violating either the law or the association's registered statutes, they may order a correction of the association's conduct, issue a reprimand, or apply to the registration court for further actions. The court may mandate various sanctions ranging from issuing reprimands, to annulling the contested action, to ordering the dissolution of the association, in case the violation of the law or the statutes is permanent, flagrant, and seemingly incorrigible.[5]

By contrast, foundations must provide annual reports of their activities to the Ministry that the registration court has determined as the relevant Ministry to supervise the foundation's activities. If a foundation acts only within one *voivodship*, the annual report must also be submitted to the *Voivod*. Annual reports of foundations should also be made available to the public. The relevant Ministry or *Voivod* may apply to the court to investigate whether a foundation acts in accordance with the law and its statutes and to annul decisions of the board of the foundation if such a decision is in gross violation of the law, the foundation's statutes, or its declared purpose.

§ 18.7   BUSINESS ACTIVITY

Because the relevant regulations for associations, foundations and various other NGOs were enacted before or just at the time of the sudden economic revolution that brought market principles into a previously state-controlled economy, the area of business activities is regulated in a very inconsistent way in Poland, leaving many doubts as to whether business activities are in accordance with the law.

With respect to foundations, the Law on Foundations of 1984 stipulates that economic activity (*dzialalnosc gospodarcza*) is permissible only if specifically authorized in the foundation's statutes. If the pursuit of economic activities was not originally intended and foundations plan to engage in such activities in the future, a respective amendment of the statutes is required. These requirements of the law aim at putting the scope of business activities of foundations under the control of the courts and also helping to insure the safety of business transactions, since foundation statutes as well as such obligatory amendments have to be filed with the central court in Warsaw. As further requirements, foundations may perform business activities only to serve their statutory goals, which in effect limits the scope of such activities, and have to set aside at least 1000 zlotys in assets, which, in 1991 when the relevant amendment was made, equaled the capital requirement set forth for limited liability companies.

The regulation pertaining to business activities of associations is far more liberal than in the case of foundations. Article 34 of the Law on Associations grants all associations the right to conduct economic activity subject only to the limitation that the income from business activities must be used for the statutory aims of the association and cannot be distributed among members. Article 34 also holds that the exercise of this right is subject to the general regulations on business activities as stipulated by other applicable laws. However, this provision refers to the Law on Economic Activity of January 23, 1988 with further amendments, which in its first article states that "the undertaking of economic activity is free and allowed to everybody on equal rights within the limits set up by the law." As a consequence, despite the fact that associations are statutorily defined as organizations with nonprofit (*niezarobkowe*) goals, economic activities of associations,

[5] Article 29.3, LA 1989.

which often develop into large enterprises, are practically unrestricted and even unregistered. This liberal regulation of the business activities of associations, and particularly the lack of any registration of such activities, has sparked intense criticism. New legislation has been drafted to remedy this situation, but, at this writing, has not yet passed.

§ 18.8   OTHER FUNDING RESTRICTIONS

In Poland, there are binding legal regulations in effect pertaining to street and door-to-door charitable collections as well as certain other kinds of fund-raising activities, such as lotteries, which require organizations to apply to local or national administrative authorities for prior authorization of such activities. Usually, organizations must seek permission from the local authorities, unless they perform activities at the regional or national levels, such as nationwide charitable collections or lotteries. If the latter is the case, a permit from either the *voivodship* or Ministry of Finance is necessary. On the other hand, there are no ceilings for fund-raising or administrative costs under Polish law.

§ 18.9   POLITICAL ACTIVITY

In general, nonprofit organizations in Poland are largely free to engage in political activities, although there are certain regulatory differences among different types of nonprofit organizations.

The Law on Associations of 1989 in its preamble lists, *inter alia*, the provision of opportunity for active participation in public life as one of the inherent purposes of associations. In pursuance of this, article 1.3 of the law explicitly grants *associations* "the right to express themselves in public matters" regardless of the association's stated goals or activities. It is generally understood, moreover, that in practice there are no limitations on the political activities of associations. Associations can even take part in elections through elective committees, which are the legal form required for this purpose by the electoral laws.

Similar to associations, *trade unions* are also permitted to take part in political activities under Polish law. They can therefore take part in local and national elections through their electoral committees, and express themselves on political issues more generally.

Although associations and unions are in this way permitted to take part in political elections, *political parties*, as defined by the Law on Political Parties of July 28, 1990, are considered the proper focus of political activity per se. Political parties are registered in a special register; can be dissolved only upon verdict of the Constitutional Court; are granted some tax exemptions; and are subject to public transparency in terms of their finances.

Concerning the political activities of *foundations*, it should be kept in mind that the Law on Foundations of 1984 provides a list of exemplary areas of permissible activities, which does not include political activities. However, political activities may be subsumed under the category of "socially useful purposes," which is the more general scope of acceptable activities. Although there are no specific regulations that prohibit foundations from entering into the sphere of political activity, foundations are, however, obligated to pursue exclusively the scope of activities and objectives defined in their registered statutes, which stands in stark contrast to the general right of public expression granted to associations by the Law on Associations of 1989. Foundations seeking to engage in political activities consequently need to make sure their statutes allow for this.

§ 18.10 KEY OUTSTANDING ISSUES

Although the key issues at present involve all the main aspects of the operation of the nonprofit sector, there are some issues that have become the subject of public controversies, administrative actions, and legislative initiatives and that should therefore be noted here. In particular:

(a) Business Activity

The largely unrestricted freedom of associations to engage in business activities without having to register such activities remains a very controversial issue, further complicated by the fact that neither the legislature nor the judicial interpretation have yet developed clear and concise conceptual definitions of profit, nonprofit, and business (economic) activities and the respective differences among these.

(b) Government Foundations

Another currently debated issue is the legal status and public accountability of foundations established by the government with endowments from the public budget. Under current law, once established, such foundations become independent and operate on the same principles as any other private foundation.

CHAPTER NINETEEN

The Russian Federation[*]

§ 19.1 LEGAL CONTEXT

The Russian Federation (RF) is a civil law country with a constitution that guarantees freedom of association and freedom of religion. In response to decades of constitutionally mandated Communist Party dominance, the RF Constitution guarantees the equality of public associations and religious organizations before the law.[1]

The legal framework for nonprofit organizations (NPOs) rests not only on the RF Constitution, but also on the RF Civil Code, legislation governing specific categories of NPOs, and other laws and normative acts addressing issues relevant to NPO activity. The Civil Code provides a general framework for NPO activity; other laws develop this framework by providing more detailed regulation. These include the laws "On NPOs" (1996), "On Labor Unions" (1996), "On Public Associations" (1995), "On Charitable Activity and Charitable Organizations" (1995), "On Consumer Cooperatives" (1992), and "On Religious Freedom" (1990).[2]

RF law encourages federal and local governments to support NPOs through tax advantages, special privileges, competitive grants, and direct financial assistance.[3] The federal government sometimes uses NPOs as instruments for implementing state programs. The government can also reorganize a public agency as an NPO in order to facilitate fund raising and to increase cooperation with individuals and organizations outside of the government; one of the more prominent examples of this is the Russian Cultural Foundation, which was reorganized as an NPO in January 1996.[4] A governmental body, however, may not be a founder,

---

[*] Country Rapporteurs: Nina Belyaeva, J.D., Moscow State University; Ph.D., Institute for State and Law; President, Interlegal International Charitable Foundation and Jeffrey A. Trexler, Ph.D., Duke; J.D., Yale; Associate, Gardner, Carlon and Douglas.

[1] RF Constitution, articles 13, 14, 30 (1993).

[2] RF Law No. 10-FZ, "On Trade Unions, Their Rights, and Guarantees for Activity" (January 12, 1996); RF Law No. 7-FZ, "On NPOs" (January 12, 1996); RF Law No. 135-FZ, "On Charitable Activity and Charitable Organizations" (August 11, 1995) (hereinafter "On Charitable Activity"); RF Law No. 82-FZ, "On Public Associations" (May 19, 1995); RF Law No. 3085-1, "On the Consumers' Cooperative in the RF" (June 12, 1992); RSFSR Law, "On Religious Freedom" (October 25, 1990).

[3] RF Law No. 7-FZ, "On NPOs," article 31; RF Law No. 135-FZ, "On Charitable Activity," article 18; RF Law No. 82-FZ, "On Public Associations," article 18; RF Law No. 98-FZ, "On State Support of Youth and Children's Public Associations" (June 26, 1995); RF Administration Resolution No. 837, "On Support of Public Movement in Protecting Consumers' Rights" (August 26, 1995).

[4] RF Presidential Decree No. 15, "On State Support for the Russian Cultural Foundation" (January 6, 1996).

member, or participant in a public association.[5] Nor may governmental bodies, enterprises, or institutions found a charitable organization.[6]

Local governments have played a significant role in supporting NPOs and developing NPO law. For example, years before the federal government passed the law "On NPOs," Moscow had established its own standards for registering NPOs and regulating their activity. These procedures will remain in effect until the federal government finalizes its procedures for registering NPOs.[7] Moscow also has its own law on charitable organizations, which requires an organization to undergo a rigorous certification process in order to receive charitable status.[8] The Moscow city government keeps regular contact with NPOs through its City Charitable Council as well as the Commission of the Moscow Administration on NPO Concerns.

§ 19.2   ELIGIBILITY

(a) Types of Organizations

The First Part of the RF Civil Code recognizes two main categories of legal entities: commercial organizations and NPOs. Under the Civil Code, there are five basic types of NPOs: consumer cooperatives, public and religious organizations, foundations, institutions, and associations of legal entities.[9] Laws supporting the Civil Code can establish additional types of NPOs within these categories. For example, the law "On NPOs" provides the legal basis for nonprofit partnerships and autonomous NPOs, while the law "On Public Associations" provides for public movements and community action groups.

RF legislation also recognizes types of NPOs not specifically defined in the Civil Code or the law "On NPOs." One fast-growing form of NPO activity is the nongovernmental pension fund, which is an organization that receives funds designated for private pension plans, transfers the money to a legally distinct company for investment, and then receives the profit from the investment company for distribution as pension payments. Other prominent types of NPOs include chambers of commerce, condominium partnerships, and stock and commodities exchanges.[10]

The classification of NPOs in the Russian Civil Code is based on several different factors, including membership, fundamental purposes, and property interests. Thus, the defining characteristic of a *public or religious organization* is

---

[5] RF Law No. 82-FZ, "On Public Associations," article 19.

[6] RF Law No. 135-FZ, "On Charitable Activity," article 8.

[7] Moscow Mayor's Directive No. 598-RM, "On Establishing the Regulation on the Order of Registration of NPOs in Moscow" (December 29, 1992).

[8] Moscow Law No. 11-46, "On Charitable Activity" (July 5, 1995).

[9] First Part of the RF Civil Code, article 50 (November 30, 1994); see also articles 116–23.

[10] RF Presidential Decree [NPFs]; RF Presidential Decree No. 2275, "On Establishing the Temporary Regulation on the Condominium" (December 23, 1993); RF Law No. 5340-1, "On Chambers of Commerce and Industry" (July 7, 1993); RF Law No. 2383-1, "On Commodities Exchanges and Exchange Trade" (February 20, 1992); RSFSR Administration Resolution No. 78, "On Establishing the Regulation on the Issuance and Return of Stocks and Stock Exchanges in the RSFSR" (December 28, 1991).

that it is based on its members' or participants' common interest in providing for spiritual and other nonmaterial needs. In contrast, a *consumer cooperative* consists of members who unite on the basis of contributions that go toward satisfying the members' material needs.[11]

Relation to property is a primary defining characteristic in several other types of NPOs. A *foundation* is a nonmembership NPO formed on the basis of voluntary contributions of money or property that go toward socially beneficial goals. Another nonmembership NPO formed on the basis of voluntary contributions of money or property is the *autonomous NPO*; however, the autonomous NPO aims specifically at providing services.[12] A *nonprofit partnership* is a membership organization in which the members combine assets in order to engage in nonprofit activity. The members are not liable for the partnership's debts, but they retain the right to receive a portion of its assets when they leave the organization. An *institution* is an NPO created by a property owner for administrative, educational, or other nonprofit functions; the institution, such as a hospital or school, manages the property, but the founder retains full ownership rights.[13]

An additional important defining characteristic is the place where the NPO conducts its activity. For example, a *public movement* is a nonmembership public association that operates over a large area; it is a "mass" movement of people and organizations working together to serve social, political, and other publicly beneficial goals.[14] A *community action group* is also a nonmembership public association, but it serves the interests of individuals in a place of residence, work, or study.[15] RF law additionally provides for classifying a public association in terms of its territorial sphere of operation: local, regional, interregional, or all-Russian (i.e., has offices in more than half of the RF's constituent territories).[16]

(b) Types of Purposes

RF law defines an NPO as an organization that does not have profit-earning as a fundamental goal and does not distribute profit among its participants.[17] The scope of the term *NPO* includes any purpose that does not primarily involve the sale of goods and services. Legitimate nonprofit purposes include administration, research, conflict resolution, public health and athletic development, the protection of citizens' rights and legal interests, and the fulfillment of social, cultural, charitable, educational, and other publicly beneficial goals.[18]

Some NPOs can also qualify as "charitable organizations." An NPO is charitable if it meets the standards set by the law "On Charitable Activity." A chari-

---

[11] First Part of the RF Civil Code, articles 116–17; RF Law No. 82-FZ, "On Public Associations," article 5 (May 19, 1995).

[12] First Part of the RF Civil Code, articles 116–18, RF Law No. 7-FZ, "On NPOs," articles 6–8, 10 (January 12, 1996).

[13] First Part of the RF Civil Code, article 120; RF Law No. 82-FZ, "On Public Associations," article 11; RF Law No. 7-FZ, "On NPOs," articles 8–9.

[14] RF Law No. 82-FZ, "On Public Associations," article 9.

[15] Ibid., article 12.

[16] Ibid., article 14.

[17] First Part of the RF Civil Code, article 50; RF Law No. 7-FZ, "On NPOs," article 2.1.

[18] RF Law No. 7-FZ, "On NPOs," article 2.2.

table NPO is one that serves public interests through the gratuitous transfer of assets, performance of services, or rendition of other assistance to citizens or legal entities. "Gratuitous" signifies that the action was either uncompensated or rendered on terms advantageous to the recipient. Legitimate charitable purposes include giving aid to the poor, helping people recover from catastrophes and conflicts, promoting peace, strengthening the family's role in society, protecting the environment, and conducting activity in the educational, scientific, artistic, and cultural spheres. The law specifically excludes activity aimed at rendering assistance to commercial organizations or supporting political parties or campaigns.[19]

(c) Other Requirements

The law "On NPOs" states that there are no limitations on the number of persons founding an NPO, except as provided by other federal laws.[20] Under the law "On Public Associations," all public associations, with the exception of labor unions and political parties, must have at least three individual founders.[21]

An NPO is subject to a minimum capital contribution only if its charter provides for conducting for-profit ("entrepreneurial") activity. An NPO whose charter authorizes engaging in entrepreneurial activity must have charter capital equal to no less than one-hundred times the monthly minimum wage. In contrast, a commercial company must have charter capital of at least one thousand times the monthly minimum wage.[22]

(d) Registration Procedures

A bill establishing uniform registration procedures for all legal entities, including NPOs, is reportedly close to becoming law. When this bill is signed into law, NPOs will obtain legal entity status by registering with the RF Ministry of Justice in Moscow or one of its branch offices. However, at present, RF legislation has provided Ministry of Justice registration procedures only for public and religious associations.[23] In the absence of a law providing for a uniform procedure for registration, many NPOs have had to obtain legal entity status by registering with chambers of commerce or special local government offices. However, in many localities officials have made no provisions for the registration of NPOs. In addition, certain types of NPOs, such as nongovernmental pension funds or exchanges, must also obtain licenses in order to conduct their chartered activity.

[19] RF Law No. 82-FZ, "On Charitable Activity," article 2.

[20] RF Law No. 7-FZ, "On NPOs," article 15.2.

[21] RF Law No. 82-FZ, "On Public Associations," articles 18.

[22] RF Presidential Decree No. 1482, "On Establishing State Registration of Enterprises and Entrepreneurs on RF Territory" (July 8, 1994).

[23] First Part of the RF Civil Code, article 51; RF Law No. 7-FZ, "On NPOs," article 3; RF Ministry of Justice Order No. 19-47-94-9. "The Registration of Charters of Political Parties and Other Public Associations in the RF Ministry of Justice," § 2 (September 16, 1994); RF Ministry of Justice Order No. 19-01-159-94, "On Establishing in a New Version the Rules for the Registration of Charters (Regulations) of Religious Associations" (November 30, 1994).

Registration provides an NPO with civil law rights, including property rights, the right to enter into contracts, the right to open a bank account, and the right to conduct entrepreneurial activity that furthers the attainment of the NPO's chartered goals.[24]

Perhaps the most important registration requirements are those governing an NPO's name and charter. The name must indicate the organization's non-profit legal status as well as the nature of the activity and the charter serves as the legal basis for all of the NPO's activity. An NPO conducting activities not authorized by its charter will receive a written warning from its registering body and, after failing to respond to two warnings, the NPO can be dissolved by court order.[25]

Individuals have the right to establish a public association without registering with the state.[26] However, an unregistered public association is not a legal entity.

Following registration as a legal entity, an NPO must register with the RF State Committee for Statistics. This state agency publishes statistical reports on the country's economic development, including the activity of commercial entities and NPOs.[27]

An NPO need not undergo a preliminary certification process in order to obtain charitable status and to be eligible for tax privileges. An NPO can obtain charitable status simply by including charitable purposes in its charter and registering as a charity with the Ministry of Justice.

§ 19.3   INTERNAL GOVERNANCE

RF law generally gives NPOs latitude in determining the precise nature of their governing bodies and decision-making procedures. These are required to be spelled out, however, in the organization's charter.[28] In addition, the law establishes specific guidelines for several types of public associations.

Thus, a public organization, which has members, and a public movement, which does not, both have as their highest governing body a convention, conference, or general meeting. The highest governing body can select ongoing governing bodies responsible to the said highest governing body.

A public foundation, on the other hand, can be governed by the founder, the founder's appointees, or administrators appointed at a convention, conference, or general meeting of participants in the foundation's activity. In the case of a "public institution," the governing body is to be chosen by participants who are neither founders of the institution nor users of its services.[29]

---

[24] RF Law No. 7-FZ, "On NPOs," article 6.
[25] RF Law No. 7-FZ, "On NPOs," articles 4, 33.
[26] RF Law No. 82-FZ, "On Public Associations," articles 3, 21.
[27] "Regulation on the Order of Presentation of State Statistical Accounting in the RF," established by the RF State Committee on Statistics Resolution No. 130 (August 14, 1992).
[28] RF Law No. 7-FZ, "On NPOs," article 14.3.
[29] RF Law No. 82-FZ, "On Public Associations," articles 8–11.

§ 19.4 TAX TREATMENT

(a) Tax Treatment of Organizations

RF law recognizes a wide range of tax privileges for NPOs, most notably with regard to the Enterprise Profits Tax, the VAT and the Enterprise Assets Tax. Registration as the type of NPO specified in the pertinent legislation is in itself sufficient to enable the organization and its supporters to claim the exemption or deduction. An NPO need not go through a separate process of certification with the tax authorities in order to qualify for tax benefits.

(i) *Enterprise Profits Tax.* NPO's are generally exempt from the profits tax on all income except that received from entrepreneurial activity. This includes income received in the form of designated gifts, foreign grants, membership dues, and participants' deposits designated for the NPO's use. By contrast, revenue from an NPO's entrepreneurial activity is subject to taxation, as is revenue received through partnerships or joint ventures with commercial organizations. In addition, the government has the right to confiscate from the NPO the amount of income from foreign grants or designated gifts not used according to the designated purpose.[30]

Religious organizations and public organizations for the disabled are generally exempt from the profit tax. Moreover, the taxable profit of enterprises owned by artistic unions is reduced by the amount applied to fulfilling the parent organization's chartered activity.[31]

Generally, inasmuch as the law does not sanction entrepreneurial activity that does not correspond to the NPO's chartered purposes, it does not provide for an unrelated business income tax (UBIT).

(ii) *Value-Added Tax.* Resources received in the form of designated budgetary financing and foreign grants are not subject to VAT. Also not subject to the VAT are goods and services sold by public organizations for the disabled, services of a nonprofit educational nature, services of religious associations, and services of cultural and artistic institutions, such as theaters, museums, libraries, and clubs.[32] NPOs must pay VAT when they purchase goods and services subject to VAT, which is not deductible and thus represents a cost for them.

(iii) *Enterprise Assets Tax.* Assets used exclusively for the needs of education and culture are not subject to taxation, as are the assets of NPOs devoted to certain other specified types of activity. While religious and public organizations

---

[30] RF State Tax Service Instruction No. 37, "On the Order of Calculation and Payment into the Budget of the Tax on the Profit of Enterprises and Organizations," § 2.12 (August 10, 1995); RF State Tax Service Explanation No. VG-4-01/145N, Ques. 87 (September 14, 1993).

[31] Ibid., §§ 4.3, 4.6.

[32] RF State Tax Service Instruction No. 39, "On the Order of Calculation and Payment of the Value-Added Tax," § 12m (November 3, 1995).

for the disabled are generally exempt, other public associations are exempt only if they do not engage in entrepreneurial activity.[33]

(b) Tax Treatment of Contributions—Domestic Organizations

Deductibility of donations is granted to both individuals and corporations, though to varying degrees. Prior to a December 1994 amendment to the personal income tax law, individuals could deduct up to 100% of the year's income for donations made toward charitable goals. However, as a result of the 1994 amendment, deductibility is now limited to contributions made to certain organizations that receive state subsidies. Specifically, individuals can deduct up to 100% of the year's income for donations "for charitable goals to enterprises, associations, and organizations of culture, education, health, and social protection located in RF territory, partially or fully financed from the corresponding [state] budgets."[34]

Corporate donors can deduct contributions made "for charitable purposes" in computing their enterprise profits tax liabilities. Contributions to specific types of NPOs are also deductible. The level of the deduction is calculated in terms of a percentage of taxable "net profit," which is the amount remaining after costs are subtracted from the organization's total revenue.[35] However, the sum of certain tax concessions, including, for instance, the investment tax credit, loss carryforwards, and deductions of charitable contributions, cannot reduce taxable profit by more than 50%.

A corporate donor can deduct up to 5% of its net profit for contributions to charitable organizations working in Chernobyl-related projects. The 5% deduction is also available for contributions to governmental institutions and organizations of culture and art, cinematography, archival service, artists' unions, and other associations of artistic workers.[36]

A corporate donor can deduct up to 3% of its net profit for contributions for charitable purposes connected with the realization of programs for retraining military officers and other soldiers. The 3% deduction is also available for contributions to the following charitable organizations:

1. Ecological and reform foundations for restoring objects of cultural and natural heritage
2. Public organizations of the disabled as well as their subsidiaries
3. All-Russian public associations, specializing in issues of national development and international relations
4. Foundations for the support of education and art
5. Public associations for children and youth
6. Registered religious organizations and associations
7. Sports enterprises, institutions, and organizations

---

[33] RF State Tax Service Instruction No. 33, "On the Order of Calculation and Payment into the Budget of the Tax on the Assets of Enterprises," § 5 (June 8, 1995).
[34] State Tax Service Instruction No. 35, "On Implementing the RF Law, 'On Individual Income Tax,' " § 14(a) (June 29, 1995).
[35] RF State Tax Service Instruction No. 37, "On the Order of Calculation and Payment into the Budget of the Tax on the Profit of Enterprises and Organizations," § 4.1.3.
[36] Ibid.

8. Nature preserves
9. National parks
10. Botanical gardens

(c) Tax Treatment of Contributions—Foreign Organizations

The latest State Tax Service personal income tax instruction restricts the charitable deduction for contributions to organizations operating within the Russian Federation. Profits Tax regulations neither specify such a limit nor provide separate rules governing contributions to non-Russian organizations, although they do note that donations to both domestic and international Chernobyl-related charities are deductible. Foreign legal entities receive the same tax deductions for their contributions as Russian legal entities.

Grants to Russian organizations from foreign charitable organizations are not subject to VAT or profits tax. The organization receiving the grant must provide the Tax Service a description of the program being financed as well as documentation confirming the charitable status of the foreign grantor. Humanitarian aid is generally exempt from customs tariffs and VAT, but donors must make certain that the aid conforms to the latest customs regulations.[37]

§ 19.5 PERSONAL BENEFIT RESTRICTIONS

NPOs in the RF are generally subject to the nondistribution constraint, that is, they cannot distribute profit among their participants.[38] A charity cannot provide goods or services to its founders or members on more favorable terms than it offers to other persons.[39]

(a) Remuneration of Directors

The members of an NPO's highest governing body are prohibited from receiving compensation for their services, with the exception of reimbursement of expenses incurred in direct relation to their work.[40] The members of a charity's highest governing body are furthermore prohibited from holding office in commercial or nonprofit organizations which the charity itself has founded or joined.[41] Founders and directors of a public foundation are prohibited from using its assets in their own interests.[42]

(b) Conflicts of Interest

Members of an NPO's governing body as well as officers must disclose conflicts of interest to the governing body. An individual with a conflict of interest must

---

[37] See Appendix to R.F. State Customs Committee Order No. 142 (March 15, 1996), "Order of Customs Formulation for Products Imported as Humanitarian and Technical Aid to R.F. Customs Territory."

[38] RF Law No. 7-FZ, "On NPOs," article 2.1.

[39] RF Law No. 135-FZ, "On Charitable Activity," article 16.

[40] RF Law No. 7-FZ, "On NPOs," article 29; RF Law No. 135-FZ, "On Charitable Activity," article 10.3.

[41] RF Law No. 135-FZ, "On Charitable Activity," article 10.4.

[42] RF Law No. 82-FZ, "On Public Associations," article 10.

act in the NPO's best interests and must inform the governing body of the conflict. The governing body must then specifically approve the transaction involving a conflict of interest and the individual with the conflict is not prohibited by law from voting on this decision. However, courts have the authority to nullify any transaction involving an individual with a conflict of interest, and the individual with the conflict is liable for any losses incurred as a result of his or her actions.[43]

§ 19.6   OBLIGATIONS TO THE PUBLIC

Like a commercial entity, an NPO must generally maintain financial records, make statistical reports in accordance with the standards set by RF legislation, and submit its books for review to the State Tax Service. It must furthermore keep separate accounts on its use of income received from entrepreneurial activity, foreign grants, designated gifts, membership dues, and participants' deposits. An NPO cannot claim that its financial records are a trade secret. A foundation must publish an annual report concerning the use of its assets.[44]

Public and charitable NPOs are subject to somewhat more exacting requirements. A public association must (1) publish or otherwise make accessible to the public an annual financial report; (2) annually report to its registering agency the ongoing location of its governing body as well as the names and addresses of its directors; (3) present a record of its governing body's decisions or the NPO's tax reports, at the request of the registering body; and (4) grant officials from the registering body access to any of its activities. If a public association fails to present the requisite reports to the registering agency over a three-year period, a court can dissolve the organization and order its name removed from the state register of legal entities.[45]

A charitable organization must present to its registering body an annual report that includes information concerning its finances, personnel, charitable programs, and the content and results of its activity. Both the registering agency and the charitable organization are to guarantee open access to these reports. The amount a charitable organization spends in publishing its annual report constitutes an expenditure for charitable purposes.[46]

§ 19.7   BUSINESS ACTIVITY

An NPO has the right to engage in entrepreneurial activity that serves the attainment of, and corresponds to, its chartered goals. Under Russian law, an activity is entrepreneurial if it is applied toward systematically receiving profit from the use of property or the sale of goods or services.[47] This includes the right to receive unearned income through stock ownership, interest on bank deposits, or a trust.[48]

---

[43] RF Law No. 7-FZ, "On NPOs," article 27.
[44] Ibid., articles 7, 32.
[45] Ibid., article 29.
[46] RF Law No. 135-FZ, "On Charitable Activity," article 19.
[47] First Part of the RF Civil Code, article 2.1.
[48] RF Law No. 7-FZ, "On NPOs," article 24.2.

An NPO may also raise funds by conducting lotteries that support its programs or serve charitable purposes.[49] Besides conducting entrepreneurial activity itself, an NPO can also have separate commercial subsidiaries, although charities are prohibited from being a co-founder, joint participant, or partner of a commercial organization.[50]

Profits from entrepreneurial activity that an NPO conducts itself are subject to the profits tax. An NPO involved in a joint venture or partnership is subject to taxation based on the actual amount of profit derived from the activity.

The commercial subsidiary of an NPO is generally subject to profits tax just as any commercial organization, but there are several important exceptions. Profits earned by enterprises owned by artistic unions, public charitable foundations, and religious organizations are tax-exempt to the extent that they are used to fund the parent NPO's chartered goals. In addition, the profits of commercial subsidiaries of public organizations for the disabled are tax-exempt.[51]

The law recognizes a distinction between certain NPOs' entrepreneurial activity and their fundamental activity. For example, fee-for-service activities offered by a nongovernmental educational institution are not considered entrepreneurial if the revenue goes entirely toward the educational process.[52] Likewise, fee-for-service activity of a cultural NPO is not considered entrepreneurial if it implements, and is applied to, the fundamental chartered activity.[53]

§ 19.8 OTHER FUNDING RESTRICTIONS

(a) Spending Restrictions

A charitable organization is prohibited from spending more than 20% of its assets for the fiscal year on the salaries of administrative personnel. However, this limitation does not apply to personnel involved in implementing a charitable program. Unless established otherwise by the terms set by a donor or a charitable program, a charity must apply toward its charitable goals no less than 80% of a cash donation within a year of its receipt. In addition, a charity must apply toward financing specific charitable programs no less than 80% of its unearned income, contributions from commercial subsidiaries, and income received from entrepreneurial activity.[54]

(b) Donations

The Second Part of the RF Civil Code establishes that an individual or organization need not obtain any sort of permission or agreement in order to accept a

---

[49] RF Law No. 135-FZ, "On Charitable Activity," article 15; Temporary Regulation, "On Lotteries in the RF," in Presidential Decree No. 955 (Sept. 15, 1995), § 35.

[50] RF Law No. 7-FZ, "On NPOs," article 24.2; RF Law No. 135-FZ, "On Charitable Activity," article 12.3.

[51] RF State Tax Service No. 37, "On the Order of Calculation and Payment into the Budget of the Tax on the Profit of Enterprises and Organizations," §§ 2.12, 4.3, 4.7.

[52] RF Law No. 12-FZ, "On the Introduction of Amendments and Additions to the RF Law 'On Education,' " article 46 (January 13, 1996).

[53] RF Law No. 3612, "On Fundamentals on Culture," article 47 (October 9, 1992).

[54] RF Law No. 135-FZ, "On Charitable Activity," articles 16–17.

donation. While this also applies to NPOs, an NPO accepting a donation must keep separate account of how the donation is used. A donor, the donor's heirs, or other legally authorized individuals have the right to demand the return of a donation not used in accordance with its designated purpose. If a change in circumstances makes fulfilling the original designated purpose impossible, the donation can be used for other purposes only with the agreement of the donor. If the donor is dead or, if a legal entity, no longer in existence, only a court can change the donation's original purpose.[55]

(c) Liability

Except for institutions and associations of legal entities, an NPO is not liable for the debts of its founders, members, or participants, and vice versa. An institution answers for its obligations from the funds at its disposal. If these funds are insufficient, the owner of the property used by the institution bears secondary liability. NPOs belonging to an association of NPOs bear secondary liability for the association's debts.[56]

(d) Dissolution

The assets of a dissolved NPO must first go toward satisfying its creditors. Then, with the exception of institutions and nonprofit partnerships, and in accordance with the NPO's charter, the remaining assets are to be applied toward charitable goals and toward goals serving the interests for which the NPO was founded. In a nonprofit partnership, remaining assets go toward these goals only after each partner has received assets equivalent to the value of his or her contribution. The assets of a nonprofit institution go to the institution's property owner following the satisfaction of creditors.[57]

§ 19.9   POLITICAL ACTIVITY

There are few limitations on the political activity of NPOs. However, a public association cannot work for the violent overthrow of the RF's fundamental constitutional order or the destruction of its unity, or pose a threat to state security, create armed forces, or incite social, racial, national, or religious discord. In enforcing these restrictions, the state cannot treat working for social justice as an incitement of social discord.[58]

Political parties, which are public associations, can participate in elections only if registered with the RF Ministry of Justice at least six months before election day.[59] A charitable organization cannot use its resources to support political parties, movements, groups, and campaigns.[60] A religious association is prohibited from contributing to the election fund of a candidate or political party.[61]

---

[55] Second Part of the RF Civil Code, article 582 (January 26, 1996).
[56] RF Law No. 7-FZ, "On NPOs," article 9.2, 11.2.
[57] Ibid., article 20.
[58] RF Law No. 82-FZ, "On Public Associations," article 16.
[59] RF Law No. 56-FZ, "On Basic Guarantees of RF Citizens' Election Rights," article 2 (December 6, 1994); RF Law No. 76-FZ, "On Elections for President of the RF," article 28 (May 17, 1995).
[60] RF Law No. 135-FZ, "On Charitable Activity," article 12.5.
[61] RF Law No. 56-FZ, "On Basic Guarantees of RF Citizens' Election Rights," article 28.

§ 19.10   KEY OUTSTANDING ISSUES

(a) Federal Law and Local Regulation

RF law affords local governments wide latitude in regulating and taxing NPOs. This means that the status of NPOs can differ considerably throughout the RF; in many areas, NPOs have no way even to register as a legal entity. There is also significant variation in how regional and local governments utilize NPOs in implementing public programs. An important question with regard to local regulation is how local governments will attempt to safeguard the integrity of the nonprofit legal form. This is especially true with respect to charities; the Moscow law on charity reflects a concern that federal law makes it too easy for *de facto* commercial organizations to obtain charitable status.

(b) Development of the Civil Law Framework

The revolution in NPO legal reform is far from over. In addition to the law establishing uniform procedures for registering as a legal entity, legislators and NPO leaders have been developing new laws on foundations, political parties, artistic unions, lobbying, freedom of religion, and the use of NPOs in implementing state programs.

(c) Tax Reform

The RF government has made numerous modifications of the tax law over the past five years, but it is now in the process of adopting a completely new tax code. NPO leaders have especially focused on persuading legislators to increase the tax incentives for businesses to contribute to charitable activity. Another priority is to reform the personal income tax in order to allow deductions for charitable donations made to organizations that do not receive state subsidies. In addition, a particular concern of many American advisors has been that the new tax code include the Unrelated Business Income Tax, although its appropriateness in the RF context is open to question.

(d) Consistency in Applying Federal Law

That new laws have been passed is no guarantee that government officials will implement them consistently. Such problems grow more acute the further an NPO is from major urban areas such as Moscow or St. Petersburg, where city leaders have made considerable efforts to educate government officials and employees on the legal status of NPOs. It is not uncommon, for example, for NPOs to encounter officials at local branches of the State Tax Service who do not understand the tax privileges granted NPOs and donors. In fact, one can never guarantee that a tax inspector will even know that such tax advantages exist. In order to overcome such problems, NPOs are working to educate government officials and ordinary citizens on the rights and privileges contained in the law.

CHAPTER TWENTY

South Africa*

§ 20.1 LEGAL CONTEXT

Historically, South African nonprofit law has been substantially derived from Roman-Dutch common law, except to the limited extent that it has been codified by statute. Roman-Dutch common law refers to a system known as "Rooms-Hollands-Recht," which prevailed in Holland during the seventeenth and eighteenth centuries, being a synthesis of the Roman civil law system, and Dutch customary law, including legislative enactments then applicable within the states of Holland and West Friesland. Roman-Dutch law was introduced into South Africa in 1652, when the permanent settlement of the Dutch East India Company was first established at the Cape.

The statutory component of South African nonprofit law includes some measures enacted by the former Apartheid regime, which were intended to enable that government to gain knowledge of, and thereby to control, sources of funding of nonprofit organizations, including the ability to suspend their right to receive foreign funds.

With the ending of the Apartheid era, some of this oppressive legislation has been repealed. Following a four year negotiation process, and a transitional period of multiparty government during which an "interim" constitution was in force, South Africa has finally adopted its new constitution, which binds all legislative, executive and judicial organs of the State, and operates as the supreme law of the land.[1] This final constitution includes a Bill of Rights which has broad application to both natural and juristic persons, and includes a number of provisions which have particular reference to nonprofit organizations. Thus, for example, section 18 of the constitution states that "everyone has the right to freedom of association." Other provisions affirm the right to freedom of conscience, religion, thought, belief and opinion;[2] to freedom of expression;[3] to freedom to engage in political activity;[4] and to freedom to form, join and maintain cultural, religious, and linguistic associations and other organs of civil society.[5] The Bill of Rights prescribes that all administrative actions and decisions must be "lawful, reasonable and procedurally fair," and stipulates for a right to written reasons

---

* Country Rapporteur: Richard Rosenthal, a South African attorney specializing in nonprofit and development law.
[1] The Constitution of the Republic of South Africa Act, No. 108 of 1996.
[2] *Id.*, Section 15.
[3] *Id.*, Section 16.
[4] *Id.*, Section 19.
[5] *Id.*, Section 31.

(thereby facilitating judicial review) where administrative actions have adversely affected individual rights.[6]

Government has responded to widespread disaffection and a prevailing disregard for the requirements of erstwhile apartheid-era legislation, by appointing task groups and commissions to review, *inter alia*, the whole body of laws governing nonprofit organizations (NGOs) and by announcing its intention to introduce new legislation in respect of the nonprofit sector as speedily as possible.

This chapter therefore reviews the current status of South African law as affecting nonprofit organizations, against the backdrop of anticipated substantive changes within the relatively short term.

§ 20.2 ELIGIBILITY

(a) Types of Organizations

There are three types of legal structures available to nonprofit organizations in South Africa: (1) *voluntary associations*, which are predominantly governed by the common law; (2) *trusts*, which are governed by a combination of common and statute law;[7] and (3) *incorporated associations*, or Section 21 companies, which are the product of statute law.[8]

(i) Voluntary Associations. The voluntary association form is undoubtedly the most commonly used legal structure and is particularly suitable for small-scale public benefit initiatives as well as other activities, including sporting clubs, societies, and community-based organizations, which do not involve the ownership and management of substantial assets or cash-flows. The principal advantage of this type of structure is the absence of prescribed formality. The mere fact of agreement between three or more persons with a common purpose involving charity or public interest is sufficient, and even a written constitution is not necessary. As indicated, there is no statute that currently regulates the registration of voluntary associations, whose legal status and powers are derived from their constitutions, interpreted against a background of common law.

Two classes of voluntary associations do exist, however: those with separate legal personality and those without. The former are characterized by the common law term *"universitas."* An association in this class must meet three basic prerequisites: (1) the constitution must make provision for "Perpetual Succession," denoting a process for the accession and succession of new members; (2) the constitution must include provisions regarding the association's capacity to own property separately from its members; and (3) its agreed purpose must not be for gain. In return, the association is enabled in its own name, and separately from its members, to incur liabilities, acquire assets, and engage in financial activities.

(ii) Trusts. A trust may be defined as an arrangement through which the ownership and control of property is vested in one or more persons (trustees) for

---

[6] *Id.,* Section 33.
[7] The Trust Property Control Act, No. 57 of 1988, as amended.
[8] The Companies Act, No. 46 of 1973, as amended (Section 21).

the benefit of another or others, or for some public benefit. Trusts are largely governed by the Trust Property Control Act, No. 57 of 1988, as amended. However, the common law, which includes a considerable body of English law judicially "imported" to amplify Roman-Dutch law, also applies to trusts with respect to matters not specifically dealt with by South African statute.[9]

According to the Trust Property Control Act, a trust may only be brought into being by virtue of a "Trust Instrument," which denotes "a written agreement, or testamentary writing, or Court Order."[10] Trusts established by wills or other testamentary documents are also subject to particular prescribed formalities.[11] Trusts established by agreement in writing are frequently (but not essentially) attested by a notary public. The statute requires that in each instance a copy of the Trust Deed be filed and registered with the Master of the Supreme Court having jurisdiction at the place where the majority of the trust property is located. The statute likewise applies to the acts of any person appointed outside the Republic to administer trust property within the Republic.[12]

(iii) Incorporated Associations (Companies).   The commonly used term is "a Section 21 Company" which denotes an "Incorporated Association not for Gain in terms of Section 21" of the Companies Act.[13] Such associations are incorporated as companies limited by guarantee. Their main object must involve "promoting religion, arts, sciences, education, charity, recreation, or any other cultural or social activity, or communal or group interests." The further requirements of the statute are that (1) the payment of a dividend to members is prohibited; (2) all income and property must be applied solely toward the promotion of the stipulated main object; and (3) upon winding-up or dissolution, any net assets must be transferred to some other institution having similar purposes. Section 21A of the Act also makes provision for the registration as incorporated associations of the South African branches of qualifying foreign companies.

As a so-called "public" company, a Section 21 Company must have at least seven members. Each member must undertake a guarantee commitment that in the event of the financial failure of the association, such member will make payment to the association of a stipulated (nominal) amount. Persons subsequently admitted as members are likewise required to undertake similar guarantee obligations. As in the case of ordinary companies, the Memorandum and Articles of Association of a Section 21 Company makes provision for a "two-tiered" structure, involving, at one level, its membership, and at another level, its executive organ. Frequently names other than "members" and "directors" may be assigned to these functional categories.

---

[9] This comingling of statute and common law has resulted in some degree of ambiguity. For example, a legal debate continues with regard to the issue of whether a trust can have separate "legal personality" apart from its trustees. The dominant view is that a trust in fact does not have such personality, and that all rights, aggrements, and formal acts are therefore vested in the trustees, rather than in the trust as a distinct legal entity.

[10] Section 1.

[11] The Wills Act, No. 7 of 1953, as amended.

[12] Section 8.

[13] Companies Act, No. 61 of 1973, as amended.

(b) Types of Purposes

With respect to *voluntary associations*, the only common law prescription as to purpose is that it must be lawful and not for profit. Similarly, there is no legal prescription concerning the purpose of a *trust*, except that it must be lawful. The statute on companies requires that Section 21 Companies, have purposes and a main object which involves "promoting religion, arts, sciences, education, charity, recreation, or any other cultural or social activity, or communal or group interests." Whichever form of legal structure is adopted, the precise formulation of particular purposes is crucial and likely to have a decisive impact upon the organization's eligibility for tax exemption or other fiscal privileges.

(c) Other Requirements

There are no general minimum or specific resource requirements for the establishment of a nonprofit organization, although there must be a contingent obligation in the nature of a guarantee for Section 21 Companies. However, the amount of the guarantee may be purely nominal (e.g., one cent).

With respect to membership requirements, voluntary associations must have a minimum of three members and Section 21 Companies a minimum of seven members. The creation of a trust presupposes an agreement between the prospective trustee(s) and the donor and/or the beneficiary(ies).

(d) Registration Procedures

There is at present no office of registry for all nonprofit organizations although proposals under consideration by Government envisage the establishment of such an office—with registration being either voluntary or compulsory. All nonprofit organizations are, however, subject to registration requirements insofar as their activities may fall within the ambit of the Income Tax Act.[14] The present formalities attendant upon registration of each type of legal entity are as follows:

(i) Voluntary Associations. There is, at present, no office of registry for voluntary associations and the requirements for the formation of such associations are therefore minimal. As indicated above, it is not even necessary that there be a written constitution.

(ii) Trusts. The written document ("trust instrument") establishing a trust must be lodged and registered with the appropriate Master's Office, together with a formal Acceptance of Trust by the persons nominated to serve as trustees, accompanied by a Performance Guarantee (described as "security") for the trustee duties or, alternatively, a grant of exemption from the need to provide such security, which is at the discretion of the Master provided it is permitted by the trust instrument. When the requirements of the Master have been satisfied, the trustees operate under Letters of Authority, which are subject to periodic updating with respect to changes of appointment.

Although ordinarily the nominated trustees are routinely appointed, the Master has power to refuse to effect such appointment and to remove a trustee

---

[14] Act No. 58 of 1962, as amended.

under specified circumstances, including the failure to perform the required trustee duties. If such circumstances occur, the Master may call for alternative nominations, or may override the trust instrument and appoint such person(s) the Master deems fit.[15] Any amendments to the Trust Deed, or changes in the composition of the Board of Trustees, must be notified to and sanctioned by the Master. Despite these notional powers, in practice, there is minimal practical oversight of the activities of trustees, except for the returns required by the fiscal statutes.

(iii) Section 21 Companies.   Such Companies are registered at the Central Companies Office in Pretoria, and the Companies Act requires lodgment of the original Memorandum and Articles of Association, duly subscribed by the minimum seven members, and conforming generally to the requirements of the Act, which contemplates the following:

1. A distinctive company name, followed by the words "Association incorporated under Section 21"
2. A concise statement of "the Purpose describing the Main Business," and a separate statement of the "Main Object"
3. A provision defining the powers of the company—incorporating such of the prescribed "Standard Powers" as are applicable, but excluding and qualifying those which are not applicable
4. Certain specific prescribed conditions required of all Section 21 Companies
5. A statement defining the initial members, their qualifications, rights, and prerogatives; and detailing procedures for enrollment and removal of members
6. A clause providing for resignation, disqualification, and removal of members and/or directors
7. A clause stating the formalities attendant upon the amendment of the company's constitution or a change of its name
8. Procedural clauses dealing with the conduct of general meetings and directors' meetings, including the period of notice, quorum requirements, voting, the chairperson's powers, minutes, deadlock-breaking devices, proxies, alternates, and so on
9. A statement of the minimum number of directors, their terms of office, powers of appointment, co-option, and removal
10. Provisions governing the preparation of annual financial statements and the annual general meeting
11. Indemnities exonerating directors from the consequences of decisions made in good faith

Upon lodgment of the necessary documentation, the Registrar issues a Certificate of Incorporation.

[15] Section 7 of the Trust Property Control Act, No. 57 of 1988.

§ 20.3 INTERNAL GOVERNANCE

There are minimal statute-based requirements as to internal governance of non-profit organizations. Most internal governance issues are left to the constituting documents of the organizations. However, persons serving as directors, trustees, or executives in a fiduciary capacity must at all times act scrupulously in the interests of the organization they serve, and not seek to prefer or benefit themselves, friends, or next-of-kin. Governing bodies are generally bound by the obligations (1) to observe the terms of the constitutional arrangements of the organization; (2) to avoid decisions involving private profit; (3) to avoid situations involving conflicts between duty and self-interest; (4) to exercise independent discretion in the best interests of the organization and not to act simply upon instructions or preferences of some third party; (5) to act impartially, without prejudice, bias, or discrimination; (6) to observe utmost good faith, and exercise due diligence and care; (7) to keep the organization's assets separate from their own; and (8) to ensure that proper books and records are maintained.

Certain particular categories of institutions, such as Housing Utility Companies and Housing Utility Organizations, are furthermore required under the Income Tax Act to include a Ministerial nominee on their boards in order to be eligible for tax exemption. At least 25% of the members of the Governing Body of such organizations must be persons deriving no benefit from the organization other than reasonable remuneration for services rendered. Moreover, the Director of Fund-raising habitually imposes a number of standard requirements on organizations seeking Fund-raising Authority (see below), including provisions that board decisions must be supported by a majority of board members actually present at a quorate meeting, that a quorum requires a majority of all board members, and that amendments to the constitution must be first submitted for approval by the Director of Fund-raising.

§ 20.4 TAX TREATMENT

(a) Tax Treatment of Organizations

Nonprofit organizations are subject to normal income and other taxes, unless specifically exempted in terms of certain defined categories referred to in the fiscal legislation, that is, the Income Tax Act, No. 58 of 1962, as amended.[16] The principal exempting sections with reference to nonprofit organizations relate to the following categories :

- "Religious, charitable and educational institutions of a public character"[17]
- Funding bodies, whose sole object is to provide financial support to such "religious, charitable and educational institutions of a public character"[18]

---

[16] These provisions are currently under review by the Government-appointed Katz Commission.

[17] Section 10(1)(f) of the Income Tax Act, No. 58 of 1962, as amended.

[18] Section 10(1)(fA), *id.*

- Organizations conducting scientific, technical, and industrial research, or providing necessary or useful commodities, amenities, or services to the state or members of the public[19]
- Medical, dental, blood transfusion, hospital, or nursing services; nature conservation or animal protection activities; activities regarded by the Commissioner as being of a cultural nature; organizations providing social or recreational amenities; or organizations promoting the common interests of persons carrying on particular businesses, professions, or occupations[20]
- Housing utility companies providing newly built housing or residential accommodation[21]
- Amateur sporting associations[22]
- Political parties registered under the Electoral Act[23]
- Organizations providing residential accommodation for the aged[24]
- Organizations providing residential land and facilities for indigent communities[25]
- Organizations engaged solely in trading with, and on behalf of, their individual members[26]

Organizations exempted from *income tax* are generally eligible to apply for a range of other fiscal exemptions under the relevant fiscal statutes, including, *inter alia, stamp duties* (on marketable securities and certain other documents), *transfer duty* (on property transactions), *estate duty* (on bequests), *donations tax* (on gifts), and *Value Added Tax* (VAT) (on goods donated for approved charitable purposes).

While the range of exempt organizations identified above seems quite broad, in practice, the Department of Revenue has inconsistently and often narrowly interpreted terms such as "charitable." Thus, the Department has had no difficulty in regarding poor relief or orphanages as charitable, but has refused tax-exempt status to organizations engaging in longer-term development activities such as job creation, development of small businesses, and entrepreneurship. These anomalies have provided added motivation for an overall tax review.

(b) Tax Treatment of Contributions—Domestic Organizations

Generally, donors are not entitled to deduct amounts donated to tax-exempt organizations from their taxable income. However, a very limited exception is granted to certain specific categories of donations made to universities, technical colleges, and approved educational funds. Such tax-deductible donations are limited to 2% of the taxable income of individuals, and 5% of the taxable income of companies. Donations in excess of these amounts, far from being tax exempt, are, with some exceptions, subject to a donations tax, currently at 25% of the value of

---

[19] Section 10(1)(cA), *id.*
[20] Section 10(1)(cB), *id.*
[21] Section 10(1)(cC), *id.*
[22] Section 19(1)(cB), *id.*
[23] Section 10(1)(cE), *id.*
[24] Section 10(1)(cF), *id.*
[25] Section 10(1)(cl), *id.*
[26] Section 10(1)(e), *id.*

the donation, with a tax-free allowance of R 25,000 *per annum* for natural persons, and R 5,000 *per annum* for "casual donations" by companies or juristic persons. This tax is recoverable from the donor in the first instance, although the donor is granted a right of recourse against the beneficiary. This donations tax, which in effect represents a disincentive to philanthropy, can be avoided only if the beneficiary organization is specifically exempted from donations tax at the discretion of the Commissioner. In addition, as noted under section 20.8 below, nonprofit organizations in South Africa are for the time being subjected to a Fundraising Law that imposes additional restrictions on their fund raising.

(c) Tax Treatment of Contributions—Foreign Organizations

Contributions made to or by foreign organizations are exempt from donations tax. Insofar as income tax is concerned, receipts attributable to philanthropy are treated as being of a capital nature and, therefore, tax exempt.

A foreign organization could become liable for South African income tax (which is based upon a residency principle) with respect to those parts of its income as may be earned or generated in South Africa. Such tax paying foreign organizations would be entitled to the same tax treatment in respect of donations made or received within South Africa as apply to indigenous organizations. There are stringent controls applicable to foreign exchange which substantially limit the ability of South African individuals and organizations to engage in offshore philanthropy, although Government has announced its intention to progressively remove all such controls as soon as this is perceived as financially feasible.

§ 20.5   PERSONAL BENEFIT RESTRICTIONS

(a) Remuneration

Board members and staff are subject to fiduciary constraints, which require that they act *bona fide,* in the best interests of the organization, and without self-enrichment or personal advantage other than reasonable remuneration for services rendered. The law therefore does not preclude remuneration of board members, although not infrequently the constitution of an organization may hold stipulations to that effect. The Director of Fund-raising may also impose a prohibition on remuneration of board members of organizations seeking permission to engage in public fund-raising activities, and generally requires that remunerated employees may not serve on management boards other than in an advisory capacity.

In the case of trusts, trustees are entitled by statute to reasonable remuneration, to be determined if necessary at the discretion of the Master,[27] unless the Deed disallows remuneration.

(b) Self-Dealing

Save for ordinary remuneration, contracts involving some benefit to board members, must be sanctioned by the Court, which requires evidence as to special

---

[27] Section 22 of the Trust Property Control Act.

reasons, including the best interests of the organization and the intended beneficiaries. Organizations seeking fund-raising permission are usually required by the
Director of Fund-raising to prohibit board members from benefiting from contracts entered into with the organization.

Various provisions of the fiscal statutes preclude a donor from imposing conditions which entitle such donor to retain control over, or benefit from, the subject
matter of the donation. The granting of loans to members or to Trustees is likewise
often prohibited by the Commissioner for Inland Revenue. *Bona fide* staff loans in
amounts and on terms that are reasonable would, however, be permissible.

§ 20.6   OBLIGATIONS TO THE PUBLIC

Although envisaged new legislation proposes a public right of access to information in respect of registered nonprofit organizations, it is not clear that registration as such would be enforced. Accordingly, and for the time being, there are no
general obligations to make public the accounts or reports of nonprofit organizations, including those which are tax exempt and those which engage in public
fund-raising. However, the respective offices of the Commissioner for Inland Revenue and the Directorate of Fund-raising have statutory powers to require annual
accounts, but such official disclosures are not accessible to the public.

The public does have access to the constituting documents of trusts at the
Master's Office and Section 21 Companies at the Companies Office. However, the
information filed at such offices is of a relatively formal nature, such as the identity of current office holders and auditors. No such public office or registry exists
for voluntary associations.

Concerning trusts, it is customary, though not statutorily prescribed, that
independent auditors be appointed at the behest of the Master, in the exercise of
his overall discretion. The statutory duty to notify the Master in the event of any
"material irregularity" not being rectified within a period of one month's notice[28]
is imposed upon any person who undertakes the audit of a trust.

In terms of fiduciary duties, the Trust Property Control Act stipulates that all
trustees act "with the care, diligence and skill which can reasonably be expected
of a person who manages the affairs of another."[29] Any provision which purports
to exempt a trustee from this standard of conduct is void. Similar broad obligations also apply to other nonprofit organizations.

§ 20.7   BUSINESS ACTIVITY

The Income Tax Act imposes constraints on the conduct of business activities by
certain types of tax-exempt institutions.[30] Constraints are likewise imposed

---

[28] Section 15 of the Trust Property Control Act, No. 57 of 1988, as amended.
[29] Section 9(1), *id*.
[30] For example: Funding bodies [Section 10(1)(fA)]; Utility Housing Companies [Section
10(1)(cC)]; Utility Housing Organizations [Section 10(1)(cl)], each of which is precluded from
carrying on "any business," except when authorized by the Commissioner.

administratively by the Commissioner for Inland Revenue and Director of Fund-raising, on exempt religious, charitable, or educational institutions. The bureaucratic concern appears to be to ensure that the profit sector does not face "unfair competition" from the nonprofit sector. However, such administrative decisions are being challenged, and the Courts have recently overruled the Commissioner's attempt to disallow exemptions and to tax the proceeds of a business activity supporting the charitable activities of an exempt institution.

The Income Tax Act requires that these prohibitions on business activity be actually incorporated as terms of the founding documents of the organization, and therefore, any such activity would not only be unlawful, but also beyond the powers of the organization concerned. The conduct of any business activity outside these parameters entitles the Commissioner to withdraw tax-exempt status and/or to levy tax upon profits generated from the relevant business activity.

§ 20.8   OTHER FUNDING RESTRICTIONS

In terms of funding restrictions, certain types of nonprofit organizations face a "payout requirement" in the form of statutory (in the case of funding bodies) and administrative (in the case of charitable institutions) stipulations, to the effect that at least 75% of net revenue of an exempt organization must be expended on its activities within a period of twelve months reckoned from the end of the financial year in which such revenue arises.

Pending its imminent repeal, far more severe funding restrictions are imposed on nonprofit organizations by the Fund-raising Act, No. 107 of 1978, which was devised and enforced by the Apartheid regime. This Act, which was enacted "to provide for control of the collection of contributions from the public," prescribes that: "No person shall collect contributions unless authorized thereto in terms of this Act, and unless the collection takes place in accordance with the provisions of this Act." While the term "person" includes nonprofit organizations, the term "collect" includes not only soliciting, but also the mere act of accepting contributions. The term "contributions" includes not only money, but also any other kind of valuable consideration. Although the Act is ostensibly directed at controlling contributions from the public within the Republic, the term "public" (in terms of a subdefinition) includes any person making a contribution from outside the Republic. In other words, it is not possible to receive any contribution from outside the country without a fund-raising permit.

Under this Act, nonprofit organizations have to register with the Director of Fund-raising in order to be eligible to engage in "public" fund-raising activities. The Director may, at his or her entire discretion, attach a variety of conditions to the registration and the issuance of a "Fund-raising Authority." These may relate to the type of eligible charitable activity, the area within which such activity may legitimately be carried out; the area within which contributions may legitimately be raised, and other matters affecting the organization and its governance. The Directorate also has wide powers of inspection, inquiry, oversight, and, in the event of noncompliance, closure and seizure of assets. Among the standard restrictions imposed by the Director are stipulations to the effect that fund-raising expenses should not exceed 40% of gross receipts, and that investments may only be placed with registered financial institutions or in securities listed on a licensed stock exchange.

Certain institutions are exempt from the purview of the Act, however, including religious bodies, as long as collections take place during a religious service and for the purpose of promoting "religious work." Contributions collected from a person "by virtue of his membership of the organization" are also exempt, as are contributions collected for the benefit of political parties, universities, and tertiary educational institutions.

§ 20.9   POLITICAL ACTIVITY

Under the terms of the Constitution, the right to join, campaign and participate in the activities of a political party or cause, are guaranteed (Section 19). Beyond this, there is currently no legislation which either permits or disallows political activity or advocacy by tax-exempt nonprofit organizations.

Political parties registered as such under the Electoral Act are entitled to tax exemption. In addition, the Commissioner for Inland Revenue has a wide discretion to exempt organizations engaged in activities which he considers to be "of a cultural nature," and it is conceivable that quasipolitical and public information activities, such as voter education, could be included under this rubric.

§ 20.10   KEY OUTSTANDING ISSUES

At the date of submission of this contribution (May 1997), post-Apartheid South Africa is engaged in a process of sociopolitical transformation, involving a broad-ranging review of many aspects of society, including its legal system. Nonprofit law forms part of this ongoing process of fundamental change. The prevailing legal and fiscal environment for nonprofit organizations is therefore undergoing fundamental review and is likely to be the subject of statutory innovation in the short to medium term.

Government has also appointed a special Commission of Enquiry into the Tax Structure with power to make recommendations regarding appropriate law changes. The early recommendations of this Commission, supported by the Joint Standing Committee on Finance, suggest that the present tax-exempting provisions are likely to be substantially revised and broadened to include *inter alia* a more adequate description of development organizations. Representations have been made to broaden the ambit of donor tax deductibility, but concern has been expressed by the fiscal authorities, regarding its difficulties of administration, and the possibility of abuse and loss of revenue to the state. The Commission has recommended in a split decision that trading activities of charitable, religious, and educational institutions should be tax exempt, provided these are not used for purposes of tax-avoidance schemes.

The current vigorous debate on the future of nonprofit law in South Africa is characterized by the voluble participation of large numbers of organizations and individuals involved with the nonprofit sector. A series of workshops, conferences, and study groups have been initiated both by the government and by independent civil society organizations. Government has also encouraged the formation of sectoral forums leading to the establishment of National and Provincial NGO Coalitions with which it has announced its intention to consult regarding future changes in the law.

Probably the most significant private sector initiative thus far has been that styled "The Independent Study into an Enabling Environment for NGOs," which, with support from a service NGO known as the Development Resources Centre (DRC), commissioned four expert studies on the related topics of *Civil Society and Fundamental Freedoms; The Establishment, Registration and Administration of NGOs; Fund-raising, Giving and Volunteering;* and *The Taxation of NGOs.* An organization representative of major donors, the South African Grantmakers Association (SAGA), has also been proactive in convening workshops and submitting legislative proposals.

A current outcome of this initiative is that unofficial draft legislation has been proposed with a view to consolidating all laws affecting the operation of nonprofit organizations, and establishing a unitary system of registration, regulation, and empowerment under the broad jurisdiction of a proposed nonprofit organizations Commission.

While the exact contours of new legislation are difficult to predict at the present time, there is broad agreement on the overall agenda for reform, which may be summarized as follows:

- To render the establishment, registration, and operation of nonprofit organizations easy, speedy, and inexpensive
- To retain existing legal forms and statutory structures, but also to innovate new models which are not fraught with the rigors of statute law and the uncertainties of Common Law
- To ensure that due effect is given to the relevant provisions of the Bill of Rights within the constitution
- To repeal erstwhile politically motivated constraints on registration and fund raising; but to encourage high standards of integrity and accountability for public fund-raising and fund-spending, including the avoidance of self-enrichment and conflicts of interest
- To review existing tax regimes as they affect nonprofit organizations, and to broaden the notion of "charitable purposes" to include developmental, advocacy (religious, political, and other), and other public interest activities
- To create incentives for philanthropy—including not merely donor tax deductibility, but also fiscal exemptions and advantages—while acknowledging the state's legitimate concern to protect its tax base and to order its own developmental budgetary priorities
- To dismantle residual apartheid era bureaucracies which are perceived as oppressive and restrictive, and substitute alternative structures to facilitate, enable and support the nonprofit sector

CHAPTER TWENTY-ONE

Spain[*]

§ 21.1 LEGAL CONTEXT

Spain is a civil law country with a modern Constitution, adopted in 1978, that defines Spain as "a social and democratic state ruled by law,"[1] thus providing a broad framework of civil liberties and facilitating a high degree of collective action and civic participation.[2] Moreover, the Spanish Constitution of 1978 provides institutional guarantees for certain types of nonprofit organizations by expressly guaranteeing the right to associate as well as to form foundations. Article 22 of the Constitution thus explicitly recognizes the "right of association" and holds, *inter alia*, that "associations may only be dissolved or suspended in their activities by virtue of a reasoned court order." Even more importantly, Spain was the first country to establish a constitutional right to create foundations. According to article 34, "the right to create foundations for aims of a general interest is recognized in law."

Apart from the Constitution, the Spanish Civil Code of 1889 contains some general provisions with relevance to both associations and foundations. The general clauses of the Civil Code are complemented by specific laws concerning different types of nonprofit organizations, such as public corporations, civil and mercantile companies, political parties and trade unions, sport associations, religious associations, consumer and user associations, and so on.

The most important of these laws, however, is Law 30/1994 of November 24 on Foundations and Tax Incentives for Private Participation in Activities of a General Interest (published in the Official State Gazette of November 25, 1994). This law constitutes the essential legal provision concerning foundations.[3] It replaced

* Prepared by Dr. José Luis Piñar Mañas, Professor of Administrative Law, San Pablo-CEU University, Madrid; and Dr. Alicia Real Pérez, Professor of Civil Law, Complutense University, Madrid.

[1] Article 1 of Constitution.

[2] This point has been reinforced in the important Decision 18/1984 of February 7 of the Spanish Constitutional Court, which ruled that the social clause of the Constitution means that the pursuit of aims of a general interest is not an exclusive right of the state, but one that should be performed by the state and society acting in their mutual benefit. The special importance of this decision for the definition of the third sector, civil society, and, in particular foundations, has been highlighted elsewhere (see J. L. Piñar Mañas, Régimen Jurídico de las Fundaciones: Jurisprudencia del Tribunal Constitucional v del Tribunal Supremo (Legal System of Foundations: Jurisprudence of the Constitutional Court and the Supreme Court), (Madrid: Ministerio de Asuntos Sociales, 1992, p. 9).

[3] The following regulatory provisions have been developed: (1) Royal Decree 316/1996 of February 23, approving regulations on foundations (published in the Official State Gazette on March 6); (2) Royal Decree 384/1996 of March 1, passing regulations on the registration of foundations (published in the Official State Gazette of March 29, 1996); and (3) Royal Decree 765/1995 of

the previous fragmented regulatory framework pertaining to foundations pursuing different aims, which included more than one hundred provisions successively passed from the middle of the nineteenth century.[4] This law also contains regulations pertaining to the tax status of both foundations and public interest associations.

In addition to national laws, foundations in Spain are also subject to the laws of Spain's Autonomous Communities, or *Comunidades Autónomas*. Under the 1978 Constitution, authority over a variety of fields was transferred to this local government level, and the *Protectorate* on foundations was one of these. Thus while the national Law on Foundations is basically applicable to all foundations in Spain (except those operating only within one Autonomous Community having a separate law on foundations), many Autonomous Communities have also enacted regional regulations pertaining to foundations active within their borders.[5]

In terms of fiscal regulations, the general tax system applicable to foundations and associations of public utility is laid out under Title II of the November 24, 1994 Law on Foundations. However, some Autonomous Communities have also passed certain tax provisions which are more favorable than state legislation in some respects.

§ 21.2 ELIGIBILITY

(a) Types of Organizations

(i) General Foundation and Association Regulation.   As is common in civil law countries, associations and foundations are the main types of nonprofit organizations under Spanish law. The general regulations pertaining to foundations and associations are spelled out in articles 35 through 39 of the Civil Code of 1889, which also include the general rules applicable to all bodies corporate. These articles allow separate legal status for associations and foundations and detail the capabilities of bodies corporate, the rules to which their functioning must conform, and rules governing their possible modification and liquidation.[6]

May 5, regulating certain matters in the tax incentive system for private participation in activities of a general interest (published in the Official State Gazette of May 24, 1995).

[4] See J. L. Piñar Mañas & A. Real Pérez: Legislaciòn sobre instituciones de beneficiencia particular (Legislation on private benefit institutions), Madrid: Ministerio de Trabajo, 1987.

[5] The Spanish constitution grants so-called *foral*, or special, rights to Autonomous Communities (Catalonian, Navarran, Aragonese, Balearic, Galician, and Basque), allowing them to enact certain types of civil legislation that only applies within these Autonomous Communities. Laws on Foundations passed by Autonomous Communities include Laws 44 to 47 of Navarre's New "Compilation" of 1973; Catalonian Law 1/1982 of March 3 on private foundations (modified in its articles 11.6 and 13.1 and 2 by Catalonian Law 21/1985 of November 8); Law 7/1983 of June 25 on the system of foundations of interest to Galicia (modified by Law 1/1991 of November 8); Law 1/1990 of January 29 on Canary Islands Foundations; and Law 12/1994 of June 17 on Basque Country Foundations.

[6] These include, for example, article 28, which details restrictions regarding the nationality of bodies corporate; article 41 referring to the registered address of bodies corporate; and other articles on the rights of inheritance governing specific aspects with regard to establishing some bodies corporate as heir or legatee (articles 671, 745.2, 746, 788, 953, 957, and 993).

Specific legislation regulating associations and foundations is left to the special laws respecting the principles expressed in these five articles of the Code.

(ii) Associations. Associations in general are mainly governed by Law 191/1964 of December 24 on Associations as supplemented by Decree 1140/1965 of May 20; the Order of July 10, 1965 regulating the maintenance of Association Registers; and Royal Decree 713/1977 of June 1. However, these regulations were partially repealed by the 1978 Spanish Constitution since they contradicted the broader constitutional right of association provided in article 22 of the Constitution. However, there has not been sufficient political consensus to pass a new Basic Law on Associations, leaving some aspects of association law in Spain in limbo.

Two broad types of associations can be distinguished: those that are considered of public utility; and those that are not. According to article 4 of Law 191/1964 on Associations, as amended by the thirteenth additional provision of Law 30/1994 on Foundations and Tax Incentives, to be declared a public utility association an association must: (1) have purposes that are of a general interest; (2) be nonprofit and not distribute earnings obtained from its activities; (3) be open to beneficiaries other than the associates; and (4) not pay members of its management board.[7] Associations declared as being of public utility are entitled to enjoy the same special exemptions and tax benefits as do foundations,[8] but are required to register, to render annual accounts to the Ministry of Internal Affaires, and to furnish reports on their activities to the Public Administrations on request.[9]

(iii) Foundations. According to article 1.1 of Law 30/1994, foundations are "non-profit organizations which, by the will of their creators, have their assets long lastingly earmarked to achieving aims of general interest." This legal definition, while in keeping with historic legislation as well as article 34 of the Constitution, is somewhat innovative in Spanish law, since it goes beyond the old (legal) notion of foundations as heritages assigned to fulfilling aims of a general interest by emphasizing their character as organizations. The Law on Foundations allows both individuals and bodies corporate, whether public or private, to set up foundations,[10] unless a public body corporate's statutes establish the contrary.[11]

Since the right to form foundations is derived in Spain from the constitutionally guaranteed rights to own property, a central feature of foundation law is to protect the will of the founder. However, since the legal system must equally protect the general interests which foundations serve, there are certain exceptions where these general interests may override the founder's volition. The 1994 Law on Foundations endeavors to keep the difficult balance between these opposing interests. It thus states that "foundations are governed by the founder's volition, by their statutes and, in any event, by this Law,"[12] but also holds that "any provision of the statutes of the foundation or declaration of the founder's volition contrary to this Law will be taken as not established, unless affecting the consti-

---

[7] Article 4.1. Law 191/1964 as amended by Law 30/1994.
[8] Article 4.2. Law 191/1964 as amended by Law 30/1994.
[9] Article 4.3. Law 191/1964 as amended by Law 30/1994.
[10] Article 6.1 of 1994 Law on Foundations.
[11] Article 6.4 of 1994 Law on Foundations.
[12] Article 1.2 of 1994 Law on Foundations.

tutional validity of the former. In this latter case, it will not be appropriate to register the foundation in the Foundation Register."[13] The Law furthermore allows the modification of the foundation's statutes (even if prohibited by the founder) provided such reform is beneficial to the foundation and authorized by the Protectorate.[14] It allows the founder to decide on the destination of a liquidated foundation's remaining assets provided they will be transferred to public or private bodies corporate pursuing aims of a general interest.[15] Finally, the Law commissions the Protectorate with "watching over effective fulfillment of the foundation's aims according to the founder's volition and bearing in mind fulfillment of the general interest."[16]

(b) Types of Purposes

(i) Foundations.   In keeping with the institutional guarantee of freedom to create foundations, the range of aims foundations may pursue is extremely broad. Article 2.1 of the 1994 Law on Foundations therefore holds that "foundations shall pursue aims of a general interest [such as] social assistance, civic, educational, cultural, scientific aims, sport, health, cooperation for development, defense of the environment or fostering the economy or research, promotion of voluntary services or any others of a like nature." However, in accordance with article 35.1 of the Civil Code and article 34 of the Constitution, articles 2.2 and 2.3 of the Law on Foundations stipulate that a foundation's aims must be socially important and the group of intended beneficiaries must be open and may not be limited to predetermined individuals. Foundations are thus prohibited from pursuing private interests and family foundations providing benefits to the family of the founder are prohibited.

(ii) Associations.   By contrast, associations may pursue both public and private aims. The only limit is the content of articles 22.2 and 22.5 of the Spanish Constitution, which hold that associations pursuing aims or using means classed as an offense are illegal, and that secret associations and those of a paramilitary nature are forbidden. However, associations declared as being of public utility are subject to the same regulations as foundations and required to pursue only aims of a general interest.

(c) Other Requirements

(i) Composition of Foundation Assets.   The assets of a foundation comprise all properties and rights having a financial value that are owned by the foundation at a certain time.[17] These assets must be recorded in an inventory and must be registered in the Foundation Register[18] open for public inspection. Any

[13] Article 9.2.
[14] Articles 27.1 and 28.1.
[15] Articles 31.2 and 3.
[16] Article 32.2.b.
[17] Article 17.1 of the 1994 Law on Foundations.
[18] Article 18.

changes the foundation's assets may undergo throughout the foundation's life-time must also be made public in the Register.[19]

However, not all of a foundation's assets are included in its endowment, which is particularly protected by law inasmuch as it is deemed to be the corner-stone on which the foundation is based. The endowment consists of the initial endowment at the time the foundation's deed of constitution is executed; and (1) any donations by the founders or other persons thereafter, which are given with the declared intent of increasing the endowment but not the rest of the assets,[20] and (2) any property, which the *Patronato*, or governing body, assigns to the endowment[21] either voluntarily or because they are legally bound to do so.[22]

No minimum asset size is specified for foundations. However, the endowment must be adequate and sufficient for achieving the foundation's aims. In addition, any disposition or lien involving 20% or more of a foundation's endowment must receive the prior authorization of the civil "protectorate."

(ii) Associations.   There are neither membership nor capital requirements for associations under Spanish law.

(d) Registration Procedures

(i) Foundations.   According to article 7 of the Law on Foundations, founda-tions may be set up *inter vivos* (in a public deed) or *mortis causa* (in a will). In any case, a deed of constitution and a statute are necessary for registration. Articles 7 and 10 describe the minimum content of a deed of constitution. However, the founder may prescribe additional provisions as long as these do not infringe the Law.[23] Generally, the deed of constitution must (1) identify the founder or founders; (2) indicate the founder's intentions or goal to be served by the foun-dation; (3) clarify the specifics of the endowment, including properties provided, their valuation, and the way they will be provided; (4) provide the statutes; and (5) identify the persons who will serve as the first *Patronato* of the foundation.

The statutes must include (1) the foundation's aims; (2) basic rules for apply-ing resources to fulfill these aims; and (3) regulations pertaining to the founda-tion's governing body, and so on.[24] The endowment may consist of properties and rights of any kind with a financial value,[25] which must be adequate and sufficient for achieving the foundation's aims.[26] The endowment may be successively pro-

---

[19] Article 19.4.

[20] Articles 10.2.2 and 25.1.

[21] Article 10.2.2.

[22] At least 70% of the income or any other net earnings which the foundation obtains after tax must be assigned to achieving the foundation's aims. The rest must be allocated to increasing the foundation's endowment after deducting administration costs (Article 25.1 of 1994 Law on Foundations).

[23] Articles 9.1 and 9.2.

[24] Article 9.1.

[25] Article 10.1 in relation to 10.3 and 17.1.

[26] The sufficiency of endowment as well as the fact that the foundation's aims are of a general interest will be checked by the Public Administration before registering the foundation in the Register (article 36.2 of Law 30/1994 on Foundations).

vided as long as the initial contribution[27] is at least 25% of the total and the remainder will be transferred within five years from the date of execution of the deed of constitution.[28]

Once these prerequisites are met, the foundation's deed of constitution is legally binding and irrevocable by the founder, founders, or their heirs, unless the foundation is refused registration in the Register and thus does not acquire legal personality.

Once a foundation's deed of constitution is legally valid, the foundation's *Patronato*[29] must register the deed and take charge of the assets in a way to conserve them and not to damage the foundation. If the foundation is validly registered, it will become the owner of the properties and rights and will assume the obligations taken on within the limits as indicated in article 11. If registration is refused, assets will be returned to the founder after any obligations have been met; and if the assets are not sufficient to cover debts, the *Patronato* members are jointly liable.[30]

Foundations acquire legal status with the registration in the Foundation Register.[31] Registration is a mandatory process to ensure the correct fulfillment of the legal requisites and to make the relevant documents available to the public.[32] The Register for Foundations within the state's domain, as regulated in Royal Decree 384/1996, is held by the Ministry of Justice.[33] In addition, there are separate registries in the different Autonomous Communities for foundations that are only regionally active. Registration by the authorities would be an automatic process, however, for those foundations that meet the basic requirements of the law and little discretion is left to the official registering bodies.

(ii) Associations. Associations must only publicize their establishment by being listed in a Register.

§ 21.3   INTERNAL GOVERNANCE

(a) Foundations

Spanish law vests responsibility for the management of foundations in the foundation's board, or *Patronato*, while remaining silent with respect to the decision-making procedures they will use.

---

[27] Effected together with the foundation's deed of constitution, article 10.3.

[28] Article 10.2.

[29] As indicated, the founder must appoint the first governing body or *Patronato* in the deed of constitution (article 8.3). As soon as the *Patronato* members appointed accept their posts, they will commence carrying out their functions (article 13.3).

[30] Article 11 "in fine".

[31] Article 3 of Law 30/1994.

Article 3: "1.—Foundations will have a legal status as from registration of the public deed whereby they are set up in the pertinent Foundation Register. Registration may only be denied when said deed does not conform to the Law's prescriptions.

2.—Only entities registered in the Registry to which the foregoing subparagraph refers may use the name of foundation."

[32] This system for granting status to foundations conforms with the provisions of the Spanish Civil Code.

[33] Article 36.1 of Law on Foundations.

The *Patronato* must, however, include at least three members, or *Patronos*, and must adhere to the procedures set out in the foundation's statutes with respect to the type of majorities needed both for forming the governing body (constitution quorum) and for adopting legally binding resolutions (quorum for adopting resolutions). The *Patronato* is considered the basic representative of the foundation, and is also responsible for the management of the organization and the administration of the assets, which must be used for achieving the foundation's general interest aims.[34] The decisions made by the *Patronato* in accordance with the foundation's operating rules are decisions of the foundation as a body corporate. The office of *Patrono* is voluntary and nonremunerated,[35] and both individuals or bodies corporate may hold such an office.[36] While exercising responsibility for their organizations, however, *Patronos* are allowed to delegate the management of day-to-day activities to other persons, which may be authorized by the *Patronato* for such purposes unless the statutes specify otherwise.[37] The *Patronato* may also delegate certain tasks and responsibilities to one of the *Patronos*. However, the approval of accounts or the budget or any decisions relating to acts requiring authorization from the Protectorate must be undertaken by the full *Patronato*.[38] The replacement, dismissal, and suspension of *Patronos* for any of the reasons provided for in article 16 of the Law must be accompanied by due guarantees (e.g., a hearing for the party concerned), and must be published in the Foundation Register.

The modification, merger, and liquidation of foundations is regulated in articles 27 to 31 of Law 30/1994. A foundation's modification means a modification of its statutes in cases where such a modification serves the foundation's interest (even if the founder has originally forbidden it).[39] Modification is mandatory in cases where, for unforeseeable circumstances, the foundation cannot continue to operate in a satisfactory manner.[40] By the same token, the merger of two or more foundations may be agreed to by the respective *Patronatos*.[41]

The Public Administration (the Protectorate) plays various roles in the modification and merger of foundations: the Protectorate can prohibit the modification or merger and thus override respective decisions of the *Patronato* or *Patronatos* for reasons of legality and by means of a reasoned resolution.[42] Moreover, the Protectorate may also initiate a foundation's modification if necessary to ensure the foundation's survival even if the *Patronato* does not agree;[43] or it may petition the

---

[34] Articles 12 and 17.2 of Law 30/1994.

[35] "*Patronos* will undertake their posts with no remuneration and in no event may receive retribution for their services" (article 13.4). However, they will be entitled to reimbursement of duly justified expenses incurred by them in rendering their services (article 13.6). It is also possible for *Patronos* to enter into contracts with the foundation after receiving authorization from the *Protectorate* (article 26) which will only be granted for specific activities.

[36] In this case, a body corporate must appoint the individual who will represent it (article 13.2.2nd.).

[37] Article 14.2.

[38] Article 14.1.

[39] In this case, the prior authorization of the "Protectorate" will be required.

[40] Articles 27.1 and 2.

[41] Article 28.1.

[42] Articles 27.4 and 28.1.

[43] Article 27.3.

courts to force foundations to merge.[44] Both statutory modifications and the merger of foundations must be put down in a public deed and be recorded in the Foundation Register.[45]

Regarding liquidation, the Law allows (1) an automatic liquidation if a foundation is set up only for a specified length of time;[46] or (2) a liquidation on decision of the *Patronato*. In the latter case, the Law lists three types of qualifying causes: (1) the foundation's aims have been fully achieved, or their achievement is impossible, or some other cause provided for in the deed of constitution or in the statutes;[47] (2) a reasoned legal resolution becomes necessary, for example, if the foundation's aims were to become illegal;[48] or (3) a foundation is liquidated in the course of a merger and a new one is created in its place.[49] In any event, neither the *Patronato* nor the Protectorate are empowered to arbitrarily decide on a foundation's liquidation; the final decision to liquidate a foundation is usually left to the civil courts.[50]

If liquidation is agreed upon, it will be undertaken by the foundation's governing body under the control of the Protectorate.[51] Properties resulting from liquidation will be assigned to other nonprofit entities pursuing aims of a general interest designated in the foundation's deed of constitution. Should the founder not have made such designation, the *Patronato* may do so. On default, the Public Administration will decide on the destination of the liquidated foundation's assets.[52]

(b) Associations

There are no explicit provisions concerning the internal governance of associations, except that whatever form of governance is selected must be democratic in nature.

§ 21.4 TAX TREATMENT

Part II of Law 30/1994 established a preferential tax treatment for foundations and public utility associations both in terms of exemptions for the organizations and deductibility of donations. Other associations are not eligible for such preferential treatment. Although the system is generally favorable, eligibility for this beneficial tax treatment is fairly narrowly defined. According to article 42 of the Law on Foundations, to be eligible foundations and associations of public utility must (1) pursue aims of a general interest; (2) earmark at least 70% of net income and other earnings to the pursuit of these aims; (3) testify that any majority inter-

---

[44] Articles 28.2 and 3.
[45] Articles 27.4 and 28.4.
[46] Articles 29.a and 30.1.
[47] Articles 29.b, c, and e and 30.2.
[48] Articles 29.f and 30.3 of the Law on Foundations; and articles 34.2 and 22.4 of the Spanish Constitution.
[49] Article 29.d.
[50] Article 30 of the 1994 Law on Foundations.
[51] Article 31.1.
[52] Articles 31.2 and 3.

ests held in commercial companies serve the pursuit of the aims while not infringing on the nonprofit character of the organization; (4) render accounts to the Public Administration; and, in case of dissolution, (5) apply their assets to other organizations pursuing similar aims of a general interest.

(a) Tax Treatment of Organizations

Organizations complying with the aforementioned requisites are exempted from the *corporation tax* on income obtained from activities related to the organization's object or specific purpose.[53] On income obtained from any financial undertaking other than the foregoing, a tax rate of 10% is levied,[54] although organizations that provide services free of charge may qualify for a "reduced rate" of taxation on unrelated income.[55] According to article 58 of the Law, foundations and associations of public utility are also exempted from the *real estate tax* and from the *tax on economic activities*, which are both local taxes governed by Law 39/1988 of December 28.

(b) Tax Treatment of Contributions—Domestic Organizations

(i) Donations. Both individuals and bodies corporate may make tax-deductible contributions to foundations and associations of public benefit.

Individuals may deduct up to 20% of the amount of the donation from their personal income tax. However, the sum of the amounts invested or donated cannot exceed 30% of taxable income.[56]

The Law also regards donations made by *bodies corporate* as a deductible item in determining taxable income for the corporation tax. Depending on the type of donation, this deduction may not exceed 10% or 30% of taxable income before the deduction or, alternatively, 1/1000 or 3/1000 of sales turnover. However, the application of these percentages cannot give rise to a negative taxable income in either case.[57]

Furthermore, the deductible percentages and the percentage amount of the maximum deduction limits may be increased by a maximum of 5% if the donee foundations and associations undertake activities or programs deemed as priorities in the General State Budget Laws for each year.[58]

In order for the donor to be able to deduct the donation, the donee must issue a certificate which must identify both the donor and donee and further contain:

1. The tax status of the donee entity as being included among those entitled to enjoy the favorable tax system as set by the Law
2. The date and amount of the donation in the case of cash donations
3. An authentic document accrediting the delivery of the donated asset in the case of in-kind contributions

---

[53] Article 48.

[54] Articles 50 and following of the Law take many variables into consideration with regard to determining the taxable income, which we cannot analyze in detail here.

[55] Article 55.

[56] Article 80.1 of Personal Income Tax Law 18/1991 of June 6.

[57] Article 63 of Law 30/1994.

[58] Article 67 of the Law on Foundations.

4. An explanation of how the donee will use the donated assets in compliance with its aims

5. A statement regarding the irrevocable nature of the donation[59]

(ii) Sponsorships. Sponsoring activities in the form of cooperation agreements between business companies and foundations and associations in activities of a general interest are also allowed under Spanish law. Article 68 of the Law on Foundations defines sponsoring as arrangements in which foundations or associations of public utility agree to publicize in written material the cooperator's (or sponsor's) participation in this activity in exchange for financial support for carrying out activities related to their aims of a general interest. For the sponsor, the sponsorships are deemed deductible business expenses, which are, however, subject to a limit of 5% of taxable income or 0.5 per 1000 of sales turnover. As with donations, the application of the latter percentage cannot give rise to a negative taxable income.

Recently, two new legislative items have been passed that are specifically designed to further encourage the participation of businesses in achieving aims of a general interest. The first permits businesses to claim a deduction for the actual cost of works of art donated to public entities, foundations, and associations of public utility. The second allows businesses to deduct costs arising from their participation in activities of a general interest up to a limit of 5% of taxable income or 0.5 per 1000 of sales turnover.[60] In both cases, however, the deductions cannot give rise to a negative taxable income.

(c) Tax Treatment of Contributions—Foreign Organizations

Spanish law requires representatives of foreign foundations to register in the Foundation Registry, making them eligible to receive the same tax treatment as Spanish foundations. Domestic organizations operating abroad are still eligible for fiscal benefits in Spain.

§ 21.5 PERSONAL BENEFIT RESTRICTIONS

(a) Foundations

As pointed out earlier, foundations must solely pursue aims of a general interest. Therefore, foundations benefiting founders or governing bodies are not permitted. Thus article 2 of Law 30/1994 clearly states that "the foundation's purpose must benefit generic groups of persons" and "in no event may foundations be set up with the purpose of assigning benefits to the spouses or relatives of the founder down to the fourth degree of kinship inclusive."

---

[59] Article 66 of the Law on Foundations.
[60] Such activities may include:
    (a) Performing activities or organizing public events of an assistance, educational, cultural, scientific, research, sport or social voluntary service promotional type or any other similar activity of general interest.
    (b) Undertaking activities for promoting and developing cinema, theater, music and dance, book publishing, videos and phonogrammes.

Furthermore, article 13.4 of the Law indicates that the foundation's governing body members "shall exercise their post free of charge without receiving any retribution for discharging their functions." Similarly, one of the prerequisites for favorable tax treatment, as laid down in the Law, is that the office of *Patrono* must be nonremunerated and that *Patronos* may have no financial interest in the results of the foundation's activity either directly or by proxy."[61] Members of the foundation's governing body may enter into contracts with the foundation (*autocontratación*), though only with prior authorization from the Public Administration.[62]

(b) Associations

Governing bodies of associations may receive remuneration. However, if an association wishes to be declared of public utility, it must accredit that the governing body members hold their offices without remuneration.[63] In addition, self-dealing (*autocontratación*) is not permitted in the case of associations declared of public utility.

§ 21.6   OBLIGATIONS TO THE PUBLIC

(a) Liability of the Foundation's Governing Board

The Law on Foundations requires entities to be managed professionally and lays down a system of liability for the members of governing bodies. Thus article 15 stipulates that "*Patronos* must act in their office with the diligence of a loyal representative" and that "*Patronos* are liable to the foundation for damages caused by acts performed in violation of the law or statutes or for negligently performing them." However, *Patronos* who either expressly opposed or did not participate in such acts are exempt from liability. If governing body members incur a liability, they can be dismissed from their office.[64] A declaration of liability may be demanded in the courts either by the foundation's governing body or by the Public Administration.[65]

(b) Transparency in the Activity of Foundations

In order to guarantee the transparency of the actions of foundations, the Law stipulates that the Foundation Register shall be open to the public.[66] The Law also imposes various obligations on foundations, such as the requirement to prepare and

---

[61] Article 43 of Law 30/1994.

[62] "*Patronos* may make contracts with the foundation in either their own or in a third party's name with the prior authorization of the Protectorate" (article 26 of the Law on Foundations). In developing this article, article 16 of the Royal Decree 316/1996 of February 23, approving the regulation of foundations within the state's domain, lays down that the Public Administration must refuse authorization for *self-dealing* (*autocontratación*) when (1) the deed of constitution conceals remuneration for acting as the *Patrono*; and (2) the value of the consideration the foundation receives is less than the value of the service it provides.

[63] Article 43 of Law 30/1994 and article 4 of Law 191/1964 of December 24, as modified by the 1994 Law on Foundations.

[64] Article 16.2.

[65] Article 15.3.

[66] Article 36.4 and Royal Decree 384/1996 of March 1.

make publicly available Annual Reports. Furthermore, one of the main functions of the Protectorate is "to publicize the existence and activities of foundations."[67]

(c) Associations

Similar provisions exist for associations declared of public utility.

§ 21.7 BUSINESS ACTIVITY

(a) Foundations

Generally, foundations may undertake any legal activities through which they may achieve their general interest aims. However, whatever activity they carry out, article 21 of the Law on Foundations stipulates that "foundations are obliged to: a) Exclusively earmark the assets and income to the foundation's aims, in accordance with this Law and the foundation's Statutes; b) provide sufficient information on their aims and activities for their possible beneficiaries and other persons concerned; c) act with criteria of impartiality and non discrimination in determining their beneficiaries." The Law further demands that at least 70% of income or any other net earnings the foundation obtains after tax be earmarked to the pursuit of the foundation's aims.[68]

With regard to related activities, previous legislation held that the achievement of aims of a general interest necessarily implies that foundations had to act in a beneficial fashion, effectively prohibiting foundations from charging fees for services. However, the Law of 1994 has eliminated this prohibition. Accordingly, article 24 lays down that "foundations may obtain income for their activities provided this does not involve an unjustified limitation of the sphere of their possible beneficiaries."

With regard to commercial or industrial activities, foundations may own interests in businesses, which may even be an integral part of their assets, as long as such businesses are independent and institutionally separate bodies corporate. In cases like this, the foundation would be a shareholder receiving dividends which it would earmark to achieving its aims. However, while the Law on Foundations allows foundations to hold interest, even majority stakes, in limited liability enterprises,[69] it prohibits foundations from holding interests in commercial companies which are not limited in their liability.[70] Quite similarly, foundations may themselves set up institutionally independent business ventures with the intention of using profits to further their aims, as long as the participating foundations cannot become liable for any debts arising from such businesses.[71]

---

[67] Article 32.2.

[68] Article 25.1.
Although the foundation may effectively earmark this proportion in a term of three years as from the time when obtained (article 25.2).

[69] Article 22.3.

[70] Articles 22.2 and 3.

[71] Articles 22.1 and 3.
In principal, a foundation may even act as a business enterprise itself. In practice, however, there are too many ethical and practical problems involved to make this a feasible option.

(b) Associations

The rules on business activities for associations declared of public interest are very similar to those for foundations. Regular associations can carry out commercial activities with even fewer restrictions.

§ 21.8   OTHER FUNDING RESTRICTIONS

Apart from the requirements that foundations must record all contributions received in their accounting and budget documents and must also issue a certificate accrediting the donations received, there are no other restrictions on foundations with regard to fund-raising.

However, there are some restrictions on financial transactions beyond the mere administration of a foundation's assets concerning (1) the acceptance of inheritances and donations and (2) the disposal of assets.

If properties and rights are acquired free of charge by way of inheritance, legacy, or donation, the *Patronato* may accept such gifts at its discretion and consider them "to the benefit of inventory."[72] However, if such legacies or donations come with stipulations that may distort the foundation's purpose[73] or if the *Patronato* decides to refuse an inheritance or legacy, prior authorization of the Protectorate is necessary.[74]

As regards the disposal and lien of properties and rights a foundation owns, Law 30/1994 stipulates that prior authorization of the Protectorate must be sought for any acts of disposal, lien, transaction, and undertakings in arbitration of equity relating to the properties forming the endowment, properties directly set aside for achieving the foundation's aims, and properties whose value represents more than 20% of the foundation's assets according to the latest annual balance sheet.[75] The Protectorate must be immediately notified of the same acts as applied to real estate, commercial, or industrial establishments and certain valuable objects not included in the foregoing.[76] The remaining acts of disposal may be freely undertaken by the *Patronato*, which is empowered to perform all acts of administration it may deem necessary for suitably conducting the foundation's activity.

§ 21.9   POLITICAL ACTIVITY

(a) Foundations

There are no specific restrictions on political activities of foundations in Spain. Moreover, some foundations have been created or promoted by various political parties. Although there has been some concern regarding the use of these political foundations as sources of political party finance, there is no legal limitation on the possibility of setting up foundations for political ends.

[72] Article 20.1 of the Law 30/1994 on Foundations.
[73] Article 20.2 of the Law 30/1994 on Foundations.
[74] Article 20.3 of the Law 30/1994 on Foundations.
[75] Articles 19.1 and 3 of the Law 30/1994 on Foundations.
[76] Articles 19.2 and 3 of the Law 30/1994 on Foundations.

(b) Associations

Associations are also generally free to take part in political activities in Spain.

§ 21.10 KEY OUTSTANDING ISSUES

Despite the recent growth of foundations, associations, and social enterprises in Spain, there remain some challenges which foundations and associations will face in the future.

(a) Professionalization

Among these are the need to professionalize the management of these organizations, as foundations and associations must have effective governing bodies able to manage the entity productively and effectively. So far, old notions that charitable activities should not or cannot be performed in a professional manner still prevail.

(b) Administrative Oversight

The new Law on Foundations of 1994 has been a major step forward in modernizing the foundation sector in Spain by laying down certain operating rules which foundations must respect. Unfortunately, the Law's regulations have been interpreted in a quite restrictive fashion so far, placing more emphasis on administrative functions of control than on the unrestricted development of foundations. The structure and functions of the administrative services controlling foundations (the *Protectorates*) may therefore need to be modified further to reduce their controlling functions and reinforce their support and advisory functions. Ideally, distrust and excessive control of foundations should give way to a model based on confidence in the positive contributions of nonprofit enterprises, particularly given the recognition of the right to create foundations in article 34 of the constitution. This also calls for a self-demanding, self-regulating effort on the part of the foundation sector.

(c) Transparency

The transparency of foundation activities must be strengthened. To this effect, Law 30/1994 on Foundations and Royal Decree 383/1996 of March 1 have reinforced the aspects of transparency through creation and regulation of the State Register of Foundations within the state's domain.

In conclusion, it may be stated that the situation of foundations in Spain has evolved favorably over the last few years. Their management has become more professional and their presence in social development has increased. The 1978 Constitution and 1994 Law have constituted really important foundation-modernizing elements to this effect. Associations, by contrast, still operate in legal limbo, with few regulations but also few protections.

REGULATIONS APPENDIX

The main provisions regulating foundations in Spain (as per the constitution, the state and the Autonomous Communities) are as follows:

1. 1978 Constitution: article 22 (right of association) and article 34 (right to create foundations).
2. Law 30/1994 of November 24 on Foundations and Tax Incentives for Private Participation in Activities of a General Interest (Official State Gazette of November 25, 1994).
3. Law 191/1964 of December 24, on Associations, modified by the thirteenth provision of Law 30/1994 on Foundations.
4. Royal Decree 316/1996 of February 23 whereby the Regulations on Foundations within the state's domain are approved (Official State Gazette of March 6).
5. Royal Decree 384/1996 of March 1 whereby Regulations for the Registry of Foundations within the state's domain are approved (Official State Gazette of March 29, 1996).
6. Royal Decree 765/1995 of May 5 whereby certain matters of the scheme for tax incentives for private participation in activities of a general interest are regulated (Official State Gazette of May 24, 1995).
7. Law 1/1973 of March 1 whereby the Compilation of Civil Law of Navarre is approved (Laws 44, 45, 46 and 47).
8. Catalonian Law 1/1982 of March 3 on private foundations (modified by Law 21/1985 of November 8).
9. Galician Law 7/1983 of June 22 on the system of foundations of interest to Galicia (modified by Law 11/1991 of November 8).
10. Canary Islands Law 1/1990 of January 29 on Canary Islands Foundations.
11. Basque Law 12/1994 of July 17 on Basque Country Foundations.

CHAPTER TWENTY-TWO

Sweden[*]

§ 22.1 LEGAL CONTEXT

Sweden is a civil law country with separate systems of public and private law. The legal system provides a general freedom of association, as well as a general freedom regarding religion, politics, ideology, and so on. By virtue of these general principles of freedom, any person is free to establish a nonprofit association or foundation for whatever purpose.

Generally, there is very little regulation of nonprofit organizations and foundations in terms of statutes or acts or other governmental regulations. While a general law exists on foundations, the primary source of law for associations is case law and general principles of law underlying all types of economic organizations and associations as well as the organization's own articles of association and internal rules.

The legal position of foundations is under revision, and a new Act on Foundations as part of private law took effect as of January 1, 1996. Furthermore, the tax law regulation of nonprofit associations as well as foundations will be revised within the near future.

§ 22.2 ELIGIBILITY

(a) Types of Organizations

In Swedish law, there are basically two types of organizations through which nonprofit activities can be carried out: the nonprofit association (*ideell förening*) and the foundation (*stiftelse*). Both of these types are legal entities, the essence of which is that, in principle, only the entities, and not the members or directors, are liable for the obligations of the entity in question. The fundamental distinction between a nonprofit association and a foundation is that associations have members which control the policy and activities of the association in general terms (the daily control being exercised by a board of directors), whereas foundations have no members, are independent and self-governed, and are exclusively controlled by their boards of directors, or an administrator.

In principle, there are three types of foundations in Sweden: first, the type that carries out its purposes by making grants out of the proceeds of the foundation's assets, which are normally invested in securities, real estate, or other capital investments (*avkastningsstiftelse* or *fond*); second, the type that carries out its

* Country Rapporteur: Dr. Erik Nerep, in cooperation with Dr. Sven-Erik Sjöstrand, Stockholm School of Economics, Stockholm, Sweden. This chapter is based on a legal field guide prepared for the Johns Hopkins Comparative Nonprofit Sector Project.

purposes by actually rendering services in, for example, the educational or medical sector (*verksamhetsstiftelse*, also occasionally designated as *anstalt, institut*, or *inrättning*); and third, the type that has no permanent endowment or assets but collects donations from time to time and distributes them to targeted beneficiaries (*anslagsberoende stiftelser*).

Associations and foundations are, if not the exclusive, then at least by far the most common legal forms of nonprofit organizations in practical use. Only very rarely used for nonprofit activities are the other forms of legal entities in the Swedish legal system such as public or private limited companies, partnerships (whether limited or not), or economic associations. Limited companies (*Aktiebolagslagen*), which are governed by the Company Act of 1975,[1] may—at least in theory—engage exclusively in nonprofit activities, provided that the articles of association explicitly state so. Nevertheless, there are very few limited companies in Sweden whose purpose is not to make profit. This is also true for partnerships, which are governed by the Act on Partnerships.[2] By their very nature, economic associations, the purpose of which by definition must be to make profits for their members, cannot exclusively carry out nonprofit activities.[3]

(b) Types of Purposes

Under Swedish law, it is not required that nonprofit associations or foundations serve some specific public benefit purpose in order to achieve nonprofit status. Any person having legal capacity can establish a nonprofit association or foundation, irrespective of whether the organization is an instrument for public utility, benefit, or charity. However, only nonprofit associations or foundations serving some specific public benefit purpose are usually eligible for privileged tax status (see below).

The one major restriction on nonprofit associations is that they not be principally engaged in economic activities intended to earn profit for their members. A clear legal distinction thus exists between nonprofit associations and economic associations (*ekonomiska föreningar*) under Swedish law. By definition, the purpose of economic associations is to generate profits for their members. This type of association is, therefore, part of the business sector. As such, it must register with the Swedish Patent Office to acquire the status of a legal entity. A nonprofit association that engages in economic activity for the purpose of making profits for its members and does not register as an "economic association" thus denies itself the status of a legal entity, making its board and members personally liable for the organization's actions.

(c) Other Requirements

Nonprofit associations have to have at least two members, have to operate according to majority rule, and have to treat all members equally. A further requirement, applicable only to associations seeking tax exemption, is that a nonprofit association has to be open and must accept members without other restrictions

---

[1] SFS 1975, p. 1385.
[2] SFS 1980, p. 1102.
[3] See Act on Economic Associations, or *Lag om ekonomiska föreningar*, SFS 1987, p. 667.

than those which correspond to the association's purpose. There are no capital asset requirements for foundations. However, according to the new Act on Foundations, the size of assets determines whether a foundation needs to register or not (see below).

(d) Registration Procedures

(i) Associations. In order to establish a nonprofit association, no official registration is needed. General principles of law require only the fulfillment of certain minimum conditions: the association must be formed by at least two members, and it must have an oral or written charter providing for the government of the association (board of directors with at least one member) and setting out the general provisions for decision-making and the purpose of the association.[4] If these minimum criteria are met, the association automatically becomes a legal entity without any further registration or any other acts of the state.

However, practical problems have arisen in connection to the distinction between economic associations, governed by the Act on Economic Associations, on the one hand; and nonprofit associations, which are not governed by any statutory provisions, on the other. The specific criteria for distinguishing between these two forms of associations, as developed in case law and the legal literature,[5] are the following:

- Whereas nonprofit associations do not need to register to become a legal entity, economic associations gain legal status through an official registration at the Swedish Patent Office. Consequently, prior to registration an economic association is not recognized as a legal entity.
- In order to register, economic associations must fulfill specific requirements, as set out in the Act on Economic Associations, especially with regard to the articles of association, which must define the association's purpose.
- Potentially, problems arise when associations which formally and officially regard themselves as nonprofit associations are in practice engaged in economic activities for the purpose of making profit for their members. In such cases, associations are denominated as "unregistered economic associations" under Swedish law. As a consequence, they lack legal status and all persons in the association who take part in decision making and the execution thereof will be fully responsible for all the association's obligations as a result of those decisions and executions.
- In other words, should an association be engaged in economic activities for the purpose of making profits for its members, it is incumbent upon the association's representatives to fulfill the requirements of an economic association, as laid down in the Act on Economic Associations and officially register the association as such.

---

[4] Supreme Court case NJA 1987, p. 394.
[5] C. Hemström, Organisationernas rättsliga stallning. Om ekonomiska och ideella föreninger. Norstedts Juridik (Lund: Studentlitteratur AB, 1992); H. Nial, Svensk assocociationsratt, 5:e (Lund: Norstedts, 1991).

Ultimately, these legal matters are in the hands of general courts in cases concerning personal liability, damages, and so on.

(ii) Foundations. Under the new Act on Foundations, which came into effect on January 1, 1996, a foundation is legally established when in accordance with the foundation's constitution, which must be in written form, certain property (assets) has been definitely and irrevocably assigned to a person who has pledged to administer and manage the assets in accordance with the provisions of the foundation's constitution. The foundation must also have a name which must include the word *stiftelse*. Again, registration is not necessary as a prerequisite for becoming a legal person. Nevertheless, as a matter of administrative order, all foundations that carry out business activities or have subsidiaries such as limited companies or associations which are engaged in business activities, as well as foundations with assets the value of which exceeds approximately SEK 375,000, must be registered at the County Administration in the county in which the foundation has its seat.[6]

§ 22.3 INTERNAL GOVERNANCE

As noted above, both nonprofit associations and foundations need to include minimum provisions regarding internal governance in their articles of association or charters. Associations need to provide for a board of directors with at least one member to execute the day-to-day decisions, while the ultimate control lies with the membership. Since foundations are self-governed, the ultimate control lies with the board of directors or the administrator. Whether a foundation should be governed by a board of directors or simply by an administrator depends on the respective provisions in the charter.

There are no codified rules regarding the decision-making procedures in associations. However, there are three basic principles which are extracted from case law and general legal principles concerning nonprofit organizations which are basically applicable: the *principle of majority*, the *principle of equality*, and the *principle of fairness*. While the law on nonprofit associations does not prohibit undemocratic procedures of decision making as such, the *principle of majority* prescribes that—in the absence of explicit rules to the contrary—decisions in general meetings of the members shall be taken by a simple majority of the members participating in the assembly. At the same time, it is understood that associations are free to determine independently whether some decisions require a qualified majority or a unanimous vote, and whether veto power shall be accepted. According to the *principle of equality*, all members must be treated equally in any economic or other respect. Again, in the absence of statutory provisions to the contrary, an association's membership is free to determine whether, and, if so, how this principle should be adapted. However, any attempt to provide for unequal treatment in the association's constitution must be supported by all members, or at least most members, and at the very least by those members who will be subjected to unfavorable treatment (*principle of fairness*).

---

[6] Chapter 10 of the Act on Foundations.

§ 22.4 TAX TREATMENT

(a) Tax Treatment of Organizations

(i) *Associations.*   Nonprofit associations are generally subject to taxation at the regular corporation tax rate of 28%. However, organizations of several kinds serving a public benefit are exempted from tax on their income under the condition that they use at least 80% of their income for their public benefit purposes. The VAT basically follows the income tax. Furthermore, exempted organizations do not have to pay the 0.15% net wealth tax and are also exempted from inheritance and gift taxes. However, the exemption does not normally apply to their unrelated business income. However, capital gains are tax exempt, even if related to property used in the generation of unrelated business income. The definition of public benefit, as spelled out in Section 7 of the Act of State Income Tax, or *Lagen om statlig inkomstskatt,* is very wide.[7] It encompasses any activity for the public good, provided it is of a general character and principally addressed to an unlimited number of persons, and not oriented to certain family members or to an otherwise limited circle. Any religious, charitable, social, political, athletic, artistic, and cultural purpose would be acceptable in so far as that particular purpose is the principal purpose of the association, and the activities are geared to fulfilling that purpose. Under such circumstances, all income that arises from the activities of the association is exempt from taxes, provided that such activities have a natural connection to the public benefit purpose. However, income earned from businesses unrelated to the principal public benefit purpose of the association is still subject to taxation if it amounts to more than 15% to 20% of the association's total business income. If such income exceeds this percentage, the whole of the business income will be taxed.

(ii) *Foundations.*   A vast number of foundations are also exempted from taxes, especially those foundations that serve the public good, such as foundations pursuing charitable, scientific, educational, religious, welfare, and other public or commonweal purposes.[8] To enjoy such tax exemption, a foundation must pursue these purposes exclusively or principally in its daily activities, and at least 80% of the proceeds or returns received by the foundation from its property or assets must be used for the same purposes. Family foundations, on the other hand, do not enjoy any particular tax exemptions.

(b) Tax Treatment of Contributions—Domestic Organizations

The general rule under Swedish law is that contributions to nonprofit associations or foundations are *not* exempt from income or other taxation, either for individuals or corporations. Corporate contributions may be deductible, but only to the extent that the contribution could be defined as a cost for sponsoring or marketing the company or its goods or services and thus deductible as a business expense. Furthermore, it is not likely that deductibility of contributions will be introduced in the revised tax system.

---

[7] SFS 1928, p. 370.
[8] Act on State Income Tax, Section 7, SFS 1928:370.

(c) Tax Treatment of Contributions—Foreign Organizations

Donations to foreign organizations are not deductible as well.

§ 22.5   PERSONAL BENEFIT RESTRICTIONS

In principle, there are no legal restrictions or other regulations governing the level of executive salaries or board member compensation for Swedish associations and foundations. Significantly, while the Foundation Act[9] stipulates that board members are entitled to a reasonable fee or compensation, it is also clear from the language of the Act that the provision is dispository or nonmandatory, that is, the parties concerned are free to determine the level of compensation.

With respect to self-dealing, the Act on Foundations stipulates in Chapter 2, Section 14 that board members or managing directors may not deal with matters relating to agreements, such as court and other legal actions, between themselves and the foundation, nor may they deal with matters related to agreements between the foundation and a third party if they have a considerable interest in the matter contrary to that of the foundation. Since this provision is based on a general principle of law applicable to all business organizations, it is safe to assume that the Foundation Act's provision concerning self-dealing is also applicable to nonprofit associations.

The rule on self-dealing emanates from the general legal principle that the foremost duty of representatives of associations, companies, or foundations is to protect the interests of their organization. Accordingly, board members or directors must abstain from promoting their own interests if these are in conflict with the organization's interests. Should conflicts of interest arise, the respective board member or director is disqualified from taking part in the decision-making process in order not to invalidate the decision. Furthermore, board members and directors may not directly or indirectly conduct a business that competes with the association or foundation, and are also under an obligation of secrecy with regard to confidential information and trade secrets.

The general rules on self-dealing apply similarly to members of nonprofit associations. It is generally held that a member is disqualified from participating in decisions concerning claims or legal actions against the member in question as well as in decisions regarding other individuals or legal entities in which the member has a substantial interest.[10]

Finally, foundations, but not nonprofit associations, are subject to a prohibition regarding loans. The Act on Foundations, Chapter 2, Section 6, prohibits foundations from extending cash loans to, or furnishing security in favor of, the founder, the administrator, or those who participate in the administration of the foundation, to affiliated associations or companies, or relatives of the donor or the administrator. Any violation of the prohibition may render the responsible persons, that is, those who participated in the decision to extend the loan or in the execution thereof, liable to compensate the foundation for any damages inflicted by the violation.

[9] Chapter 2, Section 15.
[10] Nial, *supra* 5, pp. 154–55.

§ 22.6   OBLIGATIONS TO THE PUBLIC

With regard to fiduciary responsibilities, there is generally a growing awareness of the fact that at least board members and managing directors of nonprofit associations and foundations engaged in economic or commercial activities may—under certain circumstances—be personally liable for the debts and obligations of the organization. This is evident from Sections 5 and 7 of the Act on Foundations, under which any board member and administrator may be held personally liable for damages inflicted upon the foundation by negligent acts of this person, and also for damages inflicted upon other persons, such as creditors, contracting parties, or employees. Personal liability also arises if board members or the administrator fail to apply immediately to the district court for an order to dissolve a foundation as soon as debts begin to exceed assets.

The legal literature generally holds that the provisions in question represent general principles of law governing all types of companies and associations, regardless of whether they are profit oriented or not, as long as they engage in economic or commercial activities of any kind. Accordingly, in regard to non-profit associations, personal liability may specifically result from the following circumstances:

1. A board member or director has—willfully or as a result of negligence—caused an association damages while performing his or her duties.
2. The board member or director has violated the Constitution or Article of Association, and has thereby inflicted damages upon a third person.
3. The board member has violated criminal law, especially those criminal laws that protect creditors, laws regarding misappropriations, or laws regarding the negligent conduct of business.[11]
4. The nonprofit association distributes profits to members, thereby losing the status of a legal person.
5. The association is used as a vehicle for normal business and commercial activities with a specific risk exposure, in which case—under very exceptional circumstances—the courts may disregard the corporate entity status and make the members personally liable. In practice, such a nonacceptance of the corporate entity status has so far only occurred in four Supreme Court rulings regarding economic associations[12] and limited companies.[13]

There are no general reporting and disclosure requirements. However, Chapters 3 and 4 of the new Act on Foundations contain provisions regarding general reporting and disclosure requirements in the case of foundations. More specifically, the requirements under Chapter 3 of the Act include, *inter alia*, the obligation to keep books and accounts in correspondence with the Swedish Accounting Act of 1976, the obligation to submit annual reports consisting of income statements, balance sheet, and an administration report, applying generally accepted

[11] See the Criminal Code, Chapter 11, Sections 1 to 3.
[12] NJA 1935, p. 81; NJA 1942, p. 473.
[13] NJA 1947, p. 647; NJA 1975, p. 45.

accounting principles, handing over such annual reports to an auditor, submitting consolidated accounts in case a foundation controls other business entities, and so on. These provisions affect all foundations that carry out business activities or control companies or associations which carry out business activities, as well as foundations with assets exceeding approximately SEK 380,000. All other foundations are under the limited obligation to keep summarized accounts of income and costs, and so on. In addition, Chapter 9 of the Act on Foundations provides that most foundations are subject to surveillance and inspection by the County Administration.

§ 22.7   BUSINESS ACTIVITY

In Swedish law, there are no specific restrictions on the business activities of nonprofit associations or foundations. Consequently, such organizations are free to own, operate, or otherwise control any type of business. However, a nonprofit association that engages extensively in business activities that benefit the members of the association is considered an "unregistered economic association" and thereby loses its status as a legal entity. Beyond this, there are tax law differences depending on whether the business activities are related or unrelated to the public benefit purpose of the organization.

(a) Associations

For nonprofit associations, business activities that are genuinely linked to the public benefit purpose of the association are tax exempt. In the case of a sports association, for instance, those profits are exempt which result from entrance fees, sales of programs or other regular items in connection with sports events, as well as specific services to members who participate in the association's activities.

Profits resulting from business activities of an unrelated nature, on the other hand, are subject to taxation. However, there are essentially unrelated business activities which have traditionally been carried out by nonprofit organizations that are accepted and regarded as related activities for tax purposes. These activities include, among others, the organization of lotteries, bingo games, festivities, bazaars, campaigns of different types, and income from corporate sponsorships. Furthermore, in cases where nonprofit associations engage both in related and unrelated business activities, the Swedish tax authorities will normally exempt profits from the unrelated activities if they do not exceed 15% or 20% of the association's total income.

Special principles apply to profits resulting from the use of real estate property of nonprofit associations. Profits from renting or leasing parts of the real estate to third parties are tax exempt only if 50% or more of the real estate is used for the association's public benefit purposes. Under this general principle, it is also possible for nonprofit associations to use the real estate for unrelated activities for less than half of the business year in order to be tax relieved for the whole year.

(b) Foundations

Foundations are relieved from taxes on capital income—including capital gains, interest, dividends, and so on—provided that at least 80% of annual proceeds are used for the foundation's public benefit purpose. With respect to the type of businesses in which a foundation engages, Sections 6 and 7 of the State Income Tax Act distinguish between foundations that are completely relieved from taxes, and foundations that are only relieved from certain taxes, but are under the obligation to pay taxes on profits resulting from business activities, regardless of the nature of the business. Those foundations which are entirely relieved from taxes are exempted by virtue of the circumstance that they are generally believed to serve the public benefit and are specifically listed in Section 7 of the Act. All other foundations are liable to taxation on profits from business activities, irrespective of whether they serve a public benefit or not.

§ 22.8   OTHER FUNDING RESTRICTIONS

There are no other funding restrictions on nonprofit organizations or limitations on fund-raising costs under Swedish law.

§ 22.9   POLITICAL ACTIVITY

Except for the general restrictions that localities place on public political demonstrations, and the general criminal laws concerning bribes, and so on, there are no restrictions on the political activities of nonprofit associations and foundations at all. Nonprofit organizations are free to engage in political activities, and there are no limits on such activities. Likewise, candidates for political office are allowed to hold positions in nonprofit organizations.

§ 22.10   KEY OUTSTANDING ISSUES

Swedish law on nonprofit organizations is fairly stable at the present time. At the same time, several issues remain somewhat unsettled and could surface for debate.

(a) The Tax Treatment of Charitable Donations

As noted, Swedish tax law provides no deductions for charitable contributions. Various efforts have been made to establish such deductions in recent years, but they have made little headway. Although a Government Tax Committee is presently formulating new tax provisions for nonprofit associations and foundations, it is not expected that these will alter the current tax treatment of contributions.

Swedish governments in the early 1990s sought to enhance the variety of forms of institutions in the health and education sectors, and in the field of scientific research, by encouraging the formation of private foundations and then channeling public funds to them. The more recent Social Democratic government has sought to recover some of these funds and dissolve the newly created foundations. This has occasioned a significant controversy with legal experts, who have generally held that under the new Act on Foundations and the fundamental principles on which it is based, a foundation once established can be dissolved only by decision of its board.

(b) Application of European Competition Law

Largely based on the competition law of the European Union, as laid down in the Rome Treaty and various regulations and directives, Sweden enacted a new Competition Act on July 1, 1993, prohibiting anticompetitive behavior on the part of Swedish organizations. The far-reaching prohibitions of the Act apply to practically any kind of organization engaged in economic and commercial activities, including nonprofit associations and foundations. However, the sections of the Act that bear specific relevance for the nonprofit field are particularly directed toward business associations, and cooperation and concerted actions of individual businesses under cover of these associations. The Act's impact on the nonprofit field is further diminished by an exemption granted to small organizations. For instance, the prohibition against anticompetitive agreements does not cover so-called small agreements which are defined as agreements between organizations which hold market shares of no more than 5% of the relevant market, and which do not have a total annual turnover of more than SEK 200 millions. While it is generally believed that this exemption covers most nonprofit associations and foundations, certain business and industry associations such as the Swedish Association of Banks are subject to the Act's provisions, and many have already modified their operations in order not to contravene the requirements of the Act.

(c) The Liability of Nonprofit Boards

A spate of bankruptcies among nonprofits over the past five or six years, especially in the field of sports, athletics, and similar activities, have led to a number of legal actions against board members and directors and consequently increased attention to the legal liabilities of board members and managing directors of nonprofit associations. While it is unclear how these cases will be resolved, it seems likely that they will lead to legislative changes to codify laws governing this aspect of nonprofit operations. This is already apparent in the new Act on Foundations, which explicitly holds board members and administrators personally liable for damages resulting from negligence on the part of the board members or administrators. Similar clarification of liability seems highly likely in the case of associations as well.

CHAPTER TWENTY-THREE

Thailand[*]

§ 23.1 LEGAL CONTEXT

Thailand is a civil law country with a body of law based heavily on the European Roman law system. The civil code, known technically as the Civil and Commercial Code, specifies the legal purpose and method of governance for all nongovernmental organizations, both for-profit and nonprofit.

Prior to the 1932 coup d'état in Thailand, the civil code made no provision for the formation of nonprofit organizations. Since that date, however, such organizations have been authorized. Indeed, Section 89 of the Constitution of 1995 explicitly establishes the right to associate and further holds that the government should promote and support social welfare activities of private organizations.

§ 23.2 ELIGIBILITY

(a) Types of Organizations

Apart from labor unions and federations of unions or employers' associations, only two other types of nonprofit organizations are legally recognized and registered by the Thai government: associations and foundations. Other terms exist, such as councils and leagues, but to acquire legal status these entities must register under one of the two legally acceptable terms. Unregistered organizations, including development and religious groups, also form part of Thailand's nonprofit sector, though they may or may not be recognized by the government.

(i) Associations.   In general, associations are governed by the Civil and Commercial Code of 1992, Sections 78 to 109. Section 78 of the Civil Code of 1992 holds that "[a] contract of association is a contract whereby several persons agree to unite for a common undertaking other than that of sharing profits. Every association must have regulations and must be registered." Besides employers' associations, there are three different types of associations: commercial associations, cremation associations, and general nonprofit associations.

- *Commercial associations* include organizations whose membership consists of commercial enterprises, but whose objectives are not profit sharing. Examples include import-export groups and commodity sales groups. They differ from other organizations in that they operate for the interest of

---

* Country Rapporteur: Dr. Amara Pongsapich, Director of Social Research Institute, Chulalongkorn University, Bangkok. This chapter is based on a legal field guide of the Johns Hopkins Comparative Nonprofit Sector Project.

members rather than for the public. Chambers of Commerce also fall into this category.

- *Cremation associations* are viewed as welfare organizations attending to the basic needs of people in matters of death and cremation. Buddhist theology prescribes ceremonies for the proper care of the bodies of the deceased. Joining a cremation association is one way to assure that the rituals are followed correctly. A separate type of cremation association is comprised of customers of the Bank of Agriculture and Agricultural Cooperatives. These groups were established as an organizing mechanism in rural areas, where the Bank conducted extensive services. Eventually, the Bank itself agreed to incorporate cremation associations as part of its normal business activities—a strategy to attract rural customers.
- *General nonprofit associations* include all associations whose objectives do not fall under the other categories. Usually, general nonprofit associations pursue cultural and social activities.

(ii) Foundations.   Foundations are governed by Sections 110 to 136 of the Civil and Commercial Code of 1992. Section 110 defines foundations as consisting of property appropriated to charitable, religious, scientific, literary or other purposes. Traditionally, foundations are established in honor of distinguished Thai citizens to provide welfare and relief assistance to the victimized populations, as well as to promote education, culture, and preservation of the cultural heritage. More recently, foundations are being established for environmental protection and economic development as well. Foundations derive their revenues primarily from individual donations and/or fund-raising drives. They are prohibited from engaging in profit-making activities.

(iii) Unregistered Associations.   In addition to the types of organizations mentioned above, unregistered nonprofit groups organize for specific purposes but do not acquire legal standing. Such organizations are known as project or working groups, units, and forums. They tend to be small and are dedicated to public welfare, community development, and campaign advocacy issues such as human rights, the environment, and cultural promotion. They may, on occasion, combine under umbrella councils or coordinating committees. A 1986 survey of developmental NGOs revealed that most of these groups are unregistered and tend to be found near colleges and universities. The issues they address appeal to young people, who are apparently more willing to work for the public interest, and are easy to recruit. Grassroots organizations and advocacy groups usually do not register with government agencies as well, often because of burdensome endowment or registration and management requirements. Beyond development and advocacy groups, various unregistered centers and institutions in Thailand operate action projects and/or research programs. Many religious organizations are also unregistered, as are most of the umbrella groups which coordinate particular projects, for example, on behalf of children, women, primary health, human rights, slum improvement, and environmental protection.

In general, unregistered associations operate the same way as registered associations, except they need not report to any authority. Many developmental groups prefer not to register in order to avoid reporting requirements. Although *all* nonprofit organizations are required to register, the National Cultural Commission, which registers associations and foundations, has neither the authority nor the manpower to monitor unregistered groups, and thus cannot initiate any actions against those that do not register.

(b) Types of Purposes

Until recently, organizations applying for registration had to specify in their application forms that the organization will not be involved in political activities. However, after a revision in 1992, this phrase may be deleted and replaced by a phrase indicating that no activities will be carried out that threaten national security. Otherwise, only gambling and other illegal activities are prohibited.

(c) Other Requirements

While there are no specific collateral requirements for associations, foundations with public interest objectives, such as educational, cultural, sports- or development-related purposes, are required to maintain at least 100,000 baht in assets and another 100,000 baht in cash. Foundations with no public interest objectives need to maintain a capital of 500,000 baht.

(d) Registration Procedures

Nonprofit associations were first ordered to register with the government under the National Cultural Act of 1942. According to this Act, the National Cultural Commission of the Ministry of Education is responsible for examining the objectives and monitoring activities of foundations and associations. However, the actual registration is under the responsibility of the Ministry of the Interior (i.e., the Police Department and the Department of Local Administration). The basic registration procedures for most associations and foundations are laid out in the relevant sections of the Civil and Commercial Code.

(i) Associations. Different types of associations are registered with different government agencies.

- *General nonprofit associations,* established for cultural and social purposes, must register with the National Cultural Commission in Bangkok or the provincial governor's office in other provinces, respectively. In order to secure registration, associations have to state among their objectives that no activities will be pursued that would threaten national security. Furthermore, the following information must be included in the application for registration: (1) the name of the association; (2) its objectives; (3) the location of its office; (4) membership requirements; (5) fees; (6) details on the election of board members, including specifications of the terms of office, the size of the board, and required meetings; (7) its management, accounting system, capital and assets; and (8) the requirements for the general annual meeting of members.
- *Commercial associations* are registered with the Department of Internal Trade, Ministry of Commerce, or with provincial governors outside of

Bangkok. Since the nature of this type of association differs from that of philanthropic and social welfare associations, they are registered under the Trade Association Act and Chamber of Commerce Act of 1966 but not under the Civil and Commercial Code. Commercial associations are under the obligation to report income and expenditures annually to the trade association registrar and also file minutes of annual meetings. Commercial associations may include among their objectives provisions for consultation and information services for members. Otherwise, the registration requirements are the same as for general nonprofit associations.

- *Cremation associations* are registered with the Department of Public Welfare formerly under the Ministry of the Interior but now under Ministry of Labor and Social Welfare. The Cremation Welfare Act of 1974 gives the Department of Public Welfare the authority to oversee activities of cremation associations throughout the country. Cremation associations must have as their exclusive objective to have members helping each other with the cremation of deceased members. No other activities are allowed.

(ii) Foundations.   The establishment of foundations involves two steps: The registration as an organization, and the registration as a legal entity. Applications to establish foundations must be submitted to the National Cultural Commission in Bangkok, or to the provincial governors' offices elsewhere, to be forwarded to the National Cultural Commission. Following an initial approval regarding the registration as an organization, founders must secure clearance and approval of certain documents from either the provincial governor's office or the Department of Police in Bangkok in order to attain legal personality for the foundation. These documents must include a profile of the foundation, its objectives, location, and other data. As is the case with associations, in the application for registration the foundation has to state that no activities are intended that threaten national security. Collateral of 200,000 baht for public-interest foundations and 500,000 baht for others must be deposited in a foundation bank account. Upon registration, foundations must submit minutes of board meetings and personal biographies of the directors. Qualifications of directors and managers, meeting schedules, and annual reports are also subject to government regulations. Furthermore, changes in the board membership are subject to notification.

§ 23.3   INTERNAL GOVERNANCE

(a) Associations

By definition, all associations, general or otherwise, must have memberships, and their boards of directors must be elected from among that membership. They must hold at least one annual meeting to which all members are invited. Further, the agenda for this meeting must include an election of the board, presentation of an annual report, an annual budget, and a statement of expenditures certified by a qualified accountant, all of which must later be submitted to the National Cultural Commission, or to the Provincial Governor. The general annual meeting is required to approve the accounting of the previous year as well as the budget for the following year. Internal regulations must be clearly identified and must include organizational objectives, membership qualifications, fees, and bylaws pertaining to association activities, such as board electoral procedures.

(b) Foundations

Foundations must have a governing board that is responsible for carrying out the foundation's activities in accordance with the specified objectives. However, the management has broad powers, including the power to change the foundation's original mission. Specifically, the board may request to revise the objectives of the foundation if necessary and appropriate, which, however, is subject to approval by the authorities. In cases like this, the board would have to provide sufficient explanations and reasons for a change. In practice, however, many foundation boards decide to amend rather than overturn the original objectives. For the financial administration, it is required that foundations have accounting systems in place that are certified by qualified accountants.

§ 23.4   TAX TREATMENT

(a) Tax Treatment of Organizations

Upon registration, associations and foundations become juristic persons and are therefore subject to corporate income tax. The corporate income tax is calculated as 10% or 2%, respectively, of gross assessable income. The 2% rate applies to income from businesses, such as commercial, agricultural, industrial, or transportation activities, while the 10% rate applies to other income, including interest, rents and dividends. However, membership fees and donations and gifts are exempt from tax. Furthermore, income from activities of private school associations or foundations established under the Private School Law is also exempt, except for income derived from selling goods or rendering services to nonstudents.

   Under the Civil and Commercial Code, the Ministry of Finance may grant a registered association or foundation the special status of "nonprofitable charity organization," in which case it is not considered to be a juristic company or partnership for the purposes of the Revenue Code and is consequently exempted from corporate income tax. To qualify for this tax-exempt status, the foundation must be in existence for more than three years and its books must be endorsed by a certified accountant during the period. To maintain registered status, and therefore tax exemption and deductibility, organizations must submit to the Revenue Department within 150 days from the closing date of an accounting period annual reports, minutes of meetings, balance sheets and statements of revenue and expenditure, and budgets, and refrain from activities that would threaten national security.

(b) Tax Treatment of Contributions—Domestic Organizations

Individual donations to registered associations and foundations that have been declared tax exempt by the Ministry of Finance are tax deductible, but only up to 10% of taxable net income. For corporations, too, donations are tax deductible only when made to public interest and charitable organizations approved by the Ministry of Finance. The ceilings are 2% of net profits for contributions to organizations with public interest purposes, and an additional 2% for education and sports activities.

(c) Tax Treatment of Contributions—Foreign Organizations

Since foreign organizations are not tax exempt under Thai law, donations to them are accordingly not deductible.

§ 23.5 PERSONAL BENEFIT RESTRICTIONS

Usually, members and/or donors are not allowed to derive personal benefits from associations and foundations. However, this issue is not very well defined and it has been questioned, for instance, whether sports clubs should be able to register as associations.

§ 23.6 OBLIGATIONS TO THE PUBLIC

Registered associations and foundations have to submit annual reports, annual budgets, and certified statements of expenditure to the National Cultural Commission or the Provincial Governor.

§ 23.7 BUSINESS ACTIVITY

Business activities are allowed but only if the income derived from such activities is used for the nonprofit objectives of the association or foundation.

§ 23.8 OTHER FUNDING RESTRICTIONS

According to the regulations of the Fund Raising Control Act, the exchange of a donation for goods or for services at specified rates is not allowed. Any fund-raising activities must be approved by the Fund Raising Committee of the government. Prohibited are fund-raising activities which threaten national security or the moral basis of society.

In general, Buddhist fund-raising is governed by religious rather than state authority. Religious donations to temples, in the spirit of "making merit" for a better future, are managed by monks and temple committees. However, foundations established in honor of a particular monk or individual to dispense funds must adhere to state regulations monitored by the National Cultural Commission.

§ 23.9 POLITICAL ACTIVITY

Up until 1992, all registered nonprofits had to be nonpolitical and had to declare themselves nonpolitical under their written statement of objectives. As mentioned above, after the revision of these rules in 1992, nonprofit organizations are required only to declare that they are not going to carry out activities which are detrimental to national security. Political parties are registered separately from associations and are, of course, allowed to have political objectives.

§ 23.10   KEY OUTSTANDING ISSUES

The 1991 interim government announced a policy to loosen control of the nonprofit sector. Since then, measures have been taken to revise registration procedures and tax regulations to promote nonprofit sector activities.

(a) Burdensomeness of the Registration Procedures

Prior to the changes in 1992, the registration process had taken about one to two years. Although in Bangkok the registration papers still have to go from the Office of Cultural Affairs to the Police and the Governor's Office, some of the steps have been shortened. Even so, the procedures generally still often take a few months. However, if well-known personalities are involved in the establishment of an association or foundation, in practice, the process is often considerably shorter since the authorities require less time to check the applicants' trustworthiness and to determine that the proposed organization would not threaten national security.

(b) Capital Requirements for Foundations

With regard to the collateral requirements for the registration of foundations, the situation actually became worse in 1992, when the Revenue Department decided to raise from 200,000 to 500,000 baht the capital required to register a charity unless proof is presented that the foundation's activities are of an educational, cultural, developmental, or sport-related nature or otherwise in the public interest. The underlying argument was to prevent the establishment of foundations without adequate funding, which would then have to carry out fund-raising activities and thus put the burden of financing the organization's purposes on the general public by means of solicitation of donations.

Overall, the legal framework for the nonprofit sector has improved only slightly since 1992 and the Revenue Department has not been convinced yet that further improvements are necessary. The fact that the nonprofit sector is generally not viewed very positively and that conservatives disapprove the advocacy role of some NGOs further complicates the situation.

CHAPTER TWENTY-FOUR

United Kingdom[*]

§ 24.1 LEGAL CONTEXT

The United Kingdom is a common law country with no written constitution. Many of the key features of law governing nonprofit, or "voluntary," organizations, as they are more commonly called in the United Kingdom, are therefore embedded in case law rather than explicit statutes. Most significantly, the common law tradition guarantees an inherent right of citizens to form associations for a wide variety of purposes, both commercial and noncommercial. Among the noncommercial purposes, moreover, the common law tradition distinguishes between "charitable" and noncharitable associations. The former are entitled to certain privileges not available to the latter, among the most significant of which are exemptions from most types of taxation and eligibility to receive tax-deductible gifts from donors.

Quite apart from whether they are charitable or not, associations in the United Kingdom can take either of two broad legal forms, depending on whether they are incorporated or not. The major difference is that corporate bodies are recognized by the law as having a personality that is distinct from the personalities of the members or officers of the body. Corporate bodies are thus legal persons in the eyes of the law. Most of them are governed by the Companies Acts. In addition, there are a variety of other statutes that govern different types of nonprofit organizations, both corporate and noncorporate. These include the Charities Acts, the Friendly Societies Acts, and the Industrial and Provident Societies Acts.

The legal provisions applicable to nonprofit or voluntary organizations in the United Kingdom are not uniform throughout the country. To the contrary, there are certain differences among the laws applicable in England and Wales, Scotland, and Northern Ireland. This chapter concentrates mainly on the law governing nonprofit organizations in England and Wales, though some of the major differences applicable to Scotland and Northern Ireland are noted at appropriate places.

§ 24.2 ELIGIBILITY

In English law there are only two types of legal entities, the individual and the corporation, and nonprofit organizations can be based on either of these two, that is, they can be unincorporated or incorporated. Each of these forms in turn

---

[*] Country Rapporteur: Dr. Geraint Thomas, B.A. (Wales), D.Phil. (Oxon.) Senior Lecturer in Law, Queen Mary and Westfield College, University of London, London, England and Barrister at Law, of 10 Old Square, Lincoln's Inn, London, England. This chapter is based on a legal field guide prepared for the Johns Hopkins Comparative Nonprofit Sector Project.

has more than one type, though not all the types are used for noncommercial purposes. The discussion below therefore details the different types of noncommercial entities permitted in English law and the major characteristics and requirements of each.[1]

(a) Types of Organizations

(i) Corporations.   A corporation is defined as a body of persons (*corporation aggregate*) or as an office (*corporation sole*) which is recognized by the law as having a personality distinct from the personalities of the members or officers of the body. Corporations, of either kind, may be ecclesiastical corporations (such as an archbishop, bishop, or vicar, each of whom is a corporation sole, or the dean and chapter of a cathedral church, who are a corporation aggregate) or lay corporations (such as the Sovereign, who is a corporation sole, or companies limited by guarantee or by shares incorporated under the Companies Acts, which are corporations aggregate).[1a] Corporations may also be statutory or nonstatutory; the rights and powers of the former are limited or circumscribed by what is authorized, directly or indirectly, by the statutes creating them, whereas the latter can do everything that an individual can do unless restricted directly or indirectly by statute.

Nonprofit organizations that choose to incorporate typically do so as *companies limited by guarantee*. This means that the incorporators guarantee to cover outstanding debts up to a certain (usually nominal) guaranteed amount. The other type of company provided for under the Companies Acts is the company limited by shares, which is usually used for commercial purposes. Since a corporation is a legal person, separate and distinct from the individual corporations or members of which it is composed, it can, in its own name, do most things that a private individual can do. Thus, it can purchase, own, and sell property in its own name; it can enter into contracts; it can be liable in tort; it can be indicted and convicted for certain criminal offenses; and so forth.

One subtype of corporations serving noncommercial purposes in English law is the "foundation." Such institutions are *eleemosynary* corporations founded by the Crown or by an individual. The law distinguishes two species of foundations, namely the *fundatio incipiens*, which may be created directly by Royal Charter or Act of Parliament, or by a private individual acting under Royal license; and the *fundatio percipiens*, or endowment, created by a gift made by a founder (e.g., certain colleges and hospitals).

(ii) Unincorporated Associations.   In addition to corporations, there are many associations and bodies which are simply aggregates of persons (whether individuals or corporations) not enjoying corporate status. These may have a purely business or commercial purpose, or they may not. However, the term

---

[1] Research is under way to find a new legal structure for charities, under the auspices of the Charity Law Unit of the University of Liverpool, the NCVO and the Charity Law Association. See also the Deakin Report, "Meeting the Challenge of Change: Voluntary Action into the 21st Century." *The Report of the Commission on the Future of the Voluntary Sector* (London: NCVO, 1996), Vol. 1, paras. 3.4.1–3.4.3, 3.5.5.

[1a] See Halsbury's *Laws of England*, 4th ed., vol. 9 (London: Butterworths: 1974), paras. 1201–1210.

"unincorporated association" is generally reserved for certain bodies which exist for noncommercial purposes. An unincorporated association has been judicially defined as "two or more persons bound together for one or more common purposes, not being business purposes, by mutual undertaking, each having mutual duties and obligations, in an organization which has rules which identify in whom control of it and its funds rests and upon what terms and which can be joined or left at will. The bond of union between members of an unincorporated association has to be contractual."[2]

This definition distinguishes unincorporated associations from corporations, individuals, partnerships, and so on. Because an unincorporated association has no legal existence separate and distinct from the members of which it is composed,[3] the property of an unincorporated association must be held by some individual(s) (perhaps the individual members themselves) on behalf of the association.[4] Furthermore, an association cannot sue or be sued in its own name: legal proceedings must usually be taken by, or be directed against, individual members or officers. Nor can an association (as opposed to an individual member or officer) be guilty of any criminal offense.

There are no statutes dealing with unincorporated associations generally, and most of the law relating to them is judge made. There are, however, certain unincorporated associations, such as registered friendly societies and registered industrial and provident societies, that are dealt with separately by statute and are regarded as "quasicorporations." Although they are not corporations in the true sense, they enjoy some of the usual attributes of incorporation.

(iii) Friendly Societies.   Friendly societies are unincorporated mutual insurance associations in which members subscribe for provident benefits for themselves and their families. They form part of a group of voluntary benefit, thrift, and provident societies (the others being building societies, cooperative societies, and trade unions). Under the Friendly Societies Act of 1974, friendly societies registered pursuant to this Act enjoy, among other things:

1. The right to hold land and other property in the name of trustees, such property passing automatically to succeeding trustees without assignment or transfer
2. The right to bring or defend actions in the names of trustees
3. Exemption from stamp duties on certain documents
4. Simplified procedures for requiring officers to account for and deliver up property
5. Nomination by members over 16 years of age of sums payable on their deaths not exceeding £1,500

Unfavorable regulatory and tax frameworks in the 1970s and 1980s led to the gradual decline of friendly societies. However, the Friendly Societies Act of 1992 permitted these societies to offer a wider range of services, but balanced the

---

[2] *Conservative and Unionist Central Office v. Burrell* [1982] 1 W. L. R. 522, at p. 525, per Lawton, L.J.
[3] *Steele v. Gourley and Davies* (1886) 3 T.L.R. 772.
[4] *Re Bucks Constabulary Widows' and Orphans Friendly Society* (No. 2) [1979] 1 W.L.R. 936.

greater freedom with a more modern form of supervision and investor protection. The Act furthermore provides for the voluntary conversion of existing registered societies to corporate bodies. However, it is too soon to see how many new friendly societies will be formed under the 1992 Act or whether existing registered societies will take advantage of the new provision for incorporation.

(iv) Industrial and Provident Societies. Industrial and provident societies were originally another type of unincorporated nonprofit organization. Governed now by the Industrial and Provident Societies Acts 1965 to 1978, they were originally societies whose purposes were to make profits by personal exertions of their members and to distribute the profits by way of provident provision for their members' future. Under the Industrial and Provident Societies Act 1965, societies may be registered for the purpose of carrying on any industry, business, or trade, whether wholesale or retail, either if the society is a *bona fide* cooperative society or if the society's business or intended business is conducted for the benefit of the community and there are special reasons for the society not to register under the Companies Act. By virtue of its registration, an industrial and provident society becomes a body corporate by its registered name, by which it may sue and be sued. It acquires perpetual succession and limited liability.[5] Registration furthermore vests in the society all property for the time being vested in any person in trust for it. The society acquires power to hold land; its members may dispose of their property in the society on death by means of nomination, and so forth.

(v) Trusts. A trust may also be described, albeit loosely, as a nonprofit entity. In truth it is more a relationship than an organization. It has been defined as "an equitable obligation, binding a person (who is called a trustee) to deal with property over which he has control (which is called the trust property), for the benefit of persons (who are called the beneficiaries or *cestuis que trust*), of whom he may himself be one, and any one of whom may enforce the obligation."[6] Where the beneficiaries of a trust are the public generally or the purpose is "charitable" in the special legal meaning of the term, trusts are a form of nonprofit body. Such trusts are enforceable by the Attorney General on behalf of the beneficiaries. In principle either individuals or corporations can be trustees.

(vi) Housing Associations. A housing association is a society, body of trustees or company (a) which is established for the purpose of, or among whose objects or powers are included those of constructing, improving, or managing or facilitating or encouraging the construction or improvement of accommodation, and (b) which does not trade for profit or whose constitution or rules prohibit the issue of any capital with interest or dividend exceeding such a rate as may be prescribed by the Treasury.[7]

---

[5] Section 3 of the 1965 Act.
[6] A. Underhill and D. Hayton, *Law Relating to Trusts and Trustees,* 15th ed. (London: Butterworths, 1995), p. 3; approved by Romer, L.J. in *Green v. Russell* [1959] 2 Q.B. 226, at p. 241.
[7] Section 1(1) of the Housing Associations Act 1985.

(b) Types of Purposes

(i) *England and Wales.*   In general, there are no specific restrictions as to the purposes of nonprofit or voluntary organizations. However, an important distinction is that between charitable and noncharitable purposes. Although the rules of law relating to charitable and noncharitable purposes of a trust or corporation are generally the same, charitable status confers the following major advantages on an organization:

- Charities, in general, enjoy a number of fiscal advantages in the form of tax exemptions or reliefs (see below) which are not granted to noncharities.
- In general, private trusts will fail for "uncertainty of object" if there are no ascertainable beneficiaries on whose behalf the courts can judge the performance of trustees. Charitable trusts, on the other hand, are considered valid because the Attorney General is charged with enforcing such trusts on behalf of the Crown.
- Charitable trusts, unlike private trusts, may be perpetual.[8]
- If a private trust or gift fails, the beneficial interest in the property results back to the settlor or donor. While this may also be the case with charitable trusts or gifts, the latter are commonly saved for charity by the application of the *cy pres* doctrine, under which the gifted property is applied toward another purpose or object which is "as near as" possible to the original or intended purpose.
- Furthermore, there are some de facto advantages: Governmental as well as private funding agencies are often more willing to support certain philanthropic purposes when they are being carried out or advanced by charitable organizations.

There is no exhaustive definition of what constitutes a charitable purpose in English law. Section 97(1) of the Charities Act 1993 (reenacting Section 46 of the Charities Act 1960) simply defines the phrase "charitable purposes" as "purposes which are exclusively charitable according to the law of England and Wales." For the definition of the basic terms, it is necessary to look to the substantial body of case law that has grown up over centuries.

If a purpose is to be charitable according to English law, it must fall "within the spirit and intendment" of the preamble to the Charitable Uses Act of 1601. The preamble provided a catalogue of charitable purposes:

[The] Relief of aged, impotent and poor People, [the] maintenance of sick and maimed soldiers and mariners, schools of learning, free schools, and scholars in universities, [the] repair of bridges, ports, havens, causeways, churches, sea-banks and highways, [the] education and preferment of orphans, [the] relief, stock or maintenance for houses of correction, [the] marriages of poor maids, [the] aid or ease of any poor inhabitants concerning payments of fifteens, setting out of soldiers and other taxes. . . .

---

[8] *Re Bowen* [1893] 2 Ch. 494, at p. 495.

The preamble is not a definition but a nonexhaustive list of purposes which, in 1601, were regarded as charitable. Subsequently, the Court of Chancery treated the objects enumerated simply as particular instances to which other purposes might properly be added from time to time if some analogy could be found between them and an object mentioned in the preamble. In time, the Courts went further and granted charitable status to an object if they could find an analogy between it and an object already held to be charitable.[9]

In 1891, the mass of case law was classified by Lord Macnaghten in *Pemsel's Case*[10] into four categories: *the relief of poverty*; the *advancement of education*; the *advancement of religion*; and *other purposes beneficial to the community* not falling under any of the preceding categories. Although it is a classification of convenience only, it has constantly been referred to in later cases. Although courts have recognized that the law of charities may have evolved since Lord Macnaghten's classification, it remains the case that purposes which are neither enumerated in the preamble nor, by analogy, deemed to be within its spirit and intendment are not charitable, even though such purposes are beneficial to the public.[11]

1. *Relief of Poverty.* The law of charities' concept of poverty is relative, taking into account the circumstances and expectations of the individuals in question. Relief may take the form of cash handouts; the provision of basic amenities such as housing, clothing, food, and fuel; setting up and supporting institutions to provide things such as soup kitchens, orphanages, and nursing homes; and even the provision of legal services and holidays. In addition, the Charity Commissioners have indicated in their *Annual Report* for 1967 that they would also consider as being for the relief of poverty grants of money in the form of special payments to relieve sudden distress, sickness, or infirmity, or to pay traveling expenses to someone entering or leaving hospital; the provision of items such as furniture, bedding, clothing, books, or tools; the payment of fees for instruction or examination; the provision of holidays for those needing to recuperate, or special food, medical aid, and so forth, to the old, sick, infirm, and handicapped.[12]

2. *Advancement of Education.* The concept of education in the law of charities has broadened considerably since 1601. It includes purposes as general as "the advancement and propagation of education and learning in every part of the world"[13] and as specific as establishing a single library or museum, a single teaching post, or a scholarship. It embraces learned societies and day nurseries for children and also recognizes the usefulness not only of the traditional educational

---

[9] *Scottish Burial Reform and Cremation Society Ltd. v. Glasgow City Corporation* [1968] A.C. 138, at p. 147, per Lord Reid.

[10] *Income Tax Special Purposes Commissioners v. Pemsel* [1891] A.C. 531, at p. 583. This classification was based, in fact, on Sir Samuel Romilly's argument in *Morice v. Bishop of Durham* [1805] 10 Ves. 522, at p. 523.

[11] *Gilmour v. Coats* [1949] A.C. 426, at p. 443, per Viscount Simonds; *A.-G. v. National Provincial and Union Bank of England* [1924] A.C. 252, at p. 265, per Viscount Cave; *Dunne v. Byrne* [1912] A.C. 407, at p. 411, per Lord Macnaghten.

[12] See Tudor on Charities, 8th ed. (London: Sweet & Movewell: 1995), pp. 30–31; Picarda on Charities, 2nd ed. (London: Butterworths, 1995), Ch. 2.

[13] *Whicker v. Hume* [1858] 7 H.L.C. 124; Picarda on Charities, Ch. 3; Tudor on Charities, pp. 20–39.

subjects but also industrial and technical subjects, cultural pursuits such as music, drama, and the fine arts, and so forth.

3. *Advancement of Religion.*   There is no definition of religion for these purposes, but it is considered that it must possess two essential attributes, namely "faith in a god and worship of that god." As between different religions, the law stands neutral. Furthermore, organizations, such as the Salvation Army or the Church Missionary Society, which exist to advance religion have also been held charitable under this category, as have been ancillary or satellite purposes, such as gifts for the erection, repair, and maintenance of a church, chapel, or meeting house, or parts thereof; gifts for the upkeep of a churchyard; as well as gifts for the support of the clergy.[14] On the other hand, social movements founded on Christian ethics, and organizations based on ethical or moral principles such as the Church of Scientology or Freemasonry, are not necessarily charitable.

4. *Other Purposes Beneficial to the Community.*   This is the residual head of charity and the one in which most new registrations by the Charity Commissioners are made. Indeed, many of the main categories of charitable purposes which have been registered in recent years would seem to fall under Lord Macnaghten's fourth head (e.g., purposes connected with social welfare, cultural purposes, conservation of the environment, and the promotion of racial harmony).[15] However, there is no satisfactory test to determine whether a particular purpose falls within it. It is not sufficient that the purpose is for the public benefit. It must also be beneficial in a way which the law regards as charitable, which means that the benefit to the public must be within "the spirit and intendment" of the preamble to the 1601 Statute, or at least closely analogous to the cases previously decided. Most purposes, objects, and organizations associated with the relief of the sick and disabled, the old, or the mentally sick, fall within this category, including housing, clinics, hospitals, homes, the promotion of nursing, the advancement of medical sciences, and the provision of advice on family planning and pregnancy. Other recognized activities include the provision of care or services for those who are disadvantaged in some way which may be, but is not necessarily, caused by poverty, old age, sickness, and so on. Hereunder, a variety of activities are held charitable ranging from the provision of orphanages to establishing and maintaining a fire brigade or a life boat service, the advancement of industry and commerce, and the promotion of good race relations, to name only a few. Even a gift to the Inland Revenue is considered charitable. Furthermore, the preservation of the countryside, or of the sea against pollution, or of the country's heritage, and the establishment and maintenance of museums, libraries, public halls, botanical gardens, observatories, and community centers have been added as modern equivalents to the "repair of bridges, ports, havens, causeways . . . sea banks and highways." Gifts for the protection and welfare of animals generally, or of a class of animals, also fall within the fourth category and are therefore charitable on the ground that they benefit humankind. Although sport and recreation are certainly not within the preamble of the 1601 Statute, the Charity Commissioners now take

---

[14] See Tudor on Charities, pp. 65–87; Picarda on Charities, Ch. 4.
[15] See Picarda on Charities, Chs. 5–13; Tudor on Charities, pp. 88–120.

the view that sport can be charitable if it is directed to some other end which benefits the public.[16] Thus, it is likely that far more recreational or sporting activities will now be registered as charities. More important, Section 1(1) of the Recreational Charities Act 1958 provides that, subject to the continuing need to satisfy the requirement of public benefit, it is charitable "to provide or assist in the provision of facilities for recreation or other leisure time occupation, if the facilities are provided in the interests of social welfare." According to Section 1(2), the social welfare requirement is satisfied if facilities improve the conditions of life for users, and either the users are in need of those facilities "by reason of youth, age, infirmity or disablement, poverty or social or economic circumstances," or the facilities are open to "the members or female members of the public at large." In general, the Act has enabled a large number of recreational concerns to claim charitable status.

5. *Further Requirements.* There are two additional requirements for purposes to be recognized in law as charitable: First, a purpose must not only be beneficial in the sense that it fits into one of the four categories, but it must also be for the benefit of the *public* or an appreciable section of the public. Second, a purpose must be *exclusively* charitable. The inclusion of noncharitable objects along with charitable ones will invalidate the entirety.[17]

The former requirement of public benefit varies in its application to each of the four heads of charity. In relation to the category of relief of poverty, the requirement of public benefit has been reduced almost to the vanishing point, so that a gift in favor of "poor relatives" or "poor employees" is capable of being charitable.[18] In relation to the advancement of education, the requirement has been more stringently applied. In determining whether an appreciable section of the public is being benefited, the courts have established that the class of beneficiaries must not be "numerically negligible" and must not be selected or determined on the basis of either a personal or contractual nexus or connection, either with the donor or between themselves. The requirement in the context of religion is similar to that for education but not as stringent. Most stringent is the requirement in relation to the fourth category, the other purposes beneficial to the community. Most purposes accepted within this category seem to be for the benefit of the public generally even though only a limited number of people may actually derive some advantage. While there may be difficulties if a purpose is limited to a particular group of persons such as the "Welsh people" or the Jews,[19] no matter how large, inhabitants of a geographical area, such as a county or town or borough, have been considered a section of the public. It has been said that the test, under the fourth category, is whether the purpose in question is extended or available to the whole community, even though it may by its very nature be advantageous only to a few, as opposed to one extended or available to a select few out

---

[16] Charity Commissioners' *Annual Report* for 1984, para. 21.

[17] *Morice v. Bishop of Durham* [1805] 10 Ves. Jr. 522; *IRC v. Baddeley* [1955] A.C. 572; *Ellis v. IRC* [1949] 31 T.C. 178.

[18] *Re Scarisbrick* [1951] Ch. 622; *Re Cohen* [1973] 1 W.L.R. 415; *Dingle v. Turner* [1972] A.C. 601.

[19] In *Williams v. IRC* [1947] A.C. 447; *Keren Kayemeth Le Jisroel v. IRC* [1942] A.C. 650.

of a larger number equally willing to take advantage of it.[20] However, in truth, there is no certain accepted test of public benefit for the fourth category.

Finally, there are a few other disqualifying factors. A purpose may fall within one of the four *Pemsel* categories and may also have an element of public benefit, but still may be held noncharitable if it is infected by some disqualifying factor, the three main ones being "self help,"[21] profit distribution, and politics.

(ii) Northern Ireland.   In Northern Ireland, the law of charity is similar to that in England and Wales. The governing statute is the Charities Act (Northern Ireland) 1964, Section 35 of which defines "charitable purposes" as "purposes which are exclusively charitable according to the law of Northern Ireland." It also defines "charity" in terms which are identical to the English definition in Section 96 of the Charities Act 1993.

(iii) Scotland.   The Elizabethan Statute of 1601 never applied to Scotland and, historically, charities were not generally controlled by the Scottish courts. Although there is a great deal of similarity between Scottish and English charity law and many purposes which are regarded as charitable in England are also regarded as charitable in Scotland, no technical meaning is attached to the words "charity" or "charitable" in the general law of Scotland. The basic distinction in Scots law is between private and public trusts. In deciding on the validity of a charitable purpose, the main difficulty in the Scottish law of charity has arisen in relation to the question of whether a gift is sufficiently certain and focused to take effect.[22] In general, the construction put upon the words "charitable purposes" in Scotland can be both wider and narrower than in England. The main significance of charitable status in Scotland is in relation to the tax advantages which it attracts; and, in the context of taxation, which is United Kingdom wide, the English law of charities is regarded as part of the law of Scotland and applied accordingly.[23]

---

[20] *IRC v. Baddeley* [1952] A.C. 572, at p. 592, per Lord Simonds.

[21] Typical examples of organizations which exist for "self help" are friendly societies, mutual insurance or benefit societies, and even trade unions.

[22] *Wink's Executors v. Tallent* [1947] S.C. 470, at pp. 481–482, per Lord Keith; *Anderson's Trustees v. Scott* (1914) S.C. 942.

[23] *Pemsel's Case*; *Scottish Burial Reform and Cremation Society v. Glasgow Corporation* [1968] A.C. 138; and *IRC v. Glasgow Police Athletic Association* [1953] A.C. 380. These differences between Scottish and English charity law are reflected in the provisions of Part I of the Law Reform (Miscellaneous Provisions) (Scotland) Act 1990. The Act creates its own terminology which has no counterpart in English charity law. The primary distinction is that between "recognized bodies" and "nonrecognized bodies." The former are subjected to various statutory duties, while the latter are prohibited from holding themselves out as charities and may be prevented from doing so by the intervention of the Lord Advocate. A "recognized body" means a body which is established under the law of Scotland or which is managed or controlled wholly or mainly in or from Scotland *and* to which the Inland Revenue have given relief from income tax under Section 505 of the Income and Corporation Taxes Act 1988 in respect of income of the body which is applicable and applied to charitable purposes. Such a body is entitled to call itself a "Scottish charity." The expression "charitable purposes" in this context has the meaning ascribed to it under English law.

(c) Other Requirements

In general, there are no further requirements for charitable or noncharitable organizations with respect to membership or capital assets. However, for the purpose of registration, both friendly societies and industrial and provident societies have to have at least seven members.

(d) Registration Procedures

(i) England and Wales. Registration requirements differ considerably between charities and noncharitable organizations.

1. *Charities.* According to Section 3(1) and (2) of the Charities Act 1993, all charities must be registered on a register maintained by the Charity Commissioners. However, there are two exceptions: exempt and excepted charities.

- *Exempt charities* are charities which are, by law, exempt from the jurisdiction of the Charity Commissioners and, therefore, cannot be registered. The Second Schedule to the Charities Act 1993 lists those institutions which are exempt. The list includes the Universities of Oxford, Cambridge, and Durham (and their respective colleges and halls); the colleges of Winchester and Eton; the University of London; and any university college or institution connected with a university college which has been declared by Order in Council to be an exempt charity. Also included in the list are the Board of Trustees of the Victoria and Albert Museum, of the Science Museum, of the Armouries, and of the Royal Botanic Gardens at Kew; the British Museum; the Church Commissioners; and any registered society within the meaning of the Friendly Societies Acts or Industrial and Provident Societies Acts; and the British Library Board.
- *Excepted charities* are charities, other than exempt charities, which are either excepted by order or regulations, such as voluntary schools, boy scouts' and girl guides' organizations, nonexempt universities, and a large number of charities connected with the advancement of religion; or are excepted on the grounds of (1) having neither a permanent endowment nor the use or occupation of any land, and (2) having income which does not in aggregate exceed one thousand pounds a year. An excepted charity is therefore excepted from the requirement of registration. However, it may be entered on the register at its own request, and shall be removed therefrom at its request.

It is the duty of the charity trustees of any charity which is not registered and not exempt or excepted from registration to apply for it to be registered. An application for registration must be accompanied by a copy of the trusts (or, if they are not set out in any extant documents, particulars of them) and such other documents or information as may be prescribed or as the Commissioners may require for the purposes of the application.[24] It is also the duty of the charity trustees, or the last charity trustees, of any institution which is for the time being registered to notify the Commissioners if it ceases to exist, or if there is any change in its trusts, or in the particulars of it entered on the register, and to supply to the Commissioners particulars of any such change and copies of any new trusts or alterations to the trusts. The Commissioners may require any person in default to make good that default. The register, and copies of particulars of the trusts of any registered charity, are open to public inspection at all reasonable times.[25] Any institution which no longer appears to the Charity Commissioners to be a charity shall be removed from the register, as shall any charity which ceases to exist or does not operate.[26]

2. *Noncharities.*   In general, noncharitable organizations are not subject to overall regulation and control. However, there are optional registration procedures for industrial and provident societies, friendly societies and housing associations.

An application to register an *industrial and provident society* must be in the prescribed form (e.g., signed by seven members and the secretary). The matters for which provision must be made in the society's rules include its name; objects; the place of its registered office; the terms of admission of members; the mode of holding meetings; the appointment and removal of committees, managers, and other officers; the audit of accounts; the mode of application of the society's profits; and so forth. A society may not be registered unless (1) it has been shown to the satisfaction of the appropriate registrar[27] to be either a *bona fide* cooperative society or a society the business of which is conducted for the benefit of the community; (2) its rules contain the above mentioned matters; (3) its registered office is within either of the appropriate registrars' jurisdiction; and (4) the number of members is not less than seven.[28]

Friendly societies become incorporated from the date of their registration by the Friendly Societies Commission's central office. Any seven or more persons may establish and register a society by agreeing upon the purposes of the society and upon the extent of its powers in a memorandum, by agreeing upon rules for the regulation of the society, and by sending three copies of the memorandum and rules to the central office. The memorandum must contain certain specified information, such as the name and address of the society's registered office, the purposes, and so forth. Similarly, the society's rules must provide for certain specified matters, such as the terms of admission of members and the manner in

---

[24] For these purposes, the word "trust" means the provision establishing the charity and regulating its purposes and administration, whether those provisions take effect by way of trust or not; and the phrase "charity trustees" means the persons having the general control and management of the administration of a charity. Thus, the directors of a charity incorporated under the Companies Acts or a management committee of a charity, as well as trustees properly so called, are "charity trustees" administering charitable "trusts."

[25] Section 3(6), (7), (8), and (9) of the Charities Act 1993.

[26] Section 3(4) of the Charities Act 1993.

[27] The appropriate registrar is the Central Office of the Registry of Friendly Societies in England, Wales, and the Channel Islands; and the Assistant Registrar of Friendly Societies in Scotland.

[28] Sections 1, 2 of the Industrial and Provident Societies Act 1965.

which membership is to cease; the terms on which a benefit is provided; the consequences of nonpayment of any subscription; procedures for calling meetings; the manner in which disputes are to be settled; and so forth.

Housing associations are eligible for registration with "the Corporation"[29] if they are (a) a registered charity or (b) a society registered under the Industrial and Provident Societies Act 1965 fulfilling certain conditions. These conditions are that the association does not trade for profit and is established for the purpose of, or has among its objects or powers, the provision, construction, improvement, or management of (a) houses to be kept available for letting, or (b) housing for occupation by members of the association, where the association's rules restrict membership to persons entitled, or prospectively entitled, to occupy a house provided or managed by the association, or (c) hostels. Additional purposes or objects are permissible. Registration criteria are established by the respective Corporation.

§ 24.3 INTERNAL GOVERNANCE

The day-to-day administration of any nonprofit organization, be it charitable or not, rests with those directly charged with that task. Their administrative and managerial powers are derived from the governing or founding instrument, as amended, perhaps, by a *cy pres* scheme, or from the relevant statutes and general law. Thus, the trustees of a charitable trust will generally have available the powers conferred on trustees by the Trustee Act 1925 and the Trustee Investment Act 1961, as well as those contained in their trust instrument. Similarly, the directors of a charitable company will be subject to the Companies Acts and to their own Articles and Memorandum, while members of an unincorporated association will generally be bound by the terms of their contract *inter se*. However, charitable organizations, as well as some noncharitable ones, are also subject to regulation and control by certain statutory authorities.

(a) Charities

(i) England and Wales. The administration of charities in England and Wales is governed largely by the Charities Act 1993,[30] the Trustee Act 1925, the Trustee Investment Act 1961, the Charities Act 1985, and the Charities Act 1992, although the general law still plays an important part.

Under these Acts, authority to supervise the administration of charitable organizations, other than exempt charities, in England and Wales is vested in the Charity Commissioners, who are appointed by the Home Secretary. Additional powers are vested in the Attorney General, the Official Custodian, Visitors, and local authorities.

1. *Charity Commissioners.* First established under the Charitable Trusts Act 1853, the Charity Commissioners are charged by the Charities Act 1993 with "the

---

[29] The Corporation, for these purposes, refers to Scottish Homes in Scotland, Housing for Wales in Wales, or the Housing Corporation elsewhere.

[30] Consolidating the Charities Act 1960, Part I of the Charities Act 1992, and the Charitable Trustees Incorporation Act 1872.

general function of promoting the effective use of charitable resources by encouraging the development of better methods of administration, by giving charity trustees advice on any matter affecting the charity and by investigating and checking abuses," and their object is "so to act in the case of any charity . . . as best to promote and make effective the work of the charity in meeting the needs designated by its trusts."[31]

The Commissioners may institute inquiries with regard to charities or a particular charity other than exempt charities, either generally or for particular purposes. They may conduct the inquiry themselves or appoint a person to conduct it and report to them; and they have a range of ancillary powers, such as the power to call for documents, to compel attendance of witnesses, to inspect documents, to furnish accounts and statements in writing, to publish the report, and so forth.[32] Where the Commissioners are satisfied at any time after they have instituted such an inquiry that there has been any misconduct or mismanagement in the administration of the charity, or that it is necessary or desirable to act for the purpose of protecting the property of the charity, they may, of their own motion, exercise a wide range of powers, including the power (1) to suspend any trustee or other person connected with the charity from the exercise of his or her office or employment; (2) to appoint additional trustees; (3) to make orders as to the vesting in, or transfer to, the official custodian of charities of the charity's property; and (4) to restrict the transactions which may be entered into by the charity without the approval of the Commissioners. The Commissioners may also remove any charity trustee or other officer or employee, or, by order, establish a scheme for the administration of the charity. However, the Commissioners do not themselves have the power to act in the administration of the charity. Furthermore, the Commissioners are not to exercise their jurisdiction in any case which is of a contentious character, or which involves any special question of law or of fact, or which the Commissioners consider more fit, for other reasons, to be adjudicated by the High Court. There are also provisions for appeals to the High Court against any order of the Commissioners, by the Attorney General, by the charity or its trustees, or by any person removed from office.[33]

Where it appears to the Commissioners that any action proposed or contemplated in the administration of a charity is expedient in the interests of the charity, they may by order sanction that action, whether or not it would otherwise be within the powers exercisable by the charity trustees in the administration of the charity. Such an order may be made so as to authorize a particular transaction, compromise, or the like, or a particular application of property, or so as to give a more general authority. It may also give directions as to the manner in which any expenditure is to be borne and as to other matters connected with, or arising out of, the action thereby authorized.[34]

2. *The Attorney-General.*   The Crown as the *parens patriae* is the guardian of charity. It is therefore the duty of the Attorney-General, who represents the Crown

---

[31] Section 1 of the Charities Act 1993.
[32] Section 8 of the Charities Act 1993.
[33] Section 6(11), (12).
[34] Section 26 of the Charities Act 1993.

for all forensic purposes, to intervene to protect charities and to give advice and assistance to the Court in the administration of charitable trusts. The Attorney-General may institute and carry on proceedings of his or her own motion; and he or she will usually do so where the Charity Commissioners inform him or her that it is desirable for the Attorney-General to take proceedings in the case of a charity which is not an exempt charity.

3. *The Official Custodian.* The Official Custodian for Charities was constituted by the Charities Act 1960 as a corporation sole having perpetual succession and using an official seal, and given the function of acting as trustee for charities in the cases provided for by the Act. Specifically, the Custodian may act as a permanent holder of charity land, thus avoiding the need to alter title whenever there is a change of trustee. He or she, however, acts only as a custodian trustee and has no power of management, so that the ordinary trustees remain responsible for ensuring that the charity's property is properly invested, maintained, and so forth. By virtue of the Charities Act 1992, the Official Custodian is required to divest himself or herself of all property held by him or her except land and property vested in the Official Custodian by Order of the Charity Commissioners for the protection of charities.

4. *Visitors.* Visitation is a form of supervision of the domestic affairs of an institution, usually a corporation (e.g., colleges or hospitals). The powers vested in a visitor usually include the power to appoint and remove members and officers of the corporation; to regulate the management of the corporation's property; to determine questions of construction arising under the statutes of the foundation; and to hear and adjudicate claims and complaints concerning the internal affairs of the corporation made by members. The exercise of visitatorial power is a juridical act, and the jurisdiction is a sole and exclusive jurisdiction. There are different visitors for different types of corporations: The ordinary is generally the visitor of ecclesiastical corporations, the Sovereign the visitor of civil corporations, and in the case of eleemosynary corporations (foundations, e.g., hospitals, colleges, and corporate schools), the founder makes express appointment of the visitor. Although visitation usually applies to corporations, the trust deed of any unincorporated charity can also appoint a visitor of the charity.

5. *Local Authorities.* The Charities Act 1993 authorizes local councils to initiate and carry out, in cooperation with the charity trustees, a review of the working of any group of local charities with the same or similar purposes in the council's area, and may make to the Commissioners such report and such recommendations as the council after consultation with the trustees think fit. In addition, any local council is authorized to make arrangements with any charity established for purposes similar or complementary to services provided by the council for coordinating their activities in the interests of persons who may benefit from those services or from the charity.

(ii) Scotland and Northern Ireland. Scottish charities are not subject to a comprehensive regulatory regime, whether under a body such as the Charity

Commissioners or otherwise.[35] Part I of the Law Reform (Miscellaneous Provisions) (Scotland) Act 1990 imposes duties in relation to certain specific points and establishes a general supervisory role for the Lord Advocate and the Court of Session. Although there are certain differences, the powers conferred on the Lord Advocate and the Court of Session are very similar to some of the powers conferred on the Charity Commissioners and the English courts in relation to English charities by the Charities Act 1993.

As the Charities Act 1993 also does not extend to Northern Ireland, the governing statute there is the Charities Act (Northern Ireland) 1964 which confers certain powers on the Department of Finance and Personnel and directs the Department to receive and consider any application made to it in writing by the trustees of any charity for the opinion or advice of the Department in relation to any matter or question concerning that charity. The Department may then give such opinion or advice as it considers proper, and trustees acting in accordance with it are deemed to have acted in accordance with the terms of their trust. If the Department considers that the institution of legal proceedings should be considered in relation to a charity, it sends a certificate to that effect to the Attorney General, who may then institute proceedings if he or she sees fit.

(b) Noncharitable Organizations

In general, noncharitable organizations are not subject to overall regulation and control. However, registered industrial and provident societies, registered friendly societies, and registered housing associations are subject to the requirements of the enactments directly applicable to them.

(i) Industrial and Provident Societies.   Once registered, industrial and provident societies must register or deposit with the appropriate registrar all applications to register amendments of rules, annual returns, applications for approval of a change of name, notices of changes of registered offices, special resolutions for amalgamations, transfers of engagements or conversions, and so on. The appropriate registrar (or a person acting on his or her behalf) may inspect any particulars in any register of members and officers of a registered society, and may appoint an accountant or actuary to inspect the society's books and report on them. On the application of one-tenth of the whole number of members of a registered society (or of 100 members if the total number exceeds 1,000), or indeed of his or her own motion, the chief registrar may appoint an inspector to examine and report on the society's affairs.[36]

(ii) Friendly Societies.   Registered friendly societies now come under the jurisdiction and control of the Friendly Societies Commission, a body corporate which shall consist of not less than four and not more than ten members to be appointed by the Treasury (who shall also appoint one member to be chairman

---

[35] The Charities Act 1993 does not extend to Scotland, except for Sections 70 and 71, and part of Section 86.
[36] Sections 44, 47, 49 of the 1965 Act.

and another to be deputy chairman).[37] The general functions of the Commission shall be to promote the protection by each friendly society of its funds; to promote the financial stability of friendly societies generally; to secure that the purposes of each friendly society are in conformity with the Friendly Societies Act 1992; to administer the system of regulation of the activities of friendly societies; and to advise and make recommendations to the Treasury and other government departments on any matter relating to friendly societies. The Commission has power to do anything which is calculated to facilitate the discharge of its functions, or is incidental or conducive to their discharge.[38]

(iii) Housing Associations. Once a housing association is registered with the Corporation,[39] it becomes subject to a wide range of controls and restrictions imposed by the Housing Association's Act 1985. The Corporation has powers to remove committee members and appoint new ones.[40] No amendment of the rules of a registered housing association which is also registered under the Industrial and Provident Societies Act, 1965, and whose registration has been recorded by the Registrar (except a change in its name or its registered office) shall be valid without the Corporation's consent.[41] The association must comply with the regulations issued under the 1985 Act and the Registered Housing Associations (Accounting Requirements) Order 1988 as to the production of annual accounts. The Corporation has furthermore power to direct an inquiry or an audit, and, if misconduct or mismanagement is found in the administration of the association, to direct the transfer of the association's land to another housing association or the Corporation.[42]

§ 24.4   TAX TREATMENT

With regard to the tax treatment of organizations and donations, two things should be noted: First, the distinction between voluntary organizations which enjoy charitable status and those which are noncharitable has considerable significance for tax purposes; and second, there are no differences between England/Wales, Scotland, and Northern Ireland.

(a) Tax Treatment of Organizations

(i) Charities. Various exemptions, reliefs, concessions and privileges are granted to charitable organizations with respect to income and corporation tax; capital gains tax; inheritance tax; value-added tax; and other taxes, rates, and charges.

---

[37] The Friendly Societies Act 1992, Section 1 and Schedule 1. See also Section 124 (Northern Ireland) and Section 125 (Channel Islands and Isle of Man).

[38] Section 1(4) and (5) of the 1992 Act.

[39] Scottish Homes in Scotland, Housing for Wales in Wales, and the Housing Corporation elsewhere.

[40] Sections 16–17 of the 1985 Act.

[41] Section 19.

[42] Sections 28 to 30.

- *Income and corporation tax*: Although there is no general exemption from income tax for charities, particular exemptions have been granted by Section 505,[42a] coupled with Section 9(4), of the Income and Corporation Taxes Act 1988. These exemptions have been increased by extrastatutory concessions and additional concessions allowed in practice. Types of income which are exempt include, for example, (a) profits arising from rents or other receipts from an estate, interest, or right in or over any land (whether situated in the United Kingdom or elsewhere) which would otherwise be taxable under Schedules A and D, to the extent that such profits (1) arise from an estate, interest, or right vested in any person for charitable purposes, and (2) are applied to charitable purposes only; (b) interest, annuities, and dividends (which would otherwise be chargeable under Case III of Schedule D); (c) income from securities or other possessions outside the United Kingdom (which would otherwise be charitable under Case IV or V of Schedule D); and (d) income consisting of dividends or distributions of a company not resident in the United Kingdom (which would otherwise be chargeable under Schedule F). In addition, if a charity carries on a trade (whether in the United Kingdom or elsewhere) profits from such trade will be exempt from income tax, but only if (1) the profits are applied solely for the purposes of the charity; and (2) either the trade is related to the primary purpose of the charity (e.g., fees for services), or the work in connection with the trade is mainly carried out by the beneficiaries of the charity (e.g., the selling of goods produced by handicapped persons). To be eligible for these and other tax exemptions, a charity must be an established institute or endowment.[43] Moreover, for income tax purposes, Section 505 of the Income and Corporation Taxes Act 1988 applies only to bodies and trusts subject to the jurisdiction of the courts of the United Kingdom.[44]
- *Capital gains tax*: Charities are generally exempt from capital gains tax under Section 256 of the Taxation of Chargeable Gains Act 1992, provided that the gains are applied for charitable purposes. However, Section 256 (2) imposes a liability if such assets cease to be held on charitable trust.[45]
- *Inheritance tax*: Many trusts created in favor of charities take the form of discretionary trusts (i.e., trusts in which no interest in possession subsists). In general, those trusts are subject to inheritance tax charges on each tenth anniversary of the creation of the trust and on any occasion on which property leaves the trust or the value of the trust is otherwise reduced (Chapter III of the Inheritance Tax Act 1984). However, property solely held for charitable purposes is exempted from this charge.[46]

[42a] As amended by Section 146 of the Finance Act 1996.

[43] *Commissioners of Special Purposes of Income Tax v. Pemsel* [1981] A.C. 531; *IRC v. Yorkshire Agricultural Society* [1928] 1 K.B. 611. See also *Trading and Charities* (London: Inland Revenue Publications, 1995).

[44] *Camille and Henry Dreyfus Foundation Inc. v. IRC* [1956] A.C.

[45] There are also complex rules governing "qualifying expenditure"; see Picarda on Charities, pp. 716–720.

[46] Section 58(1)(a) of the 1984 Act.

- *Value-added tax.* Value-added tax (which is governed by the Value Added Tax Act 1994) is levied on all goods and services supplied in the United Kingdom in the course of a business (which includes a trade, profession, or vocation). Certain supplies are "zero-rated" and certain supplies are "exempt." Charities are not generally exempt from VAT. However, charities usually supply goods and services free of charge (or at reduced cost) and are therefore "exempt" from VAT (but they are then unable to reclaim "input tax," i.e., tax paid on goods and services supplied to them).

  If a charity supplies goods and services in the course of a business carried on by the charity, and provided the volume of its taxable supplies is sufficiently large, it must register for VAT purposes and VAT is then chargeable at the standard rate (currently 17.5%). (Soliciting donations and gifts or legacies with nothing supplied in return is not a business.) However, the supply of some goods and services (which are specified in Schedule 9 to the VATA 1994) by or to charities is exempt, in which case no VAT is payable or recoverable. These include, for example, goods and supplies connected with education, health and welfare, and burial and cremation. The supply of certain other goods and services (which are specified in Schedule 8 to the VATA 1994) are "zero-rated," in which case no VAT is charged on the supply: the supplier can recover the "input tax" but does not charge any "output tax." These include, for example, the supply, repair, or maintenance of tapes, recorders, players, and ancillary apparatus to the Royal National Institute for the Blind and similar bodies; the supply of drugs, medicines, and aids for the handicapped, and so forth.[47]

- *Other taxes, rates, and charges.* The Uniform Business Rate for businesses and the Council Tax for individuals are the main local taxes. Charities are entitled to a mandatory 80% relief from the Uniform Business Rate, provided the hereditament is wholly or mainly used for charitable purposes, and local authorities have a discretion to increase the relief to 100% for charities within their own jurisdiction. The net profits of charity shops are also relieved if applied wholly or mainly to charitable purposes. The Council Tax is a local tax on individuals, but one assessed by reference to the capital value of residential dwellings, assuming that each dwelling is occupied by two eligible adults. A personal element remains, since a discount of 25% will operate in cases where there is only one eligible adult resident. Certain classes of persons are disregarded for the purposes of liability for the personal element of the Council tax. The main groups with relevance for charities are the severely mentally impaired, persons in respect of whom child benefit is claimed, hospital patients and patients in homes, care workers, residents of hostels or similar accommodations for the homeless and itinerant, and members of religious communities.[47a] Exemptions from other taxes include stamp duty and pool betting duty in respect of some types of lotteries. Charities, however, are not exempt from National Insurance Contributions.

---

[47] See Picarda on Charities, pp. 722–739.
[47a] Local Government Finance Act 1992, Section 11 and Schedule 1.

(ii) Noncharitable Organizations.   Noncharitable organizations do not generally enjoy exemptions or privileges under the fiscal legislation. Any body corporate and any unincorporated association is subject to corporation tax on their income and capital gains tax on chargeable capital gains. Despite the fact that an unincorporated association does not posses a separate legal identity, it is the association which is liable to tax, and not its individual members.[48] However, associations are not liable to tax on their membership income because it does not fall within one of the income tax schedules. Similarly, an association is not liable to tax on any surplus made in the provision of services solely to members because of the principle of mutual trading. For value-added tax purposes, an association will be a taxable person if it makes supplies in the course of its business and is not otherwise excepted. The principle of mutual trading does not apply to VAT and the provision of goods and services to members will therefore be subject to VAT even if there is no sale. Furthermore, there are certain miscellaneous privileges for certain types of noncharitable organizations such as industrial and provident societies, housing associations, and friendly societies, provided they satisfy certain limited and often unusual conditions.[49]

(b) Tax Treatment of Contributions—Domestic Organizations

There is no general relief from tax for individual and corporate taxpayers who make gifts to charity, but there are several specific reliefs which have become more numerous over the years. These include relief from income and corporation taxes for deeds of covenant, single donations, payroll deduction schemes and secondments of employees; as well as relief from inheritance and capital gains taxes.

(i) Income and Corporation Tax.

- *Deeds of Covenant.* Under a deed of covenant, the taxpayer enters into a binding legal obligation to make regularly recurring payments of fixed or variable amounts for a fixed period of time. If the fixed period exceeds three years and provided the payment is "pure income benefit" in the

---

[48] *Carlisle and Silloth Golf Club v. Smith* [1913] 3 K.B. 75; *Worthing Rugby Football Club Trustees v. IRC* [1985] 1 W.L.R. 409.

[49] For instance, a registered industrial and provident society is taxed on all sources of income, including any profit or surplus arising from transactions with its members which would be included in chargeable profits or gains if those transactions were with nonmembers (Section 486 of the Income and Corporation Taxes Act 1988). If, however, a registered society does not sell to nonmembers, or if the number of its shares is not limited by its rules or practice, it may deduct as expenses any discounts, rebates, dividends, or bonuses granted to members or other persons in respect of amounts paid or payable by or to them on account of their transactions with the society. A registered friendly society enjoys limited tax privileges, including stamp duty, which is not chargeable on (a) a letter or power of attorney granted by any person as trustee for the transfer of any money of a registered society or branch invested in his name in the public funds, or (b) a policy of insurance or appointment or revocation of appointment of an agent or other document required or authorized by the Friendly Societies Act 1974 or by the rules of a registered Society or branch (Section 105(a) and (b) of the 1974 Act). A registered friendly society or branch is also entitled to exemption from income and corporation taxes on profits arising from life or endowment business within certain specified limits.

hands of the receiving charity, the donor will actually pay a sum which is net of income tax to the charity, but he or she can set the gross amount of the covenanted payment against his or her income and claim relief against higher rate income tax (if this is relevant). The receiving charity itself can then reclaim from the Inland Revenue the basic rate income tax deducted by the donor. Similar covenants can be entered into by companies, with similar results.[50]

- *Single donations or "gift aid."* Relief from income tax is also available to individuals who make a single donation to charity, provided certain conditions are met. These conditions include the requirements that the amount of the donation must not be less than £250 net of basic rate income tax; the donor must be resident in the United Kingdom for tax purposes; the donation must be one of money, and must not be a covenanted payment; and the donation must not be linked with the acquisition of any property by the charity or the supply of services to the donor.[51] Several gifts in one year, each of which is under £250 but the total of all of which exceeds £250, may still obtain relief if the entire sum is given to an agency charity such as the Charities Aid Foundation for distribution. Gift aid is also available to companies, subject to similar conditions.

- *Payroll deduction scheme.* Under the payroll deduction scheme, an employee may authorize his or her employer to deduct sums, not to exceed £1,200 a year per employee, from his or her gross pay before deduction of income tax and pay these over to a charity agent. The scheme must be approved by the Inland Revenue and the agent must pay over the deducted sums to the charities chosen by the employee.

- *Secondments.* Companies may second employees to help charities with their general organization or management or to establish specific projects. The employees' salaries, National Insurance Contributions, pension contributions, and so forth, continue to be paid by their employers who may deduct those expenditures for tax purposes, provided that the secondment is temporary.[52]

(ii) *Inheritance Tax.* Gifts or "transfers of value" to charity, whether made during the donor's lifetime or on death, are exempt from inheritance tax, provided the gift is absolute.

(iii) *Capital Gains Tax.* If the value of an asset at the date of disposal is higher than its value at the date of its acquisition, the disposal may give rise to a charge to capital gains. If the chargeable asset is disposed of to a charity, however, it is deemed that its value is such that neither a gain nor a loss arises on the

---

[50] For corporation tax purposes, the covenant is a charge on income, and it is a common practice for trading subsidiaries of charities to use such covenants to convert their profits into exempt income. It is also common to find cases in which employees of a charity, such as members of religious orders carrying out teaching or nursing duties, covenant their salaries back to the employer, thus enabling the charity to obtain tax relief which would otherwise not be available on the gift of services.

[51] Section 25 of the Finance Act 1990, Section 67(2) of the Finance Act 1993.

[52] Section 86 of the Income and Corporations Tax Act 1988.

disposal, and thus no capital gains tax is chargeable.[53] This relief applies only to the chargeable asset and not to the proceeds of sale of an asset by the donor.

(c) Tax Treatment of Contributions—Foreign Organizations

Exemption from income tax in the United Kingdom is confined to a body of persons or trust established in the United Kingdom for charitable purposes only.[54] A body of persons or trust established in the United Kingdom enjoys the exemption notwithstanding that its operations and activities take place outside the jurisdiction, provided, of course, that its purposes are exclusively charitable according to the laws of England and Wales. Conversely, a body of persons or trust established outside the United Kingdom is excluded from the scope of exemption, even if its purposes would otherwise qualify as exclusively charitable under the laws of England and Wales and even if some of its operations and activities take place within the jurisdiction. Thus, royalties arising in the United Kingdom, but received by a corporation incorporated under the laws of the State of New York, for a purpose which would be recognized in England as being exclusively charitable, would not be exempt from income tax in the United Kingdom.[55]

Although there seem to be no specific legal provisions with respect to other taxes, it is generally assumed, in practice, that, because the expression "trust established for charitable purposes only" (or a close equivalent) has been adopted by or incorporated by reference in statutory provisions granting exemption from these other taxes (e.g., capital gains tax, inheritance tax, stamp duty and local authority taxes),[56] the same interpretation would apply (i.e., foreign bodies or trusts would not enjoy exemption from any of the other taxes either).

§ 24.5   PERSONAL BENEFIT RESTRICTIONS

It is a general principle of English law that trustees and other persons in a fiduciary position are not allowed to put themselves in a position where their own interests and their duties conflict. Thus, in the absence of an express provision to the contrary, trustees and fiduciaries are generally not entitled to make a profit out of their position. This basic principle applies to charity trustees as well as to private trustees. However, whereas a private trustee owes a duty of loyalty to his or her beneficiaries, a charity trustee owes his or her duty of loyalty to the public. One aspect of this duty of loyalty is that a trustee (or other fiduciary) must act gratuitously. Although there are statutory and anomalous equitable exceptions to this basic principle, the main exception is generally provided in the form of express authorization (e.g., in the form of a charging clause) in the instrument which creates the trust (or other document which creates the relevant fiduciary relationship). In principle, this exception would seem to apply equally to both

---

[53] Section 146 of the Capital Gains Tax Act, 1979.
[54] Income and Corporation Taxes Act 1988, Section 505.
[55] *Camille and Henry Dreyfus Foundation Inc. v. IRC* [1954] Ch. 672.
[56] See, for example, Taxation of Chargeable Gains Act 1992, Section 256(1); Inheritance Tax Act 1984, Section 272; Finance Act 1982, Section 128; and Local Government Finance Act 1988, Section 47(2).

private and charitable trusts. However, in practice, the Charity Commissioners have adopted a policy not to register trusts which provide for the remuneration of trustees, except in special circumstances.

Similarly, trustees (of private or charitable trusts) are under a duty not to profit from their trust. Thus, the purchase by a trustee of trust property ("self-dealing") is prohibited; the trustee must not sell or lend his or her own assets to the trust; and he or she must not exercise powers vested in him or her as trustee in order to benefit himself or herself (e.g., by exercising voting powers attached to trust shares to appoint himself or herself a director of a company, from which he or she then receives director's fees). If he or she is in breach of this duty, the trustee will be obliged to account as constructive trustee for the profits he or she has received.

(a) Charities

The Finance Act 1986, and subsequently the Income and Corporation Taxes Act 1988 in its Sections 505 and 506, enacted complex rules dealing with the problem of nonqualifying expenditure and the restriction of tax exemptions for charities. In short, if an extravagant or excessive amount of a charity's income is expended on administration, or on its officers, or on political campaigns, the charity will lose its income and corporation tax exemptions. Furthermore, relief will also not be granted, for example, if a charity applies all (or a substantial part) of its income toward a purpose which is not exclusively charitable, such as the education of children of employees of a particular firm.[57]

(b) Noncharitable Organizations

Housing associations registered with the Corporation are subject to personal benefit restrictions under the 1985 Act. In particular, no gift may be made, and no sum be paid by way of bonus or dividend, to a person who is or has been a member of the association or a member of such person's family, or a company of which he or she is a director. Furthermore, no payment or grant may be made to committee members.[58]

Trustees and officers of unincorporated societies and associations, including friendly societies, generally owe the same fiduciary duties of loyalty to their beneficiaries and cannot, therefore, profit from their position or exercise their powers for their own benefit (subject to the same exceptions). However, it seems clear that the trustees of such societies are not subject to all the rules of conduct which apply to ordinary trustees under the general law. For example, the members, for whose benefit the property is held by the trustees, control and manage the property (either in general meeting or through their officers). The trustees do not have the powers of investment exercisable by trustees under the general law. The statutory functions of trustees of such societies are mainly ministerial. They are removable by the members at any time. Moreover, the trustees are not generally liable to make good deficiencies in the funds of the society, and each trustee is liable only for sums actually received by him or her on account of the society. Thus,

---

[57] *IRC v. Educational Grants Association Ltd.* [1967] Ch. 123; *Campbell v. IRC* [1965] 45 T.C. 427.
[58] Sections 13–15 of the 1985 Act.

although some of the basic principles of trust law apply to such trustees, they appear nonetheless to occupy a somewhat anomalous position, one in which their duties and powers are circumscribed by the overriding circumstance that they are largely under the control and direction of their society's membership.

§ 24.6   OBLIGATIONS TO THE PUBLIC

(a) Charities

The duties of charity trustees are generally the same as those of ordinary trustees,[58a] subject to the obvious differences that, whereas private trustees owe their duties to specific beneficiaries, charity trustees owe their duties to the public (or that section of the public encompassed by the charity's purposes) and that statute has imposed a wide range of additional obligations on charity trustees.

The general duties of charity trustees include the following: a duty on appointment to acquaint themselves with the terms of their trust; a duty to observe and carry out those trusts; a duty to protect trust property; a duty to apply for a *cy pres* scheme where the circumstances require the trust property to be applied for a different and more effective purpose; a duty of loyalty (see above); a duty to register the charity (unless exempted or excepted from registration); a duty to provide information to the Charity Commissioners.

In addition, charity trustees must observe and carry out all the other duties imposed on them by the Charities Act 1993. The register of charities, which is maintained by the Charity Commissioners and which is now fully computerized, is open to public inspection (at no charge). Members of the public are entitled to request and can get essential information on the purposes of any registered charity, how to get in touch with it, whether it makes grants or provides services or is a fund raiser, and also details of the annual income of the charity, its submitted accounts, and so forth. Other kinds of information may also be available (e.g., printed reports of groups of charities). Charity trustees must therefore fulfill various obligations to supply the Commissioners with such information as is required in order to keep members of the public fully informed concerning the above matters.

Charity trustees must ensure that accounting records are kept. Such records (save where the charity is a company) must satisfy the requirements of the Charities Act 1993 and must be sufficient to show and explain all the charity's transactions, the financial position of the charity, and the charity's compliance with regulations on accounting requirements. In particular, the accounting records must contain entries showing from day to day all sums of money received and expended by the charity and a record of the assets and liabilities of the charity.[58b] Charity trustees must also prepare in respect of each financial year (unless the

---

[58a] The Deakin Report recently recommended that charity trustees' duties be clarified and codified in a new Charity Trust Act. See "Meeting the Challenge of Change: Voluntary Action into the 21st Century." *The Report of the Commission on the Future of the Voluntary Sector* (NCVO: London, 1996), Vol. 1, p. 124 and paras. 3.5.6–3.5.10.

[58b] See *Accounting by Charities: Statement of Recommended Practice* (London: Charity Commission, 1995) and SI 1995 No. 2724.

charity is a company) a statement of accounts complying with the form and contents of accounts prescribed by regulations. If the charity's gross income in any financial year does not exceed £25,000, the charity trustees may elect to prepare a receipts and payments account and a statement of assets and liabilities instead. The records must be preserved for at least six years. Charitable companies are obliged to keep accounting records under Section 221 of the Companies Act 1985.

Charities whose gross income or total expenditure exceeds £100,000 must have their accounts audited by a qualified auditor. Those whose income or gross expenditure is below that sum may elect to have their accounts examined by an independent examiner instead of being audited. However, the Charity Commissioners have the power to order an audit of accounts.

Charity trustees must prepare in respect of each financial year an annual report containing a report by the trustees on the activities of the charity during that year and such other information relating to the charity or to its trustees or officers as may be prescribed by regulations made by the Home Secretary. The report, which must be transmitted to the Commissioners within ten months of the end of the year to which it relates, is open to public inspection at all reasonable times, and must also be supplied (for a small fee) to any person who makes written request for a copy of it.[59]

(b) Noncharitable Organizations

Societies which are registered under the Friendly Societies Acts may be subject, as we have seen, to different statutory regimes. Registered societies which are friendly societies are regulated partly by the Friendly Societies Act 1974 and partly by the Friendly Societies Act 1992. Existing friendly societies may (and each new friendly society must) be registered and incorporated under the 1992 Act. Registered societies other than friendly societies are regulated solely by the 1974 Act. The precise requirements imposed on a registered society therefore vary according to the type of society and the statutory provisions and regulations to which it is subject. For example, the rules of a registered society must contain certain provisions, such as the name of the society, the address of its registered office, its mode of holding meetings, the manner in which it appoints and removes officers, and so forth. Under the 1974 Act, registered societies other than friendly societies (e.g., working men's clubs, old people's homes societies, cattle insurance societies) are required to keep books of account relating to their transactions, assets, and liabilities as are necessary to give a true and fair view of the state of their affairs. They must also appoint, in each year of account, one or more qualified auditors to audit their accounts and balance sheet for that year. They must also send to the Registrar once a year a return relating to their affairs. Similarly, under the 1992 Act, every friendly society must cause accounting records to be kept and must establish and maintain systems of control of its business and records and of inspection and report. Each year, the Committee of Management of a friendly society must send to the Friendly Societies Commission a statement of its opinion as to whether these requirements have been complied with. The accounting records of a friendly society must be kept in an orderly manner and must be sufficient to show and explain the transactions of the society and must disclose, in particular, the financial position of the

---

[59] Section 26 of the Charities Act 1993.

society at any time with reasonable accuracy and promptness and enable the Committee of Management to discharge its statutory duties and functions. The Committee of Management must also prepare an annual balance sheet. Annual accounts must conform to statutory requirements and regulations made by the Treasury and the Friendly Societies Commission. Every friendly society must also appoint an auditor at each annual general meeting.

Similar requirements are laid down in respect of registered industrial and provident societies.[60]

§ 24.7   BUSINESS ACTIVITY

As mentioned above, profits deriving from a trade a charity is carrying on are tax exempt if solely applied to the charity's purposes and if either resulting from activities related to the carrying out of a primary purpose or resulting from work carried out by the charities' beneficiaries. The latter of the two alternative requirements was apparently intended to cover economic activities such as "the basket factory of a blind asylum, the blind inmates being the beneficiaries by whose work the trade of manufacturing baskets for sale mainly is carried on." In fact, however, it has been extended by the courts to an association which organized a competitive musical festival with the competitors being regarded as the beneficiaries, and also to a school run by nuns with the nuns themselves being the beneficiaries.[61] However, profits made by a charity from common activities, such as sales of Christmas cards or of gifts, are taxable and not exempt, although profits from bazaars, jumble sales, gymkhanas, carnivals, fireworks displays and similar activities run by voluntary organizations are, by concession, not generally liable to tax.[62] It is furthermore common for charities to set up companies whose shares are owned by the relevant charity to carry on trading activities, and for the company then to covenant to make payments to the charity equal to its profits. Such payments are charges on the company's income and are therefore deductible by the company. By this means, trading income can effectively be completely exempt from income tax.

§ 24.8   OTHER FUNDING RESTRICTIONS

Legislation governing fund raising is to be found in Parts II and III of the Charities Act 1992 and in the Lotteries and Amusements Act 1976 (as amended by the

---

[60] Mainly under the Friendly and Industrial and Provident Societies Act 1968.

Thus, for example, every registered society must cause to be kept such proper books of account with respect to its transactions, assets, and liabilities as are necessary to give a true and fair view of the state of its affairs and explain its transactions. It must establish and maintain satisfactory systems of control of its books of account, cash holdings, and all receipts and remittances. Each year, each such society must prepare a revenue account; it must also appoint a qualified auditor to audit its accounts and balance sheet for that year. Again, the precise requirements are set out in detailed regulations.

[61] *IRC v. Glasgow Musical Festival Association* [1926] 11 T.C. 154; *Brighton Convent of the Blessed Sacrament v. IRC* [1933] 18 T.C. 76.

[62] Extra-Statutory Concession C4 (1988). See also (1989) 4 Trust Law & P. 98 (Hill and De Souza); S. Lloyd *Charities, Trading and the Law* (London: Charities Advisory Trust, 1995).

National Lottery Act 1993).[63] In broad terms, Part II of the 1992 Act provides a new code for the control of fund raising for a "charitable institution" by imposing restrictions on "professional fund-raisers"and "commercial participators." It is unlawful for a professional fund-raiser to solicit money or other property for the benefit of a charitable institution (defined as any institution established for charitable purposes), or for a commercial participator to represent that charitable contributions are to be given or applied for the benefit of a charitable institution, unless, in either case, he or she does so in accordance with an agreement with the institution satisfying the prescribed requirements.[64]

A professional fund raiser or commercial participator who fails to comply with the provisions of the 1992 Act and the 1994 Regulations will be guilty of an offense punishable on summary conviction by fine (at present not exceeding £5, 000).

Part III of the 1992 Act makes provision for "public charitable collections" and replaces (from a day which has yet to be determined) the provisions of the House to House Collections Act 1939, the War Charities Act 1940 and the Police, Factories, etc. (Miscellaneous Provisions) Act 1916, which, between them, dealt with street collections. In broad terms, it is an offense to conduct "a public charitable collection" in the area of any local authority without a permit issued by the local authority or an order made by the Charity Commissioners (made, e.g., where a charity proposes to promote a collection throughout England and Wales). A "public charitable collection" is defined as a "charitable appeal" which is made in any public place or by means of visits from house to house; and a "charitable appeal" means an appeal to members of the public to give money or other property (whether for consideration or otherwise) which is made in association with a representation that the whole or any part of its proceeds is to be applied for charitable, benevolent, or philanthropic purposes.[65] Anyone intending to promote a public charitable collection must therefore apply for a permit from the relevant local authority for the area in which the collection is to be made (and, if the collection is to be made in a number of different local authorities, to each one, unless the Charity Commissioners make an order rendering that unnecessary). The application must be made in accordance with regulations (yet to be made) and must include a number of specified matters, such as the period (not exceeding twelve months) for which the permit is desired to have effect. Any such permit may have attached to it such conditions as the local authority thinks fit. It is an offense (punishable by a fine) to conduct a public charitable collection without a permit or, upon an application for a permit, knowingly or recklessly to furnish any information which is false in a material particular.

Finally, the Lotteries and Amusements Act 1976[66] makes provision for raising of funds by means of lotteries and prize competitions. All lotteries in the United Kingdom which do not constitute gaming are unlawful. (A "lottery" is

---

[63] See Picarda on Charities, Ch. 45.

[64] The detailed requirements of the relevant agreement are set out in the Charitable Institutions (Fund-Raising) Regulations 1994: SI 1994 No. 3024.

[65] There are certain exceptions to these rules, such as appeals made in the course of a public meeting and appeals to members of the public to give money by placing it in an unattended receptacle.

[66] As amended by the National Lottery Act 1993.

not defined in any statute, but case law establishes that it must have three essential attributes, namely a contribution, a prize, and an element of chance.) In broad terms, a society which is established and conducted wholly or mainly (i.e., not necessarily exclusively) for charitable purposes may conduct a "society's lottery" promoted on its behalf, provided certain conditions are satisfied. The main conditions are that the lottery must be promoted in Great Britain; the society promoting it must be registered under the 1976 Act; the lottery must be conducted under a scheme approved by the society; and the lottery must be registered either with the Gaming Board or with the local authority, according to certain criteria which are laid down by these registration authorities.

§ 24.9   POLITICAL ACTIVITY

Organizations with political objectives cannot qualify for charitable status. Even if they would otherwise fall within the Preamble to the 1601 Statute, trusts and other bodies of which a direct and principal purpose is (1) to further the interests of a particular political party, or (2) to procure changes in the laws of the United Kingdom or of a foreign country, or (3) to procure a reversal of government policy or of a particular decision of governmental authorities in the United Kingdom or in a foreign country, can not be regarded as being for the benefit of the public in the manner which the law regards as charitable.[67] However, if the main objects of an organization are exclusively charitable, the mere fact that it may employ political means in their furtherance will not necessarily deprive it of charitable status. Nevertheless, the dividing line between what is objectionable and what is not is often blurred.

According to the Charity Commission in its recent guidelines,[68] charities may properly campaign to inform and mobilize public opinion and influence government policy and decisions of public bodies, provided the issues concerned are relevant to their purposes and that the means by which they do so are within their powers and consistent with the guidelines. Thus, for example, a charity must ensure that the information provided to the public in support of the campaign as a whole is accurate and sufficiently full to support its position. It must also ensure that the independence of its views is explained and understood. On the other hand, a charity must not seek to organize public opinion to support or oppose a political party which advocates a particular policy favored or opposed by the charity.

A charity may seek to influence government or public opinion through well-founded, reasoned argument based on research or direct experience on issues either relating directly to the achievement of the charity's own stated purposes or relevant to the well-being of the charitable sector. It may provide information to its supporters or the public on how individual Members of Parliament or parties have voted on an issue, provided they do so in a way which will enable its supporters or the public to seek to persuade those Members or parties to change their position through well-founded, reasoned argument rather than merely through

---

[67] *McGovern v. A.G.* [1982] Ch. 321.
[68] "Political Activities and Campaigning by Charities": CC Leaflet of July 9, 1995.

public pressure. A charity may organize and present a petition to either House of Parliament or to national or local government, provided that the material amounts to well-founded, reasoned argument. A charity may provide and publish comments on possible or proposed changes in the law or government policy and, in response to a Parliamentary Bill, may supply to Members of either House for use in debate such relevant information and reasoned arguments as can reasonably be expected to assist the achievement of its charitable purposes. A charity may also advocate (or oppose) a change in the law or public policy, or the passage of a Bill, which can reasonably be expected to help it to achieve its charitable purpose (or to hinder its ability to do so). It may comment publicly on social, economic, and political issues if these relate to its purpose or the way in which the charity is able to carry out its work.

On the other hand, a charity must not base any attempt to influence public opinion, or to put pressure on the government to adopt a particular policy, on data which it knows (or ought to know) is inaccurate or on a distorted selection of data in support of a preconceived position. A charity must not participate in party political demonstrations. It must not claim evidence of public support for its position on a political issue without adequate justification. A charity whose stated purposes include the advancement of education must not overstep the boundary between education and propaganda in promoting that purpose. It must not provide supporters or members of the public with material specifically designed to underpin a party political campaign or for or against a government or particular MPs; it must not issue material which supports or opposes a particular political party or the government; and it must not seek to persuade members of the public to vote for or against a candidate or for or against a political party. A charity must also not distort research, or the results of research, to support a preconceived position or objective.

The pursuit of improper political activities by charities is a misuse of charity funds and can lead to the loss of tax relief on funds applied for that purpose. Trustees who stray too far into the field of political activity risk being in breach of trust and can be held personally liable to repay to the charity the funds spent on such activity. In certain cases, the intervention of the Charity Commissioners may be warranted. Their action will depend upon all the circumstances of the case, but may extend from advising or removing the trustees to the deregistration of the charity.

§ 24.10 KEY OUTSTANDING ISSUES

The key outstanding issues concerning nonprofit organizations in the United Kingdom relate to the legal definition of charity, the reform of tax privileges, and the political activities of charities.

(a) The Question of Definition

A perennial issue in U. K. nonprofit law concerns the desirability of establishing a statutory definition of "charity." Because the definition of charity has developed in piecemeal fashion in the United Kingdom through the slow accretion of case law, a large number of organizations exist which are considered by many to be of considerable benefit to the public, but which are currently denied charitable status; while a substantial number of acknowledged charities are considered not to confer any substantial, or even identifiable, benefit to the public.

To remedy these anomalies, many observers have called for the development of a clear statutory definition of "charity." Thus, as far back as 1952, the Nathan Committee[69] recommended that a new statutory definition of charity should be enacted. A 1975 House of Commons Expenditure Committee echoed this recommendation, urging legislation whereby all charities should be required to satisfy the test of purposes beneficial to the community. However, in acknowledgment of the fact that such a change would not affect the great majority of charities, no real attempt was made to formulate a precise or workable definition of what kind of purpose was, or should be, beneficial to the community.[70] More generally, such suggestions run up against judicial concern about the possibility of "fresh litigation" and "undesirable artificial distinctions."[71] Thus, in 1976, the Goodman Committee rejected the idea that it was possible to formulate a definition of charity, and recommended instead that an updated version of the preamble to the 1601 Statute be produced, a reformulation of the categories of charities in simpler and more modern terms,[72] which would preserve the flexibility of the law and the mass of case law decided over past centuries. In 1989, the Government decided not to promote a legislative definition of the scope of charity,[73] and the Charities Act 1992 simply builds on existing law and does not address the issue at all. More recently, the Deakin Report[73a] proposed that the legal concept of charity be retained, but that the fourfold *Pemsel* classification be replaced with an all-embracing statutory definition based on "benefit to the community." It seems, unlikely, however that such a recommendation will be acted upon in the near future. Nevertheless, the anomalous character of current usage almost guarantees that this issue will continue to be raised.

(b) The Reform of Tax Privileges

The current treatment of charities and other voluntary organizations under tax legislation is under criticism from two directions. The first, and lesser, criticism is that the relevant tax exemptions and privileges could be extended and improved to include VAT exemption or even general exemption from all taxes.[73b] In the same context, the relevant statutory provisions could be simplified or consolidated instead of being scattered throughout various Acts and expressed in obscure language.

---

[69] *Report of the Law and Practice Relating to Charitable Trusts* (1952: Cmnd 8710), paras. 120–140.
[70] *Charity Commissioners and their Accountability* (1974–75), vol. 1, paras. 31–32, 34.
[71] *Incorporated Council of Law Reporting for England and Wales v. A.G.* [1972] Ch. 73, at p. 94.
[72] *Report on Charity Law and Voluntary Organisations* (1976), paras. 16–17, 22, 26, 29, 32, and Appendix 1.
[73] White Paper, *Charities: A Framework for the Future* (1989: Cmnd 694, London: HMSO), paras. 2.7–2.17.
[73a] "Meeting the Challenge of Change: Voluntary Action into the 21st Century." *The Report of the Commission on the Future of the Voluntary Sector* (NCVO): London, 1996), para. 3.2.6. cf. Barry Knight, *Voluntary Action in the 1990s* (London: CENTRIS Report, 1993).
[73b] See the Deakin Report, p. 124.

The second, and more important, criticism is that conferring charitable status in itself brings with it an almost automatic enjoyment of tax exemptions and privileges that in fact not all organizations recognized as charities deserve. The cases in point are, for instance, private schools and hospitals which provide services by charging fees (i.e., by way of commercial transaction), while other organizations which are "worthwhile" and beneficial to the public may not enjoy these tax privileges. This raises the question whether the former institutions should be accorded charitable status at all.[74] Accordingly, it has been argued that the law of charity may be too indulgent toward organizations which operate essentially as quasicommercial concerns, and reform might be sought in the form of confining charitable status to those that provide relief of some kind. Nevertheless, in view of the criteria applied to charities generally, it is difficult to see how the general principles could be appropriately reformulated.

An associated issue is whether such bodies should continue to enjoy the tax privileges accorded to charities, independent of whether they would retain their charitable status. To this it may be added that there are several noncharitable bodies whose purposes and activities are sufficiently beneficial to the public that they too should have the same tax privileges as charities. However, all these issues—the significance of tax privileges in determining whether charitable status ought to be granted, the denial of tax privileges to certain charities, or their extension to certain noncharitable organizations—really raise the same fundamental question: What kind of purpose is it that merits special status in law? This question is ultimately a political question to be resolved by the legislature, and not one for the courts or lawyers to determine.

(c) Political Activity

As mentioned above, charities may employ limited political means for the furtherance of their exclusively charitable purposes. However, the dividing line between what is objectionable and what is not is often blurred. The Charity Commissioners have clarified their view in their *Annual Report* for 1981 and in guidelines issued in 1986. They have recently been revised and amplified.[75] Trustees who stray too far into the field of political activity risk being in breach of trust; risk being held personally liable to repay to the charity the funds spent on such activities; and risk losing tax relief for their charity. Political activity by the trustees would not necessarily affect the charitable status of the institution or be a reason for removing it from the register, but if the trustees would claim that the expressed purposes of the institution were wide enough to cover political activities, doubt would arise whether those purposes were exclusively charitable and upon the correctness of the institution's registration. The Commissioners also provided detailed guidelines for the assistance of charity trustees in these matters. Useful though these guidelines are, it will nevertheless be difficult for some charities to steer a course between what is permissible and what is not. A way for organizations with political as well as acceptable charitable purposes to avoid the law's restriction is to divide themselves into two or more legal structures, one with a charitable purpose, such as the advancement of education, and the oth-

---

[74] Chesterman, *Charities, Trusts and Social Welfare* (London: Butterworths, 1979), pp. 336–339.
[75] "Political Activities and Campaigning by Charities": CC Leaflet of September 7, 1995.

er(s) with overtly political purposes. However, there are practical disadvantages of such a course, for the separate bodies must keep separate accounts, separate payrolls, records, and so forth.

There is little doubt that many people, and not just those directly concerned with the charities themselves, consider the restrictions on the "political" activities of certain charities to be too tightly drawn under the present law. Moreover, it is doubtful whether some objects of general public benefit, such as those connected with the control or prevention of pollution, can be pursued effectively without exerting direct pressure on political parties, governments, and public authorities. On the other hand, there may be considerable opposition to the idea that the objects and purposes of political parties are charitable (although gifts to political parties already enjoy a measure of tax relief). These again are essentially issues for public debate and resolution by means of legislation, but they are likely to dominate the law of charities in the immediate future.

CHAPTER TWENTY-FIVE

United States[*]

§ 25.1 LEGAL CONTEXT

The United States is a common law country that nevertheless has a written constitution. In addition, the country has a federal governmental structure that features a national government and 50 state governments with their own elected officials and their own authority to exercise sovereign powers. These circumstances make the legal position of the nonprofit sector far more amorphous and disjointed in the United States than the significant size and scope of this sector might suggest. No single body of law guarantees the existence of this set of institutions or defines its treatment in law as is the case with the private law of civil law countries. The closest one comes to an explicit guarantee of the right to form nonprofit organizations and associations are the rights to free speech and to assemble peaceably to petition the government that are guaranteed in the First Amendment to the U.S. Constitution. In addition, the national constitution prohibits government from interfering with religious practice, thereby granting religious organizations an inherent right to exist.

Beyond this, nonprofit organizations are governed by a wide array of state and national laws relating separately to incorporation and taxation. Generally speaking, the basic legal standing of nonprofit organizations is determined by state laws and the tax treatment of the organizations by federal law. However, states have their own taxing powers and the federal government stipulates as a condition of granting tax exemptions that the entities receiving such exemptions must be "organizations" in the legal meaning of the term.

Behind this somewhat disjointed set of legal provisions, however, lies a deep-seated philosophic belief in the absolute right of Americans to form private associations and assemble private resources to pursue any of a wide variety of peaceful ends. This belief, which reflects a deeply ingrained American aversion to concentrated governmental power, has been firmly enshrined in case law and in a variety of concrete legal provisions granting special tax and other advantages to the organizations through which this right to associate is exercised. Some of these advantages apply equally to for-profit and nonprofit organizations, but others apply especially to the latter. At base, however, the formation of nonprofit organizations is regarded as a right inherently available to citizens rather than a privilege to be bestowed, or withheld, by governmental authorities.

---

* Country Rapporteur: Bruce Hopkins, Esq., a lawyer who specializes in the representation of nonprofit organizations. This chapter is based on a legal field guide for the Johns Hopkins Comparative Nonprofit Sector Project.

§ 25.2   ELIGIBILITY

(a) Types of Organizations

As noted above, the United States has a two-step process for recognizing non-profit organizations. In the first place, organizations acquire their basic legal status at the state government level (including the District of Columbia). In the second place, they acquire their special status as tax-exempt organizations at the federal government level, although states often have exemption requirements as well. The overwhelming trend over the past 50 years has been for organizations to secure formal legal standing, and also to seek formal recognition of their status as tax-exempt entities from the federal tax authorities.

So far as organizational status is concerned, nonprofit organizations can take any of three different forms in the United States: (1) corporations; (2) unincorporated associations; or (3) trusts.

(i) Corporations. Nearly every state has a "nonprofit corporation law." A corporation is formed by filing articles of organization, termed "articles of incorporation" or "certificate of incorporation," which spell out the basic purposes of the organization and indicate who is entitled to act on its behalf. In addition, organizations are required, as a condition of incorporation, to formulate a separate set of rules, usually termed "bylaws," which detail the organizations' internal structure (officers, committees, etc.) and the rules by which they will conduct business.

The principal advantage of incorporation for nonprofit organizations is that it limits the liability of directors and officers for the acts of the organization. In addition, incorporation laws define many of the duties and responsibilities of organizations as well as of their directors and officers. It also helps the organization meet the "organizational test" that the national Internal Revenue Code sets for eligibility for federal tax exemption. As a result, most nonprofit organizations in the United States in contemporary times establish themselves as corporations under state law. This applies to most of the institutionalized portions of the non-profit sector (e.g., schools, colleges, universities, hospitals, museums, libraries, advocacy groups, day care centers, and social service agencies).

Because corporation laws in the United States are developed and implemented at the state government level, the specific details of corporate structure and obligations differ from state to state. State corporation laws govern both nonprofit and for-profit corporations, moreover. The principal difference between the two relates to the allocation, or *inurement,* of any profits derived from the operation of the organization. The for-profit corporation is operated for the benefit of its owners; any profits earned are privately inured (i.e., they are passed though to those who hold an ownership share in the corporation). Unlike the for-profit corporation, a nonprofit corporation is not generally permitted to distribute net earnings to those who control and/or financially support the organization. Rather, any such net earnings must be plowed back into the purposes pursued by the organization.

(ii) Unincorporated Associations. Although most nonprofit organizations in recent times incorporate themselves under state law, this is not required in order to function as a nonprofit organization in the United States. Rather, a group

of people can simply adopt a "constitution" and bylaws, and function as an organization without seeking formal incorporation. So long as a set of bylaws exists, such entities can satisfy the "organizational test" required to qualify for tax-exempt status under federal and state tax laws. Indeed, many academic and professional societies, as well as some clubs, continue to operate in this unincorporated status. As such, they are not bound by state laws relating to the duties and obligations of corporations. However, they are also denied the limitation on the personal liability of officers and directors that incorporated status confers.

(iii) Trusts. Nonprofit organizations can also be trusts. A trust is essentially a body of assets dedicated to a particular purpose. Trusts are established by declarations of trust or trust agreements that place the assets in the care of a trustee. A trust is a common form of nonprofit organization where an entity is created out of the estate of a decedent, where the assets in the estate are to be used for essentially charitable purposes, and where the resulting entity has a single purpose (e.g., financing scholarships). Many foundations are established as trusts, as are most employee benefit funds and all political action committees. However, the trust form does not provide the shield against personal liability that the corporate form does.

(b) Types of Purposes

Formally, organizations achieve nonprofit status in the United States by complying with the law of the state in which they are organized. This is not a difficult task. Any organization whose articles of incorporation identify a purpose other than that of distributing profits to owners or directors can normally qualify for nonprofit status under state law.

In practice, however, the real test of nonprofit status is the ability to pass muster in terms of the federal tax laws, which define a set of organizational purposes that qualify an organization for exemption from federal income taxes. Since these taxes are generally higher than state taxes, federal tax exemption becomes particularly valuable for an organization and thus the effectively operating defining feature of nonprofit status, especially since many states defer to the federal law in their own tax treatment of these organizations. Tax-exempt organizations are thus a subclass of all nonprofit organizations, though in practice the two commonly collapse into one category. This is so because the requirements for federal tax exemption are rather broad. The federal tax code stipulates more than 25 different classes of tax-exempt organizations. These can in turn be grouped under six broad headings.

Perhaps the broadest, and most well known, of the purposes that qualify an organization for exemption from federal income taxation in the United States are *charitable purposes* broadly conceived. Included here are a broad set of purposes generally regarded as "charitable" under the English common law, some of which are enumerated in the relevant section of the U.S. Internal Revenue Code (Section 501(c)(3)) and others of which are included by implication from the common law tradition. The enumerated purposes include religious, scientific, literary, and educational purposes, testing for public safety, prevention of cruelty to animals, and fostering national or international amateur sports. The implied purposes embrace a wide variety of activities considered to be principally of public benefit. Organizations eligible for tax exemption under this "charitable" set of purposes thus include universities, schools, hospitals, orchestras, art galleries, environmental groups, civic associations, day care centers, social service agencies, community development organizations, and nursing homes. As will be noted below, organizations exempted from taxation under this section of the Internal Revenue Code (IRC) not only enjoy tax exemptions themselves, but also are eligible to receive tax deductible gifts from individuals, corporations, and foundations.

Within the broad class of charitable organizations are two subgroups: (a) public charities; and (b) private foundations. U.S. law does not define what a private foundation is; it defines what it is not. Generically, however, a private foundation essentially is a charitable organization that is funded from one source (usually, an individual, family, or corporation), that receives its ongoing funding from investment income (rather than a consistent flow of charitable contributions), and that makes grants for charitable purposes to other persons rather than conduct its own programs. Organizations that are classified as private foundations, however, are subject to a battery of special rules and requirements intended to avoid misuses of the tax-exempt status for the personal benefit of directors or other "disqualified persons." Since there is no advantage to being a private foundation, charitable and like organizations usually strive to be classified as other than private foundations (i.e., as public entities, or charities that receive their support from the public at large, or from government, but not from a single source).[1]

A second type of tax-exempt organization under federal tax law are *general membership organizations*, such as business leagues, chambers of commerce, and boards of trade,[2] labor unions and agricultural groups,[3] local associations of employees,[4] social clubs,[5] and homeowners' associations.[6]

A third type of purpose that qualifies an organization for tax exemption is *fraternal*. Thus fraternal beneficiary associations, fraternities, and sororities, and veterans associations are all included as tax-exempt organizations.

Organizations created for *employee benefits* constitute a fourth type of tax-exempt organization. Included here are group legal service organizations, teachers' retirement funds, black lung benefit trusts, and the like.

Organizations serving a *mutual or cooperative* purpose constitute a fifth class of tax-exempt organizations. These include mutual insurance companies,[7] cemetery companies,[8] credit unions,[9] and farmers' cooperatives.[10]

---

[1] There are some organizations that are not "standard" private foundations and thus are treated differently under the federal tax law. A private foundation that conducts its own programs is a *private operating foundation*; it is treated in certain ways as a public charity. Private foundations that are exempt from the investment income tax and that can receive grants that do not require expenditure responsibility are *exempt operating foundations*. Foundations that are supportive of governmental colleges and universities are regarded as public charities, as are community foundations. A *conduit* private foundation is one that makes qualifying distributions, which are treated as distributions out of its assets, in an amount equal to 100% of all contributions received in the year involved.

[2] IRC § 501(c)(6).

[3] IRC § 501(c)(5).

[4] IRC § 501(c)(4).

[5] IRC § 501(c)(7).

[6] IRC § 528.

[7] IRC § 501(c)(15).

[8] IRC § 501(c)(13).

Finally, there are a variety of miscellaneous purposes that also qualify as tax-exempt purposes in the United States. Included here are certain instrumentalities of the United States, title holding companies, and political organizations.[11]

(c) Other Requirements

In addition to meeting the general requirements of state law for classification as nonprofit organizations and meeting the purpose criteria spelled out in federal laws on tax exemption, nonprofit organizations have few other requirements. State laws typically stipulate the minimum number of directors for an incorporated organization, though this can be as few as one. To meet the federal tax exemption requirements, an entity must be a separate, identifiable organization rather than a formless aggregation of individuals. In practice, this means that the entity must have an organizing instrument (e.g., a constitution or articles of incorporation), governing rules, a bank account, and regularly chosen officers.

(d) Registration Procedures

Separate procedures exist for the two steps in the process of establishing a nonprofit organization enjoying exemption from federal income taxation.

(i) Organizational Status. First, the organization must come into existence as a separate entity. This can be done either by creating a constitution (in the case of an unincorporated organization) or by seeking incorporation under state laws. The latter route involves filing incorporation papers with the Secretary of State of the state in which the organization proposes to conduct business. These papers normally include articles of incorporation specifying the purposes of the organization, its principal place of business, and the persons authorized to act on its behalf; and bylaws that spell out the organization's structure and operating rules. So long as these meet the minimum requirements set in the state's incorporation law, approval is largely pro-forma.

(ii) Tax-Exempt Status. An organization is not exempt from federal income taxation simply because it is organized as a nonprofit organization. Rather, it must meet the requirements of the particular statutory provision of the federal tax code under which it claims the exemption. In the case of "charitable" and "employee benefit" organizations, this requires an explicit recognition of tax exemption from the federal Internal Revenue Service (IRS) in response to an application. No such formal certification is required in the case of other types of organizations, but it is recommended anyway. Organizations seeking such official recognition are required to file an application with the IRS district office in the district that houses the organization's principal place of business. Particular types of applications are required for the different types of tax-exempt entities. These forms normally require a statement of activities, a copy of the organization's forming documents and bylaws, and current financial statements. In the case of charitable organiza-

[9] IRC § 501(c)(14).
[10] IRC § 521.
[11] IRC § 527.

tions, information is also requested on the sources of the organization's financial support, its fund-raising program, its governing board, the nature of its services or products, and like matters. On the basis of this information, the IRS then decides whether to issue a determination letter or certification of tax-exempt status. In cases of adverse determinations, organizations can appeal the IRS decision to an appeals office within the IRS, and ultimately to the courts.

§ 25.3   INTERNAL GOVERNANCE

(i) Board of Directors.   Nearly every nonprofit organization in the United States is governed by a board of directors (sometimes termed a board of trustees). The number and composition of these boards is largely a matter of state law. The features of a board of directors are therefore reflected in the articles of organizations and the bylaws of the particular organization.

There is almost no limit to the ways in which the composition of a board is constructed; the basic requirement of law is that whatever formula is used be reflected in the organizational documents. Some boards are elected, in whole or in part, by members of the organization. Some are self-perpetuating boards: boards that periodically reelect their membership or their successors. Some boards have *ex officio* memberships, where their members are in the board positions because of a relationship with another organization. On occasion, the board of a nonprofit organization is elected, in whole or in part, by the board of another organization.

Similarly, organizations have considerable leeway in establishing board committees and in choosing officers. Whatever the arrangement, it should be spelled out in the organizational documents. These and other organizational features are rarely featured in the document by which the organization was created (such as articles of incorporation). It is in the bylaws that these elements are provided for, usually in some detail. Often, state law will dictate internal governance rules that apply only where the articles and bylaws are silent.

(ii) Discrimination in the Selection of Clients.   For the most part, there is no specific law forbidding nonprofit organizations from discriminating on some basis in the selection of members, clients, or other constituents. However, there are federal and state civil rights laws that, under varying circumstances, forbid discrimination on bases such as race, gender, age, religion, handicap, ethnicity, or sexual preference. These laws are generally applicable to nonprofit organizations.

§ 25.4   TAX TREATMENT

Generally, in the United States, every person (individual, corporation, etc.) is subject to income taxation at the federal level and often at the state and local level as well. State and local taxation also may entail sales, use, tangible personal property, intangible personal property, and/or real property taxes. Both federal and state laws provide tax exemption for various types of nonprofit organizations.

(a) Tax Treatment of Organizations

(i) *Federal Law.* The federal law in the United States provides income tax exemption for many types of organizations.[12] These organizations are, in order of their listing in the Internal Revenue Code:

1. Instrumentalities of the United States[13]
2. Title-holding corporations[14]
3. Charitable (including religious, educational, and scientific) organizations[15]
4. Social welfare organizations (sometimes termed civic leagues)[16]
5. Local associations of employees[17]
6. Labor organizations[18]
7. Agricultural organizations[19]
8. Horticultural organizations[20]
9. Business leagues[21]
10. Chambers of commerce[22]
11. Real estate boards[23]
12. Boards of trade[24]
13. Professional football leagues[25]
14. Social clubs[26]
15. Fraternal beneficiary societies[27]
16. Voluntary employees' beneficiary associations[28]
17. Domestic fraternal societies[29]
18. Teachers' retirement fund associations[30]
19. Benevolent life insurance associations[31]
20. Mutual ditch or irrigation companies[32]

---

[12] Generally, IRC § 501(a).
[13] IRC § 501(c)(1).
[14] IRC §§ 501(c)(2) and 501(c)(25).
[15] IRC § 501(c)(3).
[16] IRC § 501(c)(4).
[17] IRC § 501(c)(4).
[18] IRC § 501(c)(5).
[19] IRC § 501(c)(5).
[20] IRC § 501(c)(5).
[21] IRC § 501(c)(6).
[22] IRC § 501(c)(6).
[23] IRC § 501(c)(6).
[24] IRC § 501(c)(6).
[25] IRC § 501(c)(6).
[26] IRC § 501(c)(7).
[27] IRC § 501(c)(8).
[28] IRC § 501(c)(9).
[29] IRC § 501(c)(10).
[30] IRC § 501(c)(11).
[31] IRC § 501(c)(12).
[32] IRC § 501(c)(12).

21. Mutual or cooperative telephone companies[33]
22. Cemetery companies[34]
23. Credit unions[35]
24. Certain insurance companies or associations[36]
25. Crop operations financing companies[37]
26. Supplemental unemployment benefit trusts[38]
27. Veterans' organizations[39]
28. Group legal services organizations[40]
29. Black lung benefit trusts[41]
30. Farmers' cooperatives[42]
31. Political organizations[43]
32. The states, political subdivisions of them, and a variety of organizations that are closely associated with the states or their political subdivisions

There are several legal rationales underlying these tax exemptions. The most basic rationale is that a democratic society is best served by encouraging a pluralistic variety of private institutions through which individuals can come together to pursue noncommercial purposes. Taxation of these organizations is perceived as inconsistent with this view. This principle is the essence of a democratic society, where people can join together to solve problems without government interference.

This general rationale is amplified in the case of charitable[44] organizations by the argument that the services provided by these organizations relieve government of burdens it would otherwise have to bear. Taxing these organizations would thus be self-defeating. Other nonprofit organizations are tax-exempt because of benefits from their operations that are primarily directed at the persons who are their members; society in general is seen as indirectly benefiting from these organizations. These organizations include trade, business, and professional associations; unions and other labor organizations; various mutual and cooperative entities, such as credit unions and rural electric cooperatives; and fraternal and veterans' organizations.

Still other legal rationales abound. Some organizations, like social clubs, are tax exempt on the thought that the members are merely doing collectively what they could do individually without taxation. Many advocacy organizations gain tax exemption as a reflection of the constitutional right to petition the government. Other organizations are tax exempt as a byproduct of legislation in other

---

[33] IRC § 501(c)(12).
[34] IRC § 501(c)(13).
[35] IRC § 501(c)(14).
[36] IRC § 501(c)(15).
[37] IRC § 501(c)(16).
[38] IRC § 501(c)(17).
[39] IRC § 501(c)(19).
[40] IRC § 501(c)(20).
[41] IRC § 501(c)(21).
[42] IRC § 521.
[43] IRC § 527.
[44] IRC § 501(c)(3).

areas: most employee benefit funds that provide workplace, pension, and other retirement benefits are exempt from taxation under this rationale. Still other organizations are tax exempt because of the services they provide, either to other nonprofit organizations (such as title-holding companies) or to the public in quasigovernmental form (such as the instrumentalities of the federal government).

In some instances, the term "tax exemption" or "tax-exempt status" is somewhat of a misnomer, even under federal law. That is, in many instances, a "tax-exempt" organization, while generally exempt from taxes, nonetheless must pay certain taxes. Examples of this include the imposition of the tax on unrelated business income,[45] the tax on net investment income applicable to private foundations,[46] and the tax on the nonmember income of social clubs.[47]

(ii) State Law

1. *Income Tax Exemption.* For the most part, state law follows federal law in the realm of tax exemption. Thus, in many states, an organization that is exempt from federal income taxation will be exempt from state income taxation. However, some states have additional criteria that a nonprofit organization must satisfy to acquire tax-exempt status.

2. *Other Tax Exemption.* With regard to sales and use taxes, however, state tax exemption is often more stringent than in the case of income taxation. For example, while any nonprofit organization that has an "educational" purpose may qualify for income tax exemption, sales and use tax exemption may be confined to operating educational institutions (schools, colleges, and universities). Likewise, exemption from tangible and intangible property taxes, which are administered at the local level, usually entails still more strenuous criteria. Real property tax exemptions tend to be available to a much narrower range of nonprofit organizations and the qualifications tend to be even more difficult.

(b) Tax Treatment of Contributions—Domestic Organizations

In addition to the tax exemption afforded to nonprofit organizations themselves, U.S. law also makes provision for the favorable tax treatment of donations to at least certain classes of these organizations. These deductions are available under both federal and state law, though state law generally follows federal usage.

(i) *Federal Law.* U.S. federal tax law embodies a complex set of provisions permitting tax deductions for contributions to certain classes of nonprofit organizations. These deductions can be taken against income, gift, and estate taxes. They apply to donations to charitable organizations, but the definition of a "charitable" organization for tax deductibility purposes is broader than it is under the income tax exemption rules. Organizations eligible to attract deductible charitable gifts include not only charitable organizations (in the tax exemption sense

---

[45] IRC §§ 511–514.
[46] IRC § 4940.
[47] IRC § 512(a)(3).

of that term,[48] but also certain veterans' organizations, fraternal societies, and cemetery companies.[49] Most governmental bodies also qualify as charitable organizations under these rules.[50] These five categories of organizations are also charitable donees for purposes of the federal gift tax[51] and the federal estate tax.[52]

Charitable contribution deductions are provided for individuals, corporations, and trusts. These deductions are subtracted from gross income (or, in the case of individuals, adjusted gross income) before computing taxable income. Charitable contributions can take the form of money, property, the right to use property, and services. Charitable gifts of the right to use property and of services are not deductible. Where property constitutes a capital asset and has been held by the donor for at least 12 months (thereby becoming "long-term capital gain property"), the charitable deduction is based on the full fair market value of the property.

There are many limits on the federal income tax charitable deduction. (There are no limits on the gift and estate tax deductions.) These limits, most of which are expressed as percentages of adjusted gross income in the case of individuals (technically, the "contribution base")[53] and of pretax net income in the case of corporations,[54] are designed to restrict the amount of a charitable contribution deduction in any one tax year. However, in most instances, the amount of "excess" deductions may be carried forward and utilized in subsequent tax years (usually up to five).

The percentages are manifold and are functions of various factors, the principal ones being: (1) the subject of the gift (money or property); (2) if the gift is of property, the nature of the property (such as capital gain property or inventory); (3) if the recipient is a charitable organization (in the tax exemption sense of the term),[55] whether the donee is a "public charity" or a "private foundation";[56] and (4) if the gift is of property, the use to which the contributed property is put (such as the unrelated use of tangible personal property or the charitable use of inventory).

A full list of these limitations is offered in an Appendix to this chapter. Some of the major ones are as follows:

- The maximum federal income tax charitable contribution deduction for a tax year for an individual is 50% of the individual's contribution base.[57]
- An individual's income tax charitable contribution deduction for a tax year cannot exceed 30% of his or her contribution base where the gift is of capital gain property that has appreciated in value and the charitable recipient

---

[48] IRC § 501(c)(3).
[49] IRC § 170(c)(2)–(5).
[50] IRC § 170(c)(1).
[51] IRC § 2522(a)(2).
[52] IRC § 2055(a)(2).
[53] IRC § 170(b)(1)(F).
[54] IRC § 170(b)(2).
[55] IRC § 501(c)(3).
[56] IRC § 509(a).
[57] IRC § 170(b)(1)(A).

is a public charitable organization;[58] or where the gift (or gifts) is of money and the charitable recipient is an entity other than a public charitable organization.[59] Where the gift is of capital gain property that has appreciated in value and the charitable recipient is an entity other than a public charitable organization,[60] an individual's income tax charitable contribution deduction for a tax year cannot exceed 20% of his or her contribution base.

- If a husband and wife file a joint return, the deduction for charitable contributions is the aggregate of the contributions made by the spouses and the percentage limitations are based on the aggregate contribution base of the spouses.

- The charitable contribution deduction for a corporation for a tax year is subject to a limitation of 10% of the corporation's pretax net income.[61]

- Where a donor makes a contribution of an item of tangible personal property that has appreciated in value to a public charitable organization, where the public charity does not use the property for a purpose that is related to its tax-exempt purposes, the donor must reduce the deduction by the entirety of the capital gain element.[62]

- Where a capital gain property gift is to or for the use of a private foundation, the amount of the charitable contribution deduction must be reduced by the amount of any long-term capital gain embodied in the property at the time of the contribution.[63]

- Where a corporate donor makes a charitable contribution of property out of its inventory (often termed "gifts in kind"), the gift deduction is generally confined to an amount which may not exceed the donor's cost basis in the property.[64]

There are other factors that determine whether, or to what extent, a charitable gift is deductible. These are (1) the nature of the interest in the money or property contributed (that is, whether the gift is outright or of a partial interest), (2) whether the charitable organization has complied with certain written substantiation rules,[65] (3) whether the donor has complied with certain recordkeeping and appraisal requirements, (4) whether the donor has received something of value in exchange for the gift (the "quid pro quo contribution"),[66] (5) the year of the gift, and (6) whether the transaction is, in whole or in part, a "gift" rather than some other form of transaction, such as a payment for a service.

As to this sixth point, while a true gift to a school is deductible, tuition payments are not. Also, while an authentic gift to a hospital is deductible, payments for health care services are not. Further, while gifts to charitable membership asso-

[58] IRC § 170(b)(1)(C)(i).
[59] IRC § 170(b)(1)(B)(i).
[60] IRC § 170(b)(1)(D)(i).
[61] IRC § 170(b)(2).
[62] IRC § 170(e)(1)(B)(i).
[63] IRC § 170(e)(1)(B)(ii).
[64] IRC § 170(e)(1)(A).
[65] IRC § 170(f)(8).
[66] IRC § 6115.

ciations are deductible, payments of dues are not. (Some of these nongift payments may be deductible under other tax provisions; for example, a dues payment may be deductible as a business expense.)[67]

Under certain circumstances, out-of-pocket expenditures made for the benefit of a charitable organization are deductible, including the costs of use of an automobile for charitable purposes.[68] However, out-of-pocket expenditures for purposes of influencing legislation are not deductible.[69] Contributions to a charitable organization for the express purpose of influencing legislation or for political campaign activities are not deductible.

There is no charitable contribution deduction for traveling expenses (including amounts expended for meals and lodging) while away from home, whether paid directly or by reimbursement, unless there is no significant element of personal pleasure, recreation, or vacation in the travel.[70] There is no charitable deduction for contributions made in an effort to sidestep the rule that denies a business expense deduction for certain lobbying or political activities.[71] The amount of a charitable contribution of works of art and the like by the creator of the work is limited to the donor's cost basis in the property.[72]

There are several obligations that the recipients of tax deductible gifts incur. For the most part, these obligations are the same as those imposed under the appropriate tax exemption provision. For example, a public charity must avoid using contributions (and other revenues) for activities such as substantial lobbying, private inurement or substantial private benefit transactions, or political campaign activities.[73]

(ii) State Law.   The laws of the states provide for an income tax charitable contribution deduction. For the most part, a charitable gift that is deductible under the federal tax law is also deductible under state tax law. However, in some instances, state law imposes additional requirements for the deduction. In addi-

---

[67] Regarding contributions of "partial interests" in property to charitable organizations, there is no charitable contribution deduction for a gift of a remainder interest in property made in trust unless the trust is one of two types of trusts (IRC § 170(f)(2)(A)). These qualifying trusts are termed "charitable remainder trusts" (IRC § 664) and "pooled income funds" (IRC § 642(c)(5)). Contributions of income interests in property transferred in trust (usually termed "charitable lead trusts") are deductible only when certain special rules are satisfied (IRC § 170(f)(2)(B)).

Most contributions of a partial interest in property, not made by a transfer in trust, are not deductible (IRC § 170(f)(3)(A)). Exceptions are available for contributions of a remainder interest in a personal residence or farm, of an undivided portion of the donor's entire interest in property, or of certain contributions for conservation purposes (IRC §§ 170(f)(3)(B); 170(h)). A charitable contribution of a remainder interest in property made by contract, where the income interest retained constitutes a "charitable gift annuity," is deductible where certain requirements are satisfied (IRC §§ 501(m)(3)(E), (5); 514(c)(5)). Charitable contributions that are made by selling an item of property to charity for less than its fair market value are termed "bargain sales"; a charitable deduction is available for the gift element of the transaction. A charitable gift of an item of property subject to debt is likely to be treated as a bargain sale.

[68] IRC § 170(i).

[69] IRC § 170(f)(6).

[70] IRC § 170(j).

[71] IRC § 170(f)(9).

[72] IRC § 1221(3).

[73] IRC §§ 170(c)(2); 501(c)(3).

tion, state inheritance tax laws usually do not apply to transfers to charitable organizations.

§ 25.5 PERSONAL BENEFIT RESTRICTIONS

(a) Executive Salaries

Charitable organizations and other nonprofit organizations that are subject to the doctrine of private inurement have restrictions on the amount they can pay as compensation to executives (and others). In particular, the compensation can be no more than is "reasonable." If one of these organizations compensates a person in an amount that is "excessive," the unreasonable portion of the compensation is considered a form of private inurement and the organization can have its tax-exempt status revoked.

Reasonableness is determined as a matter of comparability. Organizations of the same size (in terms of finances and number of employees) and location are compared, as are the educational qualifications, experience, and level of responsibility of the individual involved. These rules apply with respect to all employees of this type of nonprofit organization, as well as to all consultants and vendors.

(b) Compensation of Board Members

Federal and state law does not prohibit the compensation of members of the governing board of a nonprofit organization. However, this is not a common practice. There are situations, however, where a member of a board is also an employee of the organization, and is paid as an employee, rather than as a board member. Particularly where the private inurement doctrine is applicable, a nonprofit organization that provides compensation to a board member should be certain that the amount involved is not unreasonable.

(c) Self-Dealing

The federal tax laws embody rules against self-dealing; however, these rules apply only with respect to private foundations.[74] Persons that are involved in a self-dealing transaction with a private foundation are termed "disqualified persons," which include the founder of the organization, its directors and officers, and substantial contributors to the organization.[75] Self-dealing transactions generally are:

1. Sales or exchanges of property between a private foundation and a disqualified person
2. Leasing of property between the parties
3. Lending of money or any other extension of credit between the parties
4. Furnishing of goods, services, or facilities between the parties

[74] IRC § 4941.
[75] IRC § 4946.

5. Payment of compensation (or payment or reimbursement of expenses) by a foundation to a disqualified person
6. The transfer to, or use by or for the benefit of, a disqualified person of the income or assets of a private foundation

There are many exceptions to these self-dealing rules, however. For example, a private foundation can pay compensation (and pay or reimburse expenses) to a disqualified person for personal services which are reasonable and necessary to carrying out the exempt purpose of the foundation as long as the compensation is not excessive. An act of self-dealing (in the generic sense) may be a form of private inurement.[76]

§ 25.6 OBLIGATIONS TO THE PUBLIC

(a) Fiduciary Responsibilities

The law of charitable organizations in the United States, both federal and state, rests on the English common law of charitable trusts and property. This body of law regards the resources of a charitable organization as charitable assets and the directors of the organization as stewards of those assets. Another word for steward is *fiduciary*, and the law regards these individuals as fiduciaries.

A fiduciary is expected to act, with respect to charitable assets and income, in a way that is prudent. This means that fiduciaries are charged with acting with the same degree of judgment—prudence—in administering the affairs of the organization as they would their personal affairs. The public expects that these organizations will be administered for the public good by reason of their fiduciaries adhering to the requirements of fiduciary responsibility. This is particularly important to those members of the public who are contributors to the organization or who are members of it.

(b) Reporting Requirements

Charitable and other nonprofit organizations generally must file annual reports (Form 990) with the federal government and with the appropriate state governments. These reports are public documents. At the federal level, the report filed by a nonprofit tax-exempt organization must be made available for review by anyone who appears on the business premises and asks to see a copy of it. Also, a charitable organization soliciting contributions must register with and annually report in nearly every state in which a solicitation occurs; these filings are public documents.

---

[76] There are a few additional requirements aimed at restricting potential misuses of foundations. In particular, foundations must annually pay out, in the form of grants for charitable purposes (termed *qualifying distributions*), an amount equal to at least 5% of their investment assets (termed *minimum investment return*); may not hold more than 20% (sometimes 35%) of an active interest in a commercial business; and may not invest their income or assets in speculative investments (termed *jeopardizing investments*).

Foundations must file an annual information return (Form 990-PF) that is more complex than that required of other charitable and like organizations. In addition, foundations may not make expenditures for purposes that are non-charitable, lobbying, or political, nor make grants to individuals or organizations that are not public charities without complying with certain rules; and must exercise "expenditure responsibility" with respect to grants to organizations other than public charities. Foundations generally must also pay a 2% tax on their net investment income.

§ 25.7 BUSINESS ACTIVITY

Federal tax law in the United States imposes significant restrictions on certain business activities of nonprofit organizations. In particular, this law differentiates between business activities that are "related" to an organization's tax-exempt functions and those that are not. A related business is one that is conducted so as to advance the organization's exempt purposes; the "profits" that are earned from the operation of this type of business are used to fund the organization's exempt programs and are not taxed. An "unrelated trade or business" is one that is not substantially related to the exercise or performance of the exempt purpose or function; it is an activity carried on for commercial purposes, with profit making as the purpose. The conduct of a trade or business is not made substantially related to an organization's tax-exempt purpose simply because the organization needs the income or because it uses the income to further exempt purposes.

Nonprofit organizations are allowed to operate businesses and/or operate them in separate organizations. With regard to related businesses, there is no limit on the amount that may be operated and owned by a nonprofit organization. However, if the principal purpose of a nonprofit organization is to operate and/or own one or more *unrelated* businesses, the organization cannot qualify for tax exemption. Although, with one exception, there is no specific rule on how much unrelated activity a tax-exempt nonprofit organization may engage in, it is clear that it must be less than one-half of its total annual activity or revenue. The exception is that a title-holding corporation cannot have more than 10% of its revenue derived from unrelated business activities.[77]

While nonprofit organizations are permitted to own and/or operate unrelated businesses, however, they are not entitled to exemption from taxes on the profits of such businesses. To the contrary, income from "trades or businesses" that are unrelated to an organization's exempt purposes are taxed using the same tax and accounting concepts (including business expense deductions) as are applicable to for-profit corporations. The objective is to place tax-exempt organization business activities on the same tax basis as the nonexempt business endeavors with which they compete.

Certain limitations apply to this unrelated business income tax (UBIT). First, the income must result from a "trade or business," that is, from an activity that is carried on for the production of income from the sale of goods or the performance of services and, according to some court decisions, that is conducted with

---

[77] IRC § 501(c)(25)(G).

a "profit motive." In making a determination about the existence of such a business, the Internal Revenue Service (IRS) may fragment a nonprofit organization's operations into its component parts. This "fragmentation rule" enables the IRS to ferret out unrelated business activity that is conducted with, or as part of, related business activity.[78]

Second, for an unrelated business to be subject to taxation, it must be "regularly carried on," that is, it must be frequent and continuous, and pursued in a manner generally similar to comparable commercial activities of nonexempt organizations.[79]

Third, only those businesses not "substantially related" to a nonprofit organization's tax-exempt purposes are subject to taxation. Substantially related in this context means that the conduct of the business activity must have a significant causal relationship to the achievement of a tax-exempt purpose. Thus, for the conduct of a trade or business from which a particular amount of gross income is derived to be exempt from taxation, the production or distribution of the goods or the performance of the services from which the gross income is derived must contribute importantly to the accomplishment of the organization's exempt purposes.[80]

An asset or facility necessary to the conduct of tax-exempt functions may also be utilized in a commercial manner. This is a "dual use" arrangement. In these cases, the mere fact of the use of the asset or facility in exempt functions does not, by itself, make the income from the commercial endeavor gross income from related business. The test, instead, is whether the activities productive of the income in question contribute importantly to the accomplishment of exempt purposes.

Finally, certain types of income or activities are exempt from unrelated business income taxation. These exemptions include income:

1. In the form of interest, dividends, royalties, rents, annuities, and capital gains

---

[78] IRC § 513(a).

[79] IRC § 512(a)(1).

[80] Whether activities productive of gross income contribute importantly to the accomplishment of a purpose for which a nonprofit organization is tax exempt depends in each case on the facts and circumstances involved. In determining whether activities contribute importantly to the accomplishment of a tax-exempt purpose, the size and extent of the activities involved must be considered in relation to the nature and extent of the tax-exempt function that they purport to serve. Thus, where income is realized by a nonprofit organization from activities that are in part related to the performance of its exempt functions but that are conducted on a larger scale than is reasonably necessary for performance of the functions, the gross income attributable to that portion of the activities in excess of the needs of tax-exempt functions constitutes gross income from the conduct of unrelated trade or business. This type of income is not derived from the production or distribution of goods or the performance of services that contribute importantly to the accomplishment of any tax-exempt purpose of the organization.

Ordinarily, gross income from the sale of products that results from the performance of tax-exempt functions does not constitute gross income from the conduct of unrelated business if the product is sold in substantially the same state it is in upon completion of the exempt functions. However, if a product resulting from a tax-exempt function is utilized or exploited in business endeavors beyond that reasonably appropriate or necessary for disposition in the state it is in upon completion of tax-exempt functions, the gross income derived from these endeavors would be from the conduct of unrelated business.

2. Derived from research for government
3. Derived from research performed by a college, university, or hospital
4. From a business in which substantially all of the work is performed by volunteers
5. From a business conducted by a charitable organization primarily for the convenience of its members, students, patients, officers, or employees
6. From a business that is the sale of merchandise, substantially all of which has been received by the organization as contributions
7. From the conduct of entertainment at certain fairs and expositions, or from the conduct of certain trade shows
8. From the provision of certain services to small nonprofit hospitals
9. From the distribution of certain low-cost articles incidental to the solicitation of charitable contributions, and from the exchange or rental of mailing lists with or to charitable organizations[81]

§ 25.8 OTHER FUNDING RESTRICTIONS

Although the solicitation of charitable contributions in the United States involves practices that are recognized as being forms of free speech protected by federal and state constitutional law, nonprofit organizations in the United States face considerable regulatory requirements at the federal and state levels of government when they solicit contributions for charitable purposes.

All of the states but three have some form of legal structure by which the fund-raising process is regulated. Thirty-five states have formal charitable solicitation acts. The various state charitable solicitation acts generally contain certain features. These are:

1. A process by which a charitable organization registers or otherwise secures a permit to raise funds for charitable purposes in the state
2. Requirements for reporting information (usually annually) about an organization's fund-raising program
3. A series of organizations or activities that are exempt from some or all of the regulatory requirements
4. A process by which a professional fund raiser, professional solicitor, and/or commercial coventurer registers with, and reports to, the state
5. Recordkeeping requirements, applicable to charitable organizations, professional fund raisers, professional solicitors, and/or commercial coventurers
6. Rules concerning the contents of contracts between a charitable organization and a professional fund raiser, a professional solicitor, and/or a commercial coventurer
7. A series of so-called "prohibited acts," which provide the basis for still more regulatory requirements
8. Provision for reciprocal agreements among the states as to coordinated regulation in this field (these are, however, rarely used)

[81] IRC § 512(b).

9. A summary of the powers of the government official having the regulatory authority (usually the attorney general or secretary of state)
10. A statement of the various sanctions that can be imposed for failure to comply with this law (such as injunctions, fines, and imprisonment)

The federal government is also involved in the regulation of charitable solicitations. Indeed, regulation at the federal level is immense and growing. Federal tax law regulates the practice of fund-raising for charitable purposes in the following ways:

1. Contributions in excess of $250 generally must be "substantiated" in writing by the recipient charity
2. The donee charity must provide the estimated value of nearly every product or service received by a donor in exchange for a gift, where the amount transferred is in excess of $75
3. Most contributions of property having a value in excess of $5,000 must entail an independent appraisal
4. The IRS requires a charitable organization to summarize its fund-raising program at the time it applies for recognition of tax-exempt status
5. The IRS requires a charitable organization to report the receipts of its fund-raising activities, and to report its fund-raising expenses, on an annual basis
6. The IRS and the courts apply the unrelated business income rules in a variety of ways, so as to cause certain fund-raising practices to be characterized as unrelated businesses
7. The IRS applies the rules embodying limitations on lobbying by, and calculation of the public support of, public charities in a way that defines and encourages certain forms of fund-raising
8. The fund-raising process is "regulated" by means of interpretations and enforcement of the rules involving deductible charitable contributions
9. The IRS is engaged in a program of examination of charitable organizations that engage in fund-raising

§ 25.9   POLITICAL ACTIVITY

Significant restrictions are imposed on the "political activities" of nonprofit organizations in the United States. The word "political" in this context has a special technical meaning, referring to efforts to influence legislation ("lobbying") as well as political campaign activities, though the rules differ with respect to these two different types of political activity.

Most of these restrictions apply only to charitable[82] organizations. These organizations, as a condition of tax exemption, are not permitted to engage in any political campaign activities or to take part in legislative activities to a "substantial" extent. Other organizations are not quite so constricted. For example, tax-

[82] IRC § 501(c)(3).

exempt social welfare[83] organizations are free to lobby as long as the lobbying is in furtherance of their tax-exempt purposes; these organizations may also engage in a limited amount of political campaign activity. Most other tax-exempt organizations (such as business and professional associations, labor unions, and veterans' organizations) are not so restricted in their lobbying activities. Although these organizations are subject to a tax if they engage directly in campaign activities,[84] they can conduct such activities indirectly by means of separate political action committees.[85] Such committees are tax-exempt "political organizations."[86] As such, their exempt purpose is to influence the selection, nomination, election, or appointment of any individual to a federal, state, or local public office.[87] Most political organizations are political action committees, which raise funds and contribute them to political candidates and their campaigns.[88]

(a) Political Campaign Activity

The political campaign activities prohibition applicable to charitable organizations contains four elements, all of which must be present for the limitation to be applicable. Thus, (1) the organization must be actively "participating" or "intervening" in a political campaign; (2) the political activity that is involved must be an active "political campaign;" (3) the campaign must be with respect to an individual who is a "candidate;" and (4) the individual must be a candidate for a "public office."

A variety of activities are considered "political" but are not political campaign activities. These activities include lobbying (see below), action on behalf of or in opposition to the confirmation of presidential nominees, litigation, boycotts, demonstrations, strikes, and picketing. However, nonprofit organizations may not engage in activities that promote violence, other forms of law breaking, or other activities that are contrary to "public policy."

Charitable organizations that lose their tax-exempt status because of political campaign activities are subject to an excise tax in the amount of 10% of the political campaign expenditures and perhaps an additional 100% tax.[89] Like taxes, in the amounts of 2½% and 50%, may be imposed on the directors and officers of an organization who agreed to the making of the political campaign expenditures, unless the agreement was not willful and was due to reasonable cause.

(b) Legislative Activity

The restrictions on nonprofit lobbying are less restrictive than those on nonprofit campaign activity. Many nonprofit organizations in the United States can engage in attempts to influence legislation ("lobbying") without limitation, as long as the lobbying is in furtherance of their tax-exempt function. Most organizations in this

---

[83] IRC § 501(c)(4).
[84] IRC § 527(f).
[85] IRC § 527 organizations.
[86] As defined in IRC § 527.
[87] IRC § 527(e)(2).
[88] IRC § 527(e)(2).
[89] IRC § 4955.

category are social welfare organizations,[90] trade, business, and professional associations,[91] labor organizations,[92] and veterans' organizations.[93]

Charitable organizations are also permitted to engage in lobbying, but the amount of lobbying they can conduct is restricted. The rule is that no "substantial part" of the activities of a charitable organization may consist of lobbying activities.[94] The term "substantial," as used in this context, has never been defined. However, as a very general guideline, a charitable organization can annually expend up to 15% of its funds on lobbying. A major exception to these rules is that a private foundation generally may not engage in any lobbying activities.[95]

There are two types of lobbying recognized in U.S. law. One is "direct" lobbying, where the organization communicates directly with a legislature, a legislator, or an employee of a legislature with respect to a particular piece of legislation. The other is "grassroots" lobbying, where the organization appeals to the general public, or segments of the public, intending to cause members of the public to contact the members of a legislature or take other specific action as regards particular legislation. "Legislation" here includes bills, resolutions, appropriations measures, treaties, and Senate consideration of presidential nominations. Lobbying can be done in person (office visits and testimony before legislative committees) and by mail, telephone, print media, radio, and television.

Certain activities are excluded from the definition of lobbying, however, such as the presentation of testimony at a public hearing of a legislative committee by invitation, general education and research efforts, and monitoring the status of and nonpartisan reporting on legislation.

Organizations that are under the substantial part test and lose their tax-exempt status because of excessive lobbying are subject to an excise tax in the amount of 5% of the excess lobbying expenditures.[96] A like tax may be imposed on the directors and officers of an organization who agreed to the making of the excess lobbying expenditures, unless the agreement was not willful and was due to reasonable cause.

Most charitable organizations that are not private foundations may elect[97] to have their lobbying measured by a special set of rules[98] known as the "expenditure" test. These rules allow a charitable organization to expend up to 20% of its total expenditures (other than certain fund-raising expenses) on lobbying; this calculation is made on the basis of a four-year average. Under the expenditure test, lobbying expenditures may be 20% of the first $500,000 of expenditures, 15% of the next $500,000, 10% of the next $500,000, and 5% of the balance, with no more than $1 million expended for lobbying in any one year. However, grassroots lobbying may not be more than 25% of the total allowable lobbying amount. An organization that exceeds one or both of the lobbying amount ceilings tolerated

---

[90] IRC § 501(c)(4).
[91] IRC § 501(c)(6).
[92] IRC § 501(c)(5).
[93] IRC § 501(c)(19).
[94] IRC § 501(c)(3).
[95] IRC § 4945(d)(1).
[96] IRC § 4912.
[97] IRC § 501(h).
[98] IRC § 4911.

by the expenditure test is subject to a 25% tax on the excess lobbying expenditures. If an organization exceeds a lobbying ceiling by more than 150%, it is to be deprived of its tax-exempt status.

A nonprofit organization generally is required to disclose to its members the portion of their dues that are attributable to lobbying[99] and no business expense deduction is allowed for this portion.[100] There is no contribution deduction for an amount given to a charitable organization that conducts lobbying if (1) the lobbying activities regard matters of direct financial interest to the trade or business of the donor and (2) a principal purpose of the contribution is to avoid the business expense disallowance rule.[101]

§ 25.10   KEY OUTSTANDING ISSUES

A number of major legal developments or issues face the nonprofit sector in the United States at the present time. Three of the most important of these are: (1) the increasing commercialization of the activities of nonprofit organizations; (2) federal and state regulation of fund-raising for charitable purposes; and (3) the appropriate role of the board of directors (or trustees) of nonprofit organizations.[102]

(a) Commerciality

The lines of distinction between nonprofit organizations and for-profit organizations in the United States are blurring, and there is confusion among the public and policy makers as to what the fundamental differences are or should be. Health care institutions are at the forefront in this regard; other nonprofit entities generating this debate include credit unions and certain other financial organizations, fraternal organizations and other insurance-providing entities, and various publishing, research, training, and counseling organizations.

In development at this time, in the federal tax law of the United States, is the "commerciality doctrine." This doctrine, being formulated principally by courts, is rooted in the principle of capitalism that underlies and defines much of the way that U.S. society is structured and functions. The doctrine embodies, yet is larger than, the issue of competition between the nonprofit and for-profit sectors.

In essence, the commerciality doctrine holds that a nonprofit, tax-exempt organization, when it engages in an activity in a manner that is considered "commercial," is engaging in an inappropriate, nonexempt undertaking. If one or more commercial activities are the organization's principal functions, then the organization is likely to lose its nonprofit status and have its tax exemption revoked.

---

[99] IRC § 6113.

[100] IRC § 162(e)(3).

[101] IRC § 170(f)(9).

[102] Other important issues include: the building challenge to the tax-exempt status of nonprofit hospitals, significant developments in the fields of deductibility of charitable contributions, lobbying, and political campaign activities, disclosure of various forms of information and reporting by nonprofit organizations, application of the unrelated business income tax rules, and charitable giving for international programs. However, these developments do not entail the significance being occasioned by the first three.

Otherwise, commercial activities frequently are regarded as forms of unrelated business.

An activity is regarded as a commercial one if it has a direct counterpart in the for-profit sector. For example, a court, in assessing whether a nonprofit organization is eligible for tax-exempt status, is likely to deny that status if a significant portion of the organization's program activity consists of undertakings that are being conducted by for-profit organizations.

There are many court cases where organizations that sell products or services that are also sold by for-profit corporations are denied tax exemption for that reason; these activities include the selling of works of art, insurance, medical devices, and publications, and the provision of services in the realms of research, counseling, fitness, and educational training.

Other signs of activity conducted in a commercial manner include sales of goods or services to the general public, operation in direct competition with for-profit (commercial) organizations, setting of prices using a formula that is common in the for-profit sector, actual profit margins, use of promotional materials and other forms of advertising to induce sales, hours of operation, lack of use of volunteers, the extent of training of employees in the fields of business operations and marketing, and the absence of charitable contributions as part of the organization's revenue base.

There is almost no law, on a statutory basis, that reflects the commerciality doctrine; the one exception is the unique body of law concerning "commercial-type insurance."[103] The doctrine is emerging because the courts are uncomfortable with the prospect of tax-exempt organizations distributing products and delivering services where these products or services are simultaneously being distributed and/or delivered by organizations in the for-profit sector. As noted, this is a bias that is being reified by the capitalist philosophy. There are many judges, legislators, and other policy makers who do not want nonprofit organizations competing with for-profit organizations.

One of the ironies in this area is that the development of the tax rules concerning unrelated business activities was designed to eliminate nonprofit/for-profit competition, or at least make it economically more similar (through taxation). These rules, initiated in 1950 and significantly augmented in 1969, have not had a major impact on the element of competition. The reason for this is that this body of law focuses on the activities of nonprofit organizations that are *not related* to their exempt purpose. Today's competition, however, effects usually the activities of nonprofit organizations that are *related* to their exempt purpose.

The IRS is doing the best it can in this environment. Congress has provided very little in the way of statutory clarification; the courts are both inconsistent and developing rules that have little or no linkage with the statutory scheme.

One of the ways the IRS is attempting to implement the commerciality doctrine is by means of the "commensurate test." This is a standard articulated by the IRS in 1964 and not much applied until the late 1980s. The commensurate test basically is used to determine whether a tax-exempt organization (particularly a charitable one) is engaging in a suitable amount of exempt activity in relation to its available resources.

---

[103] IRC § 501(m).

For the time being, however, the judiciary is the most critical branch of the U.S. government in terms of development and application of the commerciality doctrine. Nonetheless, the implications of this evolving aspect of the law should not be minimized. In a sense, it is redefining the line of demarcation between the nonprofit and for-profit sectors. As such, it is the single most important aspect of the law impacting on the federal tax treatment of nonprofit organizations today.

(b) Fund-Raising Regulation

A second area of significant legal development in the United States today concerns fund-raising regulation. Originally established as a licensing system, this body of law has evolved into affirmative regulation of charitable solicitations. Intended largely as information-gathering and -dissemination laws designed to protect the general public from fraudulent and other misleading solicitations, these law requirements are beginning to sound more like ethical precepts. Today's requirements go beyond the mechanics of registration and reporting: they instruct the charities and their assisting professionals when to do various acts, and tell them how they must conduct the solicitation and what they cannot do in this regard.

From the regulators' view, the high point of this form of regulation came when the states could ban charitable solicitations by organizations with "high" fund-raising costs. This form of regulation ultimately was found to be unconstitutional, leaving the state regulators without their principal weapon. In frustration, they turned to other forms of law based on the principle of disclosure. The registration and annual reports became more extensive. The states tried, with limited success, to force charitable organizations and professional solicitors into various forms of point-of-solicitation disclosure of various pieces of information. Some states dictated the contents of the scripts of telephone solicitors.

Today, by use of these charitable solicitation acts, the state regulators are micromanaging charitable fund-raising. They are substituting their judgment for that of donors, charities, and fund-raising professionals. They are encouraging the passage of laws with more strenuous recordkeeping requirements, detailing the contents of contracts between charities and fund-raising consultants, enhancing the regulation of commercial coventures, and even injecting themselves into matters such as the selling of tickets for charitable events and solicitations by fire and police personnel.

These laws apply with respect to the locus of the solicitation, not the location of the fund-raising charitable organization. Thus, a charitable organization must register, report, and otherwise comply with the charitable solicitation act in each of the states in which it is fund-raising. A charitable organization engaging in a nationwide solicitation effort is required, therefore, to register under about 45 statutes. Some states treat charitable fund-raising as a form of "doing business," which forces annual registration and reporting under other bodies of law as well.

These developments, which continue to build, are reaching crisis proportions for U.S. charitable organizations. The resulting collection of law has become so onerous that many organizations simply do not comply or else incur immense staffing burdens as they endeavor to meet all of the requirements. (The situation is even more acute in that many counties, cities, and towns also have fund-raising regulation ordinances.) Efforts to lighten this regulatory load—such as by inject-ing some uniformity into the text of the laws, or their forms or accounting rules—have repeatedly failed, as the states cannot agree on ways in which to cooperate. Some proponents of relief in this area advocate a preemptive federal charitable solicitation statute. However, the U.S. Congress has shown no interest in enact-ment of this type of law. Indeed, more forms of regulation in this field are being developed at the federal level.

The giving public deserves protection against fraud and other abuse in chari-table giving. But the process of raising money for charitable purposes in the United States is becoming heavily weighed down by a swirl of inconsistent and unnecessary procedures and other burdens. This is evolving as the state regula-tors endeavor to outdo each other in the formulation of "tougher" laws and the federal government inches closer to the implementation of a national charitable solicitation law (which will not preempt the state laws).

This steady imposition of regulatory burdens on the good works of non-profit organizations is becoming a significant drain on charitable resources. One of the challenges for the nonprofit community in the years ahead will be to explore a new balance between the public's need for protection and the nonprofit sector's need for relief from a growing regulatory burden.

(c) Role of Directors

A third crucial issue facing nonprofit law in the United States concerns the role of directors. The law in the United States has yet to adequately articulate the stan-dard of performance for those who sit on the boards of directors (or trustees) of nonprofit organizations. This is particularly the case with respect to charitable organizations. Again, the distinction between nonprofit organizations and for-profit organizations is relevant.

An individual who is a member of the board of directors of a for-profit organ-ization is expected to act, with respect to the resources of the organization, in a reasonable manner. Wrongful appropriation of funds, misrepresentation of mate-rial facts, and inattention to fundamental responsibilities are acts considered to violate this standard.

In contrast, the standard of behavior for those individuals who are members of the board of directors (or trustees) of a nonprofit organization (particularly a charitable one) has developed from a different premise. That premise is the set of duties assigned to trustees of a charitable trust under the English common law. There, the standard was (and is) that of "prudence"—a somewhat stricter require-ment than "reasonableness." This standard imposed on trustees the requirement to treat the assets, income, and other resources of the organization in the same way that they would treat their own. Thus, the terms that came to be applied to these individuals were "fiduciaries" and "stewards."

It is fair to say that most directors of nonprofit, charitable organizations do not understand the legal underpinnings of their position. This goes beyond mat-ters of liability—most directors (and officers) of nonprofit organizations realize they are personally vulnerable to lawsuits for what they do (commissions) or not do (omissions); that is why there is so much interest in incorporation, indemnification, and insurance as ways of eliminating or limiting exposure to legal liability.

But a focus on liability is a focus on the wrong dimension; the law encourages attention to the affairs of the nonprofit organization in ways so that liability will not arise in the first instance. This means that a director of a nonprofit organization is expected to understand the programs of the entity, to understand the nature of its governance and the way its funds are invested, to know the policies for hiring and retaining employees, to comprehend its financial statements and its annual reports, in short to "know" the organization, to attend meetings of the board and committees on which he or she has agreed to serve, to ask questions when matters are in doubt, and to officially abstain from or oppose votes on policies or decisions where there is opposition or substantial doubt.

Frequently, today, individuals are placed on the board of directors of a nonprofit organization for the wrong reason, such as a reward for services previously provided (often to another organization) or as recognition for the amount of contributions made. A position on a board of directors of a nonprofit organization thus becomes a sinecure. In other cases, business executives serving on the boards of nonprofit organizations bring attitudes and approaches inappropriate to the nonprofit context, relying too heavily, for example, on the work and views of the staff, and on written reports.

Given these failings, state law is likely to change to state more explicitly the obligations and expectations of nonprofit directors (and trustees). Of greater significance is the likelihood that the federal tax law will be enhanced to impose penalties on individuals who, as directors and as fiduciaries, do not act in the best interests of the organization they are expected to serve. The contemporary term for these penalties is "intermediate sanctions."

The fact that individuals cause nonprofit organizations to violate the law is just beginning to permeate U.S. tax law. For the most part, the sanction to date for wrongdoing has been to revoke the tax-exempt status of the nonprofit organization. But as instances of sins of commission and omission at the board level mount, it is likely that penalties (in the form of taxes) will be imposed on the individuals who knowingly cause a nonprofit organization to violate the prescription of law. This could entail excessive lobbying, inappropriate political campaign activities, substantial unrelated business activities, instances of private benefit or private inurement, or other circumstances where related program activities are subservient to other undertakings.

APPENDIX 25A: LIMITS ON THE FEDERAL INCOME TAX CHARITABLE DEDUCTION

[a] The maximum federal income tax charitable contribution deduction for a tax year for an individual is 50% of the individual's contribution base (IRC § 170(b)(1)(A)).

[b] An individual's income tax charitable contribution deduction for a tax year cannot exceed an amount equal to 50% of his or her contribution base where the gift (or gifts) is of money (and/or ordinary income property and/or short-

term capital gain property) and the charitable recipient is a public charitable organization (IRC § 170(b)(1)(A)).

[c] An individual's income tax charitable contribution deduction for a tax year cannot exceed 30% of his or her contribution base where the gift is of capital gain property that has appreciated in value and the charitable recipient is a public charitable organization (IRC § 170 (b)(1)(C)(i)).

[d] An individual donor can elect to have a 50% limitation apply, where the gift is of capital gain property that has appreciated in value and the charitable recipient is a public charitable organization, by reducing the deduction by the amount of the appreciation element (IRC § 170(b)(1)(C)(iii)).

[e] An individual's income tax charitable contribution deduction for a tax year cannot exceed an amount equal to 30% of his or her contribution base where the gift (or gifts) is of money and the charitable recipient is an entity other than a public charitable organization (IRC § 170(b)(1)(B)(i)).

[f] Contributions "for the use of" a charitable organization are subject to a 30% limitation (IRC § 170(b)(1)(B)).

[g] Where the gift is of capital gain property that has appreciated in value and the charitable recipient is an entity other than a public charitable organization, an individual's income tax charitable contribution deduction for a tax year cannot exceed 20% of his or her contribution base (IRC § 170(b)(1)(D)(i)).

[h] These limitations are blended where the individual donor contributes more than one type of item (money or property) in a tax year and/or contributes to more than one type of charitable organization in a tax year.

[i] If a husband and wife file a joint return, the deduction for charitable contributions is the aggregate of the contributions made by the spouses and the percentage limitations are based on the aggregate contribution base of the spouses.

[j] The charitable contribution deduction for a corporation for a tax year is subject to a limitation of 10% of the corporation's pretax net income (IRC § 170(b)(2)).

[k] Where a donor makes a contribution of an item of tangible personal property that has appreciated in value to a public charitable organization, where the public charity does not use the property for a purpose that is related to its tax-exempt purposes, the donor must reduce the deduction by the entirety of the capital gain element (IRC § 170(e)(1)(B)(i)).

[l] Where a donor makes a contribution of an item of ordinary income property to a charitable organization, the amount of the charitable contribution deduction must be reduced by the amount of gain which would have been recognized as gain which is not long-term capital gain if the property had been sold by the donor at its fair market value, determined at the time of the contribution (IRC § 170(e)(1)(A)).

[m] Where a capital gain property gift is to or for the use of a private foundation, the amount of the charitable contribution deduction must be reduced by the amount of any long-term capital gain embodied in the property at the time of the contribution (IRC § 170(e)(1)(B)(ii)).

[n] An exception to the preceding rule applies in the case of "qualified appreciated stock." In general, this is stock (1) that is capital gain property and (2) for which (as of the date of the contribution) market quotations are readily

available on an established securities market (IRC § 170(e)(5)(B)). Because of this exception, a charitable deduction for a contribution of qualified appreciated stock to a private foundation is based on the fair market value of the stock at the time of the gift (IRC § 170(e)(5)(A)).

[o] Where a corporate donor makes a charitable contribution of property out of its inventory (often termed "gifts in kind"), the gift deduction is generally confined to an amount which may not exceed the donor's cost basis in the property (IRC § 170(e)(1)(A)).

[p] An exception to the preceding rule applies in the case of "qualified contribution" of inventory (IRC § 170(e)(3)). In this instance, the contribution deduction must be reduced by an amount equal to one-half of the amount of gain that would not have been long-term capital gain if the property had been sold by the donor at fair market value on the date of the contribution (IRC § 170(e)(3)(B)(i)). If, after this reduction, the amount of the deduction would be more than twice the basis in the contributed property, the amount of the deduction must be further reduced to an amount equal to twice the cost basis in the property (IRC § 170(e)(3)(B)(ii)). One of the principal criteria for a qualified contribution is that the property must be used by the charitable donee solely for the care of the ill, the needy, or infants (IRC § 170(e)(3)(A)(i)).

[q] The special rule for certain gifts of inventory described in the preceding rule is termed an "augmented" charitable contribution deduction. A similar augmented deduction is available for contributions of certain scientific property used for research (IRC § 170(e)(4)).

Toward A Vital Voluntary Sector: An International Statement of Principles

PREAMBLE

The past two decades have witnessed a remarkable upsurge of interest in organized private, voluntary activity throughout the world—in the developed countries of Western Europe, North America, and Asia; in the former Soviet bloc; and in the developing countries of Africa, Asia, and Latin America.

This development holds important promise for the promotion of democracy and the enhancement of human well-being. At the same time, important questions have arisen about the role and character of the voluntary organizations resulting from this activity and about the policies that should be pursued in relation to them.

Different countries will naturally resolve these questions in different ways, reflecting their own local circumstances and traditions. At the same time, a considerable consensus has formed at the international level about certain key features of this voluntary sector, and about the principles that should guide policy toward it.

The purpose of this statement is to summarize this emerging consensus so that those involved in the development of the third sector around the world can take its contents into account when framing their own policies and practices. The statement reflects the combined efforts of a sizable network of scholars, practitioners, and experts in the field of philanthropy and voluntary action from all parts of the world who have taken part in the annual conferences of the Johns Hopkins International Fellows in Philanthropy Program held in Lille, France (1991); Jerusalem, Israel (1992); and Accra, Ghana (1993). Out of their deliberations have emerged the following basic points about the nature and importance of private, nonprofit, or voluntary organizations, about government policies toward them, and about the standards and obligations that should guide their work:

I. RATIONALE AND ROLE

1. *The right to associate is a fundamental human right, as basic as the right of free speech.*

Humans are fundamentally social beings. Association with others is therefore essential to human well-being and existence. Voluntary organizations encourage a sense of engagement and efficacy and provide a vital mechanism for promoting solidarity, encouraging mutual aid, and fostering individual initiative in the solution of public problems.

Voluntary organizations thus help satisfy needs and aspirations that neither the state nor the market can satisfy on their own—needs that can be material, social, psychological, spiritual, or other. These organizations often demonstrate a degree of flexibility, responsiveness, and sensitivity that gives them special advantages in identifying new needs, experimenting with new approaches, and creating distinctive ways to cope with pressing problems. As such, they are vital to society as well as to those who take part in, or benefit from, their operations.

2. *Voluntary or nonprofit organizations are crucial for effective citizen participation in civic and social life and therefore contribute importantly to democracy.*

In addition to responding to basic human needs, voluntary organizations are a crucial mechanism through which individuals can join together to promote common concerns, to protect group and individual rights, to support particular policies, to promote particular causes, and to hold government and the private sector accountable. In this sense, they are of basic importance to the functioning of democracy and the achievement of civil society.

3. *To achieve their full potential, nonprofit organizations should enjoy significant independence from the state, be self-governing, embody a meaningful degree of voluntary activity, and serve some public purpose.*

Nonprofit organizations are private organizations that operate in the public interest. They do not distribute profits to their owners or managers. They thus provide a mechanism for citizen initiative in pursuit of public objectives. To enjoy their advantages and perform their distinctive roles, however, nonprofit organizations must operate free of state control and must serve some definable public purpose.

II. PRIVATE GIVING AND VOLUNTEERING

4. *Volunteering and private giving are crucial elements of a vital voluntary sector.*

The vitality and health of the voluntary sector depend critically on the voluntary contributions of time and resources on the part of private individuals and businesses. Such contributions give the sector an independent base from which to act. Beyond this, they engender a sense of involvement on the part of citizens and contribute usefully to the creation or perpetuation of a tradition of caring within a society.

Efforts to promote giving and volunteering must take account, however, of the multiple impulses from which these activities spring. These impulses are in part altruistic or religious. But these activities fill other needs as well. The value of volunteering can therefore not be judged solely in terms of what it contributes to the recipient. Also important is what it contributes to the giver, and this must be kept in mind in efforts to promote giving and volunteering.

5. *Care should be taken to avoid undue donor influence over the operation of voluntary organizations.*

Private donors, whether domestic or international, should take care to avoid infringing unduly on the autonomy and independence that give voluntary organizations their special character. While such organizations need private support, such support should not carry strings that undermine the basic goals of the organizations.

6. *Volunteering and private giving should be encouraged, but not required, by public and private employers.*

Work practices and policies in government and the private sector should be designed to facilitate voluntarism. But care must be taken to preserve the voluntary character of giving and volunteering. Mandatory requirements for giving and volunteering as a condition of employment are contrary to the ethos of the sector and potentially damaging to the whole concept of voluntary action.

7. *Voluntarism and private giving are not substitutes for paid staff and government resources.*

Private giving and voluntarism add extra resources to the solution of public problems. In a modern society, however, it is highly unlikely that these sources will suffice on their own to respond to human needs. Care must consequently be taken to avoid portraying voluntarism and private giving as substitutes for government, private business, or paid staff. It is more appropriate to view nonprofit organizations as potential partners with business and the state, carrying out functions the market and the state cannot perform, or cannot perform as well, and adding an extra human dimension to efforts to meet human needs.

8. *Voluntary organizations, volunteering, and private giving must all be soundly, and effectively, managed.*

Volunteers, in their roles as board members, direct service providers, and social change agents, need ongoing education, skills training, and supervision to be effective and productive. Similarly, nonprofit organizations must be equipped with competent personnel, adequately trained and, where paid staff are involved, adequately compensated, to carry out their responsibilities.

III.   GOVERNMENT AND THE NONPROFIT SECTOR

Government plays a significant role in the functioning of the voluntary sector. In general, governments should encourage, or at least not discourage, voluntary organizations while respecting their need for a significant degree of autonomy and independence. Key features of a positive government approach toward the voluntary sector include the following:

9. *The right to associate must be clearly and forcefully embedded in law.*

For the voluntary sector to operate with the degree of flexibility and independence that is vital to its existence, the right to organize must be clearly and unequivocally enshrined in a country's legal code. Such legal provisions should provide a broad guarantee of the right to associate, clear criteria for determining eligibility for nonprofit status, and certification procedures that are flexible and involve no unreasonable requirements or delays.

10. *Voluntary organizations acting in the public interest should be eligible for preferential tax treatment.*

To the extent they serve essentially public purposes, voluntary organizations should be exempted, in whole or in part, from taxes on income or expenditures connected with their public-service activities. The ability to obtain such treatment should be clearly defined in law, and the law should require basic accountability on the part of the organizations. The preferential tax treatment afforded voluntary organizations need not extend, however, to the business activities in which these organizations engage.

11. *Government should not discourage contributions by individuals and corporations to support the public-service activities of voluntary organizations, whether these contributions are in cash or in-kind.*

Charitable contributions to voluntary organizations acting in the public interest serve important public objectives. At a minimum, government should avoid actions that penalize such private contributions. Where feasible, it should act to encourage them, for example, by making them exempt from taxation, in whole or in part.

12. *Partnership arrangements between government and the voluntary sector in the delivery of needed services should be encouraged, but in ways that avoid jeopardizing the autonomy and independence of voluntary organizations.*

Government and voluntary organizations bring their own distinctive strengths to the provision of public services. Cooperation between these two sectors can often improve the way needs are met. Voluntary organizations should therefore be ensured access to government funding in a fair and impartial fashion, and Government should actively pursue opportunities to draw on the talents and capabilities of the voluntary sector to deliver publicly financed services. Care must be taken, however, to avoid undue government control over the management or activities of nonprofit organizations as a consequence of these partnership arrangements. This can best be done by encouraging multiple sources of funding.

13. *Government should avoid infringing the independence of the voluntary sector.*

Although government has a right to expect accountability from the voluntary sector in return for its legal protections, tax exemptions, and government contracts, great care must be taken to avoid infringing unreasonably on the independence that is a central strength of the sector. Unreasonable or overburdensome reporting requirements or restrictions on the ability of the nonprofit sector to exercise its advocacy role should consequently be avoided.

14. *Government policy should respect and facilitate the advocacy role of nonprofit organizations.*

One of the central functions of nonprofit organizations is to represent different perspectives in the shaping of government policy. Nonprofit organizations should therefore not be penalized for their advocacy activities. In addition, governments have an obligation to provide the information and access that this advocacy role requires.

15. *Where misuse or mismanagement of voluntary organizations is charged, organizations must have recourse to the courts.*

Misuse of the voluntary organization form, or mismanagement of voluntary organizations, should be penalized. However, the ultimate determination of such abuses and the application of appropriate sanctions should be handled by the courts, not the administrative organs of government, since only the illegality of the practice should be evaluated, not the consistency of the organization's activities with prevailing government policies. Otherwise the independence of the voluntary sector may not be sufficiently protected.

IV. STANDARDS

In return for the special tax and other advantages they often enjoy, voluntary organizations have important obligations:

16. *Voluntary organizations must serve essentially public, as opposed to narrowly private, interests.*

The basic rationale for the tax and other advantages enjoyed by voluntary organizations is the contribution these organizations make to the public interest, broadly defined. Voluntary-organization objectives should therefore be clearly stated and have a significant public-interest dimension, and the organizations should be obliged to adhere to these objectives in order to remain eligible for special treatment. The voluntary-organization form should not be used to shield essentially profit-making activities from tax and other restrictions that would otherwise apply.

17. *Voluntary organizations should regularly disclose their activities and finances, with the level of disclosure related to the level of public support.*

To demonstrate their adherence to public-interest objectives, nonprofit organizations should report at least annually on their activities and finances, and such reports should be open to public scrutiny. Disclosure requirements should bear some relation to the reasonable need for information, however, and should not be unnecessarily or unreasonably burdensome or intrusive.

18. *Nonprofit organizations should be governed in a democratic fashion and provide meaningful opportunities for beneficiary input.*

The governance of voluntary organizations should be fair and democratic. Organizations should generally be governed by self-governing independent bodies, with no financial interest in the organization's activities. Where possible, beneficiaries of the organization, whether domestic or international, should have some meaningful way to influence agency policy and direction.

19. *The staff and boards of voluntary organizations should reap no financial benefits from the operation of their organizations aside from reasonable compensation for services rendered, and agency administrative expenses should not be excessive.*

Voluntary organizations are intended chiefly to serve broad public interests. While this does not mean that agency staff and board members cannot be compensated reasonably for their efforts, it does mean that they should not otherwise benefit financially from the organization's activities. In addition, voluntary organizations should avoid unreasonable levels of administrative or fundraising expenses.

20. *Voluntary organizations must operate in a nondiscriminatory fashion and adhere to basic human standards of mutual respect, compassion, and benevolence.*

As organizations with a significant public-interest mission, voluntary organizations must operate according to high standards of human conduct. Actions that violate basic human rights or deny basic human values of compassion and decency are inconsistent with the objectives that nonprofit organizations are intended to serve and must be avoided.

CONCLUSION

The voluntary sector is an expression of important human values of independence, personal initiative, pluralism, and solidarity. As such, it is to be nurtured and encouraged, both by those within the sector and by those outside it. This requires attention not only to the privileges such organizations should enjoy, but also to the obligations they have as a consequence. Only in this way can a vital voluntary sector emerge on the global level.

Extracts from "Handbook on Good Practices for Laws Relating to Non-Governmental Organizations" (Discussion Draft) World Bank, May 1997*

Because of the growing conviction that a healthy non-governmental organization (NGO) sector makes a strong contribution to development, the Bank has initiated various studies of national NGO sectors. This work has frequently identified the imprecision, restrictiveness, arbitrariness, or unpredictable application of laws relating to NGOs as major problems hampering the development of the sector and preventing individual NGOs from achieving their potential. On the other hand, where NGO laws are lax or non-existent, it is easy for unscrupulous individuals to take advantage and to bring the sector as a whole into disrepute.

These studies have convinced the Bank of the utility of a handbook on good practices regarding NGO laws. They have also yielded a body of evidence relevant to such a task. Hence, in 1995, the Bank commissioned a specialist NGO—the International Center for Not-for-Profit Law (ICNL)—to embark on a major study of existing practice, to distill from this important principles for legislation, and to offer lessons of good practice—recognizing that the characteristics of the NGO sector and society vary from country to country, as does the capacity of governments to implement detailed legislation.

This work has led to the publication of a "discussion draft" of a handbook on NGO Law in May 1997. This will be revised in 1998 in light of comments received and from experience using the Handbook as a tool in NGO law reform. The Bank believes that restrictive NGO laws are inappropriate and would, in the long term, erode public support and confidence in national developmental objectives. The Bank hopes that the Handbook will prove useful in the drafting and debating of new legislation.

* *Source*: World Bank, 1997, "Handbook on Good Practices for Laws Relating to NGOs," Handbook, World Bank, Social Policy Division, Environment Department, Washington, D.C.

This handbook does not present a model law because the legal systems of the world differ in large and small ways, and local traditions of law drafting are also varied. It is intended, however, to set forth principles which would enable any interested and informed reader to evaluate an existing NGO law or draft a better one. Any NGO law should, of course, be suitable to the circumstances of the country and should be prepared in consultation with representatives of the NGO sector.

The extracts which follow are the basic principles set out in the Handbook. In the Handbook, each principle is discussed and qualified, and illustrations and alternatives are frequently given. The full Handbook also provides definitions of terms (in Section 1) and a discussion of the breadth of the NGO sector and its potential contributions to society and to national development. The summary below of the basic principles is intended to provide readers with an overview of the topics discussed in the World Bank's Handbook, and to illustrate the range of issues which might appropriately be addressed through NGO laws. Readers who are puzzled, or in disagreement with one or more principles set out, are urged to obtain a full copy of the Handbook (available from the NGO Unit, World Bank, Room S-10-103, 1818 H Street NW, Washington DC 20433; tel: (202) 473-1840) and read the full discussion. Similarly, anyone engaged in formulating or critiquing a specific NGO law, are invited to request a copy of the full Handbook. The Bank hopes that the handbook will prove useful in the drafting and debating of new or revised legislation.

Good Practices for Laws Relating to NGOs

Relationship of NGO Laws to Other Laws

Section 2: Relationship of Laws Governing NGOs to Other Laws in a Legal System.

(a) *Rights, Remedies, and Sanctions.* NGOs should have the same rights, privileges, powers and immunities generally applicable to legal persons, and they should be subject to the same civil law and criminal law prohibitions, procedures, and sanctions that are generally applicable to legal persons.

(b) *Administrative and Judicial Review.* All acts or decisions affecting NGOs should be subject to the same rights of administrative and judicial review that are generally applicable to legal persons. Specifically, decisions to refuse to establish an NGO, to impose fines, taxes, or other sanctions on it, or to dissolve or terminate it, should be appealable to independent courts.

(c) *Special Issues of Federal Systems.* In any federal system careful consideration must be given to which sets of legal rules NGOs should be enacted and administered at the national level and which at the state, provincial, or local level.

(d) *Conflicts of Laws Problems.* Although important, these issues are outside the scope of this Handbook.

Legal Existence of NGOs

Section 3: Establishment (Registration or Incorporation).

(a) Laws governing NGOs should be written and administered so that it is relatively quick, easy, and inexpensive to establish an NGO as a legal person. Establishment should also be allowed for branches of both foreign and domestic NGOs.

(b) The establishment of an NGO should require filing a minimum number of clearly defined documents and should be a ministerial act involving a minimum of bureaucratic judgment or discretion.

(c) The establishment rules should set reasonable time limits within which the establishment agency must act (e.g., 60 days), and it is generally a good practice to provide that failure to act within the required time results in presumptive approval.

(d) NGOs should be allowed to have perpetual existence (or limited existence, if chosen by the founders).

(e) Both natural and legal persons should be entitled to create NGOs.

(f) Individuals should be allowed to create an NGO (e.g., a foundation) by testamentary act (e.g., by a will).

(g) Both mutual benefit and public benefit organizations should be allowed to exist.

(h) As a general matter, membership in a membership organization should be voluntary, viz., no person should be required to join or continue to belong to an organization.

Section 4: Responsible Governmental Agency. The agency vested with the responsibility for establishing NGOs should be adequately staffed with competent professionals, it should be even-handed in fulfilling its role, and its decision not to establish an NGO or to terminate one should be appealable, both administratively and to an independent court.

Section 5: Amendments to Established Status. It should be possible for an NGO to amend its governing documents without having to entirely re-establish the organization.

Section 6: Amendment in the Event of Impossibility. There should be a procedure for amending the governing documents of an organization even if the organization cannot do so by its own independent action.

Section 7: Public Registry. Whether NGOs are established in one or many locations, and in addition to any local registries, there should be a single, national registry of all NGOs that is accessible to the public.

Section 8: Mergers and Split-ups. There should be clear rules allowing, but not compelling, NGOs to merge or split up. Mergers may be limited to organizations involved in similar endeavors.

Section 9: Termination, Liquidation, and Dissolution.

(a) *Voluntary termination.* An NGO should be permitted to terminate its activities and liquidate its assets upon the decision of its highest governing body.

(b) *Involuntary termination.* The supervising agency or court should be allowed to terminate an NGO's existence only for the most flagrant of violations, or repeated failure to comply with certain rules (e.g., persistent failure to file required reports). Except in the case of flagrant fraud or other abuse, NGOs should ordinarily be permitted to correct infractions rather than suffering involuntary termination; where corrections do not occur, termination may be warranted.

Structure and Governance

Section 10: Minimum Requirements of Governing Documents. The laws governing NGOs should require minimum provisions in the governing documents of an NGO, such as that the highest governing body (assembly of members or board of directors) must meet with a given frequency, that the governing body is the sole body with power to amend the basic documents of the organization or decide upon merger, split up, or termination, that it must approve the financial statement of the organization, and so forth.

Section 11: Optional Provisions and Special Requirements. Laws governing NGOs should give an NGO (through its founders or its highest governing body) broad discretion to set and change the governance structure and operation of the organization.

Section 12: Liabilities of Officers and Directors.

(a) Laws governing NGOs should provide that officers, directors, and employees of an NGO should not be personally liable for the debts, obligations, or liabilities of the NGO.

(b) Officers and directors should be liable to the organization and/or to injured third parties for willful or grossly negligent performance or neglect of their duties.

Section 13: Duties of Loyalty, Diligence, and Confidentiality.

(a) The law should provide that officers and directors of an NGO have a duty to exercise loyalty to the organization, to execute their responsibilities to the organization with care and diligence, and to maintain the confidentiality of non-public information about the organization.

(b) The NGO itself, or any affected person in the society, should be allowed to sue for redress or any violations of these duties.

Section 14: Prohibition on Conflicts of Interest.

(a) Careful consideration should be given to the extent to which the law should provide that officers, directors, and employees of an NGOs must avoid any actual or potential conflict between their personal or business interests and the interests of the NGO; laws affecting conflicts of interest for officers and directors of for-profit entities may be adapted to apply to NGOs.

(b) Potential conflicts may be avoided through recusal procedures.

(c) An NGO should be entitled to sue for redress of any harm caused by a conflict of interest.

Prohibition on Direct or Indirect Private Benefit

Section 15: Prohibition on the Distribution of Profits.   Laws governing NGOs should provide that no net earnings or profits of an NGO may be distributed as such to any person.

This principle—the principle of non-distribution—is the single most important feature distinguishing NGOs from for-profit entities.

Section 16: Prohibition on Private Inurement.

(a) The laws governing NGOs should provide that officers or employees of an NGO may be paid reasonable compensation for work actually performed for an NGO, plus reimbursement for reasonable expenses and reasonable fringe benefits. Directors would generally not be compensated.

(b) The laws governing NGOs should provide that the assets, earnings, and profits of an NGO may not be used to provide special personal benefits, directly or indirectly, (e.g., scholarships for relatives) for any person connected with the NGO (e.g., officer, director, employee, founder, or donor).

(c) In the case of a Mutual Benefits Organisation, benefits may be made available to members if they are available on a nondiscriminatory basis to all members (e.g., special educational materials or insurance plans).

Section 17: Prohibition on Self-Dealing.

(a) Laws governing NGOs should provide that any transaction (e.g., sale, lease, or loan) between an NGO and any person connected with it (e.g., officer, director, employee, founder, or donor) must be consummated, if at all, at arms'-length and for fair market value.

(b) It may be appropriate to prohibit entirely certain kinds of transactions that have a very high potential for abuse.

(c) An NGO should be entitled to sue for redress of any harm caused by self-dealing.

Section 18: Prohibition on the Reversion of Assets.

(a) Laws governing NGOs should provide that no Public Benefit Organisation should be permitted to distribute assets to its members, officers, directors, employees, or founders upon the liquidation or termination of the NGO.

(b) An exception permitting distribution of assets to members upon termination after the payment of all liabilities of the NGO may be appropriate in the case of a Mutual Benefit Organisation which never received significant contributions from the public (i.e., persons not affiliated with it as founders, donors, officers, directors, employees, or members) or significant grants, contracts, or tax preferences from the government.

Activities and Operations of NGOs

Section 19: Economic Activities. An NGO should be permitted to engage in lawful economic, business, or commercial activities for the purpose of supporting its not-for-profit activities, provided that (i) no profits or earnings are distributed as such to founders, members, officers, directors, or employees, and (ii) the NGO is organized and operated principally for the purpose of conducting appropriate not-for-profit activities (e.g., culture, education, health, and so forth).

Section 20: Licenses and Permits. Any NGO that engages in an activity (e.g., health care, education, banking) that is subject to licensing or regulation by a government agency should generally be subject to the same licensing and regulatory requirements and procedures that apply to similar activities of individuals, business organizations, or public agencies.

Section 21: Political Activities.

(a) In general, NGOs are not political parties and should not be allowed to engage in the kinds of activities normally the preserve of political parties, such as fundraising to support candidates for public office or registering candidates to qualify for public office.

(b) NGOs are often key participants in framing and debating issues of public policy, and they should have the right to speak freely on matters of public debate, even where the positions they take are not in accord with stated government policy. Appropriate intervention by NGOs in such matters includes research, education, and advocacy activities.

Fund Raising

Section 22: Solicitation—Limitations, Standards, and Remedies.

(a) An NGO should be prohibited from engaging in any misrepresentation in connection with the solicitation of funds from others, each NGO should be required to divulge, in connection with its fundraising, the extent to which its funds are used to defray the direct and indirect costs of fundraising, and licensing is appropriate for public fundraising.

(b) Lotteries, charity balls, auctions, and other occasional activities conducted primarily to raise funds for an NGO are a form of fund raising and should not be regarded as economic or commercial activities.

Reporting

Section 23: Internal Reporting and Supervision.

(a) The highest governing body of an NGO (the assembly of members or the board of directors) should be required to receive and approve reports on the finances and operations of an NGO.

(b) Some organ of the NGO (e.g., an audit committee of the board) should be required (and each member of a membership NGO should have the right) to inspect the books and records of the organization.

(c) An NGO with substantial activities or assets should be required to have its financial reports audited by an independent certified or chartered accountant.

Section 24: Reporting to and Audit by Supervising Agency.

(a) Any registered NGO that has activities that significantly affect the public interest should be required to file reasonably detailed reports annually on its finances and operations with the agency responsible for general supervision of NGOs. In certain specialized situations more frequent reporting may be appropriate.

(b) All reporting requirements should make appropriate provision to protect the legitimate privacy interests of donors and recipients of benefits as well as the protection of confidential information.

(c) The supervising agency should have the right to examine the books, records, and activities of an NGO during ordinary business hours.

(d) Small NGOs should be allowed to file simplified reports or none at all.

(e) All NGOs should be subject to random and selective audit by the supervising agency, and very large NGOs should be audited annually.

(f) Mutual Benefit Organisations can generally be exempted from reporting requirements, or required to file simplified reports, except to the extent that they engage significantly in public interest activities.

Section 25: Reporting to and Audit by Tax Authorities.

(a) It is appropriate for separate reports to be filed with the taxing authority(ies), though efforts should be made to make these reports as consistent as possible with the financial reports filed with the general supervising agency.

(b) It is generally inappropriate for the taxing authority(ies) to examine any aspects of an NGO other than those directly related to taxation (including whether the requirements for exemption from taxation have been satisfied).

(c) Small NGOs should be exempted from filing tax reports or allowed to file simplified ones.

Section 26: Reporting to and Audit by Licensing Agencies.

(a) Any NGO engaged in an activity subject to the licensing or regulatory control of an agency of the state should be required to file the same reports with that agency as individuals or business entities are required to file.

(b) A licensing agency should have the right to audit and inspect the NGO for compliance with applicable licensing or regulatory requirements, but should not generally examine or supervise other aspects of the NGO.

Section 27: Reporting to Donors. Substantial donors to an NGO should be entitled to contract for disclosure of information adequate for the donor to assess the suitability of the NGO for receipt of donations and the use(s) to which donations, or that particular donor's donations, are put.

Section 28: Disclosure or Availability of Information to the Public. Any NGO with activities that significantly affect the public interest should be required to publish or make available to the public a report of its general finances and operations;

this report may be less detailed than the reports filed with the general supervisory agency, the taxing authority(ies), or any licensing or regulatory body and should permit anonymity for donors and recipients of benefits as well as protection of confidential information.

Section 29: Special Sanctions. In addition to the general sanctions to which an NGO is subject equally with other legal persons (e.g., contract or tort law), it is appropriate to have special sanctions (e.g., fines or penalty taxes, involuntary termination) for violations peculiar to NGOs (e.g., self-dealing or improper solicitation).

Taxation

Section 30: Income Taxation Exemption of NGOs. Every NGO, whether organized for mutual benefit or for public benefit, and whether a membership or non-membership organization, should be exempt from income taxation on moneys or other items of value received from donors or governmental agencies (by grant or contract), membership dues, if any, and any interest, dividends, rents, royalties or capital gains earned on assets or the sale of assets.

Section 31: Income Tax Deductions or Credits for Donations. Within reasonably generous limits, individuals and business entities should be entitled to an income tax deduction or credit with respect to donations made to Public Benefit Organisations (but not Mutual Benefit Organisations). As a matter of tax policy, credits are preferable to deductions for individuals under a progressive income tax system, though deductions may attract more and larger gifts from wealthy donors.

Section 32: Taxation of Economic Activities. NGOs should be allowed to engage in economic activities so long as those activities do not constitute the principal purpose or activity of the organization. Any net profit earned by an NGO from the active conduct of a trade or business could be—
    (a) exempted from income taxation,
    (b) subjected to income taxation,
    (c) subjected to income taxation only if the trade or business is not related to and in furtherance of the not-for-profit purposes of the organization, or
    (d) subjected to a mechanical test that allows a modest amount of profits from economic activities to escape taxation, but imposes tax on amounts in excess of the limit.

Section 33: VAT and Customs Duties.

    (a) Public Benefit Organisations should be given preferential treatment under a value added tax (VAT).
    (b) Public Benefit Organisations should be given preferential treatment under or exemption from customs duties on imported goods or services that are used to further their public benefit purposes.

Section 34: Other Taxes.

(a) Depending upon the extent to which a government wishes to encourage NGOs, exemption from or preferential treatment under other tax laws (e.g., taxes on real or personal property, sales taxes, estate or inheritance taxes) should be considered.

(b) No NGO should be exempted or given preferential treatment under generally applicable employment or payroll taxes.

Foreign NGOs and Foreign Funds

Section 35: Establishment and Supervision of Foreign NGOs.

(a) An NGO that is organized and operated under the laws of one country but which has, or intends to have, operations, programs, or assets, in another country should generally be allowed to operate as an NGO in that other country, or to create a subsidiary or affiliated organization under the laws of that other country, and such organization or its branch, subsidiary, or affiliate should enjoy all of the rights, powers, privileges and immunities of NGOs in that other country, and be subject to all of the requirements, responsibilities, duties, and sanctions applicable to NGOs in that other country as long as the activities of the foreign NGOs are consistent with the ordre publique of the host country.

(b) Although the general restriction on political activities by NGOs, the general requirements of reporting and disclosure, and the right of the supervising agency to audit and inspect the books, records, and activities of an NGO should generally preclude (or punish) the misuse of the NGO laws of one country by entities from another, in certain rare and highly sensitive circumstances it may be appropriate to deny a foreign NGO the right to operate in another country or to impose special requirements or restrictions on it.

Section 36: Foreign Funding.

(a) An NGO that is properly established or incorporated in one country should generally be allowed to solicit and receive cash or in kind donations or transfers from another country, a multilateral agency, or an institutional or individual donor in another country, so long as all generally applicable foreign exchange and customs laws are satisfied.

(b) Although the general restriction on political activities by NGOs, the requirement to report on the receipt and utilization of funds, and the right of the supervising agency to audit and inspect the books, records, and activities of an NGO should generally preclude (or punish) the improper use of foreign funds, in certain rare and highly sensitive circumstances it may be appropriate to require advance approval for the receipt of funds or property from abroad.

Other Government—NGO Relations

Section 37: QUANGOS and GONGOS. Although there are many appropriate roles for quasi-nongovernmental organizations or government organized or controlled NGOs (e.g., museums, research institutes, special lending or credit programs), great care must be taken to prevent the use of such entities to benefit government officials, directly or indirectly, either politically or monetarily. Special care must also be taken to avoid inappropriate discrimination against independent NGOs.

Section 38: Government Grants and Contracts.   There should be an open, fair, and nondiscriminatory bidding, tender, or procurement process for all substantial grants or purchases by or contracts from a governmental body or agency for goods, services, or assets.

Section 39: Transfer of Assets and Services Out of the Public Sector.   Consideration should be given to using NGOs to transfer various government assets or programs (e.g., educational, medical, research, or cultural) out of the governmental sector and into the NGO sector if they could be run more efficiently by an NGO or if they might be supported in whole or in part through private donations.

Self-Regulation

Section 40: Self-regulation.   Self-regulation is essential to the existence of a well-ordered NGO sector.

(a) Individual NGOs should be permitted and encouraged to adopt explicit standards for regulating their own activities.

(b) Groups of NGOs should be permitted and encouraged to set higher standards of conduct and performance through self-regulation.

(c) It is appropriate to encourage the establishment of "watchdog" organizations to monitor and evaluate organizations in the NGO sector.

(d) In certain circumstances where it is appropriate to make membership in an organization mandatory, it may be appropriate for the legislature to delegate to that organization the authority to license, regulate, supervise, and sanction members.

BIBLIOGRAPHY

Amenomori, T. "Defining the Nonprofit Sector: Japan." In L.M. Salamon and H.K. Anheier (eds.), *Defining the Nonprofit Sector: A Cross-National Analysis.* Manchester: Manchester University Press, 1997.

Aristotle. *The Politics*, translated and with an introduction by Lord. Chicago: University of Chicago Press, 1984.

Atkinson, R. "Altruism in Nonprofit Organizations." 31 *Boston College Law Review* No. 3, May 1990.

Atkinson, R. *Theories of the Federal Income Tax Exemption for Charities: Thesis, Antithesis, and Syntheses.* New York: New York University School of Law, 1991.

Barber, B.R. "Jihad vs. McWorld." *The Atlantic*, March 1992.

Baron, B. ed. *Philanthropy and the Dynamics of Change in East and Southeast Asia.* New York: Columbia University, 1992.

Barron, J.A. and Dienes, C.T. *Constitutional Law.* St. Paul: West Publishing, 1986.

Baxi, U. "The 'Struggle' for the Redefinition of Secularism in India: Some Preliminary Reflections." 44 *Social Action* 1, 1994.

Bellah, R. et al. *Habits of the Heart: Individualism and Commitment in American Life.* Berkeley: University of California Press, 1985.

Bentham, J. *An Introduction to the Principles of Morals and Legislation.* Edited by J. Burns and H. Hart. New York: Clarendon Press, 1996.

Bevaart, J. "The Function and Legal Status of Foundations in the Netherlands." In van der Ploeg, T. and Sap, J., *Rethinking the Balance: Government and Nongovernment Organizations in the Netherlands.* Amsterdam: VU University Press, 1995.

Blair, H. "Civil Society and Democratic Development." Design paper prepared by the Center for Development Information and Evaluation. U.S. Agency for International Development, February 18, 1994.

Blaise, H. "*Une Transaction Sans Concessions.*" *Droit Social*, No. 5, 1988.

Blaney, D.L. et al. "Civil Society and Democracy in the Third World: Ambiguities and Historical Possibilities." 28 *Studies in Comparative International Development* 1, Spring 1993.

Bromley, E.B. "Exporting Civil Society: Confessions of a 'Foreign Legal Expert.'" International Charity Law Conference Papers. London: National Council of Voluntary Organisations, September 1994.

Chazan, N. "Africa's Democratic Challenge: Strengthening Civil Society and the State." 9 *World Policy Journal* No. 2, Spring 1992.

Chesterman, M.R. *Charities, Trusts and Social Welfare.* London: Butterworths, 1979.

Chisolm, L. "Exempt Organization Advocacy: Matching the Rules to the Rationales." 63 *Indiana Law Journal* No. 2, 1987–1988.

Clotfelter, C. *Federal Tax Policy and Charitable Giving.* Chicago: University of Chicago Press, 1985.

Clotfelter, C. and Salamon, L.M. "The Federal Government and the Nonprofit Sector: The Impact of the 1981 Tax Act on Individual Charitable Giving." 35 *National Tax Journal* No. 2, 1982.

Cohen, J. and Arato, A. *Civil Society and Political Theory.* Cambridge: MIT Press, 1992.

Commission of the European Communities. *European Treaty Series No. 124.* Strasbourg: Conseil de l'Europe, Aug. 1990.

—— *Proposal for a Council Regulation on the Statute for a European Association.* In COM(91) 273 final—SYN 386–391, March 5, 1992.

Commission on Private Philanthropy and Public Needs. *Report of the Commission on Private Philanthropy and Public Needs: Giving in America—Toward a Stronger Voluntary Sector.* [Filer Commission Report] Washington: Commission on Private Philanthropy and Public Needs, 1975.

Committee on Fundraising Activities for Charitable and Other Purposes. *Report.* Dublin: Stationary Office, 1990.

Consumer Education and Research Centre. *A Directory of Philanthropic Organizations in Ahmedabad.* Ahmedabad: Consumer Education and Research Centre, 1991.

Cook, J., Lamppon, D. E., and Quigley, K. "The Rise of Nongovernmental Organizations in China." 2 *China Policy Series* No. 8. New York: National Committee on China Relations, 1994.

Cousins, M. *A Guide to Legal Structures for Volunteering and Community Organizations.* Dublin: Combat Poverty Agency, 1994.

Dadrawala, N.H. *Handbook on Administration of Trusts.* Bombay: Centre for Advancement of Philanthropy, 1991.

Dadrawala, N. *Management of Philanthropic Organisations.* Bombay: Centre for Advancement of Philanthropy, 1996.

Dahrendorf, R. *Reflections on the Revolution in Europe.* New York: Random House, 1990.

Dale, H. "Foreign Charities." 48 *Tax Lawyer* No. 3, 1994.

David, R. and Briley, J.E.L. *Major Legal Systems in the World Today: An Introduction to the Comparative Study of Law,* 3rd ed. London: Stevens, 1990.

De Giorgi, M.V. "Associazioni–Associazoni riconosciute," In *Enciclopedia giuridica Treccani,* vol. III, Rome, 1988.

de Tocqueville, A. *Democracy in America.* New York: Vintage Books, 1945 (1840).

Diamond, L. "Rethinking Civil Society: Toward Democratic Consolidation." 5 *Journal of Democracy* No. 3, July 1994.

Duparc, C. *The European Commission and Human Rights.* Brussels: Commission of the European Communities, 1992.

Ethical Code of the Union of Bulgarian Foundations. Sofia: Union of Bulgarian Foundations, 1993.

European Commission Delegation to the United States. *The European Union: A Guide,* 1994.

Exempt Organizations Continuing Professional Education Technical Instruction Program. 16th ed. Washington: Internal Revenue Service, 1992.

BIBLIOGRAPHY

Exempt Organization Handbook. Washington: Internal Revenue Service, periodic updates.

Fearn, D. and Hondius, F. (eds.) "Glossary of Terminology in the Field of Charities, Foundations and other Non-profit Organisations." 2 *Studies in Philanthropy*. Geneva: Interphil, July 1977.

Flaherty, S.L.Q. "The Voluntary Sector and Corporate Citizenship in the United States and Japan." 2 *Voluntas* No. 1, 1991.

Fuller, J. *The Law of Friendly Societies*. 4th ed. Stevens and Sons, 1926.

Gabor, H. "Aspects of Accountability: From Theory to the Hungarian Practice." International Charity Law Conference Papers. London: National Council of Voluntary Organisations, September 1994.

Galgano, F. *Le associazioni, le fondazioni, i comitati*. Padova: Cedam, 1987.

Geremek, B. "Civil Society Then and Now." 3 *Journal of Democracy* No. 2, April 1992.

Gjems-Onstad, O. "The Proposed European Association: A Symbol in Need of Friends." International Charity Law Conference Papers. London: National Council of Voluntary Organisations, September 1994.

—— "The Taxation of Unrelated Business Income of Nonprofit Organizations." International Charity Law Conference Papers. London: National Council of Voluntary Organisations, September 1994.

Gold, T. "The Resurgence of Civil Society in China." 1 *Journal of Democracy* No. 1, Winter 1990.

Goodwin, C. et al., eds. *Beyond Government: Extending the Public Policy Debate in Emerging Democracies*. Denver: Westview Press, 1995.

Gooley, J.V. *A Guide to Corporations and Associations Law*. Sydney: Magna Carta Press, 1989.

Gross, J.T. "Poland: From Civil Society to Political Nation." In J. Banac, ed., *Eastern Europe in Revolution*. Ithaca: Cornell University Press, 1992.

Halsbury's Laws of England, 4th ed, vol. 9. London: Butterworths, 1974.

Hansmann, H. "Unfair Competition and the Unrelated Business Income Tax." 75 *Virginia Law Review* No. 3, 1989.

—— "The Role of Nonprofit Enterprise." 89 *Yale Law Journal* No. 5, 1980.

Havel, V. et al. *The Power of the Powerless*. Armonk: M. E. Sharpe, 1985.

Hemström, C. *Organisationernas rättsliga stallning. Om ekonomiska och ideella föreningar*. Norstedts juridik, Studentlitteratur AB, Lund, 1992.

Hondius, F. "Charities and International Law." International Charity Law Conference Papers. London: National Council of Voluntary Organisations, September 1994.

Hopkins, B. and Tesdahl, D. *Intermediate Sanctions: Curbing Nonprofit Abuse*. New York: John Wiley & Sons, 1997.

Hopkins B. *The Law of Fund-Raising*. New York: John Wiley & Sons, Inc., 1991.

—— *The Law of Tax Exempt Organizations*, 6th ed. New York: John Wiley & Sons, 1992.

Huntington, S. *The Third Wave: Democratization in the Late Twentieth Century.* Norman: University of Oklahoma Press, 1991.

Industry Commission. *Charitable Organizations in Australia. Report No. 45.* Melbourne: Australian Government Publishing Service, 1995.

Industry Commission. *Charitable Organizations in Australia. Report No. 45.* Melbourne: Government Publishing Service, 1984.

Inkeles, A. "Participant Citizenship in Six Developing Countries." 63 *American Political Science Review* No. 4, 1969.

Jimenez de Barros, M. "Mobilizing for Democracy in Chile: The Crusade for Citizen Participation and Beyond." In Diamond, L. (ed.), *The Democratic Revolution: Struggles for Freedom and Pluralism in the Developing World.* New York: Freedom House, 1992.

Katz, S. "Philanthropy and Democracy: Which Comes First?" *Advancing Philanthropy* 1, New York: National Society of Fund Raising Executives, Summer 1994.

Keane, J., (ed.). *Civil Society and the State: New European Perspectives.* New York: Verso, 1988.

Keane, R. *Company Law in the Republic of Ireland.* 2d ed. Dublin, Butterworths, 1991.

Kozma, G. and Petrik, F. *Társadalmi szervezetek, alapítványok létrehozása és gazdálkodása. Jogszabályok, bírói gyakorlat és ezek magyarázata.* Budapest: UNIÓ Lap-és Könyvkiadó, 1990.

Linehan, M. and Tucker, V. eds. *Co-op Guides.* Cork: Centre for Co-operative Studies, 1988.

Lloyd, S. *Charities Trading and the Law.* London: Charities Advisory Trust, 1995.

Logan, D. *U.S. Corporate Grantmaking in a Global Age.* Washington: Council on Foundations, 1989.

Lyons, M. *Private Donations and Australia's Welfare State.* CACOM Working Paper No. 15. Sydney: University of Technology, 1993.

Lyons, M. *Tax Deductibility of Donations to Community Welfare Organizations. A Report of a Survey.* CACOM Working Paper No. 17. Sydney: University of Technology, 1993.

Lyons, M. "Australia's Nonprofit Sector." In S. Saxon-Harrold and J. Kendall, eds., *Researching the Voluntary Sector.* 2nd ed. London: Charities Aid Foundation, 1994.

Lyons, M. *Reforming Australia's Community Services: A Review of Proposals.* CACOM Working Paper No. 28. Sydney: University of Technology, 1995.

Magarey, D.R. *Guide to the NSW Co-operatives Law.* Sydney: CCH Australia, 1994.

Mathew, P.D. *Law on the Registration of Societies.* New Delhi: Indian Social Institute, 1994.

Micou, A. and Lindsnaes, B. eds. *The Role of Voluntary Organizations in Emerging Democracies.* New York: Institute of International Education, The Danish-Centre for Human Rights, 1993.

Middleton, F. and Lloyd, S. *Charities: The New Law (The Charities Act 1992).* London: Jordan & Sons Ltd., 1992.

Nial, H. *Svensk associationsrätt*. 5th ed., Lund Norsteadts, 1991.

Noakes, G. and Carrabs, A. "Charities, Philanthropies and Non-profit Organizations: The Impact of Other Taxes." In R. Krever and G. Kewley, eds., *Charities and Philanthropic Organizations. Reforming the Tax Subsidy and Regulatory Regimes*. Melbourne: Monash University and Australian Tax Research Foundation, 1992.

Oomen, F.J. *Stichting & Vereniging*. Deventer: Kluwer, 1990.

Paines, A. "Charities and Europe." 136 *Solicitors Journal*, No. 16 Supplement, April 24, 1992.

Paul, K. "U.S. Corporate Philanthropy in South Africa, 1977–89: The Impact of the Sullivan Signatories and Their Projects." *Spring Research Forum Working Papers, The Nonprofit Sector (NGO's) in the United States and Abroad: Cross-Cultural Perspectives*. Washington: Independent Sector, 1990.

Perez-Diaz, V. *The Return of Civil Society: The Emergence of Democratic Spain*. Cambridge: Harvard University Press, 1993.

Picarda on Charities. 2d ed. London: Butterworths, 1995.

Piñar Mañas, José Luis. *Regimen Jurídico de las Fundaciones: Jurisprudencia del Turibunal Constitutional y del Trubunal Supremo*. Madrid: Ministerio de Asuntos Sociales, 1992.

Piñar Mañas, José Luis and Real Pérez, A. *Legislación sobre Institutuciones de Beneficia Particular*. Madrid, Ministero de Trabajo, 1987.

Pongsapich, A. and Kataleeradabhan. "Philanthropy, NGO Activities and Corporate Funding in Thailand." Final draft paper under the auspices of the Social Research Institute, Chulalongkorn University, December 1993.

PRIA (The Society for Participatory Research in Asia). *Forms of Organisations: Square Pegs in Round Holes*. New Delhi: PRIA, 1987.

PRIA (The Society for Participatory Research in Asia). *Management of Voluntary Organisations*. New Delhi: PRIA, 1989.

PRIA (The Society for Participatory Research in Asia). *Manual on Financial Management and Account Keeping*. New Delhi: PRIA, 1990.

Putnam, R., *Making Democracy Work: Civic Traditions in Modern Italy*. Princeton: Princeton University Press, 1993.

Randon, A. and G, P. "Constraining Campaigning: Legal Treatment of Advocacy." 5 *Voluntas* No. 1, 1994.

Rau, Z. ed. *The Reemergence of Civil Society in Eastern Europe and the Soviet Union*. Boulder: Westview Press, 1991.

Robert's Rules of Order: The Standard Guide to Parliamentary Procedure. London: Bantam Books, originally 1876.

Rodman, S. and McGregor-Lowndes, M. "Income Tax Exemptions for Nonprofit Associations." In M. McGregor-Lowndes, M. Fletcher and A. Sievers (eds.), Legal Issues for Nonprofit Associations. Sydney: LBC Information Services, 1996.

Rudney, G. "Tax Rules and Overseas Philanthropy." *Philanthropy Monthly*, August 1978.

Salamon, L.M. "The Rise of the Nonprofit Sector." 73 *Foreign Affairs* No. 4, July / August 1994.

Salamon L.M., "The Nonprofit Sector and Democracy: Prerequisite, Impediment, or Irrelevance?" Paper prepared for the Aspen Institute Nonprofit Sector Research Fund Symposium on "Democracy and the Nonprofit Sector." Wye, Maryland, December 14, 1993.

—— *The Nonprofit Sector: A Primer.* New York: The Foundation Center, 1992.

—— and Anheier, H.K. *The Emerging Nonprofit Sector: An Overview.* Manchester: Manchester University Press, 1996.

—— and Anheier, H.K. "In Search of the Nonprofit Sector I: The Question of Definitions." 3 *Voluntas* No. 2, 1992.

—— and Anheier, H.K. "Caring Society or Caring Sector: Discovering the Nonprofit Sector Cross-Nationally." In Schervisch P. and Hodgkinson, V. eds., *The Future of Caring and Service to the Community.* San Francisco: Jossey-Bass, 1994.

Sárközi, T. "Az alapítványok jogi szabályozása Magyarországon," In Kuti, É. (ed.), *Alapitványi Almanach.* Budapest: Magyarországi Alapítványok Szövetsége, 1991.

Seligman, A. *The Idea of Civil Society.*, Glencoe: Free Press, 1992.

Shils, E.A. "The Virtue of Civil Society." 26 *Government and Opposition* No 1, March 1991.

Siegel, D. and Yancey, J. *The Rebirth of Civil Society.* New York: Rockefeller Brothers Fund, 1992.

Sievers, A.S. *Associations and Club Law in Australia and New Zealand.* 2nd ed. Sydney: Federation Press, 1996.

Skjelsbaek, K. "The Growth of International Nongovernmental Organizations in the Twentieth Century." In R. Keohane and J. Nye (eds.), *Transnational Relations and World Politics.* Cambridge: Harvard University Press, 1972.

Smith, J., Pagnucco, R., and Romeril, W. "Transnational Social Movement Organisations in the Global Arena." 5 *Voluntas* No. 2, 1994.

Starr, F. "The Third Sector in the Second World." 19 *World Development* No. 1, United Kingdom: Pergamon Press, 1991.

—— "Soviet Union: A Civil Society." 70 *Foreign Policy* No. 1, Spring 1988.

Surrey, S. *Pathways to Tax Reform.* Cambridge: Harvard University Press, 1973.

Tax Treaties. Washington: Commerce Clearing House.

Thomas, G. "The Legal Position of the Nonprofit Sector in the U.K." *Field Guide No. 3, Johns Hopkins Comparative Nonprofit Sector Project, U.K.* Baltimore: Johns Hopkins Institute for Policy Studies, 1993.

Tismaneanu, V. ed. *In Search of Civil Society.* New York: Routledge, 1990.

Tudor on Charities, 8th ed. London: Sweet & Maxwell, 1995.

Underhill A. and Hayton, D. *Law Relating to Trusts and Trustees*, 15th ed. London: Butterworths, 1995.

The United Nations and Non-Governmental Organizations. United Nations, New York (no date given).

United Nations. ECOSOC Resolution 1296 (XLIV), Part I.

U.S. House of Representatives. H. R. 1860, 75th Cong., 3rd Sess., 1938.

Usher, P. *Company Law in Ireland.* London: Sweet and Maxwell, 1986.

van der Ploeg, Dijk, [Overes, C., van der Ploeg, T. (ed.), Schwartz, C. and van Veen, W.] Van Vereniging en Stifting, Cooperatie em Onderlinge Waarborg-maatschappij. 3d ed. Arnhem: Gouda Quint, 1997.

Van Veen, W.J.M. "Privaatrechtelijke aspecten van decentralisatie." In M.J. van Eijk *et al.* (eds.) *Gesloten of open overlegstelsel.* 's-Gravenhage: SDU juridische & Fiscale: Uitgeverij, 1993.

Verick, A. and Lamerton, J. "Tax Concessions for Charitable Bodies and Philanthropies: Administration of the Tests." R. Krever and G. Kewley, eds., *Charities and Philanthropic Organizations. Reforming the Tax Subsidy and Regulatory Regimes.* Melbourne: Monash University and Australian Tax Research Foundation, 1992.

Weigle, M.A. and Butterfield, J. "Civil Society in Reforming Communist Regimes: The Logic of Emergence." XXV *Comparative Politics* 1, October 1992.

Weisbrod, B. "Tax Policy Toward Non-Profit Organizations: An Eleven Country Survey." 2 *Voluntas* No. 1, 1991.

Weithorn, S. *Tax Techniques for Foundations and Other Exempt Organizations.* New York: Matthew Bender, 1975.

Wester, M.J. "Central Bureau on Fund Raising and how is fundraising organized in the Netherlands." In van der Ploeg, T. and Sap, J., *Rethinking the Balance: Government and Nongovernment Organizations in the Netherlands.* Amsterdam: VU University Press, 1995.

Wuthnow, R. ed. *Between States and Markets: The Voluntary Sector in Comparative Perspective.* Princeton: Princeton University Press, 1991.

Wylie, J. *Irish Land Law.* Dublin: Butterworths, 1986.

INDEX

T

INDEX

India, 11.2(a)(ii), 11.2(d)(ii), 11.3(b)
Republic of Ireland, 12.2(a)(v)
Mexico, 16.2(a)(iii)
South Africa, 20.2(a)(ii), 20.2(d)(ii)
United Kingdom, 24(a)(v)
United States, 25.2(a)(iii)

U

Union:
Egypt, 7.2(a)(iii)
France, 8.2(a)(iv)
India, 11.2(a)(iv)
United Kingdom, 1.1(a), 2.10(d)
business activity, 24.7
Charitable Trusts Act of 1853, 24.3(a)(i)
Charitable Uses Act of 1601, 2.2(b), 24.2(b)(i)
Charities Act, 24.1
1960, 24.2(b)(i), 24.3(a)(i)
1964, 24.2(b)(ii), 24.3(a)(ii)
1985, 24.3(a)(i), 24.3(b)(iii), 24.5(b)
1992, 24.3(a)(i), 24.8, 24.10(a)
1993, 24.2(b)(i), 24.2(b)(ii), 24.2(d)(i),
24.3(a)(i), 24.3(a)(ii), 24.6(a)
Charity Commissioners, 2.2(d), 24.2(b)(i),
24.2(d)(i), 24.3(a)(i), 24.3(a)(ii), 24.6(a),
24.8, 24.9, 24.10(c)
Companies Act, 24.1, 24.2(a)(i), 24.3
Convention 124 ratification, Ch. 3
Corporation Taxes Act of 1988, Sections 505
and 506, 24.5(a)
Deakin Report, 24.10(a)
Department of Finance and Personnel,
24.3(a)(ii)
eligibility, 2.2(a), 2.2(b), 2.2(d), 24.2–24.2(d)(i)
Elizabethan Statute of 1601, 24.2(b)(ii)
Finance Act of 1986, 24.5(a)
Friendly Societies Act, 24.1
1974, 24.2(a)(iii), 24.6(b)
1992, 24.2(a)(iii), 24.3(b)(ii), 24.6(b)
Friendly Societies Commission, 24.2(d)(i),
24.3(b)(ii), 24.6(b)
fund-raising restrictions, 24.8
Goodman Committee, 24.10(a)
House of Commons Expenditure Committee,
24.10(a)
House to House Collections Act of 1939, 24.8
Housing Associations Order of 1988,
24.3(b)(iii)
Income and Corporation Taxes Act of 1988,
Sections 505 and 9(4), 24.4(a)(i)
Industrial and Provident Societies Acts of
1965 to 1978, 24.1, 24.2(a)(iv), 24.2(d)(i),
24.3(b)(iii)
Inheritance Tax Act of 1984, 24.4(a)(i)
Inland Revenue, 24.4(b)(i)
internal governance, 24.3–24.3(b)(iii)
key trends and issues, 2.10(d), 24.10–24.10(c)

Law Reform Act of 1990, 24.3(a)(ii)
Lotteries and Amusements Act of 1976, 24.8
legal context, 24.1
Nathan Committee, 24.10(a)
National Lottery Act of 1993, 24.8
obligations to the public, 24.6(a)–(b)
Official Custodian for Charities, 24.3(a)(i)
Pemsel's Case, 24.2(b)(i), 24.10(a)
personal benefit restrictions, 24.5–24.5(b)
political activity, 24.9
Recreational Charities Act of 1958, Sections
1(1) and 1(2), 24.2(b)(i)
Taxation of Chargeable Gains Act of 1992,
Section 256, 24.4(a)(i)
tax treatment, 2.4(b)(i), 2.4(b)(ii), 24.4–24.4(c)
Trustee Act of 1925, 24.3, 24.3(a)(i)
Trustee Investment Act of 1961, 24.3, 24.3(a)(i)
Value Added Tax Act of 1994, 24.4(a)(i)
War Charities Act of 1940, 24.8
United Nations, 1.1(b), Ch. 3, 6.4(c)(i), 12.4,
12.4(b)
United States, 1.1(a)
business activity, 2.7(b), 25.7
charitable deduction limits, 25.4(b)(i), Ch. 25
App.
commensurate test, 25.10(a)
commerciality doctrine, 25.10(a)
Commission on Private Philanthropy and
Public Needs, 2.3
constitution, 2.1(b), 25.1
eligibility, 2.2(a), 2.2(b), 2.2(c), 2.2(d), 25.2(a)–
(d)(ii)
fund-raising restrictions, 2.8(a), 2.8(b), 25.8
internal governance, 2.3, 25.3(i)–(ii)
Internal Revenue Code
list for individual organizations, 25.4(a)(i)
Section 170, 25.4(b)(i), Ch. 25 App.
Section 501(c)(3), 2.2(b), 2.9(b), 25.2(b),
25.4(a)(i), 25.4(b)(i)
Internal Revenue Service, 2.2(a), 16.4(c),
25.2(d)(ii), 25.7, 25.10(a)
key trends and issues, 2.10(c), 25.10–25.10(c)
legal context, 2.1(b), 2.1(d), 25.1
obligations to the public, 2.6(a), 25.6(a)–(b)
personal benefit restrictions, 25.5(a)–(c)
political activity, 2.9(a)(i), 2.9(a)(ii), 2.9(b),
25.9(a)–(b)
tax treaties, Ch. 3, 16.4(c)
tax treatment, 2.4, 2.4(b)(i), 2.4(b)(ii), 2.4(b),
25.4–25.4(b)(ii)

V

Voluntarism, 1.1(b), 2.3, App. A

W

World Bank, 1.3, App. B